DEMOCRACY BY THE PEOPLE

Thanks to a series of recent U.S. Supreme Court decisions, corporations can now spend unlimited sums to influence elections, Super PACs and dark money groups are flourishing, and wealthy individuals and special interests increasingly dominate American politics. Despite the overwhelming support of Americans to fix this broken system, serious efforts at reform have languished. Campaign finance is a highly intricate and complex area of the law, and the current system favors the incumbent politicians who oversee it. This illuminating book takes these hard realities as a starting point and offers realistic solutions to reform campaign finance. With contributions from more than a dozen leading scholars of election law, it should be read by anyone interested in reclaiming the promise of American democracy.

EUGENE D. MAZO is Visiting Associate Professor of Law at Rutgers University. He is the co-editor of *Election Law Stories* (2016), a book that tells the history of the most important Supreme Court cases in election law. He serves as treasurer of the Section on Election Law and on the executive committee of the Section on Constitutional Law at the Association of American Law Schools. Mazo has taught at the law schools of the University of Baltimore, George Mason University, the University of Maryland, and Wake Forest University. A graduate of Columbia College, he holds a master's degree from Harvard University, a D.Phil. in politics from Oxford University, and a J.D. from Stanford Law School.

TIMOTHY K. KUHNER is Associate Professor of Law at the University of Auckland. He is the author of *Capitalism v. Democracy: Money in Politics and the Free Market Constitution* (2014), a book that received acclaim from Thomas Piketty, Lawrence Lessig, Erwin Chemerinsky, the *Harvard Law Review*, and the *Law and Politics Book Review*. Kuhner was previously Associate Professor of Law at the Georgia State University College of Law, a Fulbright Senior Scholar at the University of Barcelona, and a Thomas J. Watson Fellow in Latin America. He is a graduate of Bowdoin College and holds a J.D. and an LL.M. from Duke Law School.

Democracy by the People

REFORMING CAMPAIGN FINANCE IN AMERICA

Edited by

EUGENE D. MAZO
Rutgers University

TIMOTHY K. KUHNER
University of Auckland

CAMBRIDGE
UNIVERSITY PRESS

CAMBRIDGE
UNIVERSITY PRESS

University Printing House, Cambridge CB2 8BS, United Kingdom

One Liberty Plaza, 20th Floor, New York, NY 10006, USA

477 Williamstown Road, Port Melbourne, VIC 3207, Australia

314-321, 3rd Floor, Plot 3, Splendor Forum, Jasola District Centre, New Delhi - 110025, India

79 Anson Road, #06-04/06, Singapore 079906

Cambridge University Press is part of the University of Cambridge.

It furthers the University's mission by disseminating knowledge in the pursuit of education, learning and research at the highest international levels of excellence.

www.cambridge.org
Information on this title: www.cambridge.org/9781316630679
DOI: 10.1017/9781316822906

First published 2018
First paperback edition 2019

A catalogue record for this publication is available from the British Library

Library of Congress Cataloging in Publication data
Names: Mazo, Eugene D. (Eugene David), 1973– editor. | Kuhner, Timothy K., 1976– editor.
Title: Democracy by the people : reforming campaign finance in America / edited by Eugene D. Mazo (Rutgers University), Timothy K. Kuhner (University of Auckland).
Description: Cambridge, UK; New York, NY: Cambridge University Press, 2018. | ECIP d.v. | Includes bibliographical references and index.
Identifiers: LCCN 2018029874 | ISBN 9781107177635 (hardback)
Subjects: LCSH: Campaign funds – Law and legislation – United States – Congresses. | Law reform – United States – Congresses.
Classification: LCC KF4920.A75 D46 2018 | DDC 342.73/078–dc23
LC record available at https://lccn.loc.gov/2018029874

ISBN 978-1-107-17763-5 Hardback
ISBN 978-1-316-63067-9 Paperback

For our Fathers

In memory of
Eugene Boris Mazo
(1938–2016)

and

With gratitude to
Thomas Kuhner

Contents

Contributors

RICHARD BRIFFAULT is the Joseph P. Chamberlain Professor of Legislation at Columbia Law School.

YASMIN DAWOOD is the Canada Research Chair in Democracy, Constitutionalism, and Electoral Law and Associate Professor of Law and Political Science at the University of Toronto.

K. D. EWING is Professor of Public Law at King's College, London.

RONALD A. FEIN is the Legal Director of Free Speech For People.

BRENT FERGUSON is Assistant District Attorney at the New York County District Attorney's Office and former Counsel in the Democracy Program at the Brennan Center for Justice at the New York University School of Law.

DEBORAH HELLMAN is the D. Lurton Massee Professor of Law and the Roy L. and Rosamond Woodruff Morgan Professor of Law at the University of Virginia School of Law.

MICHAEL D. GILBERT is the Sullivan & Cromwell Professor of Law at the University of Virginia School of Law.

KENT GREENFIELD is Professor of Law and Dean's Distinguished Scholar at Boston College Law School.

TIMOTHY K. KUHNER is Associate Professor of Law at the University of Auckland.

CHISUN LEE is Senior Counsel in the Democracy Program at the Brennan Center for Justice at the New York University School of Law.

ADAM LIOZ is Political Director at Demos, based in Washington, D.C.

EUGENE D. MAZO is Visiting Associate Professor of Law at Rutgers University.

MAGGIE MCKINLEY is Assistant Professor of Law at the University of Pennsylvania Law School.

ÓSCAR SÁNCHEZ MUÑOZ is Associate Professor of Constitutional Law and Vice Dean for International Relations at the Faculty of Law at the University of Valladolid.

KATHERINE SHAW is Professor of Law and Co-Director of the Floersheimer Center for Constitutional Democracy at the Benjamin N. Cardozo School of Law at Yeshiva University.

GANESH SITARAMAN is Professor of Law and Director of the Program on Law and Government at Vanderbilt University Law School.

NICHOLAS STEPHANOPOULOS is Professor of Law and Marjorie Fried Research Scholar at the University of Chicago Law School.

DANIEL P. TOKAJI is the Charles W. Ebersold and Florence Whitcomb Ebersold Professor of Constitutional Law at The Ohio State University Moritz College of Law.

NICK WARSHAW is a graduate of the UCLA School of Law who practices state and federal political law in the San Francisco Bay Area.

Acknowledgments

The ideas in this book were originally debated at a symposium that was organized and generously sponsored by Free Speech For People and held in Newark, New Jersey, on April 1, 2016. FSFP is a public interest advocacy organization that has worked tirelessly to overhaul America's campaign finance system. Our foremost thanks go to its leaders, John Bonifaz and Ron Fein, as well as to their colleagues Oske Buckley, Bri Holmes, and Aspen Webster. We are profoundly grateful to them for their vision, and we are proud to be their friends and partners in the struggle to reclaim America's democracy. We also wish to express our heartfelt thanks to Mark C. Alexander, the former academic associate dean at the Seton Hall University School of Law—and now the dean of the law school at Villanova University—for hosting this symposium at Seton Hall and for warmly welcoming all of us to Newark.

We are grateful to the law schools that employed Gene while we worked on this book. The seeds for the book were planted at Wake Forest, where Michael Curtis, Sidney Shapiro, Andrew Verstein, and Ronald Wright provided warm friendship and intellectual inspiration. The proposal was written at Rutgers, to which the dynamic duo of Dean Ronald Chen and Vice Dean Reid Weisbord welcomed Gene with open arms. The manuscript was edited at George Mason, where Dean Henry Butler took a chance on a campaign finance reformer, Gene's free speech-loving colleagues extensively debated the ideas in these pages, and Paolo Saguato and Elina Treyger proved to be excellent dinner companions. Gene also briefly worked on the manuscript at Savannah, where Caprice Roberts, Joseph D'Agostino, Sonya Jackson, and Judd Sneirson provided camaraderie and introduced Gene to Southern hospitality. By the time our manuscript was in production, Gene was teaching at the University of Baltimore and the University of Maryland. We thank Dean Ronald Weich and Associate Deans Dionne Koller and Amy Sloan for bringing Gene to

Baltimore and Dean Donald Tobin and Associate Dean Barbara Gontrum for hiring him at Maryland. Ron Chen and Reid Weisbord asked Gene to return to Rutgers as this book was about to be published, prompting us to list that institution as Gene's affiliation as he completed his grand tour of the American legal academy. For housing Gene along his journey, we owe thanks to Oluwaseun Ajayi in Arlington, Virginia, Judd Sneirson in Savannah, Georgia, and Onitta Hagerman and Sam Lloyd in Baltimore, Maryland.

We also wish to recognize Tim's former colleagues at Georgia State, in particular Steven Kaminshine, Wendy Hensel, Jessica Gabel, and Pamela Brannon, whose backing for this book was invaluable. The administration at Georgia State generously granted Tim leave to pursue this project, while the Georgia State library made many materials available to him at home and abroad. The Kuhner family moved from the United States to Spain and finally to New Zealand as this book unfolded. We gratefully acknowledge the Fulbright Scholar Program of the U.S. Department of State and the University of Barcelona, where Tim was stationed during his Fulbright award in 2017–2018, as well as Doctor Juli Ponce for being a gracious host in Barcelona and a frequent source of comparative insights about corruption and democracy. We also thank Dean Andrew Stockley for bringing Tim to Auckland Law School and for ensuring his family's smooth transition to New Zealand.

We were fortunate to work with Matt Gallaway, our extraordinary editor at Cambridge University Press, whose vision and wisdom got this project off the ground and guided it to completion. Several of Matt's colleagues at Cambridge worked tirelessly to see this book through the production process. We thank Kristina Deutsch, Meera Seth, and Jackie Grant in New York and Laura Blake in the United Kingdom. We also thank Dawn Preston at Out of House Publishing in the United Kingdom for coordinating the book's production, Lisa Cornish for providing superb copyediting from London, and Susan McCarty and Jenny Rensler of the Thurgood Marshall Law Library at the University of Maryland for helping to ensure the accuracy of our sources. This book also greatly benefitted from the tutelage of Carol McGeehan and Linda Lacy, whose knowledge of the publishing world was invaluable to us, and from the excellent research assistance of Constance Cooper.

We could never have completed this book without our loving families. Gene thanks his mother, Vlada Mazo, his brother, Phil Mazo, and his in-laws, Robert and Amanda Parker, for their support. Above all, Gene is grateful for the love and boundless encouragement he received from his wife, Gwen, and his sons, Max and Leo. Tim thanks his wife, Ana, for her sense of adventure and heartfelt support during their international journey. Tim's children, Blake and Cindy, deserve recognition here too, for their joy and sense of wonder balanced out the analytical side of life as an author and editor. When they grow up and read this book, Blake, Cindy, Max, and Leo will hopefully realize that while American democracy may be inspiring, it is also highly imperfect. May they improve it in their own way throughout their lives.

Our fathers instilled a deep appreciation for democracy in each of us throughout our lives. It is only fitting that we dedicate this book to them.

Finally, we reserve our greatest thanks for the contributors to this volume. We are grateful to them for their professionalism and hard work, for their wisdom and friendship, and for being bold and provocative in advancing their proposals for reform. A few of the ideas found in these pages first appeared in other publications. Chapter 3 draws in part on Nicholas O. Stephanopoulos, *Aligning Campaign Finance Law*, 101 VA. L. REV. 1425 (2015); Chapter 8 on Ganesh Sitaraman, *Contracting Around* Citizens United, 114 COLUM. L. REV. 755 (2014); Chapter 9 on Nick Warshaw, *Forget Congress: Reforming Campaign Finance Through Mutually Assured Destruction*, 63 UCLA L. REV. 208 (2016); and Chapter 13 on Michael D. Gilbert & Emily Reeder, *Aggregate Corruption*, 104 KY. L.J. 651 (2016). We thank the editors of these journals for kindly granting us permission to republish this material in substantially revised form here.

Democracy by the Wealthy: Campaign Finance Reform as the Issue of Our Time

Eugene D. Mazo and Timothy K. Kuhner

Campaign finance is undermining democracy in the United States, and most Americans know it. In poll after poll, Democrats and Republicans alike say that money has too much influence in elections and that the United States government is controlled by special interests.[1] Regardless of political affiliation, Americans overwhelmingly support reining in large donations to political campaigns, restraining outside spending, and requiring unaffiliated groups to publicly disclose their donors when they spend money to influence an election.[2] In short, the American people want campaign finance reform.

The strong consensus among Americans that there is too much money in politics should represent a powerful call for action. Yet campaign finance reform is notoriously tricky to pull off. The campaign finance system is highly intricate and complex, and many politicians benefit from the current system. And then there is another problem still. Beyond overcoming the patterns of access, influence, and dependence created by money in politics, popular reform efforts must also account for the jurisprudence that nurtures and protects the system in the first place. Before they can advance their ideas for reform, citizens and legislators need to understand this jurisprudence and why it makes regulating campaign finance such a challenge.

1 *See, e.g.*, Nicholas Confessore & Megan Thee-Brenan, *Poll Shows Americans Favor an Overhaul of Campaign Financing*, N.Y. Times (June 2, 2015), www.nytimes.com/2015/06/03/us/politics/poll-shows-americans-favor-overhaul-of-campaign-financing.html; Michael Beckel, *Don't Support "Campaign Finance Reform?" Try Combating "Corruption,"* Center for Public Integrity (Dec. 3, 2013), www.publicintegrity.org/2013/12/03/13943/don-t-support-campaign-finance-reform-try-combating-corruption.

2 New York Times/CBS News Poll, *Americans' Views on Money in Politics*, N.Y. Times (June 2, 2015), www.nytimes.com/interactive/2015/06/02/us/politics/money-in-politics-poll.html?_r=2.

In recent years, the United States Supreme Court has issued a number of controversial campaign finance decisions that have buttressed the role of money in politics. Those decisions wrongly equate money with speech, corporations with citizens, and financial influence over lawmakers with responsive government. Declaring this to be our Constitution's view of democracy, the Supreme Court has paved the way for individual donors to give millions of dollars to candidates and party committees, given corporations the green light to use their treasury funds to influence elections, and enabled the rise of Super PACs and "dark money" groups. Through its campaign finance jurisprudence, the Supreme Court has legalized the abuses that most Americans deplore, ensuring that an elite class of donors and spenders controls our campaign finance system and that the United States is governed by an increasingly influential class of plutocrats.

As a result of these rulings, the role of big money in politics has grown, the system has become more resistant to change, and—foreseeably enough—popular frustration is on the rise. In a 2016 poll, nearly 95 percent of Americans stated that legislators are more attentive to wealthy donors than voters.[3] A solid 80 percent of those polled also added that the problem is "worse now than at any other time in their lives."[4] And essentially the same portion of respondents from both major parties—81 percent of Democrats and 79 percent of Republicans—said that they want their representatives to cross party lines in order to reduce the influence of money in politics.[5]

This rare example of bipartisan agreement in today's political climate points to something profound. Though Americans may be divided, they come together on the essential questions concerning their democracy. As Abraham Lincoln put it in his Gettysburg Address, the United States stands for a system of government of the people, by the people, and for the people.[6] When elections and lawmaking come under the dominion of a small class of wealthy individuals and interest groups, Americans rightly perceive a system of government of the wealthy, by the wealthy, and for the wealthy. Do we want democracy by the people or democracy by the wealthy? That is the essential issue bound up in campaign finance reform.

[3] Issue One-Ipsos Poll, *Americans Say Money in Politics Is a Top Five Concern This November* (June 17–20, 2016), www.issueone.org/wp-content/uploads/2016/06/issue-one-ipsos-polling-june-2016.pdf.

[4] *Id.*

[5] *Id.*

[6] *See* Michael Burgan, The Gettysburg Address 8 (2005); Garry Wills, Lincoln at Gettysburg: The Words that Remade America 191–204 (1992).

In his eighth and final State of the Union Address, delivered before Congress on January 12, 2016, President Barack Obama spoke about the public's role in addressing this problem:

> We have to reduce the influence of money in our politics, so that a handful of families or hidden interests can't bankroll our elections. And if our existing approach to campaign finance reform can't pass muster in the courts, we need to work together to find a real solution—because it's a problem.
>
> Changes in our political process—in not just who gets elected, but how they get elected—will only happen when the American people demand it. It depends on you. That's what's meant by a government of, by, and for the people.[7]

In quoting Lincoln's famous line from November 19, 1863, Obama was appealing to the hearts and minds of Americans to change their nation's broken campaign finance system. He reminded us that democracy by the people is not just the end that we all seek. It is also the means to achieving that end. The system will not change unless citizens decide to make campaign finance reform a priority. The moment has come for Americans to learn more about the problem, debate the options for reform, and take part in restoring popular government.

I. THE ISSUE OF OUR TIME

Consider the choice that voters faced in the 2016 presidential election. On the one hand, they could choose Hillary Clinton, a Washington insider who made tens of millions of dollars from her Wall Street speeches,[8] received over $623 million in large donations to her campaign, brought in $598 million more in donations to her associated political committees, and benefitted from $204 million of Super PAC spending.[9] Given these staggering sums, it is no wonder that many Americans had questions about how Wall Street and donors

[7] *See* The White House, Office of the Press Secretary, *Remarks of President Obama—State of the Union Address as Delivered* (Jan. 13, 2016), https://obamawhitehouse.archives.gov/the-press-office/2016/01/12/remarks-president-barack-obama-%E2%80%93-prepared-delivery-state-union-address.

[8] *See* Lindsey Cook, *Here's Who Paid Hillary Clinton $22 Million in Speaking Fees*, U.S. NEWS (Apr. 22, 2016), www.usnews.com/news/articles/2016-04-22/heres-who-paid-hillary-clinton-22-million-in-speaking-fees.

[9] *Money Raised as of December 31*, WASH. POST (Apr. 1, 2018), www.washingtonpost.com/graphics/politics/2016-election/campaign-finance/.

to the Clinton Foundation would influence Clinton's decision-making if she were elected President.[10]

On the other hand, voters could choose Donald Trump, an unapologetic icon of conspicuous wealth whose $66 million in self-funding for his presidential campaign and $957 million in total campaign, party, and Super PAC funding paled in comparison to what his global business holdings stood to gain if he won the presidency.[11] After his election, as if on cue, Americans watched as Trump chose a cabinet for his new administration comprised exclusively of millionaires and billionaires.[12] For Americans worried about the effects that big money has on politics, the 2016 presidential election did not provide any meaningful choice.

The same can be said for the 2016 congressional elections, where successful candidates were also either wealthy themselves or backed by wealthy interests. In 2016, the average cost of winning a U.S. Senate race hit a new high. The prior average was $10.6 million, but in 2016 that figure was reached three weeks before Election Day even arrived.[13] Outside spending on Senate races rose in 2016 as well, so that the average effective cost of a winning a Senate seat was actually over $19 million. In 2016, what it cost the average candidate to win a seat in the U.S. House of Representatives remained steady at $1.5 million,[14] but in 2017 Americans witnessed a special election in a Georgia congressional district that shattered all prior records. In that race to fill an open seat in the House, Democrat Jon Ossoff raised $23.6 million in contributions while Republican Karen Handel raised $4.5 million. However, conservative party committees and Super PACs spent a total of $18.2 million for Handel, while liberal outside groups spent only $7.6 million to support Ossoff. Altogether, $55 million was spent in this election.[15]

[10] *See* Matt Rhoades, *How the Clinton Foundation Brought Down Hillary's Campaign*, N.Y. Post (Nov. 17, 2016), http://nypost.com/2016/11/17/how-mitt-romneys-campaign-manager-took-down-hillary/.

[11] *Here's How Much of His Own Money Donald Trump Spent on His Own Campaign*, Fortune.Com (Dec. 9, 2016), http://fortune.com/2016/12/09/donald-trump-campaign-spending/; *Money Raised as of December 31*, *supra* note 9; Richard C. Paddock et al., *Potential Conflicts of Interest around the Globe for Trump, the Businessman President*, N.Y. Times (Nov. 26, 2016), www.nytimes.com/2016/11/26/us/politics/donald-trump-international-business.html.

[12] *See generally* Timothy K. Kuhner, *American Kleptocracy*, 28 King's L.J. 201 (2017).

[13] Soo Rin Kim, *The Price of Winning Just Got Higher, Especially in the Senate*, Center for Responsive Politics (Nov. 9, 2016), www.opensecrets.org/news/2016/11/the-price-of-winning-just-got-higher-especially-in-the-senate/.

[14] *Id.*

[15] Alicia Parlapiano & Rachel Shorey, *Who Financed the Georgia Sixth, the Most Expensive House Election Ever*, N.Y. Times (June 20, 2017), www.nytimes.com/interactive/2017/06/20/us/politics/georgia-6th-most-expensive-house-election.html.

In the aftermath of the Supreme Court's controversial decision in *Citizens United v. Federal Election Commission*,[16] outside spending in elections has skyrocketed. Today, corporations, unions, trade groups, political parties, and wealthy individuals all jockey to influence voters' perceptions of candidates and issues. Outside spending in federal elections never exceeded $20 million between 1990 and 1998, but it surpassed $330 million in 2008, exceeded $1 billion in 2012, and reached $1.4 billion in 2016.[17] Super PACs provided over $1 billion of that money in 2016 alone.[18] Even more worrisome than these organizations that can accept unlimited donations are "dark money" groups, which have no obligation to disclose their donors at all. The sum total of dark money in federal elections between 2010 and 2016 surpassed $800 million.[19]

If these price tags seem astounding, the bad news is that they are likely to keep rising. Outside groups spent more in the first eight months of the 2018 election cycle than they had spent over the same period in any previous election. By August 2017, outside groups had already deployed nearly $48 million to influence the November 2018 elections. That is more than double the $20.7 million that was spent in the same period during the 2016 presidential election and the $18 million spent in the same period during the midterm election of 2014.[20] Given the astronomical sums spent on campaigns and outside advertisements, it should come as no surprise that most Americans believe their elected officials listen more to their donors than to their constituents. Americans are right to believe that our system of government is no longer a democracy run by the people. Rather, it has become a democracy run by the wealthy.

The empirical evidence concerning campaign finance bears this out. Few Americans give to political candidates, parties, or PACs. Those who contribute over $200, the amount that triggers disclosure, represent an even smaller portion of the general public.[21] In 2016, for example, only 0.52 percent

16 558 U.S. 310 (2010).

17 *Total Outside Spending by Election Cycle, Excluding Party Committees*, Center for Responsive Politics, www.opensecrets.org/outsidespending/cycle_tots.php.

18 *Outside Spending*, Center for Responsive Politics, www.opensecrets.org/outside spending/fes_summ.php.

19 Ciara Torres-Spelliscy, *Dark Money as a Political Sovereignty Problem*, 28 King's L.J. 239, 239–40 (2017).

20 Robert Maguire, *Dark Money, Super PAC Spending Surges Ahead of 2018 Midterms*, Center for Responsive Politics (Aug. 25, 2017), www.opensecrets.org/news/2017/08/dark-money-super-pac-spending-surges-ahead-of-2018-midterms/.

21 *See Donor Demographics*, Center for Responsive Politics, www.opensecrets.org/overview/donordemographics.php?cycle=1990&filter=A (listing the percentage of U.S. adults who donated $200 or more in each election since 1990 and the total amount of campaign contributions provided by such donations).

of the population made contributions of $200 or more to candidates, and only 0.08 percent gave contributions of over $2,700. If we include in the denominator only the 245 million Americans who are over 18 years of age, it still turns out that only 0.68 percent of the population contributed more than $200.[22] And yet, the great majority of total campaign contributions come from those checks.[23] As though the 0.68 percent were not already a sufficiently small fraction of Americans, the percentage of campaign funds supplied by the top 0.01 percent of donors has also grown. In 1980, the top 0.01 percent of donors accounted for 15 percent of all campaign contributions, whereas by 2016 the top 0.01 percent—just 24,949 people—accounted for 40 percent of all contributions.[24] In other words, campaign finance is increasingly controlled by a few exceedingly wealthy individuals.

The members of the donor class who engage in outside spending, including spending by Super PACs and dark money groups, is even more exclusive still. Take the liberal Senate Majority PAC and the conservative American Crossroads, two of the largest Super PACs that operated in the 2014 elections. Two-thirds of the $90 million they raised came in donations of $500,000 or more, meaning that less than 200 donors provided the vast majority of their funding.[25] The same can be said of the $1.1 billion in outside spending that we saw during the 2012 elections: the top 200 donors to outside expenditure groups supplied approximately 80 percent of the money.[26] These 200 people represented just 0.000084 percent of the adult population. A similar pattern played out in Super PAC financing in 2016, when the top 100 individual donors contributed 43 percent of all Super PAC funds.[27] This miniscule group exerts tremendous influence over outside spending in American electoral campaigns.

The wealthy political donors and spenders who influence our elections are not representative of the general American population. They tend to be

[22] *Id.*

[23] *See id.* (listing the percentage of U.S. adults who donated $200 or more in each election since 1990 and the total amount of campaign contributions provided by such donations).

[24] Editorial, *The Tax Bill that Inequality Created*, N.Y. Times (Dec. 17, 2017); *see also* Adam Bonica, Nolan McCarty, Keith T. Poole & Howard Rosenthal, *Why Hasn't Democracy Slowed Rising Inequality?*, J. Econ. Persp., Summer 2013, at 103.

[25] Carrie Levine, *Surprise! No. 1 Super PAC Backs Democrats*, Center for Public Integrity (Nov. 3, 2014), www.publicintegrity.org/2014/11/03/16150/surprise-no-1-super-pac-backs-democrats.

[26] Meredith McGehee, *Only a Tiny Fraction of Americans Give Significantly to Campaigns*, Campaign Legal Center (Oct. 18, 2012), www.campaignlegalcenter.org/news/publications-speeches/only-tiny-fraction-americans-give-significantly-campaigns-zocalo-public.

[27] *2016 Super PACs: How Many Donors Give?*, Center for Responsive Politics, www.opensecrets.org/outsidespending/donor_stats.php?cycle=2016&type=B.

significantly more conservative on economic issues, in their views on government spending on social programs, and on issues like affirmative action.[28] On the whole, donors and spenders desire different laws and policies for the country. The wealthiest donors tend to oppose public education, unions and collective bargaining, universal healthcare, and a living wage. They prefer tax cuts, austerity measures, and privatization.[29] Besides ideological differences, the donor class exhibits important demographic differences as well. Donors are overwhelmingly white, predominantly male, and generally middle-aged or older.[30] In sum, they comprise a miniscule group that has little in common with most American citizens.

Despite this, donors heavily influence legislative decision-making. Politicians and political parties depend almost exclusively on private funds. To begin with, candidates rely on wealthy donors to back their electoral campaigns. Then, once elected, officeholders have no choice but to please the donors who supported them, given that the alternative is to not have enough money to run for reelection. This reality has allowed wealth and special interests to infiltrate the lawmaking process at all levels. Even well-intentioned politicians succumb to the system.

Unlike individuals, corporations cannot contribute directly to political campaigns. They can hire lobbyists to pressure legislators, however. Politicians often look to lobbyists to provide information essential to measuring the trade-offs involved in complex legislation. But most lobbyists do not have the interests of ordinary Americans in mind. Rather, they mostly advance the interests of corporations and well-connected trade groups. In 2012, corporations spent 34 times more money on lobbying than did public interest groups and unions.[31] Undoubtedly, the information these lobbyists provided to officeholders was

[28] *See* Clyde Wilcox, *Contributing as Political Participation*, *in* A User's Guide to Campaign Finance Reform 115–19 (Gerald C. Lubenow ed., 2001); *see also* Benjamin I. Page & Martin Gilens, Democracy in America? What Has Gone Wrong and What We Can Do About It (2017).

[29] *See, e.g.*, Sean McElwee, *Whose Voice, Whose Choice? The Distorting Influence of the Political Donors Class in Our Big-Money Elections*, Demos (Dec. 8, 2016), www.demos.org/publication/whose-voice-whose-choice-distorting-influence-political-donor-class-our-big-money-electi.

[30] *See* Wilcox, *supra* note 28, at 116–19. *See also* David Roberts, *Political Donors in the U.S. are Whiter, Wealthier, and More Conservative than Voters*, Vox.com (Dec. 9, 2016), www.vox.com/policy-and-politics/2016/12/9/13875096/us-political-donors; *5 Facts About U.S. Political Donations: More Affluent, Educated and Older Americans More Likely to Say They Donate*, Pew Research Center (May 16, 2017), www.pewresearch.org/fact-tank/2017/05/17/5-facts-about-u-s-political-donations/ft_17-05-11_donations_demos/.

[31] Lee Drutman, The Business of America Is Lobbying: How Corporations Became Politicized and Politics Became More Corporate 13 (2015).

skewed to privilege the financial interests of those who hired the lobbyists in the first place.

To understand the effects of lobbying, all one has to do is follow the money. The sums that corporate interests spend on lobbying each year are startling. Payments to lobbying firms more than doubled between 1998 and 2010, rising from $1.44 billion to $3.47 billion.[32] Business interests have cornered the market for lobbyists, spending vastly more than unions and public interest groups combined.[33] Today, corporate lobbyists outnumber state and federal officeholders, and the budget for corporate lobbying exceeds the budget that Congress earmarks for its own operations by a wide margin.[34] A recent report on politically active corporations found their lobbying expenditures and political donations earned them $4.4 trillion in federal support. This translates into a whopping 560 percent return on their investment.[35]

Wealthy donors have come to symbolize a new system of political exclusion in the United States. Today's system of political exclusion is no longer based on property ownership, literacy tests, or poll taxes—requirements for the franchise which have all been abolished—but rather on an increasingly rigid system of pay-to-play politics. The game is one where tremendous wealth buys one a seat right on the playing field, while ordinary wealth merely buys a seat in the stands. Meanwhile, the rest of the country only gets to watch the game on television—that is, if it even bothers to tune in. Such extreme government capture by wealthy interests in the United States would normally motivate citizens to propose drastic reforms. However, it turns out that the problem runs deeper still.

II. THE JURISPRUDENCE BEHIND CAMPAIGN FINANCE

Campaign finance law is highly complex and often not easy to understand. Because most Americans are not aware of the jurisprudence that enables the system, they are unable to come up with practical solutions for reform. In order to know why the American campaign finance system is so difficult to change, one first has to understand and appreciate the law behind it.

[32] Kay Lehman Schlozman, Sidney Verba & Henry E. Brady, The Unheavenly Chorus: Unequal Political Voice and the Broken Promise of American Democracy 593 (2012).

[33] Drutman, *supra* note 31, at 13.

[34] Lee Drutman, *How Corporate Lobbyists Conquered American Democracy*, The Atlantic (Apr. 20, 2015), www.theatlantic.com/business/archive/2015/04/how-corporate-lobbyists-conquered-american-democracy/390822/.

[35] Bill Allison & Sarah Harkins, *Fixed Fortunes: Biggest Corporate Political Interests Spend Billions, Get Trillions*, Sunlight Foundation (Nov. 17, 2014), https://sunlightfoundation.com/2014/11/17/fixed-fortunes-biggest-corporate-political-interests-spend-billions-get-trillions/.

The modern era of campaign finance regulation began in the 1970s. In 1971, Congress passed the Federal Election Campaign Act (FECA), a statute that it subsequently strengthened in 1974, in the wake of the Watergate scandal. FECA tried to regulate four different aspects of money in politics: *contributions*, or the amount that a person could donate to politicians or campaigns; *expenditures*, or the amount that candidates or campaigns could spend or that an individual could spend independently of candidates and campaigns to encourage a particular candidate's election; *disclosure*, or the amount that campaigns, committees, and donors had to report publicly; and *public financing*, which refers to the funding that a candidate for office could seek from the government. In addition, FECA entrusted the administration and enforcement of federal campaign finance law to the Federal Election Commission, a new federal agency that Congress had created.

In 1976, the constitutionality of FECA was challenged in *Buckley v. Valeo*,[36] which still stands as the seminal case of American campaign finance law. In *Buckley*, the Supreme Court allowed restrictions to be placed on campaign contributions to a federal candidate for office—at the time, the cap was $1,000; it now stands at $2,700—but the only justification it recognized for doing so was the government's desire to prevent corruption or the appearance of corruption. At the same time, the Supreme Court held that placing limits on expenditures, either by preventing a candidate from spending his own money or other people from spending their money independently of the candidate to urge his election, violated the First Amendment. In its decision, the Supreme Court specified that restrictions on expenditures should be subjected to a heightened level of scrutiny by the courts. In practice, this meant that the government would not be able to place any meaningful limits on expenditures.

Buckley only concerned the spending of money by individuals. The question of whether corporations should also be granted the protections of the First Amendment would take many more years to iron out. Between 1978 and 2003, the Supreme Court revisited this question several times, deciding the issue in inconsistent ways. Then, in 2010, in *Citizens United*, a narrow 5-4 majority of the Court held that corporations were entitled to spend unlimited amounts of money from their general treasury funds on independent expenditures to influence the outcome of elections—a holding that gave corporations some of the First Amendment rights enjoyed

[36] 424 U.S. 1 (1976).

by ordinary citizens. After *Citizens United*, spending by wealthy interests to elect candidates soared, while the average citizen's voice dwindled.[37]

Under Chief Justice John Roberts, the Supreme Court has repeatedly struck down the campaign finance restrictions that Congress and the states have enacted. In so doing, the Court has protected the role of powerful donors in our democracy, while providing political candidates more of an incentive to listen to their wealthiest supporters at the expense of their constituents. In *Davis v. Federal Election Commission*[38] and *Arizona Free Enterprise Club's Freedom Club PAC v. Bennett*,[39] the Court struck down laws that helped poorly financed candidates run against much wealthier opponents. Then, in *McCutcheon v. Federal Election Commission*,[40] the Roberts Court struck down aggregate limits on political contributions, paving the way for donors to give the maximum amount (currently $2,700) to as many candidates and political committees as they desired. Before *McCutcheon*, a single donor was not allowed to give more than $123,200 to all candidates and political committees combined in a two-year election cycle. After *McCutcheon* was decided, that same donor could give as much as $3.6 million.

In deciding these cases, the Supreme Court has imposed its own political philosophy on the nation, elucidating and elaborating on it each time it interprets how the First Amendment applies to the giving and spending of money in political campaigns. The Constitution is silent on campaign finance. And yet, under Chief Justice John Roberts, the Supreme Court has championed the idea that money is speech, that democracy is a free market, that corporations have the same rights to outside expenditures as citizens, that it is unconstitutional to limit spending in the name of political equality, that the heightened political access given to wealthy donors does not translate into corruption, and that public financing systems are unconstitutional if they reduce the effectiveness of private political spending.[41] The Court has made up these principles from scratch, all on its own, but claimed nonetheless that the Constitution requires them. In short, this undemocratic jurisprudence has made it difficult to restrain the power of big money in politics.

[37] *See* Michael Kent Curtis & Eugene D. Mazo, *Campaign Finance and the Ecology of Democratic Speech*, 103 Ky. L.J. 529 (2015).

[38] 554 U.S. 724 (2008).

[39] 564 U.S. 721 (2011).

[40] 134 S. Ct. 1434 (2014).

[41] *See* Timothy K. Kuhner, Capitalism v. Democracy: Money in Politics and the Free Market Constitution 33–136 (2014).

III. THERE IS STILL HOPE

Most legislators do not have the stomach to pass new campaign finance legislation, out of a fear that it is likely to be challenged in court and struck down for violating the Supreme Court's First Amendment jurisprudence. Under such circumstances, citizens and legislators have often turned to scholars for solutions. But most of the scholarly literature so far has been focused on explaining "the problem" inherent in our campaign finance system, while it has not offered many practical solutions. Recently, many excellent books have been published by prominent academics to explain the problem of campaign finance.[42] However, there are almost no books squarely devoted to putting forth multiple ideas for how to fix or reform the system.

Some of the solutions that scholars have proposed are unattainable, at least today. For example, Richard Hasen, one of the most serious thinkers we have when it comes to issues of campaign finance, argues that the best way to reform the campaign finance system is by changing the Supreme Court's membership. As Hasen elaborated not long ago:

> The key is to lay the groundwork for the Supreme Court to reverse *Citizens United* and other cases, returning to its role of carefully balancing rights and interests in this very difficult arena. There will come a time in the not too distant future when Justice Scalia and Justice Kennedy will leave the Court, and if a democratic president appoints their successors, the Court's campaign finance jurisprudence easily could turn back 180 degrees ...[43]

Hasen wrote those words in 2014, but his proposed solution never saw the light of day.[44] After Justice Antonin Scalia died in February 2016, a political struggle ensued over the future of the Supreme Court. Barack Obama nominated Judge Merrick Garland, a centrist Democratic sitting on the U.S. Court of Appeals for the District of Columbia Circuit, for the vacant Supreme Court seat. But the Republicans refused to hold hearings in the Senate on

[42] *See, e.g.*, ROBERT POST, CITIZENS DIVIDED: CAMPAIGN FINANCE REFORM AND THE CONSTITUTION (2014); ZEPHYR TEACHOUT, CORRUPTION IN AMERICA: FROM BENJAMIN FRANKLIN'S STUFF BOX TO *CITIZENS UNITED* (2014); LAWRENCE LESSIG, REPUBLIC, LOST: HOW MONEY CORRUPTS CONGRESS—AND A PLAN TO STOP IT (2011).

[43] Richard L. Hasen, *Three Wrong Progressive Approaches (and One Right One) to Campaign Finance Reform*, 8 HARV. L. & POL'Y REV. 21, 35 (2014).

[44] In 2016, Hasen continued to argue that changing the Supreme Court was the best strategy for campaign finance reform. *See* RICHARD L. HASEN, PLUTOCRATS UNITED: CAMPAIGN MONEY, THE SUPREME COURT, AND THE DISTORTION OF AMERICAN ELECTIONS 95 (2016) (promoting the strategy of "changing the Court as the most promising path to achieve campaign finance reform").

Garland's nomination until after the results of the 2016 presidential election were known. When Donald Trump won the presidency, he nominated Judge Neil Gorsuch of the U.S. Court of Appeals for the Tenth Circuit to fill Justice Scalia's old seat, thus restoring the Supreme Court to its former conservative majority. Then, in June 2018, Justice Anthony Kennedy announced his retirement from the Court, and Trump nominated Judge Brett Kavanaugh of the U.S. Court of Appeals for the District of Columbia Circuit to replace Justice Kennedy. Kavanaugh's confirmation would ensure that the Supreme Court remains in conservative hands for another generation.

As a result, Hasen's proposed solution is not achievable today, and may not be for a long time to come. The Supreme Court will not change in its conservative outlook anytime soon. Indeed, even before Donald Trump was elected, it was, in many ways, wishful thinking to hope that a newly Democrat-appointed Supreme Court justice would take his seat, realize the mistakes of his colleagues and predecessors, and vote to overturn the current system. Hasen's plan was a noble one, but it put all of its eggs in one basket, only to see Donald Trump win the presidency.

In this book, we seek to bring more realistic campaign finance reform solutions within the public's grasp. The solutions proposed in this volume do not call for the Supreme Court to change its jurisprudence. Rather, the volume brings together leading experts in election law to offer proposals that can be made to work within the confines of the existing jurisprudential system. Our contributors know that the Court's doctrine is unlikely to change in the near future, and yet they still believe that there are meaningful ways for Americans to reform campaign finance and reclaim democracy.

Because the Supreme Court is responsible for a fair portion of the problem, we begin the book there. Part I explains the problem in greater detail. It opens with Timothy Kuhner's exposé on plutocracy in the United States and the Supreme Court's role in justifying—even celebrating—democracy by the wealthy. From there, Deborah Hellman examines the philosophical issues that our campaign finance jurisprudence raises but leaves unanswered. Her chapter urges reformers to begin championing the liberty found in self-government alongside the liberty found in free speech. Nicholas Stephanopoulos next elucidates the ways in which our campaign finance system skews the policy positions of politicians by aligning them to the policies of their donors. Stephanopoulos argues that courts should instead work to ensure that the policy preferences of voters align with the government's policy outputs.

Part II proposes a host of reforms to our campaign finance system. Proceeding under the idea that campaign finance solutions have to be realistic, not to mention achievable, these solutions come in several stripes. The first of these includes solutions that aim to alleviate the problem of money in politics on a small scale by working within the Supreme Court's existing jurisprudential framework. These solutions do not call for overturning *Citizens United* or any other Supreme Court decision. Rather, they accept the law as given and seek to work within its confines to improve the system. The solutions found here include various ideas for implementing better public financing schemes, as Richard Briffault and Adam Lioz propose. They also include ideas for strengthening the existing disclosure regime, something that Katherine Shaw urges. And they include a reform proposal by Daniel Tokaji aimed at improving the work of the Federal Election Commission and the way its rulings are reviewed by the courts. The FEC is the federal agency tasked with enforcing the country's campaign finance laws, and it is well known in Washington for its politicized dysfunction. Tokaji recommends ending the deference that courts give to the FEC whenever it deadlocks along party lines in an enforcement action.

A second set of solutions found within Part II of the book is "extra-judicial" and "extra-statutory." Those solutions do not seek to overturn any of the Supreme Court's precedent either. Instead, they try to bypass the Supreme Court altogether. Ganesh Sitaraman explains how political candidates can enter private contracts that may influence outside independent expenditure groups to spend less money. In 2012, Democrat Elizabeth Warren and Republican Scott Brown, in their U.S. Senate race in Massachusetts, entered into such a contract and saw out-of-state independent spending decline by 84 percent. Meanwhile, Nick Warshaw explains how we can use the power of the profit motive to offer Super PAC insurance to political candidates, with the threat of an insurance payout possibly working to deter outside spending. Kent Greenfield argues that we should change corporate governance, corporate taxation, and corporate charters to make the political spending of corporations more accountable, while Maggie McKinley provides a blueprint for reforming our lobbying system. Eugene Mazo's chapter proposes that Congress use legislative recusal rules to regulate outside spending.

Next, Michael Gilbert makes a persuasive argument that one way to decrease the corrupting influences found in our campaign finance system is to bring back aggregate contribution limits in the states, given that *McCutcheon* only struck down aggregate contribution limits in federal elections. Brent Ferguson and Chisun Lee advocate for the wisdom of providing courts, whenever they consider future campaign finance cases, with better empirical evidence concerning the effects of money in politics. Part II ends with perhaps the boldest non-statutory and extra-judicial solution of all: Ron Fein's proposal to pass a constitutional amendment to overturn *Citizens United*. Fein and several of his colleagues helped craft the language of that amendment when it was last considered by the Senate, and his chapter lays the intellectual groundwork for how a future amendment could be steered through Congress.

Part III offers several comparative perspectives on U.S. campaign finance law. Keith Ewing's chapter looks at how *Buckley v. Valeo* has been received in a number of other English-speaking countries, including the United Kingdom, Canada, and Australia. Yasmin Dawood compares the campaign finance jurisprudence of the U.S. Supreme Court with that of the Supreme Court of Canada, which has readily accepted the concept of equal participation in campaign finance jurisprudence. Finally, Óscar Sánchez Muñoz elaborates on the relevant laws of several European countries, explaining how Germany, France, Italy, and other European states handle contributions, expenditures, disclosure, and public financing. It was important to us to include Part III in this book, as we believe campaign finance reformers in the United States stand to learn a great deal from the experiences of other democracies.

IV. A HISTORIC MOMENT FOR CAMPAIGN FINANCE REFORM

This book's importance springs from its historic moment. Campaign finance reform is on the national agenda, and it affects all Americans. The 2016 presidential candidates certainly got that message. During the historic 2016 presidential campaign, despite the backing of wealthy interests and raising millions herself, Hillary Clinton called for a constitutional amendment to be passed to reverse the Supreme Court's decision in *Citizens United*. Bernie Sanders, who raised more than half of his total funds from small donors, pushed for this reform even before Clinton did.[45] Both candidates championed a public financing system to combat political inequality.[46] On the other side of the aisle, Donald Trump, a candidate who was more than twice as rich than all previous U.S. presidents combined, publicly criticized our current campaign finance system and its beneficiaries with a pledge to "drain the swamp" in Washington. One presidential candidate, Harvard law professor Lawrence Lessig, even ran his campaign based entirely around that single issue: reforming the campaign finance system.

[45] *See Bernie Sanders*, CENTER FOR RESPONSIVE POLITICS, www.opensecrets.org/pres16/candidate?id=N00000528 (noting that Sanders raised 59% of his 2016 campaign funds from small donors).

[46] *See* Carrie Levine, *Sanders, Clinton Want Campaign Finance Overhaul, But Face Huge Obstacles*, CENTER FOR PUBLIC INTEGRITY (Mar. 24, 2016), www.pri.org/stories/2016-03-24/sanders-clinton-want-campaign-finance-overhaul-face-huge-obstacles.

Though public support for campaign finance reform is overwhelmingly bipartisan, surveys suggest that Americans know very little about campaign finance law and the options for improving it.[47] This book aims to familiarize Americans with both matters. We believe the country's lack of familiarity with campaign finance can be easily fixed. Indeed, this is a task that has become increasingly important as the cost of campaigns continues to rise, as the country's economic and social problems continue to grow, and as elected officials continue to be more responsive to their donors than their voters. Slowly, on their own, Americans have started to connect campaign finance to the more salient issues that concern them, such as taxes, healthcare, and the economy. They now realize that if their campaign finance system cannot be reformed, none of these other issues can be reformed either.

If the influence of money on our politics were reduced, elected officials could afford to listen to ordinary citizens. Officeholders would be able to deliberate more on the merits of the issues and not think about the financial implications facing them when the time comes to raise money for the next election. Citizens would get closer to having a system of government that works for the best interests of the people. If the influence of money were reduced, the voices and efforts of ordinary Americans could not be so easily countered by expensive ad campaigns, and maybe ordinary citizens would be able to afford to run for office themselves. Given what is at stake, it is no wonder that campaign finance reform has become such an important issue.

Understood in this greater context, this is a book about the fate of American democracy in our time. We live in an era of vast financial power and concentrated wealth. Behind this book's pragmatic aim—reducing the power of money in politics—lies the greater project of restoring to the United States a form of government consistent with its democratic ideals. The chapters that follow provide many options for achieving this goal. But this book's importance does not revolve around the authority of its contributors or the particulars found in any one chapter.

Rather, this book's center of gravity lies in the American people and their long experience with self-government, which has come under threat. The ideas for campaign finance reform found in these pages represent the possibility of changing the harmful conditions that exist in the United States today and producing a better democracy. We sought to bring together reform proposals from leading scholars who understand the intricacies of campaign finance law and have written extensively about it. We wanted to take their best ideas and place them under one set of covers. In framing this project, we were

47 *See, e.g.*, David Primo, *Public Opinion and Campaign Finance*, 7 INDEP. REV. 207, 212 (2002).

inspired by the belief that scholars can play a critical role in changing politics by connecting public demand with powerful ideas.

Our hope in offering these solutions is to provide a blueprint for social change in the United States—indeed, many blueprints. We also hope that through the ideas found in these chapters, Americans will be able to take a step toward restoring the belief among their fellow citizens that having a meaningful democracy is still possible. When it comes to their campaign finance system, it is time for American citizens to demand change. This book provides a number of unique proposals for how that change can be achieved.

PART I

Defining the Problem

1

The Third Coming of American Plutocracy: What Campaign Finance Reformers Are Up Against

Timothy K. Kuhner*

The United States is rightly famous for its political transformations. Everyone knows that we went from a backwater colony to a powerful self-governing nation, from a slave republic of propertied white men to a free land of universal suffrage, and from a pitiful stage of child labor and slums to a middle-class golden age. The trouble is that this democratic trajectory is so famous that Americans take it on faith. Our political independence, equal citizenship, and land of plenty occur to us today as foregone conclusions—we hardly need to consult reality to check their status. We tend to believe that those battles were fought and won, once and for all, and that self-government, equality, liberty, and opportunity for all could never be extinguished on our soil.

The United States is also famous for the many harvests of agitators behind its democratic trajectory. Who can forget the likes of Thomas Paine, Patrick Henry, Thomas Jefferson, Andrew Jackson, Frederick Douglass, Abraham Lincoln, Sojourner Truth, Susan B. Anthony, Franklin Delano Roosevelt, and Martin Luther King? Modern-day Americans have not forgotten their names or achievements, but many of us tell ourselves that the issues of our day are not so significant. History gives a concrete sense of right and wrong, while the present moment remains a place of doubt. That doubt, that inability to see our moment in history clearly, banishes conviction and collective action to the past.

In light of all this, ours is not a time of constitutional amendments or waves of progressive legislation. And that would be fine, if only self-government,

* Timothy K. Kuhner is Associate Professor of Law at the University of Auckland. While writing this chapter, he served as a Fulbright Senior Scholar at the University of Barcelona (2017–2018). He thanks Eugene D. Mazo, Angela P. Harris, Athena D. Mutua, and Matthew Titolo for their comments.

equality, liberty, and opportunity for all were not being extinguished on our soil.

Advancing along its present course, the United States is becoming famous for the opposite sort of political transformation as before: from self-governance to governance by a financial elite; from political inclusion regardless of race, sex, religion, or heritage to political exclusion on the basis of wealth; and from a thriving middle class to a massive underclass.

This undemocratic trajectory reveals that our legal system is incomplete. Although our laws rule out government by a monarch, a religious authority, and by a few generals or a dictator, they fail miserably when it comes to government by and for the wealthy. Plutocracy, defined long ago as "a form of government in which the supreme power is lodged in the hands of the wealthy classes,"[1] was never prohibited or eliminated in the United States. Its endurance is not, on the whole, a symptom of criminal activity or legal defiance. Rather, it is ironclad proof that American democracy was never completed in the first place. Together in their entirety, the many legal means through which financial power can be converted into political power are America's Achilles heel.

To see democracy's exceptional vulnerability to financial power up close, one need only observe how political campaigns, political parties, interest groups, and lobbyists are financed. Longstanding trends in these areas reveal the woeful state of campaign finance law—its omissions, its weak terms, its dysfunctional administration and enforcement by the Federal Election Commission, and, perhaps worst of all, its hostile treatment by the Supreme Court. Because of this structural flaw in our political architecture, a form of government hostile to democracy is being consolidated and our nation's achievements in self-governance and social mobility are being reversed. The mechanism, simply enough, is the privatization of government.

Although the privatization of government is a defining aspect of modern life, it is also one of the oldest forms of corruption under the sun. Consider the situation Romans faced roughly 1,600 years ago:

> Bribery and abuses always occurred, of course. But by the fourth and fifth centuries they had become the norm: no longer abuses of a system, but an alternative system in itself. The cash nexus overrode all other ties. Everything was bought and sold: public office … access to authority on every level, and particularly the emperor. The traditional web of obligations became a

[1] Freeman Otis Willey, The Laborer and the Capitalist 35 (1896).

> marketplace of power, ruled only by naked self-interest. Government's operation was permanently, massively distorted.[2]

As a freed slave from the period put it, such "universal corruption ... increased the influence of the rich, and aggravated the misfortunes of the poor."[3] Ultimately, the Roman Empire succumbed not just to overexpansion and invasions, but also to a market for political power.[4] Soon enough, the United States may also pay the price for privatizing government.

Still, past generations of Americans have improved upon ancient Rome. They made the President an elected figure, abolished slavery, redesigned the Senate as an elected body, and instituted a regime of universal suffrage. After economic and political inequality peaked again after abolition, Americans responded with antitrust laws, labor rights, and the New Deal. Were an ancient Roman to have our vantage point, he would see more than government in the private interest and the aggravation of the poor's misfortunes. He would see a cyclical process: universal corruption, response; universal corruption, response; universal corruption ... (response pending). Each response entailed a quantum leap for American democracy and targeted some of the wealthy interests that had captured the government at the time. But no response successfully targeted democracy's systemic vulnerability to government capture by the wealthy, and so that vulnerability has endured. As a result, plutocracy has been reincarnated multiple times throughout U.S. history.

Of course progress has been made since that early *slave republic* of white, property-owning males; of course progress has been made since that *industrializing republic* of Robber Barons and corporate trusts. But the linear view of history ignores the fact that extreme levels of economic and political exclusion keep resurfacing. The nation overcame slavery and formal disenfranchisement only to arrive at monopoly power and Jim Crow. Then the nation overcame monopoly power and vindicated the civil rights movement only to arrive at our *neoliberal republic* of wealthy donors, interest groups, and lobbyists.

We need not go back to ancient Rome in order to grasp the present moment in history. An alternative regime has nearly defeated democracy three times in the last 150 years of U.S. history alone. Its signature traits include extreme levels of economic and political inequality; behind that injustice, a concrete

2 Stephen Williams, *Corruption and the Decline of Rome*, History Today, www.historytoday.com/stephen-williams/corruption-and-decline-rome.

3 6 Edward Gibbon, The History of the Decline and Fall of the Roman Empire 60 (1788) (relaying the tearful lament of the freedman of Onegesius).

4 Ramsay MacMullen, Corruption and the Decline of Rome 122–70 (1988) (describing how power was "for sale").

set of laws and policies; behind those laws and policies, a system of government co-opted by wealthy interests; and, legitimizing this *status quo* to a surprising extent, Supreme Court case law.

The recurrence of this pattern should remove our doubts and equivocations about the present. The country now labors under the third coming of American plutocracy. If most Americans could see this and realize that democracy's survival is no more certain today than it was during slavery or the Gilded Age, then perhaps conviction, collective action, and legal reforms would reach their peak once again.

I. THE SLAVERY PLUTOCRACY

A. *Economic and Political Inequality*

The American Revolution threw off monarchy, paving the way for citizens to enjoy unprecedented rights and powers. But, slavery and mass disenfranchisement endured. As Frederick Douglass pointed out, slavery exposed America's claim of liberty, equality, and self-governance as a "hollow mockery."[5] It branded American "republicanism as sham."[6] But what gave the institution of slavery—and the massive concentration of wealth it produced—its staying power?

Slavery rested on political foundations: first, the absence of personhood, citizenship, and rights for slaves and their descendants; and second, a combination of property and contractual rights that allowed slave traders and corporations to forcibly abduct people from their homelands, bring them to market as commodities, breed them in captivity, enslave them and their offspring in perpetuity, and build an entire economy on whips and chains.

Those first two foundations generated a great deal of wealth for slave traders and slave owners, and concentrated that wealth in the upper echelons of a land-owning, person-owning elite. For example, as of 1860, the top 20 percent of Southern households earned over 62 percent of their regions' total income, while the bottom 40 percent earned roughly 8 percent of it.[7] Meanwhile, in

5 Frederick Douglass, *The Meaning of July Fourth for the Negro*, *in* 2 The Life and Writings of Frederick Douglass: Pre-civil War Decade, 1850–1860, at 192 (Philip S. Foner ed., 1950).

6 *Id.* at 201.

7 Peter H. Lindert & Jeffrey G. Williamson, American Incomes 1774–1860, at 36 tbl. 7 (Nat'l Bureau of Econ. Res., Working Paper No. 18396, 2012), www.nber.org/papers/w18396.pdf. These percentages are the average of the rates recorded for the South Atlantic, East South Central, and West South Central regions.

Northern states, the top 20 percent earned less than 50 percent of all income, while the bottom 40 percent earned roughly 15 percent.[8] The share of income obtained by the top 1 percent of Southern households was nearly twice as great as the share of income obtained by their counterparts in the North.[9] That inequality was partly a function of assets: in 1860, slaves, some 4 million in total, exceeded the value of all manufacturing and railroad companies.[10] It was also a reflection of the fact that this "human capital" was unevenly distributed. Approximately 30 percent of families in slave states held slaves,[11] but less than 1 percent of Southern whites owned over 50 slaves.[12] That inequality in ownership concentrated wealth in plantation owners and their associated industries, such as cotton, sugar, and tobacco.

Then came the third political foundation of slavery: the use of that concentrated wealth to obtain disproportionate influence over the government. Plutocracy was not just a symptom of slavery and the concentration of wealth that slavery produced. It was also a cause of slavery, or at least its endurance, and certainly a cause of the legal conditions that made slavery possible and profitable. James Ashley attributed slavery to a government "dominated over by the minority, and … administered by organized force and fraud, in the interest of a privileged class."[13] Senator Henry Wilson developed the same view at length, exposing the corruption of the United States by what he called "the slave power."[14] Beyond ownership over human beings, slavery entailed ownership of government; it voided popular sovereignty and political representation. It made the republican form of government impossible to achieve. Indeed, the government of the Confederacy, made up largely of slaveholders,[15] attempted to make its dominion permanent by seceding.

[8] *See id.* These percentages were obtained by comparing the average rates in South Atlantic, East South Central, and West South Central regions with the average rates in New England, East North Central, and West North Central regions.

[9] *Id.* This conclusion was reached by comparing the average rates in South Atlantic, East South Central, and West South Central regions with the average rates in New England, East North Central, and West North Central regions.

[10] *See* Ta-Nehisi Coates, *Slavery Made America*, THE ATLANTIC (June 24, 2014), www.theatlantic.com/business/archive/2014/06/slavery-made-america/373288/ (quoting from David Blight's course, "The Civil War and Reconstruction").

[11] ROBERT E. WEIR, CLASS IN AMERICA: AN ENCYCLOPEDIA 780 (2007).

[12] *Id.*

[13] James M. Ashley, Closing Portion of Stump Speech Delivered in the Grove near Montpelier, Williams County, Ohio (Sept. 1856). This source was quoted in Rebecca E. Zietlow, *The Ideological Origins of the Thirteenth Amendment*, 49 HOUS. L. REV. 393, 435 (2012).

[14] *See* Lea VanderVelde, *Henry Wilson: Cobbler of the Frayed Constitution, Strategist of the Thirteenth Amendment*, 15 GEO. J.L. & PUB. POL'Y 173, 176 (2017) (internal quotations removed).

[15] WEIR, *supra* note 11, at 780.

This brings to mind something written by the Reverend Henry Ward Beecher, who has gone down in history as "one of the most hated men in the Confederacy."[16] Beecher habitually objected to slavery on the grounds that it was incompatible with Christianity and American political ideals. But in 1863, Beecher objected to slavery for an additional reason: slavery concentrated wealth and power in a ruling class, which Beecher called a "plutocracy" and "the most dangerous kind of aristocracy."[17] Of those who held such "disproportioned political power," Beecher honed in on the men who "scorn the principle of universal liberty and … foam at the mouth and detestingly curse the conception of political equality."[18] Run by such men, Beecher labeled plutocracy "dangerous beyond anything that the mind can conceive."[19]

While that description readily singles out the usual suspects who controlled the South and ran the Confederacy, it also describes some unusual ones. If Supreme Court Justices are not commonly associated with the mouth foam and extreme danger that Beecher mentions, it is because we have forgotten *Dred Scott v. Sandford*.[20]

B. *Justifying Slavery*

In 1857, seven men validated slavery with the force of the Constitution. Chief Justice Roger Taney's majority opinion decided whether Dred Scott, a slave who had made it to free territory, had legal standing to sue his owner. But to decide that technical question, the Court had to resolve a profound one: whether "a negro, whose ancestors were imported into this country, and sold as slaves" could be considered a citizen.[21]

Chief Justice Taney acknowledged the scope of the inquiry, asking "whether the class of persons described in the plea … are constituent members of this sovereignty?"[22] "We think they are not," he continued, "and that they … were not intended to be included, under the word 'citizens' in the Constitution."[23] He claimed that when the Constitution was adopted they were "considered

16 Debby Applegate, The Most Famous Man in America: The Biography of Henry Ward Beecher 5 (2007).

17 Henry Ward Beecher, Freedom and War: Discourses on Topics Suggested by the Times 380–81 (1863).

18 *Id.* at 381.

19 *Id.*

20 Dred Scott v. Sandford, 60 U.S. 393, 403 (1857).

21 *Id.* at 403.

22 *Id.* at 404.

23 *Id.*

as a subordinate and inferior class of beings, who had been subjugated by the dominant race, and, whether emancipated or not, yet remained subject to their authority."[24] Slaves and their descendants were "beings of an inferior order [who] might justly and lawfully be reduced to slavery for [their] benefit."[25] Naturally, such beings were "altogether unfit to associate with the white race, either in social or political relations."[26]

These remarks justified the exclusive sovereignty of white males, not wealthy white males in particular. But by denying Scott's claim, the Court justified plutocracy indirectly. It did so, simply enough, by preserving the *status quo*.

But then the leveling came.

By the time in 1863 that Beecher's book was published, the Emancipation Proclamation had already changed enslaved people's status and disrupted the rights of contract and property bound up in slavery. Abraham Lincoln and Union forces vindicated the fundamental American ideals of which Douglass and Beecher spoke, fighting and dying for political equality. Two years later, the Thirteenth Amendment was ratified, Confederate generals surrendered, and Jefferson Davis was captured. The Civil Rights Act of 1866 and the Fourteenth and Fifteenth Amendments eviscerated the *Dred Scott* opinion, responding directly to outstanding matters of citizenship, legal standing, and suffrage. Slavery was over, but the use of wealth to influence government remained.

II. THE INDUSTRIAL PLUTOCRACY

A. *Economic and Political Inequality*

Slavery reduced labor costs and put free laborers, small employers, and small farmers at a competitive disadvantage. Emancipation removed an enormous sum of *private capital* from portfolios and sent Southern plantations and their crops to "commodity hell."[27] Still, child labor and sharecropping aided recovery.[28] And that was the bottom line: once the slaves were freed, old crops and new industries depended on cheap labor. Although mass production

24 *Id.* at 404–5.

25 *Id.* at 407.

26 *Id.*

27 Richard Follett, Sven Beckert, Peter Coclanis & Barbara M. Hahn, Plantation Kingdom: The American South and Its Global Commodities 5–6 (2016) (discussing the effect of emancipation on slave-dependent business interests).

28 *See id.* at 59 (noting that in 1905 "23 percent of all workers in Southern cotton mills were younger than 16").

methods were the innovation of the day, it was corporate consolidation and "government by campaign contributions" that tilted law and policy toward the interests of large employers and the rest of the industrial elite.[29] Both factors increased the bargaining power of wealthy interests over labor and government; both became definitive of a new era.

Describing that era, Congressman Milford W. Howard's 1895 book, *The American Plutocracy*,[30] pointed first to grossly unequal wealth distribution. Out of a population of nearly 70 million people, "[t]hirty thousand men, or fewer, own half of the wealth of this country," he noted. Scaling up to the wealthiest 250,000 men, amounting to just 0.35 percent of the population, Howard reported that they owned "almost or quite eighty percent of our total wealth."[31] Other estimates from the 1890s are not as extreme, but the data still suggest something remarkable: the antebellum era was not the high point of economic inequality in the United States.[32]

One might imagine that wealth creation arose from neutral conditions in the industrial era, such as technological change, plentiful natural resources, a large labor force, and unconquered terrains. But, as was the case with the slavery era, certain laws and policies were required in order for wealth to accumulate so severely in the hands of the few. The legal conditions behind wealth aggregation in the industrial era included corporate consolidation (or "trusts"), inhumane labor conditions with bare minimum pay, child labor, low tax burdens, the lack of an economic and social safety net, means in law and law enforcement for controlling unions and breaking up strikes, and a strong police power focused on keeping the poor in check. The "laws are such," wrote Congressman Howard, that a "vast army of people … are compelled to labor and toil in poverty in order that the few … may lead lives of idleness and luxury."[33]

Were such laws fairly produced? Were the people who made them fairly elected?

Once again, it was not that the political community had decided of its own accord to enact laws and policies favorable to the wealthy. Rather, the wealthy

[29] Jack Beatty, The Age of Betrayal: The Triumph of Money in America 1865–1900, at 218 (2008).

[30] M. W. Howard, The American Plutocracy (Holland Pub. Co., 1895).

[31] *Id.* at 12.

[32] *See* Robert E. Gallman, *Trends in the Size Distribution Trends in the Nineteenth Century: Some Speculations*, *in* Six Papers on the Size Distribution of Wealth and Income 15 (National Bureau of Economic Research, Lee Soltow ed., 1969) (noting that the data "do suggest that the share of wealth held by the very rich was substantially higher in 1890 than in the few decades before the Civil War").

[33] *Id.* at 3.

had captured the government. Congressman Howard's analysis hit the mark, moving from the conditions required for unconscionable wealth concentration to their underlying cause:

> [B]oth of the old parties are the friends of plutocracy. The leaders—a great many of them—are under plutocratic influence. Both of the old parties go to the money power for campaign funds, and put themselves under obligation to plutocracy at the very outset.[34]

But this was not a one-way street of party leaders and candidates appealing to wealthy industrialists for political funds. As an analysis of the Gilded Age that was published in 1934 put it:

> The Masters of Industry who sat in the upper chamber of congress ... or their close associates who became Representatives or governors of states, make up a long and distinguished role ... [E]very industrial group and every great monopoly was almost directly represented in the political councils of the nation.[35]

By enriching themselves at the expense of competitive capitalism, representative democracy, and the general public, these captains of industry earned the title "robber barons."[36]

By 1921, Senator Richard Pettigrew enjoyed a privileged vantage point on the period, one informed by his eleven years in the Senate:

> Within the past fifty years the wealth of the United States ... has been accumulated in the hands of a few, so that five per cent of the people own three-quarters of the nation's wealth, while two-thirds of the citizens—the workers—are practically without property ... [T]he few men who own nearly all the wealth have gained control of the machinery of public life. They have usurped the functions of government and established a plutocracy.[37]

These were among the dramatic economic and political components of plutocracy's second incarnation.

[34] Howard, *supra* note 30, at 103.

[35] Matthew Josephson, The Robber Barons 347–48 (Houghton Mifflin, 2011) (1934).

[36] *See id.* at 315–423 (chronicling the people, conditions, and anecdotes that characterize this era of history).

[37] R. F. Pettigrew, Triumphant Plutocracy 370–71 (1922). Several other notable works also gave a vivid account of the economic and political conditions of the time. *See, e.g.*, Edgar Howard Farrar, The Legal Remedy for Plutocracy (1902); Leslie Chase, Plutocracy (1910); Eli Beers, The Dangers of Plutocracy (1919); Scott Nearing, The New Slavery: Or, the World Made Safe for Plutocracy (1920); and Scott Nearing, The Course of American Empire 74–119 (1921) (discussing plutocracy).

But little by little, the leveling came.

The trusts and their monopoly power came under fire from Congress and the President in 1890 and again in 1914. The Sherman Antitrust Act addressed monopolies and other restraints on trade and competition. The Clayton Antitrust Act added specificity and additional coverage, targeting certain types of holding companies, certain mergers and acquisitions, interlocking directorates, and price discrimination. The Federal Trade Commission Act added a bipartisan federal agency dedicated to protecting consumers and promoting competition.[38]

Theodore Roosevelt's presidency also stands as an example of progressive opposition to the Gilded Age. Roosevelt prosecuted antitrust violations and broke up trusts, regulated the meat industry, urged inheritance and graduated income taxes, advocated fewer injunctions against labor unions, and empowered the Interstate Commerce Commission to control the railroads. Roosevelt also promoted democratic integrity directly, targeting the political source of corporate power. In 1905, he implored Congress to "forbid any officer of a corporation from using the money of the corporation in or about any election [and] also forbid such use of money in connection with any legislation."[39] Congress agreed in part, prohibiting contributions from corporations and national banks to federal candidates in the 1907 Tillman Act.[40] In 1910 and 1911, President William Howard Taft and Congress added disclosure requirements and spending limits for House and Senate campaigns.[41] Still, the Tillman Act, the 1910 Publicity Act, and their related amendments were hobbled by loopholes. Economic and political power continued to accrue sharply and rather exclusively in a privileged class of citizens.

The Great Depression and Franklin Delano Roosevelt's presidency catalyzed a stronger regulatory response to the Industrial Plutocracy, which continued beyond the 1920s. Indeed, in 1936, the younger Roosevelt alleged that "economic royalists" had "carved new dynasties."[42] Citing corporations and banks, he alleged that "the privileged princes of these new economic dynasties, thirsting for power, reached out for control over Government itself."[43] Roosevelt described the undemocratic control of government visible in his

[38] *What We Do*, U.S. Federal Trade Commission, www.ftc.gov/about-ftc/what-we-do.

[39] Theodore Roosevelt, *Fifth Annual Message* (Dec. 5, 1905), www.presidency.ucsb.edu/ws/?pid=29546.

[40] *See* Campaign Finance Reform: A Sourcebook 36 (Anthony Corrado et al. eds., 1997).

[41] *Id.* at 37–41.

[42] Franklin D. Roosevelt, *Acceptance Speech for the Renomination of the Presidency* (June 27, 1936), www.presidency.ucsb.edu/ws/?pid=15314.

[43] *Id.*

day as "economic tyranny" and "a new despotism."[44] He labeled "Government by organized money … just as dangerous as Government by organized mob."[45] As a step toward reducing those dangers, the 1940 Amendments to the Hatch Act limited individual contributions and party committee expenditures.[46]

Franklin Delano Roosevelt also highlighted a parallel between the Industrial Plutocracy and the Slavery Plutocracy, describing the giants of industry as having "concentrated into their own hands an almost complete control over other people's property, other people's money, other people's labor—other people's lives."[47] He believed that the "collapse of 1929 [had] showed up the despotism for what it was […] economic slavery."[48] He welcomed industrialists' support for the right to vote, but considered that "the political equality we once had won was meaningless in the face of economic inequality."[49]

Where progressives saw political inequality and domination, however, others saw market-based equality and freedom. And, as fate would have it, the others possessed the power of constitutional interpretation and judicial review.

B. *Justifying Gilded Age Capitalism*

Like the Slavery Plutocracy, the Industrial Plutocracy was kept in place for a time by the Supreme Court. The vehicle, once more, was the Fifth Amendment and, ironically enough, the parallel terms of the Fourteenth Amendment. A few steps past enslaved persons and massive profits from coerced labor, one found workers without bargaining power and massive profits from cheap labor. The Court frequently protected that *status quo* from regulation between 1895 and 1937, a period referred to as the Lochner era.

The *Lochner* Court did not always hand down anti-regulatory decisions,[50] but it operated from a worldview that tended to produce them. In the 1905 case,

44 *Id.*

45 Franklin D. Roosevelt, *Address at Madison Square Garden, New York City* (Oct. 31, 1936), www.presidency.ucsb.edu/ws/?pid=15219.

46 1940 Amendments to the Hatch Act, 54 Stat. 767 (July 19, 1940). *See* CAMPAIGN FINANCE REFORM: A SOURCEBOOK, *supra* note 40, at 47 (describing the Amendments as "impos[ing] the first yearly limit on individual contributions to federal candidates or national party committees" and limiting "the total amount a political party committee operating in two or more states could receive or spend in a year").

47 Roosevelt, *Acceptance Speech for the Renomination of the Presidency*, *supra* note 42.

48 *Id.*

49 *Id.*

50 *See* David E. Bernstein, *Lochner's Legacy's Legacy*, 82 TEX. L. REV. 1, 63 (2003) (noting that "[t]he Court also upheld a wide range of redistributive laws, ranging from antitrust laws intended to help small proprietors at the expense of large corporations to estate taxes to various ameliorative labor laws").

Lochner v. New York,[51] the Court invalidated a state law that prevented bakers from working over 60 hours per week. The law sought to protect the health of bakers and prevent bakeries from exploiting them. The Court struck down the law, deeming it an unconstitutional limitation of a right essential to the free market order. "The general right to make a contract in relation to his business is part of the liberty of the individual protected by the 14th Amendment," wrote the Court.[52] The Fourteenth Amendment, in relevant part, does not allow the state to "deprive any person of life, liberty, or property, without due process of law." Substituting unregulated economic freedom for "liberty" was the Court's idea in 1897, not the Constitution's in 1791 (when the Fifth Amendment was ratified) or 1868 (when the Fourteenth Amendment was ratified).[53]

The Lochnerian view of economic power and economic inequality is well illustrated by the 1915 case of *Coppage v. Kansas*.[54] *Coppage* gave the Court the opportunity to weigh in on a key part of the progressive movement. The State of Kansas had made it unlawful for employers to coerce, require, or influence employees to forego union membership.[55] The Kansas Supreme Court approved of the law, noting that employees were at an economic disadvantage and could be easily compelled to accept employers' "unreasonable and unjust demands."[56] The Kansas Supreme Court concluded that "such a condition … tends to reduce employees to mere serfdom"[57] and that "the state has the right to protect the freedom and independence of employees."[58]

The U.S. Supreme Court agreed that there was considerable inequality in bargaining power between employees and employers, but it reached the opposite conclusion as the Kansas Supreme Court: in order to uphold contractual and property rights, the legal order must "recogniz[e] as legitimate those inequalities of fortune that are the necessary result of the exercise of those rights."[59] The Court reasoned that prohibitions on union membership posed no constitutional problem because all men were "free to decline the employment on those terms … for 'it takes two to make a bargain.'"[60] Slaves did not possess that elementary freedom of Gilded Age employees to decline an offer

51 Lochner v. New York, 198 U.S. 45 (1905).
52 *Id.* at 53.
53 *See* Allgeyer v. Louisiana, 165 U.S. 578, 589 (1897) (making contractual freedom a constitutional right).
54 Coppage v. Kansas, 236 U.S. 1 (1915).
55 *Id.* at 6.
56 State v. Coppage, 125 P. 8 (Kan. 1912).
57 *Id.* at 10.
58 *Id.* at 11.
59 *Coppage*, 236 U.S. at 17.
60 *Id.* at 21.

or quit. In the shift from a free market for slaves to a free market for labor, the Supreme Court found a new natural order to defend from regulation.

The Court bent over backwards to reconcile this unequal natural order with equality concerns. Regarding the freedoms to offer, terminate, accept, and reject employment, the Court reasoned in *Adair v. United States* that "the employer and the employee have equality of right."[61] Building on this version of equality in *Coppage*, the Court described the right to make contracts that prohibited union membership as just "as essential to the laborer as to the capitalist, to the poor as to the rich."[62] *Coppage* considered the Kansas law "so disturbing to [this] equality of right."[63] The Court could have validated union membership and fair wages as starting points for equality and freedom. But *Adkins v. Children's Hospital* summed up the choice made by the Court throughout the Lochner era. The Court grounded the nation's constitutional order in citizens' "equal right to obtain from each other the best terms they can as the result of private bargaining."[64]

The Court's aversion to regulation was one-sided, ignoring state-sponsored advantages for the rich, such as corporate legal personhood and directors' legal duty to maximize profits for shareholders.[65] The Court's phrase, private bargaining, described a regime of contractual freedoms unfettered by public-minded regulation.

But, in 1937, the Court reversed *Adkins* and sunk a dagger into *Lochner's* heart. "The Constitution does not speak of freedom of contract," stated the 5-4 majority in *West Coast Hotel v. Parrish*. Instead of an equal right to private bargaining and legitimate inequalities of fortune, the Court now spoke of the "exploitation of a class of workers who are in an unequal position with respect to bargaining power and are thus relatively defenseless against the denial of a living wage."[66] It framed government inaction and cheap labor as "a subsidy for unconscionable employers" and insisted that the "community may direct its law-making power to correct the abuse which springs from their selfish disregard of the public interest."[67]

61 Adair v. United States, 208 U.S. 161, 175 (1908).

62 *Coppage*, 236 U.S. at 14.

63 *Id.*

64 Adkins v. Children's Hosp., 261 U.S. 525, 545 (1923).

65 On corporate legal personhood, see generally Santa Clara County v. S. Pac. R.R. Co., 118 U.S. 394 (1886). *See also* James D. Cox et al., Corporations 2–6 (2d ed. 2002). On the primary duty of corporate directors to maximize profits for shareholders, see Dodge v. Ford Motor Co., 170 N.W. 668, 684 (Mich. 1919).

66 West Coast Hotel v. Parrish, 300 U.S. 379, 399 (1937) (upholding a Washington State minimum wage law).

67 *Id.* at 399–400.

So motivated, the Court reinterpreted the liberty protected by the Fifth and Fourteenth amendments as "liberty in a social organization,"[68] not "an absolute and uncontrollable liberty."[69] The implication was simple: "freedom of contract is a qualified, and not an absolute, right" and so the law could protect more fully "against the evils which menace the health, safety, morals, and welfare of the people."[70] Arbitrary restraint remained unconstitutional but "reasonable regulations and prohibitions imposed in the interests of the community" came back into the Court's good graces.[71] Finally, the Kansas Supreme Court's concerns over serfdom received the answer they deserved: "the Legislature has necessarily a wide field of discretion … to insure … freedom from oppression."[72]

The New Deal then took its full shape and was followed by gains in education, labor, and infrastructure in the post-World War II era, and by a host of measures in Lyndon B. Johnson's Great Society. Together, these policies reduced economic inequality well below the levels that empowered the Slavery Plutocracy and the Industrial Plutocracy. Slums shrunk, palaces and mansions shrunk a bit too, and the vast American landscape known as the middle class arose and filled the gap. Today's reports on economic inequality marvel at how things played out between the 1930s and 1970s—particularly, the "long historical decline in the concentration of wealth" and the fact that "incomes across the [spectrum] grew at nearly the same pace."[73]

Still, wide-open legal channels for economic power to translate into political power remained. Seizing on that enduring vulnerability, plutocracy has come to the United States for the third time.

III. THE GLOBAL PLUTOCRACY

A. *Economic and Political Inequality*

Recall Senator Pettigrew's 1921 assessment: the richest 5 percent of the population owned 75 percent of the nation's wealth, while the bottom two-thirds of the population owned practically nothing. He laid the blame for this on the

68 *Id.* at 391.
69 *Id.* at 400.
70 *Id.* at 391.
71 *Id.* at 392.
72 *Id.* at 393.
73 Chad Stone, Danilo Trisi, Arloc Sherman & Emily Horton, *A Guide to Statistics on Historical Trends in Income Inequality* 15 (Center on Policy and Budget Priorities, Nov. 7, 2016), www.cbpp.org/sites/default/files/atoms/files/11-28-11pov_1.pdf.

plutocracy: the few men who owned nearly all the wealth, controlled public life, and usurped the functions of government.[74] Now, nearly a century after Senator Pettigrew's exposé, Americans suffer from extreme levels of economic inequality and government capture once more.

As for inequality, the richest 10 percent of the population owned 72 percent of all national wealth in 2010.[75] Meanwhile, the poorest 50 percent owned just 2 percent of national wealth.[76] And by 2013, the top 10 percent had increased their share, owning a full *three-quarters* of national wealth.[77] This brings the United States dangerously close to Pettigrew's figures from the Industrial Plutocracy. The same goes for the distribution of income from labor. The portion of total income received by the top 10 percent of earners rose to 50 percent in 2007, the highest point reached since the eve of disaster, 1928.[78] By 2002 the top 0.01 percent of income earners made more than 300 times the amount made by the average worker, the greatest degree of income inequality since 1915.[79]

As of 2010, at least 46 million Americans were living in poverty, the highest level ever recorded by the Census Bureau in the 52 years it had been keeping track.[80] To make matters worse, another 51 million Americans were near poverty, meaning that about one in three Americans were poor or in serious risk of becoming poor.[81] Yet, as of 2011, some billionaires paid a lower percentage of total income in taxes than bus drivers.[82]

Thomas Piketty describes rising inequality in the United States in a way that speaks to the undoing of the New Deal.[83] But his data from 1970 to 2010 have broader implications. They show rising inequality in a wide sample of capitalist democracies, most of which appear to be undergoing similar changes in

74 PETTIGREW, *supra* note 37, at 370–71.

75 THOMAS PIKETTY, CAPITAL IN THE TWENTY-FIRST CENTURY 257 (Arthur Goldhammer trans., 2014).

76 *Id. See also* Emmanuel Saez, *Striking It Richer, The Evolution of Top Incomes in the United States* (Sept. 3, 2013), http://eml.berkeley.edu/~saez/saez-UStopincomes-2012.pdf.

77 Stone et al., *supra* note 73, at 14.

78 Thomas Piketty & Emmanuel Saez, *Income and Wage Inequality in the United States, 1913–2002, in* TOP INCOMES OVER THE TWENTIETH CENTURY 147 (A. B. Atkinson et al. eds., 2006). *See also* Stone et al., *Guide to Statistics on Historical Trends, supra* note 73, at 12 ("[T]he share of before-tax income that the richest 1 percent of households receive has been rising since the late 1970s, and in the past decade has climbed to levels not seen since the 1920s.").

79 Piketty & Saez, *supra* note 78, at 148.

80 *See* Mark R. Reiff, *The Difference Principle, Rising Inequality, and Supply-Side Economics: How Rawls Got Hijacked by the Right*, 13 REV. PHIL. ÉCONOMIQUE 119, 124 (2012).

81 *Id.*

82 *Id.* at 128.

83 PIKETTY, *supra* note 75, at 173 (citing "the gradual privatization and transfer of public wealth into private hands in the 1970s and 1980s" and "a political context that was on the whole more favorable to private wealth than that of the immediate postwar decades").

law and policy. In short, the New Gilded Age is not confined to the United States. Rather, it is part of the international phenomenon of neoliberalism that has swept the globe over the last 48 years.

An economic and political rejection of social, ethical, and regulatory commitments, neoliberalism has brought about what Wendy Brown calls the "economization of political life" for the purpose of "capital enhancement."[84] In short, the state is repurposed by (and for) concentrated capital. David Harvey notes the new paradigm that has become increasingly dominant since the 1970s: "[d]eregulation, privatization, and withdrawal of the state from many areas of social provision."[85] Finance capital, corporate lobbies, supranational institutions, and political parties have carried out such austere measures on a global scale.[86]

There is a simple reason for such international and foreign pressure. Many sectors of the economy have been globalized—or been acquired by an exclusive class of foreign investors. The laws and policies required for maximum profit are now advanced in a coordinated fashion across the globe. It is no coincidence, as Chrystia Freeland puts it, that today's plutocrats are different from yesterday's insofar as they comprise a "transglobal community of peers who have more in common with one another than with their countrymen back home."[87] She describes today's super-rich as "increasingly a nation unto themselves."[88]

Plutocracy also had a global side at the start of U.S. imperialism in the 1890s. Maximum profits for sugar, tobacco, coffee, and shipping industries depended on annexations and policies hostile to the needs of foreign populations.[89] Now that the spread of capitalist democracy has advanced, profits do not tend to depend so heavily on imperialist violence. For exceptions, one can look to today's fossil fuels, weapons, and private military industries, true holdovers from the past. But, as a general rule, today's global industries require subtler policies for profit maximization.

Consider, for example, the law and policies favored by agribusiness, banking and finance, pharmaceuticals, private healthcare providers, automobile

84 Wendy Brown, Undoing the Demos: Neoliberalism's Stealth Revolution 17, 22 (2015).

85 David Harvey, A Brief History of Neoliberalism 2–3 (2007).

86 *See, e.g.*, Mark Blyth, Austerity: The History of a Dangerous Idea (2015); Kerry Anne Mendoza, The Demolition of the Welfare State and the Rise of the Zombie Economy (2014).

87 Chrystia Freeland, Plutocrats: The Rise of the New Global Super-Rich 5 (2012).

88 *Id.*

89 *See* Pettigrew, *supra* note 37, at 310–37 (discussing the causal role of plutocracy in imperialism).

manufacturers, real estate and construction companies, and telecommunications. As a general rule, the members of today's plutocracy pursue privatization, reductions in social spending, tax reform, tort reform, industry deregulation, the defeat of environmental protections, and the weakening of organized labor. Laws and policies to these effects expand the boundaries and profitability of capital, not those of nations or empires. But, as was the case with imperialism, a majority of voters, politicians, bureaucrats, and judges cannot be counted on to support, produce, and maintain these policies independently. Consequently, corporations, wealthy individuals, and economic interest groups devote tremendous resources to acquiring and maintaining political power.

One can hardly imagine a world in which some wealthy citizens and organized economic interests did not make such efforts. But democracy can be more or less resistant. That is a causal variable underlying each plutocracy, whether foreign or domestic, historical or present tense: insufficient resistance to government capture by wealth, open pathways even. And the evidence about the United States today warrants no doubt.

"Careful studies reveal that elected U.S. politicians, themselves often very wealthy, are much more responsive to the preferences of the rich than to the needs and hopes of middle-class or poor citizens"[90]—that was Theda Skocpol and Alexander Hertel-Fernandez's assessment in 2016. But even that word choice, "much more responsive," is mild in comparison to Martin Gilens and Benjamin Page's conclusion in 2014. On the topic of U.S. government policy, they found that "mass-based interest groups and average citizens have little or no independent influence."[91]

Gilens and Page explain the powerlessness of the general public in terms of the political dominance of economic elites and business interest groups.

> [I]t is well established that organized groups regularly lobby and fraternize with public officials, move through revolving doors between public and private employment, provide self-serving information to officials, draft legislation, and spend a great deal of money on election campaigns.[92]

[90] Theda Skocpol & Alexander Hertel-Fernandez, The Koch Effect: The Impact of a Cadre-Led Network on American Politics 1–2 (Conference Paper, Jan. 16, 2016), www.scholarsstrategynetwork.org/sites/default/files/the_koch_effect_for_spsa_w_apps_skocpol_and_hertel-fernandez-corrected_1-4-16_1.pdf.

[91] Martin Gilens & Benjamin I. Page, *Testing Theories of American Politics*, 12 PERSP. ON POL. 564 (2014).

[92] *Id.* at 567.

Money in politics is a particularly extreme factor in that equation and it is not just organized groups that have cornered the market for political finance. Today, less than 1 percent of the population supplies the great majority of those election funds. In fact, between 1990 and 2016, an average of just 0.36 percent of the adult population stood behind the great majority of federal campaign donations.[93] An even smaller percentage of Americans stands behind independent political spending. For example, data on Super PAC spending in 2012 and 2014 suggest that fewer than 200 Americans provided roughly 80 percent of the billions of dollars that these groups spent, which would mean that a mere 0.0001 percent or less of the adult population was primarily responsible for the messages of independent expenditure groups.[94]

If this elite group of donors and spenders were representative of the general population, then money in politics would be a poor explanation for the general public's lack of influence over law and policy. But it turns out that this elite class of donors and spenders is highly unrepresentative of the general public. Beyond being overwhelmingly white and wealthy, and mostly male,[95] the donor class does not want the same things from government as average citizens do. Indeed, studies suggest that conservative economic views are what most distinguish campaign donors from the rest of the population and even from other wealthy citizens.[96] Donors' conservative views on economic matters coincide with the legal and policy environment driving economic inequality. Of course there are a host of causes, but this is the environment and the outcome that monied interests have conspired to produce.[97]

That combination of extreme inequality in influence and a large divergence in preferences between donors and average citizens recalls Congressman Howard's 1895 explanation of the problem: "Both of the old parties go to the

93 *See Donor Demographics*, CENTER FOR RESPONSIVE POLITICS, www.opensecrets.org/overview/donordemographics.php?cycle=1990&filter=A (listing the percentage of U.S. adults who donated $200 or more in each election since 1990 and the total amount of campaign contributions provided by such donations).

94 On 2012 Super PAC spending, see Meredith McGehee, *Only a Tiny Fraction of Americans Give Significantly to Campaigns*, CAMPAIGN LEGAL CENTER (Oct. 18, 2012), www.clcblog.org/index.php?option=com_content&view=article&id=482:only-a-tiny-fraction-of-americans-give-significantly-to-campaigns. On 2014 Super PAC spending, see Carrie Levine, *Surprise! No. 1 Super PAC Backs Democrats*, CENTER FOR PUBLIC INTEGRITY (Nov. 3, 2014), www.publicintegrity.org/2014/11/03/16150/surprise-no-1-super-pac-backs-democrats.

95 Clyde Wilcox, *Contributing as Political Participation*, *in* A USER'S GUIDE TO CAMPAIGN FINANCE REFORM 116–19 (2001).

96 *Id. See also* Benjamin Page, Larry Bartels & Jason Seawright, *Democracy and the Policy Preferences of Wealthy Americans*, 11 PERSP. ON POL. 51–73 (2013).

97 *See, e.g.*, JEFFREY A. WINTERS, OLIGARCHY 251–54 (2011) (discussing other means, besides campaign finance, through which oligarchic power is expressed).

money power for campaign funds, and put themselves under obligation to plutocracy at the very outset."[98] Martin Gilens reached the same conclusion about candidates in 2012: "Affluent contributors … serve as a political filter mechanism; without the support of a sufficient core of well-off contributors, a prospective candidate has little chance of mounting a competitive campaign."[99] The news is no better for political parties. Skocpol and Hertel-Fernandez's 2016 analysis finds that "donor consortia," which they define as "well-organized sets of super-wealthy donors who work together over time," exercise a great deal of influence over political parties.[100] Indeed, their analysis of the Koch network suggests that the power of organized donors has advanced to the point, essentially, of forming a private political party.[101]

Next, we come to a more conventional means of legislative capture by wealthy interests: lobbying. Between 1998 and 2010, payments to lobbying firms rose 140 percent (from $1.44 billion to $3.47 billion).[102] That expanding market for political influence benefits the rich, because interest groups and lobbyists disproportionately represent business concerns. Faulting the decline of organized labor, Gilens and Page noted that "[r]elatively few [of such actors] represent the poor or even the economic interests of ordinary workers."[103] Indeed, Lee Drutman found that business interests controlled 95 of the top 100 lobbying organizations in 2012.[104] A more poetic way to put it is that the "lobbying section of the heavenly chorus … sings with an upper-crust accent."[105]

The same can be said for Congress itself. The need for vast campaign funds, the revolving door, and the increasing social ties between the political and economic elite help to explain why over half of the members of the House and Senate were millionaires as of 2013.[106] Being wealthy and having a network of

98 Howard, *supra* note 30, at 103.

99 Martin Gilens, Affluence & Influence: Economic Inequality and Political Power in America 244 (2012).

100 Skocpol & Hertel-Fernandez, *supra* note 90, at 6–7.

101 *Id.* at 8.

102 Kay Lehman Schlozman, Sidney Verba & Henry E. Brady, The Unheavenly Chorus: Unequal Political Voice and the Broken Promise of American Democracy 593 (2012).

103 Gilens & Page, *supra* note 91, at 567.

104 Lee Drutman, The Business of America is Lobbying: How Corporations Became Politicized and Politics Became More Corporate 12–13 (2015).

105 Schlozman, Verba & Brady, *supra* note 102, at 593–94.

106 Russ Choma, *One Member of Congress = 18 American Households: Lawmakers' Personal Finances Far from Average*, Center for Responsive Politics (Jan. 12, 2015), www.opensecrets.org/news/2015/01/one-member-of-congress-18-american-households-lawmakers-personal-finances-far-from-average/.

wealthy contacts certainly facilitates the task of mounting a viable campaign. It also heightens the incentives to obtain political office—a station offering considerable opportunities for personal enrichment. While the average American household experienced a 36 percent decline in net worth (even adjusted for inflation) between 2003 and 2013,[107] members of Congress gained substantial wealth.[108]

The existence of a gilded legislature constitutes an independent explanation for laws and policies favoring concentrated capital. Wealthy donors, spenders, and lobbyists may have a sympathetic audience to begin with, at least on economic issues and entitlements. All other things equal, millionaires are unlikely to raise taxes on themselves and unlikely to benefit personally from government programs—or less likely than middle- and lower-class Americans, at least. In sum, the considerable and increasing wealth of members of Congress explain part of the overlap between their policy preferences and those of donors, spenders, and interest groups, such as the U.S. Chamber of Commerce.[109]

All of this suggests government *by and for* the wealthy. But this time around, the leveling has not come. Or, more accurately, it came, but the Supreme Court fought it off.

B. *Justifying Plutocracy*

It is not surprising that extreme levels of economic and political inequality repeat themselves. As Hamilton asked rhetorically in *The Federalist Papers*, "Has it not ... invariably been found that momentary passions, and immediate interests, have a more active and imperious control over human conduct than general or remote considerations of policy, utility, or justice?"[110] In the competitive, impersonal contexts of politics and the economy, where fortune and power are won and lost, it is axiomatic that participants tend to pursue their own interests above those of others and the public at large. Unequal cumulative results predictably recur. But if Hamilton was right to posit a difference between the conduct justified by passion and interest, on the one hand, and

[107] Anna Bernasek, *The Typical Household, Now Worth a Third Less*, N.Y. TIMES (July 26, 2014), www.nytimes.com/2014/07/27/business/the-typical-household-now-worth-a-third-less.html.

[108] Choma, *supra* note 106.

[109] The Chamber has defined itself by coordinated opposition to taxes and regulations. *See* Skocpol & Hertel-Fernandez, *supra* note 90, at 3–4.

[110] THE FEDERALIST NO. 6 (Alexander Hamilton).

the conduct justified by considerations of justice on the other, then it would be unexpected for the Court to keep transforming the means to economic and political domination into constitutional rights. Surely the versions of liberty, equality, and sovereignty behind *Dred Scott* and *Lochner* have been safely confined to history …

Handed down on the nation's bicentennial, the Burger Court's per curiam opinion in *Buckley v. Valeo* responded to Congress's efforts to begin a new stage in American democracy. For nearly 200 years, no comprehensive set of campaign finance regulations could be found in the United States.[111] The Watergate scandal, which included million dollar campaign contributions,[112] was the latest of many scandals that had afflicted the country since its beginnings. But Watergate's magnitude and timing successfully brought into question the longstanding *status quo* of piecemeal regulations and privatized political finance. Passed in 1971 and expanded in 1974, the Federal Election Campaign Act (FECA) implemented the first comprehensive approach to campaign finance—including limits on how much money individuals and political action committees could give to campaigns (referred to as contributions), limits on how much money candidates and campaigns could spend (referred to as expenditures), public disclosure requirements, provisions for the voluntary public financing of presidential campaigns, and an administrative agency to enforce election law (the Federal Election Commission).[113]

The Constitution contains no provision on the financing of campaigns or elections. When the Court was asked to strike down FECA's provisions, it conducted its analysis on a blank canvass. And yet, this was not just any case of first impression on a matter untouched by the framers. *Buckley* presented the largest of all questions for a liberal democracy that had just consolidated basic civil rights. How far would political equality, public participation, and popular representation advance? What further sources of power and privilege might democracy unseat? In a nation that had finally secured universal suffrage without blatant obstacles, was there any acceptable way for elites to retain a systematic advantage in elections and policymaking?

Rather than deciding the case on narrow grounds or deferring to Congress, the Court filled the blank canvas with its own political worldview, a general approach to democracy that would orient the entire opinion. Two worldviews

[111] *See* Anthony Corrado, *Money and Politics: A History of Federal Campaign Finance Law, in* THE NEW CAMPAIGN FINANCE SOURCEBOOK 7–47 (Corrado et al. eds., 2005).

[112] Richard L. Hasen, *The Nine Lives of* Buckley v. Valeo, *in* ELECTION LAW STORIES 292 (Joshua A. Douglas & Eugene D. Mazo eds., 2016).

[113] FECA's various measures are detailed in the appendix to the *per curiam* opinion. *See* Buckley v. Valeo, 424 U.S. 1, 187–99 (1976).

were especially prominent at the time *Buckley* was drafted, two approaches to liberalism that no person of any intellectual sophistication, much less a Supreme Court Justice, could avoid contemplating.

The first approach sought liberty, political participation, and self-governance for all, and was informed by equality concerns. It was well expressed by John Rawls's A *Theory of Justice*, published in 1971 (the same year that FECA was adopted). At the time of the enforcement of the Civil Rights Act and Voting Rights Act, the country stood at the cusp of ending all categorical grounds for political exclusion. With battles over race, ethnicity, religion, and sex all fought and seemingly won, only socioeconomic status remained to be addressed. Rawls wrote:

> The constitution must take steps to enhance the value of equal rights of participation for all members of society ... those similarly endowed and motivated should have roughly the same chance of attaining positions of political authority irrespective of their economic and social class ... The liberties protected by the principle of participation lose much of their value whenever those who have greater private means are permitted to use their advantages to control the course of public debate. For eventually these inequalities will enable those better situated to exercise a larger influence over the development of legislation.[114]

Congress seemed to adopt Rawls's goals and values as legislative purposes in the 1974 installment of FECA. Besides preventing corruption, contribution and expenditure limits aimed to "[e]qualize the relative ability of all citizens to affect the outcome of elections" and slow "the skyrocketing cost of political campaigns, thereby ... open[ing] the political system more widely to candidates without access to sources of large amounts of money."[115]

In contrast to Rawls and FECA's goals, the second prominent approach to democracy sought to establish an efficient marketplace free from government intervention. As a matter of social ethos, it was hardly coincidental that Milton Friedman received the Nobel Prize and Eugene Fama published his *Foundations of Finance* in the same year that *Buckley* was handed down. The "efficient market hypothesis" associated with Friedman, Fama, and F. A. Hayek became prominent in the 1970s. As Paul Krugman explains, that was a time in which "[d]iscussion of investor irrationality, of bubbles, or destructive speculation had virtually disappeared from academic discourse."[116] Friedman

[114] John Rawls, A Theory of Justice 224–25 (1991). *See also* John Rawls, Political Liberalism 327 (1996) (elaborating a "fair value of political liberties").

[115] *Buckley*, 424 U.S. at 24–26.

[116] Paul Krugman, *How Did Economists Get It So Wrong?* N.Y. Times Mag. (Sept. 6, 2009), www.nytimes.com/2009/09/06/magazine/06Economic-t.html. *See generally* Eugene Fama,

described his work as a response to the "readiness to rely primarily on the state rather than on private voluntary arrangements to achieve objectives regarded as desirable."[117] He was inspired by what he called Adam Smith's "flash of genius," the realization that "the prices that emerged from voluntary transactions between buyers and sellers … could coordinate the activity of millions of people … in such a way as to make everyone better off."[118] This viewpoint opposed movements for economic and social justice. It emphasized that freedom, efficiency, and overall gains are best secured by free markets—and that state intervention compromises freedom.

Contribution and expenditure limits brought these two approaches into conflict. Should democracy be an inclusive community in which all, even the poor, could achieve access and influence, or should it be a free market? FECA advanced the first possibility. The *Buckley* plaintiffs advanced the second one. As the Court summarized their argument, limiting the use of money for political purposes "constitutes a restriction on communication violative of the First Amendment."[119] Agreeing with this framing of the issue, the Supreme Court focused its general approach to democracy in campaign finance cases on free speech. It found no countervailing constitutional rights implicated. That left out representative governance, equal protection, and popular participation, alternative framings of the case that could have vindicated FECA as balancing constitutional rights, not abridging them. Still, in spite of its myopic focus on free speech, *Buckley* seemed to reach a compromise between Rawls and Friedman by choosing the 1957 theory of the First Amendment given by *Roth v. United States.*[120]

1. A Democratic Rule Applied in a Gilded Fashion

Quoting *Roth* verbatim, *Buckley's* first categorical statement about the First Amendment reads: "The First Amendment affords the broadest protection to such political expression in order 'to assure (the) unfettered interchange of ideas for the bringing about of political and social changes desired by the people.'"[121] *Roth* notes that "[t]his objective was made explicit as early as 1774

THE FOUNDATIONS OF FINANCE (1976); F. A. HAYEK, THE ROAD TO SERFDOM: FIFTIETH ANNIVERSARY EDITION (1994) (featuring an introduction by Milton Friedman).

[117] MILTON FRIEDMAN, CAPITALISM AND FREEDOM 5 (2009).

[118] *See* PIERRE ROSANVALLON, DEMOCRACY PAST AND FUTURE 151 (2006) (quoting Milton Friedman).

[119] *Buckley*, 424 U.S. at 11.

[120] Roth v. United States, 354 U.S. 476 (1957).

[121] *Buckley*, 424 U.S. at 14.

in a letter of the Continental Congress,"[122] and yet, in *Buckley*, it made for a modern-day synthesis of Friedman's economic recipe with Rawls's concern over popular participation and inequalities in political power. Friedman triumphed in the means (the free market), while Rawls prevailed on the ends (democratic responsiveness), or nearly so.

Thirty-five pages after this first reference to democratic responsiveness through an open exchange of ideas, *Buckley* again quoted *Roth*. This time, the purpose of the quotation was not to introduce readers to the overall formula of market-based means producing popular ends; rather, it was to strike down expenditure limits and destroy political equality as a rationale for campaign finance limits.

Referencing the "governmental interest in equalizing the relative ability of individuals and groups to influence the outcome of elections"[123] that stood behind expenditure limits, the Court penned one of the most influential lines of constitutional law ever:

> [T]he concept that government may restrict the speech of some elements of our society in order to enhance the relative voice of others is wholly foreign to the First Amendment.[124]

The Court's support for this proposition consisted of *Roth's* First Amendment purpose of "unfettered interchange" and a complementary First Amendment purpose featured in *New York Times v. Sullivan*: the First Amendment "was designed to secure 'the widest possible dissemination of information from diverse and antagonistic sources.'"[125]

Buckley quoted *Sullivan*, but *Sullivan* itself quoted from *Associated Press v. United States*. Conspicuously, both *Buckley* and *Sullivan* omitted *Associated Press*'s full articulation of its open marketplace design.[126] That passage from 1945 gives pause:

> Th[e First] Amendment rests on the assumption that the widest possible dissemination of information from diverse and antagonistic sources is essential to the welfare of the public.[127]

[122] *Roth*, 354 U.S. at 484.

[123] *Buckley*, 424 U.S. at 48.

[124] *Id.* at 48–49.

[125] *Id.* at 49.

[126] *See* New York Times Co. v. Sullivan, 376 U.S. 254, 266 (1964) ("The effect would be to shackle the First Amendment in its attempt to secure 'the widest possible dissemination of information from diverse and antagonistic sources'"). This quotation from *Associated Press* truncates the sentence that explains why the widest possible dissemination is desirable.

[127] Assoc. Press v. United States, 326 U.S. 1, 20 (1945).

To *Roth*'s democratic responsiveness, *Associated Press* added public welfare as another instrumental purpose of the free speech principle. But *Buckley* ignored these popular purposes in analyzing the constitutionality of expenditure limits.

Having quoted the open marketplace portions of *Roth* and *Associated Press* and excluded the vital public functions of the marketplace identified in those opinions, *Buckley* made short work of expenditure limits and the political equality rationale behind them. Expenditure limits were difficult to reconcile with *Roth*'s "unfettered interchange." Limits were fetters on the strong, after all, and if "unfettered" were all we had to go by, that would seem to conclude the analysis.

Just one small opening remained: one could argue that restraints on the strong were invitations to the weak, invitations to participate alongside the wealthy on a more level playing field. Viewed in this light, expenditure limits might promote *Associated Press*'s free market formulation of "the widest possible dissemination of information from diverse and antagonistic sources."[128] Was it really so inconceivable to the Burger Court that some of society's diverse and antagonistic interests would be found on opposite ends of the economic hierarchy?

The Canadian Supreme Court's "egalitarian model of elections" rests partly on this assumption.[129] "[W]ealth is the main obstacle to equal participation,"[130] the Canadian Supreme Court wrote in *Harper v. Canada*, reasoning that it was constitutional for "the wealthy [to be] prevented from controlling the electoral process to the detriment of others with less economic power."[131] The Canadian Supreme Court's opinion in *Libman v. Quebec* also kept with *Associated Press*'s interest in information from diverse and antagonistic sources. In the words of the Canadian Supreme Court, "Spending limits are necessary to prevent the most affluent from monopolizing election discourse and consequently depriving their opponents of a reasonable opportunity to speak and be heard."[132]

Even though *Buckley* excluded *Roth*'s and *Associated Press*'s democratic purposes for the open speech marketplace, it still could have justified expenditure limits in terms of maximizing the dissemination of information from diverse and antagonistic sources. But had democratic responsiveness and the public welfare played their rightful role in expenditure limit analysis, there would have been even more powerful reasons against deeming a more level playing field wholly foreign to the First Amendment.

[128] *Id.* at 49.

[129] Harper v. Canada (Attorney General), [2004] 1 S.C.R. 827, 868, 2004 SCC 33 (Can.).

[130] *Id.* at para. 62.

[131] *Id.*

[132] Libman v. Quebec, [1997] 3 S.C.R. 569, 598–99 (Can.) (citations omitted).

First of all, the "governmental interest in equalizing the relative ability of individuals and groups to influence the outcome of elections"[133] spoke directly to producing the social and political changes desired by the people. Next came the state interest in slowing "the skyrocketing cost of political campaigns, thereby … open[ing] the political system more widely to candidates without access to sources of large amounts of money."[134] Democratic responsiveness and the public welfare might conceivably depend on greater socioeconomic diversity in the elected branches of government, or at least the inclusion on the ballot of candidates who appeal to the poor and middle class, not just to large donors and spenders. Those state interests in equality and greater ease (or accessibility) of mounting a campaign were connected to the full First Amendment formulations upon which the Court relied. But, instead of making that connection, the Court decided that limiting *quid pro quo* corruption and the appearance of corruption were the only sufficiently important state interests in play.[135]

Having found campaign expenditures, candidate expenditures, and independent expenditures not to raise any serious threat of *quid pro quo* corruption or its appearance, the Court struck them down. By focusing its analysis around the means (the open marketplace) and omitting any dutiful attention to the ends (democratic responsiveness and public welfare), *Buckley* was unfaithful to precedent. The open marketplace for speech trumped democracy only because democracy had been read out of constitutional law.

Still, a later portion of *Buckley* suggests that the Court attempted to reconcile the political marketplace with democratic responsiveness after all. Paralleling *Roth*'s stipulation that the unfettered interchange of ideas would bring about the changes desired by the people, *Buckley* assumed that "given the limitation on the size of outside contributions, the financial resources available to a candidate's campaign … will normally vary with the size and intensity of the candidate's support."[136] On the naïve assumption that poor and middle-class Americans would be able or willing to donate thousands of dollars each to political candidates and committees every election cycle, *Buckley* concluded that "[t]here is nothing invidious, improper, or unhealthy in permitting such funds to be spent to carry the candidate's message to the electorate."[137]

133 Buckley v. Valeo, 424 U.S. 1, 48 (1976).

134 *See id.* at 26 (announcing this state interest). *See also id.* at 57 (finding it insufficient to justify campaign expenditure ceilings).

135 *Id.* at 26–27.

136 *Id.* at 56.

137 *Id.*

In this hypothetical world of economic equality, campaign funds closely correlated with popular support, and a robust marketplace of diverse and antagonistic sources producing "a well-informed electorate,"[138] the unfettered interchange of ideas might actually protect the public welfare and produce the social and political changes desired by the people. On the basis of those assumptions, the Court struck down limits on expenditures by campaigns and candidates. Having registered those naïve assumptions as facts, the Court celebrated "the free society ordained by our Constitution," a legal order in which "it is not the government, but the people … who must retain control over the quantity and range of debate on public issues in a political campaign."[139] Recorded on the face of the opinion itself, that reasoning suggests that *Buckley*'s use of the market metaphor was not intended as a recipe for plutocracy.

But why was the Court engaged in such a theoretical discussion about the kind of society and free speech system the Constitution protects? That discussion came in response to the government interests behind campaign finance reform. The Court was scrutinizing those interests so closely because it had already found that limits on money in politics infringed on the First Amendment right to free political speech. And that determination did entail a recipe for plutocracy: political expenditures were political speech; indeed, money was speech itself.

Buckley approached that equivalency as if it were a matter of necessity, an inevitable concession to the times: "virtually every means of communicating ideas in today's mass society requires the expenditure of money."[140] Accordingly, the Court reasoned that congressional limits on monetary expenditures reduced the "number of issues discussed, the depth of their exploration, and the size of the audience reached."[141] Forestalling discussion about civic versus economic means for spreading ideas, and denying the distinctions between conduct and property, on the one hand, and speech on the other, the Court revealed its unwillingness to confront the inequities of the emerging neoliberal era. "[T]his Court has never suggested that the dependence of a communication on the expenditure of money … reduce[s] the exacting scrutiny required by the First Amendment,"[142] it wrote.

Political spending became First Amendment free speech, just as freedom of contract had become Fifth and Fourteenth Amendment liberty in the

[138] *Id.* at 45 n. 55.
[139] *Id.* at 57.
[140] *Id.* at 19.
[141] *Id.*
[142] *Id.* at 16 (emphasis removed).

Lochner era. Both transformations triggered rigorous scrutiny. But where was the modern-day equivalent of *West Coast Hotel*? Were all citizens in our democracy really free and equal, to paraphrase *Adkins*, on account of their right to obtain from candidates, parties, and officeholders the best terms they can as the result of private bargaining?[143] Or, to paraphrase *West Coast Hotel*, was FECA better understood as a recognition of the domination of citizens in an unequal position with respect to political bargaining power, and therefore relatively powerless to secure participation, candidates, laws, and policies that would pursue their interests?[144] *Buckley* could have interpreted political spending as a qualified right, not a nearly absolute one (subject only to concerns over *quid pro quo* corruption). The Court could have declared that the large economic transactions fueling speech were property, conduct, or liberty in social organization, all of which would be properly subject to reasonable regulations and prohibitions in the public interest. But instead, *Buckley* resurrected *Lochner* in even more dangerous terrain: the political system itself.

A number of notable scholars, including John Rawls, observed the parallel between *Lochner* and *Buckley*,[145] but nobody writing prior to the Roberts Court had seen the half of it.

2. Well beyond *Lochner*: Plutocracy Itself

In 2014, part of *Buckley* was finally overruled and its paradigm was explicitly corrected. In *McCutcheon v. Federal Election Commission*,[146] the Roberts Court struck down FECA's aggregate contribution limits, which had been preserved by *Buckley*. As of 2014, each individual campaign donor could contribute no more than $123,200 to candidates and committees per two-year election cycle.[147] Even adhering to the other limits binding upon individual donors, each individual could only give the maximum amounts for so long before running up against the aggregate two-year limits of $48,600 to federal candidates and $74,600 to other political committees.[148] On its way

143 *See* Adkins v. Children's Hosp., 261 U.S. 525, 545 (1923).

144 *See* West Coast Hotel v. Parrish, 300 U.S. 379, 399 (1937).

145 *See, e.g.*, Rawls, Political Liberalism, *supra* note 113, at 362; Cass R. Sunstein, *Political Equality and Unintended Consequences*, 94 Colum. L. Rev. 1390, 1398 (1994); Kathleen M. Sullivan, *Discrimination, Distribution and Free Speech*, 37 Ariz. L. Rev. 439, 440 (1995); James E. Fleming, *Securing Deliberative Democracy*, 72 Fordham L. Rev. 1435, 1455 (2004).

146 McCutcheon v. FEC, 134 S. Ct. 1434 (2014).

147 *See id.*

148 *Id.* at 1442. As of 2014, those individual limits were $2,600 per candidate per cycle, $32,400 per year to a national party committee, $10,000 to a state or local party committee, and $5,000 to a political action committee. *Id.*

to declaring aggregate limits unconstitutional, the Court removed *Buckley*'s stipulation about democratic responsiveness.

Recall that *Buckley* and *Roth* posited that the unfettered exchange of ideas served to produce the political and social changes desired by the people.[149] The *McCutcheon* dissenters, led by Justice Stephen Breyer, reminded the majority of precedent to this effect. Quoting a 1931 case, the dissenters tied "the opportunity for free political discussion to the end that government may be responsive to the will of the people."[150] In their view, "the First Amendment advances not only the individual's right…but also the public's interest in preserving a democratic order in which collective speech matters."[151]

The majority condemned the dissenting opinion's promotion of democratic responsiveness and the public interest. Framing the dissenters' goal as "a government where laws reflect the very thoughts, views, ideas, and sentiments [of the people],"[152] the majority concluded that "there are compelling reasons not to define the boundaries of the First Amendment by reference to such a generalized conception of the public good."[153] Those reasons included that "the will of the majority…can include laws that restrict free speech" and that the "whole point of the First Amendment is to afford individuals protection against such infringements."[154] The Court ascribed to the First Amendment the purpose of "putting the decision as to what views shall be voiced into the hands of each of us."[155]

Buckley had applauded a similar notion—that our "free society" required individuals and associations, not the government, to determine the course of the debate.[156] But *Buckley* had stipulated that political spending would be correlated with public opinion. Therefore, a free market for speech (or spending) could still be justified in terms of responsive government and the public good. Even prior to eliminating those justifications in *McCutcheon*, the Roberts Court had disagreed with *Buckley* on the relevance of a correlation between money raised or spent and popular support.

In the 2010 case *Citizens United v. Federal Election Commission*,[157] the Court struck down a prohibition on corporate general treasury spending in the weeks leading up to an election. Justice Anthony Kennedy's majority opinion

149 *See supra* note 120 and accompanying text.

150 *Id.* at 1467 (Breyer, J., dissenting) (quoting Stromberg v. California, 283 U.S. 359, 369 (1931)).

151 *Id.*

152 *Id.* at 1449.

153 *Id.*

154 *Id.*

155 *Id.* at 1448.

156 *See supra* note 139 and accompanying text.

157 Citizens United v. FEC, 558 U.S. 310 (2010).

declared: "It is irrelevant for First Amendment purposes that corporate funds may 'have little or no correlation to the public's support for the corporation's political ideas.' "[158] "All speakers," the Court announced, "use money amassed from the economic market-place"[159] and "[m]any persons can trace their funds to corporations, if not in the form of donations, then in the form of dividends, interest, or salary."[160] With these words, the Court admitted that its self-styled political marketplace operated through the economic marketplace, importing uneven outcomes in dividends, interests, and salaries into the political sphere. *McCutcheon's* elimination of the democratic purposes behind the market metaphor dovetails with this portion of *Citizens United*.

A profound question arises in light of these parts of *Citizens United* and *McCutcheon*. As a matter of constitutional law, the free market for aggregate donations and expenditures is no longer justified in terms of producing the social and political changes desired by the people. Relatedly, any lack of correlation between political spending and public support is now irrelevant. What, then, is the Court's—and therefore the Constitution's—theory of democracy? How does it conceive of the intersection between money in politics, on the one hand, and political responsiveness and the public interest on the other?

Ever since Plato, representative government has been justified on the basis of civic virtue and dedication to the public interest.[161] Classical theory holds that when those crucial features are corrupted by wealth, oligarchy arises—government in the private interest, specifically the interests of the wealthy.[162] Oligarchy has been defined in different ways over time, but once the central role of concentrated wealth is made clear, oligarchy becomes synonymous with plutocracy.[163] The portions of the Roberts Court's reasoning examined thus far merely expose the country to the risk of plutocracy. They do not enshrine plutocracy within the Constitution. But if the Court were to go further and interpret the Constitution as protecting government responsiveness

158 *Id.* at 351 (quoting Austin v. Mich. Chamber of Comm., 494 U.S. 652, 660 (1990)).

159 *Id.*

160 *Id.* (quoting *Austin*, 494 U.S. at 707 (Kennedy, J., dissenting)).

161 *See* William Doyle, Aristocracy: A Very Short Introduction 1 (2010).

162 *Id.* (discussing Aristotle's view of oligarchy). *See also* Jeffrey A. Winters, Oligarchy 3–7 (2011) (defining oligarchy not just in terms of "a tiny subset of people exercising influence grossly out of proportion to their numbers," but also in terms of massive concentrations of personal wealth and the politics of "wealth defense"). The ancient Greeks understood oligarchy as a system of rule by the few, whose purpose was moneymaking. *See* David Edward Tabachnick & Toivo Koivukoski, *Preface: Understanding Oligarchy*, *in* On Oligarchy: Ancient Lessons for Global Politics ix (David Tabachnick & Toivo Koivukoski eds., 2011).

163 Winters, *supra* note 162, at 1–26 (examining the conceptual confusion surrounding oligarchy).

to wealth, then systemic corruption would exist *de facto* and *de jure*. If plutocracy ruled the nation pursuant to law, rather than as a form of corruption or a constitutional gray area, it would be an official system of government, one ordained by the Constitution via its lawful interpreter.

The question is: What was the Roberts Court doing when it erased *Buckley*'s stipulations about democratic responsiveness and money in politics being correlated with public support? One possibility is that the Court was merely being honest and transparent about how *Buckley*'s stipulations were applied in practice. After all, those stipulations were mere formalities in *Buckley*, where expenditure limits fell and contribution limits were sustained only out of concern for *quid pro quo* corruption and its appearance. The other possibility is that the Court was gearing up for regime change, an ideological coup d'état to discredit democracy and justify plutocracy. The Roberts Court's reaction to the Rehnquist Court's expanded definition of corruption revealed the truth.

In the 1990 case *Austin v. Michigan Chamber of Commerce*,[164] the Rehnquist Court upheld the Michigan Campaign Finance Act, despite its prohibition on expenditures from corporate general treasury funds.[165] Justice Thurgood Marshall's majority opinion conceded that "the use of funds to support a political candidate is 'speech'" and that corporate status "does not remove … speech from the ambit of the First Amendment."[166] But then, the majority opinion validated a new compelling state interest, one quite separate from preventing *quid pro quo* corruption. It described the Michigan law as targeting a "different type of corruption in the political arena: the corrosive and distorting effects of immense aggregations of wealth that are accumulated with the help of the corporate form and that have little or no correlation to the public's support for the corporation's political ideas."[167] Here, in *Austin*, *Buckley*'s conclusory statement about the correlation between political spending and popular support became part of a compelling state interest—something to be ensured, not merely assumed. *Austin* did the same for *Buckley*'s cursory mention of "bringing about of political and social changes desired by the people."[168] Because of its lack of correlation with public support, corporate political spending promised to bring about the political and social changes desired by corporations and the wealthy, not those desired by the people. That is what made political expenditures from corporate general treasury funds "corrosive and distorting" of democracy.

[164] 494 U.S. 652 (1990).
[165] *See id.* at 655 (defining those expenditures).
[166] *Id.* at 657.
[167] *Id.* at 660.
[168] *See supra* note 120 and accompanying text.

This new type of corruption centered on the entanglement between the economic marketplace and the political marketplace in a nation where money is so unevenly distributed. In Justice Marshall's words, corporations may "use 'resources amassed in the economic marketplace' to obtain 'an unfair advantage in the political marketplace.'"[169] The Rehnquist Court expanded on this reasoning 13 years after *Austin* in *McConnell v. Federal Election Commission*. There the Court gave its blessing to Congress's interest in curbing "undue influence on an officeholder's judgment, and the appearance of such influence."[170] These cases bring to mind Reverend Beecher's description of plutocracy: "disproportioned political power" that "gives into the hands of a few the power of a whole state."[171] *Austin* and *McConnell* construed the new concentration of wealth that began in the 1970s as posing a mortal danger to democracy.

The Roberts Court's reason for striking down *Austin* and the related portion of *McConnell* was as elegant as it was mind-blowing: "*Austin* interferes with the 'open marketplace' of ideas protected by the First Amendment."[172] Unlike the Burger Court and the Rehnquist Court, the Roberts Court refused to tie the open marketplace to democratic responsiveness. But that was not all. In a series of interrelated statements, *Citizens United* consecrated a plutocratic version of political responsiveness. First, "The fact that speakers [employing corporate general treasury funds] may have influence over or access to elected officials does not mean that these officials are corrupt."[173] That narrowed the definition of corruption, ruling out *Austin*'s and *McConnell*'s historically grounded view to the contrary. Second, "Favoritism and influence are not … avoidable in representative politics."[174] Beyond normal and unavoidable, the Court construed political responsiveness to wealth as natural. "It is in *the nature* of an elected representative to favor certain policies, and, by necessary corollary, to favor the voters *and contributors* who support those policies,"[175] opined the Court.

Justice Kennedy's majority opinion then converted these sad reflections on political life, indeed some of the very reasons for campaign finance reform in the first place, into a necessary *status quo*, a formal redefinition of democracy:

169 *Id.* at 658–59 (quoting FEC v. Mass. Citizens for Life, 479 U.S. 238, 257 (1986)).

170 540 U.S. 93, 150 (2003).

171 Beecher, *supra* note 17, at 381. Beecher's work provided some of the intellectual foundations for the abolition of slavery. Thurgood Marshall, meanwhile, was partly responsible for desegregation, having argued *Brown v. Board of Education*. It is hardly coincidental that both men offered meaningful opposition to the plutocracies of their respective eras.

172 Citizens United v. FEC, 558 U.S. 310, 354 (2010).

173 *Id.* at 359.

174 *Id.*

175 *Id.* (emphasis added).

> It is well understood that a substantial and legitimate reason, if not the only reason, to cast a vote for, *or to make a contribution to*, one candidate over another is that the candidate will respond by producing those political outcomes the supporter favors. Democracy is premised on responsiveness.[176]

That was the third and final step. Democracy is now premised on responsiveness to the large donors and spenders, the sort who bring constitutional challenges to campaign finance regulations, that is.

After *Citizens United*'s constitutional protection of corporate general treasury expenditures, *McCutcheon v. Federal Election Commission* was the other paradigmatic case on big money.[177] Freeing individual donors to give millions of dollars in the aggregate, the majority opinion confirmed the official conversion of democracy into plutocracy:

> [G]overnment regulation may not target the general gratitude a candidate may feel toward those who support him or his allies, or the political access such support may afford. 'Ingratiation and access … are not corruption.' They embody a central feature of democracy—that constituents support candidates who share their beliefs and interests, and candidates who are elected can be expected to be responsive to those concerns.[178]

In the context of *McCutcheon*'s facts, this passage refers to financial allies, financial constituents, and economic support. As such, it makes the Roberts Court's view perfectly clear: responsive governance now means responsiveness by officeholders and candidates to their financial contributors.

To ensure that this plutocratic design would not be disturbed, the Court insisted that corruption is only the "exchange of an official act for money."[179] The Court also reminded state and federal governments that equality objectives would not be tolerated:

> No matter how desirable it may seem, it is not an acceptable governmental objective to 'level the playing field,' or to 'level electoral opportunities,' or to 'equalize the financial resources of candidates.'[180]

This suggests that the *status quo*—this market-determined, inheritance-determined hierarchy of political influence according to wealth—has been constitutionally enshrined.

[176] *Id.* (emphasis added).
[177] 134 S. Ct. 1434 (2014).
[178] *Id.* at 1441 (quoting *Citizens United*, 558 U.S. at 360).
[179] *Id.* at 1441.
[180] *Id.* at 1450.

Additional proof of wealth's officially sanctioned role came in Justice Samuel Alito's majority opinion in the 2008 case *Davis v. Federal Election Commission*.[181] There, the Court struck down the Millionaires' Amendment, a provision of the Bipartisan Campaign Reform Act that helped candidates who ran against wealthy, self-financing opponents. The problem was the provision's function of leveling the power of wealth.[182] "Leveling electoral opportunities," wrote Justice Alito for the majority, "means making and implementing judgments about which strengths should be permitted to contribute to the outcome of an election."[183] He went on to list candidates' strengths: "[s]ome are wealthy; others have wealthy supporters who are willing to make large contributions. Some are celebrities; some have the benefit of a well-known family name."[184] That was Justice Alito's exhaustive list. There was no mention of democratic strengths, only those that relate to wealth, fame from the entertainment industry, and family privilege. The amendment was held unconstitutional in its attempt "to reduce the natural advantage that wealthy individuals possess in campaigns for federal office."[185]

The following year, the Court struck down a powerful public financing system, Arizona's matching funds provision. In *Arizona Free Enterprise Club's Freedom Club PAC v. Bennett*, the Court reasoned that the system burdens the exercise of the "First Amendment right to make unlimited expenditures," because it enables one's opponents to raise more money.[186] From the perspective of a donor, spender, or privately financed candidate, that burden arises from his opponents' ability to use matching funds "to finance speech that counteract[s] and thus diminishe[s] the effectiveness of [his] own speech."[187] The resulting principle of constitutional law can be called optimal speech effectiveness, meaning that the government must not disrupt the natural, market-determined level of political power sanctified by *Davis*.[188] Access to lawmakers and elected office itself, plus influence over candidates and officeholders, now officially parallels pre-existing inequalities in wealth. In response to the matching funds law enacted by popular referendum, the

181 554 U.S. 724 (2008).
182 *See id.* at 744–45.
183 *Id.* at 742.
184 *Id.*
185 *Id.* at 741 (quoting Brief for Appellee at 33, Davis v. FEC, 554 U.S. 724 (2008)).
186 Ariz. Free Enter. Club's Freedom Club PAC v. Bennett, 564 U.S. 721, 736 (2011).
187 *Id.* (quoting Davis v. FEC, 554 U.S. 724, 736 (2008)).
188 *See* Timothy K. Kuhner, *Consumer Sovereignty Trumps Popular Sovereignty: The Economic Explanation for Arizona Free Enterprise v. Bennett*, 46 Ind. L. Rev 603, 612–32 (2013) (elaborating a theory of optimal, market-determined speech effectiveness within *Arizona Free Enterprise*).

Supreme Court chastised the people of Arizona: "the whole point of the First Amendment is to protect speakers against unjustified government restrictions on speech, even when those restrictions reflect the will of the majority. When it comes to protected speech, the speaker is sovereign."[189]

Sovereignty is ultimate power and control: the King possesses it in a monarchy, the dictator in a dictatorship, God and the high religious authority in a theocracy, the people in a democracy, and the wealthy in a plutocracy. *Buckley*, *McCutcheon*, *Citizens United*, *Davis*, and *Arizona Free Enterprise* all enthrone well-financed candidates, wealthy candidates, big donors, big spenders, and corporations. Justice Elena Kagan, for instance, rightly described the law at issue in *Arizona Free Enterprise* as "designed to sever political candidates' dependence on large contributors … [and] ensure that their representatives serve the public, and not just the wealthy donors who helped put them in office."[190] In other words, the law sought to reinstate popular sovereignty. When the Supreme Court responds that the will of the majority is unconstitutional and speakers are sovereign it means—quite plainly on the facts of the case—that large donors and spenders and wealthy candidates are sovereign, and the public may not abolish that scheme.

That brings us back to the 1896 definition of plutocracy with which we began: "a form of government in which the supreme power is lodged in the hands of the wealthy classes."[191] The natural advantage and sovereignty of the wealthy adds the final touches to a political system in which money is considered speech, democracy is construed as an open market, corruption is limited to specific instances of bribery, and ingratiation, access, and influence on the basis of wealth have obtained constitutional protection and ideological justification from the highest court in the land.

IV. THE POTENTIAL OF THE PRESENT MOMENT

Plutocracy has come again to America. This time around, in its third incarnation, it features some important innovations, beginning with its scope. First, unlike the Slavery Plutocracy or the Industrial Plutocracy, the Global Plutocracy knows no boundaries. Neoliberalism, at base, is the subjugation of all republics—all governmental forms even—to global capital. While the slave trade was international and some other American economic interests waged an international struggle for increased profits in the nineteenth and twentieth

[189] *Ariz. Free Enter.*, 564 U.S. at 754.
[190] *Id.* at 784 (Kagan, J., dissenting).
[191] WILLEY, *supra* note 1, at 35.

centuries, today's plutocracy has a broader reach and a more coordinated, more sophisticated set of policy demands. And where standard global capitalism and international economic institutions have a harder time taking hold, as in Chinese state capitalism, Russian oligarchy, and the least developed parts of Africa and Asia, government by or for the wealthy nonetheless surfaces, albeit in more authoritarian and kleptocratic varieties.[192] U.S. campaign finance reformers may not acknowledge it, but they are engaged in a major front of the global struggle for democracy's survival.

Second, on that home front, plutocracy has won an unprecedented victory. The *Dred Scott* opinion validated slavery and the sovereignty of the white race. The Lochner era validated some essential components of the Gilded Age. Both cases legitimized domination and exploitation, but neither explicitly defended the plutocracy that demanded and sustained those injustices. Our era represents the first time in American history that the Supreme Court has made plutocracy the official system of government. Never before has constitutional law defined money as speech, corporations as political speakers entitled to full First Amendment protection, democracy as political responsiveness to a natural order of wealthy sovereigns, and corruption as limited to the exchange of an official act for money.

Third, the fundamentally misguided case law of our era has lasted longer than its historical counterparts. *Dred Scott* was good law for less than a decade. The Lochner era lasted for 40 years. The Court's current plutocratic era has already lasted longer. Thirty-eight years passed between *Buckley* (1976) and *McCutcheon* (2014), and now, four years later, there is no sign that the Supreme Court will have a change of heart. Americans must not only confront the Court's stance; we must also act on the assumption that it will not change anytime soon.

Still, the commonalities between our three homegrown plutocracies outweigh their differences. None of these three moments in history has really been democratic or even republican. Consider what has happened each time: Popular participation has been officially restricted or unofficially neutralized by allowing elites disproportionate political influence. Economic and political inequalities have skyrocketed. Officeholders have indeed been responsive, but mainly to their own interests and those of their most powerful constituents. Representation has been repurposed. Government itself has been repurposed, becoming a private institution for the realization of the private interest.

[192] *See generally* Sarah Chayes, *Trump and the Path Toward Kleptocracy*, BLOOMBERG (May 22, 2017), www.bloomberg.com/view/articles/2017-05-22/trump-and-the-path-toward-kleptocracy.

In light of these crushing differences and similarities, some hopelessness is inevitable. The entire progression of abolition, universal suffrage, and the civil rights movement came and went without making campaign finance reform a top priority. The New Deal, post-World War II era, and the Great Society also came and went without making campaign finance reform a top priority. The historical lesson can be easily misinterpreted in this way: the people insist on universal suffrage, bare bones civil rights, and a modest, minimum floor of economic regulations and social entitlements, but they will demand nothing more. In fact, they will sit back while regulations and entitlements are reversed and voting rights are gradually hollowed out.[193] Americans will remain content to exercise their freedoms within a political system that has been comprehensively tilted away from liberty, equality, self-government, and representation for all.

But an alternative interpretation is more faithful to history. Slavery and Gilded Age capitalism were more oppressive regimes than American plutocracy is today, and yet Americans defeated those tyrannical regimes. When progressive elements banded together, they tapped into massive popular energy. And because those movements succeeded each time, history suggests that popular energy is more powerful than any economic or political disfiguration. At the outset, progress depends on the people awakening to their own predicament and the political tradition to which they belong. That tradition is not one of domination, but one of overcoming domination—a tradition of political transcendence.

It took nearly two centuries to achieve universal suffrage without state-sponsored obstacles. That is the time that unfolded between the Revolutionary War and the enforcement of the Voting Rights Act and Civil Rights Act in the early 1970s. That long trajectory began by overthrowing a colonial government to arrive at self-governance by our own crop of property-owning white men. The American political trajectory then progressed through many stages, including the abolition of the property requirement, the abolition of slavery, African American suffrage, female suffrage, civil rights and voting rights legislation in the mid-1960s, and the enforcement of that legislation in the following decade. Of course each progressive struggle left something undone for subsequent generations of Americans, but most generations embraced the tasks that fell to them. That collaboration across time—that intergenerational struggle to vindicate the same fundamental values across changing circumstances—is the finest, most virtuous part of American history.

[193] *See, e.g.*, JESSE H. RHODES, BALLOT BLOCKED: THE POLITICAL EROSION OF THE VOTING RIGHTS ACT (2017).

It is not difficult to locate what the past has left undone for the present. The political deformation that smiled upon slavery, child labor, mass poverty, and political exclusion—the systematic corruption driving these injustices—has never been singled out for elimination. Plutocracy's recurrence shows that a crucial piece of the democratic architecture has yet to be completed. This categorical, structural flaw has prevented gains in equality and self-governance from taking root, century after century.

Worse still, new and improved systems of domination will keep arising until Americans finally rule out plutocracy as a matter of law and public values. What could be worse than the Global Plutocracy? Surely, a global kleptocracy backed by authoritarian populists and dictators.[194] But even the comparatively gentle, neoliberal plutocracy could be consolidated, and public values more deeply altered, to the point at which submission and revolution would become the only viable options.

We cannot blame those who won the Revolutionary War, won the Civil War, redesigned the Senate, and achieved universal suffrage for failing to complete an effective regulatory structure for money in politics. Nor can we blame those who recovered from the Great Depression, created entitlements and restructured the economic system, defeated global fascism, and mounted a civil rights movement against disenfranchisement, segregation, and discrimination. They completed the biggest and costliest steps of the American journey.

Besides watching over and protecting the gains they made, those two and a half centuries' worth of committed Americans left us a monumental task. If we could only identify with them, see the world through the values we claim to share with them, and merge our public lives with theirs, then we might become protagonists in that one great American trajectory and guide self-governance to its next stage. That would prove the historical rule in full: that it is not just plutocracy, but also a triumphant progressive movement that is reborn time and time again.

In this third plutocratic cycle, progressive reformers are in a unique position. The momentous defeats suffered by the Slave Plutocracy and the Industrial Plutocracy stripped away the crude tools and value systems bound up with slavery, wholesale political exclusion, the unregulated workplace, and the unregulated economy. Reformers in the United States today do not have to penetrate the armor of slavery, partial suffrage, child labor, sweatshops, and corporate trusts in order to draw plutocracy's blood. Those institutions have been cast off and their racist, sexist, and classist justifications are finally wearing

[194] *See* Timothy K. Kuhner, *American Kleptocracy*, 28 KING'S L.J. 201 (2017); Chayes, *supra* note 192.

thin.[195] Government by and for the wealthy now steps naked into the light, out in the open at last. Plutocracy is especially vulnerable—in fact, for the first time in American history, the people are in a position to abolish it. That is the ultimate potential of campaign finance reform today: to fix democracy's greatest remaining structural flaw and end the vicious cycle of government in the private interest.

[195] Naturally, political inclusion requires more than just campaign finance reform. A partial list of other necessary measures would include: ending partisan redistricting, securing voting rights against retrenchment, facilitating voter registration, establishing a national holiday for voting in federal elections, abolishing (or reforming) the Electoral College, reforming sentencing laws to eliminate racial and class biases, and abolishing (or severely curtailing) felon disenfranchisement.

2

Liberty, Equality, Bribery, and Self-Government: Reframing the Campaign Finance Debate

Deborah Hellman*

I. INTRODUCTION

Campaign finance law is often framed as a tension between liberty and equality. On one side is the freedom of speech, which the Supreme Court has interpreted to include the freedom to give and spend money in connection with elections.[1] On the other is democratic equality and the idea that we are each entitled to an equal vote in choosing our representatives. Yet people have and spend vastly different amounts of money to influence that vote—a fact which seems to threaten the equality on which democracy rests. If this is the tension that underlies the current jurisprudence, it would appear that liberty has won out and equality has been vanquished. Ever since *Buckley v. Valeo*,[2] the Supreme Court has voiced skepticism about equality, asserting that "[t]he concept that government may restrict speech of some elements of our society in order to enhance the relative voice of others is wholly foreign to the First Amendment."[3] In the years since *Buckley*, especially recently, the Supreme Court has become more and more protective of the liberty interest that people have to give and spend money on elections.

* Deborah Hellman is the D. Lurton Massee Professor of Law and the Roy L. and Rosamond Woodruff Morgan Professor of Law at the University of Virginia School of Law. The author would like to thank both Gene Mazo and Tim Kuhner for their very thoughtful comments and feedback on this chapter.

1 While the Supreme Court in *Buckley v. Valeo* recognizes that expenditure and contribution limitations both implicate fundamental First Amendment interests, the Court treats the two as significantly different, subjecting expenditure restrictions to strict scrutiny review and contribution restrictions to intermediate scrutiny. The Court reasons that expenditure limitations substantially restrain the quantity and diversity of political speech, while contribution limitations still allow political expression of support and association. Buckley v. Valeo, 424 U.S. 1, 20–21 (1976).

2 424 U.S. 1 (1976).

3 *Id.* at 48–49.

But appearances can be deceiving. This facile contrast between liberty and equality overstates both what *Buckley* and subsequent cases have held, and it ignores the ways in which different understandings of these values are present in other aspects of our constitutional jurisprudence. A recognition of these other ways of understanding both equality and liberty allows us to see that the existing jurisprudence is both more complex and less definitive than it might, at first, appear. First, consider what exactly the Supreme Court had to say about equality. In *Buckley*, the Court: (1) rejected the idea that equality justifies restricting speech; and (2) did so because it rejected the view that equality is a foundational First Amendment value. These two positions, while significant, constituted only a partial rejection of equality, however, for the value of equality also underlies what one might call the Supreme Court's democracy jurisprudence. In particular, the requirement that voting districts be equal in size and the prohibition on charging voters a fee to vote both rest on the Equal Protection Clause and specifically on the idea that people are entitled to participate equally in electing their representatives. Thus while some campaign finance cases distance themselves from the value of equality, they can never stray too far. The equality that undergirds democracy is always nearby, and stands ready to exert a gravitational pull on the campaign finance cases.

What the campaign finance cases have to say about liberty is also not as straightforward as one might be tempted to assume. Campaign finance cases treat giving and spending money in connection with elections as protected by the First Amendment's Free Speech Clause. The freedom or liberty that is at issue here is an individual's freedom to be left alone, to be free from governmental interference regarding what the individual does with her money. While a very important aspect of individual liberty, the freedom from governmental interference is not the only type of liberty that our constitution protects. Nor is it the only type of liberty of historical significance. When Patrick Henry issued the famous call to "give me Liberty or give me death,"[4] the liberty he referred to was not the liberty to be left alone but instead the liberty of self-government. This liberty of self-government is central, not foreign, to the First Amendment.

This chapter argues that the constitutional doctrine relevant to campaign finance reform is broader than simply the list of cases dealing directly with laws limiting money in politics. It includes the equality-based doctrines governing political participation and the liberty-based commitment to self-government.

[4] Patrick Henry, *Give Me Liberty or Give Me Death* (Mar. 23, 1775), *in* THE AVALON PROJECT AT YALE LAW SCHOOL, www.avalon.law.yale.edu/18th_century/patrick.asp. Jane Mansbridge reminded me that Henry's reference to liberty refers to liberty as self-government.

This is important for two reasons. First, legislators and advocates can and should draw on these resources to support campaign finance restrictions. Second, when courts consider whether campaign finance laws are constitutional, they should remember that the equality of political participation and the liberty of self-government are also important constitutional values that can be brought to bear, along with the liberty of free speech, when deciding whether campaign finance restrictions can be upheld under current law.

II. EQUAL VOICE, EQUAL VOTE, AND EQUAL PARTICIPATION

At a superficial level, the Supreme Court's campaign finance cases reject the importance of equality. In particular, *Buckley v. Valeo* rejects the idea that some people's speech may be curtailed to ensure that others have an equal voice. In the 2014 case *McCutcheon v. Federal Election Commission*,[5] the Supreme Court quoted the passage from *Buckley* referred to above and reaffirmed its view that laws which restrict giving or spending money on elections cannot be justified by the desire "to enhance the relative voice of others."[6]

But before we abandon equality altogether, we should take care to parse exactly how the Supreme Court rejects equality and what sort of equality it rejects. Let us look at the famous passage from *Buckley* again: "[t]he concept that government may restrict speech of some elements of our society in order to enhance the relative voice of others is wholly foreign to the First Amendment."[7] What the state cannot do, according to this passage, is restrict speech to enhance voice—silence one person to better hear another. Taken at face value, this idea makes a lot of sense. Imagine telling a presidential candidate like Barack Obama that because he happens to be a skilled orator, he should speak less so that his opponent has a better chance to get the opponent's message out.

Nonetheless, some scholars have challenged the proposition that silencing some voices in order to hear others is anathema to the First Amendment. Public teachers tell some students to be quiet so that their less assertive classmates may be heard. Legislatures and courts follow rules that determine who may speak when and for how long. Perhaps an election is like these speech situations. If that were the case, laws that govern how much money can be spent on speech so that other speakers may be heard would be similarly justified.[8]

5 134 S. Ct. 1434 (2014).

6 *Id.* at 1450 (quoting *Buckley*, 424 U.S. at 48–49).

7 *Buckley*, 424 U.S. at 48–49.

8 *See* C. Edwin Baker, *Campaign Expenditures and Free Speech*, 33 HARV. C.R.-C.L. L. REV. 1 (1998).

Yet even if we accept the assertion in *Buckley* regarding equality and free speech, we should recognize that equality is rejected in only one domain—speech. The Court holds that we cannot silence to better hear, that we cannot restrict speech to enhance voice. But the Court does not, indeed cannot, reject the importance of equality as a constitutional value. After all, the Equal Protection Clause of the Fourteenth Amendment surely protects equality. So, while *Buckley* held that restrictions on giving and spending money on politics implicate the First Amendment freedom of speech, neither that case nor any other has said that freedom of speech is the only constitutional right at issue.

No one disputes that the Equal Protection Clause also has something to say about whether voting procedures are constitutional. For example, in the 1964 case of *Reynolds v. Sims*,[9] the Supreme Court held that the fact that the voting districts for the Alabama legislature were of vastly different sizes was a violation of equal protection. The Supreme Court explained its holding this way:

> [I]f a State should provide that the votes of citizens in one part of the State should be given two times, or five times, or 10 times the weight of votes of citizens in another part of the State, it could hardly be contended that the right to vote of those residing in the disfavored areas had not been effectively diluted… Of course, the effect of state legislative districting schemes which give the same number of representatives to unequal numbers of constituents is identical… Weighting the votes of citizens differently, by any method or means, merely because of where they happen to reside, hardly seems justifiable.[10]

This ruling, grounded in the constitutional mandate of equal protection, requires that state voting districts be of equal population in order to insure the equal weight of each citizen's vote.[11]

In addition, the Supreme Court has explicitly rejected laws that condition the right to vote on wealth or ability to pay on equal protection grounds. In *Harper v. Virginia State Board of Elections*,[12] the Supreme Court invalidated a state poll tax in Virginia, explaining that "a state violates [equal protection] whenever it makes the affluence of the voter or payment of a fee an electoral standard."[13] Moreover, the Twenty-Fourth Amendment to the

[9] 377 U.S. 533 (1964).

[10] *Id.* at 562–63.

[11] *Wesberry v. Sanders*, decided the same year, held that federal congressional districts also must be apportioned so that they have equal population. This case was decided on the basis of Article I, Section 2 of the Constitution rather than under the Equal Protection Clause. Wesberry v. Sanders, 376 U.S. 1, 17–18 (1964).

[12] 383 U.S. 663 (1966).

[13] *Id.* at 666.

U.S. Constitution similarly provides that the right to vote in federal elections may not be "denied or abridged by the United States or any State by reason of failure to pay any poll tax or other tax."[14] The rejection of malapportioned voting districts and poll taxes establish the constitutional norm that each person's vote should have equal weight and that wealth should not affect the exercise of this vote.[15]

If we bring these two strands of constitutional doctrine together, we might say that the Constitution demands that people have an "equal vote" but not an "equal voice." It is a nice distinction, if it holds. But recent Supreme Court cases put it in doubt. The campaign finance line of cases begins, as we saw, with the claim that people need not have an equal ability to speak so that they can give voice to their ideas. In addition, these cases assert that giving and spending money are aspects of speaking (voice) such that laws aimed at equalizing the way money affects politics are anathema to the First Amendment. Yet in two relatively recent cases, *McCutcheon v. Federal Election Commission*[16] and *Citizens United v. Federal Election Commission*,[17] the Supreme Court describes the act of contributing to a campaign as substantially similar to voting.

Consider *McCutcheon* first. In that case, the Supreme Court struck down "aggregate contribution limits"—legal regulations on the total amount of money that a person may give to all candidates and party committees in a given period of time. Chief Justice John Roberts, writing for the Court in *McCutcheon*, defended this decision on the ground that "there is no right more basic in our democracy than the right to participate in electing our political leaders," and went on to explain that the ways people participate in democracy includes the following: "They can run for office themselves, vote, urge other to vote for a particular candidate, volunteer to work on a campaign and contribute to a candidate's campaign."[18] The fact that the Chief Justice described "contributing" to a campaign as an act of political participation that is similar to running for office and voting is significant—it begins to sound more like voting than voice.

[14] U.S. CONST. amend. XXIV.

[15] There are exceptions to this norm which are provided for explicitly in the Constitution: the fact that both states with large and small populations are represented by two senators and the ways in which the Constitution provides election of the President and Vice President using the electoral college. U.S. CONST. art. II, § 1, cl. 2; *id.* art. I, § 3, cl. 1.

[16] 134 S. Ct. 1434 (2014). Chief Justice Roberts announced the judgment of the Court in an opinion joined by Justices Scalia, Kennedy, and Alito. *Id.* at 1440. Justice Thomas filed an opinion concurring in the judgment. *Id.* at 1463.

[17] 558 U.S. 310 (2010).

[18] 134 S. Ct. at 1440–41.

In *Citizens United v. Federal Election Commission*, the Supreme Court invalidated a law that restricted the ability of corporations and unions to spend money on elections.[19] Justice Anthony Kennedy, writing for the Court, described the importance of contributing to campaigns in a similar way: "It is well understood that a substantial and legitimate reason, if not the only reason, to cast a vote for, or to make a contribution to, one candidate over another is that the candidate will respond by producing those political outcomes the supporter favors. Democracy is premised on responsiveness."[20] But if contributing is a form of political participation that is like voting, then the constitutional norms that govern voting, rather than the constitutional norms that govern speaking, ought to apply.

In the case of speaking, the First Amendment forbids silencing some so that others may be heard. In the case of voting, the Equal Protection Clause requires that the weight of each person's vote be equal and especially forbids restrictions on voting based on wealth. But where does the political participation, comprised of giving and spending money, fit in? While *Buckley* characterized these activities as being similar to speaking, *McCutcheon* and *Citizens United* treated them as more akin to voting. If giving and spending money on elections are a form of political participation that is more like voting than speaking, then the Equal Protection Clause's guarantee of a right to participate equally in democratic governance ought to control.

Where does this leave us? Campaign finance cases explicitly reject the idea that the equalization of voice allows the government to restrict the speech of some to better hear others. Yet this doctrine exists alongside a robust democracy jurisprudence that recognizes the importance of equal participation in the political process. The activities of giving and spending money on elections sit uneasily between speech and voting; they are forms of political participation that are both expressive and participatory.

III. FREEDOM FROM GOVERNMENT AND FREEDOM TO GOVERN

The freedom protected by the U.S. Constitution includes two types of liberty.[21] First, there are the individual liberties defined by the Bill of Rights as

[19] 558 U.S. at 310.

[20] *Id.* at 359 (quoting his opinion in McConnell v. FEC, 540 U.S. 93, 297 (2003) (concurring in the judgment in part and dissenting in part), *overruled by* Citizens United v. FEC, 558 U.S. 310 (2010)).

[21] This material draws in part from Deborah Hellman, *Resurrecting the Neglected Liberty of Self-Government*, 164 U. Pa. L. Rev. Online 233 (2016), www.pennlawreview.com/online/164-U-Pa-L-Rev-Online-233.pdf. As explained there, the reference to two types of

well as the unenumerated rights guaranteed by the Fourteenth Amendment. The Court has interpreted these as including the right to use contraception or to abort a nonviable fetus, for example.[22] These are rights to be free from governmental interference in individual decisions and actions. This is a freedom *from* or what some scholars call a negative liberty.

In addition, the U.S. Constitution protects the liberty of self-government. When Patriots in Boston leading up to the Revolution called for "no taxation without representation,"[23] they asserted this form of liberty, a right to collectively and democratically determine the laws by which they would be governed. This liberty imbues the whole of the Constitution, but most especially the clauses that set out the manner in which representatives are elected and the powers they wield.[24] This is a liberty *to* govern ourselves, a form of self-determination, or what some scholars might call a positive liberty.

These "two concepts of liberty"[25]—freedom from and freedom to—together animate the U.S. Constitution. Both are also at issue when either federal or state legislatures enact campaign finance regulations.

Our campaign finance jurisprudence currently emphasizes only the first form of liberty. The freedom from state interference protects an individual's decision to spend her money to express her own views and to contribute her money to candidates, associations, and political parties of her choice.[26] But the second form of liberty—the freedom to govern ourselves—is also present in these cases. Its most ardent defender on the Supreme Court is Justice Stephen Breyer.[27] In his book, *Active Liberty*, Justice Breyer describes these two dimensions of liberty and emphasizes that we must not forget the second: "The United States is a nation built upon principles of liberty. That liberty means not only freedom from government coercion but also the freedom to participate in the government itself."[28]

liberty draws from Isaiah Berlin, *Two Concepts of Liberty*, *in* FOUR ESSAYS ON LIBERTY 118 (1969).

22 Griswold v. Connecticut, 381 U.S. 479 (1965); Roe v. Wade, 410 U.S. 113 (1973).

23 *See, e.g.*, DANIEL A. SMITH, TAX CRUSADERS AND THE POLITICS OF DIRECT DEMOCRACY 176 n. 13 (1998).

24 U.S. CONST. art. I, § 2, cl. 1; *id.* art. I, § 3, cl. 1; *id.* art. I, § 8.

25 This is the title of Berlin's essay. *See* Berlin, *supra* note 21. By "positive liberty," I mean here Berlin's early definition of the concept as self-government. *Id.* at 131–34. I do not accept the implications of his later argument, which stretches that concept to cover other meanings.

26 The freedom has been extended to corporations as well in *Citizens United*, an extension that remains controversial.

27 *See, e.g.*, McCutcheon v. FEC, 134 S. Ct. 1434, 1467 (2014) (Breyer, J., dissenting).

28 STEPHEN BREYER, ACTIVE LIBERTY: INTERPRETING OUR DEMOCRATIC CONSTITUTION 3 (Knopf 1st ed. 2005).

There are two ways in which the recognition of the constitutional importance of the liberty of self-government is relevant to campaign finance regulation. First, campaign finance legislation helps to secure the conditions that make self-government possible. Because the use of money by some individuals and entities may skew outcomes, campaign finance regulation helps to ensure self-government by making sure that the representatives chosen are those the people actually want and that the policies adopted are those people actually favor. If money, rather than the genuine preferences of voters, determines who is elected and what policies elected representatives support, our ability to govern ourselves is substantially compromised. When wealthy individuals and institutions spend large amounts of money on speech, their messages can dominate others and skew the outcome of democratic politics. In addition, when some individuals lack the funds to get their messages out, their views remain unheard.

The fact that money can skew democratic politics has been recognized in campaign finance law. For example, in *McConnell v. Federal Election Commission*,[29] the Supreme Court explained that "[j]ust as troubling to a functioning democracy as classic *quid pro quo* corruption is the danger that officeholders will decide not on the merits or the desires of their constituencies, but according to the wishes of those who have made large financial contributions valued by the officeholder."[30] While current doctrine seems to have rejected this line of thought, that rejection is not as definitive as one might think. Prior cases, including *McConnell*, located this concern about the influence of money on policymakers within their discussions about corruption. What sort of corruption is sufficiently compelling to justify restrictions on speech, these cases asked? *McConnell* and other cases concluded that distortions of influence and of officeholder judgment are forms of corruption.[31] In *Citizens United v. Federal Election Commission*, however, the Court narrowed the sort of corruption that justifies restrictions on speech to what it called "*quid pro quo* corruption."[32]

But the distortion of democracy that money in politics creates is not, or is not only, a matter of corruption. It is a threat to self-government as well. So, while the Supreme Court has rejected the distorting effect of money on judgment as a

[29] 540 U.S. 93 (2003).

[30] *Id.* at 153.

[31] For a discussion of these two conceptions of corruption and the case support for each, see Deborah Hellman, *Defining Corruption and Constitutionalizing Democracy*, 111 MICH. L. REV. 1385, 1396–402 (2013).

[32] Justice Kennedy, writing for the Court, states that corruption is "limited to *quid pro quo* corruption." Citizens United v. FEC, 558 U.S. 310, 359 (2010).

form of corruption, that holding is limited. When we are no longer talking about corruption, these cases no longer apply. Regulating money in politics not only prevents corruption, it also protects the liberty of self-government. This liberty is constitutionally significant. When laws involve both the freedom from governmental interference and the freedom to govern ourselves, the two liberties must both be given weight.

It was precisely this idea that led a three-judge federal district court to uphold the restrictions that Congress put in place to prevent foreigners from giving and spending money on elections. In *Bluman v. Federal Election Commission*,[33] the U.S. District Court for the District of Columbia considered a First Amendment challenge to campaign finance restrictions preventing foreigners from spending money to influence U.S. elections. While the District Court agreed that foreigners residing in the United States have First Amendment rights, it also found that because foreigners were not part of our political community, their rights to engage in certain sorts of activities could be limited. The court in *Bluman* drew on a line of cases restricting aliens from "voting, serving as jurors, working as police or probation officers or working as public school teachers."[34] According to the District Court's analysis, the principle that underlies those cases is this: "It is fundamental to the definition of our national political community that foreign citizens do not have a constitutional right to participate in, and thus may be excluded from, activities of democratic self-government."[35]

The relevant question then becomes whether giving and spending money in connection with elections is more like pure speech (a right that foreigners residing in the United States retain) or more like voting or serving on a jury (rights which they don't have). The district court in *Bluman* has no trouble answering that question: "In our view, the answer to that question is straightforward: Political contributions and express-advocacy expenditures are an integral aspect of the process by which Americans elect officials to federal, state, and local government offices."[36] The court in *Bluman* does not deny that expressive activity is at issue as well. The negative liberty to be free from governmental interference is certainly at issue for these aliens. But this case also implicates the collective liberty of self-government. When the two liberties are both involved, a court must balance them. This is precisely what the district court did in concluding that "the United States has a compelling interest for purposes of First Amendment analysis in limiting the participation of foreign citizens in

33 800 F. Supp. 2d 281 (D.D.C. 2011), *aff'd mem.*, 565 U.S. 1104 (2012).

34 *Id.* at 287.

35 *Id.* at 288.

36 *Id.*

activities of American democratic self-government."[37] Though it did not issue a written opinion, the Supreme Court summarily affirmed the district court's reasoning in *Bluman*.[38]

Campaign finance regulation aims to enhance self-government. As a result, courts considering the constitutionality of these laws must consider not only their effect on the liberty of free speech but also their effect on the liberty of self-government. The issue of how one treats contributions by foreigners brings this issue home, as we just saw. While non-citizens clearly have freedom of speech, if we mean by that the freedom to say what they wish without sanction, this freedom does not include the freedom to contribute money to candidates or to spend money to advocate on behalf of candidates. Why not? Because spending money on these activities also implicates the liberty of self-government, which as foreigners to our polity they have no right to enjoy. To preserve this liberty for members of the political community, foreigners are permissibly forbidden from contributing to candidates and from spending money to advocate on their behalf. The lesson we learn when we focus on contributions by foreigners is that giving and spending money on elections implicates both forms of liberty—the freedom from governmental interference and the freedom to govern ourselves.

The liberty of self-government is relevant to campaign finance laws in a second way as well. Besides the fact that campaign finance laws help to secure the conditions for self-government, such laws may constitute *fundamental* exercises of self-government itself.

The enactment of any law implicates the liberty of self-government to some degree. After all, the decision to adopt the law is an exercise of self-government. But some laws implicate this value more than others. One of the central decisions a polity makes is to set the boundaries of what is, and is not, for sale. For example, in our society today most goods and real estate are for sale. Yet some things are not; it is not permissible to sell votes, judicial decisions, and political decisions, for example. When the legislature determines that electoral, judicial, and political decisions may not be exchanged for money or other things of value, that choice should be afforded great weight because it is a *fundamental* exercise of self-government.

What do I mean by this? I use the expression "fundamental" to mirror the distinction between fundamental and non-fundamental liberties. The freedom from governmental interference is arguably also at issue any time a law is enacted that restricts what a person may do. Yet, as any first-year law

[37] *Id.*

[38] Bluman v. FEC, 565 U.S. 1104 (2012).

student knows, only some of these liberties are constitutionally protected—those that are "fundamental." My freedom to drive my car 80 miles per hour is limited by a state law that says I may travel no more than 65 miles per hour. The fact that the law limits liberty is not a constitutional problem because the liberty to drive fast is not constitutionally guaranteed. Why not? Because it is not a fundamental liberty. Similarly, every time a state or the federal government enacts a law, that polity exercises the positive liberty of self-government. All of these enactments should not command judicial deference.[39] Rather, some laws constitute *fundamental* exercises of the liberty of self-government and those that do are entitled to some degree of deference. These include decisions about the reach or scope of the economic market, determinations of what things are not, in our society, for sale.

The choice to wall off certain domains from the economic market is accomplished through two distinct bodies of law: criminal laws governing political bribery and campaign finance laws limiting giving and spending money on elections. Because both types of laws constitute fundamental exercises of self-government, both should be afforded deference by courts.

IV. THE UNCERTAIN RELATIONSHIP BETWEEN BRIBERY LAW AND CAMPAIGN FINANCE LAW

Bribery laws and campaign finance laws both govern when and how officials may accept money and other things of value. These bodies of law are related and have the potential to exert influence on each other in both good ways and bad. Yet how they are connected and how they affect each other is complex and underappreciated.[40] A better understanding of this relationship will illuminate how campaign finance doctrine may influence bribery law in ways that are problematic and will allow campaign finance reformers to see how they might use bribery law to exert influence on campaign finance doctrine.

People are legally permitted to give money to elected officials and candidates, and officials and candidates are allowed to accept this money so long as the money given is a campaign contribution. There are limits on the amount that may be given and accepted and rules that govern how the money is recorded and reported. At the same time, a person who "corruptly gives, offers, or promises anything of value to a public official," with the intent to

39 If it did, the power of judicial review would be eviscerated.

40 *See* George D. Brown, *Applying* Citizens United *to Ordinary Corruption: With a Note on* Blagojevich, McDonnell, *and the Criminalization of Politics*, 91 N.D. L. REV. 177 (2015).

"influence an official act," commits bribery.[41] Since a campaign contribution is surely something of value, the only way to distinguish the constitutionally protected campaign contribution from the criminal act of bribery is that the latter is given "corruptly." What makes such a gift "corrupt?" That is not easy to say.

I have attempted to provide an answer elsewhere.[42] For now, I want to highlight one specific way in which the two bodies of law intersect; understanding it offers opportunities for campaign finance reformers.

Ever since *Buckley*, the Supreme Court has held that restrictions on giving and spending money are restrictions on speech and are therefore justified only by a compelling governmental interest. In addition, the Supreme Court has held that the only governmental interest that is sufficiently compelling to justify such restrictions—*Bluman*'s treatment of foreign contributions and expenditures excepted—is avoiding "corruption" or its appearance. In the years since *Buckley* (which was decided in 1976), the Supreme Court has sometimes defined corruption broadly and sometimes narrowly. When it adopted a broad definition of corruption, campaign finance regulations were generally upheld. When it adopted a narrow definition, these laws were generally struck down.[43] Today we are in a narrow period. For example, in *Citizens United*, Justice Kennedy, writing for the Court, states that corruption is "limited to *quid pro quo* corruption."[44] In particular, the Supreme Court also emphasized that "[i]ngratiation and access, in any event, are not corruption."[45]

When these cases define what "corruption" is, they do so in order to answer a specific question. That question is this: what type of corruption is sufficiently compelling to avoid that preventing it justifies restrictions on giving and spending money on elections. The answer the Supreme Court provides is: only *quid pro quo* corruption, but not ingratiation and access.

This answer leaves open an important question. What if there is a *quid pro quo* exchange of money for access? Suppose an elected official and a prospective contributor make the following explicit agreement. The contributor offers to make a contribution if the elected official agrees that she will see the contributor whenever the contributor wishes. Is this *quid pro quo* exchange an instance of corruption? Or, because what is sought is (merely) access rather than something else, is it not corruption? In other words, when the Supreme

41 18 U.S.C. § 201(b) (2012).

42 I offer such an account in Deborah Hellman, *A Theory of Bribery*, 38 CARDOZO L. REV. 1947 (2017).

43 *See generally* Hellman, *supra* note 31.

44 Citizens United v. FEC, 558 U.S. 310, 359 (2010).

45 *Id*. at 360.

Court emphasizes that access is not sufficient for corruption, does it mean to say only that the fact that an officeholder provides access to contributors—voluntarily after a contribution has been made, for example—is not corruption *so long as* there is no *quid pro quo* exchange? Or does the Supreme Court mean to adopt the stronger view that an agreement to exchange money for access would not be corruption? The campaign finance cases do not clearly answer this question.

Now consider the criminal law side of this issue. The law of bribery (and other related offenses) determines what "official acts" office holders are forbidden to exchange for money or other things of value. These laws prohibit *quid pro quo* exchanges in which anything of value, including campaign contributions, is exchanged for an official act. This formulation gives rise to a question: can a legislature determine what exchanges are prohibited in any way it thinks best? And in particular, can a state explicitly prohibit the sale of access using a clearly defined bribery statute? I think the best answer to this question is probably "yes" but the recent case invalidating the conviction of the former Governor of Virginia, Robert McDonnell, on bribery charges muddies the water somewhat. Let us examine that case more closely.

On the last day of the 2016 term, a unanimous Supreme Court vacated the conviction of Virginia's former Governor Robert McDonnell.[46] McDonnell was charged with trading luxury items, including a Rolex watch and a shopping trip for his wife, in exchange for both setting up meetings and hosting events (access) for the owner of a dietary supplement company, as well as exerting pressure on public officials to make decisions that would benefit that company and its owner. Unfortunately, the jury instructions did not separate these two sorts of agreements—the agreement to provide access in exchange for goods versus the agreement to pressure other public officials to make particular decisions in exchange for such goods. The Supreme Court found that the first exchange (access for a Rolex, for example) would not violate the statute while the second exchange (pressure for a Rolex) would. Because there was no way to know whether the jury had found that the second type of exchange occurred, the Supreme Court invalidated the conviction.

In this opinion, the Supreme Court found that the exchange of money for access did not constitute bribery. However, the opinion is somewhat unclear about the basis for that holding. The decision might rest on an unremarkable exercise in statutory interpretation, as the opinion explains that the best understanding of the term "official act" in the federal bribery statute does not

[46] McDonnell v. United States, 136 S. Ct. 2355 (2016).

include merely setting up a meeting or hosting an event.[47] If statutory interpretation is the basis of the Court's decision, then Virginia or any other state could pass a new statute that clearly prohibits the exchange of money, goods, or campaign contributions for political access.

If *McDonnell* rests on statutory grounds, then the case suggests that a state could define bribery differently and, in particular, a state could determine that an agreement to exchange access for money constitutes bribery. Yet, in the campaign finance area, the Supreme Court has said that "ingratiation and access … do not constitute corruption." Do we have a conflict? Not necessarily. As I explained above, the pronouncement in the campaign finance cases could merely refer to access granted voluntarily after, or as a result of, a campaign contribution but not in exchange for it. If so, an agreement to exchange a campaign contribution for access would constitute both bribery (under our hypothetical statute) and corruption (according to the definition adopted in *Citizens United*).

In addition, the two bodies of law are, at least ostensibly, answering different questions. Bribery law sets out the legislature's view about what exchanges are impermissible. In the case of political bribery, or bribery of public officials, this is a view about what kinds of exchanges undermine democratic governance. The campaign finance cases are not addressing that question. Rather, these cases determine the sort of corruption that justifies restrictions on speech.

While there is no direct conflict between these two bodies of law if *McDonnell* rests on statutory grounds, understanding the relationship between them provides a way for legislatures to prohibit the sale of access by elected officials and, perhaps, to influence campaign finance doctrine using bribery law. Were a state or Congress to pass a law defining bribery as an agreement to exchange something of value, including a campaign contribution, for access to an elected official, the existence of this criminal law would make two important contributions. First, it would prohibit the sale of access—a desirable goal. Second, it would allow the public to contribute to the conversation about what exchanges are, in its view, corrupting democratic governance. These contributions could exert influence on the conception of corruption in campaign finance doctrine.

[47] The opinion draws in part on the language of the relevant statute and cannons of interpretation in order to give content to such terms as "question" or "matter" in the statute. *Id.* at 2368–72 (explaining that "question" and "matter" should be read using the "familiar interpretive canon *noscitur a sociis*, 'a word is known by the company it keeps,'" to conclude that those terms, like "cause," "suit," "proceeding," and "controversy," should be interpreted to relate to a "formal exercise of governmental power"). As a result, the Court concludes that "[s]etting up a meeting, talking to another official, or organizing an event (or agreeing to do so)—without more—does not fit that definition of 'official act'" from the federal bribery statute. *Id.* at 2370.

McDonnell does not rest unequivocally on statutory grounds, however. There is a suggestion, albeit tentative, that "[i]n addition to being inconsistent with both text and precedent, the government's expansive interpretation of 'official act' [to include access, for example] would raise significant constitutional concerns."[48] The Chief Justice appears to worry that interpreting the bribery statute to outlaw the exchange of value for access would "cast a pall of potential prosecution" over normal interactions between constituents and their representatives if those constituents had also made campaign contributions.[49]

The Chief Justice's worry illustrates the influence of campaign finance doctrine on the law of bribery. This is an unfortunate development. It is one thing for the Supreme Court to hold that the access money gives rise to is not the sort of corruption that is important enough to justify restrictions on speech. But it is quite another for the Court to conclude that a legislature may not prohibit the sale of such access. While the *McDonnell* opinion hints at a constitutional limit on the way that statutes may define bribery, these suggestions are for the moment only dicta.

V. CONCLUSION

The values of liberty and equality are both at stake when state or federal legislatures enact campaign finance regulation. The dominant way courts currently understand such regulations is by focusing on the fact that laws that restrict money in politics restrict the liberty of free speech. Because the freedom of speech is protected by the First Amendment, these laws can only be justified by a compelling governmental interest. And the Supreme Court has insisted that equalizing the ability of speakers to be heard is not a compelling governmental interest; indeed, it is not even legitimate. Our campaign finance jurisprudence would thus seem to represent the triumph of liberty over equality.

But that analysis is both superficial and partial. Equality remains a constitutional value. The Equal Protection Clause not only protects individuals from discrimination by the state, it also ensures that our electoral process is fair, that each person's vote counts equally, and that wealth, in particular, does not affect political participation. This democracy jurisprudence, animated by the value of equality, exists alongside the campaign finance jurisprudence and exerts some pressure on it. After all, campaign finance regulations involve both the freedom of speech and democratic equality. While the Supreme Court has rejected the idea that the First Amendment allows equalizing voice, it has at the same time embraced the idea that the Fourteenth Amendment's guarantee

[48] *Id.* at 2372.

[49] *Id.*

of equal protection requires that citizens have an equal ability to participate in electoral politics. Recent Supreme Court cases recognize that contributions to political candidates and expenditures on political speech sit precisely at the juncture between these two domains. These activities are a form of political participation that is between voice and vote. As a result, both freedom of speech and democratic equality are relevant to assessing the constitutionality of such laws.

Campaign finance cases have indeed emphasized liberty, stressing that giving money to political candidates and causes and spending money to speak both implicate the freedom of speech protected by the First Amendment. It is because "virtually every means of communicating ideas … requires the expenditure of money"[50] that the Supreme Court protects giving and spending money on elections. While it is certainly true that speaking often requires money and that the liberty to speak freely is at stake when laws limit political contributions and expenditures, this liberty is not the only relevant liberty at issue in these cases. Also relevant is the liberty of self-government. The liberty to govern ourselves is implicated in campaign finance laws in two distinct ways. First, campaign finance regulations help to secure the conditions for true self-government. By limiting the influence of money in politics, these laws help to ensure that the candidates elected and the policies they adopt are those that the people actually have chosen. Second, campaign finance laws are themselves fundamental exercises of self-government. Among the most important decisions a society makes are the decisions about what is, and is not, for sale. When legislatures determine that political decisions and votes are not for sale, they wall off politics from market influences. This foundational choice about the kind of society citizens want should be afforded special deference.

Citizens determine what is and is not for sale in their society indirectly through campaign finance laws and directly through criminal bribery laws. These two bodies of law are importantly related and therefore have the potential to influence each other—a fact that has not attracted significant attention thus far. This influence can go in either direction. The narrow definition of corruption adopted in recent campaign finance cases could affect what exchanges are considered bribery under criminal law. This would be an unfortunate result. But influence is possible in the other direction as well. Criminal laws could explicitly define the sale of access as bribery. These laws would then exert pressure on how corruption can be defined in campaign finance cases. Recognition of the interconnected nature of these bodies of law thus offers a possible strategy, within the boundaries of the current jurisprudence, to advance the cause of campaign finance reform.

50 Buckley v. Valeo, 424 U.S. 1, 19 (1976).

3

Aligning Campaign Finance Law

Nicholas Stephanopoulos*

I. INTRODUCTION

Here are some facts about money and politics in today's America. At the federal level, campaign spending totaled $8.7 billion in 2016.[1] Almost all of this funding came from individual donors, not corporations or unions.[2] Individuals gave about half of their contributions to specific candidates, a quarter to political parties, and a quarter to PACs and Super PACs.[3] These donors were in no way representative of the country as a whole. They were heavily old, white, male, and, of course, wealthy.[4] They also were far more polarized in their political views than the general population.[5] Most Americans were moderates in 2012, but most donors were staunch liberals or conservatives.[6]

However, there is no evidence that much of this money is traded explicitly for political favors. Proof of *quid pro quo* transactions is vanishingly

* Nicholas Stephanopoulos is Professor of Law and the Herbert and Marjorie Fried Research Scholar at the University of Chicago Law School.

1 *See Statistical Summary of 24-Month Campaign Activity of the 2015–2016 Election Cycle*, FEDERAL ELECTION COMMISSION (Mar. 23, 2017), www.fec.gov/updates/statistical-summary-24-month-campaign-activity-2015-2016-election-cycle/ [hereinafter *FEC 2016 Summary*].

2 *See* Stephen Ansolabehere et al., *Why Is There So Little Money in U.S. Politics?*, J. ECON. PERSP., Winter 2013, at 105, 109; Adam Bonica, *Avenues of Influence: On the Political Expenditures of Corporations and Their Directors and Executives*, 14 BUS. & POL. 367 (2016).

3 *See FEC 2016 Summary*, *supra* note 1.

4 *See* PETER L. FRANCIA ET AL., THE FINANCIERS OF CONGRESSIONAL ELECTIONS: INVESTORS, IDEOLOGUES, AND INTIMATES 16 (2003); Adam Bonica et al., *Why Hasn't Democracy Slowed Rising Inequality?*, J. ECON. PERSP., Summer 2013, at 103, 111.

5 *See* Joseph Bafumi & Michael C. Herron, *Leapfrog Representation and Extremism: A Study of American Voters and Their Members in Congress*, 104 AM. POL. SCI. REV. 519, 536 (2010); Michael Barber, *Representing the Preferences of Voters, Partisans, and Donors in the U.S. Senate*, 80 PUB. OPINION Q. 225, 237 (2016).

6 *See id.*

rare,[7] and studies that try to document a link between PACs' contributions and politicians' votes typically come up empty.[8] But there *is* evidence that politicians' positions reflect the preferences of their donors to an uncanny extent.[9] The ideal points of members of Congress—that is, the "unique set[s] of policies that they 'prefer' to all others"—have almost exactly the same bimodal distribution as the ideal points of individual contributors.[10] They look nothing like the far more centrist distribution of the public at large.

Suppose a jurisdiction is troubled by this situation and decides to enact some kind of campaign finance reform. What reason might it give? One option is preventing the corruption of elected officials. But the Supreme Court has recently narrowed the definition of corruption to *quid pro quo* exchanges,[11] and, as just noted, such exchanges do not occur with any regularity in contemporary America. Another possibility is avoiding the distortion of electoral outcomes due to the heavy spending of affluent individuals (and groups). But the Court has emphatically rejected any governmental interest in ameliorating "'the corrosive and distorting effects of immense aggregations of wealth.'"[12] Yet another idea is equalizing the resources of candidates or the electoral influence of voters. But this equality interest has been deemed invalid in even more strident terms. "[T]he concept that government may restrict the speech of some elements of our society in order to enhance the relative voice of others is wholly foreign to the First Amendment."[13]

So is our reformist jurisdiction out of luck? Not quite. This chapter's thesis is that there is an additional interest, of the gravest importance, that both are threatened by money in politics and is furthered by (certain) campaign finance regulation.[14] This interest is the promotion of *alignment* between voters' policy preferences and their government's policy outputs. Alignment operates at the levels of both the individual constituency and the jurisdiction as a whole. Within the constituency, the views of the district's median voter

7 *See* McConnell v. FEC, 540 U.S. 93, 149 (2003).

8 *See, e.g.*, Ansolabehere et al., *supra* note 2, at 116.

9 *See* Bafumi & Herron, *supra* note 5, at 536–37; Barber, *supra* note 5, at 236–37; Bonica, *supra* note 2, at 27.

10 Chris Tausanovitch & Christopher Warshaw, *Measuring Constituent Policy Preferences in Congress, State Legislatures, and Cities*, 75 J. Pol. 330, 331 (2013).

11 *See* McCutcheon v. FEC, 134 S. Ct. 1434, 1450 (2014) (plurality opinion); Citizens United v. FEC, 558 U.S. 310, 359 (2010).

12 *Citizens United*, 558 U.S. at 348 (quoting Austin v. Mich. Chamber of Comm., 494 U.S. 652, 660 (1990)).

13 Buckley v. Valeo, 424 U.S. 1, 48–49 (1976).

14 In earlier work, I have applied the alignment approach to election law as a whole. *See* Nicholas O. Stephanopoulos, *Elections and Alignment*, 114 Colum. L. Rev. 283 (2014).

and the district's representative should align. One step up, the preferences of the *jurisdiction's* median voter and the *legislature's* median member should correspond. Moreover, at the jurisdictional level, the median voter's views should be congruent not only with the median legislator's positions, but also with actual policy outcomes. *Preference alignment* refers to the former sort of congruence; *outcome alignment* to the latter.

Alignment is a significant—indeed, compelling—interest because of its tight connection to core democratic values. At the district level, it follows directly from the delegate theory of representation. A delegate "must do what his principal would do, must act as if the principal himself were acting … must vote as a majority of his constituents would," as Hanna Pitkin wrote in her landmark work.[15] In other words, a delegate must align his own positions with those of his constituents. Likewise, at the jurisdictional level, alignment is essentially another term for majoritarianism. To say that policy should be congruent with the preferences of the median voter is to say that it should be congruent with the preferences of the *majority*. Of course, majoritarianism is not our only democratic principle. But, as Jeremy Waldron has argued, it *is* "required as a matter of fairness to all those who participate in the social choice."[16]

Despite its intuitive appeal, some scholars claim that alignment is a forbidden interest—a slick repackaging of the anti-distortion and equality interests that the Court already has rejected.[17] This charge misses its mark. The distortion that cannot justify campaign finance regulation, in the Court's view, is the skewing of *electoral* outcomes due to large *expenditures*. The Court has never suggested that the warping of *policy* outcomes due to large *contributions* (or their equivalent) is an illegitimate basis for regulation. The distortion of *voters* is different from that of *representatives*.

Alignment also is distinct from equality (in all its guises). One form of equality is the leveling of candidate resources. But candidates need not be equally funded to produce alignment, nor does alignment follow from evenly sized war chests. Another kind of equality is equal representation for all voters. But it is only the *median* voter, not *every* voter, who is entitled to congruence under the alignment approach. Alignment at the median can arise only if there is *mis*alignment at all other points in the distribution. A final type of equality

15 Hanna Fenichel Pitkin, The Concept of Representation 144–45 (1967).

16 Jeremy Waldron, *Five to Four: Why Do Bare Majorities Rule on Courts?*, 123 Yale L.J. 1692, 1718 (2014).

17 *See* Richard L. Hasen, *Is "Dependence Corruption" Distinct from a Political Equality Argument for Campaign Finance Laws? A Reply to Professor Lessig*, 12 Election L.J. 305, 308 (2013).

is equal voter influence over the political process. But equal influence is, at most, a *means* to achieving alignment. It is not the end itself. Alignment also is possible under conditions of unequal influence, and equal influence does not necessarily result in alignment.

Assume, then, that alignment is a compelling interest that is not identical to goals the Court already has rebuffed. We are not done yet. The next step is to determine whether money in politics can generate misalignment, and whether campaign finance reform can promote alignment. According to a burgeoning political science literature, the answer to both questions is yes, at least sometimes. The relevant empirical evidence fits into two main categories.

First, as noted at the outset, politicians and donors have nearly identical ideal point distributions: highly bimodal curves in which they cluster at the ideological extremes and almost no one occupies the moderate center. Voters' views, in contrast, exhibit a normal distribution whose single peak is in the middle of the political spectrum. It is fair to say that donors receive exquisitely attentive representation—and that voters receive virtually no representation at all. It is also reasonable to surmise that the relationship between campaign funding and misalignment is causal, not correlational. The link remains intact even after controls are included for voters' preferences and non-monetary forms of participation.[18]

Second, campaign finance regulation can be aligning *or* misaligning based on its implications for how candidates raise their money. Tight individual contribution limits reduce the funds available from polarized individual donors. They therefore encourage candidates to shift toward the ideological center, the home of the median voter. Conversely, stringent *party* or PAC contribution limits have the opposite effect. Both parties and PACs are relatively moderate in their giving patterns—parties because their chief goal is winning as many seats as possible, PACs because they want access to incumbents of all political stripes. Reducing the funds available from these more centrist sources thus incentivizes candidates to move toward the ideological fringes. As for public financing, its impact hinges on its treatment of individual donors. "Clean money" schemes that provide block grants to candidates after they receive enough individual contributions are misaligning because of the extremism of the donors who initially must be wooed. But multiple-match systems that offer high matching ratios for small contributions may be aligning because of the more representative pool of donors they attract.[19]

[18] *See infra* section III.A.

[19] *See infra* section III.B.

What do these findings mean for the constitutionality of different policies? Individual contribution limits would sit on sturdy legal ground under the alignment approach. Whatever their link may be to the prevention of corruption, they demonstrably further the governmental interest in alignment. Unlike under current law, individual *expenditure* limits also might survive judicial scrutiny. Since politicians mirror the views of not only individuals who donate directly to them, but also individuals who spend on their behalf, no great significance would attach to the contribution/expenditure distinction. Public financing that relies on individual donors who resemble the general population (or that does not rely on individual donors at all) would be valid as well. On the other hand, contribution and expenditure limits for parties and PACs could not be sustained by reference to alignment. Since these entities are relatively moderate, their funds exert little misaligning pressure. Public financing that requires entreaties to polarized individual donors also could be justified only on the basis of other interests.

The chapter proceeds as follows. Part I introduces the alignment interest, describing the different forms it can take as well as the reasons why it is an attractive aim. Part II argues for the distinctiveness of alignment. It compares alignment to the interests the Court already has rejected—anti-distortion and equality—and shows that it is different from each of them. Part III conveys the current state of knowledge about alignment. It summarizes the many studies on the misaligning influence of money in politics, as well as the fewer studies on the aligning impact of (certain) regulation. Lastly, the conclusion assesses the implications of this literature for the validity of different campaign finance policies.

II. THE ALIGNMENT INTEREST

The term *alignment* is unhelpful until it is clear *what* should be aligned and *where*. In this part, then, I identify two axes that can be used to categorize different types of alignment. The first refers to the governmental output that should be aligned with voters' preferences; the second to the governmental level where the alignment should occur. After defining the alignment interest, I address a series of related issues: its democratic appeal, its administrability, its novelty, and its legal and practical limitations.

I note that my survey of alignment is quite brisk. This is because I have elaborated on the interest elsewhere, in work arguing for the adoption of alignment as an overarching principle of election law.[20] There is no reason to

[20] *See generally* Stephanopoulos, *supra* note 14.

repeat all of that analysis here. But there *is* reason to say more about alignment in the campaign finance context specifically. The interests the Court currently recognizes in this domain are insufficient to sustain much regulation, and the misalignment caused by money in politics is steadily worsening. The bulk of the chapter thus examines the intersection of alignment and campaign finance. Only this section deals with alignment more generally.

Starting with taxonomy, there are three kinds of governmental outputs that should be congruent with voters' preferences. The first is a representative's partisan affiliation. If a representative belongs to the party preferred by the median voter,[21] then there is *partisan alignment*. The second is a representative's policy views. If a representative has the same ideal point as the median voter, then there is *preference alignment*. And the third is actual policy outcomes. If enacted policy corresponds to the wishes of the median voter, then there is *outcome alignment*. Of these three variants, I address only the latter two in this chapter (and depict only them in Figure 1). Asymmetric campaign spending *can* cause partisan misalignment, by shifting electoral outcomes from what they would have been under conditions of more equal outlays.[22] But this is the one form of misalignment that the Court's precedent unambiguously rules out as an acceptable basis for regulation.[23]

Next, there are two governmental levels at which alignment should occur. The first is the individual constituency, in which the preferences of the district's median voter and the district's representative should be congruent. Since districts have (almost) no policymaking authority, only partisan alignment and preference alignment are sensible concepts at this level. The second is the jurisdiction as a whole, in which governmental outputs should match the preferences of the jurisdiction's median voter. With respect to partisan alignment and preference alignment, the relevant outputs are, in turn, the partisan affiliation and the ideal point of the median legislator. With respect to outcome alignment, the relevant output is enacted policy. As discussed below, both *dyadic* and *collective* alignment should be deemed valid rationales for regulation.

Why, then, is alignment an attractive value? The most important answer is that it is implied by several widely accepted theories of democracy. At the

21 The median voter is the voter at the *midpoint* of the relevant distribution. Only this voter necessarily represents the views of a majority of the electorate, and so cannot be outvoted by any other group.

22 *See* Stephanopoulos, *supra* note 14, at 338–39. In this case, misalignment ensues between the median *actual* voter and the median *hypothetical* voter exposed to more equal outlays. *See id.*

23 *See, e.g.*, Ariz. Free Enter. Club's Freedom Club PAC v. Bennett, 131 S. Ct. 2806, 2825 (2011); Citizens United v. FEC, 558 U.S. 310, 348 (2010); Davis v. FEC, 554 U.S. 724, 741–42 (2008); Buckley v. Valeo, 424 U.S. 1, 54 (1976).

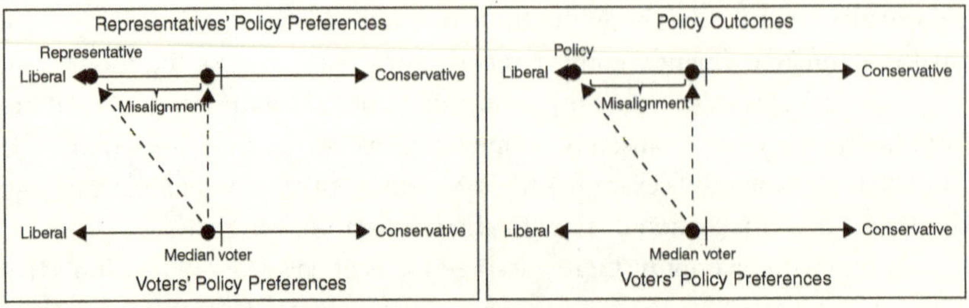

FIGURE 1: Illustrations of Preference and Outcome Misalignment

dyadic level, one of the classic conceptions of the representative's role is the delegate model. As the earlier quote from Hanna Pitkin illustrates, a delegate is supposed to act in accordance with the wishes of his constituents—to "do what his principal would do."[24] In the words of two other theorists, "The delegate theory of representation … posits that the representative ought to reflect purposively the preferences of his constituents."[25] Both of these formulations necessarily entail alignment. If a delegate does what his constituents want, he must be aligning his positions with theirs.

Likewise, at the collective level, one of the pillars of American democratic thought is majoritarianism. Madison stated in *The Federalist Papers* that the "fundamental principle of free government" is that the "majority … would rule."[26] Hamilton declared it a "poison" to "subject the sense of the greater number to that of the lesser."[27] In more recent times too, Alexander Bickel has remarked that we are "a nation committed to … majoritarian democracy,"[28] and Jesse Choper has written that throughout "this nation's constitutional development from its origin to the present time, majority rule has been considered the keystone of a democratic political system."[29] Once again, alignment follows from these arguments. If the wishes of the collective majority (embodied in the median voter) are heeded by officeholders, then governmental outputs must be congruent with those wishes.

To be sure, there are other theories of democracy with which alignment is in tension. The trustee model of representation holds that elected officials should exercise their own independent judgment, not abide by the preferences of

[24] PITKIN, *supra* note 15, at 144–45.

[25] Donald J. McCrone & James H. Kuklinski, *The Delegate Theory of Representation*, 23 AM. J. POL. SCI. 278, 278 (1979).

[26] THE FEDERALIST NO. 58 (James Madison).

[27] THE FEDERALIST NO. 22 (Alexander Hamilton).

[28] ALEXANDER M. BICKEL, THE LEAST DANGEROUS BRANCH: THE SUPREME COURT AT THE BAR OF POLITICS 188 (1962).

[29] JESSE H. CHOPER, JUDICIAL REVIEW AND THE NATIONAL POLITICAL PROCESS 4 (1980).

their constituents.[30] Pluralists argue that "minorities rule" as they join together in ever-shifting combinations.[31] Minimalist democrats downplay congruence in favor of retrospective accountability based on politicians' records in office.[32] And so forth. But the point here is not that alignment is *required* by democratic theory. It is only that alignment is *consistent* with key conceptions of democracy—and thus that jurisdictions should have the discretion to invoke it if they so desire. Alignment may not be an *obligatory* state interest, but surely its democratic origin makes it a *permissible* one

The other advantage of alignment is that it is more determinate than concepts such as corruption, distortion, and equality. As I explain in Part II, the Court has struggled for nearly 40 years to construe these terms, lurching unpredictably from one definition to another. In contrast, alignment quite plainly refers to the correspondence of a given popular input with a given governmental output. Per the above taxonomy, it is true that there are different inputs and outputs that can be aligned at different levels. But this only means that there are several kinds of alignment. It does not undermine the clarity of the idea itself. If "[a]n ounce of administrability is worth a pound of theoretical perfection," as David Strauss has quipped about justifications for campaign finance reform, then alignment may tip the scale.[33]

A skeptic might retort that alignment is theoretically determinate but practically hopeless. How, after all, are voters' policy preferences and their government's policy outputs even supposed to be measured, let alone compared to each other? Not long ago, this objection might have been fatal. But in the last few years, political scientists have made great strides in quantifying both public opinion and the activities of elected officials.[34] The most promising new work takes advantage of questions answered by *both* voters and representatives to plot their positions in a common policy space.[35] To the extent they pertain to money in politics, these studies are discussed in Part III. In sum, this scholarship leaves little doubt that, as a group of political scientists has written, "methodological advances [now] allow us to evaluate the congruence between voters and legislators across districts and time."[36]

[30] *See* PITKIN, *supra* note 15, at 127.

[31] ROBERT A. DAHL, A PREFACE TO DEMOCRATIC THEORY 132 (1956).

[32] *See* JOSEPH A. SCHUMPETER, CAPITALISM, SOCIALISM, AND DEMOCRACY 272 (2d ed. 1947).

[33] David A. Strauss, *Corruption, Equality, and Campaign Finance Reform*, 94 COLUM. L. REV. 1369, 1386 (1994).

[34] *See* Stephanopoulos, *supra* note 14, at 308 n. 102.

[35] *See id.* at 309 n. 103.

[36] Thad Kousser et al., *Reform and Representation: A New Method Applied to Recent Electoral Changes*, POL. SCI. RES. & METHODS 2 (Nov. 4, 2016).

But while the indeterminacy charge falls flat, there are other critiques (or, rather, caveats) that ought to be acknowledged. First, the alignment interest does not always support the lawfulness of campaign finance regulation. Policies that exert an *aligning* influence may be defended on this basis. But policies whose effects are ambiguous or misaligning—of which there are many—must be tethered to other interests or else face invalidation. Alignment does not give a free pass to challenged laws. Second, while no other scholar has argued explicitly for alignment as a compelling interest, the idea that money in politics may disrupt the link between public opinion and public policy is not new. It has appeared in the work of, among others, Richard Briffault, Bruce Cain, Samuel Issacharoff, and Lawrence Lessig.[37] What *is* new here is the framing of the issue as well as the systematic treatment of the theory, doctrine, and empirics of alignment.

Third, alignment is not, of course, the only available interest in the campaign finance context. The prevention of (a constricted notion of) corruption remains a valid basis for regulation, and the Court also recognizes an informational interest in providing voters with data about campaign contributions and expenditures.[38] Moreover, the anti-distortion and equality rationales may have been "orphaned," in Richard Hasen's phrase, but their resonance cannot be denied in a democracy that adheres to the principle of one person, one vote.[39] Fourth, it is important to be clear that money in politics is only one of many causes of misalignment in today's America. Even if the misaligning effects of campaign funds were eliminated entirely, significant noncongruence would persist thanks to franchise restrictions, partisan pressures, legislative rules, gerrymandered districts, etc. Misalignment is a complex phenomenon with no simple solution.

Finally, *perfect* alignment is an inherently unattainable goal. Even a jurisdiction (or representative) that cares about nothing else might lack information about voters' preferences on certain subjects, or be unable to change policies (or policy stances) at exactly the same rate at which public opinion shifts.[40] Voters' preferences on particular matters also might be weak, uninformed, or

[37] *See, e.g.*, LAWRENCE LESSIG, REPUBLIC, LOST: HOW MONEY CORRUPTS CONGRESS—AND A PLAN TO STOP IT 151 (2011); Richard Briffault, *Issue Advocacy: Redrawing the Elections/Politics Line*, 77 TEXAS L. REV. 1751, 1772 (1999); Bruce E. Cain, *Moralism and Realism in Campaign Finance Reform*, 1995 U. CHI. L. FORUM 111, 138; Samuel Issacharoff, *On Political Corruption*, 124 HARV. L. REV. 118, 126 (2010).

[38] *See* Citizens United v. FEC, 558 U.S. 310, 366–67 (2010).

[39] *See* Richard L. Hasen, Citizens United *and the Orphaned Antidistortion Rationale*, 27 GA. ST. U. L. REV. 989, 990 (2011).

[40] Alignment is thus not a recipe for stagnation or stasis because voters' preferences can and do *change*. In the face of shifting preferences, alignment can be achieved only if representation and policy change as well.

unstable—and so less worthy of respect from a democratic perspective (and more difficult to heed from a practical one). *Overall* ideological alignment, then, is more important than alignment on each individual issue that appears on the political agenda. Likewise, *persistent* misalignment is more objectionable than misalignment that is temporary and soon resolves.

III. THE DISTINCTIVENESS OF ALIGNMENT

In an ordinary field of constitutional law, the discussion could end here. Alignment is a weighty enough interest that a jurisdiction should be able to assert it in defense of a challenged policy. Campaign finance, though, is no ordinary field. It is unique, rather, because of the hostility the Supreme Court has evinced toward two other interests—anti-distortion and equality—that might, on their face, seem significant enough that a jurisdiction should be free to invoke them. Far from countenancing these interests, the Court has *proscribed* them, declaring them forbidden goals for a regulation of money in politics.

How alignment relates to anti-distortion and equality is therefore vitally important. If it is indistinguishable from them, as some critics allege, then the Court cannot be expected to recognize it (barring a doctrinal revolution). Accordingly, in this part, I explain why alignment in fact is quite distinct. With respect to distortion, the term (as used by the Court) refers to the skewing of electoral results due to asymmetric campaign spending. It has nothing to do with how money in politics may affect officeholders' positions or policy outcomes.

Similarly, equality comes in various forms, but none of them is synonymous with alignment. Equality of candidate resources is an entirely orthogonal goal; there is no reason why evenly funded candidates should be any more aligned with voters than unevenly funded ones. Equality of representation actually is inconsistent with alignment. For there to be any kind of congruence with the median voter, there must be *non*congruence with voters at all other points in the spectrum. And equality of voter influence may be conducive to the achievement of alignment, but it is just one of several possible means, not the end itself. It also is neither a necessary nor a sufficient condition for alignment to be realized.

A. *Anti-Distortion*

Notwithstanding its present pariah status, the prevention of electoral distortion has a long pedigree in the campaign finance case law. This interest first emerged in early decisions such as *United States v. Automobile Workers*, in which the Court expressed concern about the "deleterious influences on federal elections resulting from … large aggregations of capital."[41] It also turned up in decisions in the first decade after *Buckley v. Valeo*, in which the Court worried that the "corrosive influence of concentrated corporate wealth" would undermine the "integrity of the marketplace of political ideas."[42] But the interest did not come into its own until the 1990 case of *Austin v. Michigan Chamber of Commerce*,[43] which upheld Michigan's ban on campaign expenditures by corporations. The Court famously expounded on the "corrosive and distorting effects of immense aggregations of wealth … that have little or no correlation to the public's support for the corporation's political ideas."[44] *Austin*, however, stood for only two decades. Its holding that corporate expenditures could be limited was reversed in *Citizens United v. Federal Election Commission*—and the anti-distortion interest on which its holding rested was rejected as well.[45]

For present purposes, the crucial point about distortion is that, at least as understood by the Court, it refers to the skewing of *electoral* outcomes due to large *expenditures*. Distortion occurs, in the Court's view, when wealthy entities spend heavily during a campaign and thus induce some number of voters to cast their ballots differently than they would have under conditions of more even outlays. This conception explains why the *Austin* Court concluded its opinion by warning of the "threat that huge corporate treasuries … will be used to influence unfairly the outcome of elections."[46] It also explains why the Court, in other cases, highlighted the "governmental interest in reducing … the influence of wealth on the outcomes of elections"[47] and the risk that "wealthy and powerful" entities "may drown out other points of view" and "exert an undue influence on the outcome of a … vote."[48] As Julian Eule has observed, *Austin*'s theory was that "corporations spoke too loudly and wielded too much influence on the electorate."[49]

The definition of distortion matters because if the term denotes the skewing of electoral outcomes due to large expenditures, then it does *not* denote misalignment. Misalignment, again, is the lack of fit between voters' policy

[41] United States v. Auto. Workers, 352 U.S. 567, 585 (1957).
[42] FEC v. Mass. Citizens for Life, 479 U.S. 238, 257 (1986).
[43] 494 U.S. 652 (1990).
[44] *Id.* at 660.
[45] Citizens United v. FEC, 558 U.S. 310, 348–56 (2010).
[46] *Austin*, 494 U.S. at 669.
[47] Davis v. FEC, 554 U.S. 724, 755 (2008) (Stevens, J., dissenting).
[48] First Nat'l Bank of Bos. v. Bellotti, 435 U.S. 765, 789 (1978).
[49] Julian N. Eule, *Promoting Speaker Diversity: Austin and Metro Broadcasting*, Sup. Ct. Rev. 105, 109 (1990).

preferences and key governmental outputs. It accepts voters' preferences as they are, without seeking to convert them to some sort of pure or unadulterated state. It also compares voters' preferences to products of the political process such as officeholders' positions and actual policy outcomes. In contrast, *Austin*-style distortion does not take voters' views as it finds them. Its central aim is to determine how asymmetric spending *changes* these views relative to a hypothetical benchmark of more even outlays. *Austin*-style distortion also is indifferent to the positions that representatives adopt and the policies that in fact are enacted. Public opinion is its sole focus—not, as with misalignment, merely one side of the equation. Accordingly, it seems clear that *Austin*-style distortion and misalignment are not the same thing. The former cares only about the effect of campaign money on voters; the latter only about its impact on officeholders.

To be sure, *Austin*-style distortion is not the *only* kind of distortion that one could imagine. For instance, one could define an aligned political system—a system in which voters' policy preferences are congruent with key governmental outputs—as an undistorted state. Then any divergence from this state (that is, any misalignment) would constitute distortion. But the availability of such conceptual moves is not particularly relevant. The anti-distortion interest does not encompass every sort of skew that a commentator can concoct. Rather, it includes only the specific phenomenon that the Court has described in its decisions on money in politics: the shifting of voters' preferences as a result of lopsided campaign spending. Whatever the case may be for other types of distortion, *this* phenomenon simply is not misalignment.

B. *Equality*

Another key interest in the campaign finance case law—one long championed by liberals but never accepted by a majority of the Court—is equality. In *Buckley*, the Court considered equality justifications for expenditure limits on candidates and on individuals.[50] It spurned the justifications in both cases, declaring in perhaps the field's best-known line that "the concept that government may restrict the speech of some elements of our society in order to enhance the relative voice of others is wholly foreign to the First Amendment."[51] The Court adhered to its position on candidate equality in subsequent cases such as *Davis v. Federal Election Commission*[52] and *Arizona Free Enterprise*

[50] Buckley v. Valeo, 424 U.S. 1, 39–59 (1976).

[51] *Id.* at 48–49.

[52] 554 U.S. 724 (2008).

Club's Freedom Club PAC v. Bennett.[53] In *Arizona Free Enterprise*, faced with a "trigger" provision that allocated matching funds to publicly financed candidates if their opponents spent heavily, the Court commented that "it is not legitimate for the government to attempt to equalize electoral opportunities in this manner."[54] The Court also stuck to its guns on individual equality in *Citizens United*. Quoting *Buckley*, it reaffirmed that "the Government has [no] interest 'in equalizing the relative ability of individuals and groups to influence the outcome of elections.'"[55]

From these decisions (as well as the academic literature), we can glean three kinds of equality. The first is equality of candidate resources, referred to by Hasen and Daniel Lowenstein as equality of *outputs*.[56] This sort of equality is present when candidates have the same amount of money to spend in their campaigns, but is absent when one candidate enjoys a financial advantage over her opponent. The second, only hinted at in the doctrine but developed more fully by scholars such as Yasmin Dawood and Kathleen Sullivan, is equality of *representation*. This variant exists when every voter is represented equally, but not when "elected officials are disproportionately responsive" to their constituents.[57] And the third is equality of voter influence over the political process, dubbed equality of *inputs* by Hasen and Lowenstein.[58] Voters have equal influence (at least from a financial perspective) when they each are able to donate and spend the same amount of money. But they lack it when some voters are able to deploy greater resources than others.

Are any of these forms of equality equivalent to alignment? If so, then alignment would be an illegitimate interest under the Court's precedent, but I believe the answer is no. To begin with, equality of candidate resources (i.e., output equality) is an essentially unrelated concept. A candidate may disburse just as much money as her opponent during a campaign, but then flout her constituents' preferences once in office. Conversely, a candidate may outspend her opponent (or be outspent), but then abide by voters' wishes after being elected. There is no logical link between a candidate's relative spending and her subsequent alignment with her constituents. In fact, there is not

53 131 S. Ct. 2806 (2011).

54 *Id.* at 2826.

55 Citizens United v. FEC, 558 U.S. 310, 350 (2010) (quoting *Buckley*, 424 U.S. at 48).

56 *See* Hasen, *supra* note 17, at 312; Daniel Hays Lowenstein, *A Patternless Mosaic: Campaign Finance and the First Amendment After Austin*, 21 Cap. U. L. Rev. 381, 393 (1992).

57 Yasmin Dawood, *Classifying Corruption*, 9 Duke J. Const. L. & Pub. Pol'y 103, 125 (2014); *see also* Kathleen M. Sullivan, *Political Money and Freedom of Speech*, 30 U.C. Davis L. Rev. 663, 678 (1997).

58 *See* Hasen, *supra* note 17, at 312; Lowenstein, *supra* note 56, at 393.

even much of a *correlation* between these variables. Even if equal spending produces more competitive races, candidates who squeak into office are only barely more aligned with voters than candidates who prevail in landslides.[59] In addition, the effect of public financing systems that equalize candidate resources has been to *increase* misalignment, not to reduce it.[60]

Next, equality of representation actually is profoundly at odds with alignment. Alignment is the congruence of governmental outputs with the views of the median voter. As long as voters diverge in their opinions, such congruence can be achieved only if there is *non*congruence with the views of voters at all other points in the distribution. Alignment at the median requires misalignment at all other locations. Moreover, this conclusion holds even if we use Dawood or Sullivan's formulation of equal *responsiveness*. When the preferences of the median voter change, governmental outputs must change in tandem in order to maintain alignment. But when voters' preferences shift without affecting the position of the median, governmental outputs must not shift at all. Alignment thus is possible only if "elected officials" indeed "are disproportionately responsive" to their constituents.[61]

This leaves us with equality of voter influence, which is precisely the concept that Hasen claims is indistinguishable from alignment. Alignment, in his view, amounts to "a call for equality of *political inputs*," an effort to "reduce the voice of some to enhance the relative voice of others."[62] Hasen clearly is correct that equality of voter influence and alignment are related. To see why, assume that candidates' positions are entirely a product of the money that voters donate to them or spend on their behalf. (Assume also that candidates aim to maximize the sum of these donations and expenditures.[63]) Under the *status quo*, different voters deploy vastly different resources, and so candidates' positions gravitate toward the voters with the most funds to offer. But in a regime in which all voters offered the *same* funding possibilities, candidates would have a powerful incentive to shift their stances toward the median. The median is where candidates would be able to secure the most money, and, by stipulation here, resource maximization drives candidate positioning. Alignment thus would follow naturally from equal voter influence.

[59] *See* Stephen Ansolabehere et al., *Candidate Positioning in U.S. House Elections*, 45 Am. J. Pol. Sci. 136, 145 (2001).

[60] *See infra* section III.B.

[61] Dawood, *supra* note 57, at 125.

[62] Hasen, *supra* note 17, at 312.

[63] Assume further that all campaign resources are supplied by voters (and not by parties, corporations, unions, etc.).

Despite this connection, alignment and equal voter influence are not equivalent, largely for reasons that have been alluded to already. First, even if equal voter influence is a necessary and sufficient condition for alignment to arise, it still is just a condition, not the actual objective. It may *yield* alignment by inducing candidates to move toward the median, but yielding something is not the same as *being* something. It thus is beside the point that a regulation that promotes equal voter influence also may promote alignment. As Justice Elena Kagan pointed out in her dissent in *Arizona Free Enterprise*, "No special rule of automatic invalidation applies to statutes having some connection to equality; like any other laws, they pass muster when supported by an important enough government interest."[64]

Second, equal voter influence is *not* a necessary condition for alignment to arise. Imagine that a jurisdiction randomly selects half of its voters and gives each of them a sum of money that they must donate or spend during the next campaign. Imagine also that the jurisdiction bans the other half of its voters from deploying any electoral resources at all. The inequality of voter influence in this example could not be starker. Yet alignment still would ensue because candidates still would have a strong incentive to shift their positions toward the median. The random selection would make the distribution of subsidized voters identical to that of *all* voters, and thus would preserve the median as the point at which candidate funding is maximized.

Third, equal voter influence is not a sufficient condition for alignment either. If candidates' stances are wholly a function of the funds deployed by voters on their behalf, *and* if there are only two candidates in a race, then convergence at the median occurs under conditions of perfect input equality. But the introduction of additional candidates causes this relationship to break down. With three or more contestants, resource-maximizing candidates garner more funds by positioning themselves at different points along the spectrum, not by clustering in the middle (where they can be outflanked by their opponents). As Gary Cox has explained, "when there are more than two candidates competing under [standard American rules], equilibria are noncentrist; rational [resource]-seeking politicians have an incentive to avoid bunching at the median."[65]

Finally, the assumption on which the link between equal voter influence and alignment relies—that candidates' positions stem from the funds donated

64 Ariz. Free Enter. Club's Freedom Club PAC v. Bennett, 131 S. Ct. 2806, 2845 (2011) (Kagan, J., dissenting).

65 Gary W. Cox, *Centripetal and Centrifugal Incentives in Electoral Systems*, 34 Am. J. Pol. Sci. 903, 912 (1990).

to or spent for them by voters, and from nothing else—is obviously wrong. Candidates' positions actually stem from all sorts of other sources too: their own ideologies, their parties' platforms, franchise and party regulations, the views (rather than dollars) of their primary and general electorates, etc. In the real world, then, alignment does not necessarily follow from equal voter influence, even if candidates are hungry for resources and there are only two candidates per race. Equal voter influence may have an aligning *effect*, but so too may several other factors, and its impact easily may be offset by forces pushing in the opposite direction. Accordingly, equal voter influence has no stronger claim to constituting alignment itself than do any of the other aligning elements that dot the electoral landscape. It simply is one such element among many.

IV. THE EMPIRICS OF ALIGNMENT

It is not enough, though, to show that alignment is conceptually distinct from the anti-distortion and equality interests. No matter which interest is asserted in a campaign finance case, the Court carefully scrutinizes the *connection* between the interest and the policy that is being defended.[66] For alignment to serve as a viable rationale, it thus must be established that money in politics produces misalignment, and that the regulation of such money promotes alignment. The burden of proof also is heavier for alignment than for other, more familiar interests. As the Court made clear in *Nixon v. Shrink Missouri Government PAC*, "The quantum of empirical evidence needed to satisfy heightened judicial scrutiny … will vary up or down with the novelty and plausibility of the justification raised."[67]

In this part, then, I survey the empirical evidence on both the misaligning effects of campaign finance and the aligning effects of campaign finance *reform*. This evidence—most of which has emerged only in the last few years—falls into two main categories. First, several studies examine the relationship between governmental outputs and the preferences of donors and non-donors. Their results are quite unequivocal: The sway of donors dwarfs that of non-donors. Second, a handful of very recent analyses explore how regulations of money in politics influence alignment. They conclude that individual contribution limits and certain kinds of public financing are aligning, but that party and PAC contribution limits and other kinds of public financing are misaligning.

[66] *See, e.g.*, Nixon v. Shrink Missouri Gov't PAC, 528 U.S. 377, 387–88 (2000).
[67] *Id.* at 391.

A. *The Influence of Donors*

Beginning with the literature on donors, if there is one thing that political scientists have learned about the small slice of Americans who give money to candidates, it is that they are nothing like their peers who do *not* give money. With respect to demographics, surveys carried out by Peter Francia et al.,[68] Clyde Wilcox et al.,[69] and the Institute for Politics, Democracy, and the Internet[70] all have found that individuals who contribute at least $200 to federal candidates are "overwhelmingly wealthy, highly educated, male, and white."[71] In 2004, for example, 58 percent of these donors were male, 69 percent were older than 50, 78 percent had a family income above $100,000, and 91 percent had a college degree.[72] In 2012, these donors amounted to just 0.4 percent of the population, but supplied 64 percent of the funds received by candidates from individuals.[73]

Likewise, with respect to ideology, study after study has concluded that donors hold more extreme views than the public at large. While the ideal point distribution for the public is normal, with a single peak in the moderate middle,[74] the distribution for donors is strikingly bimodal, with one peak in the far left and another in the far right. This result is robust to multiple analytic approaches. It holds for donors to congressional candidates, whom Joseph Bafumi and Michael Herron[75] and Jesse Rhodes and Brian Schaffner[76] both surveyed. It holds for donors in all fifty states, as reported by Michael Barber based on the Cooperative Congressional Election Study.[77] And it holds as well if donors' views

68 *See* Francia et al., *supra* note 4.

69 *See* Clyde Wilcox et al., *With Limits Raised, Who Will Give More? The Impact of BCRA on Individual Donors, in* Life After Reform: When the Bipartisan Campaign Reform Act Meets Politics 61 (Michael J. Malbin ed., 2003).

70 *See* Inst. for Pol., Democracy, and the Internet, Small Donors and Online Giving: A Study of Donors to the 2004 Presidential Campaigns (2006) [hereinafter IPDI Study].

71 Francia et al., *supra* note 4, at 16.

72 *See* IPDI Study, *supra* note 70, at 12; *see also* Francia et al., *supra* note 4, at 28; Wesley Y. Joe et al., *Do Small Donors Improve Representation? Some Answers from Recent Gubernatorial and State Legislative Elections* 19 tbl. 1 (Aug. 28–31, 2008); Wilcox et al., *supra* note 69, at 65.

73 *See Donor Demographics*, Center for Responsive Politics, www.opensecrets.org/bigpicture/donordemographics.php?cycle=2012&filter=A.

74 *See* Bafumi & Herron, *supra* note 5, at 536–37.

75 *See id.* at 537.

76 *See* Jesse H. Rhodes & Brian F. Schaffner, *Economic Inequality and Representation in the U.S. House: A New Approach Using Population-Level Data* 34 (Apr. 7, 2013), http://people.umass.edu/schaffne/Schaffner.Rhodes.MPSA.2013.pdf.

77 *See* Michael Barber, *Ideological Donors, Contribution Limits, and the Polarization of State Legislatures*, 78 J. Pol. 296, 306 (2016).

are determined not through survey responses but rather through the ideologies of the candidates to whom they choose to contribute. Using this last approach, Barber, Adam Bonica, Nolan McCarty, and others have produced charts that reveal the bimodality of donor opinion in arresting detail.[78]

The distinctiveness of donors would matter less if they gave money for non-ideological reasons (such as personal connections or a desire for access). In this case, the *recipients* of the contributions would not necessarily be ideologically extreme, and the contributions would not necessarily exert a misaligning influence. But surveys carried out by Barber,[79] Wesley Joe et al.,[80] and Wilcox et al.[81] all found that the most important reason given by donors for their contributions is candidates' ideological proximity to them. As Barber put it, "ideological considerations are more likely to be rated as extremely important by donors than access-related motivations or motivations related to personal connections to the candidate."[82] In addition, studies by Barber, Michael Ensley, Bertram Johnson, Raymond La Raja, Walter Stone, and others all determined that the more extreme candidates are, the more money they raise from individual donors.[83] Donors' survey responses, then, are more than mere words. Their replies are corroborated by their tendency actually to contribute more heavily to candidates who share their immoderate views.

In combination, donors' abundant resources, policy extremism, and ideological giving contribute to severe misalignment in their favor. Bafumi and Herron used the voting records of members of Congress and the survey responses of donors to plot their ideal point distributions in a common policy space.[84] Bonica used data on who gave and received all disclosed campaign

[78] *See* Nolan McCarty et al., Polarized America: The Dance of Ideology and Unequal Riches 162 (2006); Barber, *supra* note 77, at 308; Michael Barber, Access Versus Ideology: Why PACs and Individuals Contribute to Campaigns 11 (Dec. 3, 2013) (unpublished manuscript) (on file with author); Bonica, *supra* note 2, at 27; Bonica et al., *supra* note 4, at 115.

[79] *See* Barber, *supra* note 78, at 307; Michael Barber et al., *Presidents, Representation, and Campaign Donors* 18–24 (Aug. 28–31, 2014), https://eslkevin.files.wordpress.com/2015/02/d5a48-apsa2014_donors_draft3.pdf.

[80] *See* Joe et al., *supra* note 72, at 22 tbl. 3.

[81] Wilcox et al., *supra* note 69, at 68.

[82] Barber, *supra* note 78, at 8.

[83] *See* Barber, *supra* note 77, at 308; Michael J. Ensley, *Individual Campaign Contributions and Candidate Ideology*, 138 Pub. Choice 221, 227 (2009); Bertram Johnson, *Individual Contributions: A Fundraising Advantage for the Ideologically Extreme?*, 38 Am. Pol. Res. 890, 899 (2010); Raymond J. La Raja & Brian F. Schaffner, Do Party-Centered Campaign Finance Laws Increase Funding for Moderates and Challengers? 19–20 (Jan. 8–11, 2014), https://polsci.umass.edu/people/faculty/ray-la-raja/working-papers; Walter J. Stone & Elizabeth N. Simas, *Candidate Valence and Ideological Positions in U.S. House Elections*, 54 Am. J. Pol. Sci. 371, 381 (2010).

[84] *See* Bafumi & Herron, *supra* note 5, at 522–26.

contributions to do the same.[85] Both studies found that the distributions of donors and members of Congress are more or less identical.[86] Their distributions are distinctly bimodal, again in marked contrast to the normal distribution of the general public.[87] Similarly, Barber used roll call votes and survey responses to determine the ideal points of senators, voters from each party, and all voters.[88] Senators, it turns out, are very distant ideologically from their state's median voter (who is represented only slightly better than a voter chosen at random).[89] They are substantially more aligned with the median voter from their own party.[90] But "[a]mong both Republicans and Democrats, the ideological congruence between senators and *donors* is nearly perfect."[91]

Barber's analysis suggests that the proximity of donors' and officeholders' views is causal rather than correlational. Since senators represent their donors better than their constituents or their co-partisans, the sway of campaign contributions must exceed the electoral incentive to appeal to the median voter or the partisan urge to please fellow party members. Additional evidence along these lines comes from Christopher Ellis[92] and Rhodes and Schaffner,[93] both of whom found that donors' preferences remain a significant driver of House members' voting records even after adding controls for voters' preferences and various forms of non-monetary participation. Still more such evidence comes from an experimental study recently conducted by Joshua Kalla and David Broockman.[94] They sent e-mails to House members, half from "local constituents" and half from "local campaign donors," asking to meet to discuss environmental issues.[95] Only 5.5 percent of the constituent e-mails resulted in a meeting with the House member or a senior staffer, compared to 18.8 percent of the donor e-mails.[96] More work on causation is necessary, but the existing literature does reveal a clear connection between campaign giving and misalignment.

85 *See* Bonica, *supra* note 2, at 26–28; *see also* Adam Bonica, *Mapping the Ideological Marketplace* 5–9 (June 25, 2013).

86 *See* Bafumi & Herron, *supra* note 5, at 536–37; Bonica, *supra* note 2, at 27.

87 *See id.*

88 *See* Barber, *supra* note 5, at 233–35.

89 *See id.* at 237.

90 *See id.* at 237.

91 *Id.* at 238 (emphasis added).

92 *See* Christopher Ellis, *Understanding Economic Biases in Representation: Income, Resources, and Policy Representation in the 110th House*, 65 POL. RES. Q. 938, 945 (2012).

93 *See* Rhodes & Schaffner, *supra* note 76, at 36.

94 *See* Joshua L. Kalla & David E. Broockman, *Campaign Contributions Facilitate Access to Congressional Officials: A Randomized Field Experiment*, 60 AM. J. POL. SCI. 545 (2016).

95 *See id.* at 5–7.

96 *See id.* at 9.

Lastly, the misaligning influence of individual donors may be growing over time. As noted earlier, the level of preference misalignment has surged over the last few decades (at least with respect to the U.S. House). Over the same period, the proportion of funds supplied to House candidates by individual donors has increased from about 50 percent to nearly 75 percent.[97] The share of individual donors who self-identify as ideologically extreme also has increased from around 40 percent to just over 60 percent.[98] These trends may be unrelated, but their juxtaposition still is striking. If individual donors are becoming both more vital to candidates and more radical in their views, then what we would expect for misalignment is exactly what we have witnessed: a steady, seemingly inexorable rise.

B. *The Impact of Reform*

That money in politics is misaligning, however, is only half the story. For the alignment interest to be a valid justification for campaign finance regulations, these policies actually must be *aligning*. If their effects are ambiguous (or worse), then they lack the tight connection with alignment that is necessary for them to be upheld on this basis. I conclude this Part, then, by discussing a series of very recent studies on the aligning implications of contribution limits on individuals, parties, and PACs as well as different kinds of public financing. This literature only now is emerging because the techniques for measuring voters' and officeholders' preferences previously did not exist.

But before getting to the studies' findings, it is important to complete the survey, begun above, of campaign funders' ideological inclinations. It should be clear by now that individual donors tend to be ideologically extreme, with starkly bimodal ideal point distributions. But what about the *other* two key sources of money in politics, parties and PACs? What do their policy preferences look like? Starting with parties, La Raja and Schaffner found that their views, at least as reflected in their committees' campaign contributions, are strikingly centrist. Parties donate about twice as much money to candidates in the middle of the political spectrum as they do to candidates at the edges.[99] The distribution of party giving by candidate ideology is distinctly normal,

[97] *See* Michael Barber & Nolan McCarty, *Causes and Consequences of Polarization, in* SOLUTIONS TO POLARIZATION IN AMERICA 31 (Nathaniel Persily ed., 2015).

[98] *See* Raymond J. La Raja & David L. Wiltse, *Don't Blame Donors for Ideological Polarization of Political Parties: Ideological Change and Stability Among Political Contributors, 1972–2008*, 40 AM. POL. RES. 501, 510 (2011).

[99] *See* La Raja & Schaffner, *supra* note 83, at 8, 14.

with a mode very near the ideological midpoint.[100] Of course, the *reason* for this pattern is not that parties prefer moderate over liberal or conservative policies. They plainly do not. Rather, the reason is that "parties put a premium on winning elections," and moderate candidates are more likely to prevail at the polls than extreme ones.[101]

Turning next to PACs, their ideologies (for the most part) are centrist as well. Barber[102] and Bonica[103] both used the positions of the candidates to whom PACs contribute to estimate the groups' ideal points. The resulting distributions were normal and unimodal in every case: for PACs that donated to state legislative candidates from 1996 to 2012,[104] for PACs that donated to federal candidates in 2012,[105] and for PACs that donated to *any* candidate over the 1980–2010 period.[106] Consistent with these findings, Bonica and Andrew Hall both determined that moderate candidates raise more money from PACs than do extreme ones. At the state legislative level, moderates raise about $12,000 more than liberals and about $7,000 more than conservatives.[107] At the U.S. House level, the advantage for moderates is about $46,000 over liberals and about $69,000 over conservatives.[108] PACs' ideologies, like individuals', thus are reflected in their contributions.

I noted above that PACs are centrist *for the most part*. The main exceptions to this rule are labor PACs, which are liberal in their orientation,[109] and single-issue PACs (focusing on abortion, taxes, the environment, and the like), which cluster at the ideological fringes.[110] However, these entities' donations are dwarfed by those of corporate and trade PACs, to which the rule applies in full.[111] Another caveat is that PACs' centrist ideal points may be the product not of actual moderation but rather of tactical giving to politicians from both parties aimed at securing access. There is some truth to this story; PACs give

[100] *See id.*

[101] *Id.* at 21.

[102] *See* Barber, *supra* note 78, at 9–11; Barber, *supra* note 77, at 308.

[103] *See* Adam Bonica, *Ideology and Interests in the Political Marketplace*, 57 Am. J. Pol. Sci. 294, 295–98 (2013).

[104] *See* Barber, *supra* note 77, at 308.

[105] *See* Barber, *supra* note 78, at 11.

[106] *See* Bonica, *supra* note 103, at 301.

[107] *See* Andrew B. Hall, *How the Public Funding of Elections Increases Candidate Polarization* 20–21 (Jan. 13, 2014).

[108] *See* Bonica, *supra* note 103, at 308.

[109] *See* Bonica, supra note 103, at 301, 306, 308; Bonica, *supra* note 85, at 21.

[110] *See* Bonica, *supra* note 103, at 301; La Raja & Schaffner, *supra* note 83, at 8, 14.

[111] *See Business-Labor-Ideology Split in PAC & Individual Donations to Candidates, Parties Super PACs and Outside Spending Groups*, Center for Responsive Politics, www.opensecrets.org/bigpicture/blio.php?cycle=2012.

more heavily to incumbents than to challengers,[112] and the variance of the ideologies of the candidates to whom PACs contribute is relatively high.[113] But Bonica[114] and McCarty et al.[115] both found that this variance is *not* as high as it would be if PACs actually were insensitive to candidates' views. PACs' motives for giving thus seem to be a mix of acquiring access and supporting like-minded candidates.

This typology of campaign funders' ideologies—in which individual donors are extreme, and parties and PACs are moderate—explains why certain campaign finance regulations are aligning and others are misaligning. In brief, regulations that decrease the relative importance of individual donors, or increase the relative importance of parties and PACs, are aligning. Conversely, policies that make candidates more reliant on individual donors, or less reliant on parties and PACs, are misaligning. Policies' aligning implications follow directly from their impact on the composition of candidates' funds.

Accordingly, as Barber found, contribution limits on *individuals* are aligning. The lower a state's individual limit is, the smaller the average individual donation is, the more individuals hit the contribution ceiling, and the less candidates raise from individuals.[116] As a result, a state that switches from no individual limit at all to some sort of limit can expect candidates' ideologies to shift toward the center by 0.1 to 0.3 units (on a -2 to 2 scale where -2 is extremely liberal and 2 is extremely conservative).[117] And a state that cuts its individual limit in half can expect candidates' positions to become 0.02 to 0.03 units more moderate.[118] These effects may seem modest but they actually are quite substantial. As Barber wrote about the impact of adopting individual limits in the first place, "This change represents 56% of the standard deviation of polarization scores."[119]

Next, as La Raja and Schaffner determined, contribution limits on *parties* are misaligning. Where such limits are present, state senate candidates receive a smaller proportion of their funds from parties, and a larger proportion from individual donors.[120] For moderate candidates in particular, party limits cause their share of party supplied funds to drop from above 8 percent to

[112] *See* Barber, *supra* note 78, at 15; Barber, *supra* note 77, at 307.
[113] *See* Barber, *supra* note 78, at 13.
[114] *See* Bonica, *supra* note 103, at 302.
[115] *See* McCarty et al., *supra* note 78, at 148–50.
[116] *See* Barber, *supra* note 77, at 308.
[117] *See id.* at 304.
[118] *See id.*
[119] *Id.* at 303.
[120] *See* La Raja & Schaffner, *supra* note 83, at 16, 19.

below 4 percent.[121] Consequently, party limits exert a centrifugal influence on candidates' positions, and the absence of such limits exerts a centripetal influence. Specifically, the median Democrat's ideology is 1.56 units apart from the median Republican's in state legislatures subject to party limits, but only 1.15 units apart in legislatures free from such limits (this time on a scale from -3 (very liberal) to 3 (very conservative)).[122] Party limits thus are associated with roughly a 35 percent increase in polarization.[123]

Analogously, as Barber also found, contribution limits on *PACs* are misaligning too. The tighter a state's PAC limit is, the smaller the average PAC donation is, the more PACs bump up against the contribution ceiling, and the less candidates collect from PACs.[124] As a result, a state that switches from no PAC limit at all to some kind of limit can expect candidates' ideologies to move away from the midpoint by 0.1 to 0.2 units.[125] And a state that cuts its PAC limit in half can expect candidates' positions to become 0.005 to 0.02 units more extreme.[126] These effects are sizeable as well: "[M]oving to unlimited PAC contributions shifts ... legislators' predicted ideal point ... [by] 70 percent of the standard deviation of [party] ideal points."[127]

This leaves us with public financing, two types of which have been analyzed for their aligning impact. First, Hall[128] and Seth Masket and Michael Miller[129] examined the "clean money" systems used in Arizona, Connecticut, and Maine. Under these systems, candidates who obtain a certain number of small contributions from individual donors then receive block grants that fund the rest of their campaigns. Publicly funded candidates also must abide by spending limits and accept no further donations. Despite their popularity with reformers, these schemes are misaligning because they eliminate most party and PAC contributions and make the grants contingent on candidates' appeal to individual donors. According to Hall, the gap between a Democrat and a Republican representing the same district (and the same median voter) jumps from 1.16 units to 1.51 units under clean

[121] *See id.* at 17.

[122] *See* Ray La Raja & Brian Schaffner, *Want to Reduce Polarization? Give Parties More Money*, WASH. POST (July 21, 2014), www.washingtonpost.com/blogs/monkey-cage/wp/2014/07/21/want-to-reduce-polarization-give-parties-more-money/.

[123] *See id.*

[124] *See* Barber, *supra* note 77, at 304.

[125] *See id.* at 37–39.

[126] *See id.*

[127] *Id.* at 39.

[128] *See* Hall, *supra* note 107, at 4–5.

[129] *See* Seth E. Masket & Michael G. Miller, *Buying Extremists? Public Funding, Parties, and Polarization in Maine and Arizona* 4–6 (2012) (on file with author).

money.[130] According to Masket and Miller, candidates entering the legislature after being elected with clean money often (but not always) are more polarized than their privately financed peers.[131]

Second, Elisabeth Genn et al.[132] and Michael Malbin et al.[133] uncovered tantalizing clues that New York City's multiple-match system may be aligning (though they did not measure alignment directly). Under New York City's system, contributions up to $175 from individual donors to city council candidates are matched 6-to-1 by the government.[134] Publicly funded candidates again must comply with spending limits, but they are not barred from receiving contributions from parties and PACs.[135] That these more centrist entities are not excluded from participation is one reason why multiple-match may perform differently than clean money.

The more important reason is that multiple-match transforms the pool of individual donors. Genn et al. compared donors to city council candidates to donors to New York City's state house candidates (to whom multiple-match does not apply).[136] They determined that the former are poorer (with almost the same poverty rate as the city as a whole), more racially diverse (with almost the same non-white proportion), and less educated (with almost the same share not completing high school).[137] Multiple-match thus attracts a much more representative group of donors than conventional private financing. Similarly, Malbin et al. found that city council candidates raise 63 percent of their funds from donors who give less than $250.[138] In contrast, U.S. Senate candidates raise only 14 percent of their funds from such donors, U.S. House candidates raise only 8 percent, and New York state legislative candidates just 7 percent.[139] This result also suggests that donors to city council candidates, unlike most other individual donors in American politics, may be a centripetal rather than a centrifugal force.

[130] *See* Hall, *supra* note 107, at 19.

[131] *See* Masket & Miller, *supra* note 129, at 15–19, 30.

[132] *See* Elisabeth Genn et al., Brennan Center for Justice, Donor Diversity Through Public Matching Funds (2012), www.brennancenter.org/sites/default/files/legacy/publications/DonorDiversityReport_WEB.PDF.

[133] *See* Michael J. Malbin et al., *Small Donors, Big Democracy: New York City's Matching Funds as a Model for the Nation and States*, 11 Election L.J. 3 (2012).

[134] *See id.* at 5–6.

[135] *See id.*

[136] *See* Genn et al., *supra* note 132, at 8–9.

[137] *See id.* at 14.

[138] *See* Malbin et al., *supra* note 133, at 15.

[139] *See id.*

V. CONCLUSION

This survey of the empirical literature has clear implications for the validity of the three main kinds of campaign finance policies—contribution limits, expenditure limits, and public financing—under the alignment approach. Beginning with contribution limits, they could be sustained on the basis of alignment when they apply to individuals, labor PACs, and single-issue PACs. As discussed above, these campaign funders hold ideologically extreme views and induce the recipients of their largesse to move in their ideological direction. Curbing their donations would thus have an aligning effect. Conversely, contribution limits on parties and corporate and trade PACs could *not* be justified based on alignment. These actors are ideologically moderate and push candidates who receive their funds toward the center of the ideological spectrum.

Next, it is harder to assess the lawfulness of expenditure limits since (with a few exceptions) they have not existed since *Buckley*. However, it is reasonable to assume that campaign funders have the same policy preferences whether they use their money on contributions or expenditures. It is also reasonable to assume that expenditures have an impact on candidates—albeit a smaller one than contributions, which enter their accounts directly. If these premises are correct, then donating and spending limits would have the same legal status under the alignment approach. They would rise or fall together for each category of funder. Accordingly, spending limits on individuals, unions, and single-issue groups (all ideologically extreme funding sources) would be valid, while similar restrictions on parties and businesses (both relatively moderate sources) could not be upheld by reference to alignment.

Lastly, the fate of public financing measures would also vary based on their particular design. Clean money programs could not be sustained under the alignment approach because studies have found them to be misaligning. Candidates' need to appeal to ideologically extreme individual donors to qualify for the public funds incentivizes them to shift their positions toward the ideological fringes—and away from the median voter. Conversely, generous multiple-match policies like New York City's might just be valid. It is clear that donors to city council candidates are very similar to the city's general population in terms of race, income, and education. If these donors also are *ideologically* representative (a proposition that has yet to be tested), then they would exert an aligning influence on the candidates who seek their support.

A final note is appropriate here about how doctrine would operate in a world in which the Supreme Court recognized alignment as a valid state interest. Crucially, alignment would *not* occupy the field, and jurisdictions would be free to defend their campaign finance policies on other grounds. So while contribution and expenditure limits on parties and businesses as well as clean money programs could not be justified on the basis of alignment, they absolutely could be upheld if they advanced some *other* compelling goal. One of the unfortunate hallmarks of the Court's current jurisprudence is its constriction of the range of available interests. If we are bold enough to imagine the Court acknowledging alignment as a legitimate objective, we should hope for the Court to be similarly receptive to other aims as well.[140]

[140] Note that none of this discussion would require the Court to reverse any of its earlier precedents. Since alignment has never been presented to the Court, it could be adopted without calling into question any previous decisions.

PART II

Proposed Solutions

4

Reforming Campaign Finance Reform: The Future of Public Financing

Richard Briffault*

I. INTRODUCTION

In his Seventh Annual Message to Congress on December 3, 1907, President Theodore Roosevelt proposed what he acknowledged was a "very radical measure": public funding of election campaigns. Roosevelt had previously urged a federal campaign disclosure law and restrictions on corporate contributions, and Congress had adopted a corporate contribution ban earlier that year. But Roosevelt warned that disclosure and contribution limits alone would not be enough to truly reform campaign finance. "[L]aws of this kind," that is, regulations of private campaign money, "from their very nature are difficult of enforcement," Roosevelt observed. They posed the "danger" they would be "obeyed only by the honest, and disobeyed by the unscrupulous, so as to act only as a penalty upon honest men." "Moreover," he continued, "no such law would hamper an unscrupulous man of unlimited means from buying his own way into office." Public financing would solve the problem of evasion and directly address the power of the wealthy. "The need for collecting large campaign funds would vanish," Roosevelt predicted, "if Congress provided an appropriation for the proper and legitimate expenses" of political campaigns.[1]

* Richard Briffault is the Joseph P. Chamberlain Professor of Legislation at Columbia Law School.

1 Theodore Roosevelt, Seventh Annual Message to Congress, Dec. 3, 1907, www.theamericanpresidency.us/1907.htm. Another powerful early call for the public financing of election campaigns came from Simeon Baldwin, governor of Connecticut and a founder of the American Bar Association, who emphasized the egalitarian value of public funding in opening public office to all regardless of wealth: "The cost of the struggle falls upon the man seeking the nomination … The obvious tendency of this is to shut out the poor man, unless he puts himself under what they would be apt to consider implied obligations to those who supply him the necessary funds." Simeon E. Baldwin, *State Assumption of Nomination and Election Expenses*, 23 YALE L.J. 158, 159 (1913). "We do not want a property qualification for every public office, either directly or indirectly." *Id.* at 163.

Roosevelt acknowledged "it will take some time for people so to familiarize themselves with such a proposal as to be willing to consider its adoption."[2] He was certainly right about that. The first bill proposing public funding of federal elections was not introduced into Congress until a half-century after his Seventh Annual Message.[3] It took another decade for Congress to take the idea seriously,[4] and public funding at the federal level became a reality only in 1974,[5] and even then only for the presidential election. In recent years, however, the presidential public funding system, which played a significant role in financing presidential elections in the last quarter of the twentieth century, has effectively collapsed. No significant presidential candidate in either major party accepted public funding in the 2012 or 2016 presidential elections.[6]

Public funding has made greater headway at the state and local level. At least three dozen states, counties, and cities currently provide some financial support for candidates for state or local office and, in a few jurisdictions, political parties.[7] In the last few years, candidates taking public funding won

2 Roosevelt, Seventh Annual Message, *supra* note 1.

3 *See* S.3242, Feb. 20, 1956, 84th Cong., 2d Sess.; "Federal Campaign Contributions to Relieve Officeholders of Private Obligations," 102 Cong. Rec. 2854–2855 (statement of Senator Richard Neuberger (D.-Ore.) (Feb. 20, 1956)).

4 *See* Presidential Election Campaign Fund Act of 1966, Pub. L. No. 89–809, 80 Stat. 1587–90 (1966). This measure—known as the Long Act after its principal sponsor, Senator Russell Long (D.-La.)—would have given each of the major parties $1 times one-half the total of the two-party vote in the preceding presidential election, minus $5 million. In 1964, the Democratic and Republican nominees together received 70.3 million votes. Half of that, multiplied by $1, would be $35.15 million, minus $5 million, would have been a little over $30 million for each party for the 1968 election. The Long Act was undone the following year, however, when Congress amended the law to provide that funds could be appropriated and disbursed to the political parties "only after the adoption by law of guidelines governing their distribution." Pub. L. No. 90-26, "An act to restore the investment credit and the allowance of accelerated depreciation in the case of certain real property," § 5, 81 Stat. 58 (1967). This effectively tabled the Long Act as no such guidelines were ever adopted.

5 Congress initially revived the Presidential Election Campaign Fund that had been created by the Long Act (see *supra* note 4) in 1971, only this time, it provided that payments would be made directly to presidential candidates, rather than to their parties as the 1966 law had provided. However, in a compromise with President Nixon necessary to secure the measure's enactment, its effective date was deferred until the 1976 election. Revenue Act of 1971, Pub. L. No. 92–178. Before it could take effect, the measure was significantly revamped in 1974 to provide more money to candidates, and to provide public funding for the presidential primaries and the presidential nominating conventions.

6 In 2016, Democratic aspirant Martin O'Malley qualified for primary matching funds and received a little over $1 million dollars, accounting for roughly 17% of his total funding, but he suspended his campaign after the Iowa caucus vote on February 1, 2016. Green Party candidate Jill Stein also qualified for primary matching funds and received approximately $465,000 prior to her formal nomination as the Green Party's nominee for President.

7 *See* Michael J. Malbin, *Citizen Funding for Elections* 5–6, 9 (Campaign Finance Inst., 2015).

races for governor in Hawaii[8] and Maryland;[9] Arizona, Connecticut, and Maine implemented extensive "clean elections" programs for statewide and state legislative candidates;[10] Minnesota restored a longstanding program of rebating public funds for small donations;[11] New York City, Los Angeles, and other large cities adopted and expanded programs that match small private donations to candidates for municipal office with public dollars;[12] Montgomery County, Maryland, enacted public funding for county elections;[13] and Seattle, Washington, and South Dakota voters approved "voucher" programs under which residents will be able to give public funds directly to the candidates of their choice.[14] To be sure, even at the state level public funding has suffered setbacks, with repeals of programs in North Carolina,[15] Wisconsin,[16] and Portland, Oregon,[17] and the South Dakota voucher program was undone by

8 Democrat David A. Ige received $105,164 in public funds in 2014, which accounted for roughly 5% of his total $2.03 million in expenditures. State of Hawaii, Campaign Spending Commission, Public Funds Disbursed in 2014, http://ags.hawaii.gov/campaign/statistics/public-funds-disbursed/public-funds-disbursed-in-2014/. Ige defeated both the incumbent Democratic governor in the primary and a Republican and other opponents in the general election.

9 In 2014, Republican Larry Hogan became the first candidate for governor of Maryland to run and win with public funds. He received a public grant of $2.6 million. The state Republican Party was allowed to spend an additional $1.8 million to support him. He prevailed even though he was outspent by his Democratic opponent, and the state Democratic Party spent $7 million against him. *See* Matthew Cella & Kellan Howell, *Larry Hogan Gets Unprecedented Win in Governor's Race on Public Financing*, WASH. TIMES (Nov. 5, 2014), www.washingtontimes.com/news/2014/nov/5/larry-hogan-vows-a-bipartisan-administration-in-mar/.

10 Nat'l Conf. of State Legislatures, Overview of State Laws on Public Financing, Clean Elections Programs, www.ncsl.org/research/elections-and-campaigns/public-financing-of-campaigns-overview.aspx.

11 *See* Malbin, *supra* note 7, at 7.

12 *Id.* at 5.

13 *See* Bill Turque, *Montgomery Council Approves Plan for Public Finance of Local Campaigns*, WASH. POST (Sept. 30, 2014).

14 *See* Bob Young, *'Democracy Vouchers' Win in Seattle; First in Country*, SEATTLE TIMES (Nov. 3, 2015), www.seattletimes.com/seattle-news/politics/democracy-vouchers/; Paul Blumenthal, *Voters Back Landmark Campaign Finance Reform in South Dakota*, HUFF. POST (Nov. 9, 2016), www.huffingtonpost.com/entry/2016-campaign-financereform_us_581d0d85e4b0e80b02ca2f31. *But see* Gregory Krieg, *South Dakota GOP Uses 'Emergency' Rules to Repeal Anti-Corruption Law*, CNN (Feb. 2, 2017), www.cnn.com/2017/02/02/politics/south-dakota-corruption-bill-republican-repeal/index.html.

15 *See* Adam Smith, *North Carolina Legislature Repeals Popular 'Voter Owned Elections' Program*, HUFF. POST. (July 26, 2013), www.huffingtonpost.com/adam-smith/nc-campaign-finance_b_3660472.html.

16 *See* Bill Lueders, *Campaign Financing Dead in Wisconsin*, WISCONSIN WATCH (June 30, 2011), http://wisconsinwatch.org/2011/06/campaign-financing-dead-in-wisconsin/.

17 *See* Paul A. Diller, *The Brief History of Voter-Owned Elections in Portland Oregon: If Public Financing Can't Make it There, Can it Make it Anywhere?*, 49 WILLAMETTE L. REV. 637 (2013).

the state legislature before it could take effect.[18] But overall developments at the state and local levels indicate public funding has become increasingly central to campaign finance reform.

At a time of considerable Supreme Court hostility to restrictions on private campaign money, public funding provides a clearly constitutional alternative. By subsidizing candidate spending rather than limiting it—although nearly all public funding programs require participants to abide by some limits—public funding is consistent with the Court's First Amendment framework for evaluating campaign finance laws.

Public funding addresses many of the traditional goals of campaign finance reform. By offsetting the financial role of large donors and interest groups, public financing can constrain inequality of influence within the election and, potentially, reduce the influence of large donors over government decision-making. By making it easier for challengers and political newcomers to raise money, public subsidies may make elections more competitive and diversify the pool of candidates. By reducing the need to engage in fundraising, public financing can free candidates and officeholders to focus more on meeting with voters and studying the issues, thus improving both the conduct of campaigns and the quality of governance. Some forms of public financing are geared particularly to promoting the engagement of small donors and low- and middle-income citizens in the political process, with potential benefits for expanding political participation that go beyond campaign financing.

To be sure, the key verb in the last paragraph is "may." In theory, public funding could have a lot of benefits, but it is uncertain whether and to what extent public funding in practice accomplishes these goals. That may be because the most significant public funding programs—in terms of the number of offices covered and the amount of funding providing—are few in number and relatively new in operation and so have not generated enough data to support clear conclusions. Moreover, the effects of public funding may be difficult to disentangle from other campaign finance developments, particularly the upsurge in outside money.

This chapter examines the place of public funding in democratic elections. The next Part explores the various forms of public funding and some common themes that cut across all public funding programs. Part III considers the constitutional framework that supports but also constrains public funding. Part IV reviews some of the evidence concerning public funding's effects on elections and governance. Part V concludes with an assessment of the future of public funding.

[18] *See* Krieg, *supra* note 14.

II. PUBLIC FUNDING: THEMES AND VARIATIONS

Public funding is a capacious concept. It could mean any use of public funds to cover or reduce the campaign costs of candidates or political parties. If a government were to assume responsibility for registering voters or to mandate that broadcasters provide candidates or parties with free airtime that could be considered public funding. But in contemporary American campaign finance parlance, public funding refers to the provision of government funds to candidates, parties, or voters for defined election-related purposes. Even when so limited, public funding programs exhibit considerable variation. Each jurisdiction that has adopted public funding has had to consider and make decisions concerning who should be eligible to receive public funds; how much public funding should be provided; what portion of campaign costs should public funds cover; and what conditions should apply to public funding recipients. No two programs answer these questions in exactly the same way, and the permutations among different programs are substantial, but a few generalizations are possible.

A. *Types of Public Funding Programs*

Broadly speaking, there are five types of public funding, although some jurisdictions further complicate the picture by combining elements of different types into distinctive, eclectic hybrids.

1. Full Government Funding. Full government funding of a candidate's election campaign is probably what most people think of when they hear the term public funding. In a full funding program, the government provides a qualifying candidate with a grant intended to cover all of the candidate's campaign costs. Once the candidate agrees to take the public grant, he or she generally cannot raise additional private funds or spend more on the campaign than the government grant. The presidential general election public funding program is one example of full funding. Once the candidate opts to take the grant, the candidate's general election spending is limited to that grant. The grant was set at $20 million in 1974 for major party nominees with an inflation adjustment that brought it to $96.14 million for the 2016 general election.[19] The paltry amount of the grant in light of current presidential campaign costs may

[19] A publicly funded presidential candidate may create a General Election Legal & Accounting Compliance (GELAC) Fund, and accept private contributions to the Fund which are used to cover the legal and accounting costs of complying with the rules governing public funding. In addition, the candidate's political party may engage in a limited amount of coordinated spending with the candidate.

explain why major party general election presidential candidates no longer take public funding.

State "clean money" or "clean elections" programs are also examples of full funding. Candidates qualify by raising a threshold number of small contributions. Each qualifying candidate then receives a lump-sum grant, with the amount depending on the office sought. Other than some privately raised "seed money" used to cover the expense of obtaining the qualifying donations, the public grant is intended to finance the full costs of the candidate's campaign. Candidates are required to accept a spending limit and the public grant is equal to that limit.[20]

By replacing private contributions with a large, lump-sum grant, full public funding probably comes the closest in theory to the reform goals of equalizing influence in the financing of campaigns, reducing the burdens of fundraising, and freeing government decision-making from the influence of campaign donors. But full public funding is "full" only for candidates who choose to accept it. Candidates cannot be forced to take public funding, and the decision of one candidate to take public funds cannot bind other campaign participants. Opposing candidates remain free to rely on private contributions or their personal wealth, and political parties and politically active groups and individuals are free to engage in unlimited independent spending that supports or opposes publicly funded candidates. Private money remains an appreciable part of the system.

2. Matching Funds. In this second model, the government matches small private donations to qualifying candidates up to some aggregate level. The candidate qualifies by raising a threshold number of small donations and by agreeing to certain restrictions and conditions. The presidential primary public funding program is a matching grant program. To qualify a candidate must raise at least $5,000 from donors in each of 20 states; thereafter the government will match the first $250 of each contribution with an equal amount of public funds, up to half the spending limit for the primary campaign (which is half the spending limit of the general election campaign). The public-to-private match ratio need not be limited to 1-to-1. New York City provides a $6 public grant for every private dollar for the first $175 of qualified contributions from individual city residents; this is the most generous match ratio in the country. The total amount of small-donor matching funds provided is typically capped at either a specific level or by a spending limit for participating candidates.

Matching programs assume some private donations, so they are less fully equalizing, even in theory, than full funding, and also assume continued candidate fundraising. On the other hand, matching funds programs, especially those

[20] For a list of jurisdictions providing full public funding, see Malbin, *supra* note 7, at 7.

with a multiple match ratio, can provide candidates with a powerful incentive to reach out to small donors, thereby potentially broadening and diversifying the donor pool. If full public funding scores higher on equalization, matching funds have the potential to be more effective in expanding political participation.

3. Partial Grants. Some programs are relatively modest in scope and simply offer qualifying candidates limited lump-sum grants. These are not intended to replace private funds and, because the size of the grant is not a match for small donations, they do not offer the same small-donor fundraising incentive as matching funds. The Hawaii program, for example, offers gubernatorial candidates a grant equal to 10 percent of the total campaign spending limits set by the state for candidates who take the grant, and a grant equal to 15 percent of the spending limits set by the state for publicly funded legislative candidates.[21] Other programs are more generous and may provide a grant up to half the spending limit.[22] These programs can provide a welcome boost to candidates who may initially have difficulty raising private funds but are unlikely to have transformative effects on elections or governance.

4. Rebates and Tax Incentives. Lump-sum grants pay public funds to candidates. Six states have taken a different approach, offering residents incentives to make small private donations to candidates. In five states, the incentive operates through the tax system, with the donor receiving a credit or deduction for a contribution to a candidate, or, in some states, to a political party or political committee. The incentives vary but are typically on the order of $50 dollars per tax filer (or $100 for a joint return). For a dozen years until repealed in 1986, federal law also offered tax incentives to small donors.[23] As with matching funds, tax breaks for small donations give candidates an incentive to solicit donations more broadly. The most successful of these programs has been Minnesota's, which gives donors an immediate cash rebate for donations of up to $50 per year, without requiring the donor to seek a credit or incentive through filing a state income tax return.[24]

5. Vouchers. With tax incentives (other than the Minnesota rebate, which is linked to a grant of public funds), the donors get to decide which candidates benefit from the incentive. But the donor has to provide the money upfront

[21] Haw. Rev. Stat. § 11–425.

[22] *See* Malbin, *supra* note 7, at 7.

[23] *See generally* David H. Gans, *Tax Credit for $200 in Political Giving Could Encourage Small Donors*, L.A. Times (Apr. 13, 2015), www.latimes.com/opinion/op-ed/la-oe-gans-campaign-finance-tax-credit-20150114-story.html.

[24] *See generally* Malbin, *supra* note 7, at 8–9.

and get the tax benefit later, which may limit who can participate. Moreover, incentives that work through the tax system provide a greater benefit to those with tax liabilities that can be reduced by a credit or deduction.[25] Voucher plans address these concerns. In a voucher program, the government issues eligible residents or voters vouchers worth a certain amount, which the recipients can give to candidates. The candidates, in turn, can redeem the vouchers with the government of the relevant jurisdiction for money to be used to pay for campaign expenses.[26] Like tax incentives, vouchers would enable the voters to decide who receives public support and how much, but, by giving every voter some public money for use in campaigns, vouchers are more egalitarian. In November 2015, Seattle became the first American jurisdiction to adopt a voucher plan, which was first used in Seattle's 2017 municipal elections. Four $25 "democracy vouchers" were sent to all eligible residents. The vouchers were transferrable to any "qualifying candidate" who agreed to accepted a spending limit and to limit the dollar value of donations he or she accepts from any private donors.[27] In November 2016, South Dakota voters approved Initiated Measure 22, which would have provided registered voters two $50 "democracy credits" to give to candidates who agreed to limit the use of their personal wealth and the size of the private contributions they receive; however, the South Dakota legislature subsequently repealed the plan.[28]

[25] To address the concern that tax credits disproportionately benefit the affluent, Oregon in 2014 amended its program to provide that its tax credit can be used only by those with an income below $100,000. See *id.* Of course, that may reduce the usefulness of the program to candidates.

[26] *See, e.g.*, Bruce Ackerman & Ian Ayres, Voting with Dollars: A New Paradigm for Campaign Finance (2002).

[27] *See* Seattle Democracy Voucher Program, www.seattle.gov/democracyvoucher. A qualifying candidate would also have to obtain a threshold number of ten-dollar contributions from adult residents of Seattle, agree to participate in debates, and agree to refrain from soliciting funds for an independent expenditure committee during the same election cycle. In 2017, candidates for three offices up for election—two at-large city council seats and city attorney—were eligible to participate in the voucher program. Although the office of mayor was also up for election, the voter initiative had specifically provided that in order to allow the accumulation of program funds, mayoral candidates would be unable to participate in the program in 2017. *See* Ron Fein, *The Impact of Seattle's Voucher Program on Candidates' Ability to Rely on Constituents for Fundraising*, Free Speech for People Issue Report 2018-01 (May 2018), https://freespeechforpeople.org/wp-content/uploads/2018/05/FSFP-Issue-Report-2018_1.pdf.

[28] *See* S.D. Att'y Gen. Statement on Initiated Measure (Sept. 25, 2015), https://sdsos.gov/elections-voting/assets/2016_IM_CampFinLobbyingLaws.pdf.

B. *Common Themes*

Although public funding programs have taken a range of forms, they exhibit a number of common themes.

1. SPENDING LIMITS. With a single exception, all of the programs that give public funds directly to candidates require that a candidate must agree to a spending limit to qualify for funds.[29] The Minnesota rebate plan and the Seattle voucher plan also require participating candidates to accept a spending limit.[30] A spending limit is inherent in a full public funding program. If the public grant is intended to fully replace private funds, then the amount of the grant automatically becomes a spending limit. This requirement no doubt reflects the egalitarian impetus that generally drives public funding, as spending limits tend to equalize candidate resources. Spending limits, however, are not logically entailed in other forms of public funding, which all assume that participating candidates will raise and spend some privately provided funds. And with public funding necessarily optional, a spending limit may discourage participation by candidates who fear a high-spending, privately funded opponent whom the limit may prevent them from matching. A number of jurisdictions sought to address this problem by giving publicly funded candidates additional funds—a solution that, as we will see in the next Part, the Supreme Court ultimately rejected.

2. OTHER CONDITIONS. Some jurisdictions impose additional requirements on candidates who take public funding. The most common are that candidates agree to participate in debates, that private contributions to the candidate in a partial public funding scheme are capped at a level lower than that for non-publicly funded candidates, and that the candidate limit or refrain from accepting donations from certain otherwise legal sources, such as political action committees or the candidate's own personal funds.[31] As with the spending limit, public funds are used as a carrot to induce other election reform goals.

3. CANDIDATE FOCUS. Public funding in the United States is largely focused on payments to candidates, not parties. This distinguishes American programs from other public funding programs around the world, which usually provide funds or in-kind benefits to political parties. The American approach is

[29] The sole exception is the matching grant program for candidates for municipal office in Richmond, California. *See* Malbin, *supra* note 7, at 5.

[30] *See id.* at 9; Seattle Democracy Voucher Program, *supra* note 27.

[31] *See* Malbin, *supra* note 7, at 5–6.

consistent with the candidate-centered nature of our election campaigns. It also reflects the fact that internal party elections—that is, party primaries—play a major role in selecting party nominees. Any public funding program for primaries would have to provide money to candidates, not parties.

There have been some efforts to give parties public financial support. The federal presidential public funding program originally provided grants to cover the costs of the national party nominating conventions. Over time, private funds raised by the convention city "host committees" overshadowed the public grant and in 2014 Congress repealed convention public funding[32] and replaced it with an amendment to the Federal Election Campaign Act allowing very large private donations to special accounts created by the parties to fund the conventions.[33] Some state tax-benefit programs and Minnesota's rebate provide some very modest funding for political parties. No state provides flat grants or matching funds to the parties.[34]

III. THE CONSTITUTIONAL FRAMEWORK

The Supreme Court has considered constitutional questions concerning public funding four times. In *Buckley v. Valeo*, the Court held that public financing of campaigns falls within Congress's power under the General Welfare Clause.[35] The Court determined that public funding advances three.general welfare goals: reducing "the deleterious influence of large contributions on our political process," "facilitat[ing] communication by candidates with the electorate," and "free[ing] candidates from the rigors of fundraising."[36] The Court went on to find that "public financing as a means of eliminating the improper influence of large private contributions furthers a significant government interest."[37] The Court summarily rejected the argument that giving

32 Pub. L. No. 113–94 (Apr. 3, 2014).

33 The continuing resolution omnibus budget legislation passed at the end of 2014 allowed individuals to donate up to triple the ordinary contribution limit on donations to national party committees to special accounts dedicated to funding the presidential nominating conventions, election recounts and other legal proceedings, and the national party headquarters buildings. *See, e.g.*, Matea Gold, *Spending Deal Would Allow Wealthy Donors to Dramatically Increase Giving to National Parties*, WASH. POST (Dec. 9, 2014). As a result, in 2016 individuals could donate $100,200 to each of these accounts, in addition to the $33,400 annual donation permitted to the party committee itself. *See* *Quick Answers to General Questions*, FEDERAL ELECTION COMMISSION, www.fec.gov/ans/answers_general.shtml#How_much_can_I_contribute.

34 Malbin, *supra* note 7, at 5.

35 424 U.S. 1, 90–91 (1976).

36 *Id.* at 91.

37 *Id.* at 96.

public money to candidates and parties violates the First Amendment "by analogy" to the ban on the establishment of religion.[38] So, too, it dismissed the argument that public funding would "lead to governmental control of the internal affairs of political parties, and thus to a significant loss of political freedom."[39] The Court found that public funding does "not abridge, restrict or censor speech" but instead "facilitate[s] and enlarge[s] public discussion and participation in the electoral process, goals vital to a self-governing people."[40]

Buckley upheld specific components of the presidential public funding program, including the candidate spending limit and the statutory formulas for determining which candidates are eligible to receive public funds and how much they can receive. Although the Court had determined that limits on how much candidates or independent groups can spend are unconstitutional, it easily upheld spending limits as a condition for public funding, finding them to be voluntarily accepted by the candidate rather than imposed by the government.[41] The Court also found that different-sized grants could be provided to the nominees of major and minor parties and that eligibility for public funds could be conditioned on some showing of political viability or past electoral success. In the Court's words, Congress need not "fund[] hopeless candidacies with large sums of public money" or provide assistance to "candidates without significant public support."[42]

The Court went on to consider two more public funding cases in the decade immediately after *Buckley*. In *Republican National Committee (RNC) v. Federal Election Commission*,[43] the Court summarily affirmed a three-judge court decision rejecting the claim that in practice—as evidenced by the significant participation in the presidential public funding program in the 1976 election—candidates were coerced into accepting public funds. In so doing, the Court also sustained the provision of the public funding law limiting coordinated spending by a political party whose candidate accepted public funds.[44] Five years later, in *Federal Election Commission v. National Conservative Political Action Committee (NCPAC)*,[45] the Court invalidated the provision of the presidential public funding law that limited independent expenditures in support of or opposition to a publicly funded candidate to

[38] *Id.* at 92.
[39] *Id.* at 93 n. 126.
[40] *Id.* at 92–93.
[41] *Id.* at 57 n. 65.
[42] *Id.* at 96.
[43] 445 U.S. 955 (1980).
[44] *Id.* (*aff'g* Republican Nat'l Comm. v. FEC, 487 F. Supp. 280, 283 (S.D.N.Y. 1980)).
[45] 470 U.S. 480 (1985).

$1,000. The Court simply reiterated its *Buckley* stance that independent spending poses no danger of corruption and thus cannot be limited.[46] It did not treat as relevant the fact that the candidate targeted by the spending had taken public funds and was thus subject to a spending limit.

The Court's most recent public funding case, the 2011 decision in *Arizona Free Enterprise Club's Freedom Club PAC v. Bennett*[47] (hereinafter "*Arizona Free Enterprise*"), emerged out of the efforts of a number of states to address the dilemma posed by NCPAC and the constitutional protection of campaign spending generally. Candidates are naturally reluctant to accept public funding if the limits that come with it will restrict their ability to respond to high-spending opponents and hostile independent groups. From their perspective public funding with a spending limit can operate as a form of unilateral disarmament. Candidates expecting to be in hotly contested races who also have the capacity to raise sufficient private funds are more likely to forego public funds with the attendant spending limit, so that in major contests public funding becomes an option only for weaker candidates who are less likely to have a real chance to win. The problem could be addressed by a very large public grant, but that raises the prospect of wasteful allocations of tax dollars in less hotly contested, low-cost races. As one scholar has noted, "it is exceedingly difficult to get the level of public subsidy right."[48]

To address this problem, starting in the 1990s, some state and local governments included so-called "trigger" provisions—or "fair fight" or "rescue" funds—in their public funding laws. These provided that if spending by a privately funded candidate (or, in some states, spending by a privately funded candidate together with spending by an independent committee opposed to the publicly funded candidate) exceeds a certain level, such as the level of the public funding spending limit, something happens. In a few states, the spending limit was raised, so that the publicly funded candidate could collect and spend additional private funds. More commonly, the jurisdiction would provide the publicly funded candidate with additional public funds up to a new, higher ceiling.[49] In Arizona, if a privately funded candidate spent above the public funding spending level, all publicly funded opponents of that candidate were entitled to receive an additional amount equal to the privately funded candidate's excess spending, all the way up to three times the original public

46 *Id.* at 490–500.

47 564 U.S. 721 (2011).

48 Stephen Ansolabehere, *Arizona Free Enterprise v. Bennett and the Problem of Campaign Finance*, 39 Sup. Ct. Rev. 53–54 (2011).

49 *See* Robert M. Stern, *Public Financing in the Municipalities and States, in* Public Financing in American Elections 103–5 (state chart 4) (Costas Panagopoulos ed., 2011).

funding level (minus 6 percent to account for the privately funded candidate's fundraising costs). Independent spending against a publicly funded candidate or in favor of a privately funded candidate was also counted in determining the additional funds a publicly funded candidate could receive.[50]

Prior to 2010, all but one of the lower federal courts that heard challenges to state trigger laws sustained the trigger mechanism, finding it advanced First Amendment values by increasing, not limiting, campaign speech and was justified by the governmental interest in making public funding an effective program attractive to all candidates. In *Arizona Free Enterprise*, however, a five-justice majority of the Supreme Court rejected this analysis and ruled trigger funds unconstitutional. In an opinion by Chief Justice John Roberts, the Court found that supplemental public funds burden the speech of the candidate or independent committee whose spending triggered the additional public payment. As a result, the trigger fund mechanism was treated like a spending limit and subjected to strict judicial scrutiny, which it was unable to withstand. Trigger funds could not be saved by the governmental interests in preventing corruption and its appearance as there was nothing corrupting about the spending of privately funded candidates or independent committees. The Court acknowledged that trigger funds "indirectly serve" the anti-corruption interest by encouraging candidates to take public financing instead of relying on private contributions, but it deemed the connection to preventing corruption too attenuated to justify the burden on spending by privately funded, non-participating candidates and independent committees.[51] To be sure, *Arizona Free Enterprise* reiterated *Buckley*'s statement that "governments 'may engage in public financing of election campaigns' and that doing so can further significant governmental interest[s]."[52] But the case dealt a blow to the viability of public funding programs, particularly to the "clean elections" or full funding model.

Immediately after *Arizona Free Enterprise*, courts invalidated the trigger provisions in Maine's clean money law and West Virginia's pilot program for judicial elections.[53] The Nebraska Supreme Court struck down that state's public funding law because it concluded that the trigger mechanism was not severable from the rest of the law.[54] Trigger fund mechanisms in the Connecticut and Florida public funding laws had already been invalidated while *Arizona Free*

[50] But independent expenditures for a participating candidate were not used to reduce the candidate's entitlement to extra funds.

[51] 564 U.S. at 752–53.

[52] *Id.* at 754 (citing and quoting Buckley v. Valeo, 424 U.S. at 57 n. 65, 92–93, 96).

[53] *See* Richard Briffault, *The Future of Public Funding*, 49 Willamette L. Rev. 521, 535 (2013).

[54] *See* State *ex rel.* Bruning v. Gale, 817 N.W.2d 768, 784 (Neb. 2012).

Enterprise was pending before the high court. The decision also led to sharp drops in candidate participation in both the Arizona and Maine clean elections systems, although Connecticut's program so far has weathered the storm, perhaps because the Nutmeg State provides its candidates with relatively large basic grants and because after *Arizona Free Enterprise* the state significantly eased its restrictions on political party participation in races with publicly funded candidates.[55] In 2015, Maine responded to *Arizona Free Enterprise* by enabling candidates to raise additional amounts of small contributions which would qualify them for additional clean money grants.[56]

Arizona Free Enterprise left one important constitutional issue unaddressed. The Arizona law invalidated in that case both lifted the spending limit for publicly funded candidates and also provided them with additional funds. This leaves open the possibility for a public funding program to address high levels of private spending by simply lifting the spending limit from the publicly funded candidate without providing her with more public funds. To be sure, lifting the spending limit would be a response to spending and so arguably a "penalty" for the other spender, but the Court in *Arizona Free Enterprise* seemed particularly exercised by the provision of additional public funds.[57]

IV. THE PUBLIC FUNDING DEBATE: ARGUMENTS AND EVIDENCE

Arguments for public funding have focused on its ability to: (i) make elections more competitive by making it easier for candidates who would otherwise have difficulty raising money to compete; (ii) improve the quality of campaigns by reducing the need for candidates to engage in fundraising, thereby allowing them to spend more time with voters; (iii) increase political participation by bringing more citizens into the financing process; (iv) promote greater equality in the financing of campaigns, and thus equalize voter influence on election outcomes; and (v) change policy outcomes by reducing the post-election influence of large donors.[58] Critics of public funding have expressed concerns that public funding is a waste of taxpayer dollars,

55 *See* Public Campaign, Small Donor Solutions for Big Money: The 2014 Elections and Beyond (Jan. 13, 2015), http://everyvoice.org/wp-content/uploads/2015/04/2014SmallDonorReportJan13.pdf.

56 *See* Kevin Miller, *Mainers Approve Clean Election Expansion and $100 Million in Bond Issues*, PORTLAND PRESS HERALD (Nov. 3, 2015), www.pressherald.com/2015/11/03/mainers-approve-clean-elections-measure-and-two-bond-issues/.

57 564 U.S. at 737 ("Here the benefit to the publicly financed candidate is the direct and automatic release of public money.").

58 *See generally* Malbin, *supra* note 7; Kenneth R. Mayer, *Public Election Funding: An Assessment of What We Would Like to Know*, 11 THE FORUM 365 (2013).

provides an opportunity for government to manipulate election outcomes, and promotes political polarization.[59]

A. *Arguments for Public Funding*

1. COMPETITION. The strongest evidence concerning the impact of public funding—based primarily on studies of the Arizona, Connecticut, and Maine clean elections programs and New York City's matching funds system—is that it has had a positive impact on electoral competitiveness. Specifically, it reduces the number of uncontested elections and tends to narrow incumbents' margins of victory. There is also some evidence that it results in a greater diversity of candidates, especially in lower-level races.[60] However, there is little evidence that it has reduced the incumbent reelection rate.[61] Skeptics suggest that this is because public funding is more likely to be taken up by long-shot challengers, not "quality" candidates, so that there will be more challengers but not many more challenger victories.[62] But surely more contested elections, more close races, and fewer landslide reelections help keep incumbents accountable to their constituents.

2. CAMPAIGNING. Some studies have found that public funding, particularly the "clean elections" model, reduces the time and effort candidates need to devote to fundraising and enables them to focus more on direct interactions with voters.[63] In his study of the Arizona Clean Elections program, Matthew Miller suggested this also had an impact on voter participation, particularly in lower-profile

[59] *See, e.g.*, WELFARE FOR POLITICIANS? TAXPAYER FINANCING OF CAMPAIGNS 7 (John Samples ed., Cato Inst., 2005); RAYMOND J. LA RAJA & BRIAN F. SCHAFFNER, CAMPAIGN FINANCE AND POLITICAL POLARIZATION: WHEN PURISTS PREVAIL 139–40 (2015) (contending that clean elections and matching funds programs exacerbate political polarization).

[60] *See, e.g.*, Mayer, *supra* note 58, at 371; *but cf.* Malbin, *supra* note 7, at 17–18 (research on this point is inconclusive).

[61] *See, e.g.*, Malbin, *supra* note 7, at 15–17; MICHAEL G. MILLER, SUBSIDIZING DEMOCRACY: HOW PUBLIC FUNDING CHANGES ELECTIONS AND HOW IT CAN WORK IN THE FUTURE 85–87 (2014); Mayer, *supra* note 58, at 370–74; U.S. GOV'T ACCOUNTABILITY OFFICE, GAO-10–390, REPORT TO THE SUBCOMMITTEE ON FINANCIAL SERVICES AND GENERAL GOVERNMENT, COMMITTEE ON APPROPRIATIONS, U.S. SENATE, CAMPAIGN FINANCE REFORM: EXPERIENCES OF TWO STATES THAT OFFERED FULL PUBLIC FUNDING FOR POLITICAL CANDIDATES 35–48 (2010) [hereinafter GAO REPORT].

[62] *See, e.g.*, Raymond J. La Raja & David L. Wiltse, *Money That Draws No Interest: Public Financing of Legislative Elections and Candidate Emergence*, 14 ELECTION L.J. 392 (2015).

[63] *See, e.g.*, Miller, *supra* note 61, at 64–79; Mayer, *supra* note 58, at 379; Peter L. Francia & Paul S. Herrnson, *The Impact of Public Finance Laws on Fundraising in State Legislative Elections*, 31 AM. POL. RES. 520 (2003).

contests. He found that the clean elections system was associated with less "roll off"—that is, the tendency of voters to turn out to vote in the elections at the top of the ballot but then not bother to vote in down-ballot races. He surmised that by spending less time on fundraising and more time with the voters, candidates for lower-level positions made voters more aware of those contests, more informed about the candidates, and thus more willing to vote.[64] On the other hand, Michael Malbin has argued that the effects of public funding on how campaigns are conducted is less clear, and may reflect differences among political communities.[65] Moreover, in matching fund jurisdictions, fundraising and voter contact may be combined, especially in smaller legislative districts, with candidates simultaneously seeking matchable donations and votes. There may be just as much fundraising as in privately funded elections, but relatively less "dialing for dollars" with potential large donors and more street-level activity that combines fundraising and campaigning.

3. Participation. There is evidence that small-donor match and tax credit and rebate programs that make small private donations more valuable to candidates broaden participation in the campaign finance system. New York City greatly increased the number and significance of small donors in its elections, with the number of small donors in City Council races more than doubling when the City went from a 1-to-1 to a 4-to-1 match (the subsequent shift to a 6-to-1 match had less impact).[66] In recent City Council races, roughly one-third of all private funds came from small donors, and roughly three-fifths of campaign funds consisted of small donations combined with the public match. As Malbin has explained, "[b]y multiplying the contribution's value, the matching program gives the candidate a stronger motive to devote the time and money needed to find these new donors."[67] Properly designed tax credit and rebate schemes have also increased the number of small donors,[68] although public education, outreach, and other program design features have been critical in determining the extent to which these programs are used.[69]

As the discussion of the impact of public subsidies on fundraising indicated, these programs can affect other forms of political participation. Small donor fundraising today may be based less on direct mail and more on social media

64 *See* Miller, *supra* note 61, at 71–79.

65 Malbin, *supra* note 7, at 18–19.

66 *Id.* at 20–21.

67 *Id.* at 21.

68 *Id.* at 22–23.

69 *See, e.g.*, Graham P. Ramsden & Patrick D. Donnay, *The Impact of Minnesota's Political Contributions Refund Program on Small-Donor Behavior in State House Races*, 33 State & Local Gov't Rev. 32 (2001).

and peer-to-peer networks, which can combine fundraising with other forms of political engagement. As Malbin has pointed out, "[s]urvey research makes it clear that giving a small contribution and volunteering are strongly associated with each other."[70] Although there is little hard evidence that small-donor funding has increased other forms of political participation, Malbin urges that, "[a]necdotally, there is good reason to believe that a small contribution can be a gateway toward activism for many donors."[71]

4. Equalizing Finance. By replacing private contributions with public funds, full funding programs necessarily reduce the role of large donors in financing elections. Properly designed small-donor match programs can promote political equality within the campaign finance system, too. A study conducted by the Campaign Finance Institute found that under New York City's 6-to-1 small-donor matching system, in the municipal elections of 2009, the combination of small donations and public matching accounted for 64 percent of the campaign funds of City Council candidates. Moreover, the small-donor match resulted in an enlarged donor pool that is roughly representative of New York City's population as a whole. In 2009, donors who gave $250 or less came from 89 percent of the city's census blocks. These small donors lived in neighborhoods where the average income, poverty level, racial composition, and education level were comparable to the city as a whole. By contrast, small donors provided hardly any of the funds for candidates in the privately funded elections for the New York State Assembly, even though City Council districts in New York City and State Assembly districts in New York City are of similar size and have similar constituencies.[72]

5. Impact on Public Policy. There is no proof that public financing has affected public policy in the jurisdictions that have adopted it. To be sure, there have been anecdotal arguments that clean elections laws in Maine and Connecticut led to the enactment of prescription drug price control and a bottle deposit reform law, respectively, in those states. A range of other reform measures in Connecticut—including college tuition assistance for undocumented immigrants, a transgender rights bill, and a paid sick leave mandate—have also been attributed to the clean elections program.[73] But the connection between public funding and the enactment of specific reforms have also been

[70] Malbin, *supra* note 7, at 27.

[71] *Id.*

[72] *Id.* at 23–25.

[73] Mayer, *supra* note 58, at 375. *See also Our Voices, Our Democracy: Victories Since Citizens United and the Road Ahead: Empowering Voters Over Wealthy Special Interests* 15–17 (Feb. 2016), www.citizen.org/documents/our-voice-our-democracy-report-february-2016.pdf.

challenged,[74] and it is inevitably difficult to determine whether an electoral reform has affected public policy or whether other underlying political forces were responsible for both. As Kenneth Mayer has explained, significant policy changes "involve a complex amalgam of factors: policy streams, issue entrepreneurs, diffusion, interest groups and lobbying, mobilization, public opinion, path dependency, institutional capacity, bureaucratic politics… Campaign contributions may play a role in this process, but are likely (at most) only one piece of a much more complicated puzzle."[75] Moreover, the effects of public funding may be offset by the role of private funding, particularly independent spending by interest groups, even in elections in which a significant percentage of the winning candidates have taken public funds. We do not have, and, under present constitutional doctrine, cannot have, truly fully public-funded elections. Thus, the impact of public funding on public policy and governance is bound to be limited.

B. *Arguments against Public Funding*

The older arguments against public funding were that it was unnecessary—given that there is no problem with privately funded elections—and therefore a waste of taxpayer dollars, and that it would lead to an "extreme, intrusive, and dangerous" government manipulation of our elections.[76] The argument that privately funded elections are just fine is essentially normative and turns on the degree of satisfaction, or the lack of it, with traditional private financing. There is, however, no evidence that public funding, where it exists, has interfered with the electoral process. Public funding may not have always helped challengers to be more competitive with incumbents, but it certainly has not advantaged incumbents over challengers.[77]

More recently, critics have suggested that public financing contributes to political polarization.[78] The argument has two strands. First, studies have found that campaign donors are more politically polarized than other voters. To the extent that some public funding programs—small-donor matches,

[74] Mayer, *supra* note 58, at 375–77.

[75] *Id.* at 377.

[76] *See, e.g.*, Welfare for Politicians? Taxpayer Financing of Campaigns, *supra* note 59, at 7.

[77] Malbin, *supra* note 7, at 16; Kenneth R. Mayer, Timothy Werner & Amanda Williams, *Do Public Funding Programs Enhance Electoral Competition?*, *in* The Marketplace of Democracy: Electoral Competition and American Politics (Michael P. McDonald & John Samples eds., 2006).

[78] *See, e.g.*, La Raja & Schaffner, *supra* note 59, at 139–40.

rebates and tax credits, and vouchers—bring more but not all voters into the campaign finance system, it may be that more polarized voters utilize these programs. Second, one goal of public funding is to offset the impact of traditional interest group money. Interest groups tend to be more focused on obtaining access to elected officials than on candidate ideology. By reducing the role of relatively moderate, non-polarized interest group donors, public funding could result in increased political polarization.[79]

At this point, however, there is little hard evidence that public funding contributes to polarization. Seth Masket and Michael Miller found no "substantively large or statistically significant" difference in the roll call voting behavior of clean-money funded state legislators, compared with their private-money funded counterparts, in Arizona or Maine during the decade after the clean elections programs were implemented in these states.[80] Moreover, as Michael Malbin has pointed out, although the top recipients of small donor contributions in Congressional races tend to be more ideologically extreme candidates, many other leading recipients of small donations are more mainstream. In privately funded elections, small donors may be more likely to hold politically extreme views than non-donors, but they tend to be less extreme than large donors.[81] And the increased polarization within Congress has occurred entirely without public funding. The forces driving polarization may be affected by the campaign finance system but they appear to reflect far broader political dynamics.

In short, if the case for public funding is somewhat weaker and more speculative than its advocates assume, the case against it appears to be weaker still.

V. LOOKING FORWARD: THE FUTURE OF PUBLIC FUNDING

A. *Rethinking Public Funding's Goals*

Although public funding in practice may not have accomplished, and may not be able to accomplish, all that its proponents have urged in theory, it still promises to make the financing of our election campaigns more consistent with our democratic ideals. Public financing appears to promote more contested elections and, when adequately funded and supported by appropriate regulation, can increase political participation and reduce the share of

79 *See, e.g.*, Andrew B. Hall, How the Public Funding of Elections Increases Candidate Polarization (Aug. 13, 2014) (unpublished working paper).

80 *See* Seth E. Masket & Michael G. Miller, *Does Public Election Funding Create More Extreme Legislators? Evidence from Arizona and Maine*, 15 St. Pol. & Pol'y Q. 24 (2015).

81 *See* Malbin, *supra* note 7, at 26.

funding provided by large donors. Going forward, however, we need to focus more precisely on what public funding can achieve as that will determine what kind of public funding system ought to be adopted.

The initial impetus for public funding, as reflected in the general election presidential program, was egalitarian. Public funding was meant to eliminate the role of private wealth in funding elections and to equalize the resources available to the major competitors. But the experience of the last four decades suggests that under our current constitutional regime these goals are impossible to accomplish. As long as candidates are free to decline public funding and to raise and spend unlimited amounts of private funds, and as long as outside groups are free to devote unlimited amounts in independent expenditures to support or oppose publicly funded candidates, private money will continue to play a substantial role, and the resources available to candidates will be unequal.

To be sure, if a future Supreme Court were to overturn *Arizona Free Enterprise*, the availability of trigger funds could go far to making public funding more attractive and to offset the role of private wealth. But even before *Arizona Free Enterprise* no jurisdiction that made trigger funds available committed to fully matching private spending. Much more drastic changes to campaign finance doctrine—such as approval of very low limits on private contributions and on independent spending, or requiring candidates to take public funding if it is made available—would be necessary to achieve the goals of complete equality of candidate resources and fully decoupling the campaign finance system from private wealth. Even then, it seems likely that private spending on the periphery of the campaign system—particularly spending on political issues with electoral implications—would challenge the possibility of a fully public-funded system. And such a system would require vigorous implementation and enforcement by a powerful campaign finance agency, which would be difficult to create.

Thus, in the near-term at least, public funding should focus on goals that seem more capable of realization: lowering barriers to entry and aiding challengers; redirecting fundraising efforts away from large donors and special interests to ordinary voters; enlarging and diversifying the donor pool so that it is more representative of the entire political community; and using the campaign finance system to stimulate political participation.

B. System Design

This suggests some form of small-donor-targeted public funding—either small-donor match, tax credits and rebates, or vouchers. New York City's 6-to-1 match system highlights the potential of small-donor match programs to play a major role in financing campaigns. To date, usage of tax credit and rebate programs has been quite modest, suggesting that these programs on their own are unlikely to generate much in campaign funds. The voucher model is only just being tried and so little is known about how it works in practice. There is, for example, considerable uncertainty about how many voters would use their vouchers. In the 2017 Seattle municipal election only about 15 percent of vouchers were actually used, but that election involved only city council seats and the city attorney position; participation might be higher for higher profile offices like mayor.[82] Vouchers may also favor candidates who are better known at the start of the campaign, and thus will have a head start on persuading voters to give them their vouchers.[83] But credits, rebates, or vouchers aimed at increasing voter participation in the campaign finance process could be part of a broader hybrid system that also includes a mix of flat grants and matching funds. Credits or rebates could be used to stimulate small donations generally. A candidate who obtains a threshold number of small donations could be given a foundation grant that could enable her to compete at a basic level. In a low-cost or not-too-competitive jurisdiction, that might be enough to fully fund her campaign. Beyond that, candidates could be eligible for matching funds at a multiple ratio. In higher cost or more competitive races, this would enable them to rely on public funds and would also give them an incentive to pursue small donations.

C. *Limiting Limits*

Public funding programs should stop requiring spending limits. They do not work. They are counterproductive. And they are not needed in a public funding system focused on increasing competition and political participation and decreasing the role of special interest money.

Spending limits do not work because they do not apply—and under current law cannot be applied—to privately funded candidates and independent spenders. So long as some campaign participants can engage in unlimited spending the goals of spending limits—including equalization of spending by competitors and holding down the cost of campaigns—cannot be achieved. Spending limits are counterproductive because they can discourage the most competitive candidates in the most contested races from taking public funding. And they really do not make sense in a public funding program focused on

[82] *See* Seattle Ethics & Elections Commission, Democracy Voucher Program Biennial Report 2017, at 5 (2017) (vouchers were mailed to 540,000 residents, but only 80,000 were processed), www.seattle.gov/Documents/Departments/EthicsElections/DemocracyVoucher/Final%20-%20Biennial%20report%20-%2003_15_2018.pdf.

[83] *See* Mark Schmitt, Brennan Center for Justice, Political Opportunity: A New Framework for Democratic Reform 10 (2015).

increasing competition and expanding participation by small donors. Rather, the public funding system could continue to match small donations, albeit probably at a lower ratio when the candidate's war chest grows beyond a certain level or outpaces the opposition by a certain amount. At some point, the jurisdiction might choose to stop matching but let the candidate continue to raise and spend money subject to contribution limits.

As previously noted, a number of partial public funding systems impose other restrictions on participating candidates, such as on the size and source of contributions. It is not clear if this makes sense. To be sure, a jurisdiction can and should limit which donations are matchable (or eligible for rebates and credits). Presumably, it can limit the matches it makes to relatively small sums donated by individuals (not organizations) who are residents of the jurisdiction. This would strengthen the tie between the candidate's voting constituency and her financial constituency. But some public funding programs also impose tighter limits on non-matchable contributions than apply to privately funded candidates. Such an approach would advance the goals of reducing the influence of large donors and interest groups over candidates, but could come at the price of making public funding less attractive to more serious candidates. Moreover, it is not clear what is gained by such a requirement. After all, even a partially public-funded candidate is necessarily less dependent on large private donors. If the standard donation cap is adequate to address the corruptive danger of private contributions to non-publicly funded candidates, it is hard to see why candidates who are less likely to be corrupted by private donations should be subject to a lower donation cap or special restrictions on the sources of funds. To be sure, if legal doctrine changes and restrictions may be imposed on donations to and spending by independent groups or on the candidate's use of his or her personal wealth, then public funding might become more generally attractive. In that scenario, there would be less concern over more restrictive contribution rules discouraging candidates from taking public funds. However, in that alternative constitutional universe it might make more sense to apply more restrictive rules to all candidates, not just those taking public funds.

D. Political Parties

In other countries, public funds are more likely to be provided to political parties than to candidates.[84] In our candidate-centered system, most public funds should go to candidates, but there is some argument for providing at least some public support to parties. Academic research has shown that

84 *See* Institute for Democracy and Electoral Assistance (IDEA), Political Finance Database, Are There Provisions for Direct Public Funding for Political Parties?, www.idea.int/data-tools/question-view/548.

political parties tend to channel money to the most competitive races,[85] and party organizations have long played an important role in engaging volunteers and mobilizing voters at the grass-roots level. In other words, providing public support to political parties would be fully consistent with the competition- and participation-promoting goals of public funding. Public funding would be particularly valuable for party building, organizational maintenance, and policy development functions in the months and years between elections. Moreover, political parties play a key role in organizing legislatures and developing and implementing public policy. Reducing the dependence of political parties on large donors could have broader benefits for governance.

Although parties could be supported by flat grants or matching funds programs, party assistance seems to be a particularly appropriate goal for tax-benefit and voucher plans.[86] Tax benefits could be made available in all years, not just election years. Permitting vouchers to be given to parties would make it easier for voters not certain of which candidate to support financially to use their vouchers: They could simply give their voucher to their party. Parties could then serve as agents of the voters by deploying the vouchers in the most contested races. Reliance on tax benefits and vouchers would also reduce the role of the government in deciding which parties are eligible for public support and how much public support any party can receive.

VI. CONCLUSION

Public funding surely has a central place in any system of democratic elections. It is the best, if not the only, way to reduce the dependence of candidates and parties on wealthy donors and special interest money. Public funding also makes it easier for challengers and political newcomers to compete, and it stimulates broader voter engagement with the electoral process. It is, of course, not a panacea and should not be oversold. Particularly in the current legal environment, there are constraints on what it can accomplish, and, accordingly, the design of public funding programs should probably reflect greater attention to its potential to increase competition and participation rather than a more thorough-going equalization of the system. Of course, if campaign finance doctrine were to give greater weight to equality, public funding could be able to accomplish far more. As with other electoral reforms, the success of public funding will turn on the specific details of the program and its fit with the surrounding political and legal environment.

[85] *See, e.g.*, La Raja & Schaffner, *supra* note 59, at 67, 84.

[86] *Accord*, *id.* at 139–40.

5

Raising All of Our Voices for Democracy: A Hybrid Public Funding Proposal

Adam Lioz*

I. INTRODUCTION

When Kelly Westlund decided to run for Wisconsin's 7th congressional district in 2014 she knew she would be facing a well-funded incumbent and that money would play an important role in her campaign.[1] But the former city councilor and small business owner was not prepared for how it would define her relationship to her own party. "When I went to the Democratic Party and told them I wanted to jump in," Westlund says, "their representative asked me if I could raise a quarter of a million dollars in three weeks. I laughed at him and said, 'No, have you met Northern Wisconsin?' I am a young working class person and most of my network is waitresses and teachers and firefighters and police officers. I don't have a network of millionaires and billionaires I can call .... [H]is response was 'Then, you're not viable.'" Westlund ran despite the lack of encouragement from her party. Although she lost the election, she raised nearly half of her funds from small donors and won nearly 40 percent of the vote, despite being outraised 5-to-1. "The current system," Westlund believes, "makes sure from start to finish our political process is dominated by the people with the most money ... it's no wonder there's no voice for working class people in Congress."

* Adam Lioz is Political Director at Demos, a public policy organization working for an America where everyone has an equal say in our democracy and an equal chance in our economy. He thanks Dr. Juhem Navarro-Rivera and Demos counsels Allie Boldt and Naila Awan for essential contributions to developing the proposal outlined in this chapter; and Demos Senior Advisor for Legal Strategies Brenda Wright for helpful feedback.

[1] Ms. Westlund is profiled in the 2015 report *The Money Chase*, from which all of the information in this paragraph comes. Adam Lioz & Karen Shanton, *The Money Chase: Moving from Big Money Dominance in the 2014 Midterms to a Small Donor Democracy*, DEMOS & U.S. PIRG EDUCATION FUND (Jan. 14, 2015).

Kelly Westlund is not alone. A candidate for the U.S. Senate must raise $3,300 *every single day for six years* just to be able to match the median amount raised by winning Senate candidates in 2014.[2] There is strong evidence that this big money system skews representation along race and class lines, and it skews our nation's policy outcomes as well.

This chapter details a policy proposal aimed at reducing the power of big money in American politics. It proposes a way of raising the voices of ordinary citizens and of helping the Kelly Westlunds of the world get a foothold in our political system. The structure of this chapter is as follows: First, it provides a precise definition of the problem our policy seeks to solve. It then discusses the two basic strategies for addressing the undue power of big money in our political system: lowering the ceiling by limiting contributions, and raising the floor by amplifying the power of small contributors. The remainder of the chapter will focus on the second strategy, describing how we can amplify the voices of ordinary citizens by providing public funding for public election campaigns. After briefly reviewing the three basic public funding models used in the United States, the chapter proposes the adoption of a "mixed" system of public funding for political campaigns that is targeted at addressing the particular problems we have identified while working within the aggressive restrictions the Supreme Court has placed on our ability to limit big money.

II. SOLVING THE RIGHT PROBLEMS

Effective policy reform must be targeted at solving the right problems. Before laying out a proposal, it is worth clarifying what the proposal does and does not aim to address. This is especially important because there are two common yet incorrect (or incomplete) definitions of the problem of money in politics.

Many—perhaps even most—Americans think there is "too much money in politics."[3] This is true in some ways. From the perspective of a committed citizen like Kelly Westlund who is looking to run for office and contemplating the rising price tag for even getting into the game; and in the eyes of a swing state voter drowning in 30-second TV ads that feature plenty of ominous music but little useful information about candidates' positions on key issues, there is too much money in politics. But, in a broader sense, focusing on the

[2] *Id.*

[3] *See, e.g.*, *Reuters Poll: Most Americans Think Too Much Money in Politics*, NEWSMAX (May 24, 2012), www.newsmax.com/Newsfront/americans-money-politics-elections/2012/05/24/id/440238/; Susan Page, *Poll: Too Much Money Spent on Presidential Campaign*, USA TODAY (Oct. 29, 2008), https://usatoday30.usatoday.com/news/politics/election2008/2008-10-29-poll_N.htm.

total amount of money in the political system misses the point. Americans spent a collective $6.4 billion to influence federal elections directly in the 2016 presidential election cycle.[4] That was a lot of money. But is it a tremendous amount when what is at stake is deciding who will govern 324 million people and manage an $18 trillion economy?[5] That amount, after all, is actually less than $20 per person. As opponents of reform are fond of pointing out, we typically spend more on potato chips and Halloween candy.[6]

Far more important than the *total* amount of money in politics is who is providing it. The vast majority of political funds in the United States comes from a tiny percentage of the population—members of a wealthy "donor class" that act as gatekeepers for aspiring officeholders and enjoy significantly more responsiveness to their policy preferences than do average voters.[7] In the 2012 election cycle, for example, more than a quarter of all disclosed federal contributions came from just 31,385 people—what political scientist Lee Drutman has termed "the one percent of the one percent."[8] Just 25 people put more than $600 million into 2016 federal election campaigns.[9]

This matters because the donor class does not look or think like the rest of America. In addition to being much wealthier, it is overwhelmingly white and disproportionately male; and its members have very different priorities, especially when it comes to the role that government should play in

4 *Cost of Election*, Center for Responsive Politics, www.opensecrets.org/overview/cost.php.

5 The U.S. population on November 8, 2016, was 324,013,789, according to the U.S. Census Bureau's "U.S. and World Population Clock"; 2015 U.S. GDP (last year available) was $18.037 trillion according to the World Bank, GDP (current US$), https://data.worldbank.org/indicator/NY.GDP.MKTP.CD?end=2015&locations=US&start=1960.

6 *See, e.g.*, *Naming Names*, Economist (Nov. 24, 2012), www.economist.com/news/leaders/21567092-limiting-role-money-politics-hard-full-disclosure-would-be-welcome; Maxim Lott, *What Campaign Spending? Americans Spend More on Halloween than on Midterms*, Fox News (Oct. 31, 2014), www.foxnews.com/politics/2014/10/31/what-campaign-spending-americans-spend-more-on-halloween-than-on-all-midterm.html; Chris Cillizza, *The 2014 Election Cost $3.7 Billion. We Spend Twice that Much on Halloween*, Wash. Post (Nov. 6, 2014), www.washingtonpost.com/news/the-fix/wp/2014/11/06/the-2014-election-cost-3-7-billion-we-spend-twice-that-much-on-halloween/?utm_term=.92ecdedb7981.

7 Blair Bowie & Adam Lioz, *Billion Dollar Democracy: The Unprecedented Role of Money in the 2012 Elections*, Demos & U.S. PIRG Education Fund (2013); Spencer Overton, *The Donor Class: Campaign Finance, Democracy, and Participation*, 153 U. Pa. L. Rev. 73 (2004).

8 Lee Drutman, *The Political 1% of the 1% in 2012*, Sunlight Foundation (June 24, 2013), http://sunlightfoundation.com/blog/2013/06/24/1pct_of_the_1pct/.

9 *Top Individual Contributors: All Federal Contributions*, Center for Responsive Politics, www.opensecrets.org/overview/topindivs.php.

shaping the economy.[10] This results in skewed policy outcomes that favor the rich.[11]

From this perspective, the key problem with money in politics is not so much that there is too much of it, but rather that too much of it is coming from too few people. In other words, the problem is *big money*, not money itself. After all, if every person living in the United States were to contribute $25 in the next presidential election, we would have more money in politics than we do now, but fewer of the problems that come with the current system. And if just 30,000 people were to buy anywhere close to $6.4 billion worth of potato chips and Halloween candy—well, they would have some serious health problems on their hands. In a similar way, the heavy concentration of campaign funding has undermined the health of our democracy.

The second incomplete definition of the problem at hand is held not by the public but rather by the Supreme Court. Over four decades, the justices have ruled in several cases that the only reason that "we the people" or our representatives may limit what the wealthiest among us can spend on or contribute to election campaigns is to fight corruption or its appearance.[12] Most people think of corruption fairly broadly, and they believe efforts to prevent corruption should include curtailing the special access that big donors have to legislators. But over the past decade, the Roberts Court has severely narrowed the legal definition of the term "corruption" so that it now is essentially equivalent to bribery—which is already illegal, and which few donors and politicians are foolish enough to engage in explicitly.[13] So the only reason we can restrict money in politics is to prevent bribery, or something akin to it. The Court's narrow concept of corruption does not even come close to capturing the full range of concerns that arise when big money enters the realm of politics. Nobody was bought off in Kelly Westlund's race for Congress, and yet big money (or lack thereof) formed a critical barrier to entry for Westlund and thousands of similar candidates who lack access to networks of wealthy donors.

[10] Adam Lioz, *Stacked Deck: How the Racial Bias in Our Big Money System Undermines Our Democracy and Our Economy*, DEMOS (2014); Sean McElwee, *Whose Voice, Whose Choice? The Distorting Influence of the Political Donor Class in Our Big-Money Elections*, DEMOS (2016).

[11] *See generally* MARTIN GILENS, AFFLUENCE & INFLUENCE: ECONOMIC INEQUALITY AND POLITICAL POWER IN AMERICA (2012); David Callahan & J. Mijin Cha, *Stacked Deck: How the Dominance of Politics by the Affluent & Business Undermines Economic Mobility in America*, DEMOS (2013).

[12] Adam Lioz, *Breaking the Vicious Cycle: How the Supreme Court Helped Create the Inequality Era and Why a New Jurisprudence Must Lead Us Out*, 43 SETON HALL L. REV. 1227 (2013).

[13] *Id.*

Rules governing the use of money in politics are about whether we should allow wealthy individuals and interests to translate economic might directly into political power. The debate surrounding these rules is about whether democracy will write the rules for capitalism or the other way around. It is about whether a narrow set of wealthy donors can drown out the voices of the vast majority of Americans. Concern over money in politics is about whether we will continue to allow disparities in wealth shaped by centuries of racial hierarchy to play out in reduced representation for people of color.[14] It is about whether we can build a democracy that inspires our collective faith in government.[15] Ultimately, it is about whether all Americans truly have equal access to our political system regardless of wealth, gender, or race. The Supreme Court's current approach does not permit us to address these broad concerns directly. For this reason, the Court has taken many important policy tools off the table.[16] Happily some remain viable, as this chapter details.

III. LOWERING THE CEILING OR RAISING THE FLOOR

Now our campaign finance system's problem has been properly defined as too much big money coming from too few wealthy donors. This phenomenon creates barriers to participation, undermines our core American value of political equality, and threatens the integrity of our democracy in myriad ways. But what are the solutions? There are two main strategies to put people, rather than big money, at the center of political campaigns. On the one hand, we can limit the amount that wealthy individuals or institutions can contribute to or spend on electoral campaigns. On the other, we can amplify the voices of ordinary citizens, giving more people more of a stake in the political process. In other words, one strategy lowers the ceiling, putting a cap on the total amount that top donors can pump into the system and their favorite candidates can spend; while the other raises the floor—increasing the amount of money that Americans of modest means can direct toward elections and the level of funding candidates without access to networks of wealthy donors can garner to run effective campaigns.

The Supreme Court has made the first strategy impossible to implement effectively on its own. While the Court has upheld limits on the amount

[14] *See generally* Lioz, *Stacked Deck*, *supra* note 10.

[15] *See generally* Robert C. Post, Citizens Divided: Campaign Finance Reform and the Constitution (2014); Daniel I. Weiner & Benjamin T. Brickner, *Electoral Integrity in Campaign Finance Law*, 20 NYU J. Leg. & Pub. Pol'y 101 (2017).

[16] Adam Lioz, *Breaking the Vicious Cycle: Rescuing Our Democracy and Our Economy By Transforming the Supreme Court's Flawed Approach to Money in Politics*, Demos 14 (2015).

donors may contribute directly to candidates, it has struck down limits on the total amount wealthy donors can give to all candidates, parties, and PACs combined in a given election cycle.[17] It has also eliminated any limits on direct spending on elections by individuals, candidates, or corporations.[18] Following the Supreme Court's dubious logic, lower courts have struck down limits on contributions to entities that spend directly on elections but do not contribute to candidates or parties, known as Super PACs.[19]

In this twisted legal landscape, contribution limits are easy to evade. A wealthy donor may only be permitted to give $500 or $1,000 directly to support George Smith for governor; but he can give an unlimited gift to a Super PAC that exists solely to support candidate Smith's campaign, or just write a big check directly to a consulting company to make his own ad attacking candidate Smith's opponent. The Supreme Court decisions that have limited lawmakers' policy options have resulted in large part from the fundamental misidentification of the problem of money in politics described above. For this reason, to effectively pursue the "lower the ceiling" strategy, it is essential to transform the Supreme Court's approach to money in politics to allow for reasonable limits on giving and spending political money.[20]

Financing election campaigns for public office in part with public funds serves the latter strategy—raising the floor of available resources by amplifying the voices of ordinary Americans who cannot afford to make large contributions, or perhaps any contributions at all. Done right, these programs can recenter politics around ordinary voters rather than large donors. The next section explores the basics of public funding systems, examines how they have worked in the United States, and then suggests a specific model system aimed at achieving these changes.

IV. PUBLIC FUNDING FOR PUBLIC ELECTION CAMPAIGNS

Choosing leaders in a democracy requires resources. At the most basic level, someone has to administer primary and general elections, and this is done entirely with public funds.[21] This makes sense because free and fair elections

17 *Id.* at 14.

18 *Id.*

19 *Id.*

20 Effective limits are also important to set the right context for pursuing the "raising the floor" strategy. It is easier to boost the voices of small donors and candidates so they can be heard when wealthy donors and interests aren't using million-dollar megaphones to drown them out.

21 In the past party primaries were considered private choices and hence were funded by the parties themselves. But, we have come to recognize that these so-called private choices (which

are the ultimate "public good"—they benefit everyone and without them no one can live in a democracy and enjoy all of the attendant benefits.[22] But the costs of running elections don't end there. Voters need some way to learn about the parties and candidates competing for elected office. And, in a free society, these parties and candidates need some way to get their messages out to voters, to work to convince people that they have the right vision for the country. In other words, to have meaningful elections we need campaigns. And campaigning costs money. Political campaigns do not necessarily have to cost anywhere near as much as TV-based campaigning in the United States does today. But, even shoestring, grassroots-style campaigning requires some funds: markers to make signs, gasoline to drive canvassers to key neighborhoods, clipboards to sign up supporters, and printing and copying for brochures. In most modern democracies, campaigning is also considered a public cost—at least in part. Most democratic governments provide some type of public financing to parties or candidates to help cover the cost of campaigning.[23] In the vast majority of jurisdictions in the United States, however, we have made the somewhat odd decision to completely privatize this aspect of campaigning. This system of highly unequal private funding for elections for public office has created the problems highlighted above.

Some far-sighted jurisdictions, however, have chosen to provide various levels of public funding for election campaigns. There have been dozens of programs tried across the country at the local, state, and federal levels. They range from small-scale pilot programs that apply to just a few races to more comprehensive programs that cover campaigns for legislative and statewide

were often marred by racial discrimination) determined voters' choices in selecting public officials; so we now treat party primaries as public elections and pay for them accordingly. This is especially appropriate given that our dominant voting system (single member, winner-take-all districts without ranked choice voting) ensures a two-party system so that voters dissatisfied with primary results functionally have nowhere else to go.

U.S. elections also used to be funded by poll taxes on voters; but we came to recognize that this practice unfairly raised wealth as a barrier to democratic participation and eliminated poll taxes through the 24th Amendment in 1964.

22 A public good is an economic concept defined as something that: (1) is impractical to exclude any member of the community from enjoying; and (2) for which one person's enjoyment of that good does not diminish another's, known as being "nonrivalrous." *See, e.g.*, Tyler Cowen, *The Concise Encyclopedia of Economics: Public Goods*, LIBRARY OF ECONOMICS & LIBERTY, www.econlib.org/library/Enc/PublicGoods.html

23 *See, e.g.*, Karl-Heinz Nassmacher, *The Established Anglophone Democracies*, *in* FUNDING OF POLITICAL PARTIES AND ELECTION CAMPAIGNS: A HANDBOOK ON POLITICAL FINANCE 269–73 (IDEA 2014), www.idea.int/sites/default/files/publications/funding-of-political-parties-and-election-campaigns.pdf; *Money, Politics and Transparency: In Law, There Is Direct Public Funding For Electoral Campaigns*, SUNLIGHT FOUNDATION, https://data.moneypoliticstransparency.org/indicators/1/.

office.[24] All of these programs are voluntary—meaning candidates running for office may choose to participate in the public funding program or else to opt-out of it and raise only private funds. This is in large part because mandatory public financing would not survive judicial scrutiny under the Supreme Court's current jurisprudence.[25]

In jurisdictions where public financing programs exist, they typically provide candidates for elected office with the option of funding their campaigns through a combination of small contributions from private actors and public funds. This candidate focus stands in contrast with programs outside of the United States; due to different legislative models, electoral systems, and campaigning styles, public funding programs in other countries typically provide campaign funding to political parties rather than to individual candidates.[26]

In typical U.S.-based systems, candidates must demonstrate a threshold level of public support to qualify to receive public funds, usually from within the jurisdiction they seek to represent. This ensures that public money goes to serious candidates with an established base of support rather than being wasted on fringe campaigns. Participating candidates are usually required to operate under certain restrictions intended to further focus their campaigns on ordinary constituents rather than large donors. Examples of the restrictions placed on candidates include limiting how much private money a candidate may raise from individual contributors, restricting what types of entities may contribute to the candidate's campaign, and placing a limit on how much a candidate may spend on her campaign overall or from her own personal wealth.

In the United States, there have been three basic models for how public funds are allocated to campaigns: grant-based programs; matching programs; and voucher, refund, or tax credit programs.[27] All of these programs fight corruption and its appearance by making candidates less dependent upon a narrow segment of large donors. Well-designed public-funding programs can

[24] *See, e.g.*, *Overview of State Laws on Public Financing*, National Conference of State Legislatures, www.ncsl.org/research/elections-and-campaigns/public-financing-of-campaigns-overview.aspx

[25] Even if advocates succeed in transforming the Supreme Court's approach to money in politics, mandatory public financing still presents interesting questions regarding how people other than candidates and political parties can make their voices heard in the context of election campaigns.

[26] D. R. Piccio, *Northern, Western, and Southern Europe*, in Funding of Political Parties and Election Campaigns, *supra* note 23, at 220–25.

[27] In an accompanying chapter in this volume, Richard Briffault breaks these systems down into five categories, separating vouchers from tax credits and refunds and dividing partial from full grant-based systems.

also boost political equality, make representation more reflective of the public at large by race, gender, and class, and help communities exercise political power that is independent of the major political parties.[28] Good public funding programs should aim to foster policy outcomes that reflect the views and priorities of average voters. They should lead to more gender, racial, and wealth diversity among candidates and elected officials. They should also enable participating candidates to raise a greater percentage of their money from large pools of small donors who reside in their communities rather than in large contributions from a handful of wealthy donors. Finally, well-designed public funding programs should sustain high rates of candidate participation and engender a more open and competitive political system writ large.[29]

A. *Grant-Based Programs*

Grant-based programs provide candidates who raise a threshold number of very small contributions (often as low as $5) to prove viability with a lump-sum grant of public funding to fuel the remainder of their campaigns—no further fundraising is required (or allowed), and every participating candidate in a competitive race has equal financial resources with which to campaign. This is often referred to as a "clean money" model of public financing, and several states—including Maine, Arizona, and Connecticut—use variations of this type of program.[30] Maine passed the first such program in 1996 and recently updated its system in 2015; Arizona passed a program like this in 1998; and Connecticut passed the newest (and thus-far most successful) program in 2005.[31]

Grant-based programs' biggest strength is that they generally ensure that participating campaigns are funded by the highest percentage of very small contributions and public money, versus large contributions. Hence, in addition to fighting corruption, these programs also come closest to providing an equal political voice to even the least well off. Grant-based programs also free

[28] *Designing Public Financing Systems to Advance Equity and Independent Political Power*, DEMOS (2016), www.demos.org/sites/default/files/publications/Public%20Financing.pdf. This paper was published by Demos without attribution; it was a collaborative effort among Demos colleagues, most notably Juhem Navarro-Rivera and this author.

[29] *Id.*

[30] *Overview of State Law on Public Financing*, NATIONAL CONFERENCE OF STATE LEGISLATURES, www.ncsl.org/research/elections-and-campaigns/public-financing-of-campaigns-overview.aspx.

[31] *See* Maine Commission on Governmental Ethics & Election Practices, *The Maine Clean Elections Act*, www.maine.gov/ethics/mcea/; Arizona Citizens Clean Elections Commission, *What Is a "Clean Election"?*, www.azcleanelections.gov/en/what-is-a-clean-election; Connecticut State Elections Enforcement Commission, *Citizens' Election Program*, www.ct.gov/seec/cwp/view.asp?a=3548&Q=489606.

candidates from spending the majority of their time raising money, since a candidate's fundraising is complete once the candidate qualifies for the grant (except for supplemental funding provided in some modern versions of these programs).[32] Finally, grant-based programs are best at providing candidates (versus voters) with an equal opportunity to get their messages out by giving them the same amount of money to conduct their campaigns—so campaigns can function as contests of ideas promoted at roughly equal volume.[33]

The most significant weakness of the grant-based model is that, in the current legal-constitutional landscape, these programs can sometimes leave participating candidates vulnerable to wealthy opponents and outside attacks. Participation in these programs is voluntary and those participants that do opt for the public funding may not be permitted to raise or spend money beyond the limited public grant they receive—and so can easily be outspent by an opt-out candidate backed by wealthy donors. Moreover, due to a misguided Supreme Court ruling from 2011 called *Arizona Free Enterprise Club's Freedom Club PAC v. Bennett*, participants are also not eligible to receive additional public funds to match the spending of their non-participating opponents.[34] In 2015, Maine updated its law with a strategy for addressing this problem by allowing candidates to qualify for supplemental public funds by raising additional small-dollar contributions.[35] For example, a candidate for Maine state House who receives a public grant and judges this to be insufficient could collect up to an additional 120 $5 qualifying contributions from private donors to qualify for $10,000 in additional funds from the state.[36]

Even with this adjustment, candidates must take the risk that available public funding (and the corresponding spending limit) will be adequate to keep up with a big money-backed non-participating opponent. The system does not self-adjust by allowing candidates to keep raising small dollars to meet an unexpected surge of opposition spending. Another weakness in

32 Maine's system now allows candidates to raise supplemental funding beyond the initial grant to help them keep pace with a big money opponent or outside spending. *See* Maine Clean Elections Act, ME. REV. STAT. tit. 21-A, ch. 14; Initiated Bill 1 (2015).

33 Generally major party candidates in competitive districts will receive equal funding, but not all candidates necessarily get equal grants. In Connecticut's system, for example, candidates can qualify for one-third or two-thirds grants by meeting lower qualifying thresholds. Connecticut State Elections Enforcement Commission, *Citizens' Election Program Overview* (2016), www.ct.gov/seec/lib/seec/CEPOverview2018.pdf.

34 Ariz. Free Enter. Club's Freedom Club PAC v. Bennett, 131 S. Ct. 2806 (2011).

35 *See* Initiated Bill 1, *supra* note 32.

36 The candidate turns the qualifying contributions over to the fund, so receives a total of $10,000 rather than $10,600. *See* Maine Commission on Governmental Ethics and Election Practices, *Supplemental Payments* (2016).

some people's minds is that grant-based systems are more candidate-focused than voter- or donor-focused and do not prioritize sustained small donor outreach and participation throughout the campaign.[37] Others would say this is a strength, since in theory candidates can turn their focus to voters rather than donors, thereby arguably reaching a broader spectrum of constituents.

Connecticut's grant-based program, enacted in 2005 and implemented in 2008, has been the most successful to date. It has robust candidate participation rates, has increased candidate racial diversity, and strong anecdotal evidence suggests that the system has led to policy outcomes that are more aligned with voter preferences and less skewed by donor priorities.[38]

Programs in other states have seen somewhat more mixed results. Participation in Arizona's system has dropped off significantly since its 1998 enactment, due in large part to two factors. First, the 2011 *Arizona Free Enterprise* Supreme Court case eliminated states' ability to provide candidates with matching funds triggered by her opponent's spending or by outside spending in the opponent's favor.[39] And, contribution limits to candidates were raised significantly in 2013, making it more difficult for those who participate in the public funding system to compete with privately funded opponents. Nonetheless, the Arizona program did have some success while it was fully active. Evidence shows that qualifying contributors in Arizona had been more racially and economically diverse than those who contributed to the candidates who opted out of Arizona's public financing system.[40] The state also experienced an initial increase in Latino and Native American candidates. However, as participation dropped off, so too did the program's benefits.[41]

In the wake of the Supreme Court's elimination of the "triggered match," participation in Maine's grant-based public funding program fell sharply; just over half of general election candidates opted into the system in 2014. In response, supporters of Maine's program passed a ballot initiative in 2015 to tweak the policy to address the threat of outside spending, allowing

37 *See, e.g.*, Spencer Overton, *The Participation Interest*, 100 Geo. L.J. 1259 (2012).

38 Public Campaign, Small Donor Solutions for Big Money: The 2014 Elections and Beyond (January 13, 2015), https://everyvoice.org/wp-content/uploads/2015/04/2014SmallDonorReportJan13.pdf; J. Mijin Cha & Miles Rapoport, *Fresh Start: The Impact of Public Campaign Financing in Connecticut*, Demos (2013), www.demos.org/publication/fresh-start-impact-public-campaign-financing-connecticut.

39 Public Campaign, *surpra* note 38.

40 Nancy Watzman, Public Campaign, All Over the Map: Small Donors Bring Diversity to Arizona's Elections (2008), www.publicampaign.org/sites/default/files/%20aotm_report_05_20_08_final_0.pdf

41 California Clean Money Campaign, *Arizona Clean Money*, www.caclean.org/solution/arizona.php.

participating candidates to raise supplemental funds as described above.[42] As a result, participation recovered in 2016, increasing to 62 percent of candidates.[43] Maine's program appears to have encouraged more women to run in that state.[44]

B. Matching Programs

The second major type of program matches each small contribution to a qualifying candidate with public funds according to a specified ratio, which can be as high as 6-to-1 (in existing programs) or 9-to-1 (in a proposed bill).[45] This means that a $50 contribution from an individual donor can actually be worth $350 or more to a participating candidate. Under this system candidates continue to raise funds from small donors throughout their campaigns, citizens control the allocation of public funding with their own contributions, and candidates with more grassroots support will end up with more campaign funds than their rivals. Several states and local governments provide some type of matching program.[46] New York City and Los Angeles are the leading municipal programs. Montgomery County in Maryland also recently passed a robust matching program. At the federal level, the Government by the People Act is the leading legislative proposal.[47]

Matching programs' biggest strength is that they amplify the dollars (and voices) of low- and middle-income voters compared with wealthy donors; so are focused on parity between voters rather than candidates. Contributors have more control over which candidates get what volume of public funding than with grant-based programs. And a large enough match changes candidates' incentive structures—encouraging them to campaign and reach out for contributions in moderate-income neighborhoods they generally would not find worth visiting to solicit $10 or $20 contributions absent a match.

42 *See* Initiated Bill 1, *supra* note 32.

43 Assoc. Press, *More Maine Candidates Use Clean Election Funds* (Oct. 1, 2016), http://mainepublic.org/post/more-maine-candidates-use-clean-election-funds#stream/0.

44 Maine Commission on Governmental Ethics and Election Practices, 2007 Study Report: Has Public Funding Improved Maine Elections? (2007), www1.maine.gov/ethics/pdf/publications/2007_study_report.pdf.

45 Most programs limit the total amount of public funds available to each participating candidate, so contributions that a particular candidate raises after exhausting her public allowance are not matched. This ensures that public funding programs have a finite cost.

46 *Overview of State Laws on Public Financing*, *supra* note 30. Many of these programs are out-of-date and/or do not provide enough evidence of impact to be considered in this analysis.

47 Adam Lioz, *The Government By the People Act*, Demos (2014), www.demos.org/publication/government-people-act.

The biggest weakness of these programs is that they may not effectively serve the most vulnerable members of society. First, voters need disposable income to participate effectively, and so many are left out altogether. Next, a $5 contribution is more meaningful in a grant-based program than a matching program since in the former it helps a candidate qualify for a substantial lump-sum grant rather than being worth $35 or $50 at most. In addition, a 6-to-1 match actually exacerbates the disparity between a $100 and a $5 contribution; it makes the $100 contribution worth $700 and the $5 contribution worth $35 (for a total differential of $665 versus $95). For these reasons, matching programs privilege middle- or working-class contributors over those on the very bottom of the socioeconomic latter. That said, a substantial match of only small contributions greatly reduces the disparity between a $100 and a $1,000 contribution, and therefore the disparity of influence between high- and moderate-income constituents—which is likely more important with respect to overall fairness and potential to skew policy.

Evidence suggests that matching programs' success depends upon the match ratio and the surrounding contribution limits. Successful programs must make soliciting truly small contributions worthwhile for candidates and parties.[48] New York City has increased its match ratio over the years to 6-to-1, and its program enjoys high levels of participation and appears to have diversified the donor base for New York City political races, and led to fewer uncontested primaries.[49] Both New York and Los Angeles have city councils even more diverse than their overall populations, suggesting that matching programs can be successful at reducing barriers to entry for candidates of color.[50]

C. *Vouchers, Refunds, and Tax Credits*

Finally, some systems allocate public funding through contributors themselves by providing vouchers, refunds, or tax credits. Voucher programs

48 One obscure but potentially important provision in the federal Government by the People Act is a "clawback" provision that ensures that only truly small contributions ($150 per election) are matched as opposed to the first $150 of a much larger contribution. Without this provision, candidates are still incentivized to seek the largest contributions allowed under the program, and the government ends up matching the first part of relatively large contributions from wealthy donors with public funds. See Lioz, *supra* note 47.

49 *See, e.g.*, Lioz, *Stacked Deck*, *supra* note 10, at 22–23, 36; New York City Campaign Finance Board, *Impact of Public Funds*, www.nyccfb.info/program/impact-of-public-funds; ANGELA MIGALLY & SUSAN LISS, BRENNAN CENTER FOR JUSTICE, SMALL DONOR MATCHING FUNDS: THE NYC ELECTION EXPERIENCE 16 (2010).

50 *Designing Public Financing Systems to Advance Equity and Independent Political Power*, DEMOS (2016).

provide "coupons" to individuals who can contribute them to a candidate (or sometimes to a party or political committee), and the candidate then redeems the voucher for campaign funds.[51] A refund program reimburses a contributor directly after she makes a contribution. A tax credit reduces a contributor's tax liability (including below zero if the credit is refundable) by the amount of a contribution (for a full credit), or some percentage of the contribution (for a partial credit). The federal government and various states have experimented with various tax credit and refund programs.[52] In 2015, voters in Seattle passed the nation's first voucher system by ballot initiative, which will go into effect in 2017.[53] In 2016, voucher-based systems were defeated on the ballot in Washington State and enacted on the ballot in South Dakota—although the South Dakota state legislature later repealed the law.[54]

Vouchers are the most promising of these contributor-based programs. While difficult to assess without an active system in place, in theory voucher programs combine the benefits of grant-based and matching systems. They provide a meaningful opportunity for participation for even the least wealthy constituents without requiring disposable income for participation, and they give these constituents control over where public funding is directed so that candidates are incentivized to reach out to a broad range of people throughout their campaigns. Outstanding questions about voucher programs include figuring out how to distribute vouchers in a robust and equitable manner,[55] ensuring that a high percentage of those eligible for vouchers will actually use them, and guaranteeing that vouchers are not bought or traded on a secondary underground market.

[51] *See, e.g.*, Richard L. Hasen, *Clipping Coupons for Democracy: An Egalitarian/Public Choice Defense of Campaign Finance Vouchers*, 84 Cal. L. Rev. 1 (1996); Bruce Ackerman & Ian Ayres, Voting with Dollars: A New Paradigm for Campaign Finance (2002).

[52] Thomas Cmar, *Toward a Small Donor Democracy: The Past and Future of Incentives for Small Political Contributions*, U.S. PIRG Education Fund (2004).

[53] Daniel Beekman, *Seattle Initiative Drive Seeks Public Campaign Financing, Reform*, Seattle Times (Apr. 3, 2015), www.seattletimes.com/seattle-news/politics/seattle-initiative-drive-seeks-public-campaign-financing-reform/.

[54] Alan Durning, Kristen Eberhard & Margaret Morales, *2016 Democracy Reform Ballot Initiative Roundup*, Sightline Institute (Nov. 8, 2016), www.sightline.org/2016/11/08/2016-democracy-reform-ballot-initiatives-roundup/; Amber Phillips, *South Dakota Republicans Just Got Rid of the State's First Independent Ethics Commission*, Wash. Post (Feb. 3, 2016), www.washingtonpost.com/news/the-fix/wp/2017/01/24/south-dakota-republicans-are-about-to-get-rid-of-the-states-first-independent-ethics-commission/?utm_term=.b9a244e0750d.

[55] Seattle's system makes vouchers available to all eligible contributors, but only actively distributes them to registered voters; this could have important equity implications for who actually uses them.

Research on tax credit and refund programs suggests that the closer these programs come to resembling a voucher system the more successful they are likely to be. Programs that offer full as opposed to partial tax credits; that provide for tax credits that are fully refundable so may be used by constituents who have no tax liability; and that may be solicited by the maximum number of political actors such as candidates, parties and PACs are likely to have the highest participation rates.[56] Oregon has had a tax credit program in place in some form since 1969, and its program enjoyed especially high participation during a brief point during the 1990s when its tax credit was paired with strong contribution limits and candidate eligibility depended upon abiding by spending limits.[57] Minnesota's political contribution refund program provided refunds to contributors within only a few weeks (as opposed to requiring donors to wait until tax time). As a result, Minnesota's program came closer to eliminating income as the primary factor driving whether constituents contributed to political campaigns.[58]

D. *Public Financing at the Federal Level*

For decades the federal government has had in place versions of some or all of the programs described above. In the wake of the Watergate scandal, Congress amended the Federal Election Campaign Act (FECA) to create a mixed public financing system for presidential elections—a matching system for the primaries coupled with a full grant program for the general elections.[59] For decades, presidential candidates from both major political parties used the system without exception.[60] Although not perfect, the system functioned largely as intended—it reduced candidates' dependence on wealthy donors and special interests and expanded voter choice by giving "outsider" candidates who lacked establishment support but could build a small donor base a platform to press their ideas both inside and outside of the major political parties.[61]

[56] Cmar, *supra* note 52, at 5–6.

[57] *Id.* at 20–21.

[58] *Id.* at 24–25.

[59] Adam Lioz, *Buckley v. Valeo at 40*, Demos 2 (2015), www.demos.org/sites/default/files/publications/buckley_at_40%20(2).pdf.

[60] Tarini Parti, *Will 2012 Be the End of the Presidential Public Financing System*, Center for Responsive Politics (2011), www.opensecrets.org/news/2011/08/the-end-of-presidential-public-financing/.

[61] *Fact Sheet on the Presidential Public Financing System*, Democracy 21 (Jan. 21, 2011), www.democracy21.org/archives/whats-new/fact-sheet-on-the-presidential-public-financing-system/.

George W. Bush became the first candidate to opt out of the primary matching system in 2000; but even with his prodigious fundraising operation, Bush participated in the full grant part of the program in the general election.[62] In 2008, Barack Obama opted out of the entire system, calculating (accurately) that he would be able to raise more money privately.[63] A system that had served our democracy for decades was doomed by the lack of political will needed to update it to meet modern political campaign conditions.

From 1972 to 1986, the federal government maintained various tax credit and deduction programs for those taxpayers who contributed to federal election campaigns.[64] At its peak more than 7 percent of eligible tax filers claimed these credits, before the program was ultimately repealed as part of Reagan's Tax Reform Act.[65] Lack of public education and awareness and shortcomings in program design—such as providing only partial rather than full credit for contributions—prevented these programs from having a transformational impact on federal elections; but the significant peak participation rate showed promise.

E. Common Factors Affecting Success

In reviewing the history of public financing programs in the United States, my colleagues at Demos and I have identified several factors critical to their success that are consistent across models and types.[66] Most of these concern whether candidates will have confidence that they can participate in the public funding system and still compete successfully against privately funded opponents.

First, there must be adequate funding available both in the aggregate and on a per-candidate basis. Most systems include both a cap on the amount of public funds any single candidate may receive and a system-wide limit, generally as a way to control costs. If per-candidate funding hits a ceiling at a level that is well below the cost of a competitive race, candidates will fear that the system may leave them insolvent just when they most need access to funding. If the total allocation for the system is inadequate, candidates will fear that

[62] Parti, *supra* note 60.

[63] *Id.*

[64] Cmar, *supra* note 52, at 12–20.

[65] *Id.* at 15.

[66] *See Designing Public Financing Systems to Advance Equity and Independent Political Power*, *supra* note 28.

money they qualify to receive will not actually materialize. Today, public financing systems also need provisions to help candidates remain competitive in a post-*Citizens United* world in which they may face an onslaught of unlimited outside spending at any time. The Supreme Court made responding to this problem more difficult when it struck down triggered matching fund systems in 2011,[67] but lawmakers have responded by designing innovative provisions to bolster programs in spite of restrictions imposed by the Court—such as allowing candidates to raise matching funds beyond their initial public funding cap in exchange for forgoing the ability to hold any money over to the next election cycle.[68]

Second, the restrictions candidates must accept to participate in the program must not be so onerous as to undermine their competitiveness with opt-out candidates. For example, many systems require participating candidates to agree to an overall spending limit. This can be helpful in keeping costs and barriers to entry down. But if the spending limit is too low, candidates will worry about locking themselves in, as their restricted spending will make them vulnerable to a high-spending opt-out opponent or to a barrage of attack ads by outside groups. Similarly, public funding systems that require participating candidates to accept lower contribution limits than are imposed on opt-out candidates must ensure that incentives to participate are sufficiently strong. One way to do this is to provide a large enough match such that small contributions made to participating candidates are actually worth as much or more than large contributions made to privately funded candidates.

The campaign finance laws that apply to candidates outside the public funding system are also critical to the success of a public funding program. Since public funding programs are always voluntary, they are always competing with a private funding option. Contribution limits that are too high for opt-out candidates undermine incentives for certain types of candidates to participate, such as those with access to networks of large donors, and hurt the prospects of those who do. Participation in Arizona's system declined, for example, when the state increased contribution limits. It can be important for a successful public financing system to reduce contribution limits for all candidates across the board.

Finally, local political culture can make a difference. Public funding programs depend upon robust participation from political stakeholders for their success—candidates to participate, constituents to make small contributions, and PACs and parties to recruit donors where permitted. They will tend to

[67] Ariz. Free Enter. Club's Freedom Club PAC v. Bennett, 131 S. Ct. 2806 (2011).

[68] Lioz, *supra* note 47.

thrive in participatory cultures with strong community infrastructure, while they may take longer to take root in places with strong anti-government sentiment or without a history of citizen engagement.

V. A POLICY PROPOSAL: THE BEST OF ALL WORLDS

The unique policy proposal offered here aims to combine the strengths of each type of public financing system while shoring up its weaknesses.[69] It is a voucher-based system that uses matching to incentivize giving to in-district candidates and political parties and also provides start-up grants to lower initial barriers to entry for political candidates. The details described below pertain to the federal election system, but can easily be adjusted to meet state or local conditions. The voucher, match, and grant levels are intended for federal elections and targeted to be paired with reasonable limits on contributions and outside spending, based upon what a broad swath of Americans can afford to give or spend—tighter than would be permitted under the Court's current approach to money in politics. They would likely need to be adjusted up to account for the higher contributions limits currently in place at the federal level and unlimited outside spending currently mandated by the Supreme Court. At the state level, these requirements could be adjusted to account for local conditions, including local contribution limits and outside spending trends.

A. *The Basics of the Proposal*

1. VOUCHER. The heart of the system proposed here is a $150 voucher provided each calendar year to every person who is at least 18 years old and eligible to make a contribution under existing federal law.[70] Contributors may give voucher gifts to candidates, parties, or political action committees (PACs) in any fraction. For example, a person could give $20 each to five candidates, and then $25 to a political party and another $25 to a PAC. To prevent fraud, vouchers cannot be spent directly through vendors or exchanged for anything of value. To qualify

[69] This policy proposal was developed in close collaboration with Allie Boldt, with helpful input and feedback from Naila Awan and several other Demos colleagues.

[70] The population eligible to contribute includes anyone who is *eligible* to vote (not just people who are registered), as well as incarcerated individuals, individuals on probation and parole, formerly incarcerated individuals, and permanent legal residents.

to receive voucher contributions, a candidate must submit signatures from 200 people in the district she is running to represent in Congress. Presidential candidates would need to submit these signatures in each state to qualify to receive vouchers from eligible contributors who reside in that state.

2. MATCH. Voucher contributions given to political parties, presidential candidates, and in-district congressional candidates (including in-state Senate candidates) are matched with additional public funds at a three-to-one ratio, or greater depending upon the surrounding contribution or spending limits and other local conditions. To qualify to receive the match, candidates would need to raise a threshold number of contributions of at least $5, and at least 75 percent of these contributions would have to come from contributors who reside within the district.[71] Voucher contributions of at least $5 count toward qualifying for the match. Parties would need to have at least one federal candidate on the ballot in the state where the contribution originates in order to have their voucher receipts matched.
3. GRANTS. Micro-grants of $30,000 to assist with start-up costs would be available to congressional challengers who raise contributions of at least $5 from 200 contributors.[72]

To reduce candidate dependence on wealthy donors across the board and facilitate maximum candidate participation in this hybrid public financing program, contribution limits to participating and non-participating candidates would ideally be lowered significantly from the current $2,700 per election (or $5,400 per cycle). The influx of public funds from the hybrid system would enable participating candidates to raise enough funds to compete with both opt-out candidates and outside spending. Limits might have to be somewhat higher for non-participating candidates in order to pass muster with the Supreme Court's current approach, but to maximize incentives to participate

[71] The thresholds would be 750 contributors for House candidates, 1,000 for Senate, and 1,000 in each of 20 states for presidential candidates. Restricting out-of-district contributions generally is a policy that should be a constitutional means of insuring elected officials are accountable to their constituents, but has been challenged under current Supreme Court doctrine. *See, e.g.*, Thompson v. Dauphinais, Case No. 3:15–218 (D. Alaska 2016). Qualifying contributions for a voluntary public financing program are a separate matter, however, and should be easily upheld even under the Court's current, restrictive approach.

[72] This provision could be adjusted to provide micro-grants of up to $30,000 to any candidate who has less than this amount in her campaign account if the policy is being pushed in the legislature rather than on the ballot, or if the courts object to a provision that provides differential benefits to challengers.

these limits should not be higher than the limit of $1,000 per election that was in place prior to the Bipartisan Campaign Reform Act of 2002.[73] If contribution limits are not lowered, policymakers should consider increasing the size of the voucher or the match to ensure that participating candidates can compete effectively with opt-out opponents backed by large donors.

Finally, the voucher level or the match ratio would be reduced incrementally if and when substantially more people start to use their vouchers to ensure that public funds are not driving up the costs of elections. Reductions can be tied to total House candidate voucher receipts (as a relatively stable measure across presidential and midterm elections). For example, we might reduce the voucher by $25 after each cycle in which House candidates raised a minimum combined $500 million in voucher receipts. Another way to look at it is if more people than anticipated start to use their vouchers and so the initial $150 voucher level matched at 3-to-1 for in-district candidates enables congressional candidates to start raising significantly more than the $1.6 million spent by the average 2016 open seat race winner, we would know that we are pumping an unnecessary amount of public funds into our elections and so can start to lower the value of the voucher each eligible donor receives (say to $125 or $100) or lower the ratio at which we match voucher contributions to eligible candidates (say to 2-to-1). Either will result in less public money going into the system.[74]

B. *Brief Rationale*

The system described above uses the strengths from each model. Vouchers are optimally decentralized and do not require participants to have any disposable income. Vouchers are also targeted to maximize both participation and equality of voice for even the least well off. They also fight corruption by reducing candidate dependence upon a narrow segment of donors thereby reducing the chances of *quid pro quo* arrangements while not placing any

[73] The 2006 Supreme Court case *Randall v. Sorrell*, 548 U.S. 230 (2006), lays out the current guidelines for contribution limit levels. Unfortunately Justice Breyer's opinion accepts the common but incorrect assumption that lower contribution limits tend to harm challengers. While it is true that extremely low limits that prevent candidates from raising the basic resources to campaign would likely entrench incumbents, social science research suggests that low but reasonable limits actually help challengers by reducing the overwhelming fundraising advantage incumbents enjoy with high-dollar donors. *See, e.g.*, Adam Lioz & Brenda Wright, *Contribution Limits: No Harm to Challengers*, State PIRGs' Democracy Program & National Voting Rights Institute (2006).

[74] *Different Races, Different Costs*, Center for Responsive Politics, www.opensecrets.org/overview/incad.php.

restrictions on political spending by any actor; and so clearly pass muster under even the Roberts Court's narrow-minded approach to money in politics. Making the widest range of legitimate political players eligible to receive voucher contributions—including recipients such as PACs and parties—helps to maximize participation (since most vouchers will likely be contributed in response to solicitation). Some would bristle at making PACs eligible for voucher contributions since PACs often serve as tools for increasing the power of corporations and other special interests.[75] But in addition to helping maximize donor participation, allowing donors to contribute their vouchers to PACs ensures that issue-specific associations such as environmental or immigrants rights organizations have a robust voice in the electoral process. Distributing vouchers to every eligible contributor puts the focus on maximizing the ability of constituents to play a more robust role in the elections process regardless of their income.

The proposed mixed system respects and rewards organizing, and it provides a good way for people to register the intensity of their preferences, for instance by allowing them to bundle contributions from friends and neighbors. As such, organizations with strong bases of community support would be able to effectively engage their members in the electoral process.

Matching voucher contributions 3-to-1 incentivizes contributions to local candidates and parties to ensure they have a strong voice in their own campaigns and that local support is critical to their success. Conversely, it incentivizes candidates to solicit funds from and depend upon the constituents they hope to represent rather than out-of-district or out-of-state donors. Matching only voucher contributions rather than private funds avoids one pitfall of matching programs—that public matching funds actually increase inequality between moderate-income donors who can afford to chip in $25 or $50 and truly poor Americans who can only spare $5 or nothing at all. Voucher amounts or match levels can be adjusted to account for surrounding contribution limits and outside spending patterns.

Micro-grants give new candidates with local grassroots support the resources to set up small dollar fundraising operations to take advantage of the rest of the system. They can help qualified community leaders get over the first and sometimes highest hurdle to running for office, which is raising enough funds to get a campaign started and off the ground.

The combined system would make it easier for low-income candidates to run competitive campaigns for public office—both by helping them get into the game and by enhancing the giving capacity of low-income constituents who

[75] For more on this question, see the *Questions and Answers* section below.

often provide a natural base of support. It would enhance racial equity by reducing dependence on existing unjust property distributions resulting from years of discriminatory public policies and general oppression of people of color.

The mixed system described here is also inherently adaptable to the fact that some races are more competitive than others and so require more fundraising. There is no fixed lump-sum grant, which can be excessive for a non-competitive race in a cheap media market and at the same time insufficient for candidates facing stiff opposition in a large city with expensive media costs. Notably there is no spending limit for participating candidates—in contrast to many systems currently in place. This makes the system self-adjusting and responsive to conditions on the ground. Candidates facing big money opposition can continue to raise funds to keep pace. And given that successful campaigns will build a strong cohort of supporters who give voucher contributions (but not necessarily their own private funds at first) they will have a natural base of support to solicit as races heat up and more resources are required. A candidate in a highly competitive race can go back to her voucher contributors in September or October and say, "you've already invested in my campaign with your voucher dollars and now we're really close to the end—I need $20 of your money to help put me over the edge."

C. *Questions and Answers about the Proposal*

1. How Much Public Money Will This Proposal Inject into the System?

The amount of public money in the system will depend upon several factors, including the exact levels of the voucher and match, how many people use their vouchers (the "uptake rate"), and the percentage of voucher contributions given to parties or in-district candidates that qualify for the match. With $150 vouchers and a 3-to-1 match, voucher use could inject approximately $2.34 billion of public funds to candidates and parties per election cycle, at least in the early stages. This estimate is based upon an initial uptake rate of 3 percent, which would constitute a 50 percent increase over estimated current contribution rates. This increase seems reasonable given that contributors would not have to lay out any of their own money.[76]

[76] Uptake rates for Seattle's voucher program will be very helpful in making accurate estimates. In the program's initial 2017 cycle, according to one estimate, 3.4% of Seattle's adult population used vouchers. This is one indication that the estimate of a 3% uptake rate is reasonable. Berk Consulting & City of Seattle Ethics and Elections Commission, Seattle Democracy Program Evaluation 22 (April 20, 2018), www.seattle.gov/ethics/meetings/2018-05-02/item2.pdf. Analysis of past tax credit and refund programs strongly suggest that minimizing the need to lay out funds should increase participation rates. Cmar, *supra* note 52.

The 3-to-1 match on vouchers could add an additional $3.94 billion in public funds, assuming that the proportion of contributions directed to in-district candidates increases by about 25 percent in response to the incentive created by the match, so that 56 percent of all voucher contributions are matched 3-to-1. Finally, the start-up grants could add up to $66.2 million per election cycle, based on an estimate of 2,205 candidates running for federal office and using the grants. This estimate comes from the 2010 federal election cycle, which had the highest number of both House and Senate candidates since the year 2000. That number includes both challengers and incumbents, which makes it generous, but not unreasonable, because we expect more challengers to run under circumstances that offer more start-up support and robust public funding to help them compete with often-prohibitive incumbent war chests.

Put together, the system might inject approximately $6.45 billion of public funds into federal elections initially. This is approximately equal to the entire reported cost of the 2016 federal elections—meaning that we would be pumping a substantial amount of public funds into the political system to balance out the current influx of large contributions and unlimited spending.[77] Of course, the estimate provided here is highly dependent upon the voucher uptake rate. We would hope that over time that rate would increase substantially and so public funds would eventually significantly outweigh the amount of private money in the system. For example, if the voucher uptake rate were ever to reach as high as 11 percent (say by the fifth election cycle of operation), this proposal would be injecting more than $12 billion of public money in to federal elections. This level of public funding could substantially alter the power dynamic in congressional and presidential elections.[78]

2. Would Adding Billions of Public Dollars into the System Backfire?

If we add several billion dollars of public funds without capping private contributions and expenditures, will we overload the system, subjecting voters to an unnecessary flood of TV ads, and will we potentially undermine public support for the system I just proposed? I think the answer is no.

As discussed above, there is not necessarily "too much money in politics." But we also need to bear in mind that there is a reasonable limit to the total amount of money that should be injected into our electoral system overall.

77 *Cost of Election*, Center for Responsive Politics.

78 As noted in the section above on basic program design, reductions in the value of the voucher or the size of the match can keep the cost of the program reasonable if and when voucher uptake rates increase substantially.

People already feel like too much money is spent on elections, and if the additional influx of public funds translated into twice as many electoral ads, public support for public financing might start to wane.

However, we should not expect there to be a one-to-one correlation between increased money in the system and increased electoral ads, for several reasons. First, it may not be possible to spend twice as much money on TV ads, as there may not be enough bandwidth available on network or cable TV at the peak of an election season to handle the increased demand.[79] Second, some of the additional funds would likely be spent on revised versions of ads that are already running but are not captured in total election spending figures reported to the Federal Election Commission (FEC). This would include money spent on so-called issue ads that are intended to influence elections but cannot be considered electoral in nature under the Supreme Court's current restrictive doctrine.[80]

Third, the program described here should lead to a jump in the number of candidates launching campaigns in any given cycle—in fact reducing barriers to entry is one of its primary objectives. Of course, some of these "new" candidates might purchase electoral ads, thereby increasing the total number of electoral ads faced by the public. But these candidates would likely also be spending funds on voter registration drives, efforts to get voters to the polls, candidate travel, compliance, and other types of spending that are less of a nuisance than electoral ads.

Perhaps most importantly, a good portion of the money in the system would likely be directed to PACs, particularly over time as PACs become more sophisticated at raising money under the program. Political consultants recognize that there are diminishing returns on TV ads. For this reason, if PACs run by organizations like the Sierra Club or the National Rifle Association had significantly more resources at their disposal, at some point they would likely decide to spend some of their PAC money in other ways. This might mean more sophisticated voter targeting, more voter registration and get-out-the-vote efforts, and other creative ways to influence elections. To the extent that these efforts are targeted toward increasing participation, they would be

[79] Cecilia Kang & Matea Gold, *With Political Ads Expected to Hit a Record, News Stations Can Hardly Keep Up*, WASH. POST (Oct. 31, 2014), www.washingtonpost.com/business/technology/with-political-ads-expected-to-hit-a-record-news-stations-can-hardly-keep-up/2014/10/31/84a9e4b4-5ebc-11e4-9f3a-7e28799e0549_story.html?utm_term=.391b8f0e5a42 (quoting a local station manager as saying "…when you have that kind of tidal wave of advertising interest over the top, it puts pressure on the station when we have limited inventory").

[80] FEC v. Wis. Right to Life, 551 U.S. 449 (2007).

helpful to the political process. If returns on electoral spending on the whole diminish sufficiently, these organizations might even decide that some PAC resources would be better spent trying to influence policy or create a more opportune environment for favored candidates in other ways—like producing reports, organizing a march against climate change, or lobbying in favor of looser gun restrictions.[81] Organizations with PACs might start strategizing about their advocacy efforts in a more holistic way, and would not necessarily use all of the resources at their disposal on electoral advocacy. In this way, an ancillary benefit of the influx of public funds is that it could democratize the civic organizing space, which is currently dominated by big money from wealthy individuals, corporations, foundations, and other sources.

3. Would the Cost of the System Be too High?

If uptake rates climb steadily and reach about 11 percent after five cycles, this program could cost around $13 billion per cycle, or around $6.5 billion per year. This sounds like a lot of money, and is about twice as much as all (disclosed) 2016 federal election spending. But, to put it in perspective, $6.5 billion is less than one quarter of 1 percent of our annual federal budget of about $3.9 trillion.[82] It is also a tiny fraction of what we spend on other public goods. For example, it is slightly more than 1 percent of discretionary defense spending and less than 10 percent of what the federal government spends on education in a single year.[83] This is not to say we should spend as much on elections as defense or even education, but it demonstrates how comparatively cheap investing in the public good of fair elections would be. Fair elections are just as important as these other public goods because the representatives chosen in our elections set policy priorities and make policy decisions in all other substantive areas of our democracy. Fair elections help ensure that decisions about how we allocate money to other public goods are being made by representatives who are responsive to the people as a whole, and not to a wealthy donor class that has different policy positions and priorities than the public at large.

Further, the ramping down of voucher and match levels would ensure that the cost of our campaign finance system would not continue to rise unabated

[81] Facilitating this development might require adjusting regulations that tax entities organized under Section 527 of the Internal Revenue Code (such as PACs) for expenditures that are not intended to influence elections.

[82] *See* Congressional Budget Office, *Budget*, www.cbo.gov/topics/budget.

[83] *See* U.S. Office of Management and Budget, Fiscal Year 2015 Budget of the U.S. Government 61, 71 (2015), https://files.eric.ed.gov/fulltext/ED555246.pdf.

as the system achieves its ultimate goal, which is to have more participation from more donors so that a greater percentage of eligible contributors have a say and a stake in the direction of public policy.

4. How Would Vouchers Be Distributed?

Creating the most efficient and equitable voucher distribution system presents a challenge, especially at the federal level. There is no single nationwide database of every eligible voter's address and we would not want to create one for this program. Therefore, voucher distribution should be decentralized and handled by state agencies rather than the Federal Election Commission (FEC) or another national entity. The FEC could create numeric voucher codes and distribute them to states in bulk, along with grants that cover the costs of dissemination. States would identify agencies that have the necessary information to distribute these vouchers to eligible contributors. Any eligible contributor who does not receive a voucher automatically would be permitted to opt in to the system by filling out a form attesting to eligibility. The FEC would retain an oversight function to ensure that the program is implemented as uniformly as possible across state lines.

Distribution would be simpler at the state or local levels. Jurisdictions can look to the Seattle program as a starting point, and look for ways to improve equity by automatically distributing to as many eligible contributors as possible.[84]

5. Why Make Voucher Contributions Available to PACs?

Political action committees (PACs) are organizations that exist specifically to raise and spend money on elections. There are two types of PACs at the federal level. Traditional PACs can accept contributions of up to $5,000 from individuals or other political committees and can make contributions of up to $5,000 to candidates, parties, or other PACs or spend an unlimited amount advocating the election or defeat of any candidate. They can be independent, or can be run by a corporation or nonprofit to serve its shareholders or members. Super PACs—created in the wake of *Citizens United v. Federal Election Commission*—can accept unlimited contributions from individuals, corporations, unions, or other political committees. They are not permitted to

[84] Seattle's program automatically distributes four $25 "Democracy Vouchers" to all Seattle registered voters. Eligible contributors who are not registered to vote may affirmatively request vouchers. *See How Your Democracy Vouchers Work*, HONEST ELECTIONS SEATTLE, http://honestelectionsseattle.org/.

make direct contributions to candidates or parties, but may spend an unlimited amount advocating the election or defeat of candidates.

Because both types of PACs can accept contributions that are significantly larger than most Americans can afford to make, they largely serve as tools to increase the power of the wealthy and have a bad name as vehicles for special interests wielding power in Washington. But, in essence, PACs are tools for organizing and aggregating political power, and they could be structured differently. For example, Colorado has small donor committees (sometimes called "People PACs") that raise contributions of $50 or less and can then give larger contributions to candidates than regular PACs.[85] Citizens organized around causes rather than candidates have a legitimate role to play in the electoral process and making PACs more dependent upon large bases of small donors rather than $5,000 checks is good for democracy. Ideally the strength of people's voices should depend not upon the size of their wallets but rather on the number of other people they can rally to their cause. For example, someone who cares a lot about fighting climate change and wants to elect candidates who favor clean energy should have more power to do so if she can bring together thousands or millions of people who agree, not because she happens to be wealthy herself. PACs that derive all or much of their support from many people making small contributions of their own money or directing voucher contributions can be great tools to facilitate this type of civic engagement.

VI. CONCLUSION

In the long run the Supreme Court must transform its approach to money in politics. We the People should be able to limit the undue power of wealthy donors over elections and policy. But we do not need to wait for the Supreme Court to allow ordinary people to amplify their voices in the political process. Public financing programs have been working successfully in various states and localities across the country. By taking the best pieces of each successful model, we can imagine a system that not only fights corruption but also helps achieve our core American value of political equality.

[85] Lioz, *supra* note 47, at 19–20.

6

Reorienting Disclosure Debates in a Post-*Citizens United* World

Katherine Shaw*

I. INTRODUCTION

Disclosure is often an afterthought in debates about money in politics. Reformers have tended to take disclosure for granted, devoting little time to developing and refining the affirmative case for it. They have also tended to assume that the current disclosure regime is an effective one, at least as far as it goes. Reformers *have* devoted substantial attention to the holes in the current regime in the post-*Citizens United* era—so-called "dark" and "gray" money[1]—and have considered ways to bring such activity into the light. Yet even if they are successful, such expansion efforts would only bring more dollars under the auspices of a disclosure regime in need of both stronger conceptual architecture and substantial practical improvements. So closing the gaps in the system is only one aspect of the task.

Consistent with the mission of this volume, this chapter will first survey the doctrine, practice, and empirics of disclosure. It will then turn to a number of proposals for reforming the reach, quality, and impact of this mode of campaign finance regulation.[2]

* Katherine Shaw is Professor of Law and Co-Director of the Floersheimer Center for Constitutional Democracy at the Benjamin N. Cardozo School of Law at Yeshiva University.

1 Chisun Lee, Katherine Valde, Benjamin T. Brickner & Douglas Keith, Brennan Center for Justice, Secret Spending in the States 5 (Sept. 2016), www.brennancenter.org/sites/default/files/analysis/Secret_Spending_in_the_States.pdf (defining dark money as "election spending by entities that do not publicly disclose their donors," and "gray money" as spending "by entities that disclose donors in a way that makes the original sources of money difficult or perhaps impossible to identify.").

2 Many of these proposals are drawn from my previous work with sociologist Jennifer Heerwig. Jennifer A. Heerwig & Katherine Shaw, *Through a Glass, Darkly: The Rhetoric and Reality of Campaign Finance Disclosure*, 102 Geo. L.J. 1443, 1449 (2014).

II. THE DOCTRINE AND PRACTICE OF DISCLOSURE

A. Doctrine

"Campaign finance disclosure" generally refers to laws that require both reporting and public dissemination of information about political actors' fundraising and spending. The term can be further divided into a few distinct but related activities: the *reporting* of information about contributions and expenditures; the public *dissemination* of that information; and *disclaimers*, which provide the public with information about the sponsors of particular political messages ("e.g., paid for by the ABC Committee.")[3]

Mandatory disclosure has long been a feature of our law of campaign finance. The Supreme Court's analytical framework for disclosure is traceable, like much in the law of campaign finance, to *Buckley v. Valeo*,[4] the Court's foundational consideration of the constitutionality of the Federal Election Campaign Act (FECA).[5]

In addition to upholding FECA's contribution limits and invalidating the law's expenditure limits, the *Buckley* Court upheld FECA's disclosure requirements in full (though subject to several important limiting principles).[6] The relevant provisions of law required "political committees"[7] to register with the Federal Election Commission (FEC), and to keep records of expenditures and contributions.[8] The law also required candidates and political committees to provide the FEC with detailed reports, which the FEC would then make available "for public inspection and copying."[9] Beyond its candidate and political committee provisions, the law required *all* individuals or groups that made independent expenditures above a certain amount "for the purpose

3 Heerwig & Shaw, *supra* note 2, at 1449; Ciara Torres-Spelliscy, *Hiding Behind the Tax Code, The Dark Election of 2010 and Why Tax-Exempt Entities Should be Subject to Robust Federal Campaign Finance Disclosure Laws*, 16 CHAP. J.L. & POL'Y 59, 79 (2010–2011).

4 Buckley v. Valeo, 424 U.S. 1 (1976).

5 Federal Election Campaign Act (FECA) of 1971, Pub. L. No. 92–225, 86 Stat. 3 (1972), *amended by* Federal Election Campaign Act Amendments of 1974, Pub. L. No. 93–443, 88 Stat. 1263 (codified as amended at 2 U.S.C. § 431 (1974)).

6 *Buckley*, 424 U.S. at 63–64.

7 When *Buckley* was decided, FECA defined a political committee as "a group of persons that receives 'contributions' or makes 'expenditures' of over $1,000 in a calendar year ... 'for the purpose of ... influencing' the nomination or election of any person to federal office." *Id.* at 62–63 (citing 2 U.S.C. § 432 (Supp. IV 1970)).

8 *Id.* at 63 (citing 2 U.S.C. § 432 (Supp. IV 1970)).

9 *Id.*

of … influencing the … election, of any person to Federal office" to file a statement with the FEC.[10]

The *Buckley* Court began its discussion with an acknowledgment that mandatory disclosure "can seriously infringe on privacy of association and belief guaranteed by the First Amendment."[11] This meant that disclosure requirements could not be justified "by a mere showing of some legitimate governmental interest,"[12] but would have to survive "exacting scrutiny," which required both a sufficiently important government interest and a substantial relationship between the governmental interest and the disclosure requirement.[13] The Court then identified three governmental interests that, taken together, *did* satisfy the "exacting scrutiny" the Constitution required.[14] The first has come to be known as the "informational" interest:

> [D]isclosure provides the electorate with information as to where political campaign money comes from and how it is spent by the candidate in order to aid the voters in evaluating those who seek federal office. It allows voters to place each candidate in the political spectrum more precisely than is often possible solely on the basis of party labels and campaign speeches. The sources of a candidate's financial support also alert the voter to the interests to which a candidate is most likely to be responsive and thus facilitate predictions of future performance in office.[15]

Next, the Court explained that disclosure furthered an important interest in preventing both corruption and the appearance of corruption, reasoning that "exposing large contributions and expenditures to the light of publicity" was likely to "discourage those who would use money for improper purposes either before or after the election,"[16] as well as to equip the public to detect "any post-election special favors that may be given in return."[17]

Finally, the Court concluded that disclosure was justified by an "enforcement interest"—that is, that the law's "recordkeeping, reporting, and

[10] *Id.* at 145 (citing 52 U.S.C. § 30101, formerly § 434(e)); *accord Buckley*, 424 U.S. at 63–64.

[11] *Id.* at 64. To underscore the significance of this interest, the Court pointed to cases like *NAACP v. Alabama*, 357 U.S. 449, 466 (1964) (holding that Alabama could not compel the state chapter of the NAACP to disclose the names of its staff and members), and *Bates v. Little Rock*, 361 U.S. 516, 527 (1960) (holding that the City of Little Rock could not demand lists of NAACP members and staff).

[12] *Buckley*, 424 U.S. at 64.

[13] *Id.* (internal quotation marks omitted).

[14] *Id.* at 64–66.

[15] *Id.* at 66–67 (internal quotation marks omitted).

[16] *Id.* at 67.

[17] *Id.*

disclosure requirements" were necessary to police compliance with FECA's other provisions.[18]

The Court found these interests "sufficiently important to outweigh the possibility of infringement [of First Amendment rights], particularly when the 'free functioning of our national institutions' is involved."[19] But it left the door open to future as-applied challenges, where there was a demonstrated "reasonable probability" that disclosure would result in "threats, harassment, or reprisals."[20]

In addition to affirming the availability of as-applied challenges, the Court limited the sweep of disclosure requirements in two ways. First, it limited the definition of *political committee* to organizations whose "major purpose … is the nomination or election of a candidate."[21] This meant, among other things, that only such entities were subject to the law's committee disclosure requirements. And second, it narrowed the independent-organization disclosure requirements to "contributions earmarked for political purposes or authorized or requested by a candidate or his agent," and "expenditures for communications that expressly advocate the election or defeat of a clearly identified candidate."[22]

The Court cited disclosure requirements in generally approving terms in a number of post-*Buckley* cases.[23] But it was not until the 2003 case *McConnell*

[18] *Id.* at 67–68.

[19] *Id.* at 66 (quoting Communist Party v. Subversive Activities Control Bd., 367 U.S. 1, 97 (1961).

[20] *Id.* at 74. This discussion occurred primarily in the context of the Court's evaluation of the argument that a blanket exemption to the disclosure requirements was warranted for independent and third-party candidates, but its general interest-balancing analysis has been understood to apply more broadly. *See id.* at 72–74. In *Brown v. Socialist Workers '74 Campaign Committee*, 459 U.S. 87, 102 (1982), the Court found that the Socialist Workers Party *was* entitled to such an exemption from Ohio's campaign finance disclosure law.

[21] *Buckley*, 424 U.S. at 79.

[22] *Id.* at 80. The Court tied this limiting definition to an earlier definition of "express advocacy" as involving "express words of advocacy of election or defeat, such as 'vote for,' 'elect,' 'support,' 'cast your ballot for,' 'Smith for Congress,' 'vote against,' 'defeat,' 'reject.'" *Id.* at 44 n. 52.

[23] *See, e.g.*, Buckley v. Am. Constitutional Law Found., Inc., 525 U.S. 182, 223 (1999) (O'Connor, J., concurring in part and dissenting in part) ("[T]otal disclosure has been recognized as the essential cornerstone to effective campaign finance reform and fundamental to the political system.") (internal quotation marks and citations omitted); FEC v. Mass. Citizens for Life, Inc., 479 U.S. 238, 262 (1986) (invalidating FECA's independent corporate expenditure limitations as applied to a nonprofit ideological corporation, but also citing with approval the disclosure provisions that continued to apply to the plaintiff group, and noting that "[t]hese reporting obligations provide precisely the information necessary to monitor MCFL's independent spending activity and its receipt of contributions"); First Nat'l Bank of Bos. v. Bellotti, 435 U.S. 765, 791–92 & n. 32 (1978) (invalidating Massachusetts's limitations on corporate spending on ballot initiatives, and remarking that "the people in our democracy are entrusted with the responsibility for judging and evaluating the relative merits of conflicting arguments,"

v. Federal Election Commission that it again addressed disclosure in depth.[24] The *McConnell* Court split 5-4 on the constitutionality of many of the substantive provisions of the 2002 Bipartisan Campaign Reform Act (BCRA).[25] But the Court was nearly unanimous in upholding the law's expanded disclosure requirements.[26] The Court explained that "the important state interests that prompted the *Buckley* Court to uphold FECA's disclosure requirements—providing the electorate with information, deterring actual corruption and avoiding any appearance thereof, and gathering the data necessary to enforce more substantive electioneering restrictions—apply in full to [the disclosure requirements created by] BCRA."[27]

In three cases in the last eight years, the Court has again reaffirmed the constitutionality of broad disclosure requirements. In *Citizens United v. Federal Election Commission*, which began as a case largely about disclosure, eight Justices resoundingly upheld the constitutionality of BCRA's expanded disclosure requirements, finding those requirements plainly justified by the "informational interest" in disclosure. (Because the Court credited this interest, it found no need even to discuss the other government interests that might be implicated.) Justice Anthony Kennedy wrote that "The First Amendment protects political speech; and disclosure permits citizens and shareholders to react to the speech of corporate entities in a proper way. This transparency enables the electorate to make informed decisions and give proper weight to different speakers and messages."[28]

Though disclosure was not directly at issue in *McCutcheon v. Federal Election Commision*, in which the Court considered the constitutionality of the aggregate limits on contributions to candidates and committees, the Court in that case went out of its way to reaffirm that "[d]isclosure of contributions minimizes the potential for abuse of the campaign finance system …

and that "[i]dentification of the source of advertising may be required as a means of disclosure, so that the people will be able to evaluate the arguments to which they are being subjected").

24 540 U.S. 93 (2003).

25 Bipartisan Campaign Reform Act (BCRA) of 2002, Pub. L. No. 107–155, 116 Stat. 81 (codified at (codified at 52 U.S.C. § 30101, formerly 2 U.S.C. § 431 (2002)), *invalided in part by* Citizens United v. FEC, 558 U.S. 310 (2010).

26 *See McConnell*, 540 U.S. at 190–92 (opinion of Justices Stevens and O'Connor, joined by Justices Souter and Ginsburg) (rejecting challenge to BCRA's expanded disclosure requirements), *id.* at 231 (opinion of Rehnquist, C.J., joined in relevant part by all Justices but Thomas) (BCRA's disclosure provisions bear "a sufficient relationship" to the important governmental interest of " 'shed[ding] the light of publicity' on campaign financing") (internal quotations omitted).

27 540 U.S. at 196.

28 *Citizens United*, 558 U.S. at 370 (citations and internal quotations omitted).

disclosure … offers a particularly effective means of arming the voting public with information."[29]

Doe v. Reed, though not a campaign finance case, represents the Court's last major foray into disclosure in recent years.[30] *Doe* involved a referendum petition to put to a popular vote a state same-sex domestic partner benefits bill. Following the signature drive, a number of groups sought access to the referendum petitions under the state's public records law. Both the sponsor and certain petition signatories brought a First Amendment challenge to the public-records law. Construing the case as a facial challenge, the Court held that the law, though it did implicate First Amendment interests, was justified by the government's compelling interest in "preserving the integrity of the electoral process."[31] Justice Antonin Scalia concurred separately, setting forth the view, not by its logic limited to the referendum signature context, that "[r]equiring people to stand up in public for their political acts fosters civic courage, without which democracy is doomed."[32]

As this discussion makes clear, a strong majority of the Court has struck a remarkably pro-disclosure note in a number of cases, including in recent years, making disclosure a noteworthy exception to the strongly deregulatory arc of the Roberts Court in campaign finance regulation more broadly.[33] And both state and lower federal courts have followed the Supreme Court's lead, for the most part rejecting challenges to disclosure requirements. But, importantly, in *all* of the campaign finance cases discussed above, disclosure challenges have come before the Court paired with challenges to other, more substantive forms of campaign finance regulation; perhaps for that reason, the Court's disclosure discussions have generally been fairly cursory, often without particularly developed reasoning.[34] This means that the constitutional politics of disclosure may be less stable than the excerpts above suggest.[35]

B. Practice

The preceding section walked through the Supreme Court's major encounters with disclosure. But there is a sizable gulf between the Court's rhetoric when

[29] McCutcheon v. FEC, 134 S. Ct. 1434 (2014).
[30] 561 U.S. 186 (2010).
[31] *Id.* at 197.
[32] *Id.* at 228 (Scalia, J., concurring).
[33] Richard L. Hasen, *Election Law's Path in the Roberts Court's First Decade: A Sharp Right Turn but with Speed Bumps and Surprising Twists*, 68 Stan. L. Rev. 1597, 1604–05 (2016).
[34] Katherine Shaw, *Taking Disclosure Seriously*, Yale J.L. & Pol'y Inter Alia 18, 19 (2016).
[35] *Id.*

it comes to disclosure, and the on-the-ground reality of our disclosure system. Accordingly, this part provides a (necessarily abbreviated) overview of the current practice of disclosure, highlighting the ways in which current practice fails to align with the Court's rhetoric.[36]

1. Dark Money and Gray Money

First, much of the money that flows through American elections today is either not subject to public disclosure at all ("dark money"), or is disclosed in a way that obscures the true sources of election spending ("gray money").[37]

For the most part, the term "dark money" refers to money spent on elections by social welfare groups organized under section 501(c)(4) of the Internal Revenue Code (and to a lesser extent other exempt organizations organized under sections 501(c)(5) and 501(c)(6) of the Code—I refer to all of these as "social welfare" organizations throughout). Such organizations are tax exempt, but, unlike section 501(c)(3) organizations, they are not prohibited from engaging in political activity.[38] Rather, the IRS has advised that a social welfare organization may engage in political activity "so long as that is not its primary activity."[39] Many such organizations have interpreted this guidance to mean that "as long as expenditures on these activities do not exceed fifty percent of the organization's expenditures … anything goes … regardless of the nature of the political activities and whether they are in furtherance of the organization's social welfare purposes."[40] And, though such entities must report their expenditures on an IRS Form 990 as part of

[36] The picture painted in this section is primarily of the federal system; space limitations preclude any real consideration of the practice in the states.

[37] LEE ET AL., *supra* note 1, at 5.

[38] Rev. Rul. 81–95, 1981-1 C.B. 332 ("In order to qualify for exemption under section 501(c)(4) of the Code, an organization must be primarily engaged in activities that promote social welfare. Although the promotion of social welfare within the meaning of section 1.501(c)(4)-1 of the regulations does not include political campaign activities, the regulations do not impose a complete ban on such activities for section 501(c)(4) organizations. Thus, an organization may carry on lawful political activities and remain exempt under section 501(c)(4) as long as it is primarily engaged in activities that promote social welfare"; *see also Social Welfare Organizations*, IRS.GOV, www.irs.gov/charities-non-profits/other-non-profits/social-welfare-organizations. *See generally* Terence Dougherty, *Section 501(c)(4) Advocacy Organizations: Political Candidate-Related and Other Partisan Activities in Furtherance of the Social Welfare*, 36 SEATTLE U. L. REV. 1337 (2013).

[39] Rev. Rul. 81–95, 1981-1 C.B. 332. *See also* Ellen P. Aprill, *Political Speech of Noncharitable Exempt Organizations after* Citizens United, 10 ELECTION L.J. 363, 381 (2011).

[40] Dougherty, *supra* note 38, at 1339.

their annual tax filings, contributors to such entities are not made publicly available.[41]

The relevant campaign finance statutes do not distinguish between for-profit and non-profit entities. But they limit meaningful disclosure in two distinct ways. As to any entity that makes an "independent expenditure" of over $250 per year, the law requires the filing of certain reports with the FEC. But, though federal statutes contain arguably conflicting directives about what those reports must contain,[42] the FEC has determined that independent spenders must report the identity of contributors *only* for contributions "made for the purpose of furthering the reported independent expenditure."[43] Since most contributors do not earmark their contributions in any way, under this interpretation there is essentially no disclosure of contributor identity.

Similarly, in the case of "electioneering"—ads that name a candidate without expressly urging any action, like a vote for or against that candidate—federal law would *seem* to require full disclosure of expenditures and contributors above a certain level. A federal statute requires entities that spend over $10,000 per year to disclose "names and addresses of all contributors who contributed an aggregate amount of $1,000 or more to the person making the disbursement" during the election cycle.[44] But an FEC regulation limits such disclosure, like independent expenditure disclosure, to contributions made "for the purpose of furthering electioneering communications,"[45] so such contributors also typically go undisclosed.

So the IRS permits tax-exempt organizations to engage in campaign-related activity; and the FEC requires the disclosure of contributors only where the contributions are specifically earmarked for political activity (and they rarely are). All of this means that a great deal of outside money is subject to no real transparency at all. According to one study, "Dark money ads amounted to nearly 14 percent of all ads aired in the 2012 cycle, and 47 percent of all interest group ads."[46]

The term "gray money" is typically used to refer to the activities of groups known as "Super PACs." These entities cropped up in the wake of the

[41] The IRS Form 990 requires the inclusion of contributors above $5,000, but such contributors are not subject to public disclosure. *See Instructions for Form 990 Return of Organization Exempt From Income Tax*, IRS.GOV, www.irs.gov/pub/irs-pdf/i990.pdf; *see also* Aprill, *supra* note 39.

[42] *Compare* 52 U.S.C. § 30104(c)(1) *to* 52 U.S.C. § 30104(c)(2)(C).

[43] 11 C.F.R. § 109.10(e)(1)(vi).

[44] 52 U.S.C. § 30104(f).

[45] 11 C.F.R. § 104.20(c)(9). *See also* Van Hollen v. FEC, 811 F.3d 486 (D.C. Cir. 2016).

[46] Travis N. Ridout, Michael M. Franz & Erika Franklin Fowler, *Sponsorship, Disclosure, and Donors: Limiting the Impact of Outside Group Ads*, 68 POL. RES. Q. 154, 156 (2015).

decision of the U.S. Court of Appeals for the D.C. Circuit in *SpeechNow.org v. Federal Election Commission*, which read the logic of *Citizens United* as condemning limits on contributions to political committees that make exclusively independent expenditures.[47] Super PACS, though they can accept unlimited contributions under *SpeechNow*, are still PACs, which means they are required to provide detailed information to the FEC (in contrast to the nonprofits described in the preceding section). But, importantly, the donors whose identities they are required to report are often other entities—including 501(c)(4) organizations, which can give to PACs and then shield their own donors as described above. So Super PAC disclosure, though in theory quite robust, frequently provides little meaningful information about the sources of PAC funds.

2. Hard Money: Flaws and Limitations

So the under-inclusiveness of our system of disclosure is one major problem. But even money that *is* subject to disclosure—the "hard money" spent by campaigns, parties, and regular PACs—suffers from flaws when it comes to the collection of meaningful, high-value information of the sort voters need if disclosure is to achieve the objectives the Supreme Court has identified.

Federal law requires campaigns and committees to provide the FEC with the first and last name, occupation, employer, and address of any individual who makes a contribution over $200. Despite this requirement, FEC records reflect a number of problems, which sociologist Jennifer Heerwig has grouped into three categories: selective compliance (donors who comply with some but not all disclosure requirements—that is, leaving particular fields blank); the provision of information that is vague (providing one's occupation as "self-employed," say, or "slumlord"[48]), and dissimulation (supplying information that masks one's true identity or interests).[49] Perhaps more important, under the current disclosure regime it is extraordinarily time-consuming to track the activity of particular donors across elections and over periods of time. All of this means that FEC records are often far less informative than they might be.

47 599 F.3d 686, 689 (D.C. Cir. 2010).

48 *See* Eric Lichtblau, *White Supremacist Who Influenced Charleston Suspect Donated to 2016 G.O.P. Campaigns*, N.Y. Times (June 22, 2015), www.nytimes.com/2015/06/22/us/campaign-donations-linked-to-white-supremacist.html.

49 Jennifer Heerwig, *Diagnosing Disclosure: A Social Scientific Perspective on the Disclosure Debate*, 34 Yale L. & Pol'y Rev. Inter Alia 8, 10 (2016).

3. Accessibility and Impact

To be sure, developments in technology have made information about hard money more accessible than ever before. While FEC files once needed to be reviewed in hard copy, they are now available for anyone with an internet connection (though subject to some of the limitations identified above). Interested members of the electorate can now use the FEC's website to access information about contributions made by specific individuals, as well as to view graphics containing information about both congressional and presidential races. But as a general matter, the data is not presented by the FEC in a fashion that facilitates its use by ordinary voters.

C. *Empirical Research*

For many years, disclosure debates unfolded without the benefit of much research on either the costs or the benefits of disclosure.[50] Social scientists have begun to remedy that state of affairs, though much work remains to be done. This part briefly walks through what the data show with respect to both the costs and benefits of disclosure.

1. Quantifying Benefits

Research on the informational benefits of campaign finance disclosure remains limited, but several studies stand out.[51] First, a classic political science text by Arthur Lupia assessed the impact of disclosure on voters in a California ballot initiative.[52] On the ballot were five distinct propositions, all related to car insurance.[53] Three separate interest groups—the insurance industry, trial

[50] John C. Fortier & Michael J. Malbin, *An Agenda for Future Research on Money in Politics in the United States*, 11 THE FORUM 455, 473 (2013) ("Current research on disclosure is fairly sparse, pointing to contrary results."). *Cf.* Daniel P. Tokaji & Renata E. B. Strause, *How Sausage Is Made: A Research Agenda for Campaign Finance and Lobbying*, 164 U. PA. L. REV. ONLINE 223, 228 (2016) ("Advocates of reform should … set aside the theoretical debate in order to engage in an empirical assessment of the effects that present-day independent spending is actually having on elections and governance.").

[51] I should note that the other interest courts have credited in the disclosure realm—preventing corruption and the appearance of corruption—remains essentially untested as an empirical matter. *Cf.* DANIEL P. TOKAJI & RENATA E. B. STRAUSE, THE NEW SOFT MONEY: OUTSIDE SPENDING IN CONGRESSIONAL ELECTIONS (2014) (reporting the results of several months of interviews with members of Congress, candidates, and staff members, regarding the impact of outside spending on campaigns and governance).

[52] Arthur Lupia, *Shortcuts Versus Encyclopedias: Information and Voting Behavior in California Insurance Reform Elections*, 88 AM. POL. SCI. REV. 63 (1994).

[53] *Id.* at 64.

lawyers, and consumer groups—had weighed in to either support or to oppose various propositions. The study found that where voters could identify the interest group backing a particular proposition, even poorly informed voters were able to mirror the decision-making processes of their more well-informed peers.[54] This means, the author concluded, that, at least in the ballot-initiative context, information about the sources of support may provide voters with valuable data they can then use to cast better-informed votes.[55]

More recently, findings from a 2013 experimental study by political scientist Michael Sances suggest that disclosure about political money can supply voters with a useful guide to candidate ideology.[56] Participants in Sances' study were shown an edited political ad in support of a candidate. The ad discussed job creation, typically a non-partisan issue, and made no mention of political party.[57] Some participants were also shown a disclaimer indicating that a fictional organization, "Americans for Change," was responsible for the advertisement.[58] Two groups were also shown text that purported to list the top contributors to "Americans for Change": one, the "Labor Disclosure" group, was shown a list of five labor unions; the other, the "Business Disclosure" group, was shown a list of five corporations.[59] Participants were then asked how likely they were to vote for the candidate. Compared to subjects who were not provided disclosures listing the top contributors to the fictional organization, Republican subjects were significantly less likely to register support for the candidate when shown the labor contributors; Democratic subjects were less likely to indicate support for the candidate when informed that the top contributors were corporations.[60]

In another recent piece, Conor Dowling and Amber Wichowsky similarly attempted to test the effects of disclosure by assessing whether, and how, disclosing the funders of political messages might impact the effectiveness of those messages (here, negative or "attack" ads). In one experiment, the authors found that where participants were shown an attack ad alone, that ad tended to erode support for the candidate being attacked; *but* where participants were also provided with information about the donors to the entity responsible for the ad—in this instance the group American Crossroads—the disclosure

54 *Id.* at 72.
55 *Id.*
56 Michael W. Sances, *Is Money in Politics Harming Trust in Government? Evidence From Two Survey Experiments*, 12 Election L.J. 53, 54 (2013).
57 *Id.* at 56.
58 *Id.* at 56.
59 *Id.* at 56–57.
60 *Id.* at 57–59.

moved "aggregate opinion roughly back to where it would have been had participants not watched the ad in the first place."[61] Those findings were confirmed by another, similar study by Travis Ridout, Michael Franz and Erika Fowler; though its findings were more complex, the authors concluded that information about the contributors to the group responsible for an attack ad had, in some cases, a significant impact on the perceived credibility of the ad, and thus its effectiveness.[62] And a recent piece by Abby Wood suggests that the informational benefits of disclosure may include supplying voters with high-value information about candidate positions on transparency itself.[63]

Taken together, these pieces suggest that individuals *do* utilize information about the sources of support in elections (whether candidate elections or ballot initiatives). But it is clear, from these studies and others, that the form in which the information is presented is of paramount importance. For example, another finding of the Dowling and Wichowsky study discussed above is that where individuals learned about the supporters of particular ads by reading news accounts, rather than via some other mechanism, that information had no impact on viewers' reactions to the ad.[64] This is consistent with a finding by David Primo—that mock newspaper articles containing disclosure information had no statistically significant impact on voters' ability to identify the positions of interest groups on a ballot issue.[65]

2. Evaluating Costs

So disclosure does appear, from the limited empirical work on the topic, to provide voters with informational benefits (though the form of disclosure matters). But what about the other side of the equation? Does disclosure

[61] Conor M. Dowling & Amber Wichowsky, *Does It Matter Who's Behind the Curtain? Anonymity in Political Advertising and the Effects of Campaign Finance Disclosure*, 41 Am. Pol. Res. 965, 978 (2013).

[62] Ridout et al., *supra* note 46. The impact of the particular disclosure varied significantly—information that an unknown entity was responsible for an attack ad made the ad more effective than it would have been had the opposing candidate been responsible, but information that even a small grass-roots group was responsible for the ad made the ad *less* credible than if there had been no disclosure at all.

[63] Abby K. Wood, Campaign Finance Disclosure and Voter Competence, Working Paper (on file with author).

[64] Dowling & Wichowsky, *supra* note 62, at 981 ("[W]hile identifying the top five donors in a table format resulted in participants being more supportive of the attacked candidate compared to only viewing the ad, we find no statistically significant evidence that reading a news article discussing the donors to American Crossroads moved opinion").

[65] David M. Primo, *Information at the Margin: Campaign Finance Disclosure Laws, Ballot Issues, and Voter Knowledge*, 12 Election L.J. 112, 114, 126–27 (2013).

impose serious costs—in particular, does it deter individuals from giving political money, as some have assumed?[66] To date, there is no real support for the proposition that disclosure acts as a *major* deterrent to political contributions, though some scholarship confirms the hypothesis that mandatory disclosure will have at least some deterrent effect.

Political scientist Ray La Raja, noting that we currently lack both "a theoretical framework and empirical research"[67] for evaluating the costs and benefits of disclosure, recently reported the findings of an experimental study designed to determine whether potential donors were deterred from giving by the prospect of publicity.[68] His results were mixed: although the prospect of public disclosure had little to no impact on would-be donors' willingness to make contributions,[69] information about specific thresholds above which contributions would be publicized *did* result in smaller overall contributions.[70] And, significantly, individuals who faced "strong interpersonal cross-pressures from people around them"[71]—that is, those who reported that they were not surrounded by like-minded individuals—were found to be "most likely to stop giving or donate at considerably smaller amounts to avoid the threshold amount,"[72] likely because they feared the social or other costs that might result from revealing their political preferences.

An even more recent piece by Abby Wood and Douglas Spencer relied on reported state-level contribution data across states that both did and did not expand state-level disclosure requirements over the period of the study. Wood and Spencer found that contributors were "only slightly less likely to contribute in future elections in states that increase the public visibility of campaign contributions, relative to contributors in states that do not change their disclosure laws or practices over the same time period," and noted that for the most part these changes in contribution behavior were negligible.[73]

66 *See, e.g.*, Van Hollen v. FEC, 811 F.3d 486, 488 (D.C. Cir. 2016) ("Disclosure chills speech"); Michael Gilbert, *Campaign Finance Disclosure and the Information Tradeoff*, 98 Iowa L. Rev. 1847, 1849 (2013) (arguing that in addition to its informational benefits, disclosure can actually "chill speech").

67 Ray J. La Raja, *Political Participation and Civic Courage: The Negative Effect of Transparency on Making Small Campaign Contributions*, 36 Pol. Behav. 753, 754 (2014).

68 *Id.* at 755.

69 *Id.* at 762.

70 *Id.* at 768.

71 *Id.* at 770.

72 *Id.* at 770.

73 Abby K. Wood & Douglas M. Spencer, *In the Shadows of Sunlight: The Effects of Transparency on State Political Campaigns* 15 Election L.J. 302, 311 (2016) (estimating one "chilled" donor per candidate).

Beyond this scholarly work, both case law and the popular press make clear that the targeting of individuals for harassment or retaliation based on disclosure of political contributions does occur. In *Brown v. Socialist Workers '74 Campaign Committee*,[74] the Court sustained a minor party's as-applied challenge to compelled disclosure, citing "numerous instances of recent harassment" by both private parties and the government.[75] More recently, in the course of considering a challenge to the broadcasting of the trial over California's Proposition 8, the 2008 ballot initiative in which California voters amended their state's constitution to recognize "only marriage between a man and a woman," the Court noted allegations of harassment, including death threats and vandalism, against Proposition 8's supporters.[76] And press accounts suggest that Mozilla CEO Brendan Eich resigned after his financial support for Proposition 8 was made public.[77] But neither the prevalence of this sort of activity, nor its impact on the behavior of active or prospective donors, is yet clear.

III. MAKING DISCLOSURE WORK

The preceding sections surveyed the current disclosure landscape. In this section, I make a number of recommendations, ranging from the practical to the theoretical, for improving this important and underappreciated element of our system of campaign finance regulation. I am guided in this effort by a succinct summation offered by Michael Malbin and Thomas Gais two decades ago. Campaign finance disclosure can only work, they wrote, if: "(1) Most candidates and political organizations report what they do accurately; (2) Such reports in fact comprise most of the activities and relationships of importance to voters; (3) The reports are available in a useful format, and at an accessible location; (4) Interested, knowledgeable people read and interpret the reports and then make useful information available in a timely way to voters; (5) Voters are able and willing to use the information as a basis for making an election decision."[78] The recommendations offered below would bring us significantly closer to achieving these objectives.

74 459 U.S. 87 (1982).

75 *Id.* at 100–1.

76 Hollingsworth v. Perry, 130 S. Ct. 705, 707 (2010) (per curiam).

77 Alistair Barr, *Mozilla CEO Brendan Eich Steps Down: Attention Focused on his Support of Anti-Gay Marriage Ballot Proposal*, WALL ST. J. (Apr. 3, 2014).

78 MICHAEL MALBIN & THOMAS L. GAIS, THE DAY AFTER REFORM: SOBERING CAMPAIGN FINANCE LESSONS FROM THE STATES 36 (1998).

A. *Expanding Disclosure*

One obvious gap in the current system is the amount of political money that is currently not subject to meaningful disclosure. Several fixes are possible here. First, the IRS could limit the ability of social welfare organizations to engage in political activity. Even if it did not ban such activity outright, as it does with 501(c)(3) charitable organizations,[79] it might impose a much stricter limit than it currently allows; Ellen Aprill has suggested that such organizations might appropriately be limited to devoting 10–15 percent of their total activities to politicking rather than the *de facto* 50 percent ceiling that is currently in effect.[80] Alternatively, it could make public the information it already collects from social welfare organization via IRS Form 990; since those entities are already required to report contributions above $5,000, it would be a simple fix to make such information publicly available.[81]

But a far better solution would be to bring all entities that engage in election-related spending under the same disclosure regime—and, short of the creation of a new entity, the best organization to oversee all disclosure would be the FEC. One way to achieve this would be to expand the definition of a PAC in order to sweep in all entities that engage in campaign spending. This could be challenging: notwithstanding the Supreme Court's general approval of disclosure, the Court has evidenced some concern about what it perceives as the burdens posed by the requirements of the PAC form. Justice Kennedy's majority opinion in *Citizens United*, in rejecting the argument that the option to speak through a PAC mitigated any constitutional concerns about the corporate speech limitation, wrote that "PACs are burdensome alternatives; they are expensive to administer and subject to extensive regulations."[82] But, critically, that statement was made in the context of a discussion that was predicated on the existence of meaningful disclosure by non-PAC entities. In light of the obvious shortcomings of that assumption,

[79] In theory, the IRS could go further by simply aligning the standards of the tax exempt organizations that currently engage in political activity with 501(c)(3)s—in other words, by prohibiting social welfare organizations from engaging in any political activity at all. The Court explained in *Regan v. Taxation without Representation*, 461 U.S. 540, 545–46 (1983), that the government has no obligation to subsidize political activities, like lobbying, by nonprofit organizations. But in the post-*Citizens United* era, it is not clear that a categorical ban of this sort would pass constitutional muster. *See* Brian Galle, *Charities in Politics: A Reappraisal*, 54 Wm. & Mary L. Rev. 1561 (2013).

[80] Aprill, *supra* note 39, at 382.

[81] Such information already appears on Schedule B of IRS Form 990. *See id.* at 403–4 & n. 327.

[82] Citizens United v. FEC, 558 U.S. 310, 337 (2010).

the Court could well come to a different conclusion about the permissibility of imposing PAC-like requirements on all independent campaign spenders.[83]

Three other possibilities bear mentioning. First, a movement has cropped up in recent years to use the Securities and Exchange Commission to require public companies to provide shareholders with information about campaign spending.[84] Second, at least one academic proposal suggests that the Federal Communications Commission could use existing authorities to require independent spenders to engage in disclosure as a condition of the purchase of advertising airtime.[85] Third, state nonprofit law may be another site of possible reform, and states like California have already begun requiring nonprofits that engage in political activity to provide the state with information about the sources of their contributions.[86] But these proposals, though constructive, are limited in scope; they would also result in the addition of new government entities as well as new sites of information to the regulatory mix.

B. *Improving Disclosure*

Several simple fixes to our hard-money system could significantly improve the quality of campaign-finance data on what is still the most important source of money in federal elections.[87] First, the use of standardized forms at the FEC, perhaps with drop-down menus of the sort used in the Census long form, would facilitate the provision of more useful information, and eliminate the prospect of evasive or non-responsive answers. Second, donors should be given unique ID numbers, which would facilitate identification—by scholars, journalists, and interested and engaged voters—of the largest and most significant donors.

83 *Cf.* Marcia Coyle, *Justice Anthony Kennedy Loathes the Term Swing Vote*, NAT'L L.J. (Oct. 27, 2015), www.nationallawjournal.com/id=1202740827841/Justice-Anthony-Kennedy-Loathes-the-Term-Swing-Vote?slreturn=20160905224907.

84 Lucian A. Bebchuk & Robert J. Jackson, *Shining Light on Corporate Political Spending*, 101 GEO L.J. 923, 925 (2013) (arguing that "the SEC should develop rules requiring public companies to disclose political spending to shareholders").

85 Lili Levi, *Plan B for Campaign-Finance Reform: Can the FCC Help Save American Politics After* Citizens United?, 61 CATH. U. L. REV. 97, 101 (2011) (arguing that the FCC can use existing authority "to require third-party purchasers of airtime for political and advocacy advertising to disclose their major direct and indirect funding sources and principal directors, officers, or operators").

86 *See* Linda Sugin, *Politics, Disclosure, and State Law Solutions for 501(c)(4) Organizations*, 91 CHI.-KENT. L. REV. 895 (2016).

87 Jennifer Heerwig, *supra* note 49, at 10 (2016). *See also* RACES IN WHICH OUTSIDE SPENDING EXCEEDS CANDIDATE SPENDING, 2014 ELECTION CYCLE, CENTER FOR RESPONSIVE POLITICS, www.opensecrets.org/outsidespending/outvscand.php?cycle=2014 (showing that in the 2014 congressional campaigns, outside groups outspent candidates in 28 races, but that candidates spent more in the remaining 443).

These two simple fixes would considerably improve the quality of data the FEC collects and maintains.

C. *Delivering Disclosure*

The FEC has made significant strides in making its data publicly available in recent years, including the very recent launch of a more interactive web portal. But a still more effective disclosure regime would allow voters to use the FEC's website to explore the vectors of political influence—perhaps, for example, by showing voters how much money a particular official has received from high-dollar contributors, or the industries or sectors from which most donations to a particular candidate come.

Even a vastly improved FEC website, however, would have limited impact, as only a small subset of the electorate engages directly with such data. If disclosure is actually to impact the behavior of voters, it needs to be presented to voters at a time and in a format that could actually affect voting behavior. Although American citizens are not going to become perfectly informed voters anytime soon, individuals with limited information are certainly capable of making informed choices.[88] The challenge, then, is how best to provide voters with information that might empower and enable them to do that.

Archon Fung, Mary Graham, and David Weil, the authors of the seminal text *Full Disclosure: The Perils and Promise of Transparency*,[89] describe restaurant-hygiene disclosure as a paradigmatic example of successful disclosure. As they explain, hygiene grades ("A," "B," "C"), typically posted in restaurant windows, "have become highly embedded in customers' … decisional processes. A restaurant's grade is available *when* users need it … *where* they need it … and in a *format* that makes complex information quickly comprehensible."[90]

How, then, to deliver campaign finance information to voters in a way that mirrors what is so effective about restaurant sanitation grades? Disclaimers,

[88] *See* Elizabeth Garrett & Daniel A. Smith, *Veiled Political Actors and Campaign Disclosure Laws in Direct Democracy*, 4 Election L.J. 295, 296 (2005) ("No voter needs to acquire all available information to competently make a reasoned decision. Instead, she can rely on particular pieces of information, connected non-accidentally to accurate conclusions about the consequences of her vote, and still vote competently.")

[89] Archon Fung, Mary Graham & David Weil, Full Disclosure: The Perils and Promise of Transparency (2007). Specifically, they write, "Successful policies focus first on the needs and interests of information users, as well as their abilities to comprehend the information provided by the system.…They seek to embed new facts in the decision-making routines of information users and to embed user responses in the decision making of disclosers," *Id.* at 11.

[90] *Id.* at 83.

which appear as part of political advertisements, are one obvious site of potential reform. At present, a provision of federal law upheld in *Citizens United* requires independent spenders to include in their ads disclaimers that read "____ is responsible for the content of this advertising," both spoken and displayed on the screen for at least four seconds.[91] (Candidates' own ads are subject to similar requirements.[92]) But because such entities typically use names that are benign, patriotic-sounding, and generally uninformative,[93] the disclosed information does not ordinarily communicate much of value.

Justin Levitt has proposed the creation of a "Democracy Facts" label to appear within campaign communications, "emphasizing simple proxies for the quantity and fervor of local support for a particular communication," including the number of supporters in a given jurisdiction, as well as the percentage of support supplied by top donors.[94] This sort of detail could make disclaimers more genuinely informative. Another possibility would be to require organizations to craft a mission or policy statement for inclusion in their disclaimers. As research like the Lupia study described above shows, information about the supporters of particular causes and messages *can* equip voters to make choices that better align with their preferences. Of course, choosing between two or more candidates is quite distinct from the decision about where to eat dinner. But the general point—that information should be delivered near in time to voting and in an accessible format—seems entirely applicable.

D. *Testing and Theorizing Disclosure*

Another important task is more academic: the need to engage in additional empirical research on how best to design and deliver disclosure, and, relatedly, to develop a more fully realized set of arguments that emphasize the constitutional values advanced by disclosure. As a number of scholars have noted,[95] in the post-*Citizens United* era, opponents of campaign finance regulation have begun to focus on challenging the premises of disclosure

91 2 U.S.C. § 441d(d)(1)(B) (2002).

92 *Citizens United*, 530 F. Supp. 2d at 280 (citing 2 U.S.C. § 441d(a)(3) (2002)). The law also requires the sponsors of ads to provide in the disclaimers identifying information that includes the name, address, and phone number or website of the sponsor.

93 Heerwig & Shaw, *supra* note 2, at 1496.

94 Justin Levitt, *Confronting the Impact of* Citizens United, 29 Yale L. & Pol'y Rev. 217, 227–28 (2010). For a visual representation of Levitt's "Democracy Facts," see http://electionlawblog.org/archives/DemocracyFacts.html.

95 Michael Kang, *Campaign Disclosure in Direct Democracy*, 97 Minn. L. Rev. 1700, 1700 (2013) ("[C]ampaign disclosure laws now are under legal and political attack as never before.").

laws;[96] meanwhile, the affirmative case for disclosure has lagged behind. Establishing a solid theoretical and empirical framework is critical both to designing better disclosure and to successfully defending disclosure against attack.[97]

E. *Taking Privacy Seriously*

Finally, any attempts to improve disclosure along the lines described above should take seriously the privacy concerns disclosure implicates.[98] One way to address privacy concerns is to explore partially de-identifying campaign finance data before public release. Bruce Cain has written in favor of what he calls "semi-disclosure";[99] noting that the government already employs a kind of semi-disclosure in the case of the census, aggregating identifying information to avoid revealing sensitive personal details, he suggests that we ought to do the same with campaign finance data. This insight has a definite appeal; at the very least, in the internet age, the benefits of requiring donors to supply a physical address seems outweighed by the potential privacy threats represented by the availability of such information online. One additional possibility is the creation of a tiered system in which data about small donors are available only in the aggregate, while the identity of donors above a certain threshold, which is of additional informational value, would be revealed.[100]

IV. CONCLUSION

For many years, disclosure has played a largely ancillary role in debates about money in politics. But any serious reform proposal today should include disclosure—both because it has genuine potential for improving our democracy, and because a functioning system of disclosure may well be a necessary predicate to building the case for other sorts of substantive campaign finance reform.

[96] *See, e.g.*, Bradley A. Smith, Scott Blackburn & Luke Wachob, *Compulsory Donor Disclosure: When Government Monitors its Citizens*, www.heritage.org/research/reports/2015/11/compulsory-donor-disclosure-when-government-monitors-its-citizens; Cleta Mitchell, *Donor Disclosure: Undermining the First Amendment*, 96 MINN. L. REV. 1755, 1759 (2012) ("Disclosure is the next frontier for those of us who toil in these vineyards—it will constitute the next wave of legal jurisprudence in the campaign finance arena. In the same way litigants challenged these substantive prohibitions on certain kinds of speech, over time we have to make the case and build a record about the threat posed by disclosure.").

[97] Abby Wood has compiled an excellent list of possible directions for future empirical work. *See* Wood, *supra* note 63, at 14–15.

[98] *See* McIntyre v. Ohio Election Comm'n, 514 U.S. 334 (1995) (holding that Ohio prohibition on anonymous pamphleteering fails to satisfy exacting scrutiny).

[99] Bruce Cain, *Shade from the Glare: The Case for Semi-Disclosure*, CATO UNBOUND (Nov. 8, 2010), www.cato-unbound.org/2010/11/08/bruce-cain/shade-glare-case-semi-disclosure.

[100] Heerwig & Shaw, *supra* note 2, at 1494.

7

Beyond Repair: FEC Reform and Deadlock Deference

Daniel P. Tokaji*

I. INTRODUCTION

No regulatory system can be better than the institutions responsible for implementing the law. From this perspective, the United States' campaign finance system is a colossal failure. The Federal Election Commission (FEC) is the administrative agency responsible for enforcing campaign law. Composed of six commissioners, three aligned with each of the major political parties, the FEC consistently stalemates on important questions.[1] Party line deadlocks have become increasingly common over the past decade, reflecting the larger phenomenon of partisan polarization that infects the American political system. The two major parties now have sharply divergent positions on campaign finance regulation, with Republican-aligned members of the commission routinely voting not to proceed with enforcement over the objection of the Democratic-aligned commissioners. Prominent among the topics of disagreement are the disclosure obligations of non-party groups receiving so-called "dark money." While the FEC's perceived impotence has long caused the reform community to brand it the "Failure to Enforce Commission,"[2]

* Daniel P. Tokaji is the Charles W. Ebersold and Florence Whitcomb Ebersold Professor of Constitutional Law, The Ohio State University Moritz College of Law. The author thanks Ann Ravel, Peter Shane, and Chris Walker for their incisive comments on an earlier draft, particularly their tutelage on administrative law and its implementation. Thanks also to Alex Szaruga for his diligent research assistance and Eugene Mazo for his careful editing. All errors are the author's alone.

1 Public Citizen, *Roiled in Partisan Deadlock, Federal Election Commission Is Failing* (July 19, 2016), www.citizen.org/documents/fec-deadlock-update-april-2015.pdf; Ann M. Ravel, Dysfunction and Deadlock: The Enforcement Crisis at the Federal Election Commission Reveals the Unlikelihood of Draining the Swamp (Feb. 2017) (on file with author).

2 Fred Wertheimer & Don Simon, *The FEC: The Failure to Enforce Commission*, Am. Const. Soc'y (Jan. 2013), www.democracy21.org/wp-content/uploads/2013/02/Wertheimer-and-Simon-The-Failure-to-Enforce-Commission-.pdf.

those complaints have much greater credibility now than in decades past as deadlocks have become more common and partisan disagreements more intransigent.

On the other hand, regulatory skeptics have a point in arguing that the FEC's bipartisan structure was designed to prevent campaign finance enforcement from being used as a political weapon.[3] Campaign finance laws can do great damage if their implementation is slanted to advantage one of the major parties, potentially infringing on the constitutionally protected free speech and association rights of those with a different viewpoint. By creating a bipartisan commission and requiring a majority vote for most of its actions, Congress sought to prevent either major party from unfairly targeting its chief adversary.[4] In addition, the mechanism for selecting commissioners was designed to ensure accountability to the major parties and to Congress,[5] a structure borne of concern that agency enforcement would otherwise be overly aggressive.[6]

That said, the paralysis that grips the FEC today is far beyond anything Congress envisioned. With its persistent stalemates on critical questions, the FEC is no longer capable of performing its basic functions. That includes not only enforcement of federal campaign finance law, but also clarification of the law so that conscientious candidates, parties, and outside groups can follow it.[7]

During the FEC's four-plus decades, there have been repeated calls to replace or restructure the agency. While various alternatives have been suggested, the most prominent would create an odd-numbered body that can take action without votes from the minority party.[8] The major advantage of this proposal

3 Scott Blackburn, *Delusions about "Dysfunction": Understanding the Federal Election Commission*, Center for Competitive Politics (Oct. 5, 2015), www.campaignfreedom.org/2015/10/05/delusions-about-dysfunction-understanding-the-federal-election-commission/.

4 Donald J. Simon, *Current Regulation and Future Challenges for Campaign Financing in the United States*, 3 Election L.J. 474, 485 (2004).

5 *See* Robert E. Mutch, Campaigns, Congress, and Courts: The Making of Federal Campaign Finance Law 87–88 (1988).

6 For background on the FEC's creation and subsequent challenges to its independence, see *id.* at 83–92 (1988) (describing history of FEC's creation and subsequent challenges to its independence). *See also* Meredith McGehee, *Fix the FEC: Background Memorandum on New Bipartisan Legislation to Address a Dysfunctional Agency*, The Campaign Legal Center (Sept. 17, 2015), www.campaignlegalcenter.org/news/publications-speeches/fix-fec-background-memorandum-new-bipartisan-legislation-address-0 (summarizing history of FEC).

7 This chapter uses the terms "outside groups" and "outside spending" to refer to entities engaging in federal campaign activities that are not formally affiliated with federal candidates or political parties. *See* Daniel P. Tokaji & Renata E. B. Strause, The New Soft Money: Outside Spending in Congressional Elections (2014).

8 *See, e.g.*, McGehee, *supra* note 6; Restoring Integrity to America's Elections Act, H.R. 2931, 115th Cong. (2015).

is that it would end the stalemates that so often result in non-enforcement—although robust enforcement would only occur when Democrats have a majority of seats on the commission, given current political realities. Such structural reform is unlikely absent unified Democratic control of government, but even if an odd-numbered commission were politically realistic, there are good reasons to fear its consequences. If the FEC were under the effective control of one party, it could enforce campaign finance laws in a way that systematically disadvantages the minority party. This possibility should give even the most ardent reformer pause about the wisdom of restructuring the FEC. In an era of intense partisan polarization, we must ask whether it is really desirable to give one of the major parties effective control over the agency responsible for regulating the flow of money into federal elections. To do so might transform an ineffectual agency into a truly dangerous one.

Fortunately, there is an alternative. Instead of trying to repair a broken agency, tiebreaking authority should be given to the federal institution with the greatest insulation from partisan politics: the judiciary. Federal courts now defer to FEC non-enforcement decisions even when they result from a party line split. This deference arises from decades of precedent from the D.C. Circuit, which has appellate jurisdiction over these cases.[9] The upshot of so-called "deadlock deference" is that FEC decisions not to pursue enforcement—as well as the legal reasoning that supports them—are difficult to overturn.[10]

This chapter argues that deadlock deference should be abandoned because it is wrong as a matter of law and harmful as a matter of policy. The D.C. Circuit's precedent rests on a misunderstanding of the *Chevron* doctrine of judicial deference to agency interpretations.[11] Where the FEC declines to take action due to the absence of a majority, it is not acting with the "force of law" and its decisions are therefore not entitled to judicial deference at *Chevron* "Step Zero."[12] Federal courts should not defer to the controlling commissioners' interpretation of the law in an enforcement matter, when the commission rejects the complaint with fewer than four votes. Abandoning deadlock deference would not only bring the D.C. Circuit into conformity with Supreme Court precedent, but also help remedy the worsening problem of party line stalemates on the FEC. Where there is no majority position on whether to

[9] *See infra* Part IV.

[10] *Statement of Vice Chair Ann M. Ravel and Commissioner Ellen L. Weintraub on Judicial Review of Deadlocked Commission Votes*, FEDERAL ELECTION COMMISSION (June 17, 2014), http://eqs.fec.gov/eqsdocsMUR/14044354045.pdf.

[11] Chevron U.S.A., Inc. v. Nat. Res. Def. Council, Inc., 467 U.S. 837 (1984).

[12] Thomas W. Merrill, *Step Zero after* City of Arlington, 83 FORDHAM L. REV. 753 (2014).

pursue enforcement—including circumstances where the commission is divided along party lines—the federal courts would decide the question *de novo*. Because Article III judges rather than partisan commissioners would break the tie, ending deadlock deference would reduce the risk of a dominant major party manipulating the rules to its own advantage.

The remainder of the chapter explains the circumstances that have led to the FEC's present troubles, the obstacles to reforming the FEC, and the reasons why deadlock deference should be abandoned. Part II discusses the FEC's history, enforcement process, and present state of dysfunction. Part III considers proposals for restructuring the FEC, assessing the pitfalls of the most commonly suggested model. Part IV argues that a better approach is to end deadlock deference. It traces the roots of this doctrine, showing that it arose from a misunderstanding of *Chevron* doctrine that subsequent Supreme Court precedent—most notably the decision in *United States v. Mead Corporation*[13]—has revealed. Rather than trying to fix the FEC, reform advocates would be better served focusing on how judicial review of the agency might be improved.

II. TWO MUSKOXEN

Campaign finance regulation advocates have lambasted the FEC for decades, calling it "dithering," "ineffectual," "impoten[t]," or even worse.[14] Animal metaphors are especially popular, with critics complaining that the agency is a "toothless tiger"[15] or—as Harry Reid claimed on the Senate floor three decades ago—a "toothless … lap dog,"[16] though regulatory skeptics have countered that the FEC is really a "toothless anaconda."[17] Whatever one's preferred dentally impaired species, the FEC's weak bite is not accidental. From the moment of its creation, some members of Congress were anxious to avoid creating an agency that could be dominated by one major party or the other. A strong

13 533 U.S. 218 (2001).

14 DEMOCRACY 21 EDUCATION FUND, PROJECT FEC, NO BARK, NO BITE, NO POINT 5 (2002), www.democracy21.org/uploads/%7BB4BE5C24-65EA-4910-974C-759644EC0901%7D.pdf.

15 Amanda S. LaForge, Note, *The Toothless Tiger: Structural, Political, and Legal Barriers to Effective FEC Enforcement*, 10 ADMIN. L.J. AM. U. 351 (1996).

16 Statement of Sen. Reid, 133 CONG. REC. 5125 (Mar. 10, 1987). Senator Reid continued: "To the extent we in Congress have drawn those fangs, or failed to provide them, we are responsible for this tame poodle. If, as some say, a camel is a horse designed by the Congress, perhaps the FEC is our version of a bulldog." *Id.*

17 Bradley A. Smith & Stephen M. Hoersting, *A Toothless Anaconda: Innovation, Impotence, and Overenforcement at the Federal Election Commission*, 1 ELECTION L.J. 145 (2002).

argument can therefore be made that the FEC was functioning more-or-less as intended for its first three decades. But the partisan disagreement on the FEC has become more bitter and rigid over the last decade, rendering the agency incapable of resolving significant disputes or clarifying the scope of federal campaign finance laws. The agency is now more dysfunctional than ever thanks to persistent stalemates over critical questions, such as the disclosure obligations of outside groups that have proliferated since *Citizens United v. Federal Election Commission*.[18] This Part discusses the FEC's history, enforcement process, and present state of disrepair, setting the stage for the discussion of structural reforms in Part III and judicial review in Part IV.

A. *How the FEC Came to Be*

The FEC was created in the wake of Watergate as part of the landmark Federal Election Campaign Act (FECA) Amendments of 1974.[19] Under the original version of FECA adopted in 1971, administrative and enforcement responsibilities were divided among three federal entities: the General Accounting office (for presidential candidates), the Clerk of the U.S. House (for House candidates), and the Secretary of the Senate (for Senate candidates).[20] The scandal surrounding Watergate, which included revelations that the break-in had been financed with undisclosed donations to President Nixon's re-election committee, revealed the inadequacy of this tripartite structure and led to bipartisan calls for an independent and nonpartisan commission.[21]

In the face of opposition to such an agency, most notably from House Administration Committee Chair Wayne Hays (D-OH), a compromise was forged.[22] The 1974 FECA Amendments created a bipartisan six-member commission, consisting of three members from each party. Two of the six commissioners were appointed by the President and the remaining four by the leadership of the two major parties in both chambers of Congress.[23] The idea was to create some political independence while also giving congressional leadership a say—and, as it turned out, four of the six members of the original FEC were former members of Congress.[24] The newly established FEC was

18 558 U.S. 310 (2010).

19 MUTCH, *supra* note 5, at 86–87.

20 *Id.* at 84.

21 *Id.* at 86–87.

22 *Id.* at 82–83, 87–88.

23 *Id.* at 87.

24 *Id.* at 87–88. *See also* BROOKS JACKSON, BROKEN PROMISE: WHY THE FEDERAL ELECTION COMMISSION FAILED 10 (1990) (asserting that commissioners were mostly "political cronies and party leaders").

given civil enforcement powers but not authority over criminal enforcement, which remained with the Department of Justice.[25] Procedural protections for accused violators were also included, to assuage congressional concerns that the FEC would become "a bunch of headhunters."[26]

The FEC's original structure was invalidated in *Buckley v. Valeo*,[27] on the ground that the method of appointing commissioners violated the Appointments Clause of the U.S. Constitution. The Supreme Court concluded that the FEC's administrative and enforcement powers could only be discharged by officials appointed by the President in the manner prescribed by Article I, Section 2 of the Constitution.[28] Congress subsequently amended the statute to conform with the requirements of Article I, as understood in *Buckley*. It gave the President power to appoint all six commissioners with Congress's advice and consent,[29] with the requirement that no more than three members of the FEC be of the same political party.[30] In addition, Congress and the President reached an unwritten agreement that remains in effect to this day, under which the President defers to the congressional leaders on both sides of the aisle in making FEC appointments.[31] That effectively reconstituted the commission along the lines originally contemplated by the 1974 Amendments, though without congressional leaders formally selecting the commissioners.

B. *The Enforcement Process*

FECA requires the affirmative votes of at least four commissioners in order to take specified actions.[32] Among the actions requiring four votes are those relating to enforcement, rulemaking, advisory opinions, litigation, and reporting violations to law enforcement authorities.[33] As former FEC Commissioner Scott Thomas and Jeffrey Bowman have explained, the purpose of the four-vote requirement was to ensure that "formal action on a matter before the Commission could go forward only on the affirmative vote

25 *Id.* at 88.
26 120 Cong. Rec. 27, 473 (Aug. 8, 1974) (remarks of Rep. Mathis).
27 424 U.S. 1 (1976).
28 *Id.* at 138–41.
29 Michael M. Franz, Choices and Changes: Interest Groups and the Electoral Process 44 (2008).
30 52 U.S.C. § 30106(a)(1).
31 McGehee, *supra* note 6.
32 52 U.S.C. § 30106(c). Lauren Eber, Note, *Waiting for Watergate: The Long Road to FEC Reform*, 79 S. Cal. L. Rev. 1155, 1167 (2006).
33 52 U.S.C. §§ 30106(c), 30107(a).

of a mixed majority of Commission members" – in other words, with the votes of commissioners aligned with both major parties.[34]

The FEC's system of enforcement depends primarily on third-party complaints.[35] Anyone who believes that a FECA violation has occurred may file a complaint, signed and under penalty of perjury.[36] The filing of a complaint triggers the opening of a "Matter Under Review" (MUR), the FEC's principal means of looking into possible violations. The person or entity accused of violating the law (the respondent) then has an opportunity to respond, after which the FEC's general counsel conducts a preliminary inquiry and makes a recommendation of whether there is "reason to believe" a violation has occurred.[37] An affirmative vote of four FEC members is required to find "reason to believe" and thus to authorize an investigation.[38] Otherwise, the complaint is dismissed.[39]

Because the FEC lacks the authority to impose penalties on its own,[40] it usually pursues a conciliation agreement (a form of settlement) if there is evidence of a violation.[41] Four votes are required to find "probable cause" that there has been a violation; otherwise, the case is closed.[42] If there are four "probable cause" votes, then the FEC's general counsel must try to negotiate a conciliation agreement with the respondent.[43] If they agree to terms, then four commission votes are required to approve a conciliation agreement.[44] If the FEC and the alleged violator cannot reach a conciliation agreement, then

34 Scott E. Thomas & Jeffrey H. Bowman, *Obstacles to Effective Enforcement of the Federal Election Campaign Act*, 52 ADMIN. L. REV. 575, 590 (2000). *See also* Jennifer Nou, *Sub-Regulating Elections*, SUP. CT. REV. 135, 154 (2013) (noting that the FEC's design "likely reflect[s] congressional desire to ensure that controversial election policies do not proceed unless they serve the interests of both parties…").

35 Michael M. Franz, *The Devil We Know? Evaluating the FEC as Enforcer*, 8 ELECTION L.J. 167, 170 (2009).

36 52 U.S.C. § 30109(a)(1).

37 Federal Election Commission (FEC), Guidebook for Complainants and Respondents on the FEC Enforcement Process 9–12 (2012), https://transition.fec.gov/em/respondent_guide.pdf.

38 52 U.S.C. § 30109(a)(2); FEC, *supra* note 37, at 14.

39 FEC, *supra* note 37, at 12. Four votes are required to dismiss a matter based on "prosecutorial discretion." This type of dismissal, and a recent troubling court decision concerning it, are discussed *infra* note 158.

40 Wertheimer & Simon, *supra* note 2, at 5. An exception is the FEC's Administrative Fines Program (AFP), which allows it to impose fines for late filings. There is also an Alternative Dispute Resolution (ADR) program for minor and inadvertent violations. *See* Franz, *supra* note 35, at 172; R. SAM GARRETT, CONG. RES. SERV., NO. R44318, THE FEDERAL ELECTION COMMISSION: ENFORCEMENT PROCESS AND SELECTED ISSUES FOR CONGRESS 4 (2015).

41 FEC, *supra* note 37, at 16–18.

42 52 U.S.C. § 30109(a)(4)(A)(i); FEC, *supra* note 37, at 20.

43 52 U.S.C. § 30109(a)(4)(A)(i); FEC, *supra* note 37, at 20.

44 52 U.S.C. § 30109(a)(4)(A)(i); FEC, *supra* note 37, at 20–21.

the FEC may institute a civil action in federal court—but again, only if there are four votes.[45] The votes of four commissioners are therefore required for the initial "reason to believe" determination, a probable cause finding, approval of a conciliation agreement, and initiation of a civil action. Four votes are also required to refer a matter to the Department of Justice for criminal investigation, which may be done if there is probable cause to believe there has been a knowing and willful violation.[46] Thus, at every stage of the enforcement process, four votes are required to move to the next step. Any party aggrieved by dismissal of the complaint may bring suit in the U.S. District Court for the District of Columbia,[47] the judgment of which may be appealed to the D.C. Circuit.[48]

C. *The FEC's Degeneration*

As Commissioner Ellen Weintraub has observed, the FEC's structure "has long been criticized as a recipe for gridlock."[49] The reality, however, is that deadlocked enforcement votes were uncommon until fairly recently. Michael Franz analyzed MURs between 1996 and 2006, finding tie votes in only 2.4 percent with unanimous 6-0 votes occurring in 55 percent of cases in which there was a full complement of commissioners.[50] While these stalemates tended to occur in especially controversial enforcement matters, one study found that less than two-thirds of the 3-3 splits on MURs were along party lines.[51] Franz found some evidence that the party affiliation of commissioners affected their votes and that incumbent candidates who were the subject of complaints fared better than challengers.[52] But on the whole, he concluded

[45] 52 U.S.C. § 30109(a)(6). The remedy in a civil action may include a request for injunctive relief as well as civil penalties of up to $5,000 or the amount involved in the alleged violation (whichever is greater). 52 U.S.C. § 30109(a)(6)(A) & (B). The court may impose greater penalties for knowing and willful violations: $10,000 or 200% of the contributions or expenditures involved, whichever is greater. 52 U.S.C. § 30109(a)(6)(C).

[46] 52 U.S.C. § 30109(a)(5)(C); FEC, *supra* note 37, at 20–21.

[47] 52 U.S.C. § 30109(a)(8).

[48] 52 U.S.C. § 30109(a)(9). Judicial review of FEC enforcement is discussed at greater length in Part IV.

[49] Ellen L. Weintraub & Samuel C. Brown, *Following the Money: Campaign Finance Disclosure in India and the United States*, 11 Election L.J. 241, 258 (2012).

[50] Franz, *supra* note 35, at 176. Franz found that there was a 3-2 vote (and therefore the absence of the four votes required to take action under the statute) in 0.4% of cases in which there was a full complement of commissioners. In cases where only five commissioners were sitting, there were only 4.3% of cases in which the four-vote threshold was not reached. *Id.*

[51] *Id.* at 177.

[52] *Id.* at 179–83.

that deadlocks were rare and that the FEC was functioning better than some of its critics claimed.[53]

That pattern changed markedly in the late-aughts, when party line splits spiked. A Congressional Research Service (CRS) report found substantive deadlocks in approximately 13 percent of publicly available Matters Under Review in 2008 and 2009, on such matters as political committee status, reporting violations, and the permissibility of contributions and expenditures.[54] A subsequent CRS report found deadlocks in 24.4 percent of closed MURs in 2014.[55] Public Citizen's analysis found that split enforcement votes (i.e., votes in which there were fewer than four votes for either side) increased sharply, going from less than 2 percent each year between 2003 and 2007 to 10 percent in 2008.[56] They have remained at or above that level since then, peaking at over 22 percent in 2013.[57] The conflict on the FEC mirrored the partisan divide in Congress, where a stalemate over the confirmation of nominees resulted in the FEC not having a quorum for several months in 2008.[58]

Most recently, the office of former Democratic Commissioner Ann Ravel issued a detailed report just before her resignation, which found that the FEC deadlocked on approximately 30 percent of substantive votes on Matters Under Review closed in 2016.[59] The report offered several examples of deadlocks, which it claimed to be illustrative. Among them were the refusal of various groups—such as Crossroads GPS, established by Karl Rove ostensibly as a social welfare nonprofit—to register as political committees,[60] Murray Energy Corporation's alleged coercion of its employees to contribute to certain candidates,[61] and Newt Gingrich's allegedly improper use of campaign funds during his 2012 presidential campaign.[62] On all these matters, the Democratic members voted to proceed with enforcement while the Republican matters voted against it. Republican Commissioner Lee Goodman responded with an

53 *Id.* at 177, 185. *See also* Todd Lochner & Bruce E. Cain, *Equity and Efficacy in the Enforcement of Campaign Finance Laws*, 77 Tex. L. Rev. 1891, 1895–96 (1999) (describing the difficulty in proving whether the FEC has been captured).

54 R. Sam Garrett, Cong. Res. Serv., No. R 40779, Deadlocked Votes Among Members of the Federal Election Commission (FEC): Overview and Potential Considerations for Congress 5, 9–10, 12 (2009).

55 Garrett, *supra* note 40, at 10.

56 Public Citizen, *supra* note 1.

57 *Id.*

58 Weintraub & Brown, *supra* note 49, at 259; Eliza Newlin Carney, *The Endless FEC Fight*, Nat'l J. (June 16, 2008).

59 Ravel, *supra* note 1.

60 *Id.* at 15.

61 *Id.* at 12.

62 *Id.* at 19.

analysis that parses the data differently, finding deadlocks in less than 10 percent of cases when non-substantive votes are included.[63]

Whatever disagreements may exist on this front, there can be no denying that both the frequency and intensity of party line deadlocks on the FEC have increased since 2007. The Democratic and Republican Commissioners, moreover, split in predictable ways with the former supporting enforcement and the latter opposing it. For those who favor robust enforcement of the law, the negative consequences are clear: because it takes four votes to move forward with any enforcement action, there are no consequences for violations of existing law. A recent example is the FEC's deadlock on whether to pursue an enforcement action against a congressional candidate who failed to refund almost $150,000 in loans from a limited liability company.[64] The Democratic commissioners voted to follow the general counsel's recommendation to pursue conciliation, but the Republican commissioners opposed it, effectively killing the case.[65]

Even if one is not an ardent reformer, party line deadlocks are still troubling, because they prevent the agency from clarifying important questions of law. Some of the most prominent deadlocks in recent years involve the applicability of federal disclosure requirements to groups engaged in political spending. Federal law treats organizations as "political committees" if their major purpose is to influence federal elections, triggering the requirement that they disclose their donors as well as their expenditures.[66] Reform groups frequently allege that certain groups have the major purpose of influencing federal elections but have failed to register as political committees, fueling the increase in so-called "dark money." The FEC has repeatedly deadlocked on this question with respect to such groups as Crossroads GPS, Americans for Job Security, and the Commission on Hope, Growth and Opportunity.[67]

63 Ashley Balcerzak, *Ann Ravel's Parting Shot*, CENTER FOR RESPONSIVE POLITICS (Feb. 23, 2017), www.opensecrets.org/news/2017/02/ann-ravels-parting-shot/ (noting Commissioner Goodman's finding that 9.7% of closed cases were dismissed on a 3-3 vote).

64 Kenneth P. Doyle, *FEC Deadlocks on Flemming Campaign Loan Case*, BLOOMBERG BNA MONEY & POLITICS REP. (June 9, 2017).

65 *Id.* Because the commission had only two Democratic commissioners, with former Commissioner Ravel's seat remaining unfilled, the vote was two in favor and three against.

66 52 U.S.C. §§ 30101(4), 30104(a). The "major purpose" test derives from *Buckley*, which limited FECA's definition of political committees to organizations "the major purpose of which is the nomination or election of a candidate." 424 U.S. 1, 79 (1976).

67 Kenneth P. Doyle, *Judge Won't Order FEC to Pursue Conservative Nonprofit*, BLOOMBERG BNA MONEY & POL. REP. (Feb. 24, 2017); Kenneth P. Doyle, *FEC Faulted for Failure to Enforce Disclosure on Nonprofits*, BLOOMBERG BNA MONEY & POL. REP. (Sept. 20, 2016); Kenneth P. Doyle, *FEC Deadlocks on Crossroads GPS Case*, BLOOMBERG BNA MONEY & POL. REP. (Jan. 25, 2016); Kenneth P. Doyle, *FEC Enforcement Deadlocks on Two Conservative Groups*, BLOOMBERG BNA MONEY & POL. REP. (July 14, 2014).

Other disclosure disputes focus on whether particular ads have the electoral content necessary to subject to disclosure requirements.[68]

Another subject on which the FEC has had multiple party line deadlocks is coordination between Super PACs and federal candidates. While Super PACs are allowed to make unlimited *independent* expenditures in federal elections, *coordinated* expenditures are treated as contributions under federal law. A 2015 analysis found that the commission deadlocked in 8 of 29 cases alleging illegal coordination by Super PACs.[69] The FEC has also deadlocked on whether an outside group's use of so-called "b-roll"—video footage created by a federal candidate's campaign—constitutes the republication of campaign materials and should therefore be treated as an in-kind contribution.[70]

The effect of FEC deadlocks is to leave a cloud of legal uncertainty over these practices. Given the D.C. Circuit's practice of deadlock deference, discussed in Part IV, the ultimate consequence is for federal campaign finance law to remain nebulous. As enforcement deadlocks have increased, FEC fines have decreased, going from over $1 million per year between 2001 and 2009, to less than $600,000 in 2014.[71] The average fine in closed cases also declined to less than $13,000, the lowest level since the early 1990s.[72] There is also evidence that FEC faces an increasing backlog of cases, with many important matters left unresolved more than two years after the initial complaint.[73]

Enforcement deadlocks are just the tip of the lance in the FEC's side. Another area of partisan stalemate is the issuance of advisory opinions, which also requires four votes. FECA permits candidates and others to submit written requests concerning the applicability of its provisions to specified conduct.[74]

68 *See, e.g.*, Kenneth P. Doyle, *FEC Deadlocks in Case of 501(c)(4) Group Touting Rubio*, Bloomberg BNA Money & Pol. Rep. (Jan. 17, 2017).

69 Kenneth P. Doyle, *Analysis: Deadlocks Are Only Part of Story at FEC*, Bloomberg BNA Money & Pol. Rep. (Sept. 1, 2015). For examples of deadlocks in coordination cases, see Kenneth P. Doyle, *Republican FEC Commissioners Explain Votes to Drop Lampson Enforcement Case*, Bloomberg BNA Money & Pol. Rep. (Apr. 10, 2015); Kenneth P. Doyle, *FEC Deadlocks in Coordination Case from 2014 Senate Election in Michigan*, Bloomberg BNA Money & Pol. Rep. (Jan. 20, 2015).

70 Kenneth P. Doyle, *FEC Deadlocks on Ads Using Candidates' Video*, Bloomberg BNA Money & Pol. Rep. (Dec. 29, 2015).

71 Kenneth P. Doyle, *Decline in FEC Enforcement Actions Detailed in New Statistical Information*, Bloomberg BNA Money & Pol. Rep. (May 8, 2015).

72 *Id. See also* Garrett, *supra* note 54, at 11–12.

73 *Id.* at 11. *See also* Kenneth P. Doyle, *FEC Faulted for Failure to Enforce Disclosure on Nonprofits*, Bloomberg BNA Money & Pol. Rep. (Sept. 20, 2016); Kenneth P. Doyle, *FEC Makes Scant Progress on Enforcement Backlog*, Bloomberg BNA Money & Pol. Rep. (Sept. 17, 2015); Kenneth P. Doyle, *FEC Backlog of 191 Enforcement Cases Includes Many Matters Pending for Years*, Bloomberg BNA Money & Pol. Rep. (Mar. 4, 2015).

74 52 U.S.C. § 30108.

This procedure allows candidates, parties, and other groups to obtain the FEC's clarification of the law before engaging in arguably illegal activity. FEC advisory opinions also provide guidance to others who might want to engage in similar activity. In a study of FEC advisory opinions, Michael Franz found that commissioners were for decades able to reach bipartisan consensus on the interpretation of the law, but that consensus has crumbled in recent years.[75] He suggests that "Republican commissioners may see their role now as less about implementing the broader will of Congress ... and more about limiting the law's application for any question not explicitly covered by the statute," while "Democratic commissioner may have mobilized in opposition to ward off the perceived erosion of existing regulations by Republican commissioners."[76] Public Citizen has documented an increase in stalemates on auditing and rulemaking as well.[77] Partisan disagreement has even left the commission without a permanent general counsel since 2013, when Anthony Herman departed after a dispute with the Republican commissioners over enforcement procedures.[78] Whatever the motivations of the commissioners from each party, their rancorous disagreement shows no sign of abating.

Looking back at the agency's history through the lens of contemporary experience, one can plausibly argue that reformers exaggerated the FEC's problems during its early years. Compared to what is now happening, the FEC displayed a remarkable ability to reach agreement across party lines in its first three decades, not only on enforcement actions but also on rules, advisory opinions, and audits. Any semblance of bipartisanship has crumbled over the past decade, with the Democratic and Republican commissioners locked in a ferocious and interminable conflict, like muskoxen repeatedly butting heads on the tundra. While a weaker muskox eventually gives up, there is no hint of the commissioners on either side relenting. Instead, they are likely to continue butting heads as long as the agency retains its current structure. That is not to deny there are legitimate disagreements over the meaning of federal campaign finance laws, often ones with weighty implications. The central problem, however, is that the FEC's structure makes it practically impossible

[75] Michael M. Franz, *The Federal Election Commission as Regulator: The Changing Evaluations of Advisory Opinions*, 3 U.C. IRVINE L. REV. 735 (2013).

[76] *Id.* at 739.

[77] *See* Public Citizen, *supra* note 1.

[78] Kenneth P. Doyle, *Vacancy at Top FEC Post to Continue as Petalas Departs*, BLOOMBERG BNA MONEY & POL. REP. (Aug. 31, 2016). There was no general counsel at all for over two years. Garrett, *supra* note 40, at 12. The Commission has had an acting general counsel since 2015. Kenneth P. Doyle, *FEC Deputy Counsel Stevenson Now Acting General Counsel*, BLOOMBERG BNA MONEY & POL. REP. (Sept. 27, 2016).

for the FEC to resolve these disputes, given the reality of partisan polarization that permeates our political system.

III. BE CAREFUL WHAT YOU WISH FOR

While there is some truth to the argument that the agency was "designed to promote deadlock,"[79] the FEC's present state of dysfunction should trouble not just reform advocates but anyone who cares about legal clarity. The bitter and intractable deadlock that now grips the agency is beyond anything Congress contemplated, rendering it unable to perform core functions like interpretation and implementation of the law. Unfortunately, it is much easier to diagnose the FEC's condition than it is to find a workable remedy. This Part considers possible reforms to the commission, including the risks inherent in giving one party effective control over enforcement decisions.

A. *Institutional Trade-Offs*

To this point, my focus has primarily been on FEC deadlocks. That, however, is only part of the picture when it comes to assessing the FEC's implementation of campaign finance law. Lloyd Mayer has offered a helpful framework for evaluating administrative agencies charged with enforcing campaign finance laws.[80] Drawing on institutional choice literature, he identifies various competencies that an effective regulator should have. Among the criteria he proposes are substantive *expertise*, their *coordination* of enforcement and other activities, susceptibility to *agency capture*, *accountability* to Congress and the public, and the *compliance burden* imposed on those regulated.[81] He proceeded to apply this framework to the FEC and the Internal Revenue Service, which is responsible for enforcing tax laws restricting political activity by nonprofit organizations. On balance, he concluded that the FEC enjoyed advantages over the IRS in terms of expertise, coordination, accountability, and resources, while the IRS was less susceptible to capture.[82] Mayer judged the FEC more effective in administering disclosure requirements than the other requirements of federal campaign finance law (such as contribution limits), due to the majority vote requirement.[83]

79 McGehee, *supra* note 6.

80 Lloyd H. Mayer, *The Much Maligned 527 and Institutional Choice*, 87 B.U. L. REV. 625 (2007).

81 *Id.* at 653–56.

82 *Id.* at 669–78.

83 *Id.* at 673–76, 682.

Although published in 2007, Mayer's article anticipated some of the issues that have since arisen in the intervening years. That includes the major increase in campaign-related activities being channeled through nonprofit organizations incorporated under Section 501(c) of the Internal Revenue Code, instead of through political organizations under Section 527. He also noted the IRS's difficulties in handling the "most politically sensitive cases,"[84] a concern brought dramatically to life in the controversy over the IRS's actions with respect to certain Tea Party groups several years later. Subsequent developments, including those set forth in Part I of this chapter, should cause us to view the FEC's efficacy as an enforcer with a more jaundiced eye. Yet they should neither eclipse nor cause us to forget the advantages of the FEC's administrative structure, in comparison to an agency in the traditional model, led by a single official selected by the President. Despite its well-documented problems, most notably repeated deadlocks over major questions of law and policy, the FEC still has some advantages, expertise, and resources. Its efficacy is certainly hampered by stalemates over enforcement, advisory opinions, and other questions. But it has avoided the problem that so devastated the IRS's reputation: namely, the appearance that partisan political concerns drove the agency to target certain groups because of their political viewpoint. Whatever its failings, the FEC's bipartisan structure—including the statutory requirement that a mixed majority of members vote to initiate and pursue enforcement—avoids the liability that has so tarnished the IRS since the Tea Party controversy. By requiring approval of a mixed majority, the FEC avoids the risk of the dominant party using campaign finance enforcement as a weapon against the other major party.

All of this reveals a conundrum at the heart of the debate over FEC reform. On one hand, the FEC's bipartisan structure and majority vote requirements hinder its effectiveness. Any doubt that might once have existed over that question has evaporated over the past decade as the commission has increasingly stalemated on significant issues. On the other hand, the increasing partisan polarization that fuels this stalemate would make it even more risky to replace the current model with one that would allow commissioners aligned with one of the major parties to take action that would harm the other.

B. *The Case against Structural Reform*

Over the years, there have been multiple suggestions on how to fix the FEC. The most tenable proposals would replace the current FEC with either a

[84] *Id.* at 677.

single administrator or an odd-numbered commission. Both of these proposals would give one major party or the other functional control of the entity responsible for interpreting, enforcing, and otherwise implementing federal campaign finance laws. There are obvious advantages to this approach, most importantly that it would end the debilitating stalemate that the FEC now faces. But there are also some genuine disadvantages. Most disconcerting is the possibility that federal campaign finance law would be administered in a manner that has the intent and effect of benefitting the dominant political party. In our current era of hyperpolarized politics, this is a profound risk. As Franz has observed, the devil we don't know might be even worse than the one we know.[85]

One of the more modest suggestions, proposed by Thomas and Bowman, is to allow early stage enforcement actions—specifically, approval of a "reason-to-believe" recommendation from the FEC's general counsel—to proceed with only three votes.[86] This would only apply in cases where the general counsel recommended finding reason to believe (not where she recommended against finding reason to believe) and that recommendation garnered three votes. This proposal has the advantage of streamlining early stage enforcement while still requiring a bipartisan vote for the more consequential enforcement decisions at later stages (i.e., probable cause, conciliation, and litigation). It would at least allow for an investigation to take place before dismissal. But its effect would be limited, insofar as it would likely postpone deadlock dismissals until a later stage of proceedings rather than stopping them entirely.

Other proposals would go further, changing the composition of the commission so that one party would have effective control and thus ending partisan stalemates. One idea is to adopt a structure like that of most other federal agencies, replacing the FEC with a single administrator who would be responsible for enforcement of campaign finance laws.[87] Another proposal would create a new-three membered body with a strong chair.[88] In recent years, the reform community has coalesced around a proposal to move to a five-member body, also with augmented powers for the chair.[89] An odd-numbered commission would allow enforcement action to proceed without any votes from the non-dominant party, effectively ending the paralysis that now grips the FEC.

85 *See* Franz, *supra* note 35, at 187.
86 Thomas & Bowman, *supra* note 34, at 592.
87 Democracy 21 Education Fund, *supra* note 14, at 34.
88 Federal Election Administration Act of 2006, H.R. 5676, 109th Cong. § 101(a) (2006).
89 McGehee, *supra* note 6.

The most recent iteration of this idea is the "Restoring Integrity to America's Election Act," a bill with co-sponsors in both major parties.[90] This bill would reduce the FEC from six to five members, with no more than two affiliated with each party.[91] Only three votes would be required for the commission to take action.[92] The chair would serve a ten-year term, while the four other members would serve staggered six-year terms.[93] The bill would also establish a blue ribbon panel to recommend potential commissioners to the President.[94] The idea is to end the commission's perceived domination by party loyalists handpicked by congressional leaders.[95] It would vest some of the FEC's current powers in the chair, including the appointment and removal of high-level staff,[96] a topic on which the commission has been at loggerheads in recent years. Like other FEC reform proposals that have been floated over the years, the basic idea is to end gridlock while beefing up the commission's enforcement powers.

There is an understandable appeal to structural reform of the FEC given the increase in party line deadlocks. Yet there are also compelling reasons for caution, particularly in an age of hyperpolarized politics. Moving to an odd number of commissioners, with a bare majority empowered to take action, would curb the persistent deadlocks that have so hampered the FEC's effectiveness and prevented it from clarifying the law. But this change would replace that problem with one that is even more worrisome. Allowing the commission to take action against the wishes of minority party members would open the door to partisan administration and enforcement. The dominant party could initiate and pursue actions with the intent and effect of weakening the rival major party. For example, it could target the minority party's candidates or groups aligned with that party. The prohibition on having more than two members from any one party is not much of a hedge against biased enforcement. The President could easily evade this requirement by choosing someone who tilts toward his or her party, even though nominally "independent." Nor is the creation of a blue ribbon commission likely to be an effective check on partisan appointees, given that the authority

90 H.R. 2034, 115th Cong. (2017).

91 *Id.* § 2(a)(1).

92 *Id.* § 2(2).

93 *Id.* § 2(b).

94 *Id.* § 2(c).

95 Kenneth P. Doyle, *Bipartisan Bill Would Restructure FEC to End Gridlock*, BLOOMBERG BNA MONEY & POL. REP. (Apr. 13, 2017); "Bipartisan FEC Overhaul Bill Introduced by Reps. Derek Kilmer (D-WA) and Jim Renacci (R-OH)," (Apr. 6, 2017), www.issueone.org/bipartisan-fec-overhaul-bill-introduced-reps-derek-kilmer-d-wa-jim-renacci-r-oh/.

96 H.R. 2034, § 3(b)(1).

to appoint would ultimately lie with the President. Supporters of the most recent FEC reform bill correctly note that other federal commissions have bipartisan structures.[97] Yet there are special reasons to be concerned about one-party control of enforcement when it comes to campaign finance, given the powerful impact that the flow of political money can have on the parties' electoral fortunes.

Put more directly, each of the major parties has an overwhelmingly strong self-interest in having campaign finance rules that inure to its benefit and in those rules being implemented to its advantage. This reality makes campaign finance qualitatively different from other administrative actions. Advocates have also compared the proposed reform—specifically, the ten-year term given to the chair—to that of the FBI director, stating that "this process has worked."[98] Intervening events, most notably President Trump's firing of James Comey, should worry even the most devoted campaign finance reformers. In this age of hyperpolarized politics, we cannot presume impartiality in the president's discharge of appointment and removal duties, certainly not when it comes to campaign finance administration. We cannot even be sure that the proposed fix to the FEC would lead to more aggressive enforcement, as reformers desire. Given the current politics, the FEC would surely be a more vigorous enforcer when commissioners aligned with the Democratic Party have the majority, given that party's general stance on regulation. But when Republican-aligned commissioners have a majority, there is little reason to believe that the FEC would vigorously enforce the law. The GOP's skepticism if not hostility toward campaign finance regulation would, if anything, make it an even less effective enforcer than the current FEC were its commissioners to hold a working majority.

All this suggests that changing the FEC's structure isn't such a great idea after all. Moving to a single administrator or odd-numbered commission might end gridlock, but it would not necessarily produce more effective enforcement. Worse still, a commission dominated by one major party could enforce the law in a way that is designed to disadvantage its chief rival. While we might imagine an administrative agency that enjoys greater insulation from partisan politics than the current FEC, that agency is not likely to exist in the real world, at least not at the federal level. It is true that the states employ various kinds of agencies to implement their campaign finance laws, some of which have reputations as fair and effective regulators.[99] But it is difficult if

97 McGehee, *supra* note 6.

98 *Id.*

99 Franz, *supra* note 75, at 761.

not impossible to create genuinely nonpartisan institutions at the federal level, especially given the constitutional constraints evident in the *Buckley* Court's invalidation of the FEC's original structure. This does not mean we should consign all new proposals for reforming the FEC to the wastebasket, but it does call for extreme caution, especially in an era of hyper-partisanship.

IV. UNDUE DEFERENCE

There is a way to improve campaign finance enforcement without the grave risks involved in restructuring the FEC. This alternative path would avoid the pronounced dangers that would arise from replacing the FEC with a single administrator or odd-numbered commission controlled by one of the major parties. And because it could be accomplished without overruling Supreme Court precedent and without any legislative or administrative action, it is more realistic than congressional action to overhaul the FEC. All that's required is abandonment of D.C. Circuit precedent requiring deference to the bloc of FEC commissioners voting against enforcement when there are fewer than four votes to proceed.[100] As explained below, this precedent derives from one sentence of dictum in the footnote written by then-Judge Ruth Bader Ginsburg,[101] which the D.C. Circuit later transformed into holdings. Subsequent Supreme Court decisions have rendered these precedents obsolete but they have not been overruled. Ending deadlock deference would do more than correct an error or law. It would have the salutary effect of allowing the federal institution with the greatest insulation from partisan politics, the judiciary, to serve as a tiebreaker when the FEC deadlocks on enforcement matters.

A. *Judicial Review of FEC Enforcement*

As Part I explained, federal law requires the votes of at least four commissioners to proceed with enforcement actions, including the initial "reason to believe" determination and the subsequent "probable cause" determination. A decision *not* to proceed with enforcement is judicially reviewable under FECA, which provides that the commission's dismissal of a complaint may be reversed if "contrary to law."[102] On its face, this language authorizes the federal courts to correct erroneous legal interpretations adopted by the FEC.

[100] *See, e.g., In re* Sealed Cases, 223 F.3d 775 (D.C. Cir. 2000).
[101] Democratic Cong. Campaign Comm. v. FEC, 831 F.2d 1131, 1135 n. 5 (D.C. Cir. 1987) (DCCC).
[102] 52 U.S.C. § 30109(a)(8)(C).

In practice, however, the courts generally defer to the statutory interpretation adopted by the controlling bloc of commissioners under *Chevron v. National Resources Defense Council*,[103] even when the commission is equally divided. *Chevron* famously articulated a two-step test for determining whether an administrative agency's interpretation should receive judicial deference. First, the court is to consider whether "Congress has directly spoken to the precise question at issue."[104] If Congress's intent is clear, then the court must follow it. But if the statute is "silent or ambiguous" on the question, then the court should proceed to the second step: determining whether the agency's interpretation of the statute is "permissible."[105] The Supreme Court later added a threshold requirement for applying *Chevron*, sometimes called "Step Zero."[106] The key decision is *United States v. Mead*,[107] under which an agency interpretation only warrants *Chevron* deference if: (1) Congress delegated to the agency the authority to make legal rules with the "force of law," and (2) the agency interpretation at issue was promulgated pursuant to that authority.[108] Only administrative interpretations that satisfy this standard are entitled to *Chevron* deference, although other interpretations may still receive respectful consideration by the courts under *Skidmore v. Swift & Co.*[109] Under *Skidmore*, the weight that agency interpretations of statute receive varies, depending on such factors as the agency's care in rendering it, its consistency, formality, and the agency's expertise.[110]

The Supreme Court addressed the deference owed to FEC enforcement decisions in *Federal Election Commission v. Democratic Senatorial Campaign Committee* (DSCC),[111] a pre-*Chevron* decision. That case arose from the FEC's unanimous decision to dismiss the DSCC's complaint against the National Republican Senatorial Committee (NRSC), concerning some state parties' designation of the NRSC as their agent for the purpose of expenditures allowed by FECA.[112] In an opinion by Justice Byron White, the Supreme

103 467 U.S. 837, 842 (1984). There is an abundance of scholarship on the *Chevron* doctrine, far too much to canvass in even a cursory fashion here. For an excellent summary of the literature, see Peter M. Shane & Christopher J. Walker, *Foreword—Chevron at 30: Looking Back and Looking Forward*, 83 FORDHAM L. REV. 475 (2014).

104 467 U.S. at 842–43.

105 *Id.* at 843.

106 *See* Merrill, *supra* note 12, at 756. This term originates from Thomas W. Merrill & Kristin E. Hickman, Chevron's *Domain*, 89 GEO. L.J. 833, 836–37 (2001). *See also* Cass R. Sunstein, Chevron *Step Zero*, 92 VA. L. REV. 187 (2006).

107 533 U.S. 218 (2001).

108 *Id.* at 232, 226–27.

109 323 U.S. 134 (1944).

110 *Mead*, 533 U.S. at 228 (citing *Skidmore*, 323 U.S. at 139–40).

111 454 U.S. 27 (1981).

112 *Id.* at 29–31.

Court concluded that the FEC's construction of the relevant statute was entitled to deference under *Skidmore*. The Court observed that the FEC was "precisely the type of agency to which deference should presumptively be afforded," given that Congress had vested the agency with primary responsibility for enforcing FECA.[113] It also noted the FEC's "inherently bipartisan" character, including the requirement that no more than three of its members be affiliated with the same political party,[114] as well as the consistency of its interpretation of the statute over time. Under these circumstances, the Court concluded that the FEC's unanimous decision not to proceed with enforcement deserved judicial deference under *Skidmore*.

A few years after *Chevron*, the D.C. Circuit applied its two-part deference framework to another unanimous FEC decision not to proceed with enforcement. The underlying issue in *Orloski v. Federal Election Commission*[115] was whether corporate contributions to a picnic sponsored by a congressman were permissible under FECA. The Court faithfully applied *Chevron*'s framework, concluding that Congress had not spoken to the issue and that the FEC's interpretation of the statute was permissible, thus warranting deference.[116] Neither the *DSCC* nor the *Orloski* decision was especially remarkable, given that both faithfully followed then-prevailing precedent on deference to agency interpretations—*DSCC* applying the *Skidmore* factors and *Orloski* the two-step test articulated in *Chevron*. In both of those cases, moreover, the FEC had voted *unanimously* against pursuing enforcement. Under these circumstances, there was no reason to doubt that the agency interpretations deserved deference.

The next major decision, *Democratic Congressional Campaign Committee (DCCC) v. Federal Election Commission*,[117] was the first to involve a deadlocked enforcement vote. The DCCC alleged that the National Republican Campaign Committee (NRCC) had violated FECA by failing to allocate certain mailing expenses against its expenditure limit. Although the FEC's general counsel recommended finding "reason to believe" there had been a violation, only three commissioners so voted, with two others finding no "reason to believe" and the other abstaining.[118] Because there were not four votes to proceed with enforcement, the complaint was dismissed. The threshold question in *DCCC* was whether the FEC's dismissal due to a deadlock was reviewable at all. The FEC argued that nothing had been

[113] *Id.* at 37.
[114] *Id.*
[115] 795 F.2d 156 (D.C. Cir. 1986).
[116] *Id.* at 161–67.
[117] 831 F.2d 1131 (D.C. Cir. 1987).
[118] *Id.* at 1132–33.

decided and thus that there was nothing for the court to review.[119] Writing for the unanimous panel, then-Judge Ginsburg "demur[red] to the FEC's observation that a 3-2-1 vote decides nothing."[120] That decision might rest on up to three commissioners' determination that "prosecutorial discretion" warranted dismissal, but so could a *unanimous* decision not to proceed with enforcement. In these circumstances, the court was unwilling to eliminate the "judicial check" on the FEC that Congress had provided.[121] Given the absence of any explanation for the decision not to pursue enforcement—recall that the FEC's general counsel had recommended finding reason to believe—the D.C. Circuit ordered the case sent back to the FEC for an explanation of why three commissioners voted not to proceed.[122] Only with such an explanation in hand could a federal court intelligently evaluate whether the decision was justified or, alternatively, rested on a mistaken understanding of the law.[123]

So far, so good. Judge Ginsburg was surely right, both to conclude that the FEC's non-enforcement decision was judicially reviewable and to send the case back to the FEC so that the controlling bloc of commissioners (i.e., those who did not vote to proceed) could explain their reasoning. The problem with *DCCC* lay in a single footnote in the portion of the opinion explaining why the case should be sent back to the FEC for an explanation of reasons. The footnote said: "In the absence of prior Commission precedent … judicial deference to the agency's initial decision or indecision would be at its zenith."[124] This was pure dictum, as the D.C. Circuit's decision to remand did not in any way rest on this statement, and the court did not decide whether the agency's interpretation warranted deference. Yet this offhand statement would ultimately lead the D.C. Circuit to hold that *Chevron* deference applies in enforcement cases where the FEC deadlocks.[125]

[119] *Id.* at 1133.

[120] *Id.*

[121] *Id.* at 1134.

[122] *Id.* at 1135. *See also* Nou, *supra* note 34, at 156 (emphasizing that *DCCC* required a statement of reasons only where the FEC's general counsel recommended proceeding with enforcement but the commission deadlocked).

[123] 831 F.2d at 1132.

[124] *Id.* at 1135 n. 5.

[125] The D.C. Circuit later extended *DCCC*'s requirement that the commission provide a statement of reasons where its general counsel recommends enforcement but the commission deadlocks. Common Cause v. FEC, 842 F.2d 436 (D.C. Cir. 1988). In *Common Cause*, however, a majority of the panel declined to apply that requirement retroactively, reasoning that it would serve no purpose in the circumstances presented (including that some of the commissioners had since departed the FEC). *Id.* at 450–51. Judge Ginsburg dissented in part, concluding that the FEC's interpretation of the statute was unreasonable and thus not entitled to deference. *Id.* 451, 451 & n. 2 (Ginsburg, J., dissenting).

Two subsequent decisions transformed the *DCCC* footnote's dictum into holdings, requiring deference to the bloc of commissioners who vote against proceeding with enforcement when the FEC deadlocks. The first was *Federal Election Commission v. National Republican Senatorial Committee* (NRSC).[126] That case concerned contributions to a national party committee that were "earmarked" for certain U.S. Senate candidates, allegedly in violation of FECA and regulations the FEC had promulgated under the statute. The commission found "reason to believe" with respect to three *statutory* charges, but deadlocked 3-3 on the charge arising from an FEC *regulation* concerning a party committee's "direction or control" over the choice of recipient candidates.[127] Technically, *NRSC* was not a *Chevron* case, because it involved the agency's interpretation of a regulation rather than a statute. The D.C. Circuit nevertheless decided that deference to the controlling bloc of commissioners (i.e., those voting against enforcement) was warranted under the doctrine of *Bowles v. Seminole Rock*,[128] which accords deference to an agency's interpretation of its own regulations. In reaching this conclusion, *NRSC* relied on Judge Ginsburg's footnote in *DCCC* which, the *NRSC* court said, "strongly suggest[ed]" that deference was appropriate when the FEC deadlocks on a previously unresolved question.[129] The court saw no reason to give any less deference to the FEC's interpretation where dismissal arose from a 3-3 split on the commission (as in *NRSC*), rather than a majority or even unanimous vote for dismissal (as in the Supreme Court's decision in *DSCC*).[130] The court did not appear to consider the argument that a tie vote is less worthy of deference, because it reflects disagreement among the commission—and the absence of a majority—on how the regulation in question ought to be construed.

The second decision to instantiate deadlock deference into D.C. Circuit law was *In re Sealed Cases*.[131] That case presented the deadlock deference question in an unusual posture. The FEC had split 3-3 on whether to find probable cause that the Republican National Committee and three of its officials had violated the federal statutory prohibition on receiving contributions from foreign nationals.[132] The subsequent litigation, however, did not arise directly

[126] 966 F.2d 1471 (D.C. Cir. 1992).

[127] *Id.* at 1474 (citing 11 C.F.R. § 110.6(d)).

[128] *Id.* at 1475–76 (citing Bowles v. Seminole Rock & Sand Co., 325 U.S. 410, 414 (1945)). The doctrine of judicial deference to an agency's interpretation of its own regulations is now commonly associated with the subsequent decision in Auer v. Robbins, 519 U.S. 452 (1997).

[129] FEC v. Nat'l Republican Senatorial Comm., 966 F.2d at 1476 (citing *DCCC*, 831 F.2d at 1135 n.5) (*NRSC*).

[130] *Id.* at 1476.

[131] 223 F.3d 775 (D.C. 2000).

[132] *Id.* at 777.

from that administrative decision but instead from the Justice Department's subsequent *criminal* investigation of the same activities. As a part of their investigation, federal prosecutors secured a subpoena for certain RNC documents, which the district court ordered produced.[133] The D.C. Circuit reversed in *Sealed Cases*, concluding that the legal interpretation offered by the controlling bloc of FEC commissioners (i.e., those voting against enforcement) deserved deference in subsequent criminal proceedings.[134] According to the court, the Justice Department was seeking to rely on "an interpretation of the relevant statutes that has been rejected by the Commission in a 3-3 decision that, under the statutory voting mechanism … controls Commission enforcement."[135] The court relied in part on *NRSC's* holding that deference must be granted where the FEC splits on whether to enforce its own *regulations*, extending its reasoning to FEC splits on federal *statutes*.[136]

The D.C. Circuit's decision in *Sealed Cases* came down shortly before *United States v. Mead*, which clarified the circumstances under which agency interpretations are eligible for *Chevron* deference. The *Sealed Cases* court did, however, rely on the Supreme Court's decision in *Christensen v. Harris County*[137] (decided earlier that year). *Christensen* had articulated what might be thought of as a beta version of "Step Zero," declining to defer to the interpretation of a federal statute offered in an agency's opinion letter. Justice Clarence Thomas's majority opinion reasoned that the interpretation contained in such a letter—unlike one issued through a formal adjudication or notice-and-comment rulemaking—"lack[s] the force of law."[138] *Sealed Cases* cited the "force of law" language from *Christensen*, but came to the opposite conclusion. The D.C. Circuit thought that the FEC's probable cause determination was more like a formal adjudication than an opinion letter and therefore fell "on the *Chevron* side of the line."[139] It noted that the FEC's structure and majority vote requirements were designed to prevent "coercive Commission action in a partisan situation,"[140] by which it presumably meant situations where the FEC commissioners were divided along party lines. As in *NRSC*, the *Sealed Cases* court cited Judge Ginsburg's dictum in *DCCC*.[141] Although

[133] *Id.*

[134] *Id.* at 779.

[135] *Id.*

[136] *Id.* at 779–80. *See* Nou, *supra* note 34, at 157 (calling the *Sealed Cases* holding that courts should defer to the bloc voting against enforcement "puzzling[]").

[137] 529 U.S. 576 (2000).

[138] *Id.* at 587.

[139] *In re* Sealed Cases, 223 F.3d 775, 780 (D.C. Cir. 2000).

[140] *Id.*

[141] *Id.* at 781 (quoting *DCCC*, 831 F.2d at 1135 n. 5).

Sealed Cases quoted *Christensen*'s "force of law" language, it conspicuously failed to explain why it thought the FEC's 3-3 decision should be deemed to have the "force of law."

B. *The Case against Deadlock Deference*

The consequence of *NRSC* and *Sealed Cases* is that, in cases where fewer than four commissioners voted to proceed with enforcement, the D.C. Circuit defers to the interpretation offered by the other commissioners (i.e., those who voted against proceeding with enforcement). That includes matters on which the FEC deadlocks 3-3 along party lines, a problem that has become more pronounced in the intervening years as explained in Part II. One might plausibly argue that these decisions were correct under the law that existed at the time, but they are not defensible under current law. According *Chevron* deference to the bloc of FEC commissioners voting against enforcement in cases where there is no majority position disregards current law, as stated in *Mead*.

To see why, it is helpful to focus on how *Mead* describes the threshold requirements for *Chevron* deference: "We hold that administrative implementation of a particular statutory provision qualifies for *Chevron* deference when it appears that Congress delegated authority to the agency generally to make rules carrying the force of law, and that the agency interpretation claiming deference was promulgated in the exercise of that authority."[142] This version of "Step Zero" has two prongs: (1) that Congress "delegated authority to the agency to make rules carrying the force of law," and (2) that the interpretation in question was "promulgated in the exercise of that authority."[143]

On the first prong, the Court did not provide much clarity on what it meant by "force of law," a point that troubles some commentators.[144] But whatever "force of law" means, it surely covers some FEC actions. A clear example is the promulgation of a regulation or other rule after notice-and-comment rulemaking.[145] FEC advisory opinions would likely fall into this category as well. Recall that such opinions must be approved by at least a four-member

[142] 533 U.S. at 226–27.

[143] *Id.* The context reveals that the Court's use of the word "rules" is not limited to rules made through agency rulemaking, but also includes rules made through other administrative processes like adjudication. *See id.* at 229 ("We have recognized a very good indicator of delegation meriting *Chevron* treatment in express congressional authorizations to engage in the process of rulemaking or adjudication that produces regulations or rulings for which deference is claimed.").

[144] *See, e.g.*, Merrill, *supra* note 12, at 766.

[145] *See* Van Hollen v. FEC, 811 F.3d 486 (D.C. Cir. 2016); Ctr. for Individual Freedom v. Van Hollen, 694 F.3d 108 (D.C. Cir. 2012).

majority of the FEC. Since *Mead*, the D.C. Circuit has held that such opinions deserve *Chevron* deference, given that an advisory opinion provides a "safe harbor" not only for the party requesting it but also for others acting in materially indistinguishable circumstances.[146] Accordingly, advisory opinions have "binding legal effect" on the FEC.[147] The FEC might also be deemed to have exercised delegated authority to make rules with the force of law, when a *majority* of the FEC votes to dismiss an enforcement matter. This depends on what "force of law" means and on the effect that the determination has on subsequent cases. A majority vote not only has legal effect with respect to the parties before the commission but may also have precedential effect on parties not before it. Moreover, the statute's majority vote requirement is satisfied in cases where four or more commissioners vote to dismiss, so there is no doubt that the commission's interpretation was "promulgated in the exercise" of the authority that Congress delegated to the agency.

Whatever uncertainty exists about whether *Mead* is satisfied in cases where a *majority* of the FEC votes to dismiss an enforcement matter, it cannot be understood to cover interpretations adopted by *less than a majority* of the FEC. A dismissal in these circumstances does not meet *Mead*'s second prong: the agency has not exercised congressionally delegated authority to make rules carrying the force of law. On this point, the difference between *Christensen*'s early formulation of the standard and *Mead*'s new-and-improved version is critical. *Christensen* asked only whether the agency interpretation had the "force of law." If "force of law" means nothing more than legal effect, as the D.C. Circuit appears to have presumed in *Sealed Cases*, then it might plausibly be said that the FEC acts with the "force of law" when it dismisses an enforcement action on a tie vote. In those circumstances, the vote has binding legal effect as to the parties before the commission, though not on others (in contrast to a regulation or advisory opinion). Under *Mead*'s refined version of Step Zero, by contrast, interpretations garnering fewer than four votes cannot receive *Chevron* deference. When the FEC deadlocks, it has not exercised its authority to make rules carrying the force of law.[148] Thus, *Mead*'s second prong is not satisfied.

[146] FEC v. Nat'l Rifle Association of America, 254 F.3d 173, 185 (D.C. Cir. 2001) (*NRA*). On the other hand, there is no deference on matters where there is no majority for an advisory opinion—including cases where the commission deadlocks 3-3 on whether to issue one. Hisp. Leadership Fund v. FEC, 897 F. Supp. 2d 407 (D.D.C. 2012).

[147] *NRA*, 254 F.3d at 185.

[148] *See* Nou, *supra* note 34, at 159 ("an FEC deadlock is not an affirmative exercise of lawmaking authority according to Congress's own voting rule, but rather the result of the agency's inability to decide").

To be sure, Congress delegated to the FEC authority to make rules carrying the force of law—through rulemaking, advisory opinions, and perhaps enforcement decisions backed by a majority vote. But nothing in federal law gives the FEC the authority to "make rules carrying the force of law" *with less than a majority*. To the contrary, FECA requires four votes for any significant action. The statute imposes a rule of decision that enforcement matters on which the commissioners are deadlocked shall not proceed, but that does not mean that the commission has made any rule of law in such cases. To the contrary, the D.C. Circuit itself has long recognized that the FEC *cannot* make law in the absence of a four-commissioner majority.[149] Without a majority, FEC decisions are not "binding legal precedent or authority for future cases."[150] It follows that judicial deference is unwarranted in cases where the FEC dismisses an enforcement action with fewer than four votes. Because the FEC has not exercised any congressionally delegated authority to make rules carrying the force of law, the second prong of *Mead*'s precondition for *Chevron* deference is not satisfied. Though the D.C. Circuit's original embrace of deadlock deference was defensible in light of the precedent that existed at the time, its continuing adherence to that doctrine is not.[151]

A more difficult question is whether *Skidmore*'s weaker form of deference should apply in cases where the FEC deadlocks. Recall that *Mead* held that reasonable agency interpretations should still be given some consideration in cases where *Chevron* deference is inapplicable.[152] The weight those interpretations deserve "var[ies] with circumstances," including the thoroughness of the agency's decision, the consistency of its interpretation over time, the procedural formality of the decision in question, the agency's expertise on the topic, and the persuasiveness of its position.[153] *Mead* noted that the *Skidmore* standard has "produced a spectrum of judicial responses, from great respect on one end ... to near indifference on the other."[154] Where there is no majority position on the FEC, and especially where there is a 3-3 tie, the appropriate

[149] Common Cause v. FEC, 842 F.2d 436, 449 & n. 32 (D.C. Cir. 1988) (noting that in the case of a 3-3 deadlock, the view of a commissioner voting against enforcement is "not law" and that the "carefully balanced bipartisan structure which Congress has enacted" requires at least four votes for "any *official* Commission decision"). *See* Nou, *supra* note 34, at 159 & n.117 (noting the conflict between *Common Cause*'s holding and the practice of deadlock deference).

[150] *Common Cause*, 842 F.2d at 449 n. 32.

[151] A case in the D.C. federal district court argues that deadlocked votes have no precedential effect, and therefore don't carry the "force of law" as *Mead* requires. *See* Campaign Legal Center, Public Citizen v. FEC, www.campaignlegalcenter.org/case/public-citizen-v-fec.

[152] 533 U.S. 228, 234–35.

[153] *Id.* at 228 (citing *Skidmore*, 323 U.S. at 139–40).

[154] *Id.*

judicial response is on the non-deferential end of the spectrum. In fact, it is doubtful that *Skidmore* applies at all. Because there is no agency interpretation, there is no position that commands deference. Even if *Skidmore* does apply, it is hard to see why the views of three commissioners voting "no" should receive greater deference than the three voting "yes," although a court should certainly give respectful consideration to all the commissioners' views as well as the position of the FEC's general counsel.[155]

For similar reasons, there is scant reason to defer to a *regulatory* interpretation (as opposed to a statutory interpretation) when an FEC deadlock results in dismissal of an enforcement action. The Court has long held that an administrative agency's interpretation of its own regulations is generally entitled to a high degree of deference, a doctrine sometimes referred to as *Seminole Rock/Auer* deference.[156] The Court has yet to clarify the preconditions for this form of deference in the manner that *Mead* clarifies the preconditions for *Chevron* deference. With that caveat, it is hard to see why deadlock deference on regulatory questions is any more justifiable than it is for statutory questions. Congress delegated the FEC authority to make legally binding rulings only with a majority vote. In other circumstances, there is no agency interpretation to which a court owes deference. And even assuming arguendo that there *is* an agency interpretation, the absence of a majority position make deference inappropriate, given the FEC's statutorily defined structure and the four-vote requirement for agency action.

The above discussion explains why deadlock deference is wrong as a matter of law, but correcting a legal error is not the only reason for abandoning it. Doing so would also have the salutary effect of allowing the federal courts to serve as a tiebreaker in cases where the FEC is without a majority position, including the many cases in which it deadlocks along party lines. This would be desirable because federal courts, populated by life-tenured judges, are more insulated from partisan politics than FEC commissioners and any other plausible decision-maker. To be clear, my claim is not based on the fantasy that federal judges are completely impartial, in the sense of being free from

155 *See* Nou, *supra* note 34, at 159–65 (suggesting that courts pay attention to the views of "career staff" within administrative agencies when there is a deadlock). One empirical study finds that agencies are significantly less likely to prevail under *Skidmore* than *Chevron*. Kent Barnett & Christopher J. Walker, Chevron *in the Circuit Courts*, 116 MICH. L. REV. 1 (2017). This evidence suggests that abandonment of *Chevron* deference in cases where the FEC deadlocks would likely result in more searching review, even if some form of *Skidmore* deference were invoked.

156 *See* Auer v. Robbins, 519 U.S. 452, 461–63 (1997); Bowles v. Seminole Rock & Sand Co., 325 U.S. 410, 414 (1945).

any ideological or even partisan attachments. Rather, it is that Article III gives federal judges greater institutional independence from partisan politics than FEC commissioners. They are, accordingly, better suited to resolve stalemates over the meaning of federal campaign finance statutes and regulations than any other actor at the federal level. Abandonment of deadlock deference would allow federal courts to serve as arbiters of the meaning of federal law where FEC commissioners split on party lines.[157]

Getting rid of deadlock deference would not magically cure all of the problems with the current enforcement regime. Perhaps most notably, it would probably have little if any impact on delays in enforcement actions in cases where the FEC stalemates along party lines. For example, there might be one appeal taken from a deadlocked vote on whether there is "reason to believe," then a federal court reversal, then another deadlocked vote on whether to find "probable cause," followed by still more federal court proceedings. If Congress were interested in addressing this potential problem, it might consider the solution that Thomas and Bowman recommended years ago: that is, to allow a "reason to believe" determination (and therefore an investigation) to be made with only three votes, while retaining the four-vote requirement for subsequent enforcement actions. There are other conceivable ways of increasing the efficacy of FEC enforcement without altering its basic structure, such as giving it authority to impose penalties—which would of course be judicially reviewable—rather than limiting it to conciliation agreements and the ability to initiate federal court actions if that process fails. A strong case can thus be made for augmentation of the FEC's enforcement powers. But only the abandonment of deadlock deference can resolve party line disagreements over the interpretations of federal law, without creating the risk of biased enforcement that would inevitably arise if one of the major parties were given effective control of the commission.[158]

[157] The U.S. District Court for the District of Columbia has already held that *Chevron* deference is inappropriate in cases where the FEC deadlocks in its interpretation of a *judicial decision*. Citizens for Resp. & Ethics in Washington v. FEC, 209 F. Supp. 3d 77, 86 (D.D.C. 2016). But D.C. Circuit precedent still requires judicial deference to FEC interpretations of statutes and regulations.

[158] Shortly before this book went to press, a divided panel of the D.C. Circuit issued a decision that threatens to exacerbate the problem of FEC deadlocks defying judicial review. Judge Raymond Randolph wrote for the majority in *Citizens for Responsibility and Ethics in Washington v. FEC*, 892 F.3d 434 (D.C. Cir. 2018), joined by Judge Brett Kavanaugh. The majority held that the FEC's dismissal of a complaint on a 3–3 vote was not judicially reviewable, where the controlling group identifies prosecutorial discretion as a reason for its decision. Declaring the exercise of prosecutorial discretion to be unreviewable, without more, would be unremarkable. The problem is that the challenged FEC decision was on whether there was *reason to believe* there had been a FECA violation. At that stage, a dismissal based on

V. CONCLUSION

The FEC's present dysfunction is nearly impossible to deny, though some may still try. Protracted party line stalemates frustrate effective enforcement and leave critical questions of law unresolved. The consequence is continuing uncertainty over such pressing questions as the disclosure obligations of outside groups, the circumstances under which expenditures will be deemed coordinated, and the scope of the ban on foreign nationals' contributions and expenditures.[159] In this environment, it is tempting to endorse proposals to restructure the FEC. Moving to an odd-numbered commission would certainly end party line stalemates, but it would create an even more serious danger, opening the door to the dominant party enforcing campaign finance laws in a manner that systematically disadvantages its chief rival. In our era of hyperpolarized politics, slanted enforcement of campaign finance laws cannot be dismissed as a fantastic hypothetical. A more constructive reform is for the federal judiciary to play a more active role in reviewing FEC enforcement decisions when no interpretation commands four votes. Ending deadlock deference would correct D.C. Circuit precedents that later Supreme Court precedents have undermined. It would also allow the institution with the greatest insulation from partisan politics, the federal judiciary, to play a more prominent role in interpreting the law. Best of all, this change could be effected without amending any existing statute or regulation. All that's required is to end the practice of deferring to interpretations that command less than a majority of FEC commissioners. Rather than trying to restructure the FEC, reform advocates should focus on securing more effective judicial review of its decisions.

prosecutorial discretion requires four votes, as Judge Cornelia Pillard's dissent pointed out. *Id.*. The upshot of the majority opinion is that FEC commissioners may now cite prosecutorial discretion as their reason for dismissing, even where four votes to dismiss on this ground are lacking. If that happens, it appears the D.C. Circuit will view the dismissal as unreviewable. The decision thus appears to provide a roadmap for avoiding judicial review where the commission is split along party lines.

159 *See* Daniel Tokaji, *What Trump Jr. Did Was Bad, But It Probably Didn't Violate Federal Campaign Finance Law*, JUST SECURITY (July 14, 2017), www.justsecurity.org/43116/trump-jr-bad-didnt-violate-federal-campaign-finance-law/ (urging clarification of whether damaging information on an opponent, like that which Donald Trump, Jr. allegedly sought from a Russian lawyer, is an in-kind contribution to which the foreign nationals' contribution ban applies).

8

The People's Pledge: Campaign Finance Reform without Legal Reform

Ganesh Sitaraman*

The Supreme Court's decision in *Citizens United v. Federal Election Commission*[1] is widely considered a major roadblock to campaign finance reform. Critics have decried the decision's effect on the ability of third parties, namely corporations, to influence elections. In response to these concerns, scholars and activists have proposed a variety of public law reforms—constitutional, legislative, and regulatory—to limit the influence of third-party spending in federal elections. Some argue for a constitutional amendment to overturn the case, others for a variety of public financing options, and still others for improved disclosure of corporate political spending.

While these reformers have appropriately focused on public law options to address a public law problem, they have missed the possibility that private ordering could limit third-party campaign spending in federal elections. This chapter argues that under certain conditions, private ordering can be effective at limiting or even eliminating third-party spending. The private ordering option involves a self-enforcing contract between the opposing campaigns, in which each campaign agrees to be penalized from its own campaign treasury for any spending from an outside group that supports the candidate. In other words, if an outside group spends money on television advertisements supporting a candidate or attacking her opponent, the candidate that benefits from the advertisements must pay, as a penalty, a proportion of the value of the third party's advertising costs. Because the penalty reduces the candidate's own funds, outside supporters will restrain themselves from spending on the candidate's behalf.

* Ganesh Sitaraman is Professor of Law and Director of the Program on Law and Government at Vanderbilt University Law School. A version of this chapter appeared first as *Contracting Around* Citizens United, 114 COLUM. L. REV. 744 (2014).

[1] Citizens United v. FEC, 558 U.S 310 (2010).

While a contract structured in this manner might seem like a fanciful solution, precisely this kind of contract succeeded in keeping third parties from television, radio, and internet advertising in the most expensive Senate race of 2012: the Brown-Warren race in Massachusetts.[2] In that race, third-party groups spent millions of dollars on advertisements until Senator Scott Brown and Elizabeth Warren signed what they called "The People's Pledge" in late January 2012.[3] The People's Pledge required each campaign to pay to charity the equivalent of 50 percent of any third party's advertising costs for advertisements that benefitted their candidacy. In March, there were two minor incursions by third parties, but the pact remained intact, as the benefiting campaign paid the penalty for third-party support. The People's Pledge continued to hold until Election Day, with no other outside groups entering the race for fear of impeding their preferred candidate's campaign. And since the Brown-Warren race, there has been a small but emerging trend of other campaigns debating and in some cases adopting a variation on The People's Pledge.

Given the current context of political gridlock in implementing constitutional, legislative, and regulatory reforms to the campaign finance system, the possibility of a private ordering option is particularly important as an additional path forward for those interested in restricting third-party spending in the short term. This chapter explains the design options for a contract between opposing campaigns that is self-enforcing and restricts third-party spending, identifies the conditions under which such a contract is likely to be offered and accepted, shows how political dynamics push third parties and campaigns to adhere to the contract's spending restrictions, and discusses possible loopholes and challenges.

I. THE PEOPLE'S PLEDGE: AN INTRODUCTION

At the start of the 2012 Brown-Warren Senate race in Massachusetts, third-party groups including the League of Conservation Voters and Crossroads

2 Total spending in the Brown-Warren race amounted to $77 million, $17 million more than the second most expensive race in 2012, in which a total of $60 million was spent. *See Historical Elections: Most Expensive Races*, CENTER FOR RESPONSIVE POLITICS, www.opensecrets.org/bigpicture/topraces.php?cycle=2012&display=currcands. The Brown-Warren race was also the most expensive Senate race in history. *See, e.g.*, Chris Cillizza, *The Most Expensive Senate Races Ever—and Where Kentucky Might Fit In*, WASH. POST: THE FIX (Aug. 12, 2013), www.washingtonpost.com/blogs/the-fix/wp/2013/08/12/the-most-expensive-senate-races-ever-and-where-kentucky-might-fit-in/.

3 Scott Brown & Elizabeth Warren, The People's Pledge (Jan. 23, 2012), https://web.archive.org/web/20131231041530/; www.scottbrown.com/wp-content/uploads/2012/03/signed-agreement.pdf. The Pledge is reproduced in the Appendix.

GPS spent millions of dollars on issue advertisements until the two candidates signed The People's Pledge in late January 2012.[4] Widely considered the first major attempt to restrict third-party groups since *Citizens United*,[5] the Pledge required each campaign to pay to charity the equivalent of 50 percent of any third party's advertising costs for advertisements that supported their candidates. On two occasions in March 2012, outside groups spent relatively small amounts of money in support of Senator Brown, and Brown's campaign paid the penalty to charity.[6] After that point, the Pledge held until Election Day, with outside groups staying out of the race for fear of impeding their preferred candidate's campaign.[7]

The difference in outside spending between the Brown-Warren race and other Senate races in 2012 is striking. Outside spending made up only 9 percent of total spending in Massachusetts, compared to 62 percent, 47 percent, and 64 percent of total spending in Senate races in Virginia, Ohio, and Wisconsin, respectively (the second, third, and fifth most expensive races of 2012).[8] While the Pledge doesn't regulate donations, there were also differences in the source of donations. Small donors (giving less than $200) had more influence than big donors in Massachusetts, contributing $23.5 million to the big donors' $8 million; in Virginia, Wisconsin, and Ohio combined, the big donors dominated the small donors, $135 million to $23.8 million.[9] Compared to those in Massachusetts, television advertisements in Virginia,

4 *See* Press Release, League of Conservation Voters, LCV Launches Major Ad Buy Showing Scott Brown Has Gone Washington (Oct. 25, 2011), www.lcv.org/media/press-releases/LCV-Launches-Major-Ad-Buy-Showing-Scott-Brown-Has-Gone-Washington.html; Robert Rizzuto, *Super PAC Crossroads GPS Takes Swipe at Elizabeth Warren's Response to Latest Ad*, MassLive (Dec. 9, 2011), www.masslive.com/politics/index.ssf/2011/12/super_pac_crossroads_gps_takes.html.

5 *See, e.g.*, Adam Sorensen, *Can a Bipartisan Pact Really Disarm the Super PAC Arsenal in Massachusetts?*, Time: Swampland (Jan. 24, 2012), http://swampland.time.com/2012/01/24/can-a-bipartisan-pact-disarm-the-super-pac-arsenal-in-massachusetts/.

6 *See* Patrick Johnson, *Scott Brown Agrees to Make Charitable Donation for 'People's Pledge' Infraction After Elizabeth Warren Calls Foul over Oil Lobbying Group's Pro-Brown Ads*, MassLive (Mar. 26, 2012), www.masslive.com/politics/index.ssf/2012/03/scott_brown_agrees_to_2nd_dona.html; Steve Leblanc, *Warren Picks Charity for Ad Deal with Sen. Brown*, Real Clear Politics (Mar. 9, 2012), www.realclearpolitics.com/news/ap/politics/2012/Mar/09/warren_picks_charity_for_ad_deal_with_sen__brown.html.

7 *Cf.* Dan Eggen, *Pact on Third-Party Ads Seems to Be Working in Massachusetts*, Wash. Post (Mar. 28, 2012), http://articles.washingtonpost.com/2012-03-28/politics/35450339_1_issue-ads-massachusetts-senate-race-senator-brown.

8 Tyler Creighton, Common Cause Mass., A Plea for a Pledge: Outside Spending in Competitive 2012 U.S. Senate Races 4 (2013), www.commoncause.org/research-reports/MA_050113_Report_Plea_for_a_Pledge.pdf

9 *Id.* at 5.

Wisconsin, and Ohio were, on average, more than twice as likely to be negative advertisements — 36 percent in Massachusetts, compared to 84 percent in the other states.[10] The success of the Pledge led to its adoption in other races, such as the Lynch-Markey Senate primary and the multicandidate fifth federal congressional district primary in Massachusetts in 2013. Still others races have seen the Pledge offered but rejected.[11]

Self-enforcing contracts like The People's Pledge have a number of elements, each of which can be customized by the campaigns during contract negotiations.

A. *The Trigger and the Penalty*

In order to create the necessary incentives for third parties to stay out of the election, the contract's central provisions are the triggering and penalty provisions. The basic structure is simple: In the event that a third-party organization engages in specified election activities, the candidate that benefits from those activities shall pay a penalty. The trigger for the penalty is the third-party campaign spending, which will be readily visible to the campaigns, press, and public at large. The public nature of the trigger ensures that the campaigns will have to respond to the third-party advertising with either compliance (and payment of penalty) or breach of the contract. The penalty harms

[10] *Id.* In the other competitive states, 97% of advertisements paid for by outside groups were negative. *Id.*

[11] *See, e.g.*, Stephen F. Lynch & Edward Markey, The People's Pledge (Feb. 13, 2013), https://s3.amazonaws.com/edmarkey/docs/PeoplesPledge2013.pdf; William Brownsberger, Katherine Clark, Peter Koutoujian, Carl Sciortino & Karen Spilka, The People's Pledge (Aug. 16, 2013), www.peoplespledge2014.org/wp-content/uploads/2014/07/MA-districti-5-2013.pdf; Dakota Smith, *Eric Garcetti's SuperPAC Pledge Gets Turned Down by Other LA Mayoral Candidates*, HUFF. POST (Jan. 18, 2013), www.huffingtonpost.com/2013/01/18/eric-garcetti-superpac-pledge-candidates_n_2503641.html; Colin A. Young, *Rob Consalvo Calls on Candidates to Pledge to Eliminate Outside Special Interest Funding from Mayoral Race*, BOSTON.COM (July 14, 2013), www.boston.com/politicalintelligence/2013/07/14/consalvo-calls-candidates-pledge-eliminate-outside-special-interest-funding-from-mayoral-race/yQohpS7zBhO2ZMv6hysSjN/story.html; Darryl R. Isherwood, *Pallone Finds No Takers for "People's Pledge,"* POLITICKERNJ (June 27, 2013), http://politickernj.com/2013/06/pallone-finds-no-takers-for-peoples-pledge/; Cameron Joseph, *Honda, Opponent Spar over 'People's Pledge,'* THE HILL (Jan. 24, 2014), http://thehill.com/blogs/ballot-box/house-races/196314-honda-opponent-spar-over-peoples-pledge; Dan McGowan, *Taveras Asks Raimondo, Others to Sign Pledge to Curb Outside Spending*, WPRI.COM (Oct. 23, 2013), http://blogs.wpri.com/2013/10/23/taveras-asks-gubernatorial-candidates-to-sign-pledge-to-curb-outside-spending; Editorial, *A Worthy Campaign Pledge for Maryland*, WASH. POST (Nov. 16, 2013), www.washingtonpost.com/opinions/a-worthy-campaign-pledge-for-maryland/2013/11/16/c24a1ef6-4cac-11e3-be6b-d3d28122e6d4_story.html.

the campaign that is benefitted by the third party's spending, thereby undermining the third party's goal to help its preferred candidate. This self-inflicted punishment is what creates the incentive for the third party to refrain from election-related advertising. In the Brown-Warren campaign, for example, The People's Pledge established a penalty of 50 percent of the cost of the third party's advertising buy, and it required that the candidate benefiting from the third-party advertising pay the penalty to a charity of the opposing candidate's choice. Of course, the amount of the penalty can be varied based on the candidates' preferences.

B. *Covered Organizations*

The contract can also vary in scope with respect to the covered organizations—that is, the organizations whose activities trigger the penalty. A broader scope that includes more organizations is likely to keep out more and different types of third parties and limit election spending to the candidates themselves. A narrower scope would allow for only certain kinds of third parties to spend funds during the campaign. The People's Pledge, for example, took a broad scope by defining third-party organizations as "including but not limited to individuals, corporations, 527 organizations, 501(c) organizations, Super PACs, and national and state party committees."

Of particular note is the inclusion of national and state party committees, such as the Democratic Senatorial Campaign Committee and the National Republican Senatorial Committee. The party committees are permitted to use funds for advertisements in campaigns, and they are allowed to coordinate with the campaigns, up to a set amount.[12] Including the party committees in addition to other third-party groups as covered organizations serves two functions. First, it ensures that only the candidates themselves are running advertisements on their behalf. Second, it closes a loophole that would allow individuals and PACs to donate to party committees, and then enable the party committees to advertise during the election season, while coordinating those advertisements with the campaign.

There is also a case *against* including party committees as a covered organization in the contract. Most candidates running for federal office face severe

[12] *See* 11 C.F.R. § 109.21 (2013) (outlining parameters for permissible coordinated communication); *Contribution Limits 2013–14*, FEDERAL ELECTION COMMISSION, www.fec.gov/pages/brochures/contriblimits.shtml. Note that The People's Pledge was used prior to the Supreme Court's decision in *McCutcheon v. FEC*, 134 S. Ct. 1434 (2014), when there was an individual limit of $123,200 biennially, with a $48,000 limit to candidates and $74,000 limit to PACs and parties.

financial constraints. They need—and work hard to get—enough funding to spend on television advertisements so they can get their story and message to the public. Party committees, particularly in congressional races, often serve as the cavalry, providing essential support to help candidates get even their basic story and message out to the people when they are short of funds. Campaigns that are unable (or think they are likely unable) to raise even the minimum necessary to purchase serious advertising time in their district or state may want to exclude party committees from the terms of the contract. Note also how narrow the loophole is that allows individuals and organizations to donate to party committees and the committees to coordinate with campaigns.[13] Donations to the party committee go to the committee's general funds for campaign activity—they are not earmarked for specific races. As a result, outside groups seeking to influence a particular race through the party committee cannot predict with certainty that their donations will be directed toward that race.

C. *Covered Activities*

In addition to defining the scope of covered organizations, the contract must also consider the scope of covered activities. Third parties can engage in a wide range of election-related activities: broadcast-television, radio, cable, satellite, and internet advertising; direct mail to voters; robocalls; billboards; leaflets; organizing drives for voters and volunteers; and communications with an organization's own members. A broader scope, including more activities, will again give more power to and place more emphasis on the campaigns themselves. A narrower scope enables third parties to play a role, albeit a limited one. Perhaps the clearest line to draw is between broadcast-television, radio, cable, satellite, and internet advertising, and other activities. These activities share a common core: paid advertising distributed via a private communications channel to a wide audience. They are also the most salient; and in the case of television, the most expensive. A slightly broader category would include direct mail to voters. Direct mail involves campaigns or third parties sending electioneering materials directly to voters via the U.S. Postal Service. Like the items in the advertising category, direct mail is a distribution channel for third-party groups to convey their message. Unlike the advertising items, however, direct mail is targeted to individuals, rather than widely distributed.[14]

[13] *See* 11 C.F.R. § 109.21 (restricting campaign-committee coordination).

[14] Internet advertising is similar. For a discussion of targeted advertising, including direct mail and the Internet, see generally Michael S. Kang, *From Broadcasting to Narrowcasting: The Emerging Challenge for Campaign Finance Law*, 73 Geo. Wash. L. Rev. 1070 (2005).

D. *Identifying the Value of Covered Activities*

Deciding which activities should be covered depends in part on whether it is possible to identify the cash value of those activities. Without knowing the cash value, it is impossible to determine the amount of the penalty. Here too, certain advertising activities have an advantage over mail and other organizational activities.

First, some advertising activities are readily discernible to the public. Because television, radio, cable, and satellite advertising are broadcast to a wide audience, third-party activity can be easily identified. Internet and direct mail violations, in contrast, are harder to discover because they are targeted directly at a narrow group of individuals who may not report the activity. Second, the value of these advertising activities (generally called "ad buys") is readily discoverable. Television stations make logs of their advertising open to the public, so any member of the public can go to the station and see the amount of the ad buy and the group that purchased the airtime.[15] Additionally, most campaign ad buys go through sales representatives, who are often grouped by television affiliate or cable system (e.g., the ABC affiliates in greater Boston). These sales representatives will usually tell campaigns what the extent of ad buys are from outside groups or their opponents, and they can usually do so with greater speed than the campaign sending a representative to the station to check the logs. Discovering the value of these ad buys is becoming easier, as more and more third-party groups send out press releases describing their advertising activities. These groups seek to take credit for their efforts to further their candidate's cause. This desire for credit enables identification of the value of the advertising buys. Finally, FEC disclosure rules also make it possible to identify third-party intervention for significant "electioneering communications" and "independent expenditures," which have to be reported within 24 and 48 hours for many kinds of spending.[16] Note that the FEC disclosure regime does not include disclosure of spending on "issue advertisements"—advertisements that might mention a candidate but do not advocate for her election or defeat—prior to the 30- and 60-day timelines that govern electioneering communications.[17]

[15] *About Public Inspection Files*, FEDERAL ELECTION COMMISSION, https://publicfiles.fcc.gov/about-station-profiles.

[16] 11 C.F.R. § 100.29(a), § 100.16(a), § 104.20, § 104.4(b)(2), § 104.4(b)-(c) (2013).

[17] *Id.* § 109.21(f) (providing safe harbor for issue advertisements).

II. WHY ADOPT THE PEOPLE'S PLEDGE?

Campaigns seeking to limit third-party spending have to consider a variety of factors when determining whether to offer the contract to their opponent or, if offered a contract by the opponent, whether to accept. In different races, these factors may have different weights, and they may interact in complex and unpredictable ways. As a result, it would be difficult, if not impossible, to outline a universal formula for when campaigns should come to an agreement. Nevertheless, it is possible to identify the factors that campaigns will consider and whether those factors push toward or against creating a contract.

A. *Fundamentals of the Race*

Campaigns analyze the fundamentals of the race by relying on polling, experience, history, and perceived strengths and weaknesses of candidates. If one side thinks it will easily win the election, that counsels in favor of offering the contract to the weaker opponent. The weaker opponent, already unlikely to succeed, would then be denied the additional support that could come from third-party advertising (supportive advertising and attacks on the opponent), while the likely winner would maintain the *status quo* of her lead. The stronger candidate could make an offer, thereby taking the moral high ground of clean elections and forcing the weaker candidate either to suffer the negative press accompanying rejection of the deal or to accept the deal and forgo support from outside groups. The weaker candidate might reject the offer on the assumption that third-party spending in her favor would outweigh the stigma from rejecting the Pledge. Note also that these lopsided elections are likely to manifest more frequently with incumbents, and to favor incumbency. In addition, in these lopsided elections, third parties are less likely to enter on either side because of the low probability of their intervention making a difference. In contrast, in situations where it is clear the race will be tight or there is uncertainty as to who is the favorite to win, the dynamics of offer and acceptance are less likely to depend on the chance of victory and more likely to depend on each campaign's access to money and on other political factors.

There still might be situations, however, in which candidates who believe they are likely to win an election easily do not want to sign such a contract, based on the fundamentals of the race. For example, if the year's electoral climate is opposed to a strong candidate's party—because it is an off-year from the presidential election, there are no strong statewide candidates of the same party running in the state to help energize party supporters, or the general climate in the country is opposed to the candidate's party, leadership, or views—the candidate might think there is a higher risk to signing a contract. If the candidate's race starts to tighten (even if, for example, that tightening reduces the likelihood of victory from 90 percent to 65 percent), the candidate will want third-party spending to provide support. Third parties, who may want to support a likely winner in a tighter-than-normal race, could then intervene on the candidate's side.

B. *Availability of Money*

Perhaps the most important factor is the campaigns' perceptions of the amount of money they will have available to them in their race. It is worth distinguishing between money the campaigns raise themselves ("campaign funds") and the money outside groups could spend ("outside money"). One of the most important factors in determining whether a campaign will sign a self-enforcing contract is whether it has sufficient campaign funds to communicate with voters. Television advertising is the easiest way to increase name identification and shape the campaign's narrative, but it is also expensive. If campaigns do not have sufficient funds to run enough television advertisements to articulate that narrative to voters, they will likely not want to exclude outside groups. In other words, there is a basic threshold of campaign funds necessary to communicate with voters, and, in the absence of that level of funding, outside money is generally considered a necessary supplement. Outside money may be necessary to introduce the candidate to voters, to defend against attacks, or to launch attacks. On the other hand, there are reasons why candidates might offer or accept these contracts even if they lack sufficient funding: Some candidates run on principle, even if it might be detrimental to their electability; others might think the contract will be effective at getting them positive press coverage that could help their candidacy; still others might believe they could never get outside funds even if they tried. For mainstream, competitive campaigns worried about having enough basic funding and simultaneously concerned about outside money, there may be a possible compromise: exclude outside groups, except for party committees. Allowing party committees would enable the campaign to have additional support that is coordinated with the campaign's strategy, but would still exclude more independent third parties. Of course, allowing party committees would slightly reduce the benefits of the contract in terms of public perceptions.

If the campaigns have or expect to have sufficient campaign funds, then the next question is whether there is symmetry or asymmetry in the expected funding levels between campaigns—that is, whether one campaign has or is expected to have substantially more campaign funds than the other. For example, at the start of the Brown-Warren race in 2011, Senator Brown had $10 million in campaign funds.[18] Although the two campaigns equalized funding by the end of the race, a $10 million advantage is substantial and something that most campaigns are unlikely to erase. Campaigns must also consider whether there is symmetry or asymmetry in the expected funding levels of outside money. The likelihood of a contract depends on the *expected* funding levels on both sides. Because the contract will be concluded with comparatively little information about the overall funding levels that each candidate will have by the end of the race, each candidate will have to make assumptions about the other candidate's campaign funds and support from outside money. This information is often uncertain, making it rational for campaigns to be risk-averse and act as if there will be an asymmetry favoring the opponent. This should push campaigns generally to think more seriously about agreeing to a self-enforcing contract.

C. *Political Factors: Branding, Narrative, Timing, and Press*

A third set of factors shares as its common concern the effect the contract will have on the short- and long-term narratives in the race. Start with branding. Some candidates are tied to particular brands that might complicate their decision to agree to a contract. For example, a candidate that has robust brand identification around supporting clean government, ending corruption, and removing conflicts of interest would have a harder time refusing to sign a contract. More interestingly, a candidate who is seen as a moderate or independent might be inclined to sign a contract to avoid affiliation with extremist elements seeking to spend money in the race, for fear of being attacked for having links to these extremist elements.

A second issue is the candidate's narrative. Candidates who are relatively or even comparatively unknown might want to have time to introduce themselves to the public in a positive way, without being bombarded by negative attack advertisements from third parties. Particularly in the early stages of the campaign, a candidate seeks to inform voters of who she is and what her story is. When third parties buy advertising, they can often define the candidate before the candidate herself has an opportunity to do so. Many candidates—particularly first-time candidates with low name recognition—might therefore

[18] David Catanese, *Scott Brown's Fundraising Approaches $10 Million*, POLITICO: DAVID CATANESE BLOG (July 6, 2011), www.politico.com/blogs/davidcatanese/0711/Scott_Brown_approaching_10_million_.html.

lean toward supporting a contract if they feel that outside money will enter the race before they have a chance to introduce themselves.

A related issue is the timing of negative advertising by campaigns and third parties. Candidates attacking each other with negative advertisements do not usually "go negative" early in the race. In part, this is because they are introducing themselves and trying to build a positive narrative, and partly this is because candidates have limited resources and want to save their funds for the end of the race. But campaigns also pay a cost for going negative, in the form of press coverage of their negative advertisement and the turn from positive to negative in the race. Third parties, however, can enter the race early with negative advertisements. Although the candidate that benefits might be blamed for the negative tone of the campaign, disclosure requirements indicate clearly which advertisements the candidates approve themselves. As a result, a candidate can condemn third-party negative advertisements as destructive to the spirit of the race while still benefiting from them. The consequence is that candidates who want to be protected from negative advertising for a longer period of time may be more inclined to offer and sign a contract to keep out third parties.

The other political factor that candidates must consider is how the press will interpret their actions. In an environment with an active press corps, the candidates will face extra scrutiny and pressure. First, once the offer is made, the offeree will face immediate pressure from the media to decide whether or not to accept the offer. Failure to accept, in an environment with an entrepreneurial press corps, could lead to negative news stories in the short run, particularly if the candidate has historically supported clean government and campaign finance reform initiatives. Second, if the offeree rejects the contract, then in the long run the offeree is likely to face pressure every time outside money funds a new advertisement, because the opposing candidate can decry the advertisement and the press can blame the offeree for rejecting the contract. Additionally, the offeree will likely face pressure in a debate or in a candidate forum, in which the offeror can criticize the offeree for rejecting the contract.

D. *The Possibility of Breach*

A final consideration is to what extent the candidates believe their opponents are good faith actors. On the one hand, if a candidate believes that his opponent or her third-party allies are bad faith actors who will breach the agreement, he may still want to sign the contract. Even with future breach, the candidate would gain time without outside money being spent (particularly important if the candidate is introducing himself to the voters), and when his opponent or her third-party allies breach, the candidate will have a campaign issue to exploit.

III. WHY THE DEAL HOLDS

Assuming the two campaigns come to an agreement, critical questions remain. Will third parties respect their wishes and refrain from spending money on behalf of the candidates? If not, will campaigns respond by fulfilling the contract's penalty terms or by refusing to pay and breaching the contract?

A. *Why Outside Groups Respect the Contract Terms*

There are three main reasons why outside groups will respect the wishes of the campaigns and restrict their activities. Foremost is the preference for campaign control over third-party control. Dollar for dollar, money spent by the campaign itself is generally understood to be more valuable than money spent by third parties. The reason is simple: third parties do not know as much as the campaign about the campaign's strategy and plans, and because campaign and third-party coordination is highly regulated,[19] third parties cannot integrate their advertising and messages into the campaign's overall strategy. Third parties understand that their dollars, while helpful, might be disconnected from the campaign's strategy, and they do not want to penalize the campaign while substituting their judgment for that of the campaign. To be sure, in a campaign that is truly disastrous, third parties might be willing to substitute their judgment for that of the campaign leadership. But at the same time, it is not uncommon for truly dysfunctional campaigns to replace their leadership.

The second reason third parties might adhere to the campaigns' wishes for them to stay out of the race is that the race remains tight or their preferred candidate leads. In cases where their preferred candidate has a big lead, the third party has no need to enter the race. In situations where the race is tight, the third party will likely not want to enter the race. Although the third party's additional dollars might give a boost to its candidate, the candidate's own coffers will be depleted by the penalty, and the candidate will face a series of negative news stories. These costs to entry are serious and caution against intervention

[19] *See, e.g.*, *Coordinated Communications and Independent Expenditures*, FEDERAL ELECTION COMMISSION (June 2007), www.fec.gov/pages/brochures/indexp.shtml (last updated Jan. 2015) (describing rules governing coordinated communications and independent expenditures).

when the race is close. When the third party's candidate is losing by a significant margin, the third party might be willing to enter the race, thinking its judgment might improve the race's dynamics, even with bad news stories and losses to the campaign's treasury. More plausibly, however, the third party might hope that the candidate will breach the agreement. A desperate candidate could think that opening the floodgates of third-party spending might give her a chance to become competitive once again.

Finally, third parties might stay out of the race because it is simply infeasible to enter the race with advertising. Toward the end of a campaign, advertising time becomes increasingly unavailable, particularly in years and jurisdictions in which there are multiple competitive races. As a result, what little advertising time remains becomes extremely expensive. In effect, there is a point of no return, after which it is simply too expensive to enter the race with advertisements that will saturate the airwaves significantly enough to make a difference.

B. *Why Campaigns Fulfill the Contract*

If a third party did enter the race, the campaign that benefitted from its entry would have a choice: it could adhere to the contract and pay the penalty or breach the contract and refuse to pay the penalty. Campaigns that are considering whether to breach the contract would weigh a number of factors to determine whether the costs of breach outweigh the benefits. One factor is the cost of the advertising buy. It is possible that the entry of third parties would be of such a magnitude that it could deplete and even bankrupt the campaign to pay the penalty. A candidate that wanted to continue in the race without going into significant debt might prefer to breach the contract and continue paying her staff and executing her plans. In this case, the costs of breach (in terms of public outcry and negative press) are relatively minor compared to the benefits of breach (continuing the race while not in debt).

A campaign might also think seriously about breach if the campaign feels that the third-party advertisements are "sham ads," advertisements that appear on the surface to benefit one candidate but in fact benefit the opponent. This loophole will be addressed in the next section, but in this situation, the costs of breach may be mitigated if the candidate can argue that the third party is exploiting a loophole or if the candidate can seek to renegotiate the contract, relying on the provision that both campaigns agree to address the problem of sham ads if it arises. The benefits of breach would be significant, as the campaign that pays the penalty would be depleting its treasury for advertisements that harm it.

The central reason for campaigns to adhere to the contract is the possible political costs of breach—damage to their brand and narrative, and negative press in the short and long run. Breach provides evidence of a serious character flaw. The candidate promised, during the campaign, to adhere to the contract, and in a matter of months broke that promise because it was politically expedient. That kind of behavior, while perhaps all too common in politics, is more significant when it takes place in the course of such a short period of time and under the spotlight of the campaign. The press and the opponent may be able to attack the breaching candidate as untrustworthy or lacking in character. Note also that a candidate can benefit politically from adhering to the contract. By paying a penalty, the candidate signals his character and integrity—and commitment to clean elections.

The campaign will also consider how tight the race is and the timing of the breach. A desperate, losing campaign will be more likely to breach than a winning campaign or a campaign in a tight race. The timing of the breach might affect the candidate as well. Although some might think that breach at the end of the race would be viable because of the limited time between the breach and Election Day, the decision is more complex. On the one hand, a desperate campaign might try anything to gain advantage. On the other hand, breaching toward the end of the race, when voters and the press are paying close attention to the campaign, is more likely to focus attention on the fact of breach and on the candidate's broken promise when faced with the choice of principle versus expedience. Breaching earlier in the race is more likely to draw immediate attention, which could potentially dissipate before Election Day.

C. *Why Informal Enforcement Predominates over Formal Enforcement*

The primary reason that formal enforcement through courts is less relevant than political enforcement is the timing of the contract, breach, and enforcement action. Campaigns take place on a limited time frame, and, as organizations, campaigns have limited resources. Once the contract is signed and there is a breach, the injured party would have to bring a case in court to seek to enforce the contract terms. First, the campaign would have to decide to spend vital campaign resources in terms of funding, time, and effort on the lawsuit instead of on election-related activities. Second, consider the timing of a lawsuit. If the breach takes place early enough and the penalty rate is high enough to both damage the breaching opponent and justify the time, effort, and opportunity costs for the harmed campaign, then the campaign might consider bringing suit. If the breach takes place close to Election Day, bringing a lawsuit to get formal enforcement may not provide redress in time for formal enforcement to affect the electoral outcome, and the opportunity costs of funding and time will be greater. If the breach takes place at a time that guarantees the lawsuit will take place after the election, then the broader political dynamics suggest campaigns will not seek to enforce the agreement. Assuming the candidate that breached the contract loses the election, the victorious candidate has no need to bring suit for damages. She already won the race. Assuming the candidate who breached the contract wins the election, the losing candidate would feel wronged—but *still* might not want to bring suit. A lawsuit would again be time consuming and expensive. Moreover, in order to be meaningful to the losing candidate, a lawsuit would have to result in a court overturning the election results—an unlikely outcome indeed.

While the candidates themselves are unlikely to bring suit to enforce the contract, the more interesting possibility is that campaigns could be liable to suits from the third-party beneficiary (the charity) in certain circumstances. Under the terms of the original People's Pledge, no particular charity was identified as the beneficiary; the harmed candidate chose the charity. As a result, no particular charity would be able to argue that it was the intended beneficiary of the contract and therefore harmed by the candidate's breach. If, however, the contract is drafted to specify a particular charity or if the harmed candidate picks a charity upon the outside group's entry into the race, then the charity would be an identifiable and intended third-party beneficiary, who could likely enforce the contract.[20] There is, however, another wrinkle: In the case of a "sham ad," an advertisement that appears to benefit one candidate but actually harms that candidate, *both* campaigns might choose charities, arguing that the other benefitted from the advertisement. If both refuse to pay, then there will be a dispute about which campaign breached the contract—and a dispute about which charity is the third-party beneficiary.

IV. THE SHAM AD PROBLEM

The most challenging problem for The People's Pledge is referenced directly in the agreement, in the provision committing both sides to work together to address the problem of "sham ads." The sham ad problem emerges from the design of the triggering mechanism. Recall that the penalty is triggered when advertising supports or promotes (or attacks or undermines) one of the

[20] For a discussion of the historical developments and debates on the enforceability of contracts by third-party beneficiaries, see generally 3 E. ALLAN FARNSWORTH, FARNSWORTH ON CONTRACTS § 10 (3d ed. 2004).

candidates. The candidate that benefits must pay a penalty. The problem with this structure is that third parties could create groups and design advertisements that *appear* to benefit one candidate, while in fact harming that candidate. In that case, the candidate would be harmed by both the advertisement and the monetary penalty triggered by the contract.

A hypothetical example will help illustrate. Suppose during the Brown-Warren campaign, a third-party group calling itself "Businessmen Supporting Scott Brown" emerged and funded a television advertisement—and the true funders of the group were unknown. The advertisement features the announcer telling the viewer that "Senator Brown stood up courageously for Massachusetts businessmen, voting against the Paycheck Fairness Act, which would have given women more power to enforce equal pay for equal work. Call Senator Brown and thank him for voting against equal pay legislation. Paid for by Businessmen Supporting Scott Brown." From just the text, the ad is a positive, supportive advertisement designed to benefit Senator Brown. The organization's name indicates that it is a group of men in business who support Scott Brown. The group is opposed to the Paycheck Fairness Act and equal pay legislation and believes Senator Brown should be praised and rewarded for his vote. On its face, the advertisement would require the Brown campaign to pay a penalty. However, in the context of an electorate in Massachusetts that strongly supports equal pay for equal work,[21] the advertisement is actually a negative ad designed to undermine Brown's support with women.

Campaigns facing a sham ad have four options. First, they can pay the penalty. This is obviously not ideal given that the candidate suffers twice—from the ad *and* from the cost. Paying the cost also sets a bad precedent, one that might encourage other third parties with insincere motives to enter the race. Second, the campaign can cry foul. The campaign can attempt to persuade the press and public that the advertisement actually harms the candidate and benefits the opponent, and call for the opponent to pay (which the opponent is unlikely to do). The People's Pledge contemplates this line of action by referencing sham ads by name. That reference enables a campaign to preemptively explain the issue of sham ads to the press when the contract is signed, so that the press understands that there is a possibility of sham ads showing up during the race, and so that the press can act as referee in the event a sham ad is aired. Third, the candidate can try to renegotiate the contract,

[21] *See, e.g.*, Press Release, UMass Amherst, 2012 Exit Poll Results: MA Exit Poll Shows Women Play Major Role in Senate Race, Question 2 (Nov. 6, 2012), www.umass.edu/poll/polls/20121106b.html (noting 61% of voters polled reported equal pay was an important issue for them).

suggesting perhaps that both sides should condemn the advertisement and reiterate their call for third parties to stay out of the race. The People's Pledge contemplates this action as well, committing both campaigns to work together to address loopholes. However, it is unlikely that the opponent will agree when she can instead characterize the harmed candidate as seeking to breach the agreement. That leaves the final option: breach. The candidate can refuse to pay and breach the contract. The candidate will pay the price of negative news stories, which will be greater or lesser depending on the nature of the advertisement and the sponsoring third party and on whether the candidate has educated the press as to the possibility of sham ads. In addition, breach would mean that more outside money would enter the race.

V. CONCLUSION

The emergence of a private ordering approach to addressing the issue of third-party spending during campaigns is an important development in campaign finance law and policy. The Supreme Court's decision in *Citizens United* severely restricts the range of options for campaign finance reform at the legislative and regulatory level, and in the short run, these reforms and attempts to amend the Constitution seem unlikely to succeed. In contrast, a self-enforcing contract can be implemented immediately, and has been shown to keep third-party spending out of the most expensive Senate race in history. While self-enforcing contracts will not be adopted in every election, they are nonetheless an important innovation because they offer an option for restricting third-party spending that avoids the difficulties of congressional action and that does not run afoul of the Supreme Court's doctrine on government restrictions on speech. Reformers and practitioners should consider it more closely as a way to achieve the goals of campaign finance reform.

APPENDIX: TEXT OF THE PEOPLE'S PLEDGE

Because outside third-party organizations—including but not limited to individuals, corporations, 527 organizations, 501(c) organizations, SuperPACs, and national and state party committees—are airing, and will continue to air, independent expenditure advertisements and issue advertisements either supporting or attacking Senator Scott Brown or Elizabeth Warren (individually the "Candidate" and collectively the "Candidates"); and

Because these groups function as independent expenditure organizations that are outside the direct control of either of the Candidates; and

Because the Candidates agree that they do not approve of such independent expenditure advertisements, and want those advertisements to immediately cease and desist for the duration of the 2012 election cycle; and

Because the Candidates recognize that in order to make Massachusetts a national example, and provide the citizens of Massachusetts with an election free of third-party independent expenditure advertisements, they must be willing to include an enforcement mechanism that runs not to the third-party organizations but to the Candidates' own campaigns:

The Candidates on behalf of their respective campaigns hereby agree to the following:

1. In the event that a third-party organization airs any independent expenditure broadcast (including radio), cable, satellite, or online advertising in support of a named, referenced (including by title) or otherwise identified Candidate, that Candidate's campaign shall, within three (3) days of discovery of the advertisement buy's total cost, duration, and source, pay 50% of the cost of that advertising buy to a charity of the opposing Candidate's choice.
2. In the event that a third-party organization airs any independent expenditure broadcast (including radio), cable, satellite, or online advertising in opposition to a named, referenced (including by title) or otherwise identified Candidate, that Candidate's campaign shall, within three (3) days of discovery of the advertisement buy's total cost, duration, and source, pay 50% of the cost of that advertising buy to a charity of the opposed Candidate's choice.
3. In the event that a third-party organization airs any broadcast (including radio), cable, or satellite advertising that promotes or supports a named, referenced (including by title) or otherwise identified Candidate, that Candidate's campaign shall, within three (3) days of discovery of the advertisement buy's total cost, duration, and source, pay 50% of the

cost of that advertising buy to a charity of the opposing Candidates [sic] choice.

4. In the event that a third-party organization airs any broadcast (including radio), cable, or satellite advertising that attacks or opposes a named, referenced (including by title) or otherwise identified Candidate, the opposing Candidate's campaign shall, within three (3) days of discovery of the advertisement buy's total cost, duration, and source, pay 50% of the cost of that advertising buy to a charity of the opposed Candidate's choice.
5. The Candidates and their campaigns agree that neither they nor anyone acting on their behalf shall coordinate with any third party on any paid advertising for the duration of the 2012 election cycle. In the event that either Candidate or their campaign or anyone acting on their behalf coordinates any paid advertisement with a third-party organization that Candidate's campaign shall pay 50% of the cost of the ad buy to a charity of the opposing Candidate's choice.
6. The Candidates and their campaigns agree to continue to work together to limit the influence of third-party advertisements and to close any loopholes (including coverage of sham ads) that arise in this agreement during the course of the campaign.

9

Super PAC Insurance: A Private Sector Solution to Reform Campaign Finance

Nick Warshaw*

Ambition must be made to counteract ambition.

– James Madison, The Federalist, No. 51

I. SUPER PAC INSURANCE: A UNILATERAL PRIVATE ORDERING REFORM STRATEGY

Private ordering[1] models present a proven and viable means of reducing the influence of outside political spending in American politics.[2] Private ordering models seek to ameliorate the influence of outside expenditure groups, such as Super PACs[3] and 501(c)(4) organizations,[4] in our elections by significantly

* Nick Warshaw is a graduate of the UCLA School of Law who practices state and federal political law in the San Francisco Bay Area. The author thanks Joseph Doherty, Karen Getman, James Harrison, Justin Levitt, Thomas Willis, and Adam Winkler for their input and guidance, Timothy Kuhner and Eugene Mazo for the opportunity to contribute to this book, and Constance Cooper for her thoughtful editing.

1 Private Ordering refers to the process of setting up social norms by private actors and not by the state. Often private ordering schemes aim to achieve public goals, such as providing efficiency, enhancing the market, or protecting rights. *See, e.g.*, Steven Schwarcz, *Private Ordering*, Nw. U. L. Rev. 319 (2002).

2 Tyler Creighton, *Plea for a Pledge: Outside Spending in Competitive U.S. Senate Races*, Common Cause Massachusetts 4 (Apr. 2013), www.commoncause.org/research-reports/MA_050113_Report_Plea_for_a_Pledge.pdf.

3 Technically, the FEC calls Super PACs "independent expenditure-only committees." *See The FEC and Federal Campaign Finance Law*, Federal Election Commission, www.fec.gov/pages/brochures/fecfeca.shtml; *see also* FEC Advisory Op. 2010–11 (July 22, 2010), http://saos.fec.gov/aodocs/AO%202010–11.pdf.

4 501(c)(4) organizations are non-profit entities formed to advocate for "social welfare" causes. A significant portion of the budget of these organizations, but not a majority of it, may be devoted to political spending. *See Social Welfare Organizations*, Internal Revenue Service, www.irs.gov/charities-non-profits/other-non-profits/social-welfare-organizations.

increasing the costs of their political spending. As the previous chapter demonstrated, during their race for the U.S. Senate in 2012, Senator Elizabeth Warren and former Senator Scott Brown jointly signed a private contract, The People's Pledge. That contract required each candidate's campaign to pay half the cost of an outside advertisement in support of his or her candidacy to charity.[5] The People's Pledge dramatically lowered the amount of out-of-state spending in the 2012 U.S. Senate race in Massachusetts.[6]

The use of private contracting between candidates remains an intriguing and effective way to reduce the influence of outside money in our politics. Unfortunately, as discussed in the previous chapter, adoption of The People's Pledge has not been widespread.[7] The initial success of The People's Pledge and its limited subsequent adoption suggests the need for a private ordering model not requiring agreement between opposing candidates. A model in which a candidate can unilaterally raise the costs of outside expenditures is uniquely positioned to deter outside entities like Super PACs from spending money.

This chapter argues the creation of a new type of insurance, Super PAC insurance,[8] will satisfy the parameters of a unilateral private ordering model. Super PAC insurance will provide an innovative non-governmental response to a growing political crisis.[9] A Super PAC insurer's business model is predicated on the Cold War principle of deterrence through "mutually assured destruction."[10] A Super PAC expenditure against an insured candidate will trigger the insured candidate's insurance policy. The policy will pay up to two times the amount the insurance carrier expected Super PACs to spend against her candidacy.[11] This payout will strengthen the insured candidate's war chest, giving

5 Ganesh Sitaraman, *Contracting Around Citizens United*, 114 COLUM. L. REV. 755, 763 n. 38 (2014).

6 *Id.*

7 *Id.*

8 In the article on which much of this chapter is based, the entity offering Super PAC insurance was referred to as Level PAC. *See* Nick Warshaw, *Forget Congress: Reforming Campaign Finance through Mutually Assured Destruction*, 63 UCLA L. REV. 207, 262 (2016).

9 LAWRENCE LESSIG, REPUBLIC, LOST: HOW MONEY CORRUPTS CONGRESS—AND A PLAN TO STOP IT 131–71 (2011).

10 During the Cold War, scholars and U.S. foreign policy officials developed the theory of mutually assured destruction (MAD), which postulated that nuclear war could not occur if both the United States and Soviet Union held similar nuclear capabilities against each other. Each country knew that if it employed its nuclear arsenal, its opponent would retaliate quickly with its own nuclear strike. This potential for mutual destruction acted as a deterrent, as neither wanted to suffer the harm of a nuclear strike. *See, e.g.*, HENRY D. SOKOLSKI, GETTING MAD: NUCLEAR MUTUAL ASSURED DESTRUCTION, ITS ORIGIN AND PRACTICE (2004).

11 The premise underlying Super PAC insurance is somewhat akin to that which was adopted by the state of Arizona when it passed its Clean Elections Act. Arizona provided matching funds to candidates who accepted public financing from the state for their campaigns. These

her more money and allowing her to spend a greater amount than the Super PAC that attacked her. This simple scheme will reduce the incentive of Super PACs to spend money against insured candidates. If Super PAC insurance becomes widely adopted, it will minimize the influence of Super PACs in our political system.

Super PAC insurance harnesses the power of the profit motive to weaken the influence of Super PACs. The goal is for an insurance company both to deter Super PAC and 501(c)(4) spending and make a profit on capital invested. Investors will see a return on their investment if the amount of money collected from insurance premiums, once administrative expenses are accounted for, is greater than the amount spent on claims.[12]

There are over half a million elected officials in the United States.[13] In the 2016 election cycle, candidates, political parties, and groups like Super PACs spent an estimated $8.6 billion on elections at the federal, state, and local levels.[14] All of the candidates in this ecosystem are potential future customers for an insurance entity.

Super PAC insurance aligns investors' desire to make a profit with the societal good of reducing Super PAC influence. This arrangement is crucial to the success of Super PAC insurance, both as a business model and as a vehicle to lessen outside spending in our elections.

This chapter discusses the preferred model of Super PAC insurance, the "candidate-driven model." Under this paradigm, candidates[15] pay insurance premiums directly to the insurer. Should an insurable event occur, the candidate would receive an insurance policy payout directly to her campaign account. There are several potential variants on this basic model;[16] regardless

matching funds were triggered when a publicly financed state candidate was outspent by an opponent who had not opted to participate in the state's public financing system. The U.S. Supreme Court, however, struck down Arizona's scheme in *Arizona Free Enterprise Club's Freedom Club PAC v. Bennett*, 131 S. Ct. 2806, 2826 (2011). However, unlike the facts giving rise to *Arizona Free Enterprise*, there are no state actors in the Super PAC insurance model proposed here. This makes it significantly less likely that the Supreme Court would find any objection to Super PAC insurance, a private business, on constitutional grounds.

12 A. M. Best Co., Understanding the Insurance Industry, at iii–iv. (2014).

13 *See* Jennifer Lawless, Becoming a Candidate 33 (2012).

14 Follow the Money, www.followthemoney.org/tools/national-overview/; *see also Cost of Election*, Center for Responsive Politics, www.opensecrets.org/overview/cost.php (showing that an estimated $6.9 billion was spent at the federal level).

15 "Candidate committees" are organizations to which a candidate can contribute funds and from which a candidate can make expenditures. *See* 11 C.F.R. 101.1 (2008) (defining a candidate committee); *see also* Federal Election Commission Campaign Guide, Congressional Candidates and Committees (June 2014), www.fec.gov/pdf/candgui.pdf.

16 For alternate models of Super PAC insurance as well as a more extensive discussion on the legality of Super PAC insurance, see Warshaw, *supra* note 8, at 224–61.

of the precise mechanics of Super PAC insurance, it aims to deter Super PACs from spending money against insured candidates. This chapter proceeds by explaining the mechanics, operations, and benefits of the candidate-driven model and why the business model should reduce the corrosive influence of money in our politics.

II. THE CANDIDATE-DRIVEN MODEL

The "candidate-driven model" affords candidates the ability to defend themselves against Super PAC attacks. Super PAC insurance involves five distinct steps. The first concerns how underwriting capital will be raised for the business. The second pertains to how precise actuarial determinations will be calculated. The third step outlines how insurance policies will be purchased. The fourth piece defines what constitutes an "insurable event." Finally, the fifth part involves the process by which a candidate will receive a payout on her policy.

A company offering Super PAC insurance should remain strictly non-partisan. This is crucial both from a business model and a branding perspective. A non-partisan company will likely raise more underwriting capital and attract more public support if it is viewed as a vehicle to deter Super PAC spending, rather than a partisan tool. Moreover, a company insuring both Republicans and Democrats can create a bigger risk pool of customers. Insuring risk across the political spectrum will help safeguard against the possibility an insurer systematically miscalculated premium pricing for candidates of one party.

A. *Underwriting*

Super PACs will be deterred from spending against an insured candidate if an insurance company credibly can pay out enough to deter the Super PAC from spending to defeat an insured candidate. At least initially, the insurance company will need this capital to fully backstop the policies it issues. To this end, the insurer must seek underwriting capital for the enterprise. These underwriters, or "patriotic investors," likely will be publicly minded investors interested in reducing the influence of money in politics—and in making a profit.[17] By associating themselves with Super PAC insurance, these investors

[17] This chapter does not dispute that a traditional existing insurance carrier could create and operate Super PAC insurance; however, given Super PAC insurance's twin goals of profit-making and deterring outside Super PAC spending, it seems much more likely that a non-traditional insurance carrier may offer Super PAC insurance.

will make a profound statement: they are interested in investing in a new business to reform democracy. Investment could come from a mix of affluent and middle-class individuals interested in investing their capital in a socially driven business.

Such patriotic investment in Super PAC insurance would be the quintessential example of an investment in the growing impact investment category.[18] J.P. Morgan estimates over $15.2 billion was invested in the United States on impact investments in 2015.[19] Impact investors commit capital to social enterprises, for-profit businesses that utilize market-driven solutions to solve societal problems.[20] Major financial institutions like Goldman Sachs, J.P. Morgan, and Merrill Lynch are devoting significant resources to optimize client investment in this category.[21] Impact investment has become so pervasive that state governments are creating new types of corporations and LLCs to accommodate this growing business type.[22] Successful examples of impact businesses include eyewear seller, Warby Parker, and shoe seller, Toms.[23] As part of their business models, for every pair of eyeglasses or pair of shoes purchased, Warby Parker and Toms provide poor individuals with free pairs of eyeglasses or shoes, respectively.[24] Both companies are incredibly successful financially,[25] but financial motives are not the sole drivers of their businesses.

[18] For a guide to social-impact investing, see Robert Milburn, *Investing with Your Heart*, Barron's (Dec. 21, 2013), http://blogs.barrons.com/penta/2013/12/20/investing-with-your-heart/.

[19] J.P. Morgan Chase & Co., 2016 Annual Impact Investor Survey (6th ed. 2016), https://thegiin.org/assets/2016%20GIIN%20Annual%20Impact%20Investor%20Survey_Web.pdf.

[20] Roger L. Martin & Sally Osberg, *Social Entrepreneurship: The Case for Definition*, Stan. Soc. Innovation Rev., Spring 2007, at 29; *see also* David Chen, *Impact Investing: Transforming How We Make Money While Making a Difference*, Stan. Soc. Innovation Rev., Winter 2013, at 11.

[21] *Impact Investing*, Goldman Sachs, www.goldmansachs.com/what-we-do/investing-and-lending/impact-investing/?cid=PS_01_47_07_00_00_00_01&mkwid=9skQQQzl; *What Is Impact Investing?*, Merrill Edge, www.merrilledge.com/guidance/what-is-impact-investing; *Generating Positive Impact Alongside Financial Return*, J.P. Morgan Chase & Co., www.jpmorganchase.com/corporate/Corporate-Responsibility/social-finance.htm.

[22] For more on changes to the traditional corporate form to accommodate this growing class of business, see Dana Brakman Reiser, *Theorizing Forms for Social Enterprise*, 62 Emory L.J. 680 (2012).

[23] Christopher Marquis & Andrew Park, *Inside the Buy-One Give-One Model*, Stan. Soc. Innovation Rev., Winter 2014, at 28.

[24] *Id.*

[25] Douglas MacMillian, *Eyeglass Retailer Warby Parker Valued at $1.2 Billion*, Wall St. J. (Apr. 30, 2015), http://blogs.wsj.com/digits/2015/04/30/eyeglass-retailer-warby-parker-valued-at-1-2-billion/; Greg Roumeliotis & Olivia Oran, *Exclusive: Bain Capital to Invest*

The campaign finance market vertical is particularly ripe for impact investment. Substantial non-tax deductible donations already flow to organizations devoted to campaign finance reform.[26] Good government groups like Common Cause, Public Citizen, and the Brennan Center for Justice raise over $34 million annually in donations.[27] In 2012, Professor Lawrence Lessig's Mayday PAC—billed as the "Super PAC that wants to end all Super PACs"[28]—raised over $10 million in non-tax deductible donations from billionaires like PayPal founder Peter Thiel and LinkedIn founder Reid Hoffman.[29] Mayday supplanted these donations from affluent donors with small-dollar contributions.[30] To accomplish its goal of electing reform-minded candidates, Mayday PAC ran television advertisements supporting targeted candidates from both sides of the aisle.[31] Unfortunately, Lessig's effort largely failed to elect these reform-minded candidates to Congress.[32]

Donations to these groups demonstrate there is a latent demand for underwriting an insurance company devoted to curtailing the influence of Super PACs on America's elections. If donors are willing to contribute millions of

in Shoemaker TOMS—Sources, REUTERS (Aug. 20, 2014), www.reuters.com/article/us-toms-baincapital-idUSKBN0GK1ZZ20140820.

[26] Byron Tau & Kenneth P. Vogel, *How to Waste $10 Million*, POLITICO (Nov. 6, 2014), www.politico.com/story/2014/11/2014-elections-mayday-PAC-larry-lessig-112617.html.

[27] For more on the budgets of a sample of non-profits attempting to reform campaign finance, see the budgets below for Common Cause, Public Citizen, and the Brennan Center. Together, these three groups raise over $36 million annually. *See* Common Cause, Form 990, www.commoncause.org/about/our-impact/faq/common-cause-990.PDF; *see also* Common Cause Education Fund, Form 990, www.commoncause.org/about/our-impact/faq/education-fund-990.PDF; *see also* Public Citizen Foundation, Inc., Form 990, www.citizen.org/documents/PC%20Fdtn%20990%20Amended%20Public%20disclosure-2016.pdf; *see also* Public Citizen, Inc., Form 990, www.citizen.org/documents/PC%20INC%20990amendedpublicdisclosurecopy-2016.pdf; *see also* William J. Brennan Center for Justice, Inc., Form 990, www.brennancenter.org/sites/default/files/publications/Brennan%20Center%20Form%20990%20Ending%2006–2014.pdf

[28] *See* MAYDAY.US, https://mayday.us/about-us/; *see also* Brian Fung, *The 'Super PAC to End All Super PACs' Was Supposed to Fix Money in Politics. Here's What Went Wrong*, WASH. POST: THE SWITCH (Nov. 20, 2014), www.washingtonpost.com/news/the-switch/wp/2014/11/20/the-super-pac-to-end-all-super-pacs-was-supposed-to-fix-money-in-politics-heres-what-went-wrong/?utm_term=.b27bf241b006.

[29] Derek Willis, *Money Is Raised; Now Lessig's Super PAC Must Win*, N.Y. TIMES (July 7, 2014), www.nytimes.com/2014/07/08/upshot/money-is-raised-now-lessigs-super-pac-must-win .html.

[30] Evan Osnos, *Embrace the Irony*, NEW YORKER (Oct. 13, 2014), www.newyorker.com/magazine/2014/10/13/embrace-irony.

[31] Derek Willis, *Mayday, A Super PAC to Fight Super PACs, Stumbles in Its First Outing*, N.Y. TIMES (Nov. 17, 2014), www.nytimes.com/2014/11/18/upshot/mayday-a-super-pac-to-fight-super-pacs-stumbles-in-its-first-outing.html.

[32] *Id.*; *see also* Tau & Vogel, *supra* note 26.

dollars to non-profit efforts, they should be prepared to invest in a related for-profit reform venture as well. When giving to previous non-profit efforts, investors suffered an inevitable financial loss; by investing in Super PAC insurance, these same investors can both change democracy and make a return on their investment.

Just as Mayday PAC raised donations from affluent individuals and grassroots supporters alike,[33] a Super PAC insurance company could supplement the underwriting capital it receives from professional investors through equity crowd-funding,[34] small equity investments from grassroots supporters. In 2012, former President Barack Obama signed the Jumpstart Our Business Startups (JOBS) Act altering previous regulations prohibiting unaccredited investors from investing in private companies.[35] As a result of this legislation, non-professional investors are now permitted to invest in private start-up companies.[36] The JOBS Act affords companies like a Super PAC insurance entity the opportunity to raise capital from thousands of passionate amateur investors.[37]

The 2016 Presidential election further proved there is a market on the left and right for grassroots investment in campaign finance reform. Based in part on Vermont Senator Bernie Sanders' emphasis on campaign finance reform, he raised over $200 million in low-dollar donations.[38] President Donald Trump also campaigned against the influence of big money in politics;[39] he raised over $100 million from grassroots donors, demonstrating small-dollar donations could be raised from across the political spectrum.[40] As

33 Osnos, *supra* note 30.

34 Crowdfunding is the process by which an individual or company seeks small donations or investments from a distributed audience online. *See* Ethan Mollick, *The Dynamics of Crowdfunding: An Exploratory Study*, 29 J. Bus. Venturing 1, 1–3 (2013).

35 Jumpstart Our Business Startups Act, 17 C.F.R. §§ 200, 227, 232, 239, 240, 249, 269, 274 (2015) (prescribing rules governing the offer and sale of securities under new § 4(a)(6) of the Securities Act of 1933).

36 *Id.*

37 Christian Catalini, Catherine Fazio & Fiona Murray, *Can Equity Crowdfunding Democratize Access to Capital and Investment Opportunities?*, M.I.T. Innovation Initiative Lab for Innovation Sci. & Pol'y Rep. (2016).

38 Peter Overby, *Will the Millions of People Who Gave Money to Bernie Sanders Give to Democrats?*, NPR (Oct. 8, 2016), www.npr.org/2016/06/15/482206235/will-future-candidates-be-able-to-raise-money-the-sanders-way.

39 Ian Vandewalker & Lawrence Norden, *Small Donors Still Aren't as Important as Wealthy Ones*, The Atlantic (Oct. 18, 2016), www.theatlantic.com/politics/archive/2016/10/campaign-finance-fundraising-citizens-united/504425/.

40 Nolan D. McCaskill, *Trump's Campaign Boasts of $100 Million Small-Dollar Donations in October*, Politico (Nov. 2, 2016), www.politico.com/story/2016/11/donald-trump-100-million-donations-230649.

such, a company offering Super PAC insurance likely could receive micro-investments form a bipartisan cadre of grassroots investors.

B. *Candidate Premium Pricing*

A company offering Super PAC insurance will perform actuarial calculations to set the policies for all congressional elections. Just as in any insurance market, the cost of a customer's premium will be predicated on how much money the insurance company expects to lose on that customer.[41] In the Super PAC context, a candidate's risk will be based on how much money Super PACs and 501(c)(4)s are expected to spend against that candidate. The insurer will predict both how much is likely to be spent by Super PACs attacking the insured candidate and supporting that candidate's opponent. Candidates who are more likely to be attacked by a Super PAC will pay proportionally higher premiums than candidates who are less likely to be targeted. Candidates wishing to obtain additional protection may purchase more coverage by paying higher premiums.[42]

To insure against an event profitably, it must be predictable.[43] Different independent variables can be used to predict potential spending by Super PACs in candidate races, including whether an incumbent is running for reelection; how much money was raised by the candidate by a given date; and the partisan vote index of the district.[44] Scholarly research confirms that Super PAC spending is not random.[45] Rather, it is predictable, and it is, therefore, likely an insurable phenomenon.[46]

[41] For a formula for calculating premiums, see Howard C. Kunreuther & Mark V. Pauly, Insurance and Behavioral Economics: Improving Decisions in the Most Misunderstood Industry 46–47 (2013). The basic formula is Premium=Expected Loss / (1-Premium Loading Factor). The Premium Loading Factor is comprised of the selling and administrative costs of administering the insurance policy.

[42] *Premiums Explained*, Understand Insurance, http://understandinsurance.com.au/premiums-explained#tab.

[43] W. Kip Viscusi, *The Risky Business of Insurance Pricing*, 7 J. Risk & Uncertainty 117, 118–21 (1993).

[44] The Partisan Voter Index (PVI) measures how Republican- or Democratic-leaning a congressional district is relative to the nation. PVIs are calculated by averaging the Republican or Democratic share of the vote in a congressional district over the last two election cycles. That average is subtracted from the average national vote share of Republicans or Democrats. The absolute value is taken to create a PVI score. A seat with a PVI of R+13 is considered a safe Republican seat, whereas a seat with a PVI of D+2 leans Democratic but is considered a swing district. *See* David Wasserman, *2017 Partisan Voter Index*, Cook Political Report (Apr. 7, 2017), http://cookpolitical.com/story/10304.

[45] Warshaw, *supra* note 8, at 229–32.

[46] *Id.*; Viscusi, *supra* note 43, at 118–21.

Of course, risks can and do change in election years. Seats that once looked competitive may suddenly become safe, due to scandal or unanticipated events.[47] Conversely, seats that seemed safe can quickly become competitive.[48] By pooling risk across the political system, Super PAC insurance should be able to account for these possibilities and still make a profit.

Like other insurance carriers, a Super PAC insurance company may want to incent customer behavior through reduced premium pricing. Just as health insurers reduce the cost of insurance plans for customers leading healthy lifestyles, a Super PAC insurer could reduce the premium for a candidate who agrees to take The People's Pledge.[49] A further reduction in price could be offered if their opponent also agreed to The People's Pledge. An insurance carrier can profitably offer this incentive because The People's Pledge, as the previous chapter demonstrated, successfully reduced Super PAC spending. Such a reduction in Super PAC spending would result in the Super PAC insurance carrier paying out less on policies thereby increasing its margins. It would, therefore, be in the insurance company's interest to incent candidates to adopt The People's Pledge. The business model for Super PAC insurance again aligns with the public good of reducing Super PAC spending.

C. *Purchasing a Super PAC Insurance Policy*

Once the insurance company raises capital and sets premiums, candidates can purchase coverage. The insurer will collect premium payments from any Republican or Democratic candidate[50] who won her primary election or caucus.

Adept campaigns are likely to see purchasing a Super PAC insurance policy as a wise strategic decision. When deciding to purchase a policy, politicians and their staffs likely will weigh whether receiving a payout from an insurance policy is more valuable than an up-front outlay of campaign funds. If a Super

[47] Jeremy Pelzer, *Rob Portman Beats Ted Strickland in Ohio's 2016 U.S. Senate Race*, CLEVELAND PLAIN DEALER (Nov. 8, 2016), www.cleveland.com/politics/index.ssf/2016/11/rob_portman_beats_ted_strickla.html; John Dickerson, *Smash and Grab: Will Competitive Senate Contests in Kansas and South Dakota Lead to More Late-Breaking Races in Future Elections?*, SLATE (Oct. 20, 2014), www.slate.com/articles/news_and_politics/politics/2014/10/kansas_and_south_dakota_s_competitive_senate_races_the_rise_of_the_smash.html.

[48] Sarah D. Wire, *Rep. Darrell Issa Re-Election Bid a 'Toss Up,'* L.A. TIMES (Oct. 31, 2016), www.latimes.com/politics/essential/la-pol-sac-essential-politics-updates-rep-darrell-issa-reelection-bid-named-1476485337-htmlstory.html.

[49] *Employer Health Incentives*, HARVARD T.H. CHAN SCHOOL OF PUBLIC HEALTH, www.hsph.harvard.edu/news/magazine/winter09healthincentives/.

[50] Initially, an insurance carrier likely will limit policies to Republican and Democratic congressional nominees. Once the insurance model is proven to be successful, a company could insure third-party candidates and could expand to insuring candidates in primary election campaigns as well.

PAC attacks the insured candidate, they stand to be paid several times as much money as they paid for the policy. Similarly, if a Super PAC is deterred from spending against the insured candidate, Super PAC insurance will prove to be an excellent strategic investment for a campaign.

From the candidate's perspective, purchasing the insurance may not seem worthwhile if Super PACs would not have attacked her in the first place. Just as it is impossible to know whether one will get into a car accident before purchasing auto insurance, it is impossible to know with absolute certainty whether a Super PAC will spend against a candidate in each race. For example, the Koch Brothers, the largest donors to outside political groups, dramatically altered their expected political spending in 2016, because President Trump became the Republican Party's 2016 nominee.[51] These political unknowns should drive candidates to purchase insurance, mitigating the risk of outside spending against the candidate.

D. *Defining Insurable Events*

The criteria for what constitutes an insurable event is based on the FEC's disclosure regime and regulations.[52] A political expenditure will be considered an insurable event if: (1) money is spent by a Super PAC or a 501(c)(4) organization; (2) the FEC classifies the spending as an "independent expenditure"[53] or an "electioneering communication";[54] and (3) the aggregated amount spent is reported to the FEC. Candidates should find the linkage between claims and FEC regulations attractive; there are clearly defined and verifiable standards for claims. Furthermore, tying insurable events to spending that must be disclosed within 24–48 hours ensures the insurance entity can verify and pay out on insurance claims quickly.

1. Money Spent by a Super PAC or a 501(c)(4) Organization

Only spending from a Super PAC or a 501(c)(4) organization will be covered by companies offering Super PAC insurance. Just like a company offering auto insurance relies on its customers to inform it of accidents that occur, a

[51] Tim Alberta & Eliana Johnson, *Exclusive: In Koch World 'Realignment,' Less National Politics*, National Review (May 16, 2016), www.nationalreview.com/article/435418/koch-brothers-campaign-activity-slows; Kenneth P. Vogel, *Behind the Retreat of the Koch Brothers' Operation*, Politico (Oct. 27, 2016), www.politico.com/story/2016/10/koch-brothers-campaign-struggles-230325.

[52] 11 C.F.R. § 100.16(a) (2015); *see also* Buckley v. Valeo, 424 U.S. 1, 44 (1976).

[53] *See generally* 11 C.F.R. § 100.16 (2015).

[54] *Id.*; 11 C.F.R. § 100.29 (2014).

Super PAC insurer will rely on candidates and their campaigns to inform it if a Super PAC attacked the insured candidate or supported the candidate's opponent. Uniquely among insurance carriers, a Super PAC insurer will rely on a federal database, the FEC's Campaign Finance Disclosure Portal,[55] to verify claims.

Insuring against expenditures from Super PACs and 501(c)(4) organizations accounts for the bulk of the money spent on elections from "outside organizations."[56] This chapter defines outside organizations as entities that are legally permitted to spend money on political campaigns but are not a candidate's campaign or a political party organization.[57] In 2016, Super PACs and 501(c)(4)s accounted for approximately 87 percent of the money spent by outside organizations.[58] Therefore, insuring against these types of expenditures protects campaigns from the vast majority of the money spent against them from outside organizations.

2. Independent Expenditure or Electioneering Communication

If a Super PAC or 501(c)(4) spends money on independent expenditures and/or electioneering communications, it will meet another criterion of an insurable event. The definition of an independent expenditure is an expenditure "expressly advocating the election or defeat of a clearly identified candidate."[59] Communication is considered "express advocacy" if a reasonable person would conclude the communication supports or encourages the defeat of a "clearly identified candidate."[60]

First articulated in *Buckley v. Valeo*, express advocacy initially required an expenditure containing one of the so-called eight "magic words" or phrases. Such words included "vote for" and "defeat."[61] In *McConnell v. Federal Election Commission*, the Court broadened this definition to comprise the functional equivalents of the magic words.[62] The FEC further defined the express advocacy standard to include communication when "taken as a

[55] *Super Pac and Other Expenditure Filers*, Federal Election Commission, www.fec.gov/portal/super_pacs.shtml.

[56] *Outside Spending*, Center for Responsive Politics, www.opensecrets.org/outside spending/fes_summ.php.

[57] *Id.*

[58] *Id.*

[59] 11 C.F.R. § 100.16(a) (2015).

[60] 11 C.F.R. § 100.22(b) (2015).

[61] 11 C.F.R. § 100.16(a) (2015); *see also* Buckley v. Valeo, 424 U.S. 1, 44 (1976).

[62] McConnell v. FEC, 540 U.S. 93, 105 (2003), *overruled by* Citizens United v. FEC, 558 U.S. 310, 366 (2010).

whole...could only be interpreted by a reasonable person as containing advocacy of the election or defeat of one or more clearly identified candidates."[63]

To be considered an electioneering communication, the advertisement must meet three requirements: (1) It must "refer to a clearly identified candidate for Federal Office";[64] (2) it must be "publicly distributed" on a television or radio station 30 days before a primary election or 60 days before a general election;[65] and (3) at least 50,000 people must be capable of receiving the communication in the candidate's district.[66]

Currently, Super PAC and 501(c)(4)s devote the majority of their political spending to independent expenditures.[67] In 2016, Super PACs spent over $1.1 billion through independent expenditures accounting for 79 percent of total outside spending.[68] Therefore, insuring against independent expenditures specifically is crucial to the deterrence of Super PAC spending.

Super PACs and 501(c)(4) organizations spend comparatively much less on electioneering communications.[69] In 2016, outside organizations only spent $1.4 million on electioneering communications.[70] Although this is a small fraction of the amount devoted to independent expenditures, candidates will likely prefer a policy that guards against these type of expenditures as well. Moreover, such communications are clearly tracked on the FEC's website[71] and as such can easily be included in a Super PAC insurance policy.

3. Reporting to the FEC

The final requirements for an insurable event are that it legally must be reported to the FEC, and the Super PAC complied with relevant regulations and reported the expenditure to the FEC. Both independent expenditures and electioneering communications must be disclosed quickly. After spending more than $10,000 in independent expenditures and/or electioneering communications in a calendar year on a specific election, Super PACs and

63 11 C.F.R. § 100.22(b) (2015).

64 *Id.*; 11 C.F.R. § 100.29(a)(1) (2014).

65 *Id.*; 11 C.F.R § 100.29(a)(2) (2014).

66 2 U.S.C. § 434(f)(3)(c) (2012).

67 *2016 Outside Spending, by Group*, CENTER FOR RESPONSIVE POLITICS, www.opensecrets.org/outsidespending/summ.php?cycle=2016&chrt=V&disp=O&type=P.

68 *Id.*

69 *Id.*

70 *Outside Spending*, CENTER FOR RESPONSIVE POLITICS, www.opensecrets.org/outside spending/.

71 *2018 Electioneering Communications*, FEDERAL ELECTION COMMISSION, www.fec.gov/data/EnhancedElectioneeringCommunications.do?format=html.

501(c)(4)s become subject to 48-hour FEC reporting requirements.[72] Within 20 days of a federal election, Super PACs and 501(c)(4)s spending over $1,000 must disclose their expenditures within 24 hours to the FEC.[73]

E. Potential Gaps in Coverage and Hydraulic Effects

Due to porous campaign finance regulations, a Super Pac insurance carrier cannot easily insure against all outside spending. Advertisements are not considered electioneering communications if they run online, or are shown on television 61 days before a general election, or are issue advertisements.[74] By running a negative advertisement online, a 501(c)(4) organization could hurt an insured candidate, without triggering FEC reporting requirements or a payout from a company offering Super PAC insurance.[75]

The importance of these gaps in coverage should not be overstated. According to the Center for Responsive Politics, 87 percent of outside spending in 2016 was fully or partially disclosed.[76] Moreover, Super PAC insurance can protect candidates against some "dark money" expenditures. An expenditure is considered "dark money" if the identity of the donor is not disclosed to the public.[77] 501(c)(4) organizations can legally hide their donors' identities.[78] As discussed above, if the 501(c)(4) makes an independent expenditure or electioneering communication, it must quickly disclose the spending to the FEC, even if the donor's identity remains unknown. As long as the law requires 501(c)(4) organizations to report their expenditures, the insurer will be able to protect candidates from some "dark money" expenditures.

Arguably, the existence of Super PAC insurance will push more political spending to expenditures that are not insurable. This argument, known in

[72] 11 C.F.R. §§ 104.4(b)(2), 104.4(f), 109.10 (b)-(e) (2015).

[73] 11 C.F.R. § 104.20(b).

[74] Federal Election Commission, Electioneering Communications: Exemptions (2010), www.fec.gov/pages/brochures/electioneering.shtml.

[75] Erika K. Lunder & L. Paige Whitaker, Cong. Research Serv., R40183, 501(c)(4)s and Campaign Activity: Analysis Under Tax and Campaign Finance Laws 10 (2013), www.fas.org/sgp/crs/misc/R40183.pdf.

[76] *2016 Outside Spending, by Group*, Center for Responsive Politics, www.opensecrets.org/outsidespending/summ.php?cycle=2016&chrt=V&disp=O&type=P.

[77] Ian Vandewalker, Brennan Center for Justice, Election Spending 2014: Outside Spending in Senate Races Since *Citizens United* 1, 13 (2015), www.brennancenter.org/publication/election-spending-2014-outside-spending-senate-races-citizens-united.

[78] *See* General Instructions for Schedule B (Form 990, 990-EZ, or 990-PF), www.irs.gov/pub/irs-pdf/f990ezb.pdf. *See also* Nat'l Ass'n for Advancement of Colored People v. Alabama *ex rel.* Patterson, 357 U.S. 449 (1958) (on the necessity for organizations to protect donor identity).

the academic literature as the "hydraulic effects" of campaign finance, claims that money in politics is like water; invariably the money will flow to another path to influence the political system.[79] The hydraulic effects thesis is predicated on the notion that state actors will be the chief drivers of campaign finance reform.[80] It does not consider the possibility that a nimble private company can dynamically respond to changing political spending behavior.

If spending behavior shifts, Super PAC insurance can adjust and alter its insurance product offerings accordingly. For example, Super PAC insurance can add non-disclosed expenditures, such as issue ads, to its coverage plans. There are a number of different sources that a Super PAC insurer can draw upon to verify insurance claims besides the FEC. Companies like Campaign Media Analysis Group (CMAG) track all political advertising and sell their insights to campaigns and PACs.[81] Similarly, the Wesleyan Media Project tracks all political advertising primarily for academics.[82] This information could be used to insure candidates against expenditures that are not disclosed to the FEC or are only disclosed after an election.

Introducing Super PAC insurance into the political system likely will result in some unanticipated effects on the financing of campaigns. As a private entity, though, the insurance carrier can adjust its business model accordingly. Regardless of how political actors choose to spend their money, a political insurer can and should modify its business model to continue deterring outside spenders from influencing elections.

F. Remitting Payment to Candidates

If an insurable event occurs, the insurance company will remit payment to the candidate's campaign. The size of the payout will be a function of the amount of insurance coverage the candidate purchased and how much Super PACs were expected to spend against the insured candidate when the insurance policy is purchased.

The baseline policy will offer candidates up to two times the amount that Super PACs are expected to spend against the insured candidate. For example, if an insurer expects Super PACs to spend $150,000 against a candidate, it will

[79] *See* Samuel Issacharaoff & Pamela S. Karlan, *The Hydraulics of Campaign Finance Reform*, 77 TEX. L. REV. 1705 (1999).

[80] *Id.*

[81] *Political Advertising, Monitoring, & Evaluation*, KANTAR MEDIA, www.kantarmedia.com/us/our-solutions/advertising-monitoring-and-evaluation/political.

[82] *Advertising Analysis*, WESLEYAN MEDIA PROJECT, http://mediaproject.wesleyan.edu/about/.

pay a candidate with a baseline policy up to $300,000 if and when insurable events occur. Candidates who wish to purchase additional coverage may do so by paying a higher premium.

The 2-to-1 payout ratio is based on the success of The People's Pledge. The People's Pledge deterred an estimated 84.4 percent[83] of outside spending in Massachusetts.[84] Under The People's Pledge, Super PAC spending was effectively deterred when candidates agreed to donate $0.50 for every $1.00 Super PACs spent.[85] If this $0.50-to-$1 ratio deterred 84.4 percent of outside spending, an insurance policy which pays a candidate $2.00 for every $1.00 spent by a Super PAC should be at least as successful as The People's Pledge at deterring Super PAC spending.

Deterring 84.4 percent of outside spending would be incredibly attractive to a candidate. Assuming this deterrence ratio holds, a candidate that would normally be attacked by $150,000 in Super PAC spending would only be subject to $23,700 in Super PAC spending. With a baseline insurance policy, the candidate would receive a $47,000 payout on the $23,700 spent against her. Moreover, under this scenario, the insurance policy effectively deterred over $100,000 in Super PAC spending, making it more likely the candidate will win her race.

Crucially, the 2-to-1 payout ratio to a candidate is even more substantial than it appears because a dollar controlled by a candidate is more valuable than one controlled by a Super PAC.[86] The Federal Communications Commission (FCC) mandates candidates receive the "lowest unit charge" from television stations.[87] Under this rule, candidates receive the same discount that a television station provides bulk commercial advertisers.[88] The candidate receives this discount regardless of how much they spend on television advertising.[89]

83 This 84.2% figure is derived from a comparison of the average outside spending levels in three other highly competitive Senate races in 2012 with outside spending levels in Massachusetts while The People's Pledge was in effect. In Virginia, Wisconsin, and Ohio, outside groups spent 62%, 64%, and 47% of the total amount spent in those respective states. Therefore, on average, outside groups spent 57.666% of the total spending in those competitive states. In Massachusetts outside groups accounted for 9% of total spending. A 9% share of total spending constitutes an 84.392% reduction in outside spending from a 57.6% share.

84 Creighton, *supra* note 2, at 4.

85 *Id.*

86 Shane Goldmacher, *Jeb Bush Loses TV Ad Edge to Marco Rubio*, POLITICO (Nov. 17, 2015), www.politico.com/story/2015/11/marco-rubio-jeb-bush-super-pac-215962.

87 47 C.F.R. § 73.1942 (1992).

88 David Oxenford, *Political Broadcasting Reminder Part 1—The Basics of Lowest Unit Charges*, BROADCAST LAW BLOG (Sept. 10, 2012), www.broadcastlawblog.com/2012/09/articles/political-broadcasting-reminder-part-1-the-basics-of-lowest-unit-charges/.

89 *Id.*

In contrast, television stations have complete discretion when charging Super PACs for advertising time.[90] This makes a material difference in the amount of money spent per commercial.[91] In the weeks leading up to the 2016 Iowa caucuses, for example, Secretary Hillary Clinton's campaign purchased advertisements during the 10:00 pm newscast for $1,500 per 30-second advertisement.[92] In contrast, Governor Jeb Bush's Super PAC, Right to Rise, spent 100 percent as much for the same type of advertising on identical channels.[93] Another study estimated that on average PACs, including Super PACs, spend 40 percent more on advertising than candidates for similar advertising spots.[94] This discrepancy is explained by the lowest unit charge mandate.[95]

Moreover, a dollar controlled by a candidate is operationally more valuable than a Super PAC dollar. A candidate has complete discretion over how to spend her campaign funds. A candidate usually knows her strengths and weaknesses better than Super PACs. As a result, a candidate is better positioned to make strategic spending decisions on her race than a Super PAC. By law, a Super PAC cannot coordinate with a candidate or her campaign[96] and therefore is not as well positioned as the candidate's campaign to make strategically wise spending decisions.

This eccentricity in federal communications law makes the candidate-driven model of Super PAC insurance incredibly attractive to candidates and should result in even greater deterrence of Super PAC spending. An insured candidate who is attacked by a Super PAC will receive a $2.00:1.00 payout in actual dollars. In reality this $2.00:1.00 payout is the equivalent of a $2.80–4.00:1.00 payout in Super PAC dollars.[97] This massive discrepancy in effective campaign dollars should be extremely concerning to Super PACs. They should fear their spending will trigger a sizable payout, in candidate dollars, to the candidate it opposes. As demonstrated with The People's Pledge, this incentive structure likely will deter Super PACs from spending as much against insured candidates.

90 *Id.*

91 Melissa Yeager, *The High Cost of Television Ads for Super PACs*, Sunlight Foundation (Dec. 22, 2015), https://sunlightfoundation.com/blog/2015/12/22/the-high-cost-of-television-ads-for-super-pac/.

92 *Id.*

93 *Id.*

94 Sarah Moshary, Price Discrimination Across PACs and the Consequences of Political Advertising Regulation 3 (unpublished Ph.D. dissertation, Mass. Inst. of Tech., Nov. 10, 2014), http://economics.mit.edu/files/10195.

95 *Id.*

96 11 C.F.R. § 109.21 (2015).

97 Moshary, *supra* note 94, at 3; Yeager, *supra* note 91.

While it may seem that the insurance company's remittance of payment to a candidate is an impermissible corporate contribution to a federal candidate,[98] the FEC would likely treat the payout on an insurance policy as a "service" not a corporate "donation."[99] Candidates are permitted to purchase and procure various services for their campaigns.[100] Such services range from accounting, package delivery, and liability insurance.[101] Corporations, however, are banned from making direct contributions to candidates.[102] Contributions include "any direct or indirect payment, distribution, loan, advance, deposit, or gift of money, or any services, or anything of value."[103] This definition of a contribution extends to "in-kind" contributions as well, which are defined as donations of services to candidates for less than the "usual and normal charge" that a candidate would pay in the market.[104] The FEC considers a charge usual and normal if the cost of the services is set "at a commercially reasonable rate" at the time services were performed.[105] Previously, when the FEC evaluated innovative business models, its legality turned on whether the candidate paid the "usual and normal charge" for the service rendered.[106]

In 1985, the FEC explicitly permitted the National Conservative Political Action Committee (NCPAC) to purchase a key person insurance policy[107] on their Chairman's life.[108] If NCPAC's Chairman died, NCPAC would receive a payout on the policy.[109] The FEC found that such a payout on an insurance policy "would not be viewed as a contribution to NCPAC from the insurer,"

98 Citizens United v. FEC, 558 U.S. 310, 366 (2010).

99 *Citizens Guide*, FEDERAL ELECTION COMMISSION, www.fec.gov/pages/brochures/citizens.shtml.

100 FEC Advisory Op. 1985-34 (Nov. 22, 1985), http://saos.fec.gov/saos/searchao?SUBMIT=continue&PAGE_NO=0.

101 Scott Jefferson, *Six Reasons Every Political Campaign Should Have Insurance*, CLARKE SAMPSON BLOG (Jan. 21, 2014), www.clarkeandsampson.com/blog/six-reasons-every-political-campaign-should-have-insurance; *AIG Introduces Coverage for Political Campaign Committees*, INS. J. (Sept. 26, 2007), www.insurancejournal.com/news/national/2007/09/26/83740.htm.

102 52 U.S.C. § 30118(a) (1976).

103 52 U.S.C. § 30118(b) (1976).

104 11 C.F.R. § 100.52(d)(1) (2014).

105 11 C.F.R. § 100.52(d)(2) (2014).

106 FEC Advisory Op. 2014-09 (Aug. 14, 2014), http://saos.fec.gov/saos/searchao;jsessionid=4A902D46538FBA4D093564C501C0192D?SUBMIT=continue&PAGE_NO=0.

107 A key person insurance policy provides a company or entity with a cash benefit if a crucial member of the company's leadership team dies. See *Key Person Insurance*, NATIONWIDE, www.nationwide.com/key-person-life-insurance.jsp; *Key Person Insurance*, ENTREPRENEUR, www.entrepreneur.com/encyclopedia/key-person-insurance (Apr. 27, 2017).

108 FEC Advisory Op. 1985-34 (Nov. 22, 1985), http://saos.fec.gov/saos/searchao?SUBMIT=continue&PAGE_NO=0.

109 *Id.*

and that the committee could use "proceeds from the policy … for any lawful purpose."[110] The policy was deemed permissible provided that NCPAC was not sold the insurance policy at a below-market rate.[111]

Super PAC insurance would be analogous to the NCPAC's key person insurance policy. The cost of every Super PAC insurance policy will be solely predicated upon actuarial determinations. In no way will an insurer favor one candidate over another, nor will it provide more favorable terms to one political party over another.

Although Super PAC insurance would be a unique form of insurance, the business model is comparable to other types of insurance that political campaigns procure, like liability insurance.[112] Such coverage protects campaigns against property damage or personal injury.[113] An insurance payout to a candidate should be treated just like every other payout made by an insurer to a candidate's campaign—that is, as a service, not a donation.

Unlike other insurers, a Super PAC insurance carrier would only offer a product in one market. Other carriers, like American International Group (AIG) or Geico, insure customers in numerous markets.[114] This is relevant because the FEC generally evaluates the reasonableness of a service based upon whether the business treats political and non-political clients alike.[115] There are exceptions to this general rule. For example, the FEC permitted AT&T to have a unique discounted rate structure for all of its political clients. Such a rate was permitted, because the rates reflected "commercial considerations," not political considerations.[116] Thus, a company that seeks to offer Super PAC insurance must set its rates in a way that is predicated on commercial considerations, rather than political ones if it wants to pass FEC scrutiny. A Super PAC insurer should not have any problems meeting these parameters.

[110] *Id.*

[111] *Id.*

[112] *See* Jefferson, *supra* note 101; *AIG Introduces Coverage for Political Campaign Committees*, Ins. J. (Sept. 26, 2007), www.insurancejournal.com/news/national/2007/09/26/83740.htm.

[113] *Id.*

[114] *Insurance for Individuals and Families*, AIG, www.aig.com/individual/insurance; Geico, www.geico.com/landingpage/go168.htm?soa=50805&43700014829300867&p14829300867&gclid=COnCoMSrltMCFYO1wAodFoAPPA&gclsrc=aw.ds&dclid=CKz17cSrltMCFYFUAQodHroE3g.

[115] FEC Advisory Op. 2014-09.; FEC Advisory Op. 1994-10 (June 9, 1994); FEC Advisory Op. 2010–11 (July 22, 2010).

[116] FEC Advisory Op. 2012–31 (Sept. 20, 2012), www.fec.gov/pages/fecrecord/2012/october/ao2012-31.shtml.

G. *Return on Investment*

Just like other insurance companies, a Super PAC insurer will make a profit if the amount of money collected in premiums exceeds the money paid out for insurable events plus administrative costs.[117] At the end of each election cycle, after accounting for costs, patriotic investors could cash out their investments. Each investor will receive a pro-rata share of the profits, based on the amount of capital they committed. Alternatively, the patriotic investor can leave her investment capital in the insurance company to be used in the next election cycle. Investors who opt to leave their money in will receive preferred equity when the insurer raises funds for the next election cycle.

Like other impact investors, patriotic investors hope to create "blended value" from their investment.[118] These investors seek investment opportunities that generate a financial return but also intentionally aim to improve social conditions.[119] In the case of Super PAC insurance, the twin goals of making a profit and deterring Super PAC spending are aligned. If the insurance company is even modestly profitable, it means it successfully deterred Super PAC spending. Patriotic investors ought to be pleased with this type of return on their investment.

H. *Attractiveness of the Candidate-Driven Model*

Super PAC insurance would provide candidates the opportunity to protect themselves from Super PAC expenditures. By paying a premium from their campaign coffers, they will receive protection from Super PACs. As former Indiana Senator Evan Bayh noted, the single greatest fear of incumbent politicians today is Super PAC expenditures.[120] Currently, there is not a mechanism for candidates to mitigate this fear; Super PAC insurance offers a private ordering solution to fill that void.

The candidate-driven model will be attractive to candidates. If an insurer's deterrence assumptions are correct, candidates will see a dramatic reduction in the money spent against them. The knowledge that a candidate is carrying

[117] *See* Understanding the Insurance Industry, *supra* note 12; *see also* Kunreuther & Pauly, *supra* note 41, at 46–47.

[118] Antony Bugg-Levine & Jud Emerson, Impact Investing: Transforming How We Make Money While Making a Difference 10–12 (2011).

[119] *Id.*

[120] Lawrence Lessig, *What's So Bad About a Super PAC?*, Medium (June 4, 2014), https://medium.com/@lessig/whats-so-bad-about-a-superpac-c7cbcf617b58.

Super PAC insurance will decrease the incentives for Super PACs to spend against insured candidates.

Ultimately, candidates must decide if they want to make an initial outlay of campaign funds in exchange for an insurance policy. Most campaigns should take this tradeoff and purchase a policy. If the model is correct, they are partially insulated from Super PAC attacks. In the unlikely event that the insurance policy is unable to discourage outside spending, the candidate will receive a significant payout on her insurance policy. Campaigns should like this model, as it will provide them with crucial additional resources to respond to a Super PAC attack. Widespread candidate adoption of this attractive product should result in a dramatic reduction in Super PAC spending.

III. CONCLUSION

As The People's Pledge demonstrated, Super PACs tend to behave rationally.[121] If their spending harms their preferred candidate, they will not engage in self-defeating behavior.[122] The idea behind Super PAC insurance builds on the success of The People's Pledge. Super PAC insurance improves private contracting, by allowing a candidate to influence the activities of her opponent's supporters without the consent of her opponent. Unlike the terms of The People's Pledge, candidates can unilaterally choose to devote resources to deterring Super PAC spending. This structure should result in the reduction of Super PAC spending across the political system.

Founding Father James Madison's principle in *The Federalist Papers* forms the basis for a Super PAC insurer's business model. Madison famously wrote: "Ambition must be made to counteract ambition."[123] The patriotic investor's desire to make a profit, coupled with candidates' goals of winning their elections should provide sufficient capital to deter Super PACs from spending against insured candidates. By harnessing candidates and investor's ambitions, Super PAC insurance will counteract the stranglehold Super PACs have on our democracy.

[121] Sitaraman, *supra* note 5, at 783–87.

[122] *Id.*

[123] ALEXANDER HAMILTON, JOHN JAY & JAMES MADISON, THE FEDERALIST 268 (George W. Carey & James McClellan eds., 2001).

10

Constraining and Channeling Corporate Political Power in Trump's America

Kent Greenfield*

After the Supreme Court decided *Citizens United v. Federal Election Commission* in 2010, it quickly joined the rogue's gallery of most-despised Supreme Court decisions in modern history. Most of the opponents of the decision have focused their energy on one matter of constitutional theory and one matter of strategy. The first has been to challenge the constitutional rights of corporations generally; the second has been to marshal support for a constitutional amendment to overturn the ruling.

I, too, believe *Citizens United* was wrongly decided, at least in rationale if not on its facts. I have nevertheless questioned many of the arguments of those who oppose corporate constitutional rights and I have also expressed reservations about an amendment remedy.[1] My support for corporate constitutional rights is hardly absolute, and my skepticism about an amendment is as much strategic as substantive. I also believe that it is reasonable to worry about the influence of corporate power in our elections and in our democracy generally. But I have been a contrarian among the ideological and academic left in how to respond to these difficulties.

* Kent Greenfield is Professor of Law and Dean's Distinguished Scholar at Boston College Law School. The author thanks Timothy Kuhner and Eugene Mazo for the invitation to contribute to this volume, and Sheila Krumholz for assistance with, and access to, data of corporate independent expenditures. The author also thanks Anna E. Sanders for excellent research assistance.

1 *See, e.g.*, KENT GREENFIELD, CORPORATIONS ARE PEOPLE TOO (AND THEY SHOULD ACT LIKE IT) (2018); Kent Greenfield, *In Defense of Corporate Persons*, 30 CONST. COMMENT. 309 (2015) (hereafter *Corporate Persons*); Kent Greenfield, *Let Us Now Praise Corporate Persons*, THE WASHINGTON MONTHLY (Jan./Feb. 2015); Kent Greenfield, *Why Progressives Should Oppose A Constitutional Amendment to End Corporate "Personhood,"* HUFF. POST (Jan. 26, 2012); Kent Greenfield, *How to Make the Citizens United Decision Even Worse*, WASH. POST (Jan. 19, 2012).

My contrariness toward the most full-throated critiques of *Citizens United* has been two-fold. First, I have argued that the question of corporate constitutional rights is more complicated than most critics acknowledge.[2] Protecting the ability of corporate entities to bring constitutional claims—that is, protecting corporate constitutional "personhood"—is a valuable element in constraining the arbitrary exercise of governmental power. *Citizens United* was incorrectly decided not because it recognized the constitutional right of corporations to speak; rather it was incorrect in applying a simplistically libertarian view of free speech to campaign finance reforms and by rejecting compelling governmental interests in constraining the power of money in politics. Second, the best way to ameliorate the problems of corporate power in American electoral and political processes is through adjustments in corporate law rather than constitutional law.[3] The problem of corporate involvement in politics is not that corporations speak. The problem is that they speak not for all their stakeholders but for a sliver of the financial and managerial elite. And that problem is best addressed through corporate law rather than constitutional law.

The purpose of this chapter is to flesh out three concrete examples of how corporate law and other areas of business regulation might be adjusted to mitigate some of the harmful effects of corporate political involvement. One can disagree with, or be agnostic toward, my (limited) defense of corporate constitutional rights and still find these concrete examples intriguing. If we worry about corporate power in democracy, we need not limit ourselves to constitutional remedies alone.[4] Non-constitutional remedies are worthy of our attention and our efforts as well.

The first of the three concrete suggestions focuses on the obligations and structure of corporate governance. If corporations are to act as citizens in a democracy, we can require corporations to import democratic norms within their governance structures. If corporations were more democratically structured so that the interests and concerns of all their important stakeholders were taken into account with regard to corporate decisions, it would be less

[2] Greenfield, *Corporate Persons*, *supra* note 1, at 315–27.

[3] *Id.* at 327–30.

[4] Though in some instances the advocates of a constitutional amendment have marshaled arguments that include an attentiveness to the interests of shareholders. This has made it appear that some opponents of *Citizens United* have signed onto the corporate governance notion of shareholder primacy, a highly contested view of corporate governance usually associated with the ideological right. As I discuss below, shareholder primacy is part of the problem and should not be part of the solution. *See* Greenfield, *Corporate Persons*, *supra* note 1, at 330–32 (describing how opponents of corporate personhood are bolstering shareholder primacy).

problematic for them to participate in the public sphere. In other words, if corporations spoke less for the financial and managerial elite and more for others who contribute to their success, their involvement would more likely reflect a pluralistic perspective and pose less risk of skewing the public debate.

The second policy idea relates to taxation. We know that the government can condition tax benefits on the agreement of recipients to do or not do certain things. Non-profit charitable organizations, for example, are prohibited from engaging in core political speech as a condition of beneficial tax status.[5] This legal tool is subject to important constraints, most notably a doctrine that limits the ability of government to condition benefits on the recipient's waiver of constitutional rights. This rule is known as the "doctrine of unconstitutional conditions," and its contours have bedeviled the courts and scholars for decades.[6] But I believe a provision can be crafted that would limit corporate political activity and withstand constitutional scrutiny.

The third idea is to use state law to include limitations on corporate political activity within the foundational chartering documents of corporations in their state of incorporation. This idea, like the second, uses the fact that government can impose conditions on government benefits. This idea is frankly more problematic as a matter of constitutional law than the second idea, for reasons I will explain. But it is worth exploring further, and I believe that there are ways to impose limits on corporate political activity with this mechanism that will pass constitutional muster.

But before sketching these ideas, this chapter will first grapple with the implications of Donald Trump's recent election for the debate on corporate political power.

5 Regan v. Tax'n with Representation of Wash., 461 U.S. 540 (1983).

6 The Court has not been clear as to when government benefits can be conditioned on the waiver of a constitutional right. *Cf.* Agency for Int'l Dev. v. Alliance for Open Soc'y Int'l, Inc., 570 U.S. 205(2013) (striking down condition on funding); Rumsfeld v. Forum for Acad. & Inst. Rts., Inc., 547 U.S. 47 (2006) (upholding conditions on funding). Academic commentary on the question is abundant. For a sampling see, for example, Mitchell N. Berman, *Coercion Without Baselines: Unconstitutional Conditions in Three Dimensions*, 90 GEO. L.J. 1 (2001); David Cole, *Beyond Unconstitutional Conditions: Charting Spheres of Neutrality in Government-Funded Speech*, 67 N.Y.U. L. REV. 675 (1992); Richard A. Epstein, *The Supreme Court, 1987 Term—Foreword: Unconstitutional Conditions, State Power, and the Limits of Consent*, 102 HARV. L. REV. 4 (1988); Robert L. Hale, *Unconstitutional Conditions and Constitutional Rights*, 35 COLUM. L. REV. 321 (1935); Frederick Schauer, *Too Hard: Unconstitutional Conditions and the Chimera of Constitutional Consistency*, 72 DENV. U. L. REV. 989 (1995); Kathleen M. Sullivan, *Unconstitutional Conditions*, 102 HARV. L. REV. 1413 (1989); Cass R. Sunstein, *Why the Unconstitutional Conditions Doctrine Is an Anachronism*, 70 B.U. L. REV. 593 (1990).

I. CORPORATE POWER AND DONALD TRUMP

In November 2016, the seismic political event of the twenty-first century occurred. To say the election of Donald Trump as President of the United States came as a surprise is a profound understatement. That someone of his insincerity and intellectual laziness, with his violent, race-baiting rhetoric, misogyny, and xenophobia could be elected to the most powerful political office in the world was a shock. Indeed, for those who had hoped the United States would rise to its better nature rather than succumb to its baser instincts, it felt like a crushing blow. Legal scholars, political scientists, journalists, sociologists, and historians will study the election of 2016 for decades. It may be quite some time before we can make sense of what happened.

At first glance, one might suggest that the election of 2016 poses a counter example to those scholars who have been warning of the power of money in elections. The Super PAC money in 2016 was not on Trump's side.[7] Democratic nominee Hillary Clinton spent more money overall,[8] and more than twice as much independent money was spent in opposition to Trump than in opposition to Clinton.[9] Indeed, Trump used free media exposure masterfully, spent relatively little money early on, and did not start running television ads for the general election until August of 2016, a strikingly late date.[10] In the general election, many of the traditional sources of large contributions abandoned Trump,[11] including the Koch Brothers.[12] While Trump's contributions and spending surged late,[13] there is little doubt that Hillary Clinton's campaign and her supporters spent much more money than Trump and his supporters. So in the end, the candidate who spent the most money was the progressive

[7] Anu Narayanswamy, Darla Cameron & Matea Gold, *Election 2016: Money Raised as of Dec. 31*, WASH. POST (Feb. 1, 2017), www.washingtonpost.com/graphics/politics/2016-election/campaign-finance.

[8] Fredreka Schouten, *How Trump Won by Spending Half as Much Money as Clinton*, USA TODAY (Nov. 10, 2016), www.usatoday.com/story/news/politics/elections/2016/2016/11/09/another-way-trumps-bid-changed-politics/93565370/.

[9] *2016 Outside Spending, by Candidate*, CENTER FOR RESPONSIVE POLITICS (Nov. 28, 2016), www.opensecrets.org/outsidespending/summ.php?cycle=2016&disp=C&type=R.

[10] Arnie Seipel, *Trump Campaign to Run First General Election TV Ads*, NPR (Aug. 16, 2016), www.npr.org/2016/08/16/490294221/trump-campaign-to-run-first-general-election-tv-ads.

[11] Jonathan Martin, Alexander Burns & Maggie Haberman, *Cut Ties to Donald Trump, Big Donors Urge R.N.C.*, N.Y. TIMES (Oct. 14, 2016), www.nytimes.com/2016/10/14/us/politics/republican-donors-trump.html?_r=0.

[12] Andy Kroll, *Trump Might Be a Dream Come True for Megarich Campaign Donors*, MOTHER JONES (Jan./Feb. 2017), www.motherjones.com/politics/2016/11/donald-trump-dark-money-election.

[13] Russ Choma, *Millions of Dollars Pouring in for Trump at Last Minute*, MOTHER JONES (Nov. 7, 2016), www.motherjones.com/politics/2016/11/last-seven-days-money.

and the Democrat, and she lost the election (or at least, most importantly, the vote of the Electoral College).

If one focuses more particularly on the role of *corporate* money in the 2016 presidential cycle, there too one could tell the story that the critics of *Citizens United* have been misdirecting their efforts. In the 2012 election, we saw the bulk of independent expenditures originate not from corporate treasuries but from high net-worth individuals. In the 2016 cycle, corporate money again stayed largely on the sidelines.[14] Indeed, according to data provided by the Center for Responsive Politics, only one publicly traded company contributed $1 million or more to a Super PAC supporting a presidential candidate in 2016. And that was from a clean energy company to Jeb Bush, who dropped out in February of that year.[15] Both of the major party's nominees were polarizing and few corporations wanted to risk alienating millions of voters by aligning with one candidate or the other. Trump's candidacy was particularly disruptive and incendiary. A number of corporations withdrew their sponsorship connections with the Republican National Convention after it became clear that Trump had accumulated the delegates necessary for the nomination.[16]

A reasonable case could be made, then, that the election of 2016 indicates that the worst predictions of the implications of *Citizens United* have not come true. Corporate money has not flooded into presidential politics. Independent expenditures have not been so massive as to dictate outcomes at the national level. And worries that *Citizens United* would create an ideological skewing of the electoral "marketplace of ideas" toward the political right have not been borne out. It is quite likely, in fact, that Clinton's defeat would have

[14] According to the *New York Times*, as of February 2016, in the heat of the primary season, 87 donors had given at least $1 million to a candidate or a candidate's Super-PACs. Of those 87, only nine donors were for-profit corporations. Of those, only one was publicly traded. Of the eight private companies, most appear to be dominated by a single owner. *See* Wilson Andrews et al., *Million-Dollar Donors in the 2016 Presidential Race*, N.Y. Times (Feb. 9, 2016), www.nytimes.com/interactive/2016/us/elections/top-presidential-donors-campaign-money.html; Theo Francis, *Despite Citizens United, Corporate Super PAC Contributions Trail Individuals, Study Finds*, Wall St. J. (Nov. 2, 2016), www.wsj.com/articles/despite-citizens-united-corporate-super-pac-contributions-trail-individuals-study-finds-1478059201; The Landscape of Campaign Contributions (Committee for Econ. Dev. of the Conf. Board, Nov. 2016), www.ced.org/pdf/Election_Spending_Report_-_Nov_2016.PDF.

[15] Right to Rise USA, Contributors, 2016 Cycle, Center for Responsive Politics, www.opensecrets.org/pacs/pacgave2.php?cycle=2016&cmte=C00571372. *See also 2016 Top Donors to Outside Spending Groups*, Center for Responsive Politics, www.opensecrets.org/outsidespending/summ.php?cycle=2016&disp=D&type=O&superonly=N.

[16] Zachary Mider & Elizabeth Dexheimer, *More Companies Opt to Sit Out Trump's Coronation in Cleveland*, Bloomberg Pol. (June 16, 2016), www.bloomberg.com/politics/articles/2016-06-16/more-companies-opt-to-sit-out-trump-s-coronation-in-cleveland.

been larger if her campaign had not been bolstered by her advantage in independent spending.

Indeed, one might say that *Citizen United*'s protection of corporate speech rights will be quite important in Trump's America. Corporations certainly have their ideological commitments and biases that do not always correlate with the public interest. But their commitments rarely include the racism, Islamophobia, homophobia, xenophobia, and misogyny that was evident at Trump's rallies (and continue, in my view, to be evident in his Presidency). Corporations are often inclusive in ways that many Americans living in homogeneous, culturally anxious, economically distressed, insular tribes are not. Corporate marketing evidences this pluralistic impulse. A current Cover Girl wears a hijab. A recent commercial for Amazon features a priest and an imam sharing tea. A Coca-Cola ad running in the months after Trump's election featured a diverse array of Americans singing "America the Beautiful" in a multitude of languages.

It is no coincidence that these commercials contain an inclusive vision of America that looks quite different from what we saw from the Trump campaign.[17]

It is unlikely, for example, that large corporations will become supporters of legislative embodiments of the nationalist urges that found voice in the Trump campaign. Nor will large corporations likely support large-scale deportations or efforts to weaken international trade agreements. And many large corporations have spoken out forcefully against proposed retreats on affirmative action or on protections for LGBTQ Americans.[18]

[17] A 2016 television advertisement for Amazon shows an elderly Catholic priest and an elderly Muslim imam sharing tea and later ordering knee pads for the other; the commercial ends with both kneeling in prayer. *See* Elizabeth Weise, *Amazon Ad May Be First to Feature a Muslim Cleric*, USA Today (Nov. 16, 2016), www.usatoday.com/story/tech/news/2016/11/16/amazon-ad-may-first-feature-muslim-cleric/93944166/. Coca-Cola ran ads during 2016 that showed a diverse array of Americans singing "America the Beautiful" in a variety of languages. *See* MPR Group, *Coca Cola—America the Beautiful—Super Bowl Ad*, YouTube, www.youtube.com/watch?v=xYVu7tRXuoM. The new "Cover Girl" is Muslim, and wears a hijab. Sarah Larimer, *She's One of the New Faces of CoverGirl, And She's Wearing a Hijab*, Wash. Post (Nov. 8, 2016), www.washingtonpost.com/news/acts-of-faith/wp/2016/11/08/shes-one-of-the-new-faces-of-covergirl-and-shes-wearing-a-hijab/.

[18] Abby Jackson, *Fortune 100 Companies Tell the Supreme Court Why America Still Needs Affirmative Action*, Bus. Insider (Nov. 6, 2015), www.businessinsider.com/fortune-100-companies-issue-amacus-brief-in-support-of-affirmative-action-at-university-of-texas-2015-11; *See Updated List: Who Has Spoken for, against NC's New LGBT Law*, Charlotte Observer, www.charlotteobserver.com/news/business/article69251877.html; Andrés Martinez, *Give Corporations More Political Power—Seriously*, Time Mag. (July 10, 2015).

In other words, large corporations may provide a brake on some of Trump's worst political tendencies. Of course, a small number of businesses that align themselves with Trump's kleptocracy may enrich themselves in the short term. The financial industry may support deregulation even if not in the public interest, and Exxon is hardly the company to trust to educate the new President about climate change. But most businesses, like most Americans, have too much at stake over the long term in a global economy to rest their fortunes on a xenophobic, narrow-minded, isolationist president.

But the story I have just told is too sanguine about the role and power of corporations. In fact, the election of Donald Trump is in some ways the result of the misuse of corporate power.

Even if it is unclear whether independent spending (or corporate independent spending) has affected *outcomes* in a material way, contributions and independent spending have certainly affected *politicians*. There is little doubt that contributions (and presumably independent spending) affects access to politicians. If you give money to candidates or spend money on their behalf, you will have their ear. Instead of looking only at how campaign money affects electoral outcomes, it is more important to look at how it affects lobbying efforts. And studies show that campaign contributions lead to lobbying success.[19]

And though corporations may be shy about weighing in too heavily in presidential politics, they do not shy away from spending money in congressional races. They do so not only through direct corporate contributions but also through trade groups and corporate PACs and by way of donations from individual executives.[20] And corporations then layer on billions of dollars of lobbying expenses. Most years, over $3 billion is spent lobbying Congress—most from corporations and trade groups of businesses.[21]

This advantageous access and the legislative success it engenders add to the public perception that the system is "rigged." The public's disassociation from

[19] *See* Raquel Alexander, Stephen W. Mazza & Susan Scholz, *Measuring Rates of Return on Lobbying Expenditures: Empirical Case Study of Tax Breaks for Multinational Corporations*, 25 J.L. & POL. 401 (2009); Brad Plumer, *The Outsized Returns from Lobbying*, WASH. POST (Oct. 10, 2011), www.washingtonpost.com/blogs/ezra-klein/post/the-outsized-returns-from-lobbying/2011/10/10/gIQADSNEaL_blog.html?utm_term=.3fddf4974cf3.

[20] *See Top PACs*, CENTER FOR RESPONSIVE POLITICS, www.opensecrets.org/overview/toppacs.php?cycle=2016; *Top Organization Contributions: All Federal Contributions*, CENTER FOR RESPONSIVE POLITICS, www.opensecrets.org/overview/toporgs.php; *Hot Races*, CENTER FOR RESPONSIVE POLITICS, www.opensecrets.org/overview/hotraces.php.

[21] *See Top Spenders*, CENTER FOR RESPONSIVE POLITICS, www.opensecrets.org/lobby/top.php?indexType=s&showYear=2016; *Lobbying Database*, CENTER FOR RESPONSIVE POLITICS, www.opensecrets.org/lobby/index.php.

and disgust with mainstream politics gave momentum not only to Trump but also to the "outsider" candidacy of Bernie Sanders in the Democratic Party. In this view, *Citizens United* did not lead to Trump's victory in any direct sense but added to the overall distrust of the political system and its loyalty to financial and corporate elites, which created the context in which Trump's victory was possible. Notwithstanding the (ironic) short-term benefits of the decision within the 2016 election and during the Trump presidency, it could indeed be that Trump would not be President but for *Citizens United* and the corporate elitism and prerogatives it embodied. At the very least, *Citizens United* reflected and furthered the larger obtuseness of the American political system to the interests of working-class Americans, and those chickens finally came home to roost. (The irony of Americans disillusioned by elitism putting their faith in a putative-billionaire-casino-and-golf-resort-magnate is a topic for another day.)

Another thing to note is that the frustration and anger of Americans who resorted to voting for Trump (and for Sanders) was not simply a political anger. The system was not only "rigged" politically. There was significant economic frustration as well, and Trump's diatribes against trade agreements and Sanders's remonstrations against economic inequality found eager listeners.

These frustrations are not unrelated. There is a link between corporate political advantage and economic stagnation. The privileged access granted to those who contribute financially to politicians not only skews the legislative process but the economic marketplace as well. In fact, often the very purpose of lobbying efforts is to affect the economic marketplace. Lobbying efforts add to or even take the place of efforts to win competitive advantage by improving goods, services, or pricing. Business advantage gained politically—by disadvantaging competitors or gaining ways to externalize costs onto employees, customers, communities, or the environment—has the same impact on the balance sheet as business advantage gained in the marketplace. Yet from the standpoint of society's balance sheet, the two are not identical at all. Unfair political advantages frequently create unfair economic advantages, which individual businesses see as net gain but which society suffers as deadweight losses. This means that successful campaign finance reforms should not only be thought of as fixes for democracy. They will be economically beneficial as well, because it will focus corporations on gaining competitive advantage through economic markets, not through the political market.[22]

Having said that, there is now virtually no chance that the Supreme Court will change in the near term in a way that will lead to a weakening of

[22] *See generally* GREENFIELD, CORPORATIONS ARE PEOPLE TOO, *supra* note 1.

Citizens United and the rest of the Court's campaign finance jurisprudence. Though Trump's campaign gave voice to the frustrations of the economically dispossessed, his nominees to the Supreme Court (like his first, Neil Gorsuch) will likely be from the jurisprudentially conservative mainstream. Unless the Court moves significantly to the left, which is quite unlikely now, there is little likelihood that the Court will abandon its flawed campaign finance jurisprudence. Limitations on contributions and independent expenditures in elections will continue to receive strict scrutiny. Existing jurisprudence, mistaken as it is, will need to be taken as given for quite some time. Changes will have to come from elsewhere.

To those ideas we now turn.

II. IDEA NUMBER ONE: CHANGE CORPORATE GOVERNANCE

The problem of corporate power in elections is an iteration of the larger problem of corporate power more generally. Compared to those of other nations, the social contract of American corporations is thin. The executives who run American corporations do not generally think of themselves as having obligations to the public. The concerns of employees, communities, consumers, the environment, and the public interest in general matter only to the extent they have implications for the company's bottom line and share price. Otherwise, they are elbowed aside. Corporations tend to be managed aggressively to maximize shareholder return. As a result, the risks they run—whether of oil spills in the Gulf or of financial crises erupting from Wall Street—are often unrecognized until too late. And corporate involvement in politics—and corporate speech more generally—is often used in service of corporations' narrow, shareholder-focused, managerially driven obligations.

A cycle has been created. The Court's increasing deference to corporate speech rights offers corporations another tool through which to exercise their considerable economic power. Their economic power is then used to bolster further their political power, which is brought to bear to increase their economic power.

Efforts to overturn *Citizens United* by way of doctrinal change or constitutional amendment work on the political side of this cycle. Those efforts face conceptual and tactical obstacles and major change is likely foreclosed in the immediate future. That is not to say that scholars and activists should cease their work on the political power of corporations. Scholars are doing important work,[23] and activist pressures

[23] *See, e.g.*, John C. Coates, IV, *Corporate Politics, Governance, and Value Before and After Citizens United*, 9 J. EMP. LEGAL STUD. 657 (2012); Ciara Torres-Spelliscy, *Corporate*

on corporations to disclose their political involvement are having an impact.[24]

But the cycle might also be weakened by focusing on the corporate side of the loop. The fact that corporations exert their considerable economic and political power in the service of a narrow group of managerial and financial elites is not a function of constitutional law or corporate "personhood." It is a function of—indeed a fundamental flaw of—corporate law.[25] As a problem of corporate law it can be fixed by corporate law.

For about 100 years, the central failure of corporate governance in the United States has been the requirement—enforced through both law and norms—that corporations must be managed to further the interests of shareholders. Scholars disagree on whether, in practice, these corporate governance rules provide more protection for shareholders or managers. But one thing is absolute: corporate law in the United States—and by that I mean the corporate law of Delaware[26]—cares not at all about employees, communities, customers, or other stakeholders, except insofar as shareholders also gain. If there is a conflict, shareholders must win. As Leo Strine, the Chief Justice of the Delaware Supreme Court, recently wrote, executives who take care of an "interest other than stockholder wealth" breach their fiduciary duties.[27]

A number of corporate scholars have challenged these assumptions for some time, arguing that corporations should be seen as having robust social and public obligations that cannot be encapsulated in share prices.[28] These

Democracy from Say on Pay to Say on Politics, 30 CONST. COMMENT. 431 (2015); Maggie McKinley, *Lobbying and the Petition Clause*, 68 STAN. L. REV. 1131 (2016).

24 *See* THE 2016 CPA-ZICKLIN INDEX OF CORPORATE POLITICAL DISCLOSURE AND ACCOUNTABILITY (2016), http://files.politicalaccountability.net/index/2016_Index.pdf.

25 *See* KENT GREENFIELD, THE FAILURE OF CORPORATE LAW: FUNDAMENTAL FLAWS AND PROGRESSIVE POSSIBILITIES (2006).

26 Kent Greenfield, *End Delaware's Corporate Dominance*, 39 DEMOCRACY: A JOURNAL OF IDEAS, Winter 2016, https://democracyjournal.org/magazine/39/end-delawares-corporate-dominance/

27 *See* Leo E. Strine, *The Dangers of Denial: The Need for a Clear-Eyed Understanding of the Power and Accountability Structure Established by the Delaware General Corporation Law*, 50 WAKE FOREST L. REV. 761 (2015).

28 For a selection, see LYNN A. STOUT, THE SHAREHOLDER VALUE MYTH: HOW PUTTING SHAREHOLDERS FIRST HARMS INVESTORS, CORPORATIONS, AND THE PUBLIC (2012); LAWRENCE E. MITCHELL, PROGRESSIVE CORPORATE LAW (1995); Brett McDonnell, *Strategies for an Employee Role in Corporate Governance*, 46 WAKE FOREST L. REV. 429 (2011); Timothy P. Glynn, *Communities and Their Corporations: Towards a Stakeholder Conception of the Production of Corporate Law*, 58 CASE W. RES. L. REV. 1067 (2009); Judd F. Sneirson, *Green Is Good: Sustainability, Profitability, and a New Paradigm for Corporate Governance*, 94 IOWA L. REV. 987 (2009); Cynthia A. Williams & John M. Conley, *An Emerging Third Way?: The Erosion of the Anglo-American Shareholder Value Construct*, 38 CORNELL INT'L L.J. 493 (2005); Marleen A. O'Connor, *The Human Capital Era: Reconceptualizing Corporate*

"progressive" corporate scholars argue that the fiduciary duties of managers should be extended to employees and other corporate stakeholders, or to the company as a whole defined as those who meaningfully invest in the collective success of the firm.[29]

One way to make these obligations operational is to make the decision-making structure of the company itself more pluralistic. In a number of European countries, for example, companies have "codetermined" board structures that require representation of both shareholders and employees.[30] Even with these management structures, corporations continue their focus on building wealth—that is the core purpose of the corporate form—but not only for a narrow sliver of equity investors. And it works. Germany, where codetermination is strongest, is the economic powerhouse of Europe. The CEO of the German company Siemens argues that codetermination is a "comparative advantage" for Germany. And a senior managing director of the U.S. investment firm Blackstone Group said that codetermination was one of the factors that allowed Germany to avoid the worst of the financial crisis.[31]

If corporations were held to a more robust social contract and governed themselves more pluralistically, their involvement in the political arena would be less worrisome. A possible cure for the fact that American corporations have become a vehicle for the voices and interests of a small managerial and financial elite is more democracy *within* businesses—more participation in corporate governance by workers, communities, shareholders, and consumers. If corporations were more democratic, their participation in the nation's political debate would be of less concern and they could even become a force for positive political change.

Ironically, many opponents of *Citizens United* make arguments that seem to cut against these governance reforms. Skeptics of corporate "personhood" often characterize corporations as having a narrow social role; because of that narrow role, the argument goes, they owe it to shareholders to stay out of politics. These arguments implicitly—and sometimes explicitly—bolster shareholder primacy.

Law to Facilitate Labor-Management Cooperation, 78 CORNELL L. REV. 899 (1993); David Millon, *Redefining Corporate Law*, 24 IND. L. REV. 223 (1991).

29 *See generally* GREENFIELD, *supra* note 25.

30 ALINE CONCHON, BOARD-LEVEL EMPLOYEE REPRESENTATION RIGHTS IN EUROPE: FACTS AND TRENDS (2011), www.etui.org/Publications2/Reports/Board-level-employee-representation-rights-in-Europe. *See also MAP: Board-Level Representation in the European Economic Area*, WORKER-PARTICIPATION.EU, www.worker-participation.eu/National-Industrial-Relations/Across-Europe/Board-level-Representation2/MAP-Board-level-representation-in-the-European-Economic-Area2.

31 CONCHON, *supra* note 30, at 8.

Take for instance Justice John Paul Stevens's dissent in *Citizens United* itself. He argued, among other things, that corporate speech should be limited in order to protect shareholders' investments. Shareholders are seen as owners, as "those who pay for an electioneering communication," and are assumed to have "invested in the business corporation for purely economic reasons."[32] Stevens argued that corporate political speech did not merit protection because:

> [T]he structure of a business corporation … draws a line between the corporation's economic interests and the political preferences of the individuals associated with the corporation; the corporation must engage the electoral process with the aim to enhance the profitability of the company, no matter how persuasive the arguments for a broader … set of priorities.[33]

Even more revealing, Stevens cites as support a set of corporate governance principles adopted by the prestigious American Law Institute. These principles were the product of compromise, both asking corporations to look after shareholder interests and allowing them to act with an eye toward "ethical" and "humanitarian" purposes. But Stevens quoted only the language embodying shareholder primacy: "A corporation … should have as its objective the conduct of business activities with a view to enhancing corporate profit and shareholder gain."[34]

Some opponents of *Citizens United* are following Stevens into the shareholder-rights trap. Common Cause has a "featured campaign" for "strengthening shareholder rights."[35] The Brennan Center for Justice is supporting a "shareholder protection act" and calls shareholders "the actual owners" of corporations."[36] Professor Jamie Raskin of American University (now a United States Congressman) is one of the smartest and most energetic academic opponents of *Citizens United*, yet he says that corporations should not be spending in elections because, "after all, it's [shareholders'] money."[37]

[32] Citizens United v. FEC, 558 U.S. 310, 475–76 (2010) (Stevens, J., dissenting).

[33] *Id.* at 469–70 (Stevens, J., dissenting) (internal citations omitted).

[34] *Id.* at 470 (Stevens, J., dissenting) (quoting A.L.I., PRINCIPLES OF CORPORATE GOVERNANCE: ANALYSIS AND RECOMMENDATIONS, § 2.01(a) 55 (1992)). *See also* Melvin Aron Eisenberg, *An Overview of the Principles of Corporate Governance*, 48 BUS. LAW. 1271 (1993).

[35] *Money in Politics*, COMMON CAUSE, www.commoncause.org/issues/money-in-politics/.

[36] Elizabeth Kennedy, *Protecting Shareholders after Citizens United*, BRENNAN CENTER FOR JUSTICE (July 13, 2011), www.brennancenter.org/blog/protecting-shareholders-after-citizens-united.

[37] Jamie B. Raskin, *A Shareholder Solution to 'Citizens United,'* WASH. POST (Oct. 3, 2014), www.washingtonpost.com/opinions/a-shareholder-solution-to-citizens-united/2014/10/03/5e07c3ee-48be-11e4-b72e-d60a9229cc10_story.html.

This is all shareholder primacy language brought to bear in fighting *Citizens United.*

Wall Street loves talk of shareholder rights. To be sure, many Americans are shareholders through our retirement accounts and the like. But "widows and orphans" are still the minority; most stock held in American businesses is owned by the very wealthy. (The richest 5 percent of Americans own over 2/3 of all stock assets. The bottom 40 percent—125 million working class people—essentially own nothing in terms of stock.[38]) So when opponents of *Citizens United* focus on shareholder rights, they are singing Wall Street's tune.

I wish this shareholder-protective rhetoric was just that, but it is not. Corporate personhood opponents urge, as an intermediate measure short of a constitutional amendment, that corporations be required to seek shareholder approval before spending corporate money on political campaigns.[39] There is something tempting in this position, if only because such a rule would help ensure executives do not spend corporate monies on issues and candidates opposing company interests. But that benefit is probably marginal and comes at the risk of validating corporate involvement in the political process in furtherance of shareholder value and to the detriment of other stakeholders. A rule that corporations could speak out in favor of Wall Street but not employees could be worse, not better, than our current broad allowance of corporate speech.

Instead, corporations should be constrained by requirements within corporate law itself that their managers take into account the interests of all of the company's major stakeholders. Companies should not be contributing their monies and their voices only to further the interests of their wealthiest investors. If corporations were required to think of their social obligations as broader and more robust than simply maximizing shareholder value, then their involvement in politics would more likely be in furtherance of the interests of their stakeholders. It would be less "them" and more "us." There is nothing inherently undemocratic in corporate speech, unless corporations themselves are undemocratic. Essentially, we could take the *Citizens United* Court at its word and seek to make corporations themselves more like the "associations of citizens" that the Court assumed they are.[40]

[38] *Wealth Groups' Shares of Assets, by Asset Type, 2010*, ECON. POL'Y INST. (Aug. 20, 2012), www.stateofworkingamerica.org/chart/swa-wealth-table-6-6-wealth-groups-shares/; *Wealth Groups' Shares of Total Household Stock Wealth, 1983–2010*, ECON. POL'Y INST. (Aug. 24, 2012), www.stateofworkingamerica.org/chart/swa-wealth-figure-6g-wealth-groups-shares/.

[39] Ciara Torress-Spelliscy, *Corporate Campaign Spending: Giving Shareholders A Voice*, BRENNAN CENTER FOR JUSTICE, www.brennancenter.org/publication/corporate-campaign-spending-giving-shareholders-voice.

[40] Citizens United v. FEC, 558 U.S. 310, 356 (2010).

Is this change too much of a long shot? In a sense it is—if only because it would require a profound change in how we conceptualize corporations. Corporations would shift from pieces of property owned by a sliver of the financial elite into collective enterprises benefitting from the contributions of stakeholders who have a role in governing the company because of their stake in the company's long-term wellbeing. Once this conceptual change takes hold, the legal adjustments are straightforward and much less demanding than a constitutional amendment. A national corporate governance law would require a simple majority vote in Congress followed by the president's signature. In fact, a national law need not be the first step. Because corporate governance has traditionally been a function of state law, many of these changes could take place one state at a time.[41]

Citizens United recognized the corporate right to speak in the American public square. Now, that poses a major problem for our democracy because corporations amplify the voices of a tiny number of the financial and managerial elite—the notorious 1 percent. If companies gave voice to a more diverse and pluralistic set of interests, the fact that corporations speak would not undermine democracy. On the contrary, corporate speech would amplify it.

III. IDEA NUMBER TWO: CHANGE CORPORATE TAX LAW

Because the Supreme Court's decision in *Citizens United* was based on its reading of the First Amendment, the legislative options are quite narrow. Congress cannot, of course, simply overturn the decision by statute. But one legislative option is still open as a constitutional matter: to limit political activity as a condition of favorable tax status.

Consider first the fact the Supreme Court—in the 1983 case of *Regan v. Taxation with Representation of Washington*—has expressly upheld limits on the political activity of certain charitable corporations.[42] Under section 501(c)(3) of the Internal Revenue Code, organizations with charitable, religious, or educational missions can be exempt from income taxes, and donations to them are deductible by donors. As a condition of this very valuable tax benefit, such charitable organizations may not participate in lobbying or partisan political activities. In *Regan*, the Court upheld conditioning the benefit of special

[41] States would merely have to resist Delaware's dominance and assert the authority to govern the corporations based in their own jurisdictions. *See* Kent Greenfield, *Democracy and Dominance of Delaware in Corporate Law*, 67 LAW & CONTEMP. PROBS. 135 (2004).

[42] Regan v. Tax'n with Representation of Wash., 461 U.S. 540 (1983).

tax status on the voluntary relinquishment of a right to engage in political activity by corporate groups.

Note how serious an infringement of political speech this is. Charities are often organized around political, social, or economic ideas. Limits on their electioneering and lobbying go to the heart of why they exist and what they stand for. But the Court nevertheless upheld these limits as constitutional. Tax deductibility was seen as a subsidy, and the Court held that the government was under no obligation to subsidize the groups' political activities.[43] Implicit in the Court's reasoning was that these restrictions were optional; if the founders of an organization wanted it to be politically active, they could operate under a separate part of the IRS Code. Alternatives were available for those institutions that wanted to engage in politics.

Regan is among a number of cases in which the Court considers the notoriously tricky question of "unconstitutional conditions." The Court has not always been clear about which conditions survive and which do not.[44] The Court seems to apply two analytical touchstones. First, the Court looks at the degree of connection between the benefit offered and the right waived, limited, or conditioned. The closer the nexus the more likely the condition will be upheld.[45] Additionally, the Court is attentive to the level of pressure applied. Conditions cannot coerce; they should be voluntary.[46] This analytical touchstone operates independently from the nexus consideration, so not every

43 *Id.* at 544.

44 *Cf.* Speiser v. Randall, 357 U.S. 513 (1958) (striking down condition); Fed. Comm. Comm'n v. League of Women Voters of Cal., 468 U.S. 364 (1984) (same); Rust v. Sullivan, 500 U.S. 173 (1991) (upholding condition); Legal Servs. Corp. v. Velazquez, 531 U.S. 533 (2001) (striking down condition); Rumsfeld v. Forum for Acad. and Inst. Rts., Inc., 547 U.S. 47 (2006) (upholding condition); Agency for Int'l Dev. v. Alliance for Open Soc'y Int'l, Inc., 570 U.S. 205(2013) (striking down condition). Also relevant are spending clause cases conditioning government benefits to states on the states' willingness to further certain federal policies. *See, e.g.*, South Dakota v. Dole, 483 U.S. 203 (1987) (upholding condition as not coercive); Nat'l Fed'n of Indep. Bus. v. Sebelius, 567 U.S. 519 (2012) (striking down condition as coercive).

45 Open Soc'y Int'l, 570 U.S. at 215 (describing problem of limiting speech beyond the "contours of the program itself"); Nat'l Fed'n of Indep. Bus., 567 U.S. at 580 (describing problem that conditions on Medicaid funds on the states "tak[e] the form of threats to terminate other significant independent grants") (plurality). But the Court does not always follow this principle, especially when the second rule of avoiding coercion does not apply. See Rumsfeld v. Forum for Acad. and Inst. Rts., Inc., 547 U.S. 47 (upholding condition on entire federal funding going to universities on whether subparts of those universities accept military recruiters); Dole, 483 U.S. 203 (upholding condition on federal highway funds to states on states' willingness to change drinking age).

46 See Open Soc'y Int'l, 570 U.S. at 221 (policy requirement "compels" the affirmation of belief); Nat'l Fed'n of Indep. Bus., 567 U.S. at 581 (describing Medicaid condition as "a gun to the head") (plurality); Dole, 483 U.S. at 211 (conditions cannot be structured so that "pressure turns into compulsion").

condition will both be coercive and impose attenuated limitations. But when a condition has a loose nexus and imposes such pressure on the beneficiary that it has no genuine choice, there is a good chance the condition will be struck down.

Even with these restrictions on the ability of government to condition benefits, it is possible to structure a fix to the worst aspect of *Citizens United*—empowering for-profit companies to engage in unlimited political activity. Congress need only apply the model used for charities to corporations. A limit on the partisan political activities of corporations can be imposed as a condition of an alternative tax status offering some kind of benefit in exchange.

As long as such tax benefit is not so great as to be coercive, and corporations can voluntarily choose to opt in, the Court would not likely strike down such a condition. That would be true even if the condition was seen to be reaching beyond the scope of the benefit to constrain political speech that had little connection with that benefit. The condition on speech upheld in *Regan* was not closely tied to the scope of the benefit—tax deductibility—yet the Court upheld it. The same would likely be true here.

In fact, this policy idea provides an opening for a bipartisan effort.

Consider that the business community has long complained about so-called "double taxation," the practice of taxing corporate profits once at the corporate level and again when distributed to shareholders as dividends.[47] Double taxation is the source of the conventional argument that it is fair to tax dividends at a lower rate than ordinary income since they have already been taxed once at the corporate level.

Congress could enact a new tax status, available for corporations to opt into. Call it Status NP—for "no politics." "NP corporations" would be subject to one benefit and one limit. The benefit would be that they will be able to deduct issued dividends from their taxable income, ending double taxation. The limit would be that they would be subject to the same constraints on political activity now applicable to 501(c)(3) charities. Because the status would be optional, there is little risk that the provision would run afoul of the doctrine of unconstitutional conditions.

The upside of this compromise could be significant. By opting into the status, corporations would be opting out of the political contribution arms race. (In fact, the law should allow exemptions to antitrust restrictions, so that corporate leaders can discuss and agree with competitors to opt-in collectively.) Shareholders could expect more dividends, since corporations can

47 *See, e.g.*, Robert C. Pozen, *Eliminating Corporate Double Taxation*, BROOKINGS (Apr. 11, 2016), www.brookings.edu/opinions/eliminating-corporate-double-taxation/.

deduct them from their taxable income. The progressive left, the most vocal critics of *Citizens United*, can use the availability of Status NP as an organizational tool for shareholder activists seeking to bring corporations to heel.

Depending on how many corporations opt in, the budgetary cost may have to be mitigated, perhaps by increasing the individual tax rate on dividends or by rationalizing the currently broken system of international corporate taxation. But it would be worth the cost. While it would not unravel all of the defects of *Citizens United*, it could make a significant impact while avoiding constitutional difficulties or requiring a constitutional amendment.

IV. IDEA NUMBER THREE: CHANGE CORPORATE CHARTERS

One element is consistent across all Supreme Court cases ruling on the First Amendment rights of corporations in politics, from *First National Bank of Boston v. Bellotti*[48] to *Citizens United*. In each case the limits on corporate spending have come as a matter of campaign finance reform, external to corporate law and outside the corporate form. In none of these cases did the limits on corporate rights arise as an organic matter within the corporate form itself. That is, in every case the role and power of the corporate parties were taken as given, and the Court (rightly) assumed the corporations were asserting rights that they could properly exercise as a matter of corporate law and prerogative.

This opens a third possibility for reform: imbed limitations on corporate political activity within the corporate form as a matter of corporate law.

Business corporations are creatures of state law, chartered as legal forms to engage in business for profit. States identify the powers of corporations chartered in their jurisdiction and provide the laws of corporate governance for those businesses. A corporation is born only when its founders petition for a charter, which in turn bestows benefits such as separate legal personality ("corporate personhood") and perpetual existence uncoupled from their founders and investors. Their investors also receive limited liability, which protects them from the liabilities of the corporate form. All of these benefits are in reality state subsidies, bestowing financial advantages upon businesses adopting the corporate form. In theory at least, in exchange for these benefits the state receives the economic advantages derived from having thriving businesses creating goods, services, and financial profit.

The chartering document also typically identifies the purposes of the corporation and its corporate powers. For most of the early history of the nation, states chartered companies only for specific purposes and often imposed

[48] First Nat'l Bank of Bos. v. Bellotti, 435 U.S. 765 (1978).

significant constraints on the powers of those companies. For example, some states prohibited corporations from owning stock in other corporations. But beginning in the late nineteenth century, states began the so-called "race to the bottom," permitting charters for "any lawful purpose" and relaxing financial and economic limits on corporate powers.[49] Corporate charters now offer wide powers to corporations pursuant to their corporate "personhood," such as the capacity to sue and be sued, to enter into contracts and own property in their own name, and to make charitable donations.[50]

In any event, there is no doubt that corporations exist only by grace of the state. In the words of Chief Justice John Marshall, writing for the Court in *Dartmouth College v. Woodward*, "A corporation is an artificial being, invisible, intangible, and existing only in contemplation of law. Being the mere creature of law, it possesses only those properties which the charter of its creation confers upon it either expressly or as incidental to its very existence."[51]

This language and the history on which it is based suggest that the secret to limiting corporate political activity is to focus on the *source* of corporate power—the charters bestowed by state law, which outline the various powers and capacities of corporations. Because a corporation possesses "only those properties" state law bestows "expressly or as incidental to its very existence," then states may simply choose to form corporations without the legal capacity to engage in political activity. In other words, if corporations were formed under charters limiting their political capacity, any political engagement beyond the strictures of the charter would be *ultra vires* ("beyond the power") and be subject to regulation by the state or injunctive action by shareholders or state attorneys general.[52]

These limits would pose fewer constitutional problems than bans on corporate expenditures imbedded in campaign finance law. The power of states to constrain corporate authority has a constitutional pedigree that stretches back for nearly two centuries to *Dartmouth College* itself. It would be difficult for the Court to deny the prerogative of the states to define the power and legal capacities of corporations that the states themselves choose to charter. (Similar reasoning would apply if the federal government stepped into the role as provider of federal corporate charters.[53])

49 For more on the history of corporate purpose, see Kent Greenfield, *Ultra Vires Lives! A Stakeholder Analysis of Corporate Illegality (With Notes on How Corporate Law Could Reinforce International Law Norms)*, 87 VA. L. REV. 1279 (2001).

50 *See, e.g.*, DEL. CODE ANN. tit. 8, § 122 (2015).

51 Dartmouth Coll. v. Woodward, 4 U.S. (Wheat.) 518, 636 (1819).

52 For more on how the doctrine of ultra vires could work in modern times, see Greenfield, *Ultra Vires Lives!*, *supra* note 49.

53 *See* Greenfield, *End Delaware's Corporate Dominance*, *supra* note 26.

The central objection to this argument would point to the notion from *Dartmouth College* that the state cannot in fact take away powers "incidental to [the] very existence" of corporations. Some powers of corporations are so inherent in the corporate form itself that to remove them, or make them conditional, would be to erase the significance of the form itself. In this light, few statements can improve on that of then-Justice William Rehnquist, dissenting in *Bellotti*: "Since it cannot be disputed that the mere creation of a corporation does not invest it with all the liberties enjoyed by natural persons, … our inquiry must seek to determine which constitutional protections are 'incidental to its very existence.'"[54]

This inquiry must necessarily begin with a discussion of what corporations are for, what purposes they serve. This in turn draws on a broad scholarly literature, in the corporate law field for the most part, about the purpose of the corporation. There is much disagreement about the question of for whom are corporate managers trustees, that is, whether corporations should be managed primarily to serve shareholder interests or to serve a more robust set of stakeholder interests. But there is indeed broad consensus that corporations are economic entities, created for the purpose of benefiting society by creating wealth through the production of goods and services. The constitutional analysis should begin, then, with the presumption that corporations should receive the rights necessarily incidental to serving that economic purpose, and should not receive those that are not germane to that purpose. This presumption may be overcome in specific contexts or to further other constitutional values, but that is the starting place for analysis.

The best example of an incidental power would be the right of corporations to own property. A corporation without property rights is unworthy of the name. Property rights are "incidental to the very existence" of corporations. It would be impermissible to condition the grant of corporate status on the waiver of property rights. Similarly, corporations could not be required as a condition of their existence to waive their Fifth Amendment rights to be free of governmental takings without just compensation.

Notice how this analysis mimics the unconditional conditions analysis. Some conditions are permissible; some are not. Some powers are incidental to the creation of the corporate form; some are not. The best reading of *Dartmouth College* and its progeny is that the more central a corporate power is to the nature of the corporation itself, the less likely it can permissibly limit it or make it the subject of a condition. Another way to conceptualize this

54 First Nat'l Bank of Bos. v. Bellotti, 435 U.S. 765, 824 (1978) (Rehnquist, J., dissenting).

point is to say the state need not grant corporate charters, but if it does so such charters must contain the "core" rights and powers of corporations.

This begs the First Amendment question. Can states condition the grant of corporate status on the limitation of the resulting entity's speech rights? Unsurprisingly, this is a complex issue.[55] But it is the correct question to ask, and it is a different question than the Court has been asking.

The answer depends on whether the asserted right is core to, or inconsistent with, corporations' economic purpose. Sometimes it makes little sense to protect the First Amendment rights of corporations. Securities laws, for example, routinely require corporations to disclose to the public their financial well-being. If human beings were required to reveal personal finances, they would rightly object to the requirement as coerced speech, a violation of the First Amendment. But corporations' arguments along those lines would fail, and they should. On the other hand, it is closer to the core of the purpose of a corporation to have the ability to speak publicly about matters germane to its economic role. That is, speech that is "incidental" to its very existence in the marketplace should receive the protection of constitutional scrutiny. This includes commercial speech at least, and presumptively even that political speech concerning economic matters germane to the business.

There is more to be said here. The legal context is difficult, and crafting the proper level of constraint on corporate political activity may require doctrinal trial and error. But I do believe that the Court, notwithstanding *Citizens United*, could (and should) uphold organic, corporate law limits on the capacity of corporations to engage in electoral politics not germane to its business. Such limits could appear in corporate law statutes with language akin to the following:

> As a condition of these powers and privileges, no business corporation chartered under this title shall have the capacity to expend general treasury funds to influence the outcome of any federal, state, or local election, unless such expenditure pertains to matters germane to its primary business activities or takes place in the normal operations of a business corporation whose primary business activities include the dissemination of information or opinion.

V. CONCLUSION

Corporate law offers real possibilities for dealing with the harmful effects of *Citizens United*. Most opponents of corporate power have focused on

[55] And I am trying to answer it. *See* GREENFIELD, CORPORATIONS ARE PEOPLE TOO, *supra* note 1.

constitutional remedies and have ignored the potential corporate law remedies. This blind spot might originate, frankly, simply from the fact that *Citizens United* was a constitutional case and most constitutional law professors do not claim expertise in corporate law. Constitutional law is public law; corporate law is seen as private law. Not many legal scholars bridge this gap. But the need to do so is clear and should no longer be ignored. Indeed, the purposes of campaign finance reform would be well served by such bridges.

11

Reforming Lobbying

Maggie McKinley*

The demand for preferably universal, and therefore equal, freedom requires universal, and therefore equal, participation in government.

– Hans Kelsen, *The Essence and Value of Democracy*

I. INTRODUCTION

Few would deny that the principle of equal participation in government is a cornerstone of American democracy. Even fewer would deny that American democracy has lost that cornerstone. Yet building political will toward reform that would ensure equal participation, while passing constitutional muster, has proved a chimera. Historically, two distinct, but complementary mechanisms aimed to facilitate equal participation in the lawmaking process: the mechanism of the vote and the mechanism of the petition. On the one hand, the electoral process provided the means by which a majority would select the membership of our lawmaking institutions. On the other, the petition process provided the means by which individuals and minorities could participate equally, publicly, and formally in the lawmaking process. Both of these mechanisms are in need of reform. However, while most reform proposals focus on campaign finance reform to protect the electoral process, very few proposals focus on how we regulate access to and participation in the lawmaking process.

* Maggie McKinley is Assistant Professor of Law at the University of Pennsylvania Law School. She thanks Monica Bell, Richard Briffault, Yaseen Eldik, Timothy Kuhner, and Eugene Mazo for close reads and thoughtful feedback on the manuscript. James Pollack provided excellent research assistance.

This chapter sketches a preliminary two-step reform proposal to ensure equal access to participation in the lawmaking process.[1] As I will show, fundamental reform of our lobbying system would allow us, under our current free speech doctrine, to reform our campaign finance system fundamentally as well. Most relevant to this discussion, regulating and formalizing the way that we access lawmakers and the lawmaking process could allow us to reform campaign finance in innovative ways, including by severing the tie between our current lobbying system and our campaign finance system. Part I of this chapter charts the recent movement to reform campaign finance by reforming lobbying and identifies a critical flaw in these efforts. Part II then outlines a two-step reform proposal that avoids this earlier flaw. Step one proposes that we institutionalize a formal petition process that would largely displace our current lobbying system as the primary means by which the public would engage with Congress. Step two then proposes to regulate campaign finance activities that disrupt that formal petition process—similar to regulations upheld by the Court protecting legislative ethics provisions, legislative procedures, and the mechanics of the voting process. Finally, in Part III, I describe how the two-step reform proposal would pass constitutional muster under our current First Amendment doctrine.

II. REFLECTIONS ON DEMOCRACY REFORM

In a republican democracy, reform often requires the expression of political will as its predicate. Because political will has proved a scarce resource around

[1] Given the inherent slipperiness of the term "equality," a point of clarification is in order: by "equality," I do not propose formal equality of policy outcomes. I propose here formal procedural equality only. As Hans Kelsen described:

> Insofar as the idea of equality is meant to connote anything other than formal equality with regard to freedom (i.e., political participation), that idea has nothing to do with democracy. This can be seen most clearly in the fact that not the political and formal, but the material and economic equality of all can be realized just as well—if not better—in an autocratic-dictatorial form of state as it can in a democratic form of state. Completely apart from the fact that the equal share of goods, which "social" democracy is supposed to guarantee to all citizens always refers to an ample share, the concepts of equality can take on such diverse meanings that it is simply impossible to link it with the concept of democracy in any fundamental way.

HANS KELSEN, THE ESSENCE AND VALUE OF DEMOCRACY 97 (Nadia Urbinati & Carlo Invernizzi Accetti eds., 2013). Moreover, the participation I describe here is specific to participation in the lawmaking process via these two formal mechanisms only. This approach is distinguished from the participation interest in equal participation in the campaign finance system—i.e., being able to offer equally meaningful campaign contributions—described in

highly technical issues like campaign finance, reformers have readily relied on scandal, and the public outrage that follows, in order to direct the mercurial attention of the American public toward reform.[2] One recent example of such a scandal arose out of the fraudulent dealings of registered lobbyist Jack Abramoff.[3] Abramoff was a federally registered lobbyist who committed such egregious acts of fraud that his actions led to an extensive corruption investigation, beginning in 2004, and to many of his associates either pleading guilty or being found guilty of crimes. Abramoff and his conspirators used personal gifts, meals, event tickets, paid vacations, and campaign contributions to allegedly gain access to members of Congress and executive officials, and to provide their clients with helpful legislative and executive actions.[4] In the end, however, Abramoff's criminal charges resulted solely from wrongdoing directed at his clients, primarily Native American Tribal Governments and their members whom Abramoff referred to with racist epithets, such as "f'ing troglodytes" and "monkeys."[5] Abramoff pleaded guilty only to conspiracy, defrauding his clients, and tax evasion.[6] Abramoff's harm of our democratic process, however, did not give rise to a charge of any kind. The public was outraged. In Washington, it seemed, buying access to the political process was simply business as usual.

The years following the Abramoff scandal gave birth to the most in-depth discussion of lobbying reform in decades.[7] While the main focus of reform discussions addressed amendments to the widely criticized Lobbying

detail by election law scholar Spencer Overton. Spencer Overton, *The Participation Interest*, 100 GEO. L.J. 1259 (2012).

2 *See, e.g.*, RAYMOND J. LA RAJA, SMALL CHANGE: MONEY, POLITICAL PARTIES, AND CAMPAIGN FINANCE REFORM 81–118 (2008) (describing two prevailing narratives of reform as "scandal" and "partisanship," respectively).

3 Elizabeth Drew, *Selling Washington*, N.Y. REV. BOOKS (June 23, 2005), www.nybooks.com/articles/2005/06/23/selling-washington/.

4 *Id.*

5 Richard L. Hasen, *Book Review: Fixing Washington*, 126 HARV. L. REV. 550, 556 (2012) (reviewing Abramoff's recent book and describing Abramoff's effort to explain away his racist epithets as "inherently incredible"). As convincingly, Abramoff cast himself as a "democracy reformer" in order to promote his book. He has since shed his reformer image in order to return to lobbying on behalf of government entities. *See* Carrie Levine, *Jack Abramoff Is Back—as a Registered Lobbyist*, CENTER FOR PUBLIC INTEGRITY (June 22, 2017), www.publicintegrity.org/2017/06/22/20942/jack-abramoff-back-registered-lobbyist.

6 Susan Schmidt & James V. Grimaldi, *Abramoff Pleads Guilty to 3 Counts*, WASH. POST (Jan. 4, 2006), www.washingtonpost.com/wp-dyn/content/article/2006/01/03/AR2006010 300474.html.

7 *See, e.g.*, Elisabeth Bassett, *Reform Through Exposure*, 57 EMORY L.J. 1049 (2008) ("By mid-April 2006, Congress had introduced fifty-one bills to reform the relationship between lobbyists and legislators."); William A. Luneburg, *Proposals to Amend the Lobbying Disclosure Act of 1995*, 31 ADMIN. & REG. L. NEWS 2 (2006).

Disclosure Act of 1995 (LDA), reformers were also quick to draw the connection between Abramoff's corruption and his abuse of the campaign finance system.[8] Responses to earlier campaign finance scandals, including the Enron scandal that provided essential momentum to the Bipartisan Campaign Reform Act,[9] aimed at ameliorating money's influence on both the electoral and the lawmaking process.[10] That is, they aimed also to regulate money's influence on electoral outcomes and the ability of well-financed voices to be heard over others during the course of a political campaign. But the Abramoff scandal narrowed the focus of the democracy reform debate to money's influence on the lawmaking process. That is, buying access to lawmakers and beneficial legislative action with campaign contributions.

In 2007, reformers were able to garner enough political support to usher the passage of the Honest Leadership and Open Government Act (HLOGA), an amendment to the Lobbying Disclosure Act that included a provision for increased disclosure requirements of certain bundled campaign contributions.[11] Following the success of HLOGA, campaign finance reformers strengthened their call to connect lobbying with campaign finance.[12] To the reform community, the success of HLOGA's passage offered a new means by which to muster the political will for campaign finance reform: harness public outrage to regulate lobbyists and thereby indirectly regulate the campaign finance system. Scandals involving lobbyists at the state level gave rise to new and innovative forms of campaign finance reform, directed primarily at lobbyists, which again bolstered calls to conflate the two.[13] The Obama campaign, and later the Obama administration, ran a historic underdog effort

[8] Mike B. Wittenwyler, *The LDA Debate a Lesson for Campaign Finance Reform?*, 31 ADMIN. & REG. L. NEWS 7 (2006).

[9] Pub. L. No. 107–155, 116 Stat. 81, enacted March 27, 2002.

[10] *See, e.g.*, Richard Briffault, *The Future of Reform: Campaign Finance After the Bipartisan Campaign Reform Act of 2002*, 34 ARIZ. ST. L.J. 1179 (2002) (describing the "core" regulations of BCRA as regulation of issue advocacy—specifically, the use of money to create advertisements—and soft money—specifically, the previously unregulated contributions to political parties). Admittedly, BCRA did also regulate for the first time fundraising on federal property—a provision aimed at ending the practice of fundraising within legislative offices. *See* 18 U.S.C. 607(a). However, the legislative process did not form the primary aim of the Act.

[11] Pub. L. No. 110–81, 121 Stat. 735, enacted September 14, 2007.

[12] *See, e.g.*, Richard Briffault, *Lobbying and Campaign Finance: Separate and Together*, 19 STAN. L. & POL'Y REV. 105 (2008); Joseph Sandler, *Lobbying and Election Law: The New Challenge*, *in* THE LOBBYING MANUAL 751 (William V. Luneberg et al. eds., 4th ed. 2009)

[13] *See, e.g.*, Memorandum of Law in Support of Defendants' and Intervenor-Defendants' Motion for Partial Summary Judgment at 12–16, Green Party of Connecticut v. Garfield, 616 F.3d 189 (2001).

aimed at "changing the way that Washington works" and laid blame at the feet of corrupting lobbyists, refusing to take their campaign contributions.[14] Lobbying and campaign finance were "separate and together"[15] and lobbying reform was christened "the new campaign finance reform."[16] Lobbying reform achieved a sort of renaissance not seen since the mid-1990s and arguably since the drafting of the first federal statute regulating lobbying in Congress in the 1940s.

However, in a constitutional republican democracy, reforms must also pass constitutional muster. In this regard, the movement soon encountered difficulty and began to slow in an overabundance of caution. Challenges to legislation limiting the campaign finance activities of lobbyists began to wind their way through the courts. Rather than litigating lobbying regulation as a distinct constitutional question, state attorneys general drew on the established campaign finance framework and argued that the involvement of lobbyists in the campaign finance system heightened the state's interest in preventing "corruption."[17] Not surprisingly, the lower courts applied the *Buckley* doctrine to strike down these reforms, which blurred the line between campaign finance and lobbying.[18] Election law scholar Richard Hasen has argued that the U.S. Supreme Court's decision in *Citizens United v. Federal Election Commission*,[19] which narrowed the corruption state interest, not only gave rise to the doctrinal conflation between campaign finance and lobbying, but likely also heralded a dark future for all lobbying reform.[20] However, to date, his predictions have not yet come to pass.

Some nascent reform proposals, born of the movement, raised constitutional concerns and thereby failed to gain enough legislative traction to reach

[14] *Obama Team Announces New Rules on Lobbyists*, NBC NEWS (Nov. 11, 2008), www.nbcnews.com/id/27665871/ns/politics-white_house/t/obama-team-announces-new-rules-lobbyists/#.WW10WzcT_BE.

[15] Richard Briffault, *supra* note 12, at 105.

[16] Heather Gerken, *Keynote Address: Lobbying as the New Campaign Finance*, 27 GA. ST. U. L. REV. 1155, 1167–68 (2011).

[17] *See* Brinkman v. Budish, 692 F. Supp. 2d 855, 858 (S.D. Ohio 2010) (proffering that the revolving door ban was passed to reduce "corruption").

[18] *See* Green Party of Conn. v. Garfield, 616 F.3d 189, 192–93 (2d Cir. 2010). While the lower courts did consistently apply the *Buckley* doctrine to regulations of lobbyist campaign activities, as legislation scholar Richard Briffault has noted, the circuits began to split on what sorts of regulations were permissible under *Buckley*. *See* Richard Briffault, *The Anxiety of Influence: The Evolving Regulation of Lobbying*, 13 ELECTION L.J. 160 (2014) (describing Ognibene v. Parkes, 671 F.3d 174 (2d Cir. 2011), *cert. den.*, 567 U.S. 935 (2012) and *Preston v. Leake*, 660 F.3d 726 (4th Cir. 2011)).

[19] 558 U.S. 310 (2010).

[20] Richard L. Hasen, *Lobbying, Rent-Seeking, and the Constitution*, 64 STAN. L. REV. 191, 196 (2012).

enactment. Most notably, the ABA Task Force on Federal Lobbying Laws proposed prohibiting a lobbyist who had lobbied a particular legislator in the past two years from engaging in campaign fundraising for that member, and further proposed more stringent annual limits on aggregate contributions by lobbyists.[21] Heather Gerken and Alex Tausanovitch proposed that we implement a robust public funding system for lobbying that would "level up" lobbyists on issue areas underfunded by the private market.[22] However, the resemblance of these ideas to those that have been proposed for campaign finance reform left them similarly vulnerable to constitutional critique.

Despite these earlier difficulties, lobbying reform still offers a potential battle flag to rally the political will for campaign finance reform. Public outrage over lobbying remains high and largely bipartisan. For example, the most recent Republican administration took office on a platform that promised to "drain the swamp" through lobbying reform.[23] Campaign finance reform efforts focused on lobbying could garner sufficient public attention to get meaningful legislation enacted. However, in order to avoid the pitfalls of earlier efforts, lobbying reform proposals must avoid simply duplicating the constitutionally fraught frameworks of campaign finance reform. Ideally, future proposals would chart a separate course and avoid the *Buckley* doctrine entirely by presenting a distinct constitutional question that does not rest on the First Amendment's Speech Clause. The petition process, a mechanism of representation codified in both Article I and the Petition Clause, offers one such distinct constitutional framework.

III. UNDERSTANDING LOBBYING BY UNDERSTANDING THE PETITION PROCESS

Earlier lobbying reform proposals struggled to articulate the normative framework and legal authority by which our current lobbying system should be

[21] Task Force on Fed. Lobbying Laws, Am. Bar Ass'n, Lobbying Law in the Spotlight: Challenges and Proposed Improvements, at vii (2011).

[22] Heather K. Gerken & Alex Tausanovitch, *A Public Finance Model for Lobbying: Lobbying, Campaign Finance, and the Privatization of Democracy*, 13 Election L.J. 75, 89–90 (2014).

[23] During his campaign, President Trump gave a speech at Gettysburg, Pennsylvania, outlining a 100-day action plan. Amita Kelly & Barbara Sprunt, *Here Is What Donald Trump Wants to Do in His First Hundred Days* (Nov. 9, 2016), www.npr.org/2016/11/09/501451368/here-is-what-donald-trump-wants-to-do-in-his-first-100-days. On his first day, half of Trump's proposed six "immediate" reforms included lobbying reform proposals. *Id.* He also promised to pursue statutory reform with the "Clean Up Corruption in Washington Act" which would enact "new ethics reforms to Drain the Swamp and reduce the corrupting influence of special interests on our politics." *Id.*

evaluated.[24] If all speech about lawmaking is political speech, protected by the First Amendment's Speech Clause, then how should we structure access to the lawmaking process within an institution with scarce time and resources? Congress has only so much attention to provide and can only review, investigate, report, and respond to a finite number of requests. Currently, Congress resolves this distributional question through ad hoc procedures. Congress has declined to formalize or regulate in any meaningful way public access to the lawmaking process—which has resulted in a gray market economy for legislative attention and resources depending on the proclivities of the individual member of Congress.

Evaluating our current lobbying system by looking to our electoral process has not provided much guidance; critics have responded that the "drowning out" of powerless voices by powerful lobbyists in Congress should no more justify the equalization of voice in Congress as it does during the electoral process. But this analogy overlooks the important fact that the problem with Congress is not simply unequal voice. Through our current lobbying system, Congress distributes government attention and resources and it distributes these resources through a wholly unequal, informal, and opaque process.[25] Imagine a system whereby only the politically powerful could vote in federal elections or a system whereby a local government distributed drivers' licenses to its supporters. Or, imagine a system in which a judge decides whether to read a complaint or throw that complaint in the trash only after first determining whether the plaintiff contributed to the judge's campaign.[26] Unlike

[24] Briffault, *supra* note 12, at 109–19.

[25] At base, the lobbying reform movement suffers from an issue of "framing," identified directly by one of the founding fathers of psycholinguistics, George Lakoff. George Lakoff & Sam Ferguson, *The Framing of Immigration*, ROCKRIDGE INSTITUTE (2006), http://afrolatinoproject.org/2007/09/24/the-framing-of-immigration-5/. The frame by which issues are defined can be powerful in directing attention toward specific kinds of reforms and away from other kinds of reforms:

> In the wake of the Jack Abramoff scandal, "lobbying reform" was all the talk in the media and on Capitol Hill. The problem defined by this frame has to do with lobbyists. As a "lobbyist" problem, the solutions focused on Congressional rules regarding lobbyists. The debate centered around compensated meals, compensated trips, access by former Congressmen (who inevitably become lobbyists) to the floor of the Senate and House of representatives, lobbying disclosure, lobbyists' access to Congressional staff and the period of time between leaving the Congress and becoming a registered lobbyists. Indeed, if the reform needed is "lobbying reform," these are reasonable solutions. But, the term "Congressional ethics reform" would have framed a problem of a much different nature, a problem with Congressmen.

Id.

[26] Maggie McKinley, *Lobbying and the Petition Clause*, 68 STAN. L. REV. 1131, 1133 (2016).

the electoral process at issue in cases like *Citizens United*, public access to the lawmaking process necessarily implicates the distribution of scarce official legislative resources. However, we have habituated so entirely to our current lobbying system that we now simply assume that it is constitutionally protected.[27] Through this habituation, we have lost all meaningful evaluative measures.

In order to understand how to reform our current lobbying system—the primary mechanism by which the public now accesses the lawmaking process—we must first understand the mechanism by which the public *historically* accessed the lawmaking process and what function and values it served in our democratic framework.[28] For much of this country's history, the public accessed Congress through a formal mechanism called the petition process.[29] Public engagement in petitioning formed an integral part of republican lawmaking by allowing the voices of individuals and minorities to be heard, by providing information to Congress on regulated populations and public concerns, and by forcing Congress to face with equal dignity those populations most aggrieved by the absence or presence of laws.[30] The petition process formed such an integral part of the Article I legislative process that the Framers protected it from disruption in the First Amendment: "Congress shall make no law … abridging the right … to petition the government for redress of grievances."[31] Once we understand how this mechanism functioned historically, we can determine how our current lobbying system fails to perform a similar function in our legislative process today.

A. *The Historical Petition Process*

On December 30, 1799, Reverend Absalom Jones joined 71 other African American petitioners in signing and submitting "The Petition of the People of Colour, free Men within the City & Suburbs of Philadelphia" to the Sixth Congress.[32] As was customary for the petition process in Congress, Representative Robert Waln of Pennsylvania read the petition aloud in

[27] *See, e.g.*, Autor v. Pritzker, 740 F.3d 176, 182 (D.C. Cir. 2014) (assuming, without much support, that lobbying is protected by the Petition Clause to strike down as unconstitutional an executive ban on lobbyists serving on certain advisory commissions).

[28] Maggie McKinley, *Petitioning and the Making of the Administrative State*, 127 Yale L.J. 1538 (2018); McKinley, *Lobbying and the Petition Clause*, *supra* note 26, at 1142–46.

[29] McKinley, *Petitioning and the Making of the Administrative State*, *supra* note 28.

[30] *Id.*

[31] U.S. Const. amend. I.

[32] Nicholas P. Wood, A "*Class of Citizens*": *The Earliest Black Petitioners to Congress and Their Quaker Allies*, 74 Wm. & Mary Q. 109, 109–44 (2017).

its entirety on the floor of the House, voicing in detail the dual grievances outlined in the petition.[33] The petition read, in pertinent part:

> The Petition of the People of Colour, Freemen within the City, and Suburbs of Philadelphia:
>
> ...
>
> That, thankful to God, our Creator, and to the Government under which we live, for the blessings and benefits granted to us in the enjoyment of our natural right to Liberty, and the protection of our Persons and property from the oppression and violence which so great a number of like colour and National Descent are subjected; ... [We] are incited by a sense of Social duty and humbly conceive ourselves authorized to address and petition you on their behalf, believing them to be objects of your representation in your public Councils, in common with ourselves and every other class of Citizens within the Jurisdiction of the United States, according to the design of the present Constitution ... We apprehend this solemn Compact is violated by a trade carried on in a clandestine manner to the Coast of Guinea...[34]

The petitioners first described "Men-stealers" who would kidnap African-Americans, under the fraudulent guise of the fugitive slave laws, selling freed men back into slavery.[35] Next, as the excerpt describes, the petitioners identified an illegal slave trade market functioning off of the coast of Guinea, in violation of the 1794 Slave Trade Act.[36] To resolve these grievances, the petitioners prayed that Congress "might exert every means in your power to undo the heavy burdens, and prepare the way for the oppressed to go free."[37] As was also customary, Representative Waln then moved to refer the petition to a committee for investigation, review, and reporting.[38]

Although the petition garnered Northern support, Southern congressmen moved quickly to reject it.[39] The grounds for the motion to reject the petition might come as a surprise, however. Rather than take issue with the race of the petitioners, the Southern congressmen quickly raised a procedural objection: petitions to Congress were to be rejected as improperly filed when the petition prayed for a remedy that fell outside of the jurisdiction of the

[33] *Id.* at 136.

[34] "The Petition of the People of Colour, Freemen within the City and Suburbs of Philadelphia," (Dec. 30, 1799), Slave Trade Committee Records (STCR), HR 6A-F4.2, National Archives (NA), Washington, D.C., www.pbs.org/wgbh/aia/part3/3h327t.html.

[35] *Id.*

[36] *Id.*

[37] *Id.*

[38] Wood, *supra* note 32, at 136.

[39] *Id.*

lawmaking body to which the petition was submitted.[40] Regulation of slavery was widely accepted at the time as falling squarely into the jurisdiction of the several states. In response, Representative Waln amended his motion to direct the committee to address only those aspects of the petition clearly within the jurisdiction of Congress—kidnapping of free African Americans and regulation of the international slave trade.[41] Recent research by historian Nicholas P. Wood has revealed that, contrary to the prevailing literature,[42] the amended motion to refer the petition was "resolved in the affirmative."[43] The reviewing committees reviewed the grievances and each reported favorably that Congress should grant the petition.[44] Both chambers of Congress agreed and, five months following the submission of the petition, Congress drafted and passed the Slave Trade Act of 1800,[45] increasing the penalties for engaging in the slave trade and holding liable those who participated even indirectly—including investors, employees, and the like.[46]

The process by which African Americans, a politically powerless minority, successfully advocated for reform was historically known as the petition process. The petition process once comprised an integral part of the lawmaking process in Congress, and it looked more like litigation in a court than the tool of mass politics that "petitioning" has become today.[47] Alongside voting, petitioning served as a fundamental mechanism of representation that allowed—as we shall soon see—for equal participation in the lawmaking process for individuals and minorities.[48]

An abridged summary of the origins and architecture of the petition process provides context about how petitioning functioned historically.[49] While

40 *Id.* at 138.

41 *Id.*

42 *Id.* Historians had mistakenly read the vote on whether to refer to a committee the emancipation grievance of the petition, which was dismissed, as a vote on whether to refer the entire petition, including all grievances. Because historians read this earlier vote to dismiss the petition entirely, and not simply in part, they missed the second vote, which resolved in the affirmative to refer the international slave trade grievance to committee for review. *Id.*

43 *Id.* at 139.

44 *Id.*

45 *Id.*

46 *Id.*

47 McKinley, *Lobbying and the Petition Clause*, *supra* note 26, at 1142–55.

48 *Id.* at 1182–85.

49 *See* Daniel Carpenter, Democracy By Petition 1–68 (unpublished manuscript, on file with author) (documenting the rise of a distinct form of American petitioning and documenting the spread of participatory democracy and the abolition of aristocracy in the antebellum era correlating with a ubiquitous peak in petitioning activity); Christine Desan, *Remaking Constitutional Tradition at the Margin of Empire: The Creation of Legislative Adjudication in New York*, 16 Law & Hist. Rev. 257 (1998) (documenting the usurpation

the framing generation mythologized American petitioning in Magna Carta and the petition of right, colonial and state governments had long developed a distinctly American form of petitioning.[50] The mechanism of American petitioning was open to equal participation by all—politically powerful and powerless alike.[51] The unenfranchised—women, Native Americans, and non-enslaved African Americans—participated in the petition process and were afforded process on par with enfranchised petitioners.[52] Congress did not demarcate petitions of the unenfranchised in any way, nor did petitions with fewer signatures receive different or lesser process.[53] The petition process in Congress was also formal. Parliamentary rules governed the procedure by which petitions were received, investigated, and reported, and a petitioner knew what process to expect in response to a petition.[54] The clerk's office in the House kept a docket book that tracked each petition from submission to reporting to disposition.[55] Finally, the petition process in Congress was public. All petition introductions were read in full on the floor, making them part of the formal legislative record, and subsequent action on a petition was recorded similarly.[56]

Petitioning served a vital role in lawmaking and ensured equal participation in the lawmaking process. Unlike the vote, which allowed a majority to decide the composition of Congress, petitioning performed a distinct and complementary function to voting: it facilitated the representation of individuals and minorities during the lawmaking process.[57] In the early- to mid-twentieth century, the petition process began to die out in Congress, and its last vestiges were effectively dismantled in 1946 by the passage of the Legislative Reorganization Act and the Administrative Procedure Act.[58] Although historians have yet to identify the exact time period, at some point in the mid- to late-twentieth century, the petition process was wholly supplanted in Congress by our current lobbying system.[59]

of public claims adjudication by colonial legislatures as a distinctly American constitutional innovation).

50 McKinley, *Lobbying and the Petition Clause*, *supra* note 26, at 1142–55.

51 McKinley, *Petitioning and the Making of the Administrative State*, *supra* note 28. Historically, the petition process facilitated what Hans Kelsen referred to as formal equality. *Id.* Namely, the ability of an individual to participate equally in the making of laws that govern her. *Id.*

52 *Id.*

53 *Id.*

54 *Id.*

55 *Id.*

56 *Id.*

57 *Id.*

58 *Id.*

59 *Id.*

B. *Evaluating Our Current Lobbying System*

Today, our lobbying system provides the primary—if not the sole—means by which the public may gain access to the lawmaking process. Although our current lobbying system has replaced our constitutionally mandated petition process, our current lobbying system fails to satisfy the same functions and values: formal, public, and equal procedural access to the lawmaking process.

Our current lobbying system lacks formal structure. There are no published parliamentary rules that govern what process a lobbyist will be afforded. Our current lobbying system is not public; rather, it evokes smoke-filled rooms. Outside of the scant self-reporting of the Lobbying Disclosure Act, there are few records on lobbying activity in Congress, and any legislative response to lobbying is not identified as responsive in the formal record—a hearing could be held in response to a lobbyist's request, but the *Congressional Record* will not identify that fact. Finally, our current lobbying system is certainly not equal. Political power and campaign contributions buy access to members of Congress and their staff during the lawmaking process, and buy more extensive process and consideration of grievances.[60] Despite the ubiquitous and explicit racism of the eighteenth century, African American petitioners were afforded more due process in the Congress of 1799 than the general public is afforded in Congress today.

Reforming our current lobbying system to comport with the function and values of the formal petition process could both protect a distinct and important form of equal participation in the lawmaking process and, conveniently, provide an avenue to then enact campaign finance reform that passes constitutional muster. The following section articulates each step of this two-step reform process in turn.

IV. PROPOSAL

A. *Step One: Reform Our Current Lobbying System*

The first step of this reform proposal focuses on reform of our current lobbying system through the reinvigoration of the petition process. Instituting this first step would involve a comprehensive overhaul of the legislative process to provide avenues for formal, public, and equal participation in lawmaking.

Although comprehensive reform of Congress has been uncommon, the institution has been successfully overhauled by statute twice in the twentieth

[60] McKinley, *Lobbying and the Petition Clause*, *supra* note 26, at 1195–97.

century. In 1946, Congress passed the first Legislative Reorganization Act,[61] which created the precursor to the Congressional Research Service, increased the staff at the legislative drafting office, restructured the committee system, provided permanent support staff to committees, and formalized their jurisdiction. The Legislative Reorganization Act also transferred much of the petition process to the administrative agencies and the federal courts.[62] Twenty-four years later, Congress passed the second comprehensive legislative reform bill of the twentieth century, the Legislative Reorganization Act of 1970.[63] This second Legislative Reorganization Act primarily focused on making the committee process more transparent and accessible—mandating that committee proceedings be made public by default, requiring committees to announce and hold regular meetings, allowing a committee member to add items to committee agendas by majority vote, and allowing the broadcasting of committee hearings.[64] In addition, the statute implemented a major infrastructure and technological change in the House: the first electronic voting system for House members.[65] Notably, prior to the passage of each Legislative Reorganization Act, Congress established a bipartisan joint committee to investigate and analyze the legislative process, and to issue a full report and recommendation for proposed reforms.[66] Now, over 40 years after our last overhaul of Congress, the institution is well overdue for reform.

There is little today on which the parties agree, but lobbying reform is the rare area of bipartisan consensus that could prove a catalyst for broad reform. Undertaking meaningful steps toward reform could provide a beleaguered and often criticized institution with some easy political wins. First, Congress should follow the three historical reform efforts described above and establish a bipartisan joint committee on legislative reorganization. The committee could begin by studying public engagement with the lawmaking process. Because our current lobbying system is entirely opaque, we have little to no data on the volume of public engagement with Congress, the process by which the public engages with Congress, and the practices that Congress undertakes

[61] 60 Stat. 812 (1946).

[62] *Id.*

[63] Pub. L. No. 91–510, 84 Stat. 1140.

[64] *Id.* at 1144–57 (outlining within the first 13 pages of the report, "Title I—The Committee System" reforms).

[65] *Id.* at 1157.

[66] *See* Judy Schneider et al., Cong. Res. Serv., No. RL31835, Reorganization of the House of Representatives: Modern Reform Efforts, at 2–7 (Oct. 20, 2003); Judy Schneider et al., Cong. Res. Serv., No. RL32112, Reorganization of the Senate: Modern Reform Efforts, at 1–12 (Oct. 15, 2003).

in response to lobbying. An internal joint committee on legislative reorganization could implement a study of member offices and committee staffs in the House and Senate to begin to sketch the contours of how Congress currently engages with the public, and the volume and types of resources already expended in responding to public requests.

In addition to the two successful joint committees that preceded the Legislative Reorganization Acts of 1946 and 1970, the joint committee could model its investigation and reporting after the executive committee that authored *The Report of the Attorney General's Committee on Administrative Procedure*, a well-respected report that provided the basis for the Administrative Procedure Act.[67] In the 1930s, when the committee began its investigation, administrative procedure was equally as vague and obscure—and likely as varied across institutions—as our current lobbying system. There is little written now on how the House and Senate respond to the public, but an internal committee, with sufficient time and funding, could provide a survey of best (and worst) practices.

With the committee report in hand, Congress could then draft and pass a new Legislative Reorganization Act based on its findings and recommendations. That new statute should include a formal, public, and equal process through which the public can access the lawmaking process. At minimum, this means that a new Legislative Reorganization Act would include a provision requiring each chamber to establish explicit parliamentary rules by which public grievances will be received, considered, reviewed, and responded to within the legislative process. These rules could be either made explicit in the statute or left to the rules committee in each chamber to determine. However, establishing the rules of public engagement in the lawmaking process should be mandatory. Regardless of who establishes the rules, the new Legislative Reorganization Act should require both the House and Senate to publish those rules: in the standing rules and manual for each chamber.

What would such a process of public engagement look like? The historic petition process could form a solid basis on which to build a formal mechanism of public engagement that takes account of modern context. First, the rules could require submission of public grievances in a written formal document—similar to a judicial complaint or historical legislative petitions—that would include the petitioner's identity, a statement of grievance, a prayer

67 *Final Report of the Attorney General's Committee on Administrative Procedure, Administrative Procedure in Government Agencies*, S. Doc. No. 8, 77th Cong., 1st Sess. 1 (1941); *see also* Louis Jaffee, *Review: The Report of the Attorney General's Committee on Administrative Procedure*, 8 U. Chi. L. Rev. 401–40 (1941).

for relief, and a signatory list. The rules could direct submission of these petitions to the clerk's office in each chamber and direct the clerk to record and review the petition. Over time, Congress could develop procedural rules by which it would evaluate each petition, including rules that mimic the pre-trial motion process in the federal courts and allow for summary disposition of petitions. For example, improperly filed petitions, petitions lacking sufficient particularity, or petitions that exceeded congressional jurisdiction could be dismissed outright by the clerk's office. Duplicate petitions could be consolidated and evaluated in the aggregate, much like the multi-district litigation model.[68] Meritorious petitions would be reported in full in the congressional record and directed to the committee with jurisdiction over the petition's prayer. For inspiration beyond the federal courts, the new Legislative Reorganization Act could draw similar mechanisms from the administrative agencies. Issues and bills on which Congress anticipates broad public concern could be announced publicly for solicitation of comments, akin to that of the APA rulemaking process.[69] Historically, committees were the engines of petition processing[70] and they could be again. The statute could provide committees with a set of rules to dispose summarily of frivolous or improperly filed petitions, alongside rules on how to review, investigate, refer, report, and provide recommendations for meritorious petitions. Either the committee to which the petition is referred or another committee could draft legislation to grant successful petitions.

Further, the statute could mandate that the modern petition process be publicly accessible – both by creating a public docket for petition actions, similar to Public Access to Court Electronic Records (PACER), and by publicizing the means by which petitioners could engage with Congress and the rules for that engagement. The federal courts provide a notably less-than-perfect, but fitting guide. At present, the U.S. Courts publish the Federal Rules of Civil Procedure, and each federal court offers its local rules and procedures on a court specific website. Similarly, Congress could publish the rules of the petition system not only in its own standing rules and manuals but also in a separate guide of petition rules and procedures for practitioners and the public. The "Federal Rules of Petitioning Procedure" could aim to provide a clear guide for the public on how to submit a petition and what sort of process ought to be expected in response.

68 *See* 28 U.S.C. § 1407 (providing consolidated pre-trial actions "involving one or more common questions of facts" and designing the procedures by which to resolve such actions).

69 *See* 5 U.S.C. § 553.

70 McKinley, *Petitioning and the Making of the Administrative State, supra* note 28.

Finally, the new Legislative Reorganization Act could ensure equal access to the petition process and mandate that review, reporting, and disposition of public grievances should be based solely on the substantive merits of the petition. Most importantly, the statute would prohibit the clerk and committees of both chambers from applying procedure arbitrarily based on the characteristics of the petitioner and, particularly relevant to this new procedure as a type of lobbying reform, could prohibit the relative political power of the petitioner from determining what procedure a petition will receive. The new Legislative Reorganization Act could require written reasons for procedural steps where abuse is most likely—for example, granting petitions for politically powerful petitioners with earlier relationships to lawmakers and committee members—and recusal for obvious conflicts of interest. In order to further ensure equal access to the lawmaking process and fair distribution of legislative resources, the statute could prohibit circumvention of the formal petition process and prohibit informal access to the lawmaking process.

Admittedly, formalizing, equalizing, and making transparent a modern petition process would require additional infrastructure within Congress. Like the earlier Legislative Reorganization Acts, the new statute would require at minimum additional staff within the clerk's office of the House and additional staff for those committees most likely to receive petitions. Moreover, the Act could further institutionalize a formal and modern petition process by creating new offices within Congress—like the Congressional Research Service—to provide neutral and bipartisan support for petition processing. Additional staff and new legislative offices will inevitably result in additional costs. However, the joint committee could, following its investigation, provide an estimate of the current amount of resources expended on our current lobbying system. It is possible that such an estimate might help to persuade fiscally conservative members of Congress that the new system could manage those resources more efficiently and, at the very least, more fairly.

B. *Step Two: Reform Campaign Finance*

A review of the literature reveals that most reform proposals for our campaign finance system have focused on one of three distinct, but often overlapping, domains. First, proposals aim to reform inequities in speech during the electoral process.[71] Growing economic inequality and the expense of modern

[71] Traditionally, reforms in this first domain consisted largely of expenditure limits. *See generally* Nicholas O. Stephanopoulos, *Aligning Campaign Finance Law*, 101 VA. L. REV. 1425, 1491–95 (2015). However, following *Citizens United*, Stephanopoulos notes that "no form

campaigns means that corporations and wealthy individuals often dominate our political discourse.[72] In this first domain, the problem is money's effect on electoral discourse—that is, it provides greater reach for the political messages of those who can afford to spend more. In the second domain, proposals aim to reform inequities in who may serve viably as a candidate. Privately funded campaigns require candidates to raise an incredible amount of money in a short period of time.[73] It goes without saying that campaigns must have basic levels of funding to compete. Moreover, fundraising benchmarks are publicized quarterly and often used to determine the popularity and viability of a candidate. In the second domain, the problem is money's effect on who can afford to run in the first place and often how those campaigns are run. Finally, proposals aim to reform inequities in access to the lawmaking process and, particularly, access to members of Congress and their staffs.[74] Because members are running for reelection every two or six years, this creates what political scientists and others have called the "permanent campaign."[75] Given the cost of campaigns and the need to raise funds for others, members of Congress often spend 30 to 70 percent of their time raising money.[76] Raising money in our current campaign finance system requires lawmakers to sell

of expenditure limit, at either the state or federal level, is permitted." *Id.* at 1492. However, earlier reform proposals argued that constitutional basis for expenditure limits derived from the same source as the one-person-one-vote principle. *See, e.g.*, Kathleen Sullivan, *Political Money and Freedom of Speech*, 30 U.C. DAVIS L. REV. 663, 671–75 (1997); David Strauss, *Corruption, Equality, and Campaign Finance Reform*, 94 COLUM. L. REV. 1369, 1383 (1994); Cass Sunstein, *Political Equality and Unintended Consequences*, 94 COLUM. L. REV. 1390, 1392 (1994).

72 *See, e.g.*, Austin v. Mich. Chamber of Comm., 494 U.S. 652 (1990) (justifying restrictions on expenditures because of distortion of electoral speech caused by "the corrosive and distorting effects of immense aggregations of wealth that are accumulated with the help of the corporate form and that have little or no correlation to the public's support for the corporation's political ideas"), *overruled by* Citizens United v. FEC, 558 U.S. 310 (2010).

73 *See, e.g.*, Jay Costa, *What's the Cost of a Seat in Congress?*, MAPLIGHT (Mar. 10, 2013), https://maplight.org/story/whats-the-cost-of-a-seat-in-congress/ (finding that winning house members during the 2012 election cycle had raised an average of $2,315 per day for a total average of $1,689,580 and that winning senators had raised an average of $14,351 per day for a total average of $10,476,451).

74 Reform proposals specific to this domain are less common. Some rare examples include a few recent HLOGA reforms to the House and Senate ethics rules, including limiting the ability of lobbyists to pay for meals that would afford them time to chat with members and their staffs and prohibiting the free trips that members and staff would take with well-heeled constituents. Pub. L. No. 110–81, 121 Stat. 735, enacted September 14, 2007.

75 *See, e.g.*, Dorie Apollonia et al., *Access and Lobbying: Looking Beyond the Corruption Paradigm*, 36 HASTINGS CONST. L.Q. 13, 13 (2008); Joe Klein, *The Perils of the Permanent Campaign*, TIME (OCT. 30, 2005), www.time.com/time/columnist/klein/article/0,9565,1124237,00.html.

76 *See* LAWRENCE LESSIG, REPUBLIC, LOST: VERSION 2.0, at 35 (2015).

access to donors through personal conversations with each donor.[77] This frequently results in lawmakers attending to only the smallest—and wealthiest—slice of their constituencies. The campaign finance reform proposal that follows focuses on this third domain.

The reform proposal advanced here assumes the implementation of a new system of public engagement with the lawmaking process as outlined in the last section. While it might be possible to pass reforms that excise the campaign finance system from our current lobbying system without first instituting a formal system of public engagement, such reforms are less likely to succeed. Because we have habituated so completely to our current lobbying system, we cannot yet see the contours of its injustice clearly. By first establishing a formal and fair means of public engagement with the lawmaking process—that is, a formal petition system—we can bring the inequities of our comingled campaign finance system and lawmaking process into sharp relief.

Instituting a formal petition system would establish a baseline by which to measure proper and improper access to the lawmaking process, and would provide a new framework to regulate conduct that circumvents or disrupts proper access to the lawmaking process. An analogy to the courts is illustrative: imagine that an elected judge holds a campaign fundraiser that required attendees to contribute $2,700 for individuals and $5,000 for PACs. The judge personally attends the fundraiser and spends about ten minutes speaking personally with each attendee. Attendees bring checks in order to gain admittance to the fundraiser and access to the judge, along with requests for the judge to hold hearings on her cases, draft orders for the judge to publish, and complaints to file in the judge's court. Each attendee hands the judge a check and then speaks with the judge for ten minutes about their pending case before her. The judge then returns to her chambers after the fundraiser, files the attendees' complaints, submits the attendees' draft orders as her own, and takes further steps on the attendees' pending cases—including calling the attendees to formal hearings to present testimony. If this occurred within our court systems, we would not only be horrified at the deprivation of due process, but would want to take concrete steps to regulate this activity through ethics and recusal rules.

Although courts and legislatures are admittedly different, they are not such profoundly different institutions that we should allow the market of our campaign finance system to drive access to the legislative process. We

77 *See, e.g.*, Nathan L. Gonzales, *Want to Run for Congress? Prepare to Ask People for Money 8 Hours a Day*, ROLL CALL (July 22, 2013), www.rollcall.com/news/rothenblog/want-to-run-for-congress-prepare-to-ask-people-for-money-eight-hours-a-day; *Are Members of Congress*

should be similarly horrified here when a lobbyist hands over draft bill text, an amendment, a set of reports, and some voting advice along with a check. However, one of Congress's distinguishing characteristics likely moderates our horror: Congress offers no other means of public engagement with the lawmaking process than through the informal gray market economy of our current lobbying system—a system that is fundamentally related to and enmeshed with our campaign finance system. Because of our current lobbying system, our campaign finance system has become a barrier to providing equal access to our lawmaking process.

Establishing a formal petition process that allows fair and equal access to the lawmaking process could remind the public that lawmaking is not simply government by the powerful and that the politically powerless will be heard in Congress when aggrieved. Access to members of Congress and their staffs, as well as review of public grievances through the petition process, is a public good that the Constitution promised to make available to all equally. Once this process is formalized, re-institutionalized, and reclaimed, the public will begin to see the injustice in allowing campaign finance to govern our petition process. It is only in the context of reforming lobbying and the petition process that we can begin to engage in truly meaningful campaign finance reform.

In 1946, Congress passed the first statute regulating lobbying at the federal level.[78] The Federal Regulation of Lobbying Act was an integral part of the Legislative Reorganization Act of 1946. Similarly, Congress could draft provisions into a new Legislative Reorganization Act that extricate our campaign finance system from our current lobbying system. These provisions could include a range of regulations from prohibitions, disclosure requirements, ethics restrictions, and recusal rules. To regulate the campaign finance system directly, the statute could include a prohibition on either formal or informal discussion of any matters pending before the formal petition process or the exchange of materials that ought to be introduced to Congress through the formal petition process—including draft statutory language—at fundraisers or during meetings procured through contributions. However, the statute could also aim to regulate

Becoming Telemarketers?, CBS NEWS: 60 MINUTES (Apr. 24, 2016), www.cbsnews.com/news/60-minutes-are-members-of-congress-becoming-telemarketers/; Ryan Grim & Sabrina Siddiqui, *Call Time for Congress Shows How Fundraising Dominates Bleak Work Life*, HUFF. POST (Jan. 8, 2013), www.huffingtonpost.com/2013/01/08/call-time-congressional-fundraising_n_2427291.html (publishing a schedule given to freshman congressmen during their orientation that included five hours of fundraising during a nine- to ten-hour workday).

78 McKinley, *Lobbying and the Petition Clause*, *supra* note 26, at 1156–62 (describing passage of the Federal Regulation of Lobbying Act, Pub. L. No. 79-601, tit. III, 60 Stat. 812, 839 (1946) (repealed 1995)).

the campaign finance system indirectly. Because the petition process would offer a formal process whereby the public could engage with the lawmaking process, then the statute could regulate the boundaries of informal engagement with Congress now governed by the campaign finance system.

To provide a few examples, the statute could, at minimum, require disclosure of informal meetings between members and the public—campaign contributors and otherwise—on matters pending in a formal petition action or on matters that could be brought in a formal petition action. Lawmakers and their staffs could be bound by ethics rules to not preference meetings and correspondences with campaign contributors. At maximum, the statute could restrict informal meetings with parties who had not appeared in a formal petition action. Further, the statute could supplement direct campaign finance regulations with ethics and recusal rules that would govern the conduct of lawmakers in a similar manner to the way ethics and recusal rules govern the conduct of judges.[79] Similar to judges, lawmakers could be bound to recuse themselves from acting on a petition submitted by their campaign contributors.[80] To focus the regulation more narrowly, the statute could require lawmakers to recuse themselves from taking action on behalf of a campaign contributor with whom they have met informally—a meeting that would be made public through a disclosure regime. Although lawmakers, like elected judges, could still raise money—their ability to do so could be circumscribed similarly—that is, through disqualification and recusal rules. Ethics rules, like those that govern judges and their clerks, would govern the informal conduct of lawmakers, their staff, and the staff of Congress.

V. PASSING CONSTITUTIONAL MUSTER

In light of an aggressive and largely successful crusade by campaign finance reform opponents to dismantle decades of campaign finance regulation, no new reform proposal can be complete without an explanation of how that proposal would fare under our current doctrinal constraints. The following sections explain how both steps of the reform proposal could pass constitutional muster.

A. *Defending the Lobbying Reforms*

A Legislative Reorganization Act that establishes a formal petition process would not only comport with the Petition Clause of the First Amendment

79 *See, e.g.*, 28 U.S.C. §§ 454, 455.

80 *See, e.g.*, Caperton v. A.T. Massey Coal Co., 556 U.S. 868, 884, 889–90 (2009).

but is also likely mandated by it.[81] In 2011, the Supreme Court made clear in *Borough of Duryea v. Guarnieri*[82] that it intended to develop a Petition Clause doctrine distinct from that of free speech, and that it would interpret the meaning of the Petition Clause in future cases by reading the right within its historical context. Although the composition of the Court has changed since 2011 with the death of Justice Antonin Scalia, the outcome of future cases is likely to remain the same for the foreseeable future. Justice Anthony Kennedy authored *Guarnieri*, an 8-1 opinion, and only Justices Thomas and Scalia wrote separately.[83] Notably, Justices Thomas and Scalia wrote separately in order to argue that the majority needed to go *farther* in its historical reading.[84] They did not tussle with the Court's proclamation that the Petition Clause involved distinct and important values from that of the Speech Clause, requiring the development of a distinct doctrine; nor did they tussle with the Court's intention to determine the meaning of the Clause by reading it in historical context.[85] The untimely death of Justice Scalia and the appointment of Justice Neil Gorsuch are unlikely to alter this doctrinal direction.[86]

Such a historical reading of the Petition Clause reveals that the Clause protects an ample right of access to the lawmaking process that began in one form in Congress and has since been siphoned off into the federal administrative agencies and the federal courts, and has in part completely disappeared.[87] This right of access was afforded to all individuals equally—regardless of the political power of the petitioner. Historically, as my earlier 1799 example illustrates, the unenfranchised—including, women, Native Americans, African Americans, and the foreign born—all engaged in the petition process and were afforded process on par with enfranchised petitioners. The right also protected access to a formal process. The historical petition process looked more like litigation in a court than the tool of mass politics that petitioning has become today. Parliamentary rules governed the petition process and the clerk's office in the House kept a docket book that tracked each petition from submission to reporting to disposition. The right also afforded access to a public process. To formally introduce a petition required reading the petition in full on the floor, making it part of the formal legislative record.

81 McKinley, *Lobbying and the Petition Clause*, *supra* note 26, at 1195–1205.

82 564 U.S. 379, 388–97 (2011).

83 *Id.* at 381, 399 (Thomas, J., concurring in the judgment), 401 (Scalia, J., concurring in part and dissenting in part).

84 *Id.* at 399–409.

85 *Id.*

86 *See, e.g.*, Max Alderman & Duncan Pickard, *Justice Scalia's Heir Apparent?: Judge Gorsuch's Approach to Textualism and Originalism*, 69 STAN. L. REV. ONLINE 185 (2017).

87 McKinley, *Petitioning and the Making of the Administrative State*, *supra* note 28; McKinley, *Lobbying and the Petition Clause*, *supra* note 26, at 1195–97.

All subsequent action on the petition—including referral, reporting, and disposition—was similarly announced and recorded. Our current lobbying system is an inadequate replacement of this right of access and fails to satisfy the fundamental function and values of the petition process. It is not formal, public, or equal. Reforming our current lobbying system to better meet the values and function of the petition process would better protect our right to petition. Should such a modern petition process face constitutional challenge, the Supreme Court would hold that such a system serves the Petition Clause and does not violate it.

A constitutional challenge brought to vindicate the rights of lobbyists prohibited from circumventing the formal petition process with informal lobbying would fare no better.

First, and most importantly, the Supreme Court has never held definitively that the right to lobby is protected by the Constitution.[88] The constitutionality of lobbying regulation—and prohibitions on that activity—remain at best an open question.[89] Moreover, under the framework delineated in *Guarnieri*, historical context should determine the reach and meaning of our future Petition Clause doctrine—and there is no protection for lobbying under our Constitution.[90] Indeed, lobbying and petitioning are wholly distinct within our historical record.[91] When the United States had a formal petition process functioning within Congress, lobbying was seen as the corrupt circumvention of that process—a corrupt circumvention to be regulated and, in some states, even criminalized.[92]

B. *Defending the Proposed Campaign Finance Reforms*

Unlike other proposals to reform campaign finance, an effort to reform our lobbying system would likely survive constitutional challenge under our current free speech doctrine and without the aid of a constitutional amendment. Although our current First Amendment doctrine has placed many campaign finance reform proposals on precarious constitutional footing, establishing a petition process for Congress—with formal rules, public processes, and equal access to the lawmaking process—and framing campaign finance reform as necessary to protect the right to petition could provide a path for reforms to circumvent the *Buckley* doctrine. The Court has yet to address the particular

88 McKinley, *Lobbying and the Petition Clause*, *supra* note 26, at 1165–68.

89 *Id.*

90 *Id.* at 1195–205.

91 *Id.* at 1154–56.

92 Zephyr Teachout, *The Forgotten Law of Lobbying*, 13 Election L.J. 4, 7 (2014).

question of whether regulation of campaign finance in the context of a formal petition process would pass constitutional muster. However, First Amendment doctrine in similar contexts gives strong hope that the reforms proposed here would survive such a challenge.

The Supreme Court has routinely held that speech rights must give way to protect the efficient operation of government processes. For example, in 2011, Justice Scalia wrote for the Court in *Nevada Commission on Ethics v. Carrigan*,[93] a case that upheld a state legislative ethics rule that required that a lawmaker recuse himself from the floor when that lawmaker had a conflict of interest. The lawmaker brought a First Amendment challenge to the Nevada ethics rule, arguing that it violated his right to free speech. However, the Court noted that the restriction, even on core political speech, was a reasonable protection of the lawmaking process: "Legislative sessions would become massive town-hall meetings if those who had a right to speak were not limited to [lawmakers] who had a right to vote… This Court has rejected the notion that the First Amendment confers a right to use governmental mechanics to convey a message."[94] Similarly, in 1997, the Court upheld a restriction on ballot information against a First Amendment challenge.[95] Again, the Court held that the restriction on core political speech was justified in order to ensure the smooth operation of the voting process: "We are unpersuaded … by the party's contention that it has a right to use the ballot itself to send a particularized message, to its candidate and to the voters, about the nature of its support for the candidate. Ballots serve primarily to elect candidates, not as forums for political expression."[96] Similarly, the regulation of speech that disrupts the functioning of the petition process would pass constitutional muster under current First Amendment doctrine. Regulations that restricted the ability of campaign contributors to obtain unequal and informal access to the lawmaking process, above and beyond that afforded to the general public through the petition process, would survive challenge under the Speech Clause.

In addition to regulations of speech that have survived challenge, there are regulations so taken-for-granted as to never face constitutional challenge

[93] 564 U.S. 117 (2011).

[94] *Id.* at 127.

[95] Timmons v. Twin Cities Area New Party, 520 U.S. 351, 362–63 (1997). In *Timmons*, a political party in Minnesota argued that the "fusion ban"—Minnesota's restriction that a candidate could not appear on the ballot as a candidate for more than one party—violated its right to Free Speech. *Id.* at 362. The party argued that the ban violated its right … to communicate its choice of nominees on the ballot on terms equal to those offered other parties, and the right of the party's supporters and other voters to receive that information." *Id.*

[96] *Id.*

in the first instance. For example, our Federal Rules of Civil Procedure are replete with restrictions on speech that are necessary to ensure the efficient operation of our federal court system.[97] Kathleen Sullivan has documented these restrictions on speech in great detail, concluding that:

> Lawyers' freedom of speech is constrained in many ways that no one would challenge seriously under the First Amendment. Rules of evidence and procedure, bans on revealing grand jury testimony, page limits in briefs, and sanctions for frivolous pleadings, to name a few, are examples of speech limitations that are widely accepted as functional necessities in the administration of justice, much like rules of order in a town meeting.[98]

Similarly, regulation that disambiguates campaign finance and a formal petition system could be justified as necessary for the efficient operation of our petition process. If these other contexts are any indication, any Speech Clause challenges to campaign finance regulation will give way to the right to petition when fundraising undermines the petition process.

97 Kathleen M. Sullivan, *The Intersection of Free Speech and the Legal Profession: Constraints on Lawyers' First Amendment Rights*, 67 Fordham L. Rev. 569, 569 (1998).

98 *Id.*

12

Regulating Campaign Finance through Legislative Recusal Rules

Eugene D. Mazo*

I. INTRODUCTION

Whenever reformers have sought to regulate campaign finance by statute, they have witnessed their efforts unravel. Each time, the Supreme Court has struck down parts of the statutory scheme. Given the hostility of the Court toward campaign finance restrictions,[1] some scholars have now come to view the legislative path as littered with pitfalls and have begun advocating campaign finance solutions that are not legislative in nature.[2]

The Supreme Court's hostility is not the only reason that the legislative path is fraught with peril. Another problem with regulating campaign finance through legislation is that all three branches of government are needed for such efforts to succeed. The two houses of Congress and the President must act in concert to pass a federal statute,[3] and that statute's fate is then left up to the courts. This does not grant Congress—the branch of government that

* Eugene D. Mazo is Visiting Associate Professor of Law at Rutgers University. The author wishes to thank Richard Briffault, Timothy Kuhner, and Charles Tiefer for comments on an earlier version of this chapter; Brennan Johnson and Michael Hess for arranging interviews in the Senate and House of Representatives; Jessica Sprigings of the U.S. Senate Library for providing unparalleled access to historical records; and Constance Cooper for superb research assistance.

[1] The Roberts Court has attempted to deregulate campaign finance in seven cases, each decided by the same slim 5-4 margin. In each case, it has struck down various aspects of campaign finance legislation. *See, e.g.*, Randall v. Sorrell, 548 U.S. 230 (2006); FEC v. Wis. Right to Life, 551 U.S. 449 (2007); Davis v. FEC, 554 U.S. 724 (2008); Citizens United v. FEC, 558 U.S. 310 (2010), Ariz. Free Enter. Club's Freedom Club PAC v. Bennett, 564 U.S. 721 (2011); Am. Tradition Partnership, Inc. v. Bullock, 567 U.S. 516 (2012); and McCutcheon v. FEC, 134 S. Ct. 1434 (2014).

[2] *See, e.g.*, Robert Yablon, *Campaign Finance Reform Without Law?*, 103 IOWA L. REV. 185 (2017).

[3] U.S. CONST. art. I, § 7.

has demonstrated the most interest and investment in campaign finance reform—the opportunity to take action on its own.

Legislative reforms have especially run into problems when they have sought to regulate the front-end "inputs" of our campaign finance system. In other words, such reforms have been held unconstitutional when they have sought to control the amount of money given to a candidate for office or else spent by an outside party on the candidate's behalf through independent expenditures. Instead, Congress's reforms should seek to regulate legislative "outputs," or the resulting actions taken by those who get elected to office.

Congress does not need to pass a statue to address the outputs of campaign finance. Instead, it can simply turn to its internal procedural rules. Such procedural rules have the benefit of being easier to pass than statutes, and they can also be designed to have many of the same regulatory effects. Moreover, given that Congress's legislative procedural rules are much harder to subject to judicial review, using legislative procedure to regulate money in politics may provide a way for Congress to get around some of the recent problems that its statutory reforms have faced.

One particular innovation that Congress can use to regulate campaign finance on its own is legislative recusal. Legislative recusal rules, enacted separately in the House and Senate, could be used to preclude members of each chamber from voting on any legislation that presents a member of Congress with a significant conflict of interest. For example, if a Super PAC spends a large sum of money to run ads on behalf of a congressional candidate and that Super PAC's funders happen to have a strong interest in a specific piece of legislation, the congressional candidate, once elected to office, would be deemed to have a conflict of interest and would be precluded from voting on such legislation.

In the early days of our republic, the first House of Representatives adopted a legislative recusal rule. Today, legislative recusal rules exist in many state legislatures. Recusal rules are also common for judges and found throughout the judiciary, both at the state and federal level. The Senate and House have very different procedural rules, and legislative recusal rules that address campaign finance would have to be adopted separately in each house of Congress. A model for what these rules might look like could be borrowed from the judiciary. Given that recusal rules already exist for judges, appropriating some of the features of our judicial recusal standards for Congress might be plausible. Moreover, because such legislative recusal rules, in regulating the vote of a member of Congress, would only control legislative "outputs," they would not interfere with the ability of donors or spenders to do what they wish with their money. As such, they would not impinge on anyone's First Amendment rights. This, it turns out, is one of the most important reasons that campaign finance reformers should champion this path.

Scholars have argued before that internal legislative rules could be used to regulate campaign finance. For example, I have written about how congressional ethics rules could be used to regulate campaign contributions.[4] The House and Senate's internal ethics rules currently regulate gifts and lobbying, and in the 1970s these rules briefly regulated campaign contributions as well.[5] Regulating campaign finance through ethics rules has advantages. First, such ethics rules are easier to adopt than statutes. Adopting an ethics rule in the House requires only a majority vote of the membership of that chamber. Second, given that there is no statute for a court to review or strike down, ethics rules are not easy targets for judicial review. Moreover, it turns out that ethics rules have some teeth. Research shows that incumbency rates for members of Congress who happen to be under an ethics investigation fall dramatically, from over 90 percent to about 54 percent. This does not make the ethics route perfect. In fact, ethics rules are hard to enforce and ethics investigations can be partisan. Nonetheless, an ethics rule that regulates campaign contributions can be used in many innovative ways. For instance, it can be designed to prevent members of Congress from receiving contributions from residents of other jurisdictions, or it can be crafted to forbid members of Congress from receiving contributions over a certain dollar amount. These practices would not be illegal. Rather, they would only be unethical. Over time, the hope is that a new behavioral norm would develop for members of Congress.

While legislative ethics rules are easier to implement than statutes, it turns out their usefulness is limited when it comes to regulating independent expenditures. To regulate independent expenditures, another parliamentary innovation is needed: legislative recusal. Like ethics rules, legislative recusal rules are also harder for courts to review. At the same time, they can be used to structure both the behavior of members of Congress and, simultaneously, the incentives of outside actors who may actively want to influence that behavior. Congress already has many well-known internal procedural rules, such as the filibuster, that work in similar ways and have similar effects.[6]

4 *See, e.g.*, Eugene D. Mazo, *The Disappearance of Corruption and the New Path Forward in Campaign Finance*, 9 Duke J. Const. L. & Pub. Pol'y 259, 293 (2014) (advocating regulating campaign finance through ethics rules).

5 *Id.* at 295, n. 153. *See also* Committee on Standards of Official Conduct, House Ethics Manual, 110th Cong., 2d. Sess., at 23–85 (2008).

6 *See, e.g.*, Howard E. Shuman, *Senate Rules and the Civil Rights Bill: A Case Study*, 51 Am. Pol. Sci. Rev. 955 (1957) (explaining how the potential use of the Senate's filibuster structured

There has recently been a growing literature on how private ordering and private action can be used to make independent expenditure spending prohibitively expensive. Ganesh Sitaraman has written about how Senate candidates Elizabeth Warren and Scott Brown entered into a private contract that depleted each campaign of its private funds whenever outside political ads ran against the other candidate.[7] Similarly, Nick Warshaw has explained how "super PAC insurance" can be used to threaten outside expenditure groups, whose spending activity would trigger an insurance premium payout to a candidate and thus provide the insured candidate with greater spending in response.[8] These and other private ordering innovations seek to make it more expensive for independent expenditure groups to influence the outcome of an electoral campaign. Private ordering schemes are designed to ratchet up the cost of independent expenditures and make it more painful for entities like Super PACs to function.

Legislative recusal rules have similar goals. By focusing on controlling "outputs"—or the actions that politicians take after being elected—recusal rules seek to diminish the influence that any particular political spender has. They do this by separating independent campaign spending from the ability of the officeholder, once elected, to vote in favor of the spender's legislative goals. If the rules of the game made it harder for politicians to vote for the financial interests of those who support them, we would have to worry less about campaign donors and spenders trying to influence politicians nefariously, for the legislative votes of the recipients of a donor's or spender's largesse would be taken away. Recusal itself is not a novel concept. Federal ethics laws already prohibit many government officials from participating in matters in which they have a financial interest. Judicial recusal rules prevent federal and state judges from doing the same. The idea here is that legislators should have to abide by similar constraints, and that the rules governing their behavior should be no different, at least when it comes to outside threats to their independent judgment.

In 2000, John Copeland Nagle wrote about how legislative recusal rules could be used to combat the possible corruption that comes from large campaign contributions.[9] Nagle argued that contributors should be allowed

strategic behavior by senators in the two parties and by outside actors concerning the passage of civil rights legislation).

7 Ganesh Sitaraman, *Contracting around* Citizens United, 114 Colum. L. Rev. 755 (2013).

8 Nick Warshaw, *Forget Congress: Reforming Campaign Finance Through Mutually Assured Destruction*, 63 UCLA L. Rev. 208 (2016) (proposing the idea of "Super PAC insurance").

9 John Copeland Nagle, *The Recusal Alternative to Campaign Finance Reform*, 37 Harv. J. on Legis. 69 (2000).

to give whatever they wish to political candidates, but successful candidates would then have to recuse themselves from voting on any legislation that directly affects those interests.[10] Although Nagle is the only scholar who has previously written seriously on this topic, other scholars have at least alluded to the benefits of using legislative recusal rules to regulate campaign finance. For example, Justin Levitt has suggested that legislative recusal rules might be used to combat independent expenditure spending by making a winning candidate "presumptively ineligible to take legislative action unusually benefiting the sponsor of the expenditure in question."[11] Despite the efforts of these able scholars, however, our understanding of how legislative recusal rules should work in practice remains largely underdeveloped and incomplete.

This chapter discusses how legislative recusal rules might be implemented in each house of Congress, how these rules could be structured to regulate campaign finance, and what advantages such rules have over statutory reforms. Part II discusses the source of Congress's internal procedural rules and how controversies concerning legislative procedure have been handled by the courts. Part III looks at the recusal rules used by the judiciary, as well as at some of the criticisms levied against current judicial recusal mechanisms. Part IV then proposes a system of regulating campaign finance through the adoption of legislative recusal rules in Congress. It addresses questions concerning when such recusal rules would take effect, what activities would trigger them, and who would make the decision of whether a legislator must recuse himself in a particular instance. Finally, Part V discusses the procedures that would need to be followed in each house of Congress for the rules proposed here to be adopted.

II. THE SOURCE OF THE CONGRESS'S PROCEDURAL RULES

A. *The Rulemaking Clause*

The ability of each house of Congress to adopt its own procedural rules comes from the Constitution. That document's so-called Rulemaking Clause, found in Article I, Section 5, Clause 2 of the Constitution, explicitly provides that "[e]ach House may determine the Rules of its Proceedings."[12] The Rulemaking

10 *Id.* at 71.

11 Justin Levitt, *Confronting the Impact of* Citizens United, 29 YALE L. & POL'Y REV. 217, 231 (2010).

12 U.S. CONST. art. I, § 5, cl. 2.

Clause was neither discussed by the framers at the Constitutional Convention nor during the public debates that followed it, when the individual states voted on whether to ratify the Constitution.[13] Indeed, the Rulemaking Clause seems to have attracted no attention during the founding era at all. Nonetheless, this provision plays a vital role in regulating our democracy today. Before Congress can make any federal laws to govern the nation, there must a set of rules in place that dictate the process according to which those laws will be debated and passed. Each house of Congress maintains sole authority to design the process by which to regulate its internal proceedings. As Josh Chafetz explains, "The ability of each chamber to determine its own cameral rules can be thought of as its authority to create its own constitution."[14] These rules are integral to Congress's lawmaking powers.[15]

During the founding era, numerous commentators recognized the importance of the Rulemaking Clause to our democracy. "No person can doubt the propriety of the provision authorizing each house to determine the rules of its proceedings," wrote Justice Joseph Story. "If the power did not exist, it would be utterly impracticable to transact the business of the nation … with decency, deliberation, and order."[16] Perhaps no individual understood the importance of having settled rules of legislative procedure more than Thomas Jefferson. Under the Constitution, the Vice President serves as the President of the Senate, though he does not vote except to break a tie.[17] When John Adams was Vice President from 1789 to 1797, Adams served as the Senate's first President, a role in which he often found himself adjudicating the Senate's procedural disputes. Adams was criticized, however, for the subjective and inconsistent manner in which he did so, a fact of which Jefferson was aware.[18] The presiding officer of the Senate, Jefferson would later explain, has to adhere to "some known system of rules," so that "he may neither leave himself free to indulge caprice or passion."[19] After Adams was elected President and

[13] *See, e.g.*, PAULINE MAIER, RATIFICATION: THE PEOPLE DEBATE THE CONSTITUTION, 1787–1788 (2010) (making no mention of the Rulemaking Clause in a 589-page book about the ratification of the Constitution).

[14] JOSH CHAFETZ, CONGRESS'S CONSTITUTION: LEGISLATIVE AUTHORITY AND THE SEPARATION OF POWERS 267 (2017).

[15] *See* MIMI MARZIANI, BRENNAN CENTER FOR JUSTICE, FILIBUSTER ABUSE 14, 15 (2010).

[16] Joseph Story, COMMENTARIES ON THE CONSTITUTION OF THE UNITED STATES § 835 (1833). *See also* MARZIANI, *supra* note 15, at 15.

[17] U.S. CONST. art. I, § 3, cl. 4.

[18] Wendell H. Ford, *Introduction*, *in* THOMAS JEFFERSON, MANUAL OF PARLIAMENTARY PRACTICE FOR USE IN THE SENATE OF THE UNITED STATES, at vi (Government Printing Office, 1993) [hereinafter JEFFERSON, MANUAL].

[19] Thomas Jefferson, *Preface*, in JEFFERSON, MANUAL, at xxxvii.

Jefferson became Vice President in 1797, Jefferson, as the new President of the Senate, took on the task of preparing a manual of legislative procedure for his own guidance. Jefferson's *Manual of Parliamentary Practice*, originally published in 1801, provided commentaries on the procedural rules that had been used in Britain's parliament, were set out in the Constitution, and had been developing in the nascent Senate. It would become an important authority on legislative practice and procedure during the decades and centuries that followed.

From the very beginning, Congress realized that legislators may have conflicts of interest. As a result, both the House and Senate contemplated adopting recusal rules shortly after the founding.[20] The House of Representative's first legislative recusal rule was adopted within a week of that chamber's first meeting in 1789, not long after the House managed to achieve its first quorum. As David Currie explains in his history of Congress during this period, the House immediately imposed a rule forbidding members from voting on matters in which they were interested.[21] "No member shall vote on any question," read the new rule, "in the event of which he is immediately and particularly interested; or in any other case where he was not present when the question was put."[22] The rule was defended on the ground that it would help legislative business proceed more fairly and efficiently.[23] Although what constituted an "interest" was not explained, the idea that legislators had certain conflicts was commonly known and accepted. John Adams even related to his colleagues how, when he served as a legislator in the Continental Congress, he had been prevented from voting on his country's independence from Britain because he had previously held office in the new government of Massachusetts and was thought to be "interested" in the question before him.[24]

In addition to the recusal rule that existed in the House, Jefferson famously called for a recusal rule to be present in the Senate. In the section of his famous *Manual* concerning "Order in Debate," Jefferson instructed that "No member may be present when a bill or any business concerning himself

[20] *See* Nevada Comm'n on Ethics v. Carrigan, 564 U.S. 117, 122 (2011) (explaining how "[w]ithin 15 years of the founding, both the House of Representatives and the Senate adopted recusal rules.").

[21] David P. Currie, The Constitution in Congress: The Federalist Period, 1789–1801, at 9 (1997).

[22] *See* 1 Annals of Cong. 99 (1789).

[23] Currie, *supra* note 21, at 9–10.

[24] *Id.* at 9–10 n. 24. *See also* Charles Francis Adams, 3 The Works of John Adams 25–28 (1851).

is debating; nor is any member to speak to the merits of it till he withdraws."[25] Jefferson, like his colleagues, understood that members of the Senate had private interests that could conflict with their legislative duties. Thus, his *Manual* provided:

> Where the private interests of a member are concerned in a bill or question, he is to withdraw. And where such an interest has appeared, his voice [is to be] disallowed, even after a division. In a case so contrary not only to the laws of decency, but to the fundamental principles of the social compact, which denies to any man to be a judge in his own cause, it is for the honor of the house that this rule of immemorial observance should be strictly adhered to.[26]

The rules put forth in Jefferson's *Manual* were never actually adopted by the Senate.[27] While Jefferson may have tried to instill the parliamentary practices he favored within the Senate while he was serving as the country's Vice President and compiling his *Manual*, the *Manual* was not published until after he had become President. Still, it is noteworthy that contemporary treatises on parliamentary practice and procedure often closely followed Jefferson's instructions and intuitions concerning legislative recusal.

For instance, Luther S. Cushing's well-known treatise on legislative practice, often referenced in the nineteenth century, explained the circumstances under which members of legislative assemblies should be precluded from voting. "No member ought to be present in the assembly, when any matter or business concerning himself is debating; nor, if present, by the indulgence of the assembly, ought he to vote on any such question," Cushing explained.[28] "Whether the matters in question concern his private interest, or relate to his conduct as a member … the member is to be heard in exculpation and then to withdraw, until the matter is settled. If, notwithstanding, a member should remain in the assembly and vote, his vote may and ought to be disallowed …"[29]

In short, legislative recusal rules that prevented a member of a legislature from voting were recognized by the great treatise writers of the nineteenth century. Forcing a legislator to withhold his vote was considered to be a kind of punishment:

[25] Jefferson, Manual, *supra* note 18, § 17.21, at 31.

[26] *Id.* § 17.22, at 31.

[27] *See* Floyd M. Riddick & Alan S. Frumin, *Riddick's Senate Procedure: Precedents and Practices*, S. Doc. 101–28, 101st Cong., 1st Sess., at 754 (explaining that "Jefferson's *Manual* is not a direct authority on parliamentary procedure in the Senate; nor is his *Manual* a part of the Senate rules.").

[28] Luther S. Cushing, Manual of Parliamentary Practice: Rules of Proceeding and Debate in Deliberative Assemblies 30 (7th ed. 1848).

[29] *Id.*

> The only punishments, which can be inflicted upon its members by a deliberative assembly of the kind now under consideration, consist of reprimanding, exclusion from the assembly, *a prohibition to speak or vote*, for a specified time, and expulsion; to which are to be added such other forms of punishment, as by apology, begging pardon … as the assembly, may see fit to impose, and to require the offender to submit to, on pain of expulsion.[30]

Modern treaties on parliamentary procedure, like their counterparts from centuries past, also contemplate recusal mechanisms when it comes to legislative voting. As Alice Sturgis explains in her *Standard Code of Parliamentary Practice*, "There are certain situations in which a member has no right to vote. As a general principle, a member having a direct personal or financial interest in a matter should not vote on it."[31]

The federal House of Representatives is not the only place where legislative recusal rules existed. Historically, legislative recusal rules could be found in many state legislatures as well. In a number of instances, these state legislative recusal rules had their origins in the common law and long predated the legislative recusal rule adopted by the House of Representatives.[32] State legislative recusal rules instructed their lawmakers on how to behave and what to do whenever a potential conflict of interest arose. States had specific regulations and procedures in place instructing legislators how to handle certain conflicts. The specific procedures could differ from chamber to chamber within a state's legislature, not to mention from state to state. In some states, a recusal rule was enshrined in a state's constitution, while in other states it was mandated by statute or, in some states, even by a simple rule of parliamentary procedure.

Today, almost every state maintains some kind of legislative recusal provision. These rules require legislators to abstain from voting on matters that present a conflict. The states themselves employ various definitions of what a "conflict of interest" entails, and these definitions guide state lawmakers. Not all state rules actually prevent a legislator from voting, although many in fact do just that. In California, a state statute mandates that "[i]f a member of the legislature has a financial interest in a matter, he cannot … [i]ntroduce

[30] *Id.* at 31. *See also* Charles Kelsey Gaines, The New Cushing's Manual of Parliamentary Law and Practice 12 (1912) (when "a question arises involving the right of a member to his seat, such member is entitled to be heard on the question [but] … he must neither take any further part in the debate, not vote on the question itself or upon any motion relating to it").

[31] *See* Alison Sturges, The Standard Code of Parliamentary Procedure 140 (4th ed. 2001).

[32] *See* Nevada Comm'n on Ethics v. Carrigan, 564 U.S. 117, 124 (2011) (explaining that a "number of States, by common-law rule, have long required recusal of public officials with a conflict").

nongeneral legislation related to that matter as a lead author; [v]ote in a legislative committee or subcommittee on related nongeneral legislation; [or p]articipate in a rollcall vote on the Senate or Assembly floor on related nongeneral legislation."[33] A state senate rule in Colorado states that a state senator cannot vote on a bill in which he has a "personal or private interest," and the rule goes on to explain that such an interest exists when the senator "[a]ccepts a gift, loan, service or other economic opportunity from someone who would be affected by or has interest in an enterprise that would be affected by the legislation."[34] A senate rule in Hawaii excuses its state senators with conflicts from voting, elaborating that "[s]ituations considered conflicts of interest include those … in which the member's right to a seat in the Senate will be affected by the outcome."[35]

Many states merely encourage legislators to recuse themselves from voting when a conflict of interest in present, but they do not mandate it. A second set of states actually forces their legislators to recuse themselves, making recusal mandatory and explicit.[36] Finally, in a third set of states legislators are required to disclose their conflicts of interest and then, after doing that, to make a formal request of the chair of their chamber asking the chair to excuse them from voting.[37] All 50 states have regulations in place explaining how conflicts of interest are to be handled by their state legislators. The vast majority of states regulate these conflicts through some kind of legislative recusal mechanism.[38]

B. *Judicial Review of Legislative Rulemaking*

One of the important reasons that legislative recusal rules constitute a powerful tool for regulating money in politics is that, unlike federal statutes, such rules are mostly resistant to judicial review.[39] The Supreme Court itself

33 Cal. Gov. Code § 87102.5 (West 2017).
34 Colo. Senate Rule 17, 41.
35 Haw. Senate Rule 71.
36 *See, e.g.*, La. Rev. Stat. §§ 1112, 1120 (requiring that a legislator with a conflict of interest "shall recuse himself from voting."); Md. Senate Rule 93 (a member "may not vote" on a measure in which he has an interest).
37 *See, e.g.*, Minn. Senate Rules 41.1., 41.2, 56.4; N.H. Senate Rules 2–21, 6–25.
38 The National Council of State Legislatures (NCSL) keeps track of the various state provisions that affect the recusal behavior of state lawmakers in each state. *See* National Council of State Legislatures, *Voting Recusal Provisions*, www.ncsl.org/research/ethics/50-state-table-voting-recusal-provisions.aspx.
39 *See* Rebecca M. Kysar, *Listening to Congress: Earmark Rules and Statutory Interpretation*, 94 Cornell L. Rev. 519, 554 (2009) (finding that "Courts generally interpret this [Rulemaking] Clause to stand for the proposition that such rules are wholly within the purview of each house, beyond scrutiny from the other branches.").

has conceded that it is powerless to assess the validity of any particular legislative procedural rule that happens to be passed under the Rulemaking Clause. "Neither … the advantages or disadvantages, the wisdom or folly, of such a rule present any matters for judicial consideration," the Supreme Court explained in *United States v. Ballin* in 1892.[40] The Court went on to state how Congress:

> may not by its rules ignore constitutional restraints or violate fundamental rights, and there should be a reasonable relation between the mode or method of proceeding established by the rule and the result which is sought to be attained. But within these limitations all matters of method are open to the determination of the house, and it is no impeachment of the rule to say that some other way would be better, more accurate, or even more just. It is no objection to the validity of a rule that a different one has been prescribed and in force for a length of time. The power to make rules is … absolute and beyond the challenge of any other body or tribunal.[41]

More than 40 years later, the Supreme Court would go on to reiterate how the power of each house of Congress to create its own procedural rules under the Rulemaking Clause was inviolate. "The Constitution commits to the Senate the power to make its own rules," the Court wrote in *United States v. Smith* in 1932, "and it is not the function of the Court to say that another rule would be better."[42] Such a view makes sense. Any other view from the courts would threaten the separation of powers, as envisioned by the framers. Lower federal courts have ruled similarly whenever they have confronted this issue.[43]

It is this way for state legislatures, too. Whenever a state's legislative procedural rules have been challenged, state courts have steadfastly refused to opine on their wisdom or to review any particular rule in question.[44] Some courts will take on the task of reviewing legislation that has not been correctly enacted as a matter of state legislative procedure, but even that is rare. Moreover, that kind of review usually only occurs in cases where a procedure for lawmaking is constitutionally mandated in the first place. Examples include the requirements

[40] United States v. Ballin, 144 U.S. 1, 5 (1892).

[41] *Id.*

[42] United States v. Smith, 286 U.S. 6, 48 (1932).

[43] *See, e.g.*, Metzenbaum v. Fed. Energy Regulatory Comm'n, 675 F.2d 1282 (D.C. Cir. 1982) (holding that a case is not suitable for judicial review if resolving the issue in question would require the court to construe the procedural rules of the House of Representatives and to impose the court's own interpretation of that chamber's rules).

[44] *See, e.g.*, Thompson v. Oklahoma, 487 U.S. 815, 877 (1988) (Scalia, J., dissenting) ("We have in the past studiously avoided … interference in the States' legislative processes, the heart of their sovereignty. Placing restraints upon the manner in which the States make their laws … is not … ours to impose.").

for bicameralism and presentment set out in the federal Constitution,[45] or the requirement set out in many states constitutions that a bill has to be read aloud three times within a legislative chamber before it can become law.[46] However, where a state's constitution is silent on legislative procedure, as most state constitutions are, courts have found it to be improper to question even controversial state legislative procedural rules. State courts in most jurisdictions have adhered to this view.[47] As the Kentucky Supreme Court explained in 2003, the state's "[c]onstitution authorizes the General Assembly to establish rules governing its own proceedings. So long as those rules do not violate some other provision of the Constitution, it is not within our prerogative to approve, disapprove, or enforce them."[48] Decisions in other jurisdictions are nearly unanimous in holding that courts cannot inquire into the wisdom of state legislative procedural rules. "It is entirely the prerogative of the legislature," explained the Iowa Supreme Court, "to make, interpret, and enforce its own procedural rules, and the judiciary cannot compel the legislature to act in accordance with its own procedural rules so long as constitutional questions are not implicated."[49]

The fact that legislative procedure is largely immune from judicial review has the potential to transform legislative procedural rules into a powerful tool for regulating campaign finance. But there is also a much more important reason why legislative procedure should interest campaign finance reformers, especially legislative procedural rules that provide for a recusal mechanism. This is because taking away a legislator's vote does not impinge on a person's First Amendment rights. The Supreme Court so held in the 2011 case of *Nevada Commission on Ethics v. Carrigan*,[50] a case that actually involved a

45 U.S. Const. art. I, § 7.

46 *See, e.g.*, Mich. Const. (1963), art. IV, § 26 ("Every bill shall be read three times in each house before the final passage thereof."); W.V. Const., art IV, § 35 ("No bill shall become a law until it has been fully and distinctly read on three different days in each branch; unless, in cases of urgency, three-fourths of the members present dispense with this rule.")

47 *See, e.g.*, Baines v. N.H. Senate President, 876 A.2d 768, 775–77 (N.H. 2005) (holding that a court can enforce lawmaking procedures required by the state's constitution but that the question of whether legislation violates the legislature's internal procedural rules is not a justiciable question). Scholars tend to agree that this is the correct position for courts to take. *See, e.g.*, Norman J. Singer, 1 Statutes and Statutory Construction § 7:4, at 609–11 (6th rev. ed. 2002); *but see* Ittai Bar-Siman-Tov, *The Puzzling Resistance to Judicial Review of the Legislative Process*, 91 B.U. L. Rev. 1915 (2011) (questioning this view).

48 Bd. of Trustees v. Atty. Gen. of Com., 132 S.W.3d 770, 777 (Ky. 2003).

49 Des Moines Register & Tribune Co. v. Dwyer, 542 N.W.2d 491, 496 (Iowa 1996); *see also* Abood v. League of Women Voters, 743 P.2d 333, 336–37 (Alaska 1987) (review of whether the Iowa legislature adhered to its own procedural rules constitutes a political question that is not judiciable); State v. Gray, 60 So. 2d 466, 468 (La. 1952) (failure of Louisiana's legislature to observe its own procedural rules does not invalidate the legislation).

50 Nevada Comm'n on Ethics v. Carrigan, 564 U.S. 117 (2011).

state recusal rule. A state ethics law in Nevada provided that public officials could not vote on any matter in which they had a conflict of interest.[51] After Michael Carrigan, a member of the city council of Sparks, Nevada, failed to recuse himself from voting for a business venture that was proposed to the city council by a company employing Carrigan's previous campaign manager, Nevada's Ethics Commission censured Carrigan. In turn, Carrigan claimed that Nevada's recusal rule violated his First Amendment rights. His case came before a divided Nevada Supreme Court, which found, in ruling for Carrigan, that a legislator's vote is protected speech and that voting "is a core legislative function."[52] However, in an important decision that is central to the argument of this chapter, the U.S. Supreme Court reversed.

Writing for the Court, Justice Antonin Scalia explained that laws restricting a legislator's vote do not implicate speech in any way. This is so because legislative recusal rules preceded the First Amendment itself, given that they were in existence before the First Amendment was adopted and ratified. Scalia compared legislative recusal rules to other laws that restrict speech, such as laws punishing libel and obscenity, which were also in existence in 1791, before the First Amendment. When the First Amendment was adopted, no one thought that laws prohibiting libel or obscenity violated the freedom of speech, and no one considered overturning libel or obscenity laws at the time.[53] Similarly, the records of Congress's earliest proceedings suggest that no one believed that the new procedural rules that the House of Representatives adopted during the first Congress, including its original legislative recusal rule, violated the constitutional rights of its members or the constitutional rights of others.[54] "Members of the House would have been subject to this recusal rule when they voted to submit the First Amendment for ratification," Justice Scalia wrote in *Carrigan*, and "their failure to note any inconsistency between the two" rules—between the new amendment protecting the freedom of speech and the rule mandating legislative recusal—"suggests that there was none."[55]

In *Carrigan*, the Court held that restrictions on a legislator's vote do not translate into restrictions on protected speech because a legislator's vote merely translates into a share of the legislature's power to pass or defeat a

[51] *See* NEV. REV. STAT. § 281A.420(2) (2007).
[52] *Carrigan*, 564 U.S. at 121.
[53] *Id.* at 122.
[54] *See* CURRIE, *supra* note 21, at 10.
[55] *Carrigan*, 564 U.S. at 123

particular legislative proposal. "The legislative power thus committed is not personal to the legislator," Scalia wrote, "but belongs to the people."[56] As such, preventing a member of Congress from voting does not impinge on one's First Amendment rights. *Carrigan* explicitly stated as much with respect to a legislator's First Amendment rights. However, whether this was also true with respect to a third party's First Amendment rights was not made clear. While this latter issue was briefly mentioned, the Court did not rule on it, given that the parties did not raise it in their litigation below.[57]

How the rights of third parties might be affected by recusal rules had to be on the Justices' minds, however, since *Carrigan* was decided only two weeks before *Arizona Free Enterprise Club's Freedom Club PAC v. Bennett*.[58] The latter case invalided a controversial public funding scheme in Arizona that came with a so-called "trigger" provision: if either a privately funded candidate's campaign spending or independent spending by third parties rose above a certain level, it triggered the disbursement of state matching funds to an opposing candidate who participated in the state's public funding system. The state provided matching funds up to three times the limit that the public funding system would have otherwise allowed the publicly funded candidate to spend. The Supreme Court invalidated this scheme, however, and held that it imposed a burden on the speech of both privately financed candidates and third-party independent expenditure groups.[59]

Though *Carrigan* and *Arizona Free Enterprise* were both decided in the same month, there are important differences between the two cases. The statutory scheme at issue in *Arizona Free Enterprise* dealt directly with the public financing of political campaigns. While Arizona's law imposed no limits on private campaign spending, it controversially allowed a benefit to be bestowed on one political candidate based purely on the spending activity of another—or on the spending activity of third parties. The Court found that Arizona was trying to "level the playing field" through its matching funds scheme, and this was a justification for campaign finance legislation that it had long ago rejected.[60] By contrast, the Nevada statute reviewed in *Carrigan*

56 *Id.* at 126.

57 *Id.* at 128. This issue was important for Justice Kennedy, who mentioned it in his concurring opinion in the case. *See id.* at 132 ("the possibility that Carrigan was censured because he was thought to be beholden to a person who helped him win an election raises constitutional issues of the first magnitude") (Kennedy, J., concurring).

58 564 U.S. 721 (2011).

59 *Id.* at 744–48.

60 *Id.* at 748. *See generally* Richard Briffault, *"More Speech" as a First Amendment Violation:* Arizona Free Enterprise Club's Freedom Club PAC v. Bennett *and the Challenge to Public Funding, in* ELECTION LAW STORIES (Joshua A. Douglas & Eugene D. Mazo eds., 2016).

did not concern campaign finance at all. Rather, that recusal statute only sought to prevent conflicts of interest from influencing the decision-making of elected public officials.

Though the Court did review a state legislative recusal statute in *Carrigan*, it is highly unlikely to review the legislative recusal rules of Congress—precisely because they would not be statutory in nature. Instead, they would be procedural rules adopted under the Rulemaking Clause. Given that courts have repeatedly said that they lack the power to review Congress's procedural rules, this distinction is crucial for our purposes here. Just like challenges to the filibuster have all been denied, so would a challenge to a recusal rule adopted pursuant to Congress's powers to design the rules of its own proceedings. A court is unlikely to opine on what procedures Congress can have or cannot, especially because doing so would raise profound separation of powers concerns.

Yet the best argument for why congressional legislative recusal is constitutional is the argument advanced by Justice Scalia: because such recusal rules were already in existence when the First Amendment was adopted. As such, from an originalist perspective, they cannot be found to violate a speaker's First Amendment rights any more than libel or obscenity laws can violate those rights. In the campaign finance context, this turns out to be an extremely important revelation. If Congress had a legislative recusal rule in place, third parties that wish to contribute to campaigns or engage in independent spending would still be able to do so. But if this legislative recusal rule happened to place a burden on that activity, the First Amendment would not be infringed. With a legislative recusal rule in place, however, third parties may be incentivized not to donate or spend quite as much as before because their desired outcome may prove much harder to attain.

Despite the intuitive attractiveness of this logic, there are many difficult issues to work through regarding how legislative recusal rules should work in practice. One place to begin to understand these issues is to examine how recusal currently works in the judicial context.

III. UNDERSTANDING JUDICIAL RECUSAL

A. *The Standards of Judicial Recusal*

Like their legislative counterparts, judicial recusal rules also have a long history. Judicial recusal rules have been applied to judges in the United States since the time of the founding, just as legislative recusal rules have been. In many ways, this is unsurprising. Early Jewish law, Roman law, and English law all recognized the need for judicial impartiality and provided a way for a judge to be disqualified from a case.[61] However, the only recusal standard that the English common law accepted was fairly narrow. Jewish law prohibited a judge from hearing a case in which a litigant was a friend, a relative, or someone the judge personally disliked.[62] Roman law allowed a judge to be disqualified from a case for his "suspicion of bias" against one of the parties.[63] However, the recusal standard of the English common law had become much more constrained by the late-eighteenth century. It called for a judge's disqualification only if he had a direct pecuniary interest in the case.[64] As Richard Flamm explains, "the common law notion of what constituted good grounds for seeking a judge's disqualification was straightforward and simple: A judge would be disqualified for possessing a direct financing interest in the cause before him, and for absolutely nothing else."[65]

In the eighteenth century, courts in the American colonies adopted this same narrow recusal standard. Forcing a judge to recuse himself based on his pecuniary interests in the matter before him was a standard that was familiar to the founding fathers, who not only accepted the English common law in their courts but also understood the need to have recusal provisions in place at the time of the country's founding. Shortly after the first House of Representatives adopted its first legislative recusal rule in 1789, Congress enacted the country's first federal judicial recusal statute in 1792.[66] As might be expected, this statute adopted the common law's disqualification standard by calling for the recusal of a judge who had a personal interest in a lawsuit—the term used in the statute was that he was "concerned in interest."[67] It also broadened the narrow pecuniary interest standard of the English common law to mandate recusal for judges in one or two other discrete instances: for example, a judge now also had to recuse himself if he had previously acted as "counsel" for either party to the case.[68]

Congress would subsequently go on to amend its federal judicial recusal statute in 1821, 1891, 1911, 1948, and 1974. Every time it did so, it expanded the grounds for seeking judicial recusal, adding new standards under which

61 Disqualification refers to the same concept as recusal. Technically, there is a difference, in that disqualification is mandatory whereas recusal is voluntary, but many scholars use the terms interchangeably. *See* Richard E. Flamm, Judicial Disqualification: Recusal and Disqualification of Judges 4 (2d ed. 2007)

62 *Id.* at 5.

63 *Id.* at 6.

64 *Id.*

65 *Id. See also* John P. Frank, *Disqualification of Judges*, 56 Yale L.J. 605, 609–12 (1947).

66 *See* Act of May 8, 1792, ch. 36, § 11, 1 Stat. 275.

67 Act of May 8, 1792, ch. 36, § 11, 1 Stat. 275, 278–79.

68 *Id. See also* Flamm, *supra* note 61, at 8.

a judge's disqualification was warranted.[69] In 1821, for example, Congress expanded the recusal standard to include situations in which the judge was "so related to, or connected with, either party, as to render it improper for him to sit."[70] In 1891, Congress added another recusal standard, this time preventing a judge from hearing an appeal of a case that the judge himself had tried.[71] In 1911, the recusal standard was expanded again, this time making any "personal bias or prejudice" on behalf of a judge a basis for judicial disqualification.[72] And in 1974, the standard was expanded yet further, this time to disqualify any judge whose "impartiality might reasonably be questioned."[73] Currently, there are numerous grounds that may be used in support of a motion for judicial recusal.

Today, at the federal level, all judicial recusal motions are governed by two statutes. These are 28 U.S.C. § 455 and 28 U.S.C. § 144.[74] Section 455 was codified by Congress in 1948 and substantially revised in 1974. That section is now divided into two parts. Subsection 455(a) contains a "catch-all" provision that mandates a judge "shall disqualify himself in any proceeding in which his impartiality might reasonably be questioned."[75] This standard, created by Congress with the intent of promoting the impartiality of judges and a positive perception in the mind of the public about the judicial process,[76] is aimed at ridding the judiciary of any "appearance of bias."[77] As a leading treatise explains, "what matters under §455(a) is not the reality of bias but it appearance."[78] Subsection 455(b), by contrast, enumerates specific circumstances when a judge's recusal is required. These include situations where a judge maintains "personal bias or prejudice concerning a party, or personal knowledge of disputed evidentiary facts concerning the proceeding";[79] where "he served as lawyer in the matter in controversy" while in private practice;[80] or where he served in government and "and in such capacity participated as counsel … concerning the proceeding or expressed an opinion concerning the merits of the particular case."[81] Other

69 *Id.* at 9, n. 8 (listing the expanded grounds for disqualification in 1821, 1891, 1911, and 1948).
70 *See* Act of Mar. 3, 1821, ch. 51, 3 Stat. 643.
71 *See* Act of Mar. 3, 1891, ch. 517, § 3, 26 Stat. 826.
72 Act of Mar. 3, 1911, ch. 231, § 21, 36 Stat. 1087.
73 Act of Dec. 5, 1974, Pub. L. No. 93–512, 88 Stat. 1609.
74 28 U.S.C. § 455 (1948); 28 U.S.C. § 144 (1948); *see* FLAMM, *supra* note 61, at 673.
75 28 U.S.C. § 455(a); FLAMM, *supra* note 61, at 698.
76 Liteky v. United States, 510 U.S. 540, 548 (1994) (calling the standard a "catch-all").
77 FLAMM, *supra* note 61, at 698–99.
78 *Id.* at 716.
79 28 U.S.C. § 455(b)(1).
80 28 U.S.C. § 455(b)(2).
81 28 U.S.C. § 455(b)(3).

grounds for recusal exist as well, such as when the judge, his spouse, or other relatives happen to be a party to the proceeding.[82]

Even though Congress has changed the standards for judicial recusal over the years, the pecuniary interest standard has never gone away. Today, Subsection 455(b)(4) specifically mandates recusal in circumstances when a judge has a financial interest in the case. This occurs when:

> He knows that he, individually or as a fiduciary, or his spouse or minor child residing in his household, has a financial interest in the subject matter in controversy or in a party to the proceeding, or any other interest that could be substantially affected by the outcome of the proceeding.[83]

The statute defines "financial interest" as the "ownership of a legal or equitable interest, however small, or a relationship as director, adviser, or other active participant in the affairs of a party."[84] Under these circumstances, Congress has stated that a judge has to recuse himself no matter how "small" his financial interest happens to be.[85] In other words, the federal statute was designed to preclude judges from making decisions in cases in which they possess *any* financial stake.[86]

A second federal judicial recusal statute, 28 U.S.C. § 144, also exists. Unlike the provisions of Section 455, however, which apply to all federal judges, Section 144 applies only to federal district court judges. This statute allows a litigant to disqualify a district court judge for any alleged bias or prejudice simply by filing a timely affidavit of bias. This filing automatically takes the recusal decision out of a judge's hands. The statute was designed to remove the choice from the judge himself. There is little doubt that Section 144 was intended to act as a preemptory disqualification provision, even though Congress later imposed certain limitations on its use.[87] This second federal statute, however, has been interpreted rather narrowly by the courts, which have successfully forced parties themselves (and not their lawyers) to be the ones to allege evidence of bias, and to do so successfully, before the recusal provisions can take effect.[88]

82 28 U.S.C. § 455(b)(5).

83 28 U.S.C. § 455(b)(4). Subsection 455(b)(4) may be divided into two prongs. Under the first, a federal judge has to disqualify himself when he has "a financial interest" in the subject in controversy. Under the second, he has to disqualify himself if he has "any other interest" that could be "substantially affected" by the outcome of the case.

84 8 U.S.C. § 455(d)(4).

85 Flamm, *supra* note 61, at 707.

86 *Id.* at 710.

87 *Id.* at 682–83.

88 *Id.* at 685; *see also* Dmitry Bam, *Our Unconstitutional Recusal Procedure*, 84 Miss. L.J. 1135, 1148 (2015).

In addition to these federal statutes, there are also judicial disqualification provisions at work in almost every state.[89] These state provisions differ significantly across jurisdictions. The most important differences between them concern how they regulate a judge's removal. In a majority of states, judges may be removed only for cause. However, in about a third of the states a party may also seek judicial recusal on a preemptory basis. This allows a party to disqualify a judge without making a showing of unfairness.[90] In some jurisdictions, the preemptory challenge works similarly to the way that preemptory strikes are used to challenge jurors in a jury pool, and neither filing an affidavit to show cause nor holding a hearing to explain the reasons for the challenge are required. That said, the states often place limits on the use of these preemptory challenges to prevent them from being abused. Typical constraints found in practice include that the challenge has to be timely, must be limited only to the parties to the case, or is available only once to each party.[91] The timeliness requirement is especially important: the targeted judge must normally be removed immediately at the start of a case, before he has had a chance to rule on any substantive issues or motions.[92]

Judicial recusal is also sometimes mandated by the Constitution. The Due Process Clause of the Fourteenth Amendment guarantees parties the right to have their cases heard by an impartial judge, and judicial recusal has been traditionally required under due process principles in two circumstances. The first, unsurprisingly, is when the judge has a financial interest in a case or could benefit financially from its outcome.[93] The second is when a judge has presided over a contempt hearing after presiding over the earlier hearing during which the alleged contempt took place.[94] In 2009, in *Caperton v. A.T. Massey Coal Company*,[95] the Supreme Court created a third situation when recusal is also mandated, namely when a judge's relationship with one of the

[89] Aside from the individual state provisions, the ABA's Code of Judicial Conduct has also been adopted in some form by 49 of the 50 states, and its provisions govern the disqualification of judges at the state level as well. Rule 2.11 of the Code requires a judge to disqualify himself in any proceeding in which his impartiality "might reasonably be questioned." *See* MODEL CODE OF JUDICIAL CONDUCT 2.11 (2011); *see also* Leslie W. Abramson, *Appearance of Impropriety; Deciding When a Judge's Impartiality "Might Reasonably Be Questioned,"* 14 GEO. J. LEGAL ETHICS 55, 55 (2000). According to Bam, disqualification under the federal statutes and the Code are similar, in that both impose an "appearance-based disqualification standard." *See* Dmitry Bam, *Making Appearances Matter: Recusal and the Appearance of Bias*, 2011 BYU L. REV. 943, 958.

[90] FLAMM, *supra* note 61, at 753–54.

[91] *Id.* at 773–75.

[92] *Id.* at 776.

[93] Tumey v. Ohio, 273 U.S. 510 (1927).

[94] *In re* Murchison, 349 U.S. 133 (1955).

[95] 556 U.S. 868 (2009).

parties creates an intolerably high "probability of bias."[96] This third scenario appears often in the context of state judicial elections.

Thirty-nine states currently use elections to select their judges. In these states, judges must campaign to earn or retain their seats, and to do that successfully they have to raise money. As big money has poured into state judicial races, these races have become more competitive, leaving judges no choice but to engage in greater fundraising efforts. Given that 90 percent of all judicial business is handled by state courts and 89 percent of all state court judges have to seek election to keep their seats, the relationship between partisan elections and judicial impartiality has come under increasing scrutiny.[97] Scholars who study this phenomenon have discovered that judges are likely to rule in favor of parties from whom they receive large campaign contributions, a finding that is in many ways unsurprising.[98]

As the role of money in judicial elections has become more pronounced, the distinctions between judges and politicians have narrowed. Much of the recent literature on judicial elections has demonstrated that the decision-making of elected judges is heavily influenced by campaign finance considerations, just like that of other elected officials. Judges appear to respond in predictable ways to the incentives of our campaign finance system, especially when running for office in partisan elections. Several recent studies by Michael Kang and Joanna Shepperd make this point.[99] At the same time, spending on judicial elections has skyrocketed. Kang and Shepperd report that during the ten-year period from 2002 to 2012, independent spending in judicial elections went from $2.7 million to $24 million.[100] While not all scholars agree that the increased spending witnessed in judicial elections is necessarily a bad thing, and some even celebrate it,[101] they are nearly unanimous in their agreement that outside spending is making judicial elections increasingly resemble legislative ones.[102] Several prominent jurists have publicly lamented this state of affairs. We live in an era when judges are "just politicians in

96 *Id.* at 887.

97 *See, e.g.*, Michael S. Kang & Joanna M. Shepperd, *The Partisan Price of Justice: An Empirical Analysis of Campaign Contributions and Judicial Elections*, 86 N.Y.U. L. Rev. 69, 71 (2011).

98 *Id.*

99 *See* Michael S. Kang & Joanna M. Shepperd, *The Partisan Foundations of Judicial Campaign Finance*, 86 S. Cal. L. Rev. 1239, 1243 (2013). *See also* Kang & Shepperd, *The Partisan Price of Justice*, *supra* note 97, at 75, 110.

100 Michael S. Kang & Joanna M. Shepperd, *Judging Judicial Elections*, 114 Mich. L. Rev. 929, 936 (2016).

101 *See, e.g.*, Melinda Gann Hall, Attacking Judges: How Campaign Advertising Influences State Supreme Court Elections (2015) (playing down worries about attack advertising in judicial elections).

102 *See* Kang & Shepperd, *Judging Judicial Elections*, *supra* note 100, at 937.

robes," as Justice Sandra Day O'Connor has said.[103] Or as Justice Stephen Breyer elaborated in a recent case: "When the political campaign-finance apparatus is applied to judicial elections, the distinction of judges from politicians dims."[104]

B. *Criticisms of Judicial Recusal*

All of this begs the question of what we should do when our elected public officials, be they judges or legislators, face conflicts of interest. If the answer is that they should be recused from participating in a case or from voting in a legislative chamber, then we have to figure out how to make this process work best in practice. Unfortunately, our current federal judicial recusal process is not able to provide a workable template because it itself suffers from a number of deficiencies. "While the substantive recusal standard has undergone substantial transformation since Congress's passage of the first federal recusal statute," explains Dmitry Bam, "the recusal procedure has largely remained the same. Just as eighteenth century judges and justices in the United States decided their own recusal motions, twenty-first century judges and justices have continued this practice."[105] When recusal is required, in most cases a judge recuses himself. He must act on his own and without request from one of the parties to the litigation.[106] Many judges recuse themselves when they have a conflict of interest without a motion from one of the parties. If they do not, a party to the litigation may file a formal motion seeking recusal, and the judge whose impartiality is challenged must then rule on the motion. In effect, the challenged judge has to rule on his own alleged bias, once evidence of it is presented by the moving party.

Recusal procedure has been a neglected topic of inquiry. The focus of the literature "has been on the substantive recusal standards, or specific recusal decisions," explains Bam, "[while] recusal procedure … has long been neglected by scholars."[107] Among the few who have studied recusal procedure, self-recusal has been widely criticized. While self-recusal is the predominant method of recusal used in our federal and state courts, scholars have found the procedure "problematic," "troubling," and a "bizarre rule."[108] Identifying

103 *See* Kang & Shepperd, *The Partisan Foundations of Judicial Campaign Finance*, *supra* note 99, at 1297 (quoting Justice O'Connor).

104 Williams-Yulee v. Fla. Bar, 135 S. Ct. 1656, 1674 (2015).

105 Bam, *Our Unconstitutional Recusal Procedure*, *supra* note 88, at 1150.

106 *Id.* at 1151.

107 *Id.* at 1136–37.

108 Louis J. Virelli III, *Congress, the Constitution, and Supreme Court Recusal*, 69 WASH. & LEE L. REV. 1535, 1554 (2012) (calling self-recusal "problematic"); Debra Lyn Bassett, *Judicial*

optimal recusal procedures is an area in which scholars, the bench, and the bar have been deficient. In a number of instances, scholars have put forth some ideas for reforming the judiciary's self-recusal system, but the courts "have largely turned a deaf ear to academia's call for procedural reform."[109] If legislators are to look to judicial recusal as the basis for the legislative recusal procedures they implement to regulate campaign finance, they need to understand the various reform proposals for judicial recusal procedure that have been proposed—and how they have been received.

The leading reform proposal for judicial self-recusal is preemptory disqualification. As mentioned, such a mechanism exists at the state level in about one-third of the states. In these jurisdictions, litigants may disqualify a judge without showing cause or giving a reason for their actions.[110] The idea behind it stems from a criminal trial, where parties from both sides are permitted to strike a certain number of people from the jury pool.[111] Among the jurisdictions that use preemptory disqualification, some require the party seeking recusal to show grounds for the judge's prejudice, while others simply allow the moving party to submit an affidavit affirming only its belief that prejudice exists. The preemptory disqualification statute in Alaska, for instance, states that "[i]f a party or a party's attorney in [an] action, civil or criminal, files an affidavit alleging … the belief that a fair and impartial trial cannot be obtained, the presiding district court or superior court judge … shall at once, and without requiring proof, assign the action to another judge in the appropriate court in the district."[112] And if no such judge is available, then "the chief justice of the supreme court shall assign a judge for the hearing or trial in the action."[113] Importantly, Alaska's courts have also added their own rule mandating that the affidavit must be timely. In Alaska, it must be filed within five days of a party's first appearance or the filing of its first pleading.[114] In Montana, each party is granted one "substitution" of a judge without cause.[115] The substitution motion must again be timely, which in Montana means it must be filed within

Disqualification in the Federal Appellate Courts, 87 Iowa L. Rev. 1213, 1237 (2002) (calling it "troubling"); John Leubsdorf, *Theories of Judging and Judge Disqualification*, 62 N.Y.U. L. Rev. 237, 242 (1987) (calling every judge's right to be the judge of his own bias a "bizarre rule"). These examples appear in Bam, *supra* note 88, at 1137 nn. 5–7.

109 *Id.* at 1151.

110 *See* James Sample, David Pozen & Michael Young, Brennan Center for Justice, Fair Courts: Setting Recusal Standards 18 (2008).

111 *Id.* at 26.

112 *See, e.g.*, Alaska Stat. § 22.20.022(a).

113 *Id.*

114 *See* Alaska Civil Rule 42(c)(3). *See also* Flamm, *supra* note 61, at 791–80.

115 *See* Sample, Pozen & Young, *supra* note 110, at 26.

30 days of the service of the summons or the appearance of a party,[116] and it must be accompanied by a fee.[117] Any untimely motion will be void.[118] While preemptory disqualification has found supporters, scholars have also expressed concern that the procedure can be abused by lawyers if they are able to engage in "judge-shopping."[119]

Another mechanism proposed to alleviate the pitfalls of self-recusal is the use of *per se* recusal rules for judges who have accepted large contributions from parties appearing before them.[120] This proposal allows all campaign contributions below a certain monetary threshold, but it imposes mandatory recusal on any judge who accepts contributions above that threshold. Since 1999, the ABA's Model Code has included language recommending that an elected judge recuse himself when the party before him or its lawyer has made aggregate contributions to the judge's campaign over a certain amount in a given year.[121] This provision is meant to eliminate the incentives of parties and their lawyers to gain favor with judges by making large contributions to their campaigns.[122]

However, there are problems with the ABA's rule that explain why the states have been slow to accept it. First, some states already place limits on campaign contributions, meaning the ABA's rule adds little to the regime that is in place in these jurisdictions.[123] Second, mandatory disqualification rules invite strategic behavior. For example, parties or lawyers could disqualify a judge they dislike by making contributions to his reelection campaign above the threshold amount. To prevent such strategic behavior, James Sample, David Pozen, and Michael Young propose a rule that would allow a party whose opponent contributed to the same judge's campaign to waive disqualification.[124] In other words, if one's opponent contributed to a judge, the non-contributing party would have the option of waiving the *per se* disqualification requirement for that judge. And if both parties contributed to a judge's election campaign, the judge would presumably not be forced to recuse himself at all. Given that lawyers often contribute to judicial campaigns, the rule

[116] MONT. CODE ANN. § 3-1-804.

[117] MONT. CODE ANN. § 25-1-201(p).

[118] *See* FLAMM, *supra* note 61, at 811.

[119] *Id.* at 757–58. *See also* Debra Lyn Bassett & Rex R. Perschbacher, *The Elusive Goal of Impartiality*, 97 IOWA L. REV. 181, 212 (2011) (explaining that an objection to preemptory recusal is "the fear of potential judge-shopping").

[120] SAMPLE, POZEN & YOUNG, *supra* note 110, at 29.

[121] *See* MODEL CODE OF JUDICIAL CONDUCT, Rule 2.11(4).

[122] SAMPLE, POZEN & YOUNG, *supra* note 110, at 29.

[123] *Id.* at 30.

[124] *Id.* at 30.

would work similarly if it turned out that, instead of the opposing party, it was the opposing lawyer who contributed to the judge's campaign.

The final proposal that scholars have put forth for reforming the judicial recusal regime is to have recusal motions adjudicated independently. The process of having a judge decide if he might be biased or have a conflict is fraught with tension, as many scholars have pointed out. For this reason, it might be wise for an independent judge or, better yet, an independent commission to decide issues of recusal.[125] In some states, when a state judge is presented with a recusal motion, the state's procedural rules mandate that he either recuse himself or request his presiding judge to find another jurist to rule on the motion. But scholars have called for states to go even further, by creating an "independent judicial recusal commission" to adjudicate judicial recusal motions, perhaps one comprised of non-judges and non-attorney members as well.[126] All recusal motions would be submitted to this commission, and it would have jurisdiction to rule on these motions. The decision of the recusal commission would be the final arbiter of the matter. The recusal commission would be a neutral decision-maker, and it would be tasked with providing independent guidance and a written opinion as to why a judge's recusal is warranted.

These various innovations seek to improve the judicial recusal system that exists in our federal and state courts. But they could also be harnessed for another task. The ideas behind them are instructive when it comes to designing effective legislative recusal mechanisms for Congress.

IV. SETTING LEGISLATIVE RECUSAL STANDARDS AND PROCEDURES

A. *Understanding Voting in Congress*

To understand how legislative recusal might work in practice, it is first necessary to know how voting works in Congress. In the Senate, there are three methods of voting: voice votes, division votes, and roll call votes.[127] Voice votes and division votes are allowed by Senate precedent. Roll call votes are governed by the Constitution and by the Standing Rules of the Senate.[128] Rule XII governs the chamber's voting procedures.[129] There are situations where the

125 *See* Matthew Menedez & Dorothy Samuels, Brennan Center for Justice, Judicial Recusal Reform: Toward Independent Consideration of Disqualification 6 (2016).

126 *Id.* at 10.

127 Martin B. Gold, Senate Practice and Procedure 115 (3d ed. 2013).

128 *See* U.S. Const. art. I, § 5.

129 Standing Rules of the Senate, Rule XII.

Standing Rules specifically require a roll call vote, such as when the Senate votes on cloture motions to prevent a filibuster.[130] Otherwise, unless either a division vote is demanded or a roll call vote is requested, a voice vote will allow the Senate to proceed with its daily business.

The kind of vote most often sought in the Senate is a voice vote. The presiding officer will ask, "All those in favor of the measure, say 'aye,' and all those opposed, say 'no.'"[131] If the measure has no opposition, it will pass. The majority of the Senate's daily business is transacted this way. When a matter is decided by voice vote, however, the public has no way of knowing how any individual senator voted. If a member of the Senate is in doubt about the outcome of the voice vote, he may call for a division vote to be taken.[132] This amounts to a request by a senator for the exact division of votes to be counted. All senators in favor of a proposition stand and their votes are counted, then those opposed stand and their votes are counted, and finally how the vote totals divide is announced. By providing an accurate count of the votes, this procedure demonstrates more accurately whether a particular proposition has been approved. However, a division vote again does not provide a record of how any individual senator voted.[133]

Before the results of a voice vote or division are announced, a senator may also call for a roll call vote to be taken. Roll call voting is entirely different from the other two methods of voting. The Constitution provides for roll call votes—which it calls "Yeas and Nays"—and requires that they be recorded in the Senate's official record.[134] In practice, any senator can ask for a roll call vote on any issue. When the senator does this, the presiding officer will ask someone to second this request. If 11 senators second it—this number constitutes one-fifth of the Senate's quorum of 51 members, again as required by the Constitution—a roll call vote will occur.[135] At that point, the clerk will call the names of the senators in alphabetical order and each will vote "Yea" or "Nay." Once a roll call commences, it may not be interrupted.[136]

[130] Standing Rules of the Senate, Rule XXII, para. 2.

[131] GOLD, *supra* note 127, at 115.

[132] *Id.*

[133] *Id.* at 116.

[134] *See* U.S. CONST. art. I, § 5, cl. 3 ("Each House shall keep a Journal of its Proceedings, and from time to time publish the same, excepting such Parts as may in their Judgment require Secrecy; and the Yeas and Nays of the Members of either House on any question shall, at the Desire of one fifth of those Present, be entered on the Journal.").

[135] GOLD, *supra* note 127, at 116.

[136] By tradition, roll call votes are set for 15 minutes, but that time may be extended. However, a senator who misses the deadline to vote may not add his name to the tally once the result has been announced. *Id.* at 117.

The Standing Rules make voting mandatory. In fact, the Standing Rules require all senators to vote unless they are excused from doing so.[137] If a senator declines to vote at the conclusion of a roll call vote, he is required to state his reason. Of all recorded roll call votes taken on the Senate floor, according to Walter Oleszek, "Senators, on average, cast votes around 95% of the time."[138] A senator may decline to vote, in committee or on the floor, only in limited circumstances. One such circumstance occurs when a senator's vote is "paired." This procedure allows a senator to withhold his vote when he knows that an absent colleague would vote the opposite way, and the two agree in advance to combine their votes and announce this. In such cases, neither the vote of the absent senator nor that of the one pairing his vote is counted. Those who give pairs are excused from the chamber's mandatory voting requirements. In addition, and importantly, mandatory voting is also excused when a senator asserts a "conflict of interest."[139]

In the House, there are four ways lawmakers vote, not three.[140] The first is through voice vote. This procedure works as it does in the Senate, with the Speaker of the House asking all in favor of a proposition to say "aye" and all opposed to say "no."[141] However, a voice vote is more difficult to administer in the House, given the chamber's membership is more than four times larger. Indeed, when a voice vote is called, it can sometimes be challenging for the Speaker to hear all of the members.[142] In these circumstances, a division vote may be requested. If the Speaker is unsure of the outcome of a voice vote or a House member demands a division vote, all in favor of the question and then all opposed will be counted.[143] A division vote in the House, as in the Senate, provides totals for the number of votes for and against a measure, although it again does not provide information about how any individual member of the House of Representatives voted.[144]

137 Standing Rules of the Senate, Rule XII.

138 Walter J. Oleszek, Cong. Res. Serv., No. 98-227, Voting in the Senate: Forms and Requirements 1 (May 19, 2008).

139 Standing Rules of the Senate, Rule XII, para. 3.

140 Walter J. Oleszek, Congressional Procedures and the Policy Process 226 (9th ed. 2014).

141 *See* Constitution, Jefferson's Manual, and Manual and Rules of the House of Representatives, 114th Cong., H. Doc. No. 113–181, 113th Cong., 2d. Sess. § 630 (2015) (referencing Rule I, cl. 6) [hereinafter House Rules and Manual].

142 Walter J. Oleszek, Cong. Res. Serv., No. 98-228, House Voting Procedures: Forms and Requirements 1 (May 19, 2008).

143 House Rules and Manual, *supra* note 141, § 1012 (referencing House Rule XX, cl. 1(a)).

144 Oleszek, House Voting Procedures, *supra* note 142, at 1.

With 435 members, the large size of the House does not always lend itself to counting votes quickly or accurately, especially if members may be moving around on the floor. For this reason, the House allows for two different types of roll call votes. The first is similar to the ordinary roll call vote used in the Senate. Any member may request a roll call vote, and if that request is seconded by one-fifth of those present, the Speaker will demand that a count of the "Yeas" and "Nays" take place.[145] When this occurs, however, it may be that a quorum of 218 members, which is necessary to transact the House's business, is absent, or at least that there is uncertainty about whether it has been reached. In such circumstances, the rules of the House allow for an innovation that does not exist in the Senate: a second kind of roll call vote known as an "automatic" roll call. If any member of the House objects to a vote being taken on the grounds that there is no quorum, then under House Rule XX the Speaker will "automatically" call a roll call vote.[146] This "automatic" roll call will then simultaneously determine whether there is a quorum and also whether there are enough votes for a given measure to pass.[147]

The final method of voting in the House is called "recorded voting," which is the term the House uses to describe voting by an electronic device. Unlike the Senate, the House's rules allow for electronic voting. First authorized by the Legislative Reorganization Act of 1970, electronic voting has been used in the House since 1973.[148] If a member requests a "recorded vote" and that request is supported by one-fifth of a quorum—or at least 44 members—the House's rules mandate that such vote shall be taken by electronic device. As Oleszek explains, the main difference between a non-electronic roll call vote and a recorded roll call vote has to do with the number of members required to support each request: it is one-fifth *of those present* for a regular roll call vote, and one-fifth *of a quorum* for a "recorded vote."[149]

Within the House, there is also a body called the Committee of the Whole.[150] The use of the Committee of the Whole as a parliamentary device originated in Britain, where the monarchy had the right to refuse the parliament's choice of a Speaker. Because any person chosen as Speaker needed the monarch's approval, the Speaker, as Chafetz explains, "was long understood to have dual loyalties, at best—and to be an agent of the Crown, at worst."[151] Eventually, the

145 U.S. Const. art. I, § 5.

146 House Rules and Manual, *supra* note 141, § 1025 (referencing House Rule XX, cl. 6).

147 Oleszek, House Voting Procedures, *supra* note 142, at 1.

148 Oleszek, Congressional Procedures and the Policy Process, *supra* note 140, at 224–25.

149 *Id.* at 226.

150 *Id.* at 201.

151 Chafetz, *supra* note 14, at 269.

British House of Commons responded to the problem of having a powerful Speaker whose loyalty might lie elsewhere by creating the Committee of the Whole. Its membership was the same as that of the entire House of Commons, but because it was technically a committee, its Chairman had to be another member of the House and could not be the Speaker.[152] This innovation made its way to the Congress of the United States. Today, the Committee of the Whole is essentially the House of Representatives reconstituted in another form. Its purpose is to facilitate debate and expedite floor action on legislation.[153] Even though every legislator is a member, the Committee of the Whole has its own rules. The Speaker does not preside over its proceedings, and only 100 members, rather than 218, need to be present for a quorum.

Voting procedures differ slightly in the Committee of the Whole. Only three methods of voting are permitted: voice votes, division votes, and recorded votes. Both kinds of roll call votes—both the type called for by the Constitution, and the "automatic" type under House Rule XX—are prohibited. If a recorded vote is requested in the Committee of the Whole, then under House Rule XVIII that request needs to be seconded by only 25 members, that is after the Committee of the Whole's 100-member quorum has been reached.[154]

As a matter of practice, legislative recusal already happens in Congress. Consider the Senate's important role in giving "advice and consent" to the President on a candidate nominated to serve in the cabinet or as an ambassador.[155] What happens when the President's nominee happens to be a sitting senator? Though the Constitution, federal law, and the Senate's own procedural rules do not prevent a sitting senator from voting for himself, senators have traditionally recused themselves from voting on their own nominations. In January 2017, Donald Trump nominated Senator Jeff Sessions of Alabama to serve as the U.S. Attorney General. The nomination was controversial, and observers expected the vote to be close. The Senate confirmed Sessions to the post along party lines, 52-47.[156] Sessions, a Republican, should rationally have voted for himself, but it turns out that he merely voted "present" on the Senate floor.[157]

152 *Id.*

153 OLESZEK, CONGRESSIONAL PROCEDURES AND THE POLICY PROCESS, *supra* note 140, at 201–2.

154 HOUSE RULES AND MANUAL, *supra* note 141, § 983a (referencing House Rule XVIII, cl. 6(e)).

155 U.S. CONST. art. II, § 2, cl. 2.

156 Eric Lichtblau & Matt Flegeheimer, *Jeff Sessions Confirmed as Attorney General, Capping Bitter Battle*, N.Y. TIMES (Feb. 8, 2017), www.nytimes.com/2017/02/08/us/politics/jeff-sessions-attorney-general-confirmation.html?_r=Oleo

157 Email from Jessica Sprigings of the Senate Library to the author (June 5, 2017).

Like Sessions, other senators have also recused themselves from voting—on the floor and in committee—when it has come to their own nominations, either due to a sense of respect for the office, out of a sense of decorum, or perhaps because of a perceived conflict of interest. In history, there have been 42 sitting senators who were nominated to the President's cabinet. Few of them until recently received a roll call vote on their nominations. Rather, in the vast majority of cases, they were confirmed by voice vote or by unanimous consent.[158] However, a roll call vote was taken on the nominations of eight senators, including Sessions. The earliest such vote took place in 1877, when Rutherford B. Hayes nominated Senator John Sherman of Ohio to be Secretary of the Treasury. Sherman was confirmed, 37-11, but he himself did not vote.[159]

It would be almost 100 years before the Senate held another roll call vote to confirm a sitting senator to a cabinet position. In 1973, Richard Nixon nominated Senator William Saxbe of Ohio to be his Attorney General. Saxbe was approved by the Senate, 75-10, but Saxby only voted "present" on the floor.[160] In 1980, Jimmy Carter nominated Senator Edmund Muskie of Maine to be his Secretary of State. At the time, Muskie was not only a sitting senator, but also a member of the Senate's Foreign Relations Committee. However, Muskie only voted "present" during the Committee's vote,[161] and after his nomination was sent to the full Senate, where he was confirmed, 94-2, Muskie only voted "present" on the Senate floor.[162]

Sitting senators nominated for cabinet positions in later administrations have likewise not voted for themselves. In 1993, Bill Clinton nominated Senator Lloyd Bentsen of Texas to be Secretary of the Treasury. Bentsen was serving on the Senate's Finance Committee at the time, which voted, 19-0, to send Bentsen's nomination to the full Senate, although Bentsen only voted "present" in the committee;[163] he was then confirmed by the Senate by voice vote.[164] In his first term, Barack Obama nominated Senator Ken Salazar of

[158] The author thanks Jessica Sprigings for confirming this point and for providing access to the historical voting records of the Senate referenced in this chapter. *See also* ROGELIP GARCIA, CONG. RES. SERV., NO. 85–1120, SENATE ACTION ON CABINET NOMINATIONS, 1789–1985 (Dec. 12, 1985); Senate, *Executive Register of the U.S.*, 1789–1902, S. Doc. 58–196; Senate, *Biographical Directory of the United States Congress*, 1774–1989, S. Doc. 100–34 (Senate Historical Office).

[159] *Senate Executive Journal* (Mar. 8, 1877), at 5.

[160] *Senate Executive Journal* (Dec. 17, 1973), at 857.

[161] *Senate Foreign Relations Committee Hearing on the Nomination of Senator Edmund Muskie to be Secretary of State*, Hearings, at 40–41.

[162] *See Senate Executive Journal* (May 7, 1980), at 281–82.

[163] *See* U.S. Congress, *PN76-2—Lloyd Bentsen—Department of the Treasury*, 103rd Cong (1993–1994), www.congress.gov/nomination/103rd-congress/76/2.

[164] *Id.*

Colorado to be his Secretary of the Interior and Senator Hillary Clinton of New York to be Secretary of State. While Salazar was confirmed by voice vote,[165] Clinton's nomination received a roll call vote. She was confirmed, 94-2, but did not vote herself.[166] In his second term, Obama nominated Senator John Kerry of Massachusetts for Secretary of State. The Senate's Committee on Foreign Relations reported favorably on Kerry's nomination by voice vote, and Kerry was confirmed by the full Senate, 94-3,[167] but he voted "present."[168] When Obama nominated Senator Max Baucus of Montana as Ambassador to China, the Committee on Foreign Relations also reported favorably on Baucus by voice vote and Baucus was then confirmed, 96-0, although he too only voted "present."[169]

Sitting senators nominated to the Supreme Court also have had the ability to vote on their own nominations. In American history, 15 senators have served as Supreme Court justices. Six of these were sitting senators at the time of their nominations: Oliver Ellsworth of Connecticut went directly from the Senate to the Supreme Court in 1796, as did Levi Woodbury of New Hampshire in 1845, Edward Douglas White of Louisiana in 1894, Hugo Black of Alabama in 1937, James F. Brynes of South Carolina in 1941, and Harold H. Burton of Ohio in 1945.[170] In each case, the senator did not cast a recorded vote on his own nomination. Oliver Ellsworth did not vote when he was confirmed, 21-1, in 1796,[171] and neither did Hugo Black when he was confirmed, 63-16, in 1937.[172] Meanwhile, Edward Douglas White in 1894,[173] James Brynes in 1941,[174] and Harold Burton in 1945 were confirmed by unanimous consent, so no roll call vote was taken.[175] Levi Woodbury

165 *See* U.S. Congress, *PN64-16—Kenneth Lee Salazar—Department of the Interior*, 111th Cong. (2009–2010), www.congress.gov/nomination/111th-congress/64/16.

166 Hillary Clinton sent a letter resigning from her Senate seat on the same day, after the vote. *See* 155 Cong. Rec. 1286 (2009).

167 *See* U.S. Congress, *PN42—John Forbes Kerry—Department of State*, 113th Cong. (2013–2014), www.congress.gov/nomination/113th-congress/42.

168 *Id.*

169 *See* U.S. Congress, *PN1295—Max Sieben Baucus—Department of State*, 113th Cong. (2013–2014), www.congress.gov/nomination/113th-congress/1295.

170 *See* U.S. Senate, *Senators Who Served on the Supreme Court*, www.senate.gov/reference/Supreme_Court.htm. John McKinley of Alabama was nominated to the Supreme Court by Martin van Buren in April 1837, a few months after he had been elected to the Senate in 1936, but McKinley resigned his Senate seat and so technically could not vote on his own nomination. *See* Jimmie Hicks, *Associate Justice John McKinley: A Sketch*, 18 Ala. Rev. 227–33 (1965); John M. Martin, *John McKinley: Jacksonian Phase*, 28 Ala. Hist. Q. 7–31 (1966).

171 *Senate Executive Journal* (Mar. 4, 1796), at 203–4.

172 *Senate Executive Journal* (Aug. 17, 1937), at 604–4.

173 *Senate Executive Journal* (Feb. 19, 1894), at 424.

174 *Senate Executive Journal* (June 12, 1941), at 292.

175 *Senate Executive Journal* (Sept. 19, 1945), at 569.

received a recess appointment to the Supreme Court in 1845 while he was a sitting senator. He was then officially confirmed by his colleagues in 1846 by voice vote,[176] but that vote took place when Woodbury was no longer officially in the Senate.[177]

There has also been one sitting senator nominated to the Supreme Court whose nomination was not acted upon by his Senate colleagues. After Justice John McKinley died in July of 1852, Millard Fillmore offered three nominations for the vacant seat but was unable to obtain confirmation for any of them, with Democrats anticipating a victory in that November's election.[178] Though Franklin Pierce won that election, Fillmore knew he would be in office until March of 1853, and he was determined to appoint a Supreme Court justice. In January of 1853, he nominated Senator George Edmund Badger of North Carolina to fill McKinley's seat, but the Senate voted to postpone voting on Badger's nomination until Franklin Pierce's inauguration,[179] which everyone knew would deny Badger the seat. Badger, however, as a sitting senator, would have been able to vote on whether his nomination should have been postponed in the first place. That vote, it turns out, was taken by roll call, with the Senate voting narrowly, 26-25, in favor of postponement.[180] Of course, Badger himself did not vote.[181]

As is evident from the history recounted here, legislative self-recusal works in Congress—or at least in the Senate—and it has been employed with dignity throughout the country's history. Given this history, how could legislative recusal now regulate campaign finance?

B. *Legislative Recusal and Campaign Finance*

Having gone over the theory and practice of legislative recusal, it is now time to explain how legislative recusal should work to regulate campaign finance. The complexities of how voting works in each house of Congress have to be understood before a workable and sensible recusal rule can be proposed. There are many difficult but important issues to work through regarding how legislative recusal should work in practice. The issues include deciding *when* recusal rules should take effect, *which* votes have to be recused, *what* kinds of

[176] *Senate Executive Journal* (Jan. 3, 1846), at 24.

[177] Vincent J. Capowski, *Levi Woodbury: 1845–1851*, *in* The Supreme Court Justices: Illustrated Biographies, 1789–1995, at 149 (Clare Cushman ed., 2d ed. 1995).

[178] *See* J. Myron Jacobstein & Roy M. Mersky, The Rejected: Sketches of the 26 Men Nominated for the Supreme Court but not Confirmed by the Senate 56 (1993).

[179] *Id.* at 58.

[180] *Senate Executive Journal* (Feb. 10, 1853), at 28.

[181] *Id.*

spending triggers recusal, and finally, but also crucially, *who* should make the determination of whether a legislator needs to recuse himself in a particular instance.

The first question—when—is perhaps the easiest. Recusal needs to take place before a legislator casts his vote. Unlike a court case, which can be retried, it is very difficult to impose a retroactive remedy on a legislative decision that has already been taken.[182] If a bill receives a sufficient number of votes to pass but the margin of victory is close, announcing after the fact that some votes should not have been counted because a lawmaker should have recused himself is a recipe for chaos. Thus if a legislator has a conflict of interest, his recusal must be sought ahead of when he casts his vote. This means that a legislator has to be given adequate notice before he is prevented from voting.

The frequency of voting in Congress and the many different types of voting that take place lead to the second issue—which votes should be subject to recusal? A careful look at Jefferson's *Manual* answers that question. Jefferson wrote that where the private interests of a member may affect "a bill or question, he is to withdraw," and "where such an interest has appeared, his voice has been disallowed, even after a division."[183] In other words, Jefferson did not believe that a recused legislator's vote should count at any time. Following this instruction, it seems that recusal rules should be used to prevent *any* type of voting in situations where a conflict of interest appears and a legislator may seek to vote. The rule, in other words, should apply to voice votes, division votes, and roll call votes, as well as to recorded electronic votes, which are used only in the House. The rule should not extend to committee votes, however, where recusal rules are difficult to enforce in practice. In that vein, recusal rules should also not apply to voting in the Committee of the Whole. Moreover, recusal rules should not affect a member's right to participate in debate. In modern legislative practice, members of the Senate and House have always been allowed to speak on their own behalf within their respective chambers, even when the member was being censured or in the midst of expulsion proceedings.

The third issue is much more complicated. What spending activities should trigger recusal in the first place? This is where the intricacies of campaign finance law are important to understand. The campaign finance jurisprudence distinguishes between contribution limits and expenditure limits.

[182] *See* Nagle, *supra* note 9, at 85–86 (making a similar point). *See also* Stephen Huefner, *Remedying Election Wrongs*, 44 HARV. J. ON LEGIS. 265 (2007) (exploring what remedies are available after an election fails).

[183] JEFFERSON, MANUAL, *supra* note 18, § 17.22, at 31.

Contributions refer to the money that a candidate for office or a political party receives from donors. For federal candidates, this amount is capped by statute. For example, in 2017–2018, a donor could contribute up to $2,700 per federal candidate per election.[184] In addition, a donor could contribute $33,900 to national party committees per calendar year.[185] Expenditures refer to the money that a candidate or a third party spends to influence the outcome of an election. The Supreme Court has applied strict scrutiny to limits on expenditures. In practice, that means that expenditures are not subject to any limits at all. In the view of many scholars, therein lies the problem with the current campaign finance system.

Most political contributions and some types of political expenditures are subject to disclosure. The Federal Election Campaign Act requires candidates, parties, and PACs to file periodic reports with the Federal Election Commission (FEC) disclosing the money they raise and spend. For example, candidates must identify all PACs and party committees that give them contributions and must identify individuals who contribute more than $200 to their campaigns in an election cycle. Federal candidates must also disclose their campaign expenditures exceeding $200 to any individual or vendor. Given that federal law already sets limits on contributions and most people do not believe that the current contribution limit of $2,700 corrupts members of Congress, there may not be a need for legislative recusal rules to target contributions.[186] Nor is there any need for them to target the expenditures of candidates or their campaigns.

However, when outside parties spend money to influence elections, the situation is different. Outside independent spending by third parties to influence the outcome of elections has skyrocketed in recent years. Moreover, such spending circumvents the restrictions placed on contributions. Candidates do not have to raise as much money as it would cost to win an election if like-minded outside entities aligned with them—such as Super PACs, 501(c) organizations, or 527 organizations—are able to get the same message out through their own independent means. We do have a disclosure regime in place, however, that forces certain types of outside independent spending

[184] 52 U.S.C. § 30116(a)(1)(A).

[185] 52 U.S.C. § 30116(a)(1)(B). In addition, certain political party committees can make contributions to Senate candidates. These contributions are currently capped at $47,400 per campaign. *See* 52 U.S.C. § 30116(h). The 2017–2018 contribution limits were published in the Federal Register on February 16, 2017, at 82 Fed. Reg. 10904.

[186] Indeed, some of the research suggests that the current contribution limit may be too low. *See, e.g.*, Nathaniel Persily & Kelli Lammie, *Perceptions of Corruption and Campaign Finance: When Public Opinion Determines Constitutional Law*, 153 U. PA. L. REV. 119 (2004).

to be reported, making it part of the public record. In most cases, this independent spending gets reported to the Federal Election Commission (or to the IRS).

Recusal rules cannot work without a regimented disclosure regime to accompany them. In this sense, any recusal mechanism by necessity has to rely on the FEC's mandatory disclosure system and its recordings of independent spending by groups such as Super PACs, 501(c) organizations, and 527 organizations. These groups differ from one another in terms of what they must disclose to the Federal Election Commission. The differences depend on the type of entity making the disclosure and whether that entity is spending money on what the law refers to as independent expenditures, electioneering communications, or issue advocacy.[187]

An independent expenditure is defined as spending on a communication "expressly advocating the election or defeat of a clearly identified candidate" for office, which is "not made in cooperation, consultation, or concert with, or at the request or suggestion of" a candidate or a political party.[188] Independent expenditures, also sometimes called express advocacy, use magic words like "vote for," "support," or "defeat," before referring to a particular candidate for office. An electioneering communication, on the other hand, is a broadcast, cable, or satellite communication that refers to a clearly identifiable candidate for federal office and is distributed within 60 days of a general federal election or within 30 days of a primary.[189] By contrast, issue advocacy refers to communications that reference broad policy issues but not specific candidates, and that due to their wording or timing do not qualify to be independent expenditures or electioneering communications. The disclosure rules mainly apply to outside spending on independent expenditures and electioneering communications. Issue advocacy receives less regulation and is not subject to disclosure when it involves certain non-profit groups.

All persons and organizations that make disbursements for independent expenditures must file reports with the Federal Election Commission. In addition, organizations that spend more than $10,000 on electioneering communications in a calendar year must file disclosure reports.[190] When such disclosure is made, the FEC and the public know how much is spent and on behalf of which candidate. Disclosure reports work to inform the public about

187 *What Super Pacs, Non-Profits, and other Groups Spending Outside Money Must Disclose about the Source and Use of their Funds*, Center for Responsive Politics, www.opensecrets.org/outsidespending/rules.php.

188 *See* 52 U.S.C. § 30101(17).

189 *See* 52 U.S.C. § 30104(f)(3).

190 *See id.* at § 30104(f).

how outside money is used to support certain candidates for office. Congress would implement its legislative recusal rules based upon these disclosure reports. Recusal would be triggered on the basis of an outside entity such as a corporation, Super PAC, 501(c) organization, or 527 organization spending more than a set amount to influence a federal candidate's election.[191]

Even if we know how much a Super PAC or 501(c) organization spends because of its disclosures, it is not immediately clear what level of spending should trigger the necessity for recusal. This would be an issue for each chamber of Congress to debate and decide on its own, and each would have to set its own limits. If a Super PAC, 501(c) organization, or wealthy individual spends a significant amount to support a candidate for office, that candidate, once elected, would then have to recuse himself from voting on all legislation of concern to that organization or individual. How the legislative recusal system's "trigger" is set, however, is a complicated issue and will be very important. For any recusal system to work, it must be activated by a recognizable trigger. That trigger needs to be based on a fair and effective recusal standard. Although determining the exact contours of this standard is beyond the scope of this chapter, and is a task being left for future determination, it is important to recognize that the devil will be found in the standard's details. There are several potential ways of arriving at the trigger. One way may be to set a maximum amount of independent expenditure spending per candidate. For example, if the Senate believes that total independent expenditure spending up to $4 million for a candidate running for the Senate is acceptable, but spending beyond that is not, then any amounts spent beyond that would trigger recusal. Once the maximum allowable amount is surpassed, a senator's vote will be recused as to all legislation affecting the largest source of independent expenditures that were spent in the previous election to help him get elected.

Another way to set the trigger is by tagging it to the identity of the spender. Here, recusal would be triggered not by a specified amount of independent expenditures spent, but by the type of entity spending it. The People's Pledge, the contract that Elizabeth Warren and Scott Brown entered to stop third-party

[191] This system would not be perfect. Who contributes money to certain outside groups is not always apparent from the current disclosure regime. While Super PACs have to report their contributors, 501(c)(4) organizations do not. This means Congress may not know who is backing a 501(c)(4) organization's spending. Disbursements spent on issue advocacy by 501(c)(4) organization are also not subject to disclosure. So money spent on communications that do not expressly advocate for the election of a clearly identifiable candidate, are aired outside the 60- and 30-day window of electioneering communications, or appear only on the Internet or social media would not have to be disclosed. As a result, non-profit groups could engage in lots of political spending that would not trigger recusal.

outside spending in their U.S. Senate race in Massachusetts in 2012, applied its prohibitions to what it called "covered organizations," which it defined broadly to include all "individuals, corporations, 527 organization, 501(c) organizations, Super PACs, and national and state party committees" that spent outside funds on the Senate race in Massachusetts in 2012.[192] As Ganesh Sitaraman explains, including national and state party committees in the list of "covered organizations" ensured that only Warren and Brown themselves would run ads on their own behalf. It also closed the loophole that would allow individuals and PACs to donate to party committees, only to witness the party committees run ads during the election.[193] It would be up to each house of Congress to determine its own appropriate recusal trigger.

Finally, there is one more very important question to iron out in all of this: Who should make the ultimate decision about whether a legislator should be recused from voting? To avoid the criticisms that have been leveled at our federal judicial recusal system, it seems obvious that legislative recusal cannot be self-regulating and self-enforcing. It will be difficult for members of the Senate or House to determine if they have a conflict of interest and then not to vote, not least because voting is a core function of their jobs. For this reason, a party other than the lawmaker himself has to determine that there is a conflict and then require recusal to take place.

Constitutionally, each chamber has the power to disallow the votes of its members. Indeed, it turns out a senator's vote has been disallowed in this way before.[194] But for a number of reasons, it would be ill-advised to ask members of the Senate and House to make decisions about whether a colleague's vote should be recused, either beforehand or after the fact. It also seems unwise to allow preemptory strikes to be used for this purpose, as they are to cast aside jurors or to remove judges in some states. Such a system could allow members of one political party to prevent the members of the other party from voting, and it would not only be seen as partisan but might be subject to abuse. There is also the added consideration that a member of Congress who has won election should be understood as having a mandate from those who elected

[192] Sitaraman, *supra* note 7, at 770.

[193] *Id.* at 771.

[194] In 1866, according to *Hinds' Precedents*, "the Senate disallowed a vote given by a senator on a question relating to his own right to a seat; but the House has never had occasion to proceed so far." 5 Hinds' Precedents of the House of Representatives § 5959, at 508–9 (1907). This occurred in relation to a vote cast by John P. Stockton of New Jersey when there was a question of whether he was properly elected and entitled to his seat. The Senate tied on the issue, 21-21, at which point Stockton asked that his name be called and voted to break the tie. Three days later, the propriety of Stockton's vote was questioned and the Senate moved to prevent his vote from being counted. *Id.* § 5959, at 509.

him to participate in the lawmaking process. While legislative recusal may be a powerful tool for confronting the ills of our campaign finance system, it should never be used to prevent officeholders from completing their mandates.[195] Rather, the goal of legislative recusal rules should only be to prevent candidates from becoming beholden to wealthy interests and from having a conflict of interest themselves in advancing the agendas of their well-to-do financiers.

Given this, recusal determinations would work best if left to a neutral third party. In the past, Congress has created several non-partisan institutions to ensure that our nation's legislature functions properly. They include the Office of the Senate Parliamentarian and the Office of the House Parliamentarian, which are charged with interpreting and enforcing the procedural rules of each chamber. They also include institutions such as the Office of Congressional Ethics in the House, which is charged with reviewing allegations of misconduct against a member. Established in 2008, this office describes itself as a "non-partisan, independent entity." It reviews allegations of misconduct and refers matters to the House Committee on Ethics, which has jurisdiction to find violations and impose punishment on House members.

In practice, the chair of each house of Congress should be the one to rule on a recusal motion in response to a point of order submitted by a member of that chamber. The most natural way to implement recusal rules would be to have rulings determined by each chamber's chair.[196] In the Senate, that would be the President *pro tempore*, who in practice always turns to the Parliamentarian of the Senate when a question is presented about the application of the Standing Rules and who does what the Parliamentarian instructs. In the House, the Speaker plays a similar role, also turning to the Parliamentarian for instructions on procedural rulings. For example, the very important "germaneness rule" in the House provides order to the chamber's proceedings by requiring there to be a relationship between any amendment proposed to a bill and the general subject of that bill.[197] Germaneness rulings

[195] Indeed, there is a greater issue lurking here that this chapter does not address: namely, the loss of democratic representation that comes from legislative recusal. In the judicial setting, another judge can always replace a judge who has been recused. But in a legislature, where each member represents a unique geographic constituency, there is no substitute for the recused lawmaker, meaning his constituents may go unpresented in the legislative process. This is a serious issue, but one which this chapter does not address adequately because of space constraints.

[196] This ensures that recusal rulings would not be automatic, and a party spending money to elect a candidate will not know ahead of time whether its candidate will be recused from voting on an issue. This distinguishes the recusal mechanism proposed here from the automatic matching funds scheme in *Arizona Free Enterprise*.

[197] House Rules and Manual, *supra* note 141, § 928 (referencing House Rule XVI, cl. 7).

are always non-partisan, based on precedent, and crucial to the ability of the House of Representatives to function. The Senate functions differently and does not have a germaneness rule, apart from when one is imposed in certain unique circumstances, such as over deliberations concerning the national budget.[198]

It may also be the case that the non-partisan Parliamentarian may not be the last authority on a point of order concerning recusal. There is also a precedent for this. For example, the Congressional Budget and Impoundment Control Act of 1974 explicitly sought to change internal congressional procedures to remedy the obstacles Congress previously faced in making the annual federal budget.[199] Each time there are rulings on budget-related points of order today, the Parliamentarian must decide whether a proposed budget resolution is valid under a budget reconciliation bill and which amendments can be offered (or not) on the floor. For this, the Parliamentarian of the House turns to the House Budget Committee, which issues an opinion on the matter backed up by cost estimates provided by the Congressional Budget Office (CBO), itself a non-partisan institution. In practice, CBO estimates provide the basis for the Parliamentarian's answer to a point of order.[200] In short, there is precedent in Congress to have the Parliamentarian act as a referee and to have that referee look to an outside institution as the basis for its rulings. In the Senate, a parliamentary innovation named after former Senator Robert C. Byrd of West Virginia, called "the Byrd rule," imposes a germaneness requirement on budget reconciliation bills.[201] The Byrd rule is an example of how the budget process has superimposed a set of new rules to ensure non-partisanship and to streamline the complex pre-existing procedures of Congress.[202]

Congress should establish an independent body similar to the CBO, calling it the Office of Legislative Recusal (OLR). The OLR would be strictly non-partisan, function independently, and be staffed by full-time professionals. The OLR would be tasked with monitoring the money spent on behalf of federal candidates, as reported through mandatory disclosure laws to the FEC. It would also have an intake system through which citizens and watchdog groups would be able to report outside spending that they are able to document. Information gathered by the OLR would be used by senators and members of the House to bring points of order regarding mandatory legislative recusal. A point of order

[198] *See* Barbara Sinclair, Unorthodox Lawmaking: New Legislative Processes in the U.S. Congress 128–30 (2017).

[199] Pub. L. No. 93-344; 2 U.S.C. §§ 601–688 (1974).

[200] Sinclair, *supra* note 198, at 130.

[201] *Id.*

[202] *Id. See also* Charles Tiefer, Congressional Practice and Procedure 891–94 (1989).

would request the President *pro tempore* of the Senate or the Speaker of the House to make a determination as to whether a particular member should be recused from voting. Rather than make this decision on his own, the President *pro tempore* of the Senate or the Speaker of the House would turn to each chamber's respective Parliamentarian. Those who receive more support from outside spenders during the course of their federal election campaigns than the Standing Rules of the Senate or the House Rules permit would be requested not to vote on a matter of interest to the spending party, as determined by the professional staff of the OLR. Whenever a point of order regarding outside spending is called, the Parliamentarian would determine whether a member of Congress is allowed to vote. The Parliamentarian's decision would be backed by evidence of outside campaign spending reported to and kept by the OLR. By design, the system would strive to keep partisanship out of all legislative recusal decisions made by the Parliamentarian and the Office of Legislative Recusal.

V. HOW LEGISLATIVE RECUSAL RULES CAN BE ADOPTED

A. *Changing the House Rules*

Now that we know what kind of recusal system would make the most sense, the next question is how to get there. The answer is by amending the existing voting rules in the House and Senate. For recusal to work, the current rules of each chamber have to change, even if the changes are going to be slight. However, the procedures for changing the rules of each house differ, and in the case of the Senate changes are difficult to implement by design. Although there is actually some guidance in the current rules of each chamber on when a member should recuse himself from voting, this guidance applies only in very narrow circumstances. The goal of the changes is to understand those circumstances and to broaden them.

Voting in the House is governed by House Rule III. That rule states that "Every Member shall be present within the Hall of the House during its sittings, unless excused and necessarily prevented, and shall vote on each question put, unless having a direct personal or pecuniary interest in the event of such question."[203] The comments to Rule III explain that the weight of past parliamentary precedent is that there is little authority to deprive a member of the House of his right to vote.[204] Though there were one or two instances

[203] House Rules and Manual, *supra* note 141, § 671 (referencing House Rule III, cl. 1).
[204] *Id.* § 672. *See also* 5 Hinds' Precedents §§ 5937, 5952, 5959, 5966, 5967; 8 Hinds' Precedents § 3072.

in the past when the Speaker made the determination that, because of a conflict of interest, a member should not vote on a question, more recently the Speaker has always ruled that the issue of whether to vote or not is one best left up to the individual member.[205] Indeed, the only place where the rules actually *mandate* recusal happens to be in House Rule XXVII, which requires a member to disclose his negotiations of future employment with a private party and "recuse himself or herself from any matter in which there is a conflict of interest or an appearance of a conflict of interest for that Member..."[206] The rule further requires that the House member "notify the Committee on Ethics of such recusal."[207]

One sensible solution would be to amend Rule III by dividing its first clause into two sub-clauses. One of the new clauses, the new Clause 1(a), would have the same text as Clause 1 does now. A new Clause 1(b) could then be added, with the following text:

> A Member, notwithstanding any other provisions of this rule, may not vote on the floor on any matter with respect to which the independence of judgment of a reasonable person could be materially affected by his commitment to the interests of others, if such interest is created by election expenditures that happen to be spent by an outside individual or group to secure the Member's election.

Similar language has been proposed concerning some of the recusal rules in the states that also aim to combat the influence of outside independent expenditure spending on the actions and judgment of their state legislators.[208] The goal in adding such language is to change the current practice of the House. As mentioned, historically the Speaker has been of the view that a member's vote may not be taken away, but it is worth pointing out that in the 100th Congress, the House did reprimand a member for allowing another person to vote in that member's place, and this lead to a change in the language of Rule III.[209] As such, there is precedent for changing the voting rules. Changing the House's rules also happens to be very easy. It requires the vote of a simple majority: 218 members. In fact, when a new Congress convenes every

[205] 5 Hinds' Precedents §§ 5950, 5951; 8 Hinds' Precedents § 3071.

[206] House Rules and Manual, *supra* note 141, § 1103a (referencing House Rule XXVII, cl. 4).

[207] *Id.*

[208] *See, e.g.*, James Marc Leas, *The "Brave Little State of Vermont" Can Overcome* Citizens United *All By Itself*, 40 Vt. L. Rev. 921, 929–31 (2015) (proposing similar language).

[209] *See* Committee on Standards of Official Conduct, House Ethics Manual, *supra* note 5, at 233–34 (explaining that historically the decision of whether to cast a vote has rested with the individual member).

two years, the new House's rules often change, while the old rules that remain are deemed to be adopted anew.

B. Changing the Senate Rules

In the Senate, by contrast, matters are much more complicated. Though it is controversial, the Senate thinks of itself as a "continuing body," one whose Standing Rules remain in effect until they are changed by a method provided by the rules themselves.[210] The only way to amend the Standing Rules of the Senate is to follow their own provisions for amendment. Those amendment provisions present high hurdles.

Standing Rule XII governs voting in the Senate. It provides that a senator "may decline to vote, in committee or on the floor, on any matter when he believes that his voting on such a matter would be a conflict of interest."[211] Conflict of interests are defined in Standing Rule XXXVII, which among other instructions provides that no senator "shall knowingly use his official position to introduce or aid the progress or passage of legislation, a principal purpose of which is to further only his pecuniary interest, only the pecuniary interest of his immediate family, or only the pecuniary interest of a limited class of persons or enterprises, when he, or his immediate family, or enterprises controlled by them, are members of the affected class."[212] This means that a senator cannot pass legislation that would only help him personally. The Senate Ethics Manual also provides definitions of what constitutes a conflict of interest. It addresses gifts, outside earned income, franking, and the like, but not campaign finance.

One proposal would be to alter Standing Rules XII and XXXVII. The third clause of Standing Rule XII could be changed to state that: "A Member, notwithstanding any other provisions of this rule, may not to vote, on the floor of the Senate, on any matter that in the eyes of a reasonable person would be viewed as a conflict of interest, particularly if that Member's commitment to that interest is created by outside election expenditures that happen to be spent by an outside individual or group to secure the Member's election." Rule XXXVII could then be changed to add, to the phrase that no senator

[210] *See* John C. Roberts, *Gridlock and the Senate Rules*, 88 Notre Dame L. Rev. 2189 (2013) 2205–7 (outlining the standing body argument and critiquing its constitutionality and wisdom); *see also* Aaron-Andrew Bruhl, *Burying the "Continuing Body" Theory of the Senate*, 95 Iowa L. Rev. 1401 (2010) (also criticizing this argument).

[211] Standing Rules of the Senate, Rule XII, para. 3.

[212] Standing Rules of the Senate, Rule XXXVII, para. 4.

"shall knowingly use his official position to introduce or aid the progress or passage of legislation, a principal purpose of which is to further only his pecuniary interest," the following: "A Member may also not vote for the pecuniary interest of an outside individual or group if, in the independence of judgment of a reasonable person, the Member's vote may be viewed as rewarding the independent expenditures of an outside individual or group that spent money to secure the Member's election." Again, the exact language to be used is somewhat beyond the scope of this chapter—it would have to be debated and settled on by the senators themselves. The goal is to present a blueprint.

While a resolution to change the Standing Rules may be adopted by a simple majority of senators present and constituting a quorum, the problem is that it would be subject to debate. When a question is subject to debate, the Standing Rules do not limit how long an issue can be debated or how long individual senators can hold the floor. A motion for unanimous consent can be used to limit the time, but such consent is unlikely to be given, in which case a motion for cloture under Standing Rule XXII would have to be called. If such a cloture motion happens to be successful, debate would be limited to 30 hours. In most cases, three-fifths of the full membership of the Senate, or 60 senators, have to vote to invoke cloture, but for changes to the Standing Rules cloture must be invoked by two-thirds of senators voting and there must also be a quorum present. In other words, the votes of 67 senators would be required.[213]

There are other obstacles to overcome as well. For example, the Senate can normally take up measures for consideration in one of two ways: by unanimous consent or by agreeing on a motion to proceed. Under the circumstances, a motion to proceed would likely be necessary. But the motion to proceed is also itself debatable and can also be filibustered. So cloture would have to be invoked on the motion to proceed first. To change the Standing Rules, as Richard Beth explains, "it might become necessary to obtain a (two-third supermajority) vote to invoke cloture on the motion to proceed to consider a rules change resolution in order to reach a (simply majority) vote on that motion, and then to invoke cloture again (by a two-third supermajority) to limit debate on the resolution itself (which can be adopted by a simple majority)."[214]

If this sounds daunting, there is more. A motion to proceed can be taken up only after it has been on the Calendar of General Orders for one "legislative day." This means the Senate has to adjourn for at least a day before the motion can be considered.[215] Moreover, a resolution reaches the Calendar of General

[213] *See* Christopher M. Davis, Cong. Res. Serv., No. 98-425, Invoking Cloture in the Senate 1 (Apr. 6, 2017); Richard S. Beth, Cong. Res. Serv., No. R42929, Procedures for Considering Changes to Senate Rules (Jan. 22, 2013).

[214] *Id.* at 4–5.

[215] *Id* at 5.

Orders only after it has been reported back from a committee, but Senate committees are not required to report on any measure referred to them for consideration.[216] On the other hand, bringing a simple resolution to the floor though an alternative procedure without going through the committee system involves its own difficulties. For example, the Senate may act on a simple motion by immediate consideration, but again only with unanimous consent.[217] If any senator objects, the motion will be "laid over" for consideration on another legislative day, and on that day it can only be considered during a two-hour period known as the "morning hour."[218] Even then, the resolution must wait until the Senate finishes considering other routine business during the morning hour, and during that period the chamber must first consider resolutions that have been awaiting morning hour consideration the longest. While the Senate may consider the resolution if time remains in this two-hour period, the simple resolution will be placed on the Calendar of General Orders if consideration happens not to be completed.[219] From there, the same supermajority requirements as above apply.

From this discussion, it is evident that any changes to the Standing Rules require 67 votes, not to mention a committee to vote in favor of the proposed changes and to send them to the Senate floor. Even if the votes to pass changes to the Standing Rules are present, there are numerous delays to be expected. Still, obtaining 67 votes for campaign finance reform is much easier than obtaining the votes of 60 senators, 218 members of the House, and the President—whose blessings all are needed for similar reforms to be enacted by statute—and then subjecting their legislation to judicial review. The 67 votes needed to make the proposal outlined here a reality do not exist in today's Senate, but there may come a day when that will change. If reformers have learned anything from their past efforts, it is that changes to our nation's campaign finance system follow on the heels of scandal.[220] Although Congress today is hostile to campaign finance reform, there will come a time, following a future scandal, when 67 senators may see things differently. And when that day arrives, senators will benefit from knowing the powerful ways in which the procedural rules of their chamber can be used to regulate outside campaign spending, free from interference by the Supreme Court.

[216] *Id.*

[217] *Id.*

[218] *Id.* at 5–6.

[219] *Id.*

[220] *See* Robert E. Mutch, Buying the Vote: A History of Campaign Finance Reform 2–11 (2014) (arguing that most significant campaign finance reforms in the United States have come as a response to a past scandal or crisis).

13

Contributions and Corruption: Restoring Aggregate Limits in the States

Michael D. Gilbert*

Since 1972, when President Nixon accepted illegal bags of cash and planted Watergate's seeds, Congress has systematically erected barriers to spending money on elections. Since 2005, when John Roberts assumed the Chief Justiceship, the Supreme Court has methodically chopped them down. The most recent cut came in a case called *McCutcheon v. Federal Election Commission*, which involved campaign contributions.[1] According to the Supreme Court, there is only one justification for limiting such contributions: to prevent corruption and its appearance.[2] For decades legislators have limited campaign contributions on that basis. Most of their effort, and nearly all scholarship, has focused on a particular kind of contribution limit called a base limit. *McCutcheon*, however, involved a different kind of restriction called an aggregate limit. That case and its subject matter are under-theorized, and a close look reveals an open road to reducing political corruption.

Base contribution limits cap the amount one can give to an individual candidate or to an individual committee or party. Aggregate limits cap what one can give to *all* candidates and groups. To illustrate, in 2013 one could give up to $5,200 to an individual candidate (the base limit) and $48,600 to all candidates (the aggregate limit) in a single, federal election cycle.[3] In *McCutcheon*, a plurality opinion authored by the Chief Justice, the Court struck down the federal aggregate limits. The plurality reasoned that such limits burden First Amendment rights and lack justification because they fail to prevent corruption or its appearance.

* Michael D. Gilbert is Sullivan & Cromwell Professor of Law at the University of Virginia School of Law. He thanks Emily Reeder for assistance with this chapter, which draws on their prior work.

1 McCutcheon v. FEC, 134 S. Ct. 1434 (2014).

2 See *id.* at 1441–42.

3 See *id.* at 1442–43.

The first part of the opinion, about burdening rights, may well ring true, but the second part falls short. Aggregate limits *must* prevent corruption, at least to some degree. Explaining why undercuts *McCutcheon*'s logic, but that is not the main purpose of what follows. The objectives instead are twofold. First, this chapter develops a richer understanding of the relationship between contributions (in all forms) and corruption, and second, it extracts a prescription: states and localities should embrace aggregate contribution limits. *McCutcheon* only foreclosed aggregate limits at the federal level. They remain available in many or even all cities and states,[4] and they can play a key role in combatting corruption.

I. CONTRIBUTION LIMITS AND *MCCUTCHEON*

The Federal Election Campaign Act (FECA) distinguished two forms of political spending, expenditures and contributions.[5] When a person spends money independently of a campaign to promote or oppose a candidate, she makes an expenditure.[6] When a person gives money directly to a candidate or to a political committee that channels money to candidates, she makes a contribution. To demonstrate, imagine a TV watcher inspired by the Democratic or Republican National Convention. When she logs on to a campaign's website and gives $20 (or $2,000), she makes a contribution.

FECA limited contributions in various ways. The base limit capped the amount one could contribute to a given candidate—at the time of the 1974 statute this was $1,000.[7] The aggregate limit capped the total amount one could contribute to candidates and political committees, like PACs and national party committees, at $25,000.[8]

In *Buckley v. Valeo*, the Supreme Court considered the constitutionality of FECA's contribution limits. The Court concluded that contributions serve as a symbolic expression of political preferences and a means of political association. Thus, limits on contributions burden First Amendment rights. However, the Court upheld the base limits at issue in *Buckley* on the ground that the government has an interest in combatting *quid pro quo* corruption—for example,

4 Many states and at least one city, Los Angeles, have or have had aggregate contribution limits.

5 For a discussion of the Act, see *Buckley v. Valeo*, 424 U.S. 1, 23–24, 39–40 (1976).

6 Coordinated expenditures, such as expenditures on a television ad made in consultation with the candidate it supports, count as contributions. *See, e.g.*, *Buckley*, 424 U.S. at 78. For a discussion of coordination, see Michael D. Gilbert & Brian Barnes, *The Coordination Fallacy*, 43 FLA. ST. U. L. REV. 399 (2016).

7 *Buckley*, 424 U.S. at 13.

8 *Id.*

dollars for votes—and that contribution limits serve that purpose. The Court also upheld aggregate contribution limits, though it spent only a few sentences explaining its reasoning on this issue:

> The overall $25,000 ceiling does impose an ultimate restriction upon the number of candidates and committees with whom an individual may associate … But this quite modest restraint upon protected political activity serves to prevent evasion of the $1,000 limitation by a person who might otherwise contribute massive amounts of money to a particular candidate through the use of unearmarked contributions to political committees likely to contribute to that candidate, or huge contributions to the candidate's political party.[9]

This is the so-called anticircumvention rationale.[10] If a contributor circumvents the base limit, directing more than $1,000 to an individual candidate, the aggregate limit provides a backstop. It places an upper limit on the flow of money from one contributor to one candidate.

By the time of the 2014 election, Congress had raised contribution limits. The base limit stood at $2,600 per election, meaning one could contribute a maximum of $5,200 to a candidate who ran in primary and general elections. The aggregate limit equaled $48,600 for contributions to candidates and $74,600 for contributions to other political committees. In total, an individual could contribute $123,200 to candidate and noncandidate committees during each two-year election cycle.[11]

Against this backdrop the Supreme Court decided *McCutcheon*. The case arose during the 2011–12 election season, when Shaun McCutcheon made contributions to 16 candidates totaling $33,088.[12] He wanted to make 12 additional contributions of $1,776 each.[13] McCutcheon also contributed $27,329 to non-candidate political committees and wanted to contribute additional money to others.[14] The aggregate limits forbade those additional contributions. Looking ahead, McCutcheon claimed that the aggregate limits would prevent him from contributing as much as he wished during the next election.[15]

9 *Id.* at 38.

10 "The aggregate limit, on the other hand, was upheld as an anticircumvention measure." *McCutcheon*, 134 S. Ct. at 1447.

11 *See id.* at 1443.

12 *Id.*

13 *Id.*

14 *Id.*

15 McCutcheon wanted to contribute at least $60,000 to various candidates and $75,000 to non-candidate political committees in the 2013–2014 election cycle. *Id.*

McCutcheon did not challenge the base limits, claiming only that the aggregate limits violated his First Amendment rights.

As in *Buckley*, the Court agreed that aggregate limits burden contributors' rights of political speech and association. Turning to the state's defense, the Court accepted that the government has an interest in preventing *quid pro quo* corruption and the appearance thereof. However, the plurality perceived a "substantial mismatch" between this objective and "the means selected to achieve it."[16] In other words, the plurality doubted that the aggregate limit prevented much corruption. This doubt rested on two arguments. First, the Court reasoned that "Congress's selection of a $5,200 base limit indicates its belief that contributions of that amount or less do not create a cognizable risk of corruption."[17] As long as one complies with the base limits, channeling no more than the limit of $5,200 to any one candidate, corruption is not a worry. Second, the plurality argued that "targeted anticircumvention measures" adopted since *Buckley* ensure compliance with the base limits.[18] In short, contributors do not and cannot channel more than $5,200 to a candidate. Thus, in the Court's view, the aggregate limits represented a "prophylaxis-upon-prophylaxis approach" that burdened speech without preventing corruption, and the Court struck them down.[19]

II. CONTRIBUTIONS AND CORRUPTION

There is much to say about *McCutcheon*, but consider first the big picture. Corruption, including the *quid pro quo* variety, harms society.[20] This explains the drive for most campaign finance regulations. To say that corruption harms, however, does not imply that it always causes equal harm. Imagine legislators accepting cash in exchange for their votes on a $20 billion defense contract. If the contract buys unnecessary or flawed equipment, the corruption causes great harm. The money could have gone to schools or infrastructure, or it could have been left in taxpayers' pockets. If, on the other hand, the contract buys vital equipment, albeit at a slightly inflated price, the corruption causes

[16] *Id.* at 1446.

[17] *Id.* at 1452.

[18] *Id.* at 1446. For example, "an antiproliferation rule prohibiting donors from creating or controlling multiple affiliated political committees" was enacted in 1976. *See id.* at 1438. This "forecloses what would otherwise be a particularly easy and effective means of circumventing the limits on contributions to any particular political committee." *Id.* at 1447 (internal quotation marks omitted).

[19] *Id.* at 1458.

[20] On the many variants of corruption, see Yasmin Dawood, *Classifying Corruption*, 9 DUKE J. CONST. L. & PUB. POL'Y 103 (2014).

relatively little harm. If a politician hires a well-qualified staffer whose resume only surfaced from the pile because of a family connection, little harm results. If a regulator accepts a payment to overlook poison in the water, society may suffer greatly. As these examples show, the costs of corruption depend on the magnitude of corrupt acts.

Now consider frequency. Corruption can happen constantly, as when border patrol demands a bribe for every crossing, or bureaucrats expect cash for every birth certificate they issue. Or it can happen rarely. Only one person in recent decades, then-Governor Rod Blagojevich, tried to extract favors for an appointment to the U.S. Senate.[21]

Together the magnitude and frequency of corruption determine its social cost. If corrupt acts individually cause great harm but happen rarely, the total costs of corruption may be small. If each corrupt act causes little harm but such acts happen routinely, total costs may be large. No lawmaker, however benevolent and determined, can eliminate corruption. The only feasible goal is to minimize the harm that flows from it, and finding that low point requires attention to both magnitude and frequency.

Now relate these ideas to campaign contributions. In general, base limits should affect the magnitude of corruption: the more a contributor can give, the more he can get in return and the greater the harm to the public. In general, aggregate limits should affect the frequency of corruption: the more politicians a contributor can support, the more favors he can buy. Thus, one may hypothesize that the combination of low base limits and no aggregate limits would yield a political system featuring many minor corrupt acts. Conversely, high base limits and low aggregate limits would yield occasional corrupt acts, each one major (or at least major on average). If the objective is to minimize the social harm from corruption, then some combination of base and aggregate limits, not the former alone, is optimal.

Though short and abstract, this discussion fills a void. Previously, anti-circumvention offered the sole rationale for aggregate contribution limits, and it involves magnitude only (the more one can convey to a candidate beyond the base limit, the bigger the favor one can buy). Now we see that aggregate limits have another justification: they can limit corruption by reducing its frequency.

The Supreme Court has never reasoned like this, and one might think that a problem. Before judges draw conclusions about contributions and

[21] Monica Davey, *Blagojevich Sentenced to 14 Years in Prison*, N.Y. Times (Dec. 8, 2011). To be precise, only one person in recent decades *got caught* trying to trade favors for a Senate seat.

corruption—conclusions based on logic, by the way, not evidence[22]—perhaps they should try to get the logic straight. On the other hand, this notion of frequency has no bite, at least in *McCutcheon*, because of the plurality's key conclusion: contributions within base limits create no "cognizable risk of corruption."[23] If individual, lawful contributions do not buy favors, then contributions to one, 100, or 1,000 candidates yield the same result: zero corruption. The next section challenges this logic.

III. SMALL-DOLLAR CORRUPTION

Suppose a buyer and seller negotiate over a car. The price will depend on the value they place on it. If the buyer values it highly, perhaps because he covets the paint job, the seller can demand a high price. Likewise, if the seller values it highly—she inherited the car from a favorite uncle—she will demand a high price. To generalize, the price of a good or service depends on the parties' go-it-alone values, that is, their respective benefits from *not* transacting. If the seller loves the car such that the benefit of keeping it instead of transacting with the seller is high, then she will demand a lot, and vice versa.

These ideas are not limited to the market for cars. They apply to exchanges involving toothpaste, tractors, and, importantly, political favors. Politicians spend a lot of time on legislation: drafting, debating, amending, and voting. Like a seller who loves her car, politicians sometimes love legislating, and when they do corruption costs a lot. A congressman of deep conviction who opposes the Affordable Care Act will relish voting against it. Buying his vote on that Act would cost an enormous sum. Likewise, a congresswoman who made an election promise to support the Act would demand a high price to change her mind.

In addition to legislating, politicians oversee the federal bureaucracy, make speeches, meet with business and community leaders, give tours to constituents, attend charity events, and engage in other activities. In all settings the same ideas apply. A politician who served in the armed forces may speak at a veterans' event every Memorial Day, no matter the other demands on her time, and getting her to change course would cost a fortune.

But what if politicians do not place a high value on staying the course? What if the benefit of not transacting—acting non-corruptly—is low? An

[22] The dissent in *McCutcheon* writes, "In the past, when evaluating the constitutionality of campaign finance restrictions, we have typically relied upon an evidentiary record amassed below." The dissent then criticizes the Court for failing to remand this case "for the further evidentiary development which has not yet taken place." *McCutcheon*, 134 S. Ct. at 1479–80.

[23] *Id.* at 1452.

incumbent congresswoman in a close race may not care about the search for a new staffer. She may tune in to a hearing involving the Environmental Protection Agency but ignore the Defense Logistics Agency. A congressman from Alaska may care very little about public works in the Gulf of Mexico. In cases like these, prices fall. Corruption is cheap.

Consider the application of these ideas to contribution limits. At the time of *McCutcheon*, base limits stood at $5,200 per election cycle. Buying a vote on the Affordable Care Act would cost a lot more than $5,200, so lawful contributions would be insufficient for that corrupt deal. One might need a briefcase full of cash. But what about buying an internship in the embattled congresswoman's office? Or buying a call from her chief of staff to the Defense Logistics Agency? How about getting Alaska's representative to speak against the public works plan in the Gulf? The owner of a valueless car will sell it for a song, and politicians with power over issues they do not care about will sell influence at a discount. Such influence can be bought for $5,200 or less. Simply put, lawful contributions can buy corruption.[24]

Evidence abounds. Judge James Hesterly pled guilty to awarding a $70,000 government contract in exchange for a $4,000 campaign contribution.[25] Judge Mike Maggio reduced the judgment against a nursing home from $5.2 million to $1 million after receiving campaign contributions from stockholders and industry lobbyists. He pled guilty to federal bribery charges.[26] One congressman was scrutinized for procuring $6 million in government contracts for a firm whose executives contributed $17,500 to his campaign.[27] Another congressman switched positions on "billboard owners' compensation" after receiving contributions of $12,000 from the billboard industry.[28] Former Congressman Michael Barnes recounts conversations with lobbyists who would remind him about the "next round of checks" before asking if he had been "following" an upcoming bill.[29] The examples keep going.[30]

The upshot of all this is clear: the *McCutcheon* plurality erred in concluding that contributions within base limits do not raise a "cognizable risk of

[24] In a recent, valuable article, Usha Rodrigues makes a similar point. *See* Usha Rodrigues, *The Price of Corruption*, 31 J.L. & Pol. 45, 49–50 (2015). For a discussion of how the point here differs from hers, see Michael D. Gilbert & Emily Reeder, *Aggregate Corruption*, 104 Ky. L.J. 651, 658 n. 53 (2016).

[25] Assoc. Press, *Former County Judge Pleads Guilty to Bribery Charge* (June 16, 2014).

[26] Benjamin Hardy & Max Brantley, *Mike Maggio Pleads Guilty to Federal Bribery Charge*, Ark. Times (Jan. 8, 2015).

[27] Matthew Mosk, *Wicker's Earmark Elicits Criticism*, Wash. Post (Jan. 16, 2008).

[28] Phillip Stern, The Best Congress Money Can Buy 151 (1988).

[29] *Id.* at 101.

[30] For more examples, see Gilbert & Reeder, *supra* note 24, at 658–59.

corruption."[31] Of course they do. Occasionally it will be big-dollar corruption, meaning the cost to society is high, but often it will be small-dollar corruption. When a congresswoman sells a job in her office or ignores a misstep by a small agency, society does not suffer terribly, it suffers a tad. But tads add up, especially without aggregate limits in place. Before *McCutcheon*, every donor of means could spend $48,600 on small-dollar corruption per federal election cycle.[32] Now those donors can spend millions.

Perhaps the prior paragraph, with its assertion that the plurality erred, treats the Court unfairly. *McCutcheon* did not actually state that lawful contributions do not cause corruption, it stated that "Congress's selection of a $5,200 base limit indicates *its belief* that contributions of that amount or less do not create a cognizable risk of corruption."[33] So the fault lies with Congress, not the Court. But one can push back. How exactly do the Justices know what Congress believes? They provide no answer, not even a citation. They simply assume that Congress—the same Congress they routinely accuse of self-dealing when it comes to campaign finance law[34]—benevolently set the base limit at the corruption-eliminating level. Would they draw the same conclusion if the base limit were set at $10,000? Or $1 million? I will return to this issue, but for now note that, whatever its source, the error persists. Lawful contributions *do* cause corruption, at least some of the time. Common sense and a raft of evidence prove it.

IV. CIRCUMVENTION AND SPILLOVER

Recall that *McCutcheon* rests on two conclusions: contributions within base limits do not cause corruption, and "targeted anticircumvention measures"[35] ensure compliance with base limits. The last section addressed the former; now consider the latter. The measures the Justices have in mind include

[31] *McCutcheon*, 134 S. Ct. at 1452.

[32] This assumes, unrealistically, that only contributions to candidates, and not to noncandidate committees and parties, can buy corrupt favors.

[33] *McCutcheon*, 134 S. Ct. at 1452 (emphasis added).

[34] For example, the Court noted in *Randall v. Sorrell*, 548 U.S. 230, 247–48 (2006), that Congress may be incentivized to set contribution limits low to magnify the benefits of incumbency. In *McCutcheon*, 134 S. Ct. at 1441–42, the plurality wrote that "those who govern should be the *last* people to help decide who *should* govern."

[35] *McCutcheon*, 134 S. Ct. at 1446. For example, "an antiproliferation rule prohibiting donors from creating or controlling multiple affiliated political committees" was enacted in 1976. *See id.* at 1438. This "forecloses what would otherwise be a particularly easy and effective means of circumventing the limits on contributions to any particular political committee." *Id.* at 1447 (internal quotation marks omitted).

antiproliferation rules, broad regulations on earmarking, and so on. These somewhat technical provisions may do what the Court says, though one wonders.[36] Regardless, another circumvention channel remains open.

Most contributions involve money, like checks at fundraisers, and the Supreme Court equates the two.[37] However, contributions can also take non-monetary forms. Anything of value given to a candidate to influence a federal election counts as a contribution. Thus, one can make a contribution by donating office furniture, offering discounted advertising, or renting a bus at below-market rates.[38] In short, the law limits the conveyance of *value*, of which money is one form.

Focusing on value casts new light on circumvention. Consider an example: a donor gives $5,200 to the Speaker of the House in Congress and the same to a member of the Speaker's party in a tight election with control of the House on the line. The checks do not change, but the value they convey does. If the candidate wins, the Speaker's power and prestige soar, thanks in part to the donor. If the candidate loses, the Speaker fizzles. This example involves high stakes, but the same idea applies elsewhere. Suppose the donor supports a party leader and a half-dozen members of the leader's party, some in close races and others not. Regardless of the outcomes of the races, the donor has increased (at least probabilistically) the leader's power. The leader's debt exceeds the face value of the checks she received. These ideas are not hypothetical. Contributions from one Congressperson to another jumped in recent decades, driven by an "increased awareness among Members of how much is at stake for them in contested elections outside their districts."[39] Contributions to leadership PACs, which are often controlled by sitting members of Congress, often go to supporting those members' allies.

36 The *McCutcheon* dissent walks through several of the ways these limits could potentially be circumvented. *See id.* at 1472–76.

37 In *McCutcheon*, the plurality wrote that "base limits … restrict how much *money* a donor may contribute to any particular candidate." *Id.* at 1442 (emphasis added). Around 30 years earlier, the Court wrote, "Elected officials are influenced to act contrary to their obligations of office by … infusions of *money* into their campaigns." FEC v. Nat'l Conservative Political Action Comm., 470 U.S. 480, 497 (1985).

38 For example, Kentucky Senate hopeful Alison Lundergan Grimes obtained her campaign bus below the market rate. *See* Manu Raju, *The Grimes Family Discount*, POLITICO (Aug. 19, 2014).

39 Anne Bedlington & Michael J. Malbin, *The Party as An Extended Network: Members Giving to Each Other and Their Parties*, *in* THE ELECTION AFTER REFORM: THE BIPARTISAN CAMPAIGN REFORM ACT MEETS POLITICS 121, 127 (Michael Malbin ed., 2003). The Democratic and Republican parties mandate inter-party giving by their members. They require contributions to campaign committees funding party incumbents and challengers. *See, e.g.*, Charles Lewis, *Himes Puts the Squeeze on Fellow Democrats*, NEWS TIMES (Nov. 24, 2013); Alex Isenstadt & Jake Sherman, *House GOP Cracks Down on Dues*, POLITICO (July 11, 2014).

Consider other settings where this idea applies. John McCain and Joe Lieberman, who sat on opposite sides of the Senate, were friends for years and members of the Gang of 14, which negotiated a compromise on judicial nominations.[40] Governor Bill Haslam of Tennessee offered financial support to incumbent Republicans facing primary challenges, saying "it does matter who serves, and even within your own party, there are some folks who have worked with us a lot better than others."[41] The President benefits when agreeable legislators, regardless of party, remain in office.

To generalize from these examples, lawmakers usually cannot act alone, and thus they benefit when surrounded by others with whom they can compromise and form consensus. This means a contributor can convey value to a lawmaker by supporting the lawmaker—*or* her allies.[42] Stated another way, contributions come with a spillover. They directly benefit the recipient, and they indirectly benefit the recipient's allies.[43]

How substantial is the spillover effect? The answer depends, of course, but consider some possibilities. Suppose a donor gives a senator and her five tepid allies $2,600 apiece. Suppose the value of a contribution to the recipient equals its size, so the senator and the others each get $2,600 in value directly. Suppose the contribution to the senator provides an indirect benefit of $100 to each of those five allies. The donor spent $15,600 and conveyed $16,100 in value, so the spillover equals $500. But perhaps this math is incomplete. If the

[40] For example, Scott Horsley details McCain's legacy of bipartisan work, including the "Gang of 14" compromise, and Mark Leibovich discusses McCain's longtime friendship with Lieberman. *See* Scott Horsley, *Retracing John McCain's Bipartisan Roots*, NAT'L PUB. RADIO (Apr. 2, 2008); Mark Leibovich, *How John McCain Turned His Clichés Into Meaning*, N.Y. TIMES MAG. (Dec. 18, 2013).

[41] Tom Humphrey, *Haslam PAC Takes Sides in GOP Legislative Primaries (A Look at Fundraising in Some Races)*, KNOXVILLE NEWS SENTINEL (July 13, 2014).

[42] The Supreme Court agrees. In *McCutcheon*, the plurality wrote, "[o]f course a candidate would be pleased with a donor who contributed not only to the candidate himself, but also to other candidates from the same party, to party committees, and to PACs supporting the party ... [w]hen donors furnish widely distributed support within all applicable base limits, all members of the party or supporters of the cause may benefit, and the leaders of the party or cause may feel particular gratitude." *McCutcheon*, 134 S. Ct. at 1461.

[43] In recent, valuable work, Michael Kang makes a related point, arguing that candidates "care not simply whether they individually receive any particular contribution, but whether a contribution, wherever it is formally received, benefits the coordinated party effort." *See* Michael Kang, *Party-Based Corruption and* McCutcheon v. FEC, 108 NW. U. L. REV. ONLINE 240, 252 (2014). Kang also criticizes the traditional "dyadic framework" that envisions corrupt "individual contributors and individual officeholders pairing off in isolation from the rest of their political world." *See* Michael Kang, *The Brave New World of Party Campaign Finance Law*, 101 CORNELL L. REV. 531, 548–49 (2016) [hereinafter Kang, *Brave New World*]. For a discussion of how the ideas in this chapter relate to Kang's, see Gilbert & Reeder, *supra* note 24, at 663 n. 77.

contribution to the senator helps her allies, one may assume the contributions to those allies help the senator. If each of the six contributions conveys $2,600 in value directly (to the recipient) and $500 indirectly (to the allies), then the donor spent $15,600 and conveyed $18,600 in value. The spillover equals $3,000.

Now suppose the senator is not so lonesome. Like Daniel Inouye and Robert Byrd, she has served in Congress for decades, occupied powerful leadership roles, and been an effective ally to members of both chambers. She owes favors to many colleagues that will become undeliverable if she loses. Now a contribution conveys $2,600 to the senator, $1,000 to her 25 closest allies, $500 to another 25 compatriots, and $100 to each of 250 members of the rank-and-file. The contributor spent $2,600 and conveyed $65,100 in value. The donor made *one* contribution, albeit to a powerful politician. Suppose the donor makes 200 contributions to candidates and additional contributions to PACs and party committees. The spillover effect grows exponentially.

Spillover can engender small-dollar corruption. The donor in the last example indirectly conveyed value to a lot of politicians, and they may reciprocate with a lot of small favors. But it can engender large-dollar, or at least larg*er*-dollar, corruption as well. A donor who supports dozens or hundreds of members of Congress may convey $2,600 directly to each recipient and, say, $4,000 indirectly. Now dozens or hundreds of members owe the donor $6,600 apiece. That sum might not buy a lot of votes,[44] but it might buy government contracts.[45]

Spillovers may multiply the value of contributions, but value alone does not prompt corruption: one also needs information. *Quid pro quo* corruption requires mutual favors, or at least the expectation of them.[46] The politician must do something *in exchange* for a benefit. If a corrupt politician knows that a person conveyed a benefit to her, perhaps by contributing directly to her campaign, she will do a favor in return. Conversely, if the politician does not know that a person helped, then she will not do a favor—even if the person in fact helped.[47] Politicians, one might argue, cannot track spillovers, so spillovers cannot corrupt.

44 *But see* STERN, *supra* note 28, at 151 (describing how a congressman switched positions on a "billboard owners compensation" law after receiving lawful contributions of only about $12,000).

45 *See* Assoc. Press, *supra* note 25.

46 Federal law prohibits corrupt exchanges and also attempts at corrupt exchanges, meaning the mere expectation or offer of a favor may violate the statute. *See* 18 U.S.C. § 201(b) (2012).

47 This idea underlies an important book that argues that masking contributions, so candidates do not know who has and has not contributed to their campaigns, would reduce corruption. *See* BRUCE ACKERMAN & IAN AYERS, VOTING WITH DOLLARS: A NEW PARADIGM FOR CAMPAIGN FINANCE (2002).

This argument is weak. At least three mechanisms help politicians track spillovers: parties, joint fundraising committees, and disclosure requirements. Regarding the first, parties coordinate fundraising and disbursements, with party leaders keeping an eye on who gave to whom and when. In exchange for support to the party, those leaders demand favors from members, even if those members did not benefit directly. As Michael Kang writes:

> The major parties centralize campaign finance for their wealthiest supporters and their candidates and officeholders. The parties carefully cultivate relationships…, maintain a legal and administrative infrastructure for campaign finance, and distribute financial support efficiently across a wide slate of candidates… [P]arties serve as a centralizing institution—a form of one-stop political shopping—through which their supporters know that they will have access to party officeholders and their financial contributions will be directed toward the party cause with the greatest expertise and effectiveness. For wealthy supporters willing to donate six-figure amounts in election cycle after election cycle, the parties are essential brokers …[48]

Joint fundraising committees (JFCs) offer another mechanism for tracking spillovers. JFCs consolidate fundraising for multiple candidates and committees.[49] Donors can write a single check to a JFC, sometimes for over one million dollars,[50] that gets disbursed in lawful increments to different candidates and committees. JFCs make spillovers transparent. To demonstrate, the "Boehner for Speaker" JFC disbursed funds to then-Speaker of the House John Boehner, 80 of his fellow Republican candidates, and the National Republican Congressional Committee.[51] Surely Boehner noticed

48 *See* Kang, *Brave New World*, *supra* note 43, at 561 ("Party candidates and officeholders, particularly the party leadership invested with the party's collective welfare, … track high-level contributors' financial support and try to reciprocate …"); *see also* Richard Briffault, *Soft Money Reform and the Constitution*, 1 ELECTION L.J. 343, 386 (2002) (noting the corruption danger is "not so much that the parties will act as conduits … but rather that the process of party fundraising will give large donors special relationships with the party's fundraisers—who are also the leaders of the party—in government").

49 FEDERAL ELECTION COMMISSION, CAMPAIGN GUIDES FOR NONCONNECTED COMMITTEES (2008) and FEDERAL ELECTION COMMISSION, SCHEDULE A ITEMIZED RECEIPTS, BOEHNER FOR SPEAKER COMMITTEE: MR. PAUL SINGER (Apr. 15, 2015) [hereinafter FEDERAL ELECTION COMMISSION, MR. PAUL SINGER].

50 Following the *McCutcheon* decision, the top tier for the RNC soared to $1.34 million per couple, and $1.6 million per couple on the Democratic side. Matea Gold & Tom Hamburger, *Political Parties Go After Million-Dollar Donors in Wake of Looser Rules*, WASH. POST (Sept. 19, 2015).

51 2014 *Financial Summary of Boehner for Speaker*, CENTER FOR RESPONSIVE POLITICS (2014). One of the largest beneficiaries of "Boehner for Speaker" JFC was the Freedom Project ($1,677,360), which supported over 100 congressional candidates and 16 Senate Republicans.

when Paul Singer contributed over $1 million to the JFC, even though Boehner himself received only $5,400 of that sum.[52] In 2014, the Boehner for Speaker Committee received $35,382,857 in contributions.[53]

Finally, disclosure helps politicians keep tabs on spillovers. At the federal level and in many states, law requires disclosure of contributions: who gave what to whom.[54] The government makes this information public, and actors like the Center for Responsive Politics organize and publicize it.[55] If a donor asks for a favor, and if a politician wonders if the donor deserves it, that politician can simply consult disclosure records. In minutes she will know how many allies that donor has supported and to what degree. Foreseeing doubt by the politician, the donor might start his pitch by pointing to disclosure records, which provide credible information on the many favors, direct and indirect, that he has done.[56]

If politicians can track spillovers, then spillovers can cause corruption, and this implicates *McCutcheon*. The plurality concluded that law prevents circumvention of base limits. Even if correct, that analysis focuses only on formal circumvention. Informal circumvention, or spillover, persists. Thus, the plurality erred in concluding that aggregate limits represent a "prophylaxis-upon-prophylaxis approach." They do important, independent work by stifling circumvention. To demonstrate concretely, suppose spillover equals 20 percent of a contribution's face value, so a contribution of $2,000 conveys $2,400 in total value to the recipient and allies. Before *McCutcheon*, one could contribute $123,200 in an election cycle, conveying $147,840 in total value. After *McCutcheon*, one can contribute $3.6 million in an election cycle,[57] conveying $4.3 million in total value.

V. THE PRESCRIPTION: EMBRACE AGGREGATE LIMITS

The last two sections uncovered problems with *McCutcheon*, but not with an eye to critique. The Court made its decision, and second-guessing is not the objective.

2014 *Summary of Contributions to Federal Candidates for Freedom Project*, CENTER FOR RESPONSIVE POLITICS (2014).

52 *See* FEDERAL ELECTION COMMISSION, MR. PAUL SINGER, *supra* note 49.

53 2014 *Financial Summary of Boehner for Speaker*, *supra* note 51.

54 For background on disclosure laws, see Michael D. Gilbert, *Campaign Finance Disclosure and the Information Takeoff*, 98 IOWA L. REV. 1847, 1854–58 (2013).

55 *See, e.g.*, opensecrets.org.

56 These arguments demonstrate a general claim that I have developed in separate work. *See* Michael D. Gilbert & Benjamin F. Aiken, *Disclosure and Corruption*, 14 ELECTION L.J. 148 (2015) (explaining how disclosure can facilitate corruption); Michael D. Gilbert, *Transparency and Corruption: A General Analysis*, U. CHI. LEGAL F. (forthcoming 2018) (same).

57 *McCutcheon*, 134 S. Ct. at 1473 (Breyer, J., dissenting).

Instead, this chapter aims to showcase the benefits of aggregate limits. Scholars and activists paid scant attention to aggregate limits before *McCutcheon*, and the Federal Election Commission hardly enforced them.[58] But such limits can stifle a lot of corruption. By restricting what one can give, they limit the number of favors—large or small, devastating to society or just pesky—that one can buy. Likewise, they dampen spillover. By capping the number of candidates one can support, they limit the favors that accrue to those candidates' allies. The informal ledgers of who owes what to whom shorten. Small-dollar corruption, and maybe the big-dollar stuff too, declines. This holds regardless of the "targeted measures" celebrated by the Court. Even if no formal circumvention of base limits takes place, aggregate limits reduce corruption.

Thanks to *McCutcheon*, these virtues are lost at the federal level, but what about in the states? Some believe the Supreme Court has foreclosed aggregate limits across the board. Following the opinion, regulators in Connecticut, Massachusetts, and elsewhere announced that they would not enforce their state-level aggregate limits.[59] But does *McCutcheon* compel that result? The case involves federal law, and the opinion itself says nothing about state law. The categorical statement in *Citizens United*—"independent expenditures … do not give rise to corruption"—has clear implications for states, but *McCutcheon* has no analogue, no declaration like, "aggregate limits do not prevent corruption or circumvention." Instead, the rationale is context-specific.

Consider the language and logic of the opinion. In explaining why *Buckley*'s holding on aggregate limits in FECA did not control, the plurality wrote:

> We are now asked to address appellants' direct challenge to the aggregate limits in place under [the Bipartisan Campaign Reform Act, or BCRA]. BCRA is a different statutory regime, and the aggregate limits it imposes operate against a distinct legal backdrop… We are confronted with a different statute and different legal arguments, at a different point in the development of campaign finance regulation.[60]

The plurality then rejected the anti-circumvention interest, not because aggregate limits *never* prevent circumvention but because "various statutes and regulations currently in effect"—all federal, and applicable only to federal

[58] *See* Lee Drutman, *Did Almost 600 Donors Break Campaign Finance Laws in 2012?*, Sunlight Foundation (May 13, 2013); *see also* Paul Blumenthal, *Campaign Contribution Limits Broken Repeatedly in 2012 Election With No FEC Oversight*, Huff. Post (May 3, 2013).

[59] *See generally* Jonathan S. Berkon & Marc E. Elias, *After* McCutcheon, 127 Harv. L. Rev. F. 373 (2014); Kenneth A. Gross et al., *Developments Regarding Aggregate Contribution Limits*, 12 Skadden Pol. L. Alert (June 17, 2014).

[60] *McCutcheon*, 134 S. Ct. at 1446.

elections—make circumvention in federal elections improbable.[61] Likewise, the plurality concluded that BCRA's aggregate limits were not closely drawn. To support this, the plurality presented evidence on contributions to candidates for federal office, and it discussed alternatives to aggregate limits "available to Congress."[62] This reads like an opinion confined to the federal setting.

Some lawmakers and courts disagree. Connecticut's Elections Enforcement Commission declared that "[i]n light of the *McCutcheon* decision" it "will not enforce" the state's aggregate limits.[63] But it provided no further explanation, no effort to distinguish the state's legal regime and history from the federal government's. In a case called *CRG Network v. Barland*, a federal district court rejected the claim that *McCutcheon* is confined to the federal level, but the reasoning seems faulty.[64] The court invalidated an aggregate limit in Wisconsin, but the limit involved contributions a candidate could *receive*—no more than 65 percent from political committees—not what a donor could give, so one wonders about *McCutcheon*'s relevance.[65] Furthermore, the court stated that *McCutcheon*'s "extended discussion of the federal regulatory scheme"—all those laws that aim to prevent circumvention, rendering aggregate limits moot—was dicta.[66] That seems obviously wrong. With respect to tailoring, the court made a point that deserves discussion.

Here is the idea behind tailoring: "fit matters."[67] The means must serve the ends without causing much collateral damage. In this context, aggregate limits must serve their purpose without unduly abridging political speech and association. *McCutcheon* concluded the aggregate limits were "poorly tailored to the Government's interest in preventing circumvention of the base limits" because other anti-circumvention measures could be adopted instead.[68] The court in *CRG Network* picked up and generalized this argument, stating that Wisconsin regulators could adopt "narrower, more closely-drawn measures to achieve their anti-corruptive purposes."[69] Assuming every state has authority to adopt such measures, then perhaps the district court is right and *McCutcheon* has broad reach after all. Regardless of their existing laws and individual histories of circumvention, states could adopt anti-circumvention laws that "fit" better than aggregate limits. Thus, all aggregate limits are void.

61 *Id.* at 1452.
62 *Id.* at 1458.
63 Connecticut State Elections Enforcement Commission, Op. No. 2014-03 (May 14, 2014).
64 CRG Network v. Barland, 139 F. Supp. 3d 950 (E.D. Wis. 2015).
65 *Id.* at 952.
66 *Id.* at 954.
67 *McCutcheon*, 134 S. Ct. at 1456.
68 *Id.* at 1457.
69 *CRG Network*, 139 F. Supp. at 955.

For this argument to work, states must have one and only one purpose when adopting aggregate limits: preventing formal circumvention. The *McCutcheon* plurality assumed this was true for Congress. Recall its statement: "Congress's selection of a $5,200 base limit indicates its belief that contributions of that amount or less do not create a cognizable risk of corruption."[70] Given that assumption—lawful contributions do not corrupt—the only possible justification for aggregate limits is anti-circumvention, preventing *un*lawful contributions that *do* corrupt. But that assumption appears from thin air. The plurality presents no evidence of Congress's "belief." Lawful contributions do not immunize one from federal bribery laws, and as discussed plenty of people have been convicted for corrupt exchanges built around lawful contributions.

In short, the plurality's claim is deeply contestable and, most importantly, confined to Congress. States may have their own "beliefs" about base limits and corruption. If they believe—as any sensible person should, and as bribery laws presuppose—that lawful contributions *can* cause corruption, then they can justify aggregate limits on anti-corruption grounds. They are not confined to the anti-circumvention argument as *McCutcheon* and *CRG Network* suggest.

All of this builds to a conclusion: *McCutcheon* has limited weight outside of the federal context. If a state has the same statutes and regulations as the federal government, the same contribution patterns observed in federal elections, a government with the same capacity as Congress and the FEC, and, critically, the same narrow purpose that *McCutcheon* imputes to Congress, then its aggregate limits violate the Constitution. For all other states, and the number 50 comes to mind, *McCutcheon* does not control.

Fifty state-level political systems, and thousands of local ones, operate in this country, and chances are good that corruption blights each one. The cost to society of that subnational corruption may swamp that which flows from the federal system. Many (but not all) states have base contribution limits, but prior to *McCutcheon* only nine contained aggregate limits, and many have since abandoned them. States should bring those aggregate limits back. Support them, enact them, enforce them. This strategy does not offer a magic bullet; enormous expenditures, "dark money," and other things reformers worry about will persist. But it does offer a hardy flyswatter. Corruption will diminish as many small, illicit exchanges, and perhaps a few large ones too, get interrupted.

70 *McCutcheon*, 134 S. Ct. at 1452.

14

Developing Better Empirical Evidence for Future Campaign Finance Cases

Brent Ferguson and Chisun Lee*

I. INTRODUCTION

In recent years, American election spending has soared but has come from fewer and fewer donors.[1] Candidates now view the support of unlimited and

* Brent Ferguson was Counsel in the Democracy Program at the Brennan Center for Justice at the New York University School of Law when this chapter was written. He is now Assistant District Attorney at the New York County District Attorney's Office. Chisun Lee is Senior Counsel in the Democracy Program at the Brennan Center for Justice at the New York University School of Law. The authors are grateful to the many people who helped guide this chapter. Scholars Michael J. Malbin, Lynda W. Powell, Michael G. Miller, and David Kimball provided extensive feedback on earlier drafts. At the Brennan Center, Ava Mehta contributed outstanding research and editing; Katherine Valde and Iris Zhang provided valuable research assistance; Lawrence Norden, Wendy Weiser, Michael Waldman, Daniel Weiner, Ian Vandewalker, and Johanna Kalb gave helpful input and suggestions; Naren Daniel provided important communications assistance; and interns Jordan Proctor, Mitchell Brown, and Kaia Austin helped with research and editing. Saul Cornell gave helpful guidance on constitutional history. The authors also appreciate the input they received on an early version of this chapter at "Democracy by the People: Reforming Campaign Finance in America Today," the symposium on which this book is based, which was sponsored by Free Speech For People and held at the Seton Hall University School of Law on April 1, 2016.

1 Total candidate and outside spending increased from $2.87 billion in the 2002 midterm election to $3.85 billion in the 2014 midterm election. Total candidate and outside spending increased by almost 12% between the 2008 and 2012 federal elections, both presidential election years (figures adjusted for inflation). *Cost of Election*, CENTER FOR RESPONSIVE POLITICS, www.opensecrets.org/overview/cost.php. Concurrently, election spending has come from fewer sources: almost half of all the early super PAC money funding the 2016 presidential election came from just 50 donors. Matea Gold & Anu Narayanswamy, *The New Gilded Age: Close to Half of All Super-PAC Money Comes from 50 Donors*, WASH. POST (Apr. 15, 2016), www.washingtonpost.com/politics/the-new-gilded-age-close-to-half-of-all-super-pac-money-comes-from-50-donors/2016/04/15/63dc363c-01b4-11e6-9d36-33d198ea26c5_story.html. For the first time since 1990, the total number of donors in 2014 declined from the previous midterm election, though total cost of the election went up. Russ Choma, *Money Won on Tuesday, But Rules of the Game Changed*, CENTER FOR RESPONSIVE POLITICS (Nov. 5, 2014), www.opensecrets.org/news/2014/11/money-won-on-tuesday-but-rules-of-the-game-changed/.

sometimes anonymous outside entities like super PACs as practically essential to compete.[2] Against this backdrop, Americans have consistently expressed the concern that wealth unfairly influences policy outcomes.[3]

As powerful as these developments may seem, it is important to remember that their legal justification emerged for the most part from just a handful of recent 5-to-4 decisions by the U.S. Supreme Court, beginning in 2007.[4] That five-justice majority has since lost one member, the late Justice Antonin Scalia. In his place, President Donald Trump nominated Neil Gorsuch, a jurist who is also skeptical of efforts to reduce the influence of money in politics. The Court will likely consider more campaign finance cases in the coming years; those cases might include both efforts to invalidate longstanding laws like contribution limits and challenges to newly enacted laws. When these cases come, they will present a significant opportunity to reshape the role that money plays in American elections.

Yet these new cases also present reformers with an opportunity. The ability to make the most of this opportunity depends less on adopting a particular advocacy stance than on being able to present the Court with objective and reliable empirical research relevant to the major issues in campaign finance law.[5] The opportunity exists because, simply put, the five-justice majority in its sweeping decisions to eradicate certain contribution limits, corporate spending bans, and public financing features, almost never considered or cited supporting evidence for its positions. Though the Court has expressed particular views about the ways politics and campaign finance regulation work, a close reading

[2] Beth Reinhard & Christopher S. Stewart, *Some Candidates, Super PACs Draw Closer*, WALL ST. J. (Oct. 25, 2015), www.wsj.com/articles/some-candidates-super-pacs-draw-closer-1445809990?mg=id-wsj. *See also* CHISUN LEE, BRENT FERGUSON & DAVID EARLEY, BRENNAN CENTER FOR JUSTICE, AFTER CITIZENS UNITED: THE STORY IN THE STATES (2014), www.brennancenter.org/sites/default/files/publications/After Citizens United_Web_Final.pdf; PAUL S. RYAN, THE CAMPAIGN LEGAL CENTER, "TESTING THE WATERS" AND THE BIG LIE: HOW PROSPECTIVE PRESIDENTIAL CANDIDATES EVADE CANDIDATE CONTRIBUTION LIMITS WHILE THE FEC LOOKS THE OTHER WAY (2015), www.campaignlegalcenter.org/sites/default/files/Testing%20the%20Waters-Full%20Paper.pdf (noting that prospective candidates waited to declare candidacies while raising money for supportive super PACs).

[3] Nicholas Confessore & Megan Thee-Brenan, *Poll Shows Americans Favor an Overhaul of Campaign Finance*, N.Y. TIMES (June 2, 2015), www.nytimes.com/2015/06/03/us/politics/poll-shows-americans-favor-overhaul-of-campaign-financing.html.

[4] *See* LAWRENCE NORDEN, BRENT FERGUSON & DOUGLAS KEITH, BRENNAN CENTER FOR JUSTICE, FIVE TO FOUR (2016), www.brennancenter.org/publication/five-four. The jurisprudence preceding 2007 was also widely criticized, often based on the Court's distinction between contributions and independent expenditures originally conceived by *Buckley v. Valeo*, 424 U.S. 1 (1976).

[5] The Brennan Center for Justice generally advocates for reasonable regulations to reduce the influence of money in politics.

of the justices' opinions reveals strikingly little consideration of the actual effects that the influx of money or campaign finance regulation has on the political process. In part, this may be because it has proven quite difficult to precisely determine the role that campaign money plays when elected officials and voters make decisions. Many factors affect political decision-making, and even when evidence exists, there is often room for genuine debate about what it means. Nevertheless, the Court's reluctance to consider relevant evidence may explain the divergence between how money in politics is viewed by the general public and by the Court.

The recent arrival of Justice Gorsuch could mean that the Court will consider making better law when presented with sound data addressing the effects of money in the political system.[6] And if opponents of campaign finance restrictions renew their efforts, developing new evidence to better understand the benefits of various campaign finance regulations may be vital to maintaining the rules that have previously been upheld by the Court.

This chapter aims to identify the key factual assumptions that underlie the Court's most important campaign finance decisions. It also seeks to catalog existing research about questions relating to these assumptions, and to suggest further ways in which they might be tested. Such studies could aid not only litigants and courts, but also policy makers.

Several notable efforts to advance empirical research about money in politics have recently emerged. In 2013, the Campaign Finance Institute and the Bipartisan Policy Center published *An Agenda for Future Research on Money in Politics in the United States*, an expansive report calling for detailed study of public financing, campaign spending disclosure, and independent spending after *Citizens United v. Federal Election Commission*.[7] One of the leaders of that charge, Michael Malbin, has also provided deep analysis of the

6 *See* Brianne J. Gorod, *The Adversarial Myth: Appellate Court Extra-Record Factfinding*, 61 Duke L.J. 1, 65 (2011) ("[I]t is unclear why factual findings should be equally stable when the world they are describing may not be, and when new research inevitably provides a better and more precise understanding of the world."). For example, in *Leegin Creative Leather Products, Inc. v. PSKS*, Inc., 551 U.S. 877, 882 (2007), the Court overruled a longstanding precedent holding that it was *per se* illegal under the Sherman Act for a manufacturer and distributor to agree on a minimum price that the distributor could charge for a manufacturer's goods. The decision to overrule precedent was made in part because "[r]espected economic analysts … conclude that vertical price restraints can have procompetitive effects." *See also* Anita S. Krishnakumar, *Textualism and Statutory Precedents*, 104 Va. L. Rev. 157 (2018) (reviewing cases in which textualist justices have advocated overturning precedent based on development of new economic data and theory).

7 John C. Fortier & Michael J. Malbin, *An Agenda for Future Research on Money in Politics in the United States*, 11 Forum 455 (2013), www.albany.edu/rockefeller/rock_images/faculty/malbin/articles/Fortier-Malbin_Report.pdf.

effects of small donor public financing systems.[8] Through a massive survey-based study, Lynda Powell has shown when and how campaign contributions affect state legislators.[9] In 2014, Renata Strause and Daniel Tokaji published an important paper urging researchers to gather legislator testimony, social science research, and press reports to demonstrate the conflicts of interest that campaign contributions and expenditures can create.[10] A systematic approach to aligning objective research with the critical legal questions surrounding the influence of money on politics serves to increase both the social value of such research and the lasting efficacy of any legal reform that might result.

II. THE COURT'S APPROACH TO EVIDENCE

The Supreme Court's approach to evaluating factual questions and evidence in campaign finance cases has varied considerably. Sometimes, as in other areas of constitutional decision-making, the justices have incorporated factual understandings into their reasoning, whether implicitly or explicitly.[11] In some cases, the Court has considered voluminous evidence submitted by the litigants, including empirical studies, legislative testimony, and evidence of public opinion. For example, in *McConnell v. Federal Election Commission*, which upheld the Bipartisan Campaign Reform Act of 2002, the Court reviewed "testimony and declarations of over 200 witnesses and 100,000 pages of material."[12] That material included studies of how often candidate advertisements contained words of express advocacy,[13] internal organizational documents of campaign spenders confirming that candidates would work closely with interest groups to sponsor issue advertisements,[14] and declarations of senators explaining that certain industry donations were the cause of "scuttled tobacco legislation" and tort reform.[15]

8 Michael Malbin, Peter W. Brusoe & Brendan Glavin, *Small Donors, Big Democracy: New York City's Matching Funds as a Model for the Nation and States*, 11 ELECTION L.J. 3 (2012).

9 LYNDA W. POWELL, THE INFLUENCE OF CAMPAIGN CONTRIBUTIONS IN STATE LEGISLATURES (2012) (finding that campaign contributions can affect the content and passage of legislation in state legislatures).

10 Renata E. B. Strause & Daniel P. Tokaji, *Between Access and Influence: Building a Record for the Next Court*, 9 DUKE J. CONST. L. & PUB. POL'Y 179 (2014).

11 *See, e.g.*, David L. Faigman, *"Normative Constitutional Fact-Finding": Exploring the Empirical Component of Constitutional Interpretation*, 139 U. PA. L. REV. 541, 556–65 (1991); *see also* Gorod, *supra* note 6, at 29 (noting prominence of legislative factfinding by appellate courts and using *Citizens United* as an example).

12 Strause & Tokaji, *supra* note 10, at 196.

13 McConnell v. FEC, 540 U.S. 93, 127, n. 18 (2003).

14 *Id.* at 127–28, 128 n. 21.

15 *Id.* at 150.

In *Randall v. Sorrell*, which struck down unusually low contribution limits in the state of Vermont, both the controlling opinion and the dissent focused on studies addressing how those limits would affect the competitiveness of elections.[16] Justice Anthony Kennedy, who authored the majority's opinion in *Citizens United*, had said in a previous case that evidence about how a system works could change his mind about the validity of a campaign finance law. He would "leave open the possibility that Congress, or a state legislature, might devise a system in which there are some limits on both expenditures and contributions."[17]

Yet *Citizens United* itself was decided on an extremely thin factual record: the Court referred to the record developed for the Bipartisan Campaign Reform Act and used in *McConnell*, but the record in *Citizens United* did not contain "a shred of evidence on how [the federal spending ban] or its state-law counterparts … affect[ed] any entity other than Citizens United."[18] Though the record lacked any empirical basis for the Court to consider whether "independent expenditures … give rise to corruption or the appearance of corruption," that did not stop the majority from concluding that they did not.[19] The recent tendency by a five-justice majority to make factual pronouncements without considering factual evidence has been a major source of disagreement on the Court.[20]

Even if we cannot change past jurisprudence, reform-minded lawyers may still be able to convince a future Court to take more seriously the need to consider evidence of actual effects when weighing the harms and benefits of particular campaign finance laws. A review of past cases yields several observations about when justices seem to have been particularly concerned about such effects; these concerns will be useful to keep in mind when framing a research agenda on the effects of money in politics. The Court has focused on the effects that campaign finance laws have on the behavior, and possibly the beliefs, of candidates, supporters, and the general public; expressed concern about laws' effects on incumbency; and repeatedly indicated that novel

16 Randall v. Sorrell, 548 U.S. 230, 253, 279 (2006).

17 Nixon v. Shrink Missouri Gov't PAC, 528 U.S. 377, 409 (2000).

18 Citizens United v. FEC, 558 U.S. 310, 400 (2010) (Stevens, J., dissenting); *see also* Zephyr Teachout, *Facts in Exile: Corruption and Abstraction in* Citizens United v. Federal Election Commission, 42 Loy. U. Chi. L.J. 295, 298 (2011) (discussing lack of record in *Citizens United*).

19 Citizens United v. FEC, 558 U.S. 310, 357 (2010).

20 *See, e.g.*, *Citizens United*, 558 U.S. at 457 (Stevens, J., dissenting); *see also* Michael M. Franz, *Addressing Conservatives and (Mis)Using Social Science in the Debate Over Campaign Finance*, 51 Tulsa L. Rev. 359, 367 (2015) (noting "frustrat[ion] … where the Roberts Court sometimes embraces and sometimes dismisses a need for evidence").

arguments for (or against) campaign finance reform may require greater supporting evidence.

A. *Effects on Behavior of Candidates, Supporters, and the General Public*

Starting with *Buckley v. Valeo*, the Court has periodically expressed concern not just about the principled justifications for and objections to a campaign finance law, but also about how and whether the law would alter actual behavior regarding elections. Striking down the Federal Election Campaign Act's limit on independent expenditures, the Court observed that the law "would make it a federal criminal offense for a person or association to place a single one-quarter page advertisement 'relative to a clearly identified candidate' in a major metropolitan newspaper."[21] When it upheld the Bipartisan Campaign Reform Act in *McConnell*, the Court relied on voluminous testimony and documentary evidence "paint[ing] a vivid picture of a Congress besieged by conflicts of interest," as Strause and Tokaji have put it, and deemed such behavior worth changing.[22] The Court took detailed note of evidence showing how national parties peddled access to candidates and officeholders.[23] In *Randall*, the justices evaluated studies concerning how proposed contribution limits would affect the ability of challengers to disseminate their message to the public.[24] Similarly, the Court has several times examined evidence of public opinion that could be affected by the law or rule at issue. In *Caperton v. A.T. Massey Coal Company*, holding that an elected judge's failure to recuse himself from a case involving a major spender violated due process, the majority noted that "over 67% of West Virginians doubted Justice Benjamin would be fair and impartial."[25]

B. *Effects on Incumbency*

Other than the concept of corruption, the theme that justices of all ideological stripes most commonly discuss is the concern that legislators enact contribution and expenditure limits to protect themselves against challengers. In

[21] Buckley v. Valeo, 424 U.S. 1, 40 (1976).
[22] Strause & Tokaji, *supra* note 10, at 210.
[23] McConnell v. FEC, 540 U.S. 93, 124–25, 148–49 (2003).
[24] Randall v. Sorrell, 548 U.S. 230, 253, 279 (2006).
[25] Caperton v. A.T. Massey Coal Co., 556 U.S. 868, 875 (2009). *See also* FEC v. Wis. Right to Life, 551 U.S. 470, 471 n. 6 (2007) (using a poll about voter knowledge to conclude that television viewers would not always conclude that ads mentioning candidates were election-related).

Randall, Justice Stephen Breyer focused heavily on incumbent protection,[26] and Justices Clarence Thomas,[27] David Souter,[28] and John Paul Stevens[29] addressed the issue in separate opinions. Incumbent protection also received attention in *Nixon v. Shrink Missouri Government PAC*,[30] in the dissent in *Austin v. Michigan Chamber of Commerce*,[31] and is commonly discussed in lower court opinions.[32] Courts have even expressed concern about incumbency advantage in evaluating a law passed by ballot initiative, as opposed to by elected officials.[33]

Justice Breyer's concern about incumbency protection is especially significant to consider for the future of campaign finance law, as he generally has been amenable to arguments for evidence-based reforms and shown a willingness to weigh empirical evidence in his decision-making. While some existing research addresses how contribution limits affect incumbency rates,[34] questions persist for other laws and other scenarios.

C. *Novel Arguments for (or against) Campaign Finance Reform*

Courts are more willing to uphold laws based on long-recognized interests or long-running problems without demanding extensive factual support, which is part of the reason that use of evidence varies between cases. In *Shrink Missouri*, for example, the Court upheld Missouri's fairly low contribution limits in spite of the state's modest evidentiary showing that these were necessary, because

26 *Randall*, 548 U.S. at 253, 255–56. Vermont's statute addressed this concern to some degree, limiting incumbents to 85% or 90% of the expenditure limits applied to challengers. *Id.* at 237–38.

27 *Id.* at 268.

28 *Id.* at 287.

29 *Id.* at 279.

30 Nixon v. Shrink Missouri Gov't PAC, 528 U.S. 377, 389 n. 4; *id.* at 402 (Breyer, J., concurring).

31 Austin v. Mich. Chamber of Comm., 494 U.S. 652, 692–93 (1990) (Scalia, J., dissenting).

32 *See, e.g.*, Lair v. Bullock, 697 F.3d 1200, 1209–11 (9th Cir. 2012); N.C. Right to Life, Inc. v. Leake, 525 F.3d 274, 305 (4th Cir. 2008). *But see* Ognibene v. Parkes, 671 F.3d 174, 192 (2d Cir. 2011) ("The doing business limits here … seek to avoid stacking the deck in favor of incumbents, to whom donors with business dealings disproportionately contribute.").

33 *See Lair*, 697 F.3d at 1209–11.

34 *See, e.g.*, Ciara Torres-Spelliscy, Kahlil Williams & Dr. Thomas Stratmann, Brennan Center for Justice, Electoral Competition and Low Contribution Limits 2 (2009), www.brennancenter.org/sites/default/files/legacy/publications/Electoral.Competition.pdf (concluding that "contribution limits of $500 or less for individual contributors and political action committees (PACs) made elections for state assembly more competitive").

contribution limits had long been recognized (in *Buckley* and since then) as a valid method to prevent corruption.[35]

Viewed another way, in the typical case, the party attempting to invalidate a commonplace restriction may bear the evidentiary burden, rather than the party seeking to justify the law.[36] In *Shrink Missouri*, after explaining that the state did not need to offer more evidence, the Court noted that the challengers had failed to show that the contribution limits would "have any dramatic[ally] adverse effect on the funding of campaigns and political associations" and that invalidating them would therefore be beneficial.[37] The plaintiffs in *Randall* did provide such evidence, and the Court invalidated Vermont's contribution limits. Significantly, Justice Breyer voted to uphold the limits at issue in *Shrink Missouri*, but voted with the plurality to invalidate Vermont's contribution limits in *Randall*.

Of course, the Court's pattern does not always hold true: as noted elsewhere in this chapter, the Court in *Citizens United* struck down a longstanding law without significant evidence to support its decision. Nevertheless, it is sensible in most circumstances to expect that extensive evidence will be needed when litigants seek to persuade the Court that new interests should be considered as justification for campaign finance laws. New research may yield new evidence that conflicts with crucial judicial conclusions or the assumptions made in prior cases. This research will have to be unassailably credible, closely relevant, and sufficiently comprehensive in scope to stand a chance of persuading even a friendly Court to uphold new laws or campaign finance restrictions that emboldened advocates may seek to pass.

III. EVIDENTIARY CONCLUSIONS AND RESEARCH QUESTIONS

The Supreme Court has reached many conclusions about the effects of money in politics and its regulation, often without citing much or any supporting evidence. Here, we describe some relevant existing research in order to provide background information, explore possible models for future studies, and suggest questions for further study in these areas. Additional research could help not only courts to consider challenged regulations, but also policy makers to craft better, more closely tailored regulations in the first place.

[35] *Shrink Missouri*, 528 U.S. at 391. In *Wagner*, the D.C. Circuit upheld the federal government's ban on contributions from contractors citing historical evidence of corruption in the contracting process starting in the 1930s. Wagner v. FEC, 793 F.3d 1, 11 (2015).

[36] *But see* McCutcheon v. FEC, 134 S. Ct. 1434, 1452–56 (2014).

[37] *Shrink Missouri*, 528 U.S. at 395.

The major campaign finance issues the Court has considered are: (1) limits on spending by candidates, independent groups, and people; (2) limits on direct contributions; (3) public financing laws; (4) disclosure laws; and (5) the role of corporations, other business entities, and unions.

A. *Political Spending*

1. Major Factual Conclusions by the Court

The Court's holding in *Citizens United* rests on a number of different factual conclusions that, upon examination, say more about the dearth of relevant evidence in the case than about the weight of it. First, the Court determined—based largely on its review of the district court opinion in *McConnell*, decided years earlier—that there was no specific evidence of political favors being traded for independent expenditures as a *quid pro quo*,[38] and that "there is only scant evidence that independent expenditures even ingratiate."[39] It also proclaimed that "[t]he appearance of influence or access … will not cause the electorate to lose faith in our democracy."[40] The dissent criticized the majority heavily for relying only on the record in *McConnell* and for failing to allow the parties to "develop[], through the normal process of litigation, a record about the *actual* effects" of the corporate and union spending ban.[41]

These conclusions call for new empirical research, not just because so little evidence went before the Court to begin with, but also because there simply has been a great deal more independent spending—and fundraising by candidates for independent spending, among other related activities—since *Citizens United*.[42] New empirical research should address all of these conclusions, starting with the Court's premise that there is no actual evidence of *quid pro quo* corruption or the appearance of corruption tied to independent expenditures. Other research should address whether nominally independent expenditures actually are independent of candidates

[38] Citizens United v. FEC, 558 U.S. 310, 360 (2010).

[39] *Id.*

[40] *Id.*

[41] *Id.* at 399 (Stevens, J., dissenting).

[42] For example, outside spending on U.S. Senate elections more than doubled between 2010 and 2014, reaching almost $500 million in 2014. Ian Vandewalker, Brennan Center for Justice, Election Spending 2014: Outside Spending in Senate Races Since Citizens United 1 (2014), www.brennancenter.org/sites/default/files/analysis/Outside%20Spending%20Since%20Citizens%20United.pdf.

in any real sense; already some information indicates that many of them are not.[43]

A variety of other empirical questions about independent spending will become relevant if the Court focuses on corruption that does not involve direct deal-making. One question involves the efficacy of independent spending in winning electoral outcomes and whether (and how) elected officials express gratitude for such spending (or fear of it). Another question would inquire into the impact of independent spending on policy outcomes. Other questions would examine any effects independent spending may have on electoral participation, including whether unlimited independent spending makes it too difficult for certain actors to be heard in the political marketplace, and whether unlimited independent spending—say, in the form of increased attack ads—causes the public to disengage from elections and even affects voter turnout. Questions also arise about whether unlimited spending by certain political actors, such as potential government contractors or lobbyists, is especially likely to influence policy outcomes.

In *Randall*, Vermont argued that candidate spending limits were necessary to allow incumbent officeholders to concentrate on their duties of office, rather than on fundraising. The Court rejected that argument with almost no discussion and no review of available data.[44] Yet data and legislator commentary demonstrate that, in our current system of unlimited candidate spending, many legislators spend between 30 and 70 percent of their time raising money.[45] Additional research could more precisely identify how the demands of fundraising affect officeholders' ability to perform their duties.

Below we describe some existing research that relates to the most legally significant empirical questions about political spending, and suggest questions for further research.

2. Effects of Political Spending on Policy Outcomes

1. EXISTING RESEARCH. Scholars have attacked the question of private money's impact on policy making in a variety of ways. Some have sought answers straight from legislators, in one case analyzing survey responses about the influence of campaign contributions from nearly 3,000 legislators representing every state,[46] and in another conducting a field experiment to test whether senior

[43] *See* LEE, FERGUSON & EARLEY, *supra* note 2.

[44] Randall v. Sorrell, 548 U.S. 230, 243 (2006).

[45] *See, e.g.*, Brent Ferguson, *Congressional Disclosure of Time Spent Fundraising*, 23 CORNELL J.L. & PUB. POL'Y 1, 13 (2013).

[46] POWELL, *supra* note 9.

congressional staffers were more accessible to donors than to non-donors.[47] Others have studied roll call votes or other outcome measures and cross-referenced these data with information about different groups' preferences and sometimes campaign contributions.[48] All of these studies found that policy makers were more responsive to the desires of donors or the wealthy than to non-donor, average constituents.

Anyone concerned about the policy making power of private money might wonder: can stronger campaign finance regulation make a difference? Intriguingly, at least one recent study indicates that it can. Political scientist Patrick Flavin examined the relationship between states' campaign finance laws and their spending priorities, finding that "states with stricter campaign finance laws devote a larger proportion of their annual budget to public welfare spending in general and to cash assistance programs in particular."[49] Yet this study does not account for independent spending regulations, and it also stops its consideration of data at 2008, raising the question of how independent spending after *Citizens United* may have changed any effect of campaign finance laws on the policy influence of wealth.

Though the question of independent spending's influence on official action remains largely unanswered, one study in 2016 found that people may *perceive* this influence to a legally meaningful degree. In simulations of grand juries and criminal jury trials, a significant majority of participants voted to indict or convict an elected official for corruption where the alleged improper payment included nothing more direct than a donation by a company with business before the official to an independent group supporting that official's

[47] Joshua L. Kalla & David E. Broockman, *Campaign Contributions Facilitate Access to Congressional Officials: A Randomized Field Experiment*, 60 AM. POL. SCI. REV. 545 (2016).

[48] Martin Gilens & Benjamin I. Page, *Testing Theories of American Politics: Elites, Interest Groups, and Average Citizens*, 12 PERSP. ON POL. 564, 575 (2014); Adam Bonica, Nolan McCarty, Keith T. Poole & Howard Rosenthal, *Why Hasn't Democracy Slowed Rising Inequality?*, J. ECON. PERSP., Summer 2013, at 103, 121 (using multiple decades' voting and contributions data to conclude that "the kinds of government policies that could have ameliorated the sharp rise in inequality have been immobilized" by several factors, including "feedback" from wealthy campaign spenders); Anne E. Baker, *Getting Short-Changed? The Impact of Outside Money on District Representation*, 97 SOC. SCI. Q. 1096 (2016) (using contribution data and ideology preference surveys to conclude that House members' dependency on out-of-district contributions draws them in a more extremely liberal or extremely conservative ideological direction than the ideological preferences of the districts they represent); POWELL, *supra* note 9; Kalla & Broockman, *supra* note 47.

[49] Patrick Flavin, *Campaign Finance Laws, Policy Outcomes, and Political Equality in the American States*, 68 POL. RES. Q. 77, 77 (2015). Flavin found no relationship between campaign finance laws and spending decisions for non-redistributive policy areas. *Id.* at 78.

reelection. The findings indicate that independent spending can give rise to an "appearance of corruption" justifying remedial reform even under the existing jurisprudence.[50]

2. QUESTIONS FOR FURTHER RESEARCH. Perhaps the largest and most legally important gap in the existing research on money in politics concerns the effects of independent spending on the political process and its substantive outcomes. To what extent has the deregulation of independent spending affected the actions of donors, candidates, and elected officials, and with what if any impact on policy? Innumerable questions about access, influence, and legislative or regulatory decisions fall under this umbrella.

As a baseline matter, it is worth interrogating the very nature of independent spending in the real world: how independent are its sources and drivers, compared to the direct contributors and campaign strategists the law already recognizes as potential collaborators in corrupting officials? Do candidates behave differently with supportive independent spenders than they do with direct contributors?

Of course the unlimited aspect of independent spending sharpens every concern about private money's influence on public officials. If the sources fueling independent spending include direct donors, government contractors, or lobbyists, should the concerns giving rise to reforms addressing these actors' campaign contributions extend to their independent spending? If so, under what circumstances? Have certain actors increased their political spending through unlimited independent channels? If so, when, why, and to what effect? Conversations with empirical scholars suggest that actors associated with heavily regulated industries and readily quantifiable interests—as opposed to ideological actors—would make for fruitful study. Such research could shed new light on the power of private wealth to gain access and influence and reveal new dimensions of the misalignment of policy with majority preferences that existing research indicates.

3. Effects of Political Spending on Participation and Political Opportunity

1. EXISTING RESEARCH. Alongside questions about substantive outcomes run questions about whether and how political spending affects participation and opportunity in the political process. Not much research exists along these

50 Christopher Robertson, D. Alex Winkelman, Kelly Bergstrand & Darren Modzelewski, *The Appearance and Reality of* Quid Pro Quo *Corruption: An Empirical Investigation*, 8 J. LEGAL ANALYSIS 1, 38 (2016).

lines, though some scholars have considered participation as a matter of civic engagement—being informed, writing a letter, contributing, voting. One survey-based study concluded that political spending does not have to rise to the level of a bribe to "corrode [citizens'] faith in the democratic process," but urged further study to determine precise effects in the age of unlimited spending on different measures of civic engagement.[51] Relatedly, a different study sought to test the notion that an unrestricted marketplace of ideas is generally best, concluding that different restrictions likely will have different effects on such phenomena as participation, but at least some restrictions may encourage more persuasive modes of speech.[52] If perception (or faith in the process) does affect participation, though, the conclusion of a different study—aggregating data from various previously conducted polls—should spur traditional campaign finance reformers to want to investigate deeply for solutions: Authors Nathaniel Persily and Kelli Lammie conclude that, while "a large majority of Americans believe that the campaign finance system contributes to corruption in government, the data do not suggest that" new laws regulating campaign finances will change people's minds about whether government is corrupt.[53]

When it comes to participation through campaign funding, research indicates that, in the years after *Citizens United*, the segment of the electorate giving money has become increasingly select. One watchdog group's report revealed that, while the 2014 midterm election was the most expensive midterm contest ever, it was the first since 1990 where fewer donors contributed than in the previous midterm election.[54] As of the second fundraising quarter of 2015, the *New York Times* reported, only 158 families accounted for nearly half of all spending for the presidential election.[55] Another investigation by the Washington Post found that by February 2016,

[51] Rebecca L. Brown & Andrew D. Martin, *Rhetoric and Reality: Testing the Harm of Campaign Spending*, 90 N.Y.U. L. Rev. 1066, 1090 (2015).

[52] Daniel E. Ho & Frederick Schauer, *Testing the Marketplace of Ideas*, 90 N.Y.U. L. Rev. 1160, 1222 (2015).

[53] Nathaniel Persily & Kelli Lammie, *Perceptions of Corruption and Campaign Finance: When Public Opinion Determines Constitutional Law*, 153 U. Pa. L. Rev. 119, 120 (2004).

[54] Russ Choma, *Final Tally: 2014's Midterm Was Most Expensive, With Fewer Donors*, Center for Responsive Politics (Feb. 18, 2015), www.opensecrets.org/news/2015/02/final-tally-2014s-midterm-was-most-expensive-with-fewer-donors/.

[55] Nicholas Confessore, Sarah Cohen & Karen Yourish, *Just 158 Families Have Provided Nearly Half of the Early Money for Efforts to Capture the White House*, N.Y. Times (Oct. 10, 2015), www.nytimes.com/interactive/2015/10/11/us/politics/2016-presidential-election-super-pac-donors.html?_r=1.

41 percent of all money raised by super PACs for the presidential election came from just 50 donors.[56]

Research suggests that recent trends in political spending have also affected the opportunity of candidates to be elected (and for their supporters to elect their chosen candidates). In a 2016 study of congressional contests from 1994 to 2014, scholars found that, after *Citizens United*, independent spending groups grew in number and diversity while increasingly promoting incumbents rather than newcomers.[57] This trend appears to contradict a commonplace claim, after the 2010 decision, that lifting limits on spending would empower new voices and expand political opportunity. In their seminal 2014 work based on interviews of principals involved in congressional campaigns, Daniel Tokaji and Renata Strause concluded that potential candidates viewed the prospect of securing support from nominally independent spenders to be a key determinant in whether to run for office.[58] Our own research into similar questions in state and local elections revealed similar reliance by candidates on nominally independent support—or fear that opponents would draw such support.[59] These recent findings follow more longstanding research showing that the demands of fundraising affect officeholders' priorities and reward candidates who are willing and able to spend, as Mark Alexander puts it, "countless hours raising money by courting a limited group of individuals, instead of meeting voters, engaging opponents, debating or voting on legislation, and the like."[60]

2. Questions for Further Research. Much research remains to be done on the effects of political spending on participation—voting, contributing,

[56] Matea Gold & Anu Narayanswamy, *The New Gilded Age: Close to Half of All Super-PAC Money Comes from 50 Donors*, Wash. Post (Apr. 15, 2016), www.washingtonpost.com/politics/the-new-gilded-age-close-to-half-of-all-super-pac-money-comes-from-50-donors/2016/04/15/63dc363c-01b4-11e6-9d36-33d198ea26c5_story.html?utm_term=.5bb6ef675558.

[57] Robert G. Boatright, Michael J. Malbin & Brendan Glavin, *Independent Expenditures in Congressional Primaries after Citizens United*, 5 Int. Groups & Advoc. 119 (2016).

[58] *See* Daniel P. Tokaji & Renata E.B. Strause, The New Soft Money: Outside Spending in Congressional Elections (2014).

[59] Lee, Ferguson & Earley, *supra* note 2.

[60] Mark Alexander, *Let Them Do Their Jobs: The Compelling Government Interest in Protecting the Time of Candidates and Elected Officials*, 37 Loy. U. Chi. L.J. 669, 676 (2006); *see also* Brief of Respondents, Cross-Petitioners at 16–19, Randall v. Sorrell, 548 U.S. 230 (2006) (Nos. 04-1528, 04-1530, 04-1697), 2006 WL 325190, at *16–19 (Vermont elected officials and donors extensively documented the amount of time candidates spent fundraising and the manner in which it affected incumbents' priorities).

advertising, or other forms of civic engagement—in the age of unrestricted independent spending. Can independent spending—often associated with negative advertising—be linked to voter disaffection or misinformation? Has unlimited independent spending affected the diversity of speakers or the price of communicating? To what extent do mere *perceptions* of wealthy donors' special access to power matter to public engagement with the political process?

Questions about the impact of political spending on political opportunity for candidates and their supporters also call for further study. Whether unrestricted independent spending has affected incumbency rates, and what amounts it takes to be actually competitive in this era, are significant questions. Are big donors more likely to see their preferred candidates elected, and small or non-donors more likely to be disappointed? Further, with candidates commonly involved in raising money for supportive independent groups, how have recent spending trends affected the already recognized time burden of candidate fundraising and with what impact on attention to constituents and substantive issues of governance?

B. *Limits on Contributions*

1. Major Factual Conclusions by the Court

In *Randall*, the Court justified its concerns about Vermont's contribution limits on the basis of a number of claims. First, reviewing conflicting studies, the Court determined that the limits would make it more difficult for challengers to compete with incumbents, because challengers would receive less money than they had in the past.[61] Implicitly, this conclusion assumes that a similar reduction in contributions to incumbents would not increase the opportunity of challengers to compete. It also presumes that candidates would be unable to offset any negative fundraising that contribution limits cause even if they try to raise additional money from more contributors. The Court also asserted that there was no evidence in the record demonstrating that low contribution limits were particularly necessary in Vermont, due to an increased threat of corruption.[62]

Invalidating the federal aggregate contribution limits in *McCutcheon v. Federal Election Commission*, the Court made several unsupported empirical pronouncements as well. Most importantly, the Court concluded that "[s]pending large sums of money in connection with elections, but

[61] Randall v. Sorrell, 548 U.S. 230, 253 (2006).
[62] *Id.* at 261.

not in connection with an effort to control the exercise of an officeholder's official duties," does not cause corruption.[63] Likewise, it does not create a risk of corruption even if large spending provides donors with "influence over or access to elected officials or political parties."[64] The Court also found that there was not a significant threat that large checks to parties or PACs would be used to circumvent the limits on contributions to existing candidates, and that "there is not the same risk of *quid pro quo* corruption or its appearance when money flows through independent actors to a candidate."[65]

New research to determine the validity of the Court's conclusions about contribution limits would be helpful, as these conclusions constrain even the narrow scope of permissible anticorruption regulation that remains. It could determine whether low limits cause candidates to raise less money than they otherwise would and disadvantage challengers. It could examine whether and to what extent donations to parties or PACs serve to circumvent limits on contributions to candidates, thus raising corruption risks similar to the candidate contribution context. Further, research on how large contributions affect policy outcomes will be relevant when the Court considers an argument that limits are justified because they prevent a type of corruption that is broader than the narrow *quid pro quo* corruption the Court now recognizes.

2. Effects of Contribution Limits on Electoral Competition

1. Existing Research. Much of the existing scholarship on contribution limits explores their effect on electoral competitiveness, yielding mixed conclusions. Likely because of the decision's recency, the body of research predates *Citizens United*. Some of it serves to establish the baseline conclusion that incumbents generally will attract more money in donations than non-incumbents.[66] Other studies use data including election results, contribution records, and details of campaign finance regulations to show that contribution limits tend to increase electoral competitiveness or at least do not advantage incumbents over challengers.[67] One scholar, examining

[63] McCutcheon v. FEC, 134 S. Ct. 1450, 1450 (2014).

[64] *Id.* at 1451 (quotation marks omitted).

[65] *Id.* at 1452.

[66] *See* Alexander Fouirnaies & Andrew B. Hall, *The Financial Incumbency Advantage: Causes and Consequences*, 76 J. Pol. 711 (2014); *Public Dollars for the Public Good: A Report on the 2005 Elections*, N.Y.C. Campaign Fin. Board 122 (2006).

[67] Torres-Spelliscy, Williams & Stratmann, *supra* note 34; Thomas Stratmann, *Do Low Contribution Limits Insulate Incumbents from Competition?*, 9 Election. L.J. 125, 126 (2010); Thomas Stratmann & Francisco Aparicio-Castillo, *Competition Policy for Elections: Do*

gubernatorial primary election spending data across a variety of campaign finance regimes, reached a neutral conclusion: contribution limits do not provide an advantage to either incumbents or challengers.[68] Finally, a number of other data-based studies conclude that contribution restrictions serve to protect incumbents.[69]

2. Questions for Further Research. The widely varying conclusions in the existing literature indicate the need for more research into the effects of contribution limits on competition. When judges voice their common suspicion that officeholders have enacted limits to help themselves, or when reformers advocate limits as a means to keep challengers from being completely outstripped in fundraising, the empirical basis for either argument remains debatable. Further, with candidate-specific independent spending groups emerging as major sources of political money after *Citizens United*, any interaction of such spending with campaign contributions and their effect on competitiveness needs to be explored. Scholars we spoke with theorized that the availability of unlimited independent support that can be harnessed to support a single candidate significantly undermines any effect of direct contribution limits.

3. The Corrupting Effect of Indirect Contributions

1. Existing Research. The Court still recognizes the corrupting effect of contributions given directly to candidates as a risk justifying regulation. But even as unlimited private money goes toward promoting candidates through nominally independent groups, the Court appears unwilling to extend the anticorruption rationale to indirect means of support. Yet most of the existing research on effects of indirect contributions indicates that these donations do influence lawmakers.

Campaign Contribution Limits Matter?, 127 Pub. Choice 177 (2006); Kihong Eom & Donald A. Gross, *Contribution Limits and Disparity in Contributions Between Gubernatorial Candidates*, 59 Pol. Res. Q. 99 (2006).

68 Kedron Bardwell examined the extent to which a range of campaign finance laws are correlated with electoral competitiveness. He concluded that "[l]evels of individual contribution limits do not provide an advantage in campaign spending to incumbents or challengers." Kedron Bardwell, *Money and Challenger Emergence in Gubernatorial Primaries*, 55 Pol. Res. Q. 653, 662 (2002).

69 John R. Lott, Jr., *Campaign Finance Reform and Electoral Competition*, 129 Pub. Choice 263, 292 (2006); Donald A. Gross, Robert K. Goidel & Todd G. Shields, *State Campaign Finance Regulations and Electoral Competition*, 30 Am. Pol. Res. 143 (2002); Adam Meirowitz, *Electoral Contests, Incumbency Advantages, and Campaign Finance*, 70 J. Pol. 681 (2008).

The record in *McConnell* offers a voluminous compilation of materials indicating that donations by "lobbyists, CEOs, and wealthy individuals" to political parties to "secur[e] influence over federal officials" had their intended effect, resulting in "manipulations of the legislative calendar, leading to Congress' failure to enact, among other things, generic drug legislation, tort reform, and tobacco legislation."[70] Since then, numerous empirical studies have established similar effects of indirect giving to PACs, or even to fellow lawmakers, on legislator decisions—ranging from the high-profile and ideological to tax rates for specific businesses.[71] One noteworthy paper aggregated the findings of some 40 empirical studies to conclude that "[o]verall, PAC contributions show relatively few effects on voting behavior";[72] but the academic literature[73] and scholars we spoke with suggest that looking primarily at voting behavior may fail to capture the equally powerful acts of amendment or simple inaction. Others have noted the ease with which donors, post-*McCutcheon*, are able to circumvent direct contribution limits to give far greater amounts indirectly.[74]

2. Questions for Further Research. One important path for further study into the corrupting effect of contributions is to explore whether unlimited contributions to parties and groups of candidates may corrupt candidates who are not direct recipients of those contributions. Also useful would be research into whether the risk of corruption increases when donors face only direct contribution limits but not aggregate limits. Michael Gilbert's chapter in this book is dedicated to examining this issue. Beyond explorations of corruption as recognized by the current Court, efforts to document other types of troubling

70 McConnell v. FEC, 540 U.S. 93, 147, 150 (2003).

71 Jennifer L. Brown, Katharine D. Drake & Laura Wellman, *The Benefits of a Relational Approach to Corporate Political Activity: Evidence from Political Contributions to Tax Policymakers*, 37 J. Am. Tax'n Ass'n 69 (2014); Christopher Witko, *PACs, Issue Context, and Congressional Decisionmaking*, 59 Pol. Res. Q. 283 (2006); Eleanor Neff Powell, Legislative Consequences of Fundraising Influence (Working Paper, 2015), www.eleanorneffpowell.com/uploads/8/3/9/3/8393347/powell__2015__-_legislative_consequences_of_fundraising_influence.pdf.

72 Stephen Ansolabehere, John M. de Figueiredo & James M. Snyder Jr., *Why Is There So Little Money in U.S. Politics?*, J. Econ. Persp., Winter 2003, at 105, 114.

73 *See, e.g.*, Witko, *supra* note 71, at 283 ("Unfortunately, [previous] studies have focused on roll-call voting to the exclusion of other forms of legislative behavior. Considering the importance of non-voting forms of committee behavior, this is a serious limitation.") (citation omitted).

74 Paul Blumenthal, *Democrats Are Proving Samuel Alito and John Roberts Wrong*, Huff. Post (Jan. 5, 2016), www.huffingtonpost.com/entry/hillary-victory-fund-campaign-finance_us_5682dcf1e4b0b958f65a9501; Bob Biersack, *How the Parties Worked the Law and Got Their Mojo Back*, Center for Responsive Politics (Feb. 19, 2016), www.opensecrets.org/news/2016/02/how-the-parties-worked-the-law-and-got-their-mojo-back/.

influence—for instance, whether legislators are more likely to vote consistent with the wishes of their donors or their average constituents, as one scholar has studied[75]—likely will benefit future regulation efforts by revealing more of the nuances of how political money really works.

C. *Public Financing and Laws to Encourage Its Use*

1. Major Factual Conclusions by the Court

In *Arizona Free Enterprise Club's Freedom Club PAC v. Bennett*, the Court relied in part on examples from the record of "specific candidates curtailing fundraising efforts, and actively discouraging supportive independent expenditures, to avoid triggering matching funds."[76] The Court also cited expert testimony that "found that privately financed candidates facing the prospect of triggering matching funds changed the timing of their fundraising activities, the timing of their expenditures, and, thus, their overall campaign strategy."[77] It also concluded that the trigger funds did not reduce corruption, because neither candidate spending nor independent spending can cause corruption.[78] The Court's opinion impliedly determined that high participation in the public financing program could not reduce corruption sufficiently to justify any burden the law created. The decision also relied on assumptions about independent spending already made in *Citizens United*: principally, that independent spending cannot cause corruption or its appearance.

Additional research would be helpful to test some of the Court's assumptions about public financing and to determine whether political spending is less likely to influence elected officials who use public financing. Some research has already addressed how public financing encourages public participation,[79] but that research could be performed in additional jurisdictions with different public financing systems.

75 Michael J. Barber, *Representing the Preferences of Donors, Partisans, and Voters in the U.S. Senate*, 80 Pub. Opinion Q. 225 (2016).

76 Ariz. Free Enter. Club's Freedom Club PAC v. Bennett, 564 U.S. 721, 744 (2011).

77 *Id.* (quotation marks omitted).

78 *Id.* at 751.

79 Elisabeth Genn et al., Brennan Center for Justice, Donor Diversity Through Public Matching Funds (2012), www.brennancenter.org/sites/default/files/legacy/publications/DonorDiversityReport_WEB.PDF.

2. Benefits of Public Financing and Effect of Trigger Laws

1. Existing Research. The bulk of existing data-based research about public financing examines its purported benefits. Some of it supports the argument that public financing enables candidates to reduce the time they spend fundraising, presumably from a select donor class, and increase the time they spend on broader public activities such as interacting directly with potential voters.[80] Other research indicates that public funding featuring a match for small private donations can result in a more diverse class of donors,[81] that public financing can increase the odds for certain challengers to take on incumbents,[82] and might incentivize candidates to rely more heavily on small donations.[83] However, one study, analyzing public surveys from several decades, concludes that public financing can have a negative effect on citizens' belief in their political power and whether officials care about their opinions.[84]

In recent years, scholars have studied whether trigger laws, such as the one invalidated in *Arizona Free Enterprise*, discourage speech by candidates or independent spenders. Several scholars studying Maine's and Arizona's public financing laws concluded that there was no evidence that trigger provisions decreased the volume of speech[85] or caused candidates to strategically avoid speech.[86] However, one study cited in the *Arizona Free Enterprise* opinion itself

[80] Peter L. Francia & Paul S. Herrnson, *The Impact of Public Finance Laws on Fundraising in State Legislative Elections*, 31 Am. Pol. Res. 520, 520 (2003); Michael G. Miller, Subsidizing Democracy: How Public Funding Changes Elections and How It Can Work in the Future 62 (2014).

[81] Elisabeth Genn et al., *supra* note 79.

[82] Kedron Bardwell, *Money and Challenger Emergence in Gubernatorial Primaries*, 55 Pol. Res. Q. 653 (2002).

[83] Michael J. Malbin, *Small Donors: Incentives, Economies of Scale, and Effects*, 11 The Forum 385 (2013).

[84] David M. Primo & Jeffrey Milyo, *Campaign Finance Laws and Political Efficacy: Evidence from the States*, 5 Election L.J. 23, 33 (2006).

[85] Michael G. Miller, Subsidizing Democracy: How Public Funding Changes Elections and How It Can Work in the Future 131–32 (2014); *see also* Brief for Municipal amici as Amicus Curiae Supporting Respondents, Ariz. Free Enter. Club's Freedom Club PAC v. Bennett, 564 U.S. 721 (2011) (Nos. 10–238, 10–239), 2011 WL 1209128; Brief for Maine Citizens for Clean Elections, Lawrence Bliss, Pamela Jabar Trinward, Andrew O'Brien & David Van Wie as Amici Curiae Supporting Respondents, Ariz. Free Enter. Club's Freedom Club PAC v. Bennett, 564 U.S. 721 (2011) (Nos. 10–238, 10–239), 2011 WL 686403.

[86] Conor M. Dowling, Ryan D. Enos, Anthony Fowler & Costas Panagopoulos, *Does Public Financing Chill Political Speech? Exploiting a Court Injunction as a Natural Experiment*, 11 Election L.J. 302 (2012); *see also* Brief for Costas Panagopoulos, Ryan D. Enos, Conor M. Dowling, & Anthony Fowler as Amici Curiae Supporting Respondents, Ariz. Free Enter. Club's Freedom Club PAC v. Bennett, 564 U.S. 721 (2011) (Nos. 10–238, 10–239), 2011 WL

found that privately financed candidates did change their campaign strategy because of the trigger law,[87] and Chief Justice John Roberts cited "examples of specific candidates curtailing fundraising efforts, and actively discouraging supportive independent expenditures, to avoid triggering matching funds."[88]

2. QUESTIONS FOR FURTHER RESEARCH. Studies of public financing have provided some answers about how such programs can affect candidate time and increase donor diversity. It would be helpful if future research more closely examined how publicly financed candidates act once elected. Are their votes and other actions more likely to align with the will of their constituents than officials who have used private funding? And are they less likely to give increased access to big political spenders? The answers to these questions will provide a basis for determining the permissible scope and incentives of new public financing programs across the country. Further, if any jurisdictions pass or enforce a modified trigger law, it will be important to study those provisions to determine how they affect spending by candidates and outside groups.

D. *Disclosure*

1. Major Factual Conclusions by the Court

The Court's conclusion, offered in *McCutcheon*, that disclosure requirements are often a sufficient substitute for limits to prevent corruption and other "abuse of the campaign finance system"[89] rests in significant part on the premise that "modern technology" has made disclosure vastly more effective than it used to be.[90] The Court's decision implicitly presumes that it is possible to craft disclosure rules applicable to corporate independent spending that will not be easy to evade. The Court in *Citizens United* seemed to think that such rules already existed in federal elections, ignoring the potential problems that would occur due to the fact that the disclosure regime did not contemplate the

686404; Anthony Gierzynski, Do Maine's Public Funding Program's Trigger Provisions Have a Chilling Effect on Fundraising? (Working Paper, 2011), www.mainecleanelections.org/sites/default/files/research/Do_Public_Funding_Program_Trigger_Provisions_Have_a_Chilling_Effect_on_Fund_Raising.pdf.

87 Ariz. Free Enter. Club's Freedom Club PAC v. Bennett, 564 U.S. 721, 744 (2011) (citing conclusion by Dr. David Primo in Petitioner's reply brief).

88 *Id.*

89 McCutcheon v. FEC, 134 S. Ct. 1450, 1459 (2014).

90 *Id.* at 1460.

significant corporate and union spending that *Citizens United* allowed. Instead of a world with lightning-fast Internet disclosure,[91] more than $800 million in dark money has been spent in federal races since 2010.[92] Such reasoning also depends on the Court's longstanding assumption (which predates even *Buckley*) that transparency actually influences how voters behave, and thus helps to prevent "the corrupt use of money to affect elections."[93] Studies on patterns of election spending and the types of information voters actually use to make decisions, among other things, could serve to illuminate the extent to which disclosure actually is a viable safeguard on its own.

2. The Effects of Disclosure Rules on Corruption and Voter Preferences

1. Existing Research. Recent studies of disclosure rules have attempted to determine how campaign finance information affects voter preferences. One study found that ads sponsored by unknown groups are more effective than those run by candidates, but that the advantage is reduced when the groups' donors are disclosed.[94] Another study concluded that potential voters rated candidates more highly if the candidate received most of his or her donations from individuals rather than interest groups.[95] A third study concluded that citizens express concern about campaign finance information in general, and they are most concerned if they learn that a candidate is funded or financed by out-of-state donors.[96]

Political scientists have also sought to determine whether disclosure law affects corruption. One examination posits that while corruption caused by campaign spending is a relatively small problem, disclosure does deter some corruption that might otherwise occur.[97] In another paper, Michael Gilbert

[91] Citizens United v. FEC, 558 U.S. 310, 370 (2010). ("A campaign finance system that pairs corporate independent expenditures with effective disclosure has not existed before today.")

[92] *See Outside Spending by Nondisclosing Groups*, Center for Responsive Politics, www.opensecrets.org/outsidespending/nonprof_summ.php.

[93] Buckley v. Valeo, 424 U.S. 1, 67 (1976) (quoting Burroughs v. United States, 290 U.S. 534, 548 (1934)).

[94] Travis Ridout, Michael M. Franz & Erika Franklin Fowler, *Sponsorship, Disclosure and Donors: Limiting the Impact of Outside Group Ads*, 68 Pol. Res. Q. 154 (2015).

[95] Conor M. Dowling & Michael G. Miller, *Experimental Evidence on the Relationship between Candidate Funding Sources and Voter Evaluations*, 3 J. Experimental Pol. Sci. 152 (2016).

[96] Conor M. Dowling & Amber Wichowsky, The Effects of Increased Campaign Finance Disclosure: Evaluating Reform Proposals (Working Paper, 2014), http://papers.ssrn.com/sol3/papers.cfm?abstract_id=2483194.

[97] Stephen Ansolabehere, *The Scope of Corruption: Lessons from Comparative Campaign Finance Disclosure*, 6 Election L.J. 163 (2007).

and Benjamin Aiken argue that because disclosure rules may instead make it easier for private actors and corrupt officials to find each other, reformers should look to other measures to prevent corruption.[98]

2. QUESTIONS FOR FURTHER RESEARCH.[99] We still do not know the extent to which disclosure laws provide voters with useful information and prevent corruption. While a few scholars have looked at whether disclosure laws deter corruption, further study should seek to determine whether strong disclosure laws reduce or increase misalignment or the ability of donors and non-donors to secure access to public officials. It would also be helpful to examine the efficacy of existing disclosure reports to determine whether current law provides the information voters want in an easily digestible fashion. Finally, the extent to which voting behavior is affected by campaign finance information has not been fully answered; new studies could seek to ascertain more precisely how many voters would be affected by certain types of donor disclosure.

E. *The Role of Corporations, Other Business Entities, and Unions*

1. Major Factual Conclusions by the Court

The Court's opinion in *Citizens United* rested partly on determinations about whether business or labor groups have distinct characteristics justifying different treatment under the law. The Court decided that because independent spending by individuals does not "give rise" to corruption, the same is true of corporate spending, despite legal advantages that distinguish corporations and unions from individuals. The Court also focused on the need for corporations to engage in electoral spending so the electorate will hear their speech, adopting the "marketplace of ideas" metaphor. Regarding that metaphor, the Court assumed the following to be true: (1) an unregulated marketplace will lead to the discovery of truth; (2) corporate spending will provide information the public does not already possess; and (3) corporate speech has the same worth as other speech in helping the electorate ascertain the truth.[100]

98 Michael D. Gilbert & Benjamin F. Aiken, *Disclosure and Corruption*, 14 ELECTION L.J. 148 (2015).

99 While this section lists several possible questions that could determine whether disclosure eliminates corruption, many of the questions in section III.A could be modified to compare similar jurisdictions with different disclosure rules.

100 Citizens United v. FEC, 558 U.S. 310, 349 (2010).

New research could look more closely at whether corporate or union spending has a distinct effect on elected officials' actions. It could also examine whether significant corporate spending affects the electorate's willingness to participate in elections.

2. Effects of Business Entity Spending

1. EXISTING RESEARCH. Several studies have looked specifically at how spending by business entities affects policy or government function. One group of scholars found that firms who give consistently to politicians, including through PACs, are likelier to pay lower taxes.[101] Another working paper found "evidence that corporations and business PACs use donations to acquire immediate access and favor."[102] In an examination of corporate political activity, one scholar concluded that large firms are more likely to engage in political activity if they are in a heavily regulated industry, and that in some firms, corporate political activity correlates negatively with corporate value.[103]

2. QUESTIONS FOR FURTHER RESEARCH. The country's reaction to *Citizens United* made clear that American citizens are especially concerned about the effect of corporate spending on elections. Existing studies tend to indicate that corporate contributions may result in substantive benefits for corporations and may lead to greater access to government officials. It would be helpful to know whether independent spending by corporations has the same effect, and whether that effect is stronger or weaker because the source of the spending is a business entity instead of an individual. Similarly, future research should explore whether issues of concern to corporations and unions differ markedly from issues of concern to the general public. Finally, scholars could examine whether heavy corporate or union spending affects voter turnout, other forms of political participation, or the prominence of certain issues discussed during a campaign.

[101] Jennifer L. Brown, Katharine D. Drake & Laura Wellman, *The Benefits of a Relational Approach to Corporate Political Activity: Evidence from Political Contributions to Tax Policymakers*, 37 J. AM. TAX'N ASS'N 69 (2014).

[102] Eleanor Neff Powell & Justin Grimmer, Money in Exile: Campaign Contributions and Committee Access (Working Paper, 2016), www.eleanorneffpowell.com/uploads/8/3/9/3/8393347/money.pdf.

[103] John C. Coates, IV, *Corporate Politics, Governance, and Value Before and After* Citizens United, 9 J. EMP. LEGAL STUD. 657 (2012).

IV. CONCLUSION

The Supreme Court will face complex and enormously consequential questions when it hears campaign finance cases in the coming years. Proponents of new laws will seek to persuade the Court that reform is beneficial and necessary to promote democratic values. Opponents of those laws will claim that they are unconstitutional attempts to prevent political participation by those who want to spend money on election-related speech. In assessing those arguments, the Court must decide whether to rely principally on evidence or on its own assumptions about how campaign finance laws actually work. If researchers make progress answering the vital questions outlined above and are able to present the Court with objective and reliable empirical research relevant to the major issues in campaign finance, it will be wise for the justices to accept the assistance that the scholarly community gives them.

15

Fixing the Supreme Court's Mistake: The Case for the Twenty-Eighth Amendment

Ronald A. Fein*

If the Supreme Court's constitutional decisions have forced our democratic system far off course, then we need to overturn those decisions. And the best way to do that is to amend the Constitution.

A fundamental principle of American democracy is "one person, one vote."[1] That principle means, in its most literal sense, that every person gets to vote once and that every person's vote counts equally. More broadly, it means *political equality*: that every person should have an equal influence in the democratic process. But when wealthy donors exert more influence than ordinary voters, that principle is mocked.

To fulfill the promise of "one person, one vote," we must bring together people of different views for important conversations about how to organize our democracy itself. But the Supreme Court has made that work vastly more difficult through its constitutional decisions in the area of campaign finance, which have hobbled our reform efforts. And to get past this problem, we must overturn the Supreme Court's constitutional decisions on campaign finance.

That is a delicate proposition in a book filled with thoughtful reform proposals that do *not* require constitutional change. But it is fundamental. After 40 years of Supreme Court decisions—some holding steady, others

* Ronald A. Fein is the Legal Director of Free Speech For People. For more information on Free Speech For People, a national non-partisan public interest advocacy organization founded on the day of the *Citizens United* decision, see www.freespeechforpeople.org. The author has been involved in some of the deliberations, debates, and drafting for issues discussed in this chapter. Thanks to John Bonifaz, Jeffrey Clements, Johannes Epke, and Jasmine Gomez, and of course this volume's editors, Eugene Mazo and Timothy Kuhner, for commenting on earlier drafts of this chapter.

1 In the early 1960s, the Supreme Court derived the "one person, one vote" principle from the forward march of "[t]he conception of political equality from the Declaration of Independence, to Lincoln's Gettysburg Address, to the Fifteenth, Seventeenth, and Nineteenth Amendments." Gray v. Sanders, 372 U.S. 368, 381 (1963).

flipping as the composition of the Court itself changes—many of the most basic policy options have been taken off the table. The beauty of our system is supposed to be that the 50 states are "laboratories of democracy." But the laboratories have been told that they cannot use certain equipment. So promising reforms that could be tried in a city government, then perhaps a small state, then a big state, and finally at the federal level, never make it past the whiteboard.

To be sure, a constitutional amendment would not by itself fix our system—it would lay the foundation for further reforms. But right now, Supreme Court precedent prevents many potentially effective reform proposals from even being tested. So a constitutional amendment that would eliminate judicially imposed obstacles to campaign finance reform deserves serious consideration.

The Twenty-Eighth Amendment would overturn *Citizens United v. Federal Election Commission* and the Supreme Court's entire line of cases starting with *Buckley v. Valeo.*[2] It would establish political equality as a legitimate public goal for campaign finance reforms, and allow federal, state, and local governments to set limits on fundraising and spending in elections.

This is as American as apple pie. When James Madison wanted to persuade the young republic to ratify the Constitution, he argued that the people who would elect Congress's House of Representatives would be "[n]ot the rich, more than the poor; … not the haughty heirs of distinguished names, more than the humble sons of obscurity and unpropitious fortune," but rather "the great body of the people of the United States."[3] At the same time, our constitutional history is the history of *improving* upon the Founders' imperfect vision. In the 231 years since the Constitution was written, we have amended the Constitution 27 times—seven times to expand democracy and the right to vote.[4] The arc of our constitutional democracy may be long, but it bends toward political equality.

Across many different polls and surveys, and literally hundreds of ballot resolutions in states red, blue, and purple, about 75 percent of Americans support a constitutional amendment to overturn *Citizens United* and

[2] *See* Citizens United v. FEC, 558 U.S. 310 (2010); Buckley v. Valeo, 424 U.S. 1 (1976) (per curiam).

[3] The Federalist No. 57, at 348–49 (James Madison) (Clinton Rossiter ed., 1961).

[4] *See* U.S. Const. amends. XIV, § 1 (guaranteeing equal protection of the laws), XV (prohibiting denial of vote based on race), XVII (providing for direct election of U.S. Senate), XIX (prohibiting denial of vote based on sex), XXIII (granting voters in the District of Columbia the ability to vote for president), XXIV (prohibiting denial of vote in federal elections based on failure to pay a poll tax), XXVI (prohibiting denial of vote to persons aged 18 or older based on age).

Buckley.[5] This depth and breadth of support defies "left" v. "right" analysis. Take just one state, Wisconsin, that was closely divided in the 2016 presidential election.[6] In that *exact same election*, 18 mostly rural Wisconsin communities passed resolutions calling for a constitutional amendment to overturn *Citizens United* by margins ranging from 65 percent to 91 percent.[7] Not much in American life has 91 percent support—even *apple pie itself* polls only at 81 percent favorable.[8]

The people understand that the Supreme Court has broken the system, and that "We the People" can fix it. Let us turn now to the case for the Twenty-Eighth Amendment.

I. THE NEED FOR AN AMENDMENT

A. *Why We Need to Overturn the Supreme Court's Constitutional Precedent*

The experience of the past century has taught us that coming up with an optimal system of campaign finance is difficult. That reflects the messy but wonderful process of democratic compromise and the complexity of human affairs. So cities, states, and occasionally Congress do their best, muddle through, and pass campaign finance reform measures that reflect the politics of the passable.

But that task has been made much more difficult by the unhelpful intrusion of the courts. If a campaign finance system is ineffective because the

5 This rough figure holds across a broad range of popular votes and polls. In the November 2012 election in Montana, the state's citizens voted for Republican presidential candidate Mitt Romney over his Democratic opponent President Barack Obama by a margin of 55% to 45%. The exact same electorate supported Initiative No. 166, calling for a constitutional amendment to overturn *Citizens United*, by 75% to 25%. In Colorado in the November 2012 election, a similar measure (Amendment 65) passed by 74% to 26%. Other direct popular votes in support of a constitutional amendment have passed by margins ranging from 52% (Brecksville, Ohio, 2012) to 91% (Monona, Wisconsin, 2017). An examination of the popular vote across multiple votes in different places and times shows a strong central tendency at about 75%. For example, examining the popular votes on amendment resolutions in 2012 local elections in Illinois, in alphabetical order by name of municipality, the first ten results are: 75%, 70%, 72%, 74%, 72%, 73%, 63%, 75%, 86%, 66%. For data on these votes, see *State and Local Support*, United For The People, http://united4thepeople.org/state-and-local-support-2/. Polls tend to produce similar results. *See Polling*, United For The People, http://united4thepeople.org/resources/#Polling, for a sample of polling data.

6 *See 2016 Fall General Election Results*, Wis. Elections Comm'n, http://elections.wi.gov/elections-voting/results/2016/fall-general (Nov. 8, 2016).

7 *See State and Local Support*, United For The People, http://united4thepeople.org/state-and-local-support-2/.

8 *See* YouGov, *Omnibus Poll*, Huff. Post (April 10–11, 2013), http://huff.to/2n5fMOp (question 1).

politics do not favor a better system, that is bad enough. But if the democratic branches (elected legislatures, or the voters through direct democracy) do enact meaningful reform, and courts selectively strike out certain elements of it, then the problem runs much deeper.

A visitor from another area of law might be surprised to see how unusual this situation is. Take, for example, environmental law, which is arguably more complex, and certainly not less important, than campaign finance. By and large, in environmental law, courts are not the final arbiters of what is possible. To be sure, there is plenty of litigation and room for critical judicial decisions. But that litigation, and the judicial role, most often involves the interpretation of a statute. If the Supreme Court rules that the Environmental Protection Agency has misinterpreted a term in the Clean Air Act, and Congress disagrees, Congress can amend the act. That is certainly not easy in our increasingly polarized politics, but at least there is a pathway to a democratic fix. At the margins, there are some limits involving the division of responsibilities between administrative agencies and the legislature, or between the federal government and states. Yet in environmental law, there are very few total gaps: policy options that, courts will say, simply cannot be done at all. Environmental policy is constrained by technology, economics, practicality, and politics (itself heavily influenced by campaign finance!). But in an important (if only theoretical) sense, almost anything is legally possible.

That is a very different scenario from campaign finance law. In a "dejudicialized" environment, we might see hundreds of different approaches, striking different balances across Congress, states and territories, and our cities and towns. Unfortunately, these efforts must contend with the additional problem that a micromanaging Supreme Court has removed critical arrows from the policy quiver. Laws that were designed with two complementary parts must function with only one. Carefully negotiated political compromises are ripped apart, leaving in their place unbalanced policies that no legislature ever enacted or ever *would* enact. Systems designed to confront one problem are shoehorned into solving another problem, and then called inadequate because they are not perfectly designed to solve the problem that was not their focus in the first place.

The net result resembles a house from which walls, studs, and joists have been removed willy-nilly. Now the house bulges in strange places, canters at odd angles, and is beset with unexpected holes in the floor and leaks in the roof. The building can be patched here and there, with scraps of plywood, jerry-rigged buttresses, and plastic sheeting. But the building is fundamentally unsound.

Imagine that you first began to think about how to address the problem of money in politics without the benefit of detailed legal advice on what the Supreme Court would permit. Perhaps you are running for city council or the state legislature, exasperated by the way that campaign funders influence and control the agenda. Suppose that you began sketching out possible ideas, without any constraints, and then presented them to a lawyer versed in campaign finance. You would quickly learn that the Supreme Court's constitutional decisions have imposed the following limitations on your ideas for how to improve the system.

1. In Most Situations, the Only Legitimate Goal of Campaign Finance Reform is Preventing "*Quid Pro Quo*" Corruption

The first question is: what is the goal? Starting from a blank slate, you might imagine a long list of goals or reasons for limiting the influence of money in politics. You might start with *equal citizenship*. As noted above, the "one person, one vote" principle is fundamental to our democracy.[9] But we increasingly see a "wealth primary," where wealthy donors select the candidates who will be allowed to present their ideas to voters, filtering out (at very early stages) those whose views, no matter how popular they might be with actual voters, are displeasing to the donor class.[10] This donor class is wealthier, whiter, older and more disproportionately male than the electorate as a whole.[11] And because it is virtually impossible for a candidate to mount a serious political campaign unless she is either herself affluent or has affluent connections, the views of the affluent are always over-represented, and the views of the masses are under-represented—if represented at all.[12]

9 *See* Gray v. Sanders, 372 U.S. 368, 381 (1963); *see also* Reynolds v. Sims, 377 U.S. 533 (1964); Baker v. Carr, 369 U.S. 186 (1962).

10 The term "wealth primary" was coined by Jamin Raskin (now a U.S. Representative) and John Bonifaz in 1993. *See* Jamin Raskin & John Bonifaz, *Equal Protection and the Wealth Primary*, 11 YALE L. & POL'Y REV. 273 (1993). The concept has been popularized recently by Lawrence Lessig. *See, e.g.*, Lawrence Lessig, "Equality," A Speech Delivered at Stetson Law School (Feb. 27, 2014), https://vimeo.com/8793140 (video). It has also been called the "money primary." *See* Ari Berman, *How the Money Primary Is Undermining Voting Rights*, THE NATION (May 19, 2015), www.thenation.com/article/how-money-primary-undermining-voting-rights/.

11 *See* Adam Lioz, *Stacked Deck: How the Racial Bias in Our Big Money Political System Undermines Our Democracy and Our Economy*, DEMOS (Dec. 2014), https://goo.gl/TJ2mQX (90% of $200+ federal contributions came from predominantly white neighborhoods); Adam Bonica et al., *Why Hasn't Democracy Slowed Rising Inequality?*, J. ECON. PERSP., Summer 2013, at 103, 111–12 (over 40% of total money contributed in federal elections comes from 0.01% of voting age population).

12 See the chapters by Timothy Kuhner and Nicholas Stephanopoulos in this book.

You might also consider *preventing systemic or institutional corruption*. Besides the election itself, in matters of *policy and legislation*, campaign funders have more influence and access than ordinary voters. Candidates and officials are likely to become biased toward, and improperly dependent upon, those funders, rather than their own constituents or any sense of the "general public interest."[13]

You might then consider a host of other worthy goals: preventing "drowning out" of less-funded voices; protecting the integrity of the electoral process; protecting the time of officials and candidates so that they may focus on legislation and constituent service rather than fundraising; and many others. As a final thought, you might also consider *preventing "quid pro quo" corruption*. Bribery—giving a politician money expressly in exchange for performance of a favor, e.g., for killing a bill in committee—is already illegal. But it can still happen. Contribution limits act as a bulwark to supplement bribery laws because the less money that can be given in the first place, the less effective it will be as a bribe.

But outside of a few very specialized contexts, such as political spending by foreign nationals, the Supreme Court has rejected *all* potential goals for regulating money in politics except the very last one on our list.[14] Nowadays, the only basis accepted by the Supreme Court for regulating political contributions and expenditures is the prevention of *quid pro quo* corruption or its appearance.[15] Although that is a legitimate goal, it should not be the *only* goal.

And the goal matters. If someone challenges a local, state, or federal campaign finance rule in court, the court must satisfy itself that the law is closely related to the goal of preventing *quid pro quo* corruption. For example, the Supreme Court has convinced itself that regulating contributions to campaigns for and against ballot measures (initiatives, referenda, voter instructions, and so on) is unconstitutional. Under the Supreme Court's analysis, there is no candidate being elected in a ballot measure and hence no risk of corruption, so contribution limits serve no legitimate goal.[16]

This is an overly cramped framework, and it does not match the way most Americans think about money in politics. If given the chance, many

[13] Lawrence Lessig describes this form of corruption as "dependence corruption." *See* LAWRENCE LESSIG, REPUBLIC, LOST: HOW MONEY CORRUPTS CONGRESS—AND A PLAN TO STOP IT 17–20, 226–47 (2011).

[14] *See* Citizens United v. FEC, 558 U.S. 310 (2010); Randall v. Sorrell, 548 U.S. 230 (2006); Buckley v. Valeo, 424 U.S. 1 (1976) (per curiam).

[15] McCutcheon v. FEC, 134 S. Ct. 1434 (2014).

[16] Citizens Against Rent Control v. City of Berkeley, 454 U.S. 290 (1981).

communities would consider adopting campaign finance laws that explicitly aim at broader goals, such as promoting equal citizenship, rather than just preventing *quid pro quo* corruption. But under Supreme Court precedent, they cannot.

2. You Cannot Set Overall Campaign Spending Limits

One of the most obvious forms of campaign finance reform is to set a maximum budget for a political campaign for a given office, and require all candidates to stick to that budget. Limiting the demand for money by capping how much can be spent takes the pressure off *raising* so much money in the first place. Election rules for high school and college student government offices often feature maximum spending limits.[17]

In other domains, it is taken for granted that spending limits can promote healthy competition and prevent dominance by big spenders. That is one reason why all four major professional sports leagues in the United States have some form of "salary cap."[18]

But we do not have to look so far for analogies. If you have ever attended a public meeting of local government—whether the traditional New England town meeting, in which the people directly debate and vote on all major proposals, or a city council hearing, in which the public can testify to city councilmembers—you have probably seen a time limit. A timekeeper announces that all speakers will have a certain amount of time to speak (five minutes is common), and then will be cut off. Presidential debates, court arguments (including at the Supreme Court), and debates in the U.S. House of Representatives all follow similar rules. Time limits ensure a fair debate by making sure that each side has an equal chance to make its case.

Putting these two principles together, some communities experimenting with campaign finance reform would like to try overall campaign spending limits. How well does this work? We do not really know, because the Supreme

[17] *See* Flint v. Dennison, 488 F.3d 816 (9th Cir. 2007) (upholding $100 candidate spending limit for state university student government).

[18] The National Football League and the National Hockey League impose "hard caps" on total team payroll. Major League Baseball imposes a "competitive balance tax" (sometimes called "luxury tax") on teams that pay more than a league-determined threshold. The National Basketball Association imposes both a "soft cap" (with certain exceptions) and a competitive balance tax. *See generally Salary Cap*, WIKIPEDIA, https://en.wikipedia.org/wiki/Salary_cap. Of course, as with sports leagues, a spending limit can have other benefits. Spending limits save money, as donors feel less obligated to engage in an arms race against other donors, and time, as candidates spend less time fundraising.

Court told us in the 1976 case of *Buckley* that it is forbidden. But we do have some clues.

In 1974, the City of Albuquerque, New Mexico enacted total campaign spending limits for candidates for mayor and city council. Two years later, the Supreme Court decided *Buckley*, which held that campaign spending limits are unconstitutional. But a funny thing happened in Albuquerque: nobody filed a lawsuit to challenge the spending limit. And courts can only decide cases that are brought to them. So for 27 years, Albuquerque conducted its municipal elections under overall campaign spending limits set at twice the annual salary of the office sought. The public and the candidates (both winning and losing) were all happy with the system. It prevented fundraising from getting out of control, and enabled years of healthy competition. Unfortunately, the system came crashing down when a mayoral candidate finally decided to challenge it in court in 2001.[19] Since the campaign spending limits were contrary to the Supreme Court's *Buckley* decision, a federal judge in New Mexico struck them down.

The accidental experiment from Albuquerque is promising. Of course, not all jurisdictions would choose a system like that. Yet if given the chance, many communities would consider adopting campaign finance laws that limit overall campaign spending. But, again, under Supreme Court precedent, they cannot do so.

3. Contribution Limits Cannot Be "too Low"

The Supreme Court allows local, state, and federal governments to set limits on contributions to political campaigns. That is the good news. But if a contribution limit strikes a judge as "too low," it will be struck down as violating the First Amendment.

That is a problem for many local and state governments. There are many reasons for contribution limits that might seem relatively low. An obvious reason is helping to protect equal citizenship. Many people cannot afford to give $27, let alone $270, let alone $2,700, to political candidates. But some can. If donors can contribute up to $2,700, then a $2,700 donor will have more influence—perhaps 100 times more influence—than a $27 donor. Setting the contribution limit at a lower limit, though, would nullify this advantage. If the contribution limit was set at $270, then the wealthy $2,700 donor has no greater financial influence than the middle class $270 donor. And if the limit was set at $27, then the wealthy donor would have no more financial influence

[19] Homans v. City of Albuquerque, 366 F.3d 900 (10th Cir. 2004).

than an unemployed or low-income worker, student, or retiree who struggles to give $27 at most.

Of course, low contribution limits may not be ideal in every situation. They presumably work best when campaign expenses are low, whether through natural market economics (e.g., a smaller jurisdiction with inexpensive campaign methods) or through legally mandated campaign spending limits (which, as noted above, the Supreme Court has rejected). They might also be viable in expensive but very high-profile races (perhaps only the presidential election) where a candidate can successfully use Internet fundraising to base an expensive campaign primarily on small grassroots donors.

These are legitimate policy debates. But they have been foreclosed by court decisions. As noted above, basing low contribution limits on a desire to protect equal citizenship is prohibited by Supreme Court precedent. They must be based on the need to prevent corruption, which is often difficult to establish.[20] And worse yet, courts now scrutinize contribution limits to determine whether they are "too low" according to a hazy set of criteria.[21]

4. You Cannot Limit Outside Spending

Not all political campaigning comes from the campaigns themselves. Sometimes, people or organizations outside the campaign want to buy advertising or otherwise indirectly fund campaigns by supporting candidate X or opposing candidate Y. In small amounts, this is as American as apple pie. Who would criticize the fifth-grader who, inspired by a local election, spends her own money to buy poster-board and markers to make handmade signs?

But as the dollars increase, outside spending tends to raise most of the same problems as direct campaign contributions and spending. And in recent years, the proportion of outside money has exploded. When the Supreme Court decided *Buckley*, big-money outside spending was a relatively uncommon phenomenon. Perhaps a wealthy individual or small group of wealthy individuals might buy a newspaper advertisement—indeed, that seems to have been the Supreme Court's exact concern in *Buckley*. But we are way past that. Back

[20] In the Court's 2014 *McCutcheon v. FEC* decision, for example, the Court essentially reasoned that, if one member of Congress cannot be corrupted by a single $2,700 contribution, then there is no risk of corruption in allowing a wealthy donor to make very large (e.g., half a million dollars) contributions to party committees, so long as those contributions could be mathematically accounted for as a set of smaller $2,700 contributions. *See* McCutcheon v. FEC, 134 S. Ct. 1434 (2014). This neat syllogism ignores how *party based* corruption can work. *See, e.g.*, Michael D. Gilbert & Emily Reeder, *Aggregate Corruption*, 104 KY. L.J. 651 (2016); Michael S. Kang, *Party-Based Corruption and* McCutcheon v. FEC, 108 NW. U. L. REV. ONLINE 240 (2014).

[21] *See* Randall v. Sorrell, 548 U.S. 230 (2006).

in 2014, it was newsworthy when twice as much of the total money spent in a Florida congressional race came from outside groups as from the candidates themselves.[22] In 2016, that ratio barely raised eyebrows; the new threshold is when *three* times as much is spent by outside groups as by candidates.[23]

Unfortunately, the Supreme Court has ruled that outside spending is largely immune from limits. There is an exception: If an outside spending group "coordinates" its spending with the official campaign team, e.g., by discussing media strategy, then the spending can be treated as if it were a contribution directly to the campaign, and subject to contribution limits. The Supreme Court's theory is that if the outside spending group is *not* coordinating its spending with the campaign, then there is no opportunity for that "*quid pro quo*" corruption to occur.

But political campaign professionals are good at toeing lines. No matter how strictly the lines against "coordination" between outside spending groups and campaigns are drawn, in the information age any reasonably competent outside spending group can figure out how to spend tens of millions of dollars in useful support of a campaign without crossing those lines. That money may not be as useful to candidates as money given directly to their campaigns—but there is so much more of it.

In today's campaign environment, outside spending is impossible to ignore.

If given the chance, many communities would consider adopting campaign finance laws that limit high-dollar outside spending. But under Supreme Court precedent, they cannot.

5. You Cannot Limit Corporate or Union Political Spending

Corporate and labor union political spending was, until 2010, prohibited or limited in federal elections, and in 24 states. Two reasons were generally offered.

First, corporations and unions should not be able to convert special state-granted legal privileges into extra political influence. Corporations, for example, can use their state-granted legal powers of limited liability and

[22] Some $12.5 million was spent in the March 2014 special election for Florida's 13th Congressional District. Of that total, the candidates (Republican David Jolly and Democrat Alex Sink) spent just 31.2%. The remainder was spent by national political party committees and various nonprofits and super PACs. *See* Michael Beckel, *Outside Groups Dwarf Candidate Spending in Florida Special Election*, Center for Public Integrity (Mar. 6, 2014), www.publicintegrity.org/2014/03/06/14337/outside-groups-dwarf-candidate-spending-florida-special-election.

[23] *See Races in Which Outside Spending Exceeds Candidate Spending, 2016 Election Cycle*, Center for Responsive Politics, www.opensecrets.org/outsidespending/outvscand.php?cycle=2016.

perpetual life to amass enormous sums of money from customers who give them money for goods or services, not to support (indeed, usually without knowing) the corporation's political spending plans. If money spent in election campaigns was thought to somehow reflect intensity or breadth of support, then corporate political spending can distort the campaign financing ecosystem by flooding elections with money that does not correlate to any public support. For example, consider a corporation with a relatively small number of employees that makes virtually all its money by exporting products to foreign customers. It might accumulate large sums of money to spend in elections, but that money does not in any meaningful way reflect public support for the corporation's political objectives. Labor unions' money generally derives from worker fees, but in some circumstances unions can similarly come to dominate political spending out of proportion from public support for their objectives.

The second rationale is that, fundamentally, corporate executives and union officials engaged in political spending are playing with other people's money. As for unions, in some cases private-sector workers are *required* to pay fees to the union. While the Supreme Court has held that unions must segregate political spending from workplace representation, and give dissenting workers the ability to opt out of the portion of a fee attributable to political spending,[24] in many cases the default is "in." In the case of corporations, the money ultimately "belongs" (at least in some senses) to shareholders, who generally do not have the ability (either legally or practically) to control, opt out of, or even *learn* management's choices for political spending.

But these reasons for restricting political spending by corporations and unions were rejected in *Citizens United* and a follow-up case, *American Tradition Partnership v. Bullock*,[25] that extended *Citizens United* to the states in 2012. As of this writing, direct corporate and union contributions to candidates can be prohibited, but corporate and union outside spending cannot be limited at all.

6. You Cannot Design a Voluntary Public Finance System with "Rescue" Provisions for Clean-Money Candidates Facing Privately Financed Opponents

Voluntary public financing systems have enjoyed some success in state and local races. These come in different versions: block grants, matching grants,

[24] *Comms. Workers of America v. Beck*, 487 U.S. 735 (1988); *cf. Janus v. Am. Fed'n of State, Cty., & Mun. Employees, Council* 31, 138 S. Ct. 2448 (2018) (invalidating agency fee requirements for public employees).

[25] Am. Tradition Partnership, Inc. v. Bullock, 565 U.S. 1187 (2012).

and in the newest variation, "citizen vouchers" given directly to voters to send to candidates. Under the right conditions, these systems can succeed.[26]

The problem comes when a clean-money candidate faces a wealthy self- or donor-funded opponent who has declined to opt into the system. One approach that had been used in federal law was to allow the clean money candidate a higher contribution limit if she faced a self-financed opponent whose spending exceeded certain levels. The Supreme Court struck that down.[27] Another approach, used in many state "clean elections" systems, was to provide additional "rescue funds" of public money to a clean-money candidate in this situation. The Court struck that down too.[28]

The remaining solutions to this problem tend to involve flooding the system with *much more* public money, so that publicly financed campaigns can compete more effectively with wealthy donor-financed or self-financed campaigns. But this puts the taxpayers in an insane financial arms race with the wealthiest 0.1 percent of the country. It may not be politically sustainable to devote so much taxpayer money to trying to outspend quixotic billionaires, and even if it is, it is a sad commentary if the only Court-approved way to make a public campaign financing system work is to divert ever-increasing amounts from the public treasury to advertising.

B. *What Is to Be Done?*

What, then, *can* we do in the face of this cramping judicial precedent? The problems identified above—tools missing from the reform toolbox, because the Supreme Court pulled them out—do not completely eliminate all possibilities for reform. Some measures, like improved disclosure rules, contribution limits, and certain limited voluntary public financing, can be designed to (hopefully) survive judicial challenge. And there are other fine reform solutions that can be pursued even in this current legal environment—this book is filled with them.

If we take the current constraints imposed by the Supreme Court as an unalterable given—if we accept that money deserves the same constitutional protections as speech, that "*quid pro quo*" corruption is the only democratic value that can justify limiting the flow of money, that spending can rarely, if ever, be limited, that corporations deserve the same protections as citizens

[26] For a fuller discussion of how the public financing of elections in the United States works, see the chapters by Richard Briffault and Adam Lioz in this book.

[27] Davis v. FEC, 554 U.S. 724 (2008).

[28] Ariz. Free Enter. Club's Freedom Club PAC v. Bennett, 564 U.S. 721 (2011).

and voters, and all the rest—then we can try to muddle through and make a terrible system marginally better.

But what if we do not have to take those constraints as given?

These shackles on reform are not inevitable. For now, we must treat them as part of constitutional law, but they are not in the Constitution itself. They were not given to us by the Founders, but imposed on us by the Supreme Court.

The Supreme Court could undo its own mischief. But it seems unlikely that the Supreme Court will be disposed to overrule *Citizens United*, let alone *Buckley*, in the next few years. And even if the composition of the Supreme Court shifts in a favorable direction, it is unlikely to overrule *Buckley* in one fell swoop. Cases have to be developed and presented, and the Supreme Court prefers to move incrementally. By the time that an opportunity to overrule *Buckley* is before the Court, the pendulum may have swung in the opposite direction. Moreover, it is unhealthy for democracy to focus on an incredibly tiny body of elite judges—really, one, since critical decisions these days tend to be 5-4—appointed in a hyper-partisan environment. In fact, such focus on the Justices replicates the injury to democracy by depriving Americans of the chance to participate in defining their own self-government, in favor of an inaccessible process centered entirely in Washington, D.C, and run by an especially elite class of judges with life tenure.[29]

The Founders gave us a sounder mechanism for amending the Constitution. And we can use it again now.

II. WHAT THE CONSTITUTIONAL AMENDMENT WILL DO

A. *What Is a Constitutional Amendment and How Do We Pass One?*

The Founders of our Constitution foresaw the need to amend it from time to time. Article V of the Constitution provides:

> The Congress, whenever two thirds of both houses shall deem it necessary, shall propose amendments to this Constitution, or, on the application of the legislatures of two thirds of the several states, shall call a convention for proposing amendments, which, in either case, shall be valid to all intents and purposes, as part of this Constitution, when ratified by the legislatures of three

[29] *See* Jeff Clements, *Justices Matter But Amendments Matter More*, THE HILL (Feb. 26, 2016), http://thehill.com/blogs/congress-blog/campaign/270766-justices-matter-but-amendments-matter-more.

> fourths of the several states, or by conventions in three fourths thereof, as the one or the other mode of ratification may be proposed by the Congress …

An amendment is written as a separate, stand-alone text that is appended to the end of the Constitution.[30] Once ratified, it becomes a full part of the Constitution, with the same force as if it had been there since 1787, but also capable of providing a new interpretive "lens" on provisions adopted before the new amendment.

Over the past 231 years, we have amended the Constitution 27 times—17 of them since the initial Bill of Rights was passed by the First Congress. Of those 17, more than half (nine) were ratified within the last century. On average, amendments have been passed about once a generation, often in batches at moments of great national significance:

- *Bill of Rights:* In 1791, with the Constitution just recently ratified and the memory of the Revolutionary War still fresh, we passed the first ten amendments, known as the Bill of Rights.[31]
- *Reconstruction Amendments:* In a five-year period during the post-Civil War Reconstruction, we passed the Thirteenth (banning slavery), Fourteenth (guaranteeing due process of law and equal protection from state governments), and Fifteenth (prohibiting denial of the vote based on race) Amendments.
- *Progressive Amendments:* During a 20-year period in the Progressive ferment of the early twentieth century, we passed six amendments, including the Sixteenth (authorizing a federal income tax), Seventeenth (requiring direct popular elections of the Senate), and Nineteenth (prohibiting denial of the vote based on sex) Amendments.[32]

[30] This was not specified in the Constitution itself. When Congress began debating the initial batch of amendments that forms our Bill of Rights, James Madison thought that the "original" text of the Constitution should be revised by amendments. But he lost that argument, and so now we have a chronological record embedded in the Constitution itself: the full original 1787 text of the Constitution, including portions of which are obsolete or repealed, followed sequentially by amendments in their order of ratification.

[31] In the decade following the ratification of the Bill of Rights, Congress passed three more amendments that might be called the Technical Correction Amendments: the Eleventh (overturning a Supreme Court decision on whether states could be sued in federal court by citizens of another state), the Twelfth (revising presidential election procedures, and itself later superseded), and the Twenty-Seventh (preventing Congress from raising its own salary mid-term), which was passed by Congress in 1789 but, due to various oversights and a remarkable historical re-discovery, not ratified until 1992.

[32] The Progressive Amendments also included Prohibition, passed by the Eighteenth Amendment and then later repealed by the Twentieth.

- *Voting Rights Amendments:* In a ten-year period during the great social upheaval of the 1960s and early 1970s, we passed the Twenty-Third (giving residents of the District of Columbia a vote for president), Twenty-Fourth (banning the poll tax in federal elections; soon after extended by the Supreme Court to state elections), and Twenty-Sixth (giving the right to vote to 18-year-olds) Amendments.[33]

Put another way, the history of our Constitution is one of constitutionally fertile "amendment eras" separated by a little over 40 years on average. Setting aside the unusual circumstances of the ratification of the Twenty-Seventh Amendment,[34] the last amendment era ended in 1971. If history is any guide, we are about due. Perhaps the paroxysm of American politics illustrated (and perhaps caused) by the election of President Trump highlights this need.

Importantly, of the 17 post-Bill of Rights amendments, seven (the Eleventh, Thirteenth, Fourteenth, Sixteenth, Nineteenth, Twenty-Fourth, and Twenty-Sixth) were passed and ratified to correct and reverse specific Supreme Court rulings with which the American public disagreed:

- The Eleventh Amendment, ratified in 1795, provides that federal courts do not have jurisdiction over a suit against a state by citizens of another state. That overturned *Chisholm* v. *Georgia*.[35]
- The Thirteenth and Fourteenth Amendments, ratified in 1865 and 1868, ban slavery and prohibit states from denying due process or equal protection of the laws. They overturned *Dred Scott v. Sandford* and *Barron v. Baltimore*.[36]
- The Sixteenth Amendment, ratified in 1913, grants Congress the authority to enact income taxes without apportioning them by state. That overturned *Pollock v. Farmers' Loan & Trust Co.*, in which the Court held that Congress lacked this power.[37]
- The Nineteenth Amendment, ratified in 1920, prohibits states from denying women the right to vote. That overturned *Minor v. Happersett*.[38]
- The Twenty-Fourth Amendment, ratified in 1964, prohibits states from conditioning the right to vote in federal elections on the payment of

[33] Over the course of the twentieth century, we also passed three amendments pertaining to presidential succession (the Twentieth, Twenty-Second, and Twenty-Fifth) after specific eye-opening problems.

[34] *See supra* note 31.

[35] Chisholm v. Georgia, 2 U.S. (2 Dall.) 419 (1793).

[36] Dred Scott v. Sandford, 60 U.S. 393 (1857); Barron v. Baltimore, 32 U.S. (7 Pet.) 243 (1833).

[37] Pollock v. Farmers' Loan & Trust Co., 157 U.S. 429 (1895).

[38] Minor v. Happersett, 88 U.S. 162 (1875).

a poll tax. That overturned *Lassiter v. Northampton County Board of Elections* and *Breedlove v. Suttles*.[39]

- The Twenty-Sixth Amendment, ratified in 1971, prohibits states from denying the right to vote on the basis of age to any citizen aged 18 or older. That overturned *Oregon v. Mitchell*.[40]

B. *What Would a Campaign Finance Amendment Say?*

Most amendment advocates agree that a constitutional amendment, to be effective, must overturn not only *Citizens United*, but *Buckley v. Valeo*, the 1976 Supreme Court decision that set the foundations for the Court's focus on "corruption," its rejection of spending limits, and what followed. Yet there are several different options for the text beyond that. Unsurprisingly, there are multiple views on how best to structure the amendment.

The first key question is whether the amendment should focus only on money in politics, or address other issues as well. The *Citizens United* case brought together two sets of issues: campaign finance, and the constitutional status of corporations. Many advocates support overturning *both* the Supreme Court's money in politics cases (going back to *Buckley v. Valeo*) *and* its cases extending constitutional rights to corporations, including outside of the context of campaign finance.[41] Others support only the first goal. Of those who support both goals, some argue that both must be accomplished in a single amendment, while others believe that passing an amendment on campaign finance alone will be more expedient than passing a combined amendment, and may indeed accelerate passage and ratification of a later amendment undoing the Court's extension of constitutional rights to corporations. And many support simultaneously addressing other democracy-related issues, such as an explicit right to vote, a national popular vote for president, or gerrymandering reforms.

The second question, with respect to money in politics, is whether the amendment should be *enabling*, *mandatory*, or *self-executing*. An enabling amendment grants Congress and the states the *power* to enact campaign finance reform and clears away judicial obstacles. A good structural model for this is the Sixteenth Amendment. In 1895, the Supreme Court ruled in

[39] Lassiter v. Northampton County Bd. of Elec., 360 U.S. 45 (1959); Breedlove v. Suttles, 302 U.S. 277 (1937).

[40] Oregon v. Mitchell, 400 U.S. 112 (1970).

[41] The details of the latter topic are beyond the subject of this chapter (or this book), but it is essential to understand the context. For more information, see ADAM WINKLER, WE THE CORPORATIONS: HOW AMERICAN BUSINESSES WON THEIR CIVIL RIGHTS (2018); JEFF CLEMENTS, CORPORATIONS ARE NOT PEOPLE (2d ed. 2014). *See also* John C. Coates, IV, *Corporate Speech & the First Amendment: History, Data, and Implications*, 30 CONST. COMMENT. 223 (2015).

Pollock v. Farmers' Loan & Trust Co. that Congress does not have the power to enact income taxes unless they are apportioned among the states based on their population.[42] The Sixteenth Amendment, which was passed to overturn *Pollock*, provides: "The Congress *shall have power* to lay and collect taxes on incomes, from whatever source derived, without apportionment among the several States, and without regard to any census or enumeration."[43] That is an enabling amendment: it provides that Congress *has the power* to tax incomes without apportionment by state, but it does not *require* Congress to do anything. Similarly, an enabling amendment for campaign finance would give Congress and the states the breathing room to take action without judicial intervention, but would not require any specific legislation.

By contrast, a *mandatory* amendment would *require* Congress and the states to pass laws limiting money in politics. Some amendment advocates argue that, after all the effort to pass an amendment, it would be deeply disappointing if Congress and the states did not actually enact any reforms under their newly restored authority. This concern is not far-fetched. By analogy, while it has been clear for over 40 years that states may enact contribution limits, 11 states choose not to do so. They allow unlimited contributions to political candidates. At the same time, a mandatory amendment raises questions as to who exactly would enforce this requirement—we do not have good legal models for how anyone can force Congress to pass a law—or what standards a court might use to determine whether the legislatures had met their requirements.

Finally, a *self-executing amendment* would impose the limits right there in the text of the constitutional amendment. This is not hard to write; for example, an amendment could specify a dollar limit on contributions to campaigns for Congress.[44] This approach eliminates the possibility of the legislature doing nothing, or of doing something inadequate. On the other hand, it locks policy into constitutional text. That means that, if Congress or the states realized that changes were needed, those later changes might require *another* constitutional amendment. This is the lesson of the Eighteenth Amendment, which enacted Prohibition as a self-executing amendment: "[T]he manufacture, sale, or transportation of intoxicating liquors within, the importation thereof into, or the exportation thereof from the United States and all territory subject

[42] Pollock v. Farmers' Loan & Trust Co., 157 U.S. 429 (1895).

[43] U.S. Const. amend. XVI (emphasis added).

[44] Such an amendment could include an inflation mechanism adjustment to avoid the problem of dollar values meaning less over time. The Seventh Amendment provides a jury trial right in federal court for certain civil suits "where the value in controversy shall exceed twenty dollars." U.S. Const. amend. VII. Twenty dollars may have been a significant figure in 1791, but at this point the $20 threshold is meaningless.

to the jurisdiction thereof for beverage purposes is hereby prohibited."[45] When the public realized that Prohibition was unsustainable, it required another constitutional amendment to undo it: The Twenty-First Amendment repealed the Eighteenth Amendment, and replaced it with an enabling provision that gave control to states.[46]

In the field of campaign finance, which changes rapidly as political fundraising and spending techniques evolve, the process of experimentation by state and local governments is critical. Arguably, if a major part of the problem thus far has been that democratic deliberation has been cramped by *supposed* constitutional mandates, it might be best not to replicate that by creating *actual* constitutional mandates that could impede healthy policy compromises.

Until 2014, there were about a dozen distinct amendment bills floating in Congress at any given time.[47] In early 2014, most of the major campaign finance reform organizations supporting an amendment converged on a consensus text, known as Democracy For All Amendment (or DFAA). Here is the full text of the DFAA, as it became amended through the Senate process, with 55 co-sponsors:

> Section 1. To advance democratic self-government and political equality, and to protect the integrity of government and the electoral process, Congress and the States may regulate and set reasonable limits on the raising and spending of money by candidates and others to influence elections.
>
> Section 2. Congress and the States shall have power to implement and enforce this article by appropriate legislation, and may distinguish between natural persons and corporations or other artificial entities created by law, including by prohibiting such entities from spending money to influence elections.
>
> Section 3. Nothing in this article shall be construed to grant Congress or the States the power to abridge the freedom of the press.

This text has several notable features.

- *Enables the consideration of broader democratic values as legitimate goals of campaign finance reform.* Through the preamble to Section 1, the DFAA explicitly advances goals beyond just corruption: democratic self-government, political equality, and the integrity of government and

45 U.S. Const. amend. XVIII § 1.
46 U.S. Const. amend. XXI.
47 *See Constitutional Amendments*, United For The People, http://united4thepeople.org/amendments/.

the electoral process. This, alone, overturns a central holding of *Buckley*, *Citizens United*, and *McCutcheon v. Federal Election Commission*:[48] that corruption (or, worse yet, only *quid pro quo* corruption) is the only basis for campaign finance legislation.

- *Enables the regulation of spending, including from non-candidates.* This overturns key holdings of *Buckley* and other cases by allowing spending limits for campaigns and outside spenders.
- *Distinguishes natural persons from artificial entities created by law.* This overturns *Citizens United* by allowing Congress and the states to treat real people differently from corporations and, if they choose, prohibit the latter from campaign spending entirely.
- *Provides a savings clause for freedom of the press.* The first two sections of the DFAA authorize Congress to set limits on fundraising and spending to influence elections. By itself, this does not authorize the government to restrict press freedoms. However, out of an abundance of caution, the DFAA includes a savings clause to make it clear that, in cases where political campaigning may tread perilously close to activities protected by the freedom of the press, the DFAA does not authorize the government to abridge that freedom.[49]

The DFAA may not be the final word. Other amendment bills are still available as vehicles.[50] In 2017, a new collaborative process entitled "Writing the 28th Amendment" was launched under the leadership of the organization American Promise.[51] That 18-month project brings together constitutional scholars, citizen leaders and elected officials from both sides of the aisle in a deliberative process that may yield a different bill or set of bills.

C. *How Would Courts Analyze Campaign Finance Laws after the Amendment?*

It is important to emphasize what would be different, and what would not be different, in the ability of the states and federal government to regulate

48 McCutcheon v. FEC, 134 S. Ct. 1434 (2014).

49 Defining the boundaries of "freedom of the press" is not a simple task, but neither is it impossible. The writings of Sonja West are an excellent starting point. *See, e.g.*, Sonja R. West, *Awakening the Press Clause*, 58 UCLA L. Rev. 1025 (2011).

50 The most prominent of these other amendment bills is the We the People Amendment, championed by Move to Amend. *See* H.R.J. Res. 48, 115th Cong. (2017), www.congress.gov/bill/115th-congress/house-joint-resolution/48/.

51 *See Writing the 28th Amendment*, American Promise, www.americanpromise.net/writing_the_28th_amendment.

campaign finance after this amendment. Some people have made the counter-intuitive claim that the DFAA would have no effect at all! They suggest that Congress and the states *already* have the power to set limits on raising and spending money to influence elections—it is just that this power is limited by the First Amendment—and that unless a new amendment repeals the First Amendment, it will have zero effect.

But this is absurd. The DFAA's explicit assertion of the power to set limits on raising and spending money to influence elections by candidates and others, coupled with the foregrounding of constitutional values besides corruption and the authority to distinguish corporations from natural persons, would clearly overrule *Buckley* and all the cases that followed, including *Citizens United*. In so doing, it would overrule the Supreme Court's interpretations of how the First Amendment applies campaign finance reform measures.

In its place, the Supreme Court would either decline to review campaign finance laws, or create a new jurisprudence. Many of the foundational theoretical questions, such as the definition and limits of political equality, have already been tackled in academic literature and (unsuccessful) legal briefs under the current constitutional framework. Other questions would be worked out as courts generally try to do: answering questions in specific factual scenarios, applying the values and principles set before them to new conditions.

This may seem like an invitation to mischief, but it is how our Constitution has always worked. The men (unfortunately, all men) who wrote and ratified the First Amendment agreed on the need to protect "the freedom of speech"; they could not have agreed on, or even considered, how a court should evaluate all the myriad hypothetical scenarios that might possibly arise under this provision in 1787, let alone in the twenty-first century. In evaluating campaign finance laws under the Twenty-Eighth Amendment, the Justices of the Supreme Court will work from, to varying degrees depending on their methodological preferences, the text (including preamble), history, and structure of the amendment, viewed in the context of the entire Constitution—including, for contrast purposes, the Court's own precedent that the amendment is clearly intended to repudiate.

It is true that sometimes, after a new amendment passes, Justices who lived through the transition can be stingy in its application. For example, the Fourteenth Amendment provides: "No State shall make or enforce any law which shall abridge the privileges or immunities of citizens of the United States." While there is some historical dispute as to the precise object of this clause, it appears likely that it was intended to make the Bill of Rights applicable against state governments as well as the federal government. But in

1873, the Supreme Court adopted an unusually cramped view of this clause, holding that it refers primarily to a narrow set of federal rights, such as the right to travel between states.[52] (That is still technically the law; the Supreme Court eventually applied the Bill of Rights to state governments through an entirely different clause that was probably not designed for that purpose.)

The same occurred shortly after the passage of the Sixteenth Amendment, which was adopted in 1913 and provides that "Congress shall have power to lay and collect taxes on *incomes, from whatever source derived,* without apportionment among the several States, and without regard to any census or enumeration."[53] The whole purpose of the Sixteenth Amendment was to overrule the Supreme Court's 1895 decision in *Pollock v. Farmers' Loan & Trust Co.* But in 1920, the Court struck down a federal income tax law, claiming that Congress could not treat stock dividends as "income" and that *Pollock* was still good law for this point![54] The Court stated that "[a] proper regard for [the Sixteenth Amendment's] genesis, as well as its very clear language, requires also that this amendment shall not be extended by loose construction."[55] Justice Oliver Wendell Holmes dissented, stating:

> I think that the word "incomes" in the Sixteenth Amendment should be read in a sense most obvious to the common understanding at the time of its adoption. For it was for public adoption that it was proposed. The known purpose of this Amendment was to get rid of nice questions as to what might be direct taxes, and I cannot doubt that most people not lawyers would suppose when they voted for it that they put a question like the present to rest. I am of opinion that the Amendment justifies the tax.[56]

Eventually, the Court came to recognize that when the people passed an amendment, they meant something by it. And it is no argument against an amendment to suggest that the Justices of the Supreme Court might ignore it—that argument proves too much, as the Supreme Court can just as easily ignore the *existing* text of the Constitution.

At the same time, it is *not* true that, after passage of the Twenty-Eighth Amendment, the Supreme Court would not apply *any* constitutional scrutiny to campaign finance legislation. Among other things, the rest of the

[52] The Slaughter-House Cases, 83 U.S. 36 (1873).

[53] U.S. CONST. amend. XVI (emphasis added).

[54] Eisner v. Macomber, 252 U.S. 189 (1920). *See also* David H. Gans & Ryan Woo, *Reversing Citizens United: Lessons from the Sixteenth Amendment*, CONSTITUTIONAL ACCOUNTABILITY CENTER (Jan. 20, 2012), www.theusconstitution.org/wp-content/uploads/2017/12/20120120_Issue_Brief_David_Gans_Ryan_Woo_Reversing_Citizens_United.pdf.

[55] *Eisner*, 252 U.S. at 206, 218.

[56] *Id.* at 219–20 (Holmes, J., dissenting).

Constitution still applies. For example, suppose a law set different spending limits for black candidates and white candidates. That would violate the Fourteenth Amendment's Equal Protection Clause. Or suppose a law set a special limit on spending money on political advertisements to promote socialism. That would violate the First Amendment's protection against abridging the freedom of speech—because the law, by singling out one particular political viewpoint to receive a special limit, is viewpoint-based.[57]

Again, the Sixteenth Amendment provides a useful analogy. Despite the different subject matter (income taxation), it is the amendment most similar in form to the DFAA, in that it authorizes the government to do something that the Supreme Court had previously said it could not. One can imagine someone in 1913 raising the objection that the Sixteenth Amendment, by granting Congress "power to lay and collect taxes on incomes," would enable Congress to discriminate by race in income tax, charging higher rates for black taxpayers than white taxpayers, or imposing special income taxes on supporters of a disfavored political party or religion. But we would see those arguments as foolish. The Sixteenth Amendment's conferral of power did not repeal the First Amendment's protection of freedom of speech or religion, or the Fourteenth Amendment's Equal Protection Clause. The same logic will apply to the Twenty-Eighth Amendment.

D. *Will the Twenty-Eighth Amendment Change the Bill of Rights?*

According to some amendment opponents, the Twenty-Eighth Amendment would amend the First Amendment. They argue that this is unprecedented,

57 Some other amendment proposals take the form of "Nothing in this Constitution shall prohibit Congress and the States from" setting limits. *See, e.g.*, *Restore Democracy Amendment*, CITIZENS TAKE ACTION, https://citizenstakeaction.org/restore-democracy-amendment/ (providing that "nothing in this Constitution shall prevent" Congress or states from imposing limits on contributions or expenditures). These formulations risk the problems described above, such as laws that set different spending limits based on viewpoint or race. To work around this problem, some amendment bills in Congress have included a "Nothing in this Constitution…" clause but then added exceptions *within* that clause. For example, one amendment bill in the 114th Congress provided that "Nothing in this Constitution shall be construed to prohibit Congress or any State from imposing *content-neutral limitations* on contributions or expenditures…" H.R.J. Res. 24 § 1, 114th Cong. (2015), www.congress.gov/bill/114th-congress/house-joint-resolution/24/text (emphasis added). This drafting approach, however, requires the amendment to include an exhaustive list of which requirements *do* apply, with the burden of writing a mini-Constitution into the amendment and the risk of omitting something important. The DFAA's formulation, by retaining all previous constitutional history, avoids this problem entirely. It is also worth noting that no constitutional amendment yet passed uses a formulation like "nothing in this Constitution."

and that this very novelty, alone, should give us strong pause. Sometimes this is reduced to the shorthand of "we have never amended the First Amendment (or the Bill of Rights) before."[58]

The Twenty-Eighth Amendment would not, however, amend the First Amendment. The portion of the First Amendment that amendment opponents believe to be at issue states that "Congress shall make no law … abridging the freedom of speech …"

Before even addressing campaign finance, it is important to step back and understand the indeterminacy of this command. The First Amendment does not say "Congress shall make no law abridging speech." It says Congress shall make no law abridging "the freedom of speech." But what is "the freedom of speech"? It is generally accepted that "the freedom of speech" does not prevent the government from regulating or prohibiting: providing national security secrets to foreign spies; child pornography; malicious libel; copyright infringement; criminal extortion; noisy amplified announcements in residential neighborhoods at 3 a.m.; and many other things that are, in some ways, "speech."

The First Amendment also does not say anything about raising or spending money in elections by individuals or corporations. The Supreme Court interpreted "the freedom of speech" to include these activities. And when the people disagree with a Supreme Court interpretation of the Constitution, a constitutional amendment is a legitimate response. The Twenty-Eighth Amendment would not change one word of the First Amendment. Rather, it would correct an *erroneous judicial interpretation* of the First Amendment with respect to raising and spending money in elections.

We have lived under *Buckley*'s functional equation of political money with "the freedom of speech" for so long that it may be hard to remember a different way of looking at things. But it is important to remember that *Buckley* itself overturned a very thoughtful decision of the U.S. Court of Appeals for the District of Columbia Circuit (a particularly influential appellate court that is sometimes called the "second highest court in the land") that rested on a very different analysis. In the D.C. Circuit, the highly respected Judge Skelly Wright drew upon two different analogies from then-recent Supreme Court law in analyzing the contribution and spending limits of the Federal Election Campaign Act.

58 For example, Senator Ted Cruz of Texas used this argument at a Senate Judiciary Committee hearing on the proposed constitutional amendment. *See Examining a Constitutional Amendment to Restore Democracy to the American People Before Sen. Comm. on the Judiciary*, www.judiciary.senate.gov/meetings/examining-a-constitutional-amendment-to-restore-democracy-to-the-american-people (video starting at 1:03).

The first analogy was the "sound truck" case, *Kovacs v. Cooper*.[59] *Kovacs* came from an era when sound trucks were a crucial part of political campaigns. These trucks would drive around a city with amplified loudspeakers and blare political messages. The problem was, with a loud sound truck circling around the neighborhood, no one else could get a word in edgewise. In *Kovacs*, the Supreme Court upheld a local noise ordinance that limited operation of these sound trucks. In the Court's view, "the freedom of speech" did not include the freedom of those with the loudest amplification technology to drown out the voices of those without. By analogy, the Court of Appeals reasoned in its original decision in *Buckley* (which was later overturned by the Supreme Court) that "the freedom of speech" does not include the freedom of those with the most money to dramatically outspend those with less and thereby drown out their influence.[60]

The second analogy was the principle of "one person, one vote" as articulated in several cases over the 1960s. Under this principle, the Supreme Court struck down arrangements in various states under which one legislative district might have a wildly different population than another, yet both would have the same number of votes in the legislature.[61] These arrangements gave voters in the less-populated districts more influence, per person, than voters in the more-populated districts. They got, in essence, more votes. By analogy, the Court of Appeals reasoned in its original decision in *Buckley* (which, again, the Supreme Court overturned), allowing a small number of major financial donors to have an outsized influence on electoral and policy outcomes violated the "one person, one vote" principle.

Of course, the Supreme Court rejected these analogies drawn by the appellate court. And the Supreme Court is authorized, as the nation's highest court, to interpret the Constitution. But when the Court reaches an interpretation with which the American people profoundly disagree, the people are entitled to respond with a counter-interpretation—as we have done seven times before.

It is sometimes said that previous amendments have been about *expanding* rights, rather than restricting them. But this argument is not quite correct. As a simple factual matter, the Eleventh Amendment took away citizens' rights to sue other states in federal court. And certainly the Sixteenth Amendment, enabling Congress to collect federal income taxes, does not expand individual rights.

59 Kovacs v. Cooper, 336 U.S. 77 (1949).

60 Buckley v. Valeo, 519 F.2d 821 (D.C. Cir. 1975), *rev'd*, 424 U.S. 1 (1976) (per curiam).

61 Reynolds v. Sims, 377 U.S. 533 (1964); Gray v. Sanders, 372 U.S. 368 (1963); Baker v. Carr, 369 U.S. 186 (1962).

But more importantly, sometimes expanding equality can be painted as diminishing a previously enjoyed, but unearned and illegitimate, "right" to dominate others. For example, the Thirteenth Amendment could be claimed to have abolished the "right" of slaveholders to own slaves—a "right" legitimated by the Constitution and the Supreme Court in *Dred Scott*. The Thirteenth Amendment therefore abolished the "right" of white people to own black people. Similarly, the Nineteenth Amendment could be claimed to have abolished the "right" of men to control elections—a "right" seemingly enshrined in the Fourteenth Amendment.[62] The Twenty-Fourth Amendment could be claimed to have abolished the "right" of citizens with enough money to pay a poll tax to control elections. And so forth.

Indeed, a slaveholder could argue that the Thirteenth Amendment actually repealed his Fifth Amendment rights! According to the Fifth Amendment, "private property" may not be "taken" by the government "without just compensation."[63] As grotesque at it seems now, in the legal framework of the *Dred Scott* era, before the Thirteenth Amendment, slaves were "private property" under the law. A slaveholder could object that the government, by freeing the slaves, was "taking" property without compensation.

To be sure, political dominance by wealthy elites through the power of their wallets is not comparable to the horrors of slavery. The point is simply that amending the Constitution to expand equality can often be portrayed as diminishing someone else's (illegitimate) advantages or "rights." What is important to understand is that the very process of amendment pronounces that the previous exercise of domination should never have been a "right" in the first place. Consider, for example, the Nineteenth Amendment. Before the Nineteenth Amendment, men had the right to vote, and also the "right" to a disproportionate exercise of power through that vote. The Nineteenth Amendment, by guaranteeing the right to vote to women, did not take it away from men—men still have the right to vote. But it did proclaim that the disproportionate political power held by men by virtue of being born male was not a "right" after all. Similarly, the Twenty-Eighth Amendment will not deprive

62 The Fourteenth Amendment includes a now mostly obsolete provision that was intended to discourage Southern states from denying the vote to black citizens by reducing a state's representation in Congress to the extent that it denied or abridged the right to vote "to any of the male inhabitants of such State, being twenty-one years of age, and citizens of the United States." U.S. CONST. amend. XIV, § 2. The mechanism of the provision, however, reinforced the presumption of male-only suffrage. The original thrust of that provision is now mostly obsolete because of the Fifteenth Amendment and the federal Voting Rights Act, and its focus on male citizens of age 21 or older is largely supplanted by the Nineteenth and Twenty-Sixth Amendments.

63 U.S. CONST. amend. V.

wealthy donors of their freedom of speech. Instead, it will represent a collective determination that the power of wealth to disproportionately influence our politics and democracy is not a right, but a form of domination.

III. HOW WE GET THERE

As noted above, Article V of the Constitution provides two formal mechanisms for initiation of an amendment: a vote by two-thirds of both houses of Congress, or a constitutional convention (sometimes called a "convention of the states") on application of two-thirds of the states. Either way, the proposed amendments must be ratified by three-fourths of the states.

This process is deliberately difficult. The primary method of amending the Constitution requires two-thirds of *both* houses of Congress, *and* ratification by three-quarters of the states—today, that would be 38 states. A secondary method, floated several times but not yet actually used, is designed to work around a recalcitrant Congress: a constitutional convention convened on application of two-thirds of the states, which can then propose amendments, which must then be ratified by three-quarters of the states. So far, all 27 amendments have been enacted by Congress; we have not had a constitutional convention since 1787.[64]

The Article V amendment process is cumbersome—indeed, it was designed to be cumbersome—and it contains many points of failure. It needs to pass two-thirds of the House of Representatives' 435 members (i.e., 290 votes) and

64 Several convention calls have come close, including as recently as the 1980s. *See generally* James Kenneth Rogers, *The Other Way to Amend the Constitution: The Article V Constitutional Convention Amendment Process*, 30 HARV. J.L. & PUB. POL'Y 1005 (2007). A close call just short of the threshold was an important factor in Congress's eventual passage of the Seventeenth Amendment, and some have suggested that convention calls "may also have played a role in leading Congress to propose the Twenty-first, Twenty-second, and Twenty-fifth Amendments." *Id.* at 1008. Within the amendment movement, some support a convention call, arguing that Congress is part of the problem and too entrenched in the existing system. *See, e.g.*, Alison Hartson, *The Logical Path to End Corruption*, MEDIUM (May 11, 2017), https://medium.com/wolf-pac/the-logical-path-to-end-corruption-a64c1d06394b. Most amendment supporters, however, oppose a constitutional convention, arguing that its unprecedented nature, combined with open questions about our ability to contain the scope of its the convention's proposals and a convention's authority to change the ratification requirements, make it dangerous under present political conditions. *See, e.g.*, *The Dangerous Path*, COMMON CAUSE, www.commoncause.org/issues/more-democracy-reforms/constitutional-convention/executive-summary.html; *Free Speech For People Statement Opposing Call for a Constitutional Convention*, FREE SPEECH FOR PEOPLE (May 18, 2017), https://freespeechforpeople.org/free-speech-people-statement-opposing-call-constitutional-convention/.

two-thirds of the Senate's 100 members (i.e., 67 votes), and then be ratified by three-fourths of the 50 states (i.e., 38 states).[65] That is not an easy process.

Some amendment skeptics cannot get past the fact that an amendment is hard to pass. But, as American history demonstrates, it is sometimes necessary and far from impossible.

The leading strategy of most constitutional amendment supporters today takes the best features from the convention call methodology—its bottom-up, state-by-state, grassroots-oriented approach—and applies them to the Congress-initiated formal mechanism. In other words, the plan is *not* to begin with Congress, lobby members of the House and Senate to pass an amendment, and *then* approach the states for ratification, but rather the other way around: *first* line up the states in support, *then* push for a Congressional vote.[66]

Toward this end, supporters have pressed for state-level resolutions—through direct popular vote where state laws allow, and through a legislative vote elsewhere—calling upon Congress to pass an amendment. As of this writing, 19 states (and over 700 cities and towns) have passed such resolutions, generally by overwhelming margins.[67]

To be clear, this strategy is *not* a call for a convention of the states. Rather, these state and local resolutions *call upon Congress* to pass an amendment and submit it to the states for ratification. While these resolutions vary from state to state, depending both on local circumstances and specific limits of state constitutions for such resolutions,[68] typically they do two things. First, they call upon Congress to pass an amendment to overturn *Citizens United*

[65] Under Article V of the Constitution, amendments must be "ratified by the legislatures of three fourths of the several states, or by conventions in three fourths thereof, as the one or the other mode of ratification may be proposed by the Congress." U.S. CONST. art. V. In practice, most amendments have not specified a particular method of ratification; of those that have, only the Twenty-First Amendment (repealing Prohibition) specified that it must be ratified by convention. *See* U.S. CONST. amend. XXI, § 3. All states but one (Nebraska) have bicameral legislatures, and generally speaking, state ratification of a constitutional amendment requires *both* state houses to ratify an amendment. Therefore, ratification by 38 states likely requires 76 different bodies to vote for ratification.

[66] In 2014, the Senate leadership decided to hold a preview test vote on the DFAA. This was a fortuitous opportunity, but ahead of schedule under this strategy.

[67] The states on record in support are California, Colorado, Connecticut, Delaware, Hawaii, Illinois, Maine, Maryland, Massachusetts, Montana, New Jersey, New Mexico, Nevada, New York, Oregon, Rhode Island, Vermont, Washington, and West Virginia. For a detailed list of the precise votes taken, see *State and Local Support by the Numbers*, UNITED FOR THE PEOPLE, http://united4thepeople.org/state-and-local-support-2/.

[68] These differences between state resolutions are not significant because each state is stating its own call to Congress and the state legislature. Obviously, when an amendment is submitted for ratification, all the states will be voting on whether to ratify the same amendment.

and allow the people to set limits on money in politics from wealthy donors, corporations, and labor unions. Second, they call upon the state legislature to ratify such an amendment once it is submitted to the states by Congress. In some cases, these resolutions express a sense of the legislature; in others, they may even qualify as voter "instructions."[69]

For example, Colorado's voters in 2012 voted for the following question:[70]

> Shall there be amendments to the Colorado constitution and the Colorado revised statutes concerning support by Colorado's legislative representatives for a federal constitutional amendment to limit campaign contributions and spending, and, in connection therewith, *instructing Colorado's congressional delegation to propose and support, and the members of Colorado's state legislature to ratify, an amendment to the United States constitution that allows congress and the states to limit campaign contributions and spending?*

This resolution is not a call for a constitutional convention of the states. Rather, it is a nonbinding resolution *calling upon Congress to pass a constitutional amendment*, and Colorado's legislature to then ratify it. This strategy has been used since 1793, when the Massachusetts and Virginia legislatures passed resolutions calling on their representatives in Congress for a constitutional amendment to overturn *Chisholm v. Georgia*, thus starting the process that led to the Eleventh Amendment.[71]

When members of Congress know that the people of their states have affirmatively and clearly expressed their desire for an amendment, then their political calculations will reflect that change. This does not mean that it will be easy; it will still be difficult, and members of Congress could still choose to defy popular will in their state or district. But the goal of the movement is to change the political conditions under which they make these decisions. And when Congress passes an amendment bill, states that have already expressed their views on this topic are likely to ratify it quickly.

69 In many states, voters have an explicit constitutional right to "instruct" their representatives, and this has often been used in the context of ratifying federal constitutional amendments. *See, e.g.*, CAL. CONST. art. I, § 3; Howard Jarvis Taxpayers Ass'n v. Padilla, 62 Cal. 4th 486, 517–18, 363 P.3d 628, 647–48 (Cal. 2016), *reh'g denied* (Feb. 24, 2016); Kris W. Kobach, *May "We the People" Speak?: The Forgotten Role of Constituent Instructions in Amending the Constitution*, 33 U.C. DAVIS L. REV. 1 (1999).

70 *Ballot Language for 2012 Amendments and Propositions*, COLO. SEC'Y OF STATE, www.sos.state.co.us/pubs/elections/Results/Abstract/2012/general/ballotLanguage.html (Amendment 65) (emphasis added).

71 *See Howard Jarvis Taxpayers Ass'n*, 62 Cal. 4th at 501–2, 363 P.3d at 636 (discussing this history).

Of course, some argue that the amendment process will get harder as it goes on—that the initial batch of states are, almost by definition, the easiest. That is not totally wrong; some states will pose more obstacles than others. But it is important to remember how broad and bipartisan the support for this amendment is. On this issue, conventional divisions between "red" and "blue" are irrelevant—at least among voters, if not pundits. This distinguishes it from many other ideas for constitutional amendments that have strong partisan resonances among the grassroots.

Furthermore, as compared to other methods of reform, this last argument proves too much. A Twenty-Eighth Amendment to overturn *Citizens United* and *Buckley* is overwhelmingly popular among voters of both parties. If amendment skeptics want to argue that it is politically impossible to pass a pro-amendment resolution in certain states, then they may be forced to concede that more modest reforms will also be politically impossible to pass in those states. Indeed, as amendment advocate Derek Cressman notes, it is often easier to organize people to do something big (like pass an amendment) than something small (like update disclosure laws).[72] More people will call their legislators, march in the streets, or take other action in support of an amendment to overturn *Citizens United* than will do so for low-profile reforms. Furthermore, many of the various modest but worthy reforms that can be passed under the current constitutional jurisprudence face their own political obstacles; for example, some people oppose public funding of elections as taxpayer subsidies for politicians and their consultants. To argue that an amendment resolution cannot pass in a given state is probably to concede that modest reforms cannot pass in that state either. In fact, experience suggests that a constitutional amendment has broader support than any specific policy measure.[73]

Finally, it is important to understand that the amendment process may experience stops and starts. The Nineteenth Amendment (granting women the right to vote) was first introduced in 1878. Its first Senate floor vote was taken in 1887, but it failed to pass. It also failed to pass the Senate in 1914, 1918, and 1919. Three months later, it was brought back to Congress in a

[72] *See* Derek Cressman, When Money Talks: The High Price of "Free" Speech and the Selling of Democracy (2014).

[73] For example, in the November 2016 election, Washington state voters simultaneously voted *for* a resolution calling for a constitutional amendment and *against* a public funding proposal. *See Election 2016 Results for national, statewide races*, Seattle Times (Nov. 22, 2016), https://projects.seattletimes.com/2016/election-results/ (noting that Initiative 735, support for a constitutional amendment, passed 63-37, while, Initiative 1464, providing for publicly funded campaigns, failed 46–54).

special session, and this time (May 1919) the amendment passed the Senate. In 1920, four decades after it was first introduced, the Nineteenth Amendment was finally ratified. (Amendment advocates plan and hope for a much faster passage than the Nineteenth Amendment, of course!)

Will passing a constitutional amendment be easy? Of course not—the process was *intended* to be hard. But in these turbulent times, with widespread public unhappiness with the influence of big money in politics and broad grassroots support, and with a President Trump-appointed Supreme Court unlikely to reverse *Citizens United* (let alone *Buckley*) any time soon, the pieces are coming together. With a determined "citizen uprising," the Twenty-Eighth Amendment could become part of our Constitution before *Buckley* turns 50.

PART III

Inspiration from Abroad

16

The Repudiation of *Buckley v. Valeo*

K. D. Ewing*

I

The U.S. Supreme Court in *Buckley v. Valeo* was right about one thing: money is speech.[1] Look at any American coin, and you will find one word: liberty. Look in contrast at the French coins before the Euro, and you will find three words: liberté, égalité, and fraternité. But although money thus conveys a message, it is unlikely that this is what the Court had in mind. On the contrary, the justices were concerned not with the idea that money speaks *to* us, but with the idea that it speaks *for* us. The more money we have, the more we can say, and the more loudly we can say it. It is nevertheless the case, however, that the way in which money is permitted to speak *for* us is not unrelated to the way in which it speaks *to* us.

So to the scholar who asked the brilliant question, "If money talks, what does it say?"[2] one answer might be: "Look at the currency, and all will be clearly revealed." True, not all money is as explicit as the American or the French about the values it puts into people's hands, pockets, and purses. Some currencies carry other labels of national identity, while others are silent. But in talking to us in simple slogans, the currency tells us something profound about the values of the nation in which it circulates, as well as the values likely to have informed the nation's constitution, and its constitutional jurisprudence. U.S. currency tells us that it buys liberty, while the old French currency spread equality (on more favorable terms than now does the Euro).

* Keith Ewing is Professor of Public Law at King's College, London.

1 Buckley v. Valeo, 424 U.S. 1 (1976). *See* J. Skelly Wright, *Politics and the Constitution: Is Money Speech?*, 85 YALE L.J. 1001 (1976).

2 *See generally* IAIN MCMENAMIN, IF MONEY TALKS, WHAT DOES IT SAY? CORRUPTION AND BUSINESS FINANCING OF POLITICAL PARTIES (2013).

The Supreme Court in *Buckley* thus speaks to us in much the same unequivocal terms as the one cent coin.[3] In doing so, it presents us with what, in comparative terms, is a rampant form of liberty to the exclusion of other electoral values, and a rampant form of liberal democracy which simultaneously reflects and sustains the rampant form of economic liberalism which the United States promotes.[4] The *Buckley* decision has been widely criticized, and if it is not the root of all evil in the U.S. campaign finance system, then it is generally believed to be a major part of the problem, not only for the ideological position it adopted, but also at a more practical level for what it struck down and the regulatory options it now prevents.[5]

Internationally, *Buckley* is most famous for striking down FECA's spending limits on candidates, campaigns, and third parties.[6] These limits had been defended on the ground that they would reduce the risk of corruption, reduce the cost of politics, and equalize opportunities by focusing on the content of the candidates' messages rather than its volume. But while the Court speaks, it does not listen, striking down spending limits with the immortal and damning line from the playbook that "the concept that government may restrict the speech of some elements of our society in order to enhance the relative voice of others is wholly foreign to the First Amendment."[7]

We will never know how spending limits would have worked in a system as vast as the American one, and we will never know if Congress's attempt to contain campaign costs would have succeeded. Had campaign finance legislation not been struck down by *Buckley* and its progeny, it is likely that conservative snipers would subsequently have been deployed in a long and debilitating guerilla campaign against it. This is a campaign that would have pushed to a breaking point the enforceability of national spending limits, which would have been waged in the partisan environment of FECA. In doing so, it would have reinforced the folly of eschewing a non-partisan enforcement agency of the kind that we see now operating in other liberal democracies.[8]

3 *See* Timothy K. Kuhner, Capitalism v. Democracy: Money in Politics and the Free Market Constitution 33–64 (2014).

4 *Id.* at 153–88.

5 For a brief account of various regulatory options, see K. D. Ewing, The Cost of Democracy: Party Funding in Modern British Politics 23–62 (2007); Party Funding and Campaign Financing in International Perspective 1–16 (K. D. Ewing & Samuel Issacharoff eds., 2006).

6 *See Buckley*, 424 U.S. at 58.

7 *Id.* at 48–49.

8 For a discussion of the role and importance of independent enforcement, see Michael Pal, *Electoral Management Bodies as a Fourth Branch of Government*, 21 Rev. Const. Stud. 85 (2016).

But it was not only interested parties in the United States who were left to lament the decision in *Buckley*. The case would go on to have a profound effect elsewhere in the world as well, as other countries adopted legislative measures similar in purpose to FECA's 1974 Amendments. The *Buckley* decision coincided with the expansion of judicial power in traditional "Westminster-style" democracies that had typically rejected a significant judicial role in the scrutiny of legislation to protect core liberal values. In the words of a leading Australian judge:

> Indeed, those responsible for the drafting of the Constitution saw constitutional guarantees of freedoms as exhibiting a distrust of the democratic process. They preferred to place their trust in Parliament to preserve the nature of our society and regarded as undemocratic guarantees which fettered its powers. Their model in this respect was, not the United States Constitution, but the British Parliament, the supremacy of which was by then settled constitutional doctrine.[9]

This chapter considers how *Buckley* has been received in other countries. The decision is important not only for its immediate effect in striking down progressive legislation, but also for its reasoning and the ideas it projected about democracy. It was a hard case to ignore, and wherever campaign finance reform has been subsequently contemplated and reform legislation drafted, *Buckley* was one of the obstacles that had to be acknowledged and overcome. Wherever campaign finance reform was subsequently being challenged in litigation, *Buckley*'s seductive rhetoric and memorable quotes presented challenges for judges throughout the world initially overawed by powerful arguments underpinned by U.S. jurisprudence.

This chapter considers specifically the way in which courts in other jurisdictions have responded to *Buckley*. The decision has loomed large in the jurisprudence of three jurisdictions addressed here, namely Australia, Canada, and the United Kingdom, all largely English-speaking countries in the common law tradition, based on the Westminster system of government, albeit with different levels of scrutiny of legislation by judges.[10] *Buckley* was initially enthusiastically embraced by young and inexperienced suitors in these countries, but this embrace was followed by a universal repudiation if not revulsion of the reasoning of U.S. Supreme Court. This chapter examines

9 Australian Capital Television Pty Ltd and New South Wales v. Commonwealth, [1992] HCA 45; (1992) 177 CLR 106, para. 23 (Austral.) (Dawson, J.). He was referring in the first sentence of this passage to the Constitution of the Commonwealth of Australia.

10 On the Westminster system, see R. A. W. Rhodes, John Wanna & Patrick Weller, Comparing Westminster (2011).

what happened and pulls together some of the speculation as to why there should have been such a decisive change of mind.

II

Buckley v. Valeo must rank as one of the most poisonous decisions of the U.S. Supreme Court, and it has been rightly condemned both nationally and internationally. It must also rank as one of America's most toxic legal exports, having spread like a virus quickly to other legal systems until a suitable antidote was developed to contain the disease to its country of origin. The United States was not the only country struggling with the problem of democracy being undermined by private wealth, and was not the only country passing legislation to deal with it.

We forget just how radical the steps taken in FECA's 1974 reforms were, though no doubt if we were legislating today, we would want to go much further. Equally radical steps were taken in Canada at the same time as FECA,[11] with the comprehensive Election Expenses Act 1974 introducing new disclosure requirements, state support for candidates and political parties, the regulation of broadcasting and the provision of free time to political parties, and most controversially the introduction of campaign spending limits. These spending limits applied to candidates, political parties, and third parties, in the last case going beyond even what FECA's 1974 amendments contemplated by ostensibly banning third-party spending altogether.[12] There were no contribution limits.[13]

Yet although the ban on third-party spending was tightened up in 1983, it did not stop all third-party activity during an election campaign when due allowance was made for legal definitions of what was an election expense. As Canada's Chief Electoral Officer pointed out, even after the amendment in 1983 Canada's legislation did not prevent "the debate or discussion of issues during an election."[14] He continued by saying that "the only thing that was not allowed was to promote directly or oppose directly a candidate or a political party," and that "any single-issue group or pressure-group could still promote its own platform," so long as it was not "promoting or opposing directly, by naming him, the candidate or a political party."[15]

[11] For the influences on campaign finance reform during this period in Canada, see generally K. D. Ewing, Money, Politics, and Law: A Study of Electoral Campaign Finance Reform in Canada (1992).

[12] *Id.* at 60–92.

[13] The reason for this is that the legislation was introduced by a minority government that relied on the labor-based New Democratic Party. *See id.* at 33–92.

[14] *Id.* at 137.

[15] *Id.*

A number of lower courts had struggled faithfully to apply the third-party limits, but following the 1983 amendments by which these limits were tightened up, they were the subject of a direct challenge, on the grounds that they violated the freedom of expression guarantees in the Canadian Charter of Rights and Freedoms. The Charter had been adopted only in 1982, eight years after Canada's campaign finance scheme had been put in place and only a year before the tightening of the regulatory screw. The legal challenge to Canada's campaign finance regulations was launched in 1984, at a time when Charter jurisprudence was fast moving but greatly undeveloped, meaning the courts had to rely heavily on foreign jurisprudence to find their way through problems simultaneously novel and complex.

Indeed, unlike in the United States, the adjudication of Charter claims in Canada requires the courts to have regard to foreign jurisprudence, with the language of the Charter itself insisting that any restrictions on Charter rights and freedoms must be "demonstrably justified in a free and democratic society."[16] It is in this context that *Buckley v. Valeo* was cited by the applicants in *National Citizens' Coalition (NCC) v. Canada*[17] in their successful action in the Alberta Queen's Bench to strike down third-party spending limits. It would have taken a courageous court to have directly repudiated *Buckley* at a time when that case was so freshly minted, and it would have taken an unusually self-confident court strongly to imply that the United States after *Buckley* was not "a free and democratic society."

At the time the decision in NCC was delivered, however, it was hardly earth-shattering, and did not have the significance in Canada that *Buckley* had in the United States. Partly this is because only third-party limits were struck down, leaving intact the spending limits on candidates and parties. Partly it was also because the issue of third-party activity in Canada had been an irritant rather than a problem. And partly too it was because those wishing to engage politically were free to make contributions rather than incur expenditures. As already pointed out, in an explicit regulatory accommodation with the way in which the labor-based New Democratic Party was then organized, there were no contribution limits in Canada.[18]

16 *See* Canadian Charter of Rights and Freedoms, § 1, Pt. I of the Constitution Act 1982, being Sch. B to the Canada Act 1982 (U.K.) 1982, c. 11 (providing that "The *Canadian Charter of Rights and Freedoms* guarantees the rights and freedoms set out in it subject only to such reasonable limits prescribed by law as can be demonstrably justified in a free and democratic society.")

17 National Citizens' Coalition, Inc. v. Canada (Attorney General), [1985] 11 D.L.R. (4th) 480 (Alberta Q.B.) (Can.). This was the first of three *Buckley* inspired challenges to third-party spending limits, all initiated in Alberta, which is regarded as the most conservative Canadian province.

18 The position has changed. *See* Ewing, The Cost of Democracy, *supra* note 5, at 197–223.

The striking down of the spending limits was nevertheless very fortuitous, coming only three years before the general election in 1988, which was in effect a Canadian referendum on NAFTA. The decision in *NCC* unleashed the biggest third-party intervention in Canadian political history, with spending by the political parties being accompanied by the so-called independent expenditures of third parties. These third-party independent expenditures were dominated by corporate Canada's desire to ensure that the Conservative party should be reelected to ensure in turn that NAFTA would prevail. Although the precise amount of third-party spending was difficult to calculate, it was clearly not insubstantial and led to the appointment of a Royal Commission to revisit the question of third-party limits.[19]

The need to revisit third-party limits led to a second attempt at legislation, which avoided a ban on third-party spending in favor of a cap. However, the cap was set very low—at $1,000 per participant on advertising "for the purpose of promoting or opposing, directly and during an election, a particular registered party or the election of a particular candidate." Perhaps unsurprisingly this too was struck down, *Buckley* being deployed this time by the Alberta Court of Appeal in *Somerville v. Canada*, another NCC-inspired challenge, where it was said that:

> Without a doubt, less intrusive means of fostering the purported objectives of this legislation are available. For example, the respondent points out that possible alternatives to third party spending limits include limiting either (or both) the source and quantity of direct contributions to political parties. It is worth noting in this respect that the U.S. Supreme Court in *Buckley v. Valeo* … upheld limits on contributions to parties and candidates. It found such limits less intrusive upon freedom of expression and association than independent third party spending limits ... Further, stringent disclosure requirements could be imposed upon third parties who advertise in relation to election campaigns; some such requirements already exist in … the *Elections Act* ... The Attorney General suggests that by confining the $1,000 limit only to direct advertising, a reasonable limit was achieved. However, it cannot rebut the fact that this financial limit amounts, in effect, to a total ban on national advertising … The $1,000 limit … cannot be viewed as the minimal impairment of freedom of expression.[20]

19 On the competing claims about how much was spent, see EWING, MONEY, POLITICS, AND LAW, *supra* note 11, at 221–25. *See also* ROYAL COMMISSION ON ELECTORAL REFORM AND PARTY FINANCING, REFORMING ELECTORAL DEMOCRACY (Ottawa: Minister of Supply and Service, 1992) [hereinafter LORTIE COMMISSION].

20 Somerville v. Canada (Attorney General), [1996] 1996 ABCA 217 (CanLII), 185 A.R. 241 at para. 83 (Can.).

III

This was only the start. Shortly after *Buckley*'s first reception in Canada, the virus mutated to Australia, where it found an altogether different host. Whether by luck or design, Australia had created what in retrospect was probably the best campaign finance regulatory system in the world. Similar (but not identical) in form to the German system,[21] the Australian federal regime eschewed both contribution and expenditure limits, thereby avoiding the intractable problems of definition, avoidance, and enforcement.[22] Instead, it banked on the simplicity of transparency, state financial support for candidates and parties, and a ban on broadcast media advertising, with broadcasting legislation similar to the British practice having been introduced by a Labor government in 1991.[23]

The broadcasting restrictions of 1991 were the last piece of a regulatory structure started in 1984. Under Australian legislation it was unlawful for broadcasters to carry political advertisements during an election period, regardless of the source of the advertisement. For these purposes a political advertisement was widely defined to mean "material containing an express or implicit reference to, or comment on," any of the following:

(a) the election or referendum concerned;
(b) a candidate or group of candidates in that election;
(c) an issue submitted to or otherwise before electors in that election;
(d) the government, the opposition, or a previous government or opposition, of the Commonwealth;
(e) a member of the Parliament of the Commonwealth;
(f) a political party, or a branch or division of a political party.[24]

But not only did Australia's legislation ban political advertising; it also imposed a duty on broadcasters, as a condition of their license, to provide free airtime to political parties and independent candidates. The airtime was to be allocated in accordance with a formula prescribed by the legislation itself. Similar to how the regime had operated in the United Kingdom since the

[21] On the German system, see MICHAEL KOSS, THE POLITICS OF PARTY FUNDING: STATE FUNDING TO POLITICAL PARTIES AND PARTY COMPETITION IN WESTERN EUROPE 103–27 (2011).

[22] For details on the Australian system, see generally JOO-CHEONG THAM, MONEY AND POLITICS: THE DEMOCRACY WE CAN'T AFFORD (2010).

[23] On the British legislation banning political advertising, see generally JACOB ROWBOTTOM, DEMOCRACY DISTORTED: WEALTH, INFLUENCE AND DEMOCRATIC POLITICS (2010).

[24] Political Broadcasts and Political Disclosures Act 1991 (Cth), § 95B (Austral.).

birth of commercial television (and before then in the case of the publicly funded BBC),[25] airtime in Australia was to be allocated to political parties for the broadcast of electoral and political messages in a way that would privilege the largest parties, based on the number of parliamentary seats held (that is to say, based on the results of the previous general election).[26]

In terms of controlling costs at elections, this was the most effective and clinical way of doing so. It simply removed the single most important item of expenditure from the equation, and at a stroke would help greatly to equalize the contest between the main parties. It is true that it privileged the larger parties and may have had a tendency toward "ossification," making it harder for new parties to break through. It is also true that it would exclude non-party electoral participants from a key medium for getting out their message and persuading voters. But what is also true is that the legal challenge to this regime came not from small parties or from interest groups, the same groups that were thought to be most prejudiced.

The first challenge to the Australian regime came in *Australian Capital Television Pty Ltd and New South Wales v. Commonwealth* (ACTV),[27] and a much overlooked feature of this case is that it was initiated by a broadcaster rather than by parties, candidates, or third parties denied an opportunity to use a particular medium of expression. In other words, it was motivated by the interests of the messenger rather than the message, the former no doubt moved by naked commercial self-interest and the loss of the opportunity to make money out of politics. Perhaps nothing so clearly reveals that speech is a commodity and that political participants must be forced to be free, even though they were not sufficiently moved by the restrictions to challenge them, and even though in the unregulated market place of ideas rationing by ability to pay would risk an even less competitive system.

The problem for the applicants, however, was that there is no First Amendment in Australia and (still) no Canadian-style Charter. Yet in a remarkable sleight of hand, the High Court of Australia implied a power to intervene to protect the freedom of political communication,[28] and this intervention seemed to be tailored specifically to the claims of the applicants: the communicator rather than the speaker. Despite the absence of any such power in the Australian federal constitution, it could nevertheless be implied from the

25 On the origins of the British system, see generally D. E. Butler, The Electoral System in Britain 1918–1951 (2d ed. 1963).

26 *See* H. F. Rawlings, Law and the Electoral Process 151–61 (1988).

27 Australian Capital Television Pty Ltd and New South Wales v. Commonwealth, [1992] HCA 45; (1992) 177 CLR 106 (Austral.).

28 *Id.*

provision made by the constitution for a system of a "responsible and representative government,"[29] for the purposes of which freedom of communication was essential if government was to be responsive to the wishes of the people.

Having thus created the power to intervene, the second question was whether the implied freedom had been violated by the contested legislation. Here the reasoning of *Buckley* was clearly evident, which was hardly surprising given that it was read, digested, and cited by the High Court of Australia on five occasions (once by Chief Justice Anthony Mason and four times by Justice Michael McHugh) in what was a 6-3 decision.[30] In a tone consistent with that of the U.S. Supreme Court, a majority in the High Court of Australia concluded that while the freedom of political communication was not unlimited, the public interest in reducing the risk of corruption and in eliminating the unfair advantage of the wealthy did not justify the restraints imposed by the broadcasting ban.

The influence of *Buckley* can be seen particularly in the explicit references by Justice McHugh. He rejected the argument that the broadcasting ban was not inconsistent with parliamentary democracy in view of the fact that paid political advertising was prohibited or restricted in a number of countries,[31] none of which had been found to have violated the free speech provisions of international treaties as a result.[32] How, then, could the legislation be seen to be inconsistent with the concept of representative democracy? Addressing the rhetorical question directly, Justice McHugh responded by saying that the answer "lies in the different contexts in which the guarantees of freedom of expression operate in those countries and in Australia,"[33] adding crucially that:

> A more valid analogy would be an instrument on which the Commonwealth placed no reliance—the Constitution of the United States of America. It is a more valid analogy because, like our Constitution, the legislative power of the central government to control elections is subject to the First Amendment guarantee of freedom of speech. In *Mills v. Alabama*, the Supreme Court said of a law that made it an offense for the editor of a paper to publish an editorial on election day urging people to vote a certain way that it would be "difficult to conceive of a more obvious and flagrant abridgment of the constitutionally guaranteed freedom of the press." In *Buckley*, the Supreme Court

[29] *Id.* at paras. 30–31 (Mason, C.J.).

[30] *Id.* at para. 19 (Mason, C.J.) and paras. 28, 37, 42, 48 (McHugh, J.).

[31] Including Austria, Belgium, Denmark, Finland, France, Ireland, Israel, Italy, Japan, the Netherlands, Norway, Sweden, Switzerland, and the United Kingdom.

[32] Notably, these treaties include the International Covenant on Civil and Political Rights and the European Convention on Human Rights (ECHR).

[33] *Australian Capital Television Pty Ltd*, [1992] HCA 45 at para. 41.

held unconstitutional laws imposing restrictions on campaign expenditures by various people notwithstanding that the object of the laws was to prevent the rich from corrupting the political process.[34]

IV

Buckley thus claimed two significant international prizes, challenging spending limits in two jurisdictions which had adopted "demand-side" initiatives as the best way to promote fair and clean elections.[35] The question now was whether a leap could be made to a third jurisdiction, this time the United Kingdom, which had pioneered spending limits. The British had introduced controls on candidate spending in 1883, and these were accompanied by third-party limits, which had been introduced in 1918.[36] *Buckley* was of course well known in Britain, and although it was not referred to in the decision of the European Court of Human Rights in *Bowman v. United Kingdom*,[37] it nevertheless provided part of the intellectual context of that decision.

Bowman was a case in which a pro-life activist, Phyllis Bowman, distributed handbills produced by the Society for the Protection of the Unborn Child at a parliamentary election, making it clear that she was not advising people how to vote, but asking them to reflect on the rival candidates' positions on abortion and related questions before doing so. The handbills also gave details of the views and voting records of the candidates on abortion as well as information about abortion procedures. About a 1.5 million of these leaflets were distributed, including 25,000 or so in the constituency (electoral district) of Halifax. As a result, Bowman was prosecuted under the Representation of the People Act 1983.

It was (and still is) an offense in Britain for anyone other than a candidate to incur an expense "with a view to promoting or procuring the election of a candidate at an election," where the expense in question related to holding public meetings or organizing any public display; issuing advertisements, circulars, or publications; or otherwise presenting to the electors the candidate or his or her views.[38] There were a number of blanket exceptions for newspapers and broadcasters, and a conditional exception for everyone else (including

34 *Id.* at para. 42 (internal citations omitted).

35 "Demand side," in this sense, refers to measures designed to reduce the demand for money by limiting the capacity to spend it, in contrast to "supply side," which measures limiting the capacity to raise it.

36 *See* Keith Ewing, The Funding of Political Parties in Britain 49–72 (1988).

37 Bowman v. United Kingdom, 1998 Eur. Ct. H.R. 4.

38 Representation of the People Act 1983, §75 (U.K.). *See also* Ewing, *supra* note 36, at 49–72.

Bowman herself) if the total spending by the individual in question did not exceed £5, a pitifully small amount that would prevent any effective electoral activity.

Given the context, it is unsurprising that this legislation should also be found to violate free speech guarantees, on this occasion to be found in the European Convention on Human Rights (ECHR), which in its Article 10 guarantees the right to freedom of expression. In contrast to the U.S. Constitution, however, Article 10(2) of the ECHR expressly permits limitations to be imposed on free speech, where these can be shown to be:

> prescribed by law and ... necessary in a democratic society, in the interests of national security, territorial integrity or public safety, for the prevention of disorder or crime, for the protection of health or morals, for the protection of the reputation or rights of others, for preventing the disclosure of information received in confidence, or for maintaining the authority and impartiality of the judiciary.[39]

On this occasion, the Court by a majority again found the statutory restraints in Britain to violate the freedom of expression guarantee and was unwilling to accept that they could be saved by the exceptions enumerated in Article 10(2). This was despite the strong argument of the government that the legislation advanced the legitimate aim of "protecting the rights of others" in three different ways:

> First, it promoted fairness between competing candidates for election by preventing wealthy third parties from campaigning for or against a particular candidate or issuing material which necessitated the devotion of part of a candidate's election budget, which was limited by law ... to a response. Secondly, the restriction on third-party expenditure helped to ensure that candidates remained independent of the influence of powerful interest groups. Thirdly, it prevented the political debate at election times from being distorted by having the discussion shifted away from matters of general concern to centre on single issues.[40]

In upholding Bowman's complaint, the Court accepted that Britain's legislation served a legitimate purpose, which was "to contribute towards securing equality between candidates,"[41] but it also found that in doing so it imposed restraints so tight that the response was disproportionate. This was nevertheless

[39] *See* Council of Europe, Convention for the Protection of Human Rights and Fundamental Freedoms, as amended by Protocols Nos. 11 and 14 (European Convention on Human Rights) (Nov. 4, 1950), E.T.S. No. 5, 213 U.N.T.S. 221, art. 10(2).

[40] Bowman v. United Kingdom, 1998 Eur. Ct. H.R. 4 at para. 36.

[41] *Id.* at para. 38.

an important turning point, for what the Court said in effect was that third-party spending limits were permitted provided they were proportionate. The unresolved question was what would be proportionate for this purpose, and what would be acceptable to the European Court of Human Rights? The response of the government was to repeal the offending provision in British law and to replace it with a measure that permits third parties to spend £500 promoting or opposing a candidate, while also prohibiting bundling by third parties.[42]

The legislative response to *Bowman* was informed by the report of the Committee on Standards in Public Life (which coincidentally had been appointed in 1998 to conduct the most intense investigation ever of party funding in the United Kingdom). But apart from adapting existing spending limits to the new jurisprudence, the Committee on Standards in Public Life proposed even wider-ranging spending limits, and Britain would soon see the introduction of spending limits on political parties as well as candidates. The Committee also proposed limits on national campaigns by third parties at election time to operate alongside the modified existing limits designed to address candidate-focused third-party activity.[43]

These proposals were accepted by the government, which introduced legislation imposing limits on the election spending of a political party incurred in the 12 months before election day, with the amount of the limit varying according to the number of candidates the party in question fielded at the election. But for the main parties, which contested every seat, it worked out at a spending limit of about £20 million, though there was no limit on the general administrative expenses of the parties. In addition, a cap was imposed on the independent expenditures of third parties, based informally on a figure of 5 percent of the permitted expenditure of the major parties, which meant a third-party limit of about £1 million for each individual or organization.[44]

V

Although the European Court of Human Rights struck down the £5 limit as being too low, the tenor of its decision in *Bowman* was nevertheless one that accepted in principle that third-party spending limits were legitimate. As

[42] Political Parties, Elections and Referendums Act 2000, § 131, amending Representation of the People Act 1983, § 75 (U.K.).

[43] Committee on Standards in Public Life, The Funding of Political Parties in the United Kingdom, *Report*, Cm 4057-1. *Buckley* was referred to five times in the Committee's comparative review of freedom of expression.

[44] Political Parties, Elections and Referendums Act 2000, Pts. V and VI.

such, the decision coincidentally mirrored a striking decision of the Supreme Court of Canada (SCC), which in 1997 began the short journey of repudiating *NCC*, and also the subsequent decision in *Somerville*, thereby restoring the right of legislatures to ensure competitive elections. The case in question was *Libman v. Quebec*,[45] and it concerned the question of spending limits in referendum campaigns, which were funded by public subsidies, and which in turn were accompanied by tight spending limits on opposing campaigns.

This was the first time the Supreme Court of Canada had assessed whether spending limits were constitutional, with little option but to conclude that the referendum regime was a violation of the Charter guarantee of freedom of expression. Under the challenged legislation, individuals and organizations could affiliate with one of the two official "national campaigns," but were prohibited from spending on their own account from their own resources. Although there were a number of minor exceptions, this regime amounted to enforcing virtually a "total ban" on third-party expenditures. But having found the referendum regime to breach Section 2 of the Charter, the Court's attention returned to Section 1 to determine whether the restriction could be justified.

At this point the weather began to change, with the Court noting that the rationale for the Canadian legislation in question was:

> first, egalitarian in that it is intended to prevent the most affluent members of society from exerting a disproportionate influence by dominating the referendum debate through access to greater resources. What is sought is in a sense an equality of participation and influence between the proponents of each option. Second, from the voters' point of view, the system is designed to permit an informed choice to be made by ensuring that some positions are not buried by others. Finally, as a related point, the system is designed to preserve the confidence of the electorate in a democratic process that it knows will not be dominated by the power of money.[46]

These compelling considerations, sympathetically articulated, were not only accepted, but they were expressly endorsed as being "highly laudable."[47]

But having accepted the justification for the restraint on freedom of expression, there was also a third question for the Court, which was whether the "total ban" was proportionate. It was here that the Court had trouble in

[45] Libman v. Quebec, [1997] 3 S.C.R. 569 (Can.); *see also* Colin Feasby, Libman v. Quebec (AG) *and the Administration of the Process of Democracy under the Charter: The Emerging Egalitarian Model*, 44 McGill L.J. 5 (1999).

[46] *Libman*, [1997] 3 S.C.R. 569 at para. 41.

[47] *Id.* at para. 42.

accepting the arguments of the government, concluding that there were better ways of reconciling freedom of expression with the "public interest" in fair campaigns. In making clear that it disagreed with the decisions of the lower courts referred to above on third-party limits in federal election law,[48] the Court signaled that one possible reconciliation of these competing interests would be to permit third-party spending but to impose a limit on how much each third party could spend, with a ban on the pooling of resources.

The ground was thus set for a defense of spending limits in election law, though it was difficult to visualize how the reasoning in *Libman* would not travel from referendums to elections. In 2000, Canada's federal government moved quickly to introduce new third-party spending limits for federal elections with further incremental adjustments after *Somerville*, set at levels that now seemed realistic rather than prohibitive, while also imposing serious restraints on the volume of speech and perhaps also the means used to spread the message. Thus, the new legislation introduced independent spending limits at the riding level of $3,000 (much higher than the amended British limits also introduced in 2000), and at the national level of $150,000 (much lower than the British equivalent).

The Supreme Court of Canada in *Harper v. Canada* subsequently rejected the inevitable third NCC challenge to these provisions,[49] endorsing the "the egalitarian model of elections" that had been identified in *Libman*, before adding that:

> This model is premised on the notion that individuals should have an equal opportunity to participate in the electoral process. Under this model, wealth is the main obstacle to equal participation. Thus, the egalitarian model promotes an electoral process that requires the wealthy to be prevented from controlling the electoral process to the detriment of others with less economic power. The state can equalize participation in the electoral process in two ways. First, the State can provide a voice to those who might otherwise not be heard. The Act does so by reimbursing candidates and political parties and by providing broadcast time to political parties. Second, the State can restrict the voices which dominate the political discourse so that others may be heard as well. In Canada, electoral regulation has focused on the latter by regulating electoral spending through comprehensive election finance provisions. These provisions seek to create a level playing field for those who wish to engage in the electoral discourse. This, in turn, enables voters to be better informed; no one voice is overwhelmed by another. In contrast, the

[48] *Id.* at para. 79 (expressly disapproving *Somerville*).
[49] Harper v. Canada (Attorney General), [2004] 1 S.C.R. 827 (Can.).

> libertarian model of elections favours an electoral process subject to as few restrictions as possible.[50]

This is a long, long way from *Buckley*. But the acceptance of a partially social democratic vision of democracy did not end the inquiry, for the Court was also required to scrutinize the restraints on electoral speech in response to complex standards which examine their justification, proportionality, and minimum impairment. There was also the issue here that we were talking about political speech in a context (elections) that demands maximum protection, and justifications for control that cannot be proved (the impact of money on electoral outcome). As the majority in *Harper* recognized, "spending limits which are overly restrictive may undermine the informational component of the right to vote."[51]

In the end, it was partly on the question of evidence and proof of harm that the Supreme Court of Canada split. Its 6-3 majority was prepared to accept that "scientific proof" of harm was not required, and that "a reasoned apprehension of that harm" based on "logic, reason and some social science evidence" was enough,[52] especially when spiced with a sense that political questions such as the design of the electoral system are best left to Parliament. In these circumstances the Court's majority was prepared to defer to the findings of a Royal Commission (the "Lortie Commission"),[53] and in particular to its assessment that third-party spending limits could be justified to promote equality in political discourse, protect the integrity of the financing regime for candidates and parties, and maintain confidence in the electoral process.

VI

Returning to the United Kingdom, the spending limits introduced in 2000 have never been challenged, and it is now inconceivable that any challenge would succeed. Indeed, the legitimacy of spending limits had been accepted by the English courts shortly before the decision in *Bowman*, with one of England's most highly respected judges commenting that there is a need:

[50] *Id.* at para. 62 (Bastarache, J.) (internal citations omitted).
[51] *Id.* at para. 73.
[52] *Id.* at paras. 77–78.
[53] See Ewing, Money, Politics, and Law, *supra* note 11, at 221–25, for the competing claims about how much was spent. *See also* Lortie Commission, *supra* note 19.

> to achieve a level financial playing field between competing candidates, so as to prevent perversion of the voters' democratic choice between competing candidates within constituencies by significant disparities of local expenditure. At the constituency level it is the voters' perception of the personality and policies of the candidates, and the parties which they represent, which is intended to be reflected in the voting, not the weight of the parties' expenditure on local electioneering.[54]

These remarks were expressed in the context of the prosecution of a Member of Parliament and her agent for filing inaccurate spending returns following the general election in 1997.

With comprehensive reform legislation enacted in 2000, the United Kingdom turned its back on *Buckley* by strengthening its commitment to spending limits, which were subsequently reduced still further by amending legislation in 2009 and again in 2014.[55] In stark contrast to the United States, the United Kingdom's regulatory route was paved with transparency and spending limits rather than transparency and contribution limits.[56] And alongside these restrictions, broadcasting restrictions were reenacted, with the qualification that the statutory ban in the United Kingdom went even further than that which had been struck down by the High Court of Australia in the *Australian Capital Television (ACTV)* case.

Since 1954, British legislation has prohibited all forms of political advertising on television and radio. A similar ban in Switzerland was successfully challenged before the European Court of Human Rights by an animal welfare group that was prohibited from countering commercial advertising undertaken by the beef industry.[57] According to the Court, the Swiss ban violated the Article 10(1) of the European Convention on Human Rights, referred to above, and could not be saved as being a proportionate restriction justified under Article 10(2). Nevertheless, when the regulation of television and radio

54 R. v. Jones, [1999] 2 Cr App R 253, 255 (U.K.).

55 Political Parties and Elections Act 2009, Pt. 2 (U.K.); Transparency of Lobbying, Non-Party Campaigning and Trade Union Administration Act 2014, Pt. 2 (U.K.).

56 As in the case of Canada above, this was a direct result of the organizational structure of a labor-based party, which was a "mixed party" in the sense that its members were organizations (trade unions and socialist societies) and individuals. Contribution caps were seen as a threat to the autonomy of the party and its right to freedom of association. The issue is now less compelling in view of recent changes to the party's organization.

57 Verein gegen Tierfabriken (VgT) v. Switzerland, 2001 Eur. Ct. H.R. 159.

was revised in the United Kingdom in 2003, the ban was reenacted, despite the government's clearly expressed concerns that it violated Convention rights.[58]

These concerns were considered by a parliamentary committee, which referred both to *Buckley* and its Australian progeny in the following manner:

> There is a different tradition in the USA and Australia which gives greater weight to the interest in fostering as much political expression as possible. But the European tradition seems to us to be preferable, in that it gives what we consider to be appropriate weight to the legitimate objective of securing equality of opportunity for political expression, at any rate in the broadcast media. In our view, this justifies restrictions on the freedom to buy advertising time for political purposes.[59]

The government was therefore to stick to its guns and to find ways to accommodate the demands of the European Court of Human Rights in the Swiss case.

Britain's approach was broadly to reenact the *status quo* and wait for the inevitable legal challenge, which duly arrived in the form of a claim by another animal welfare body, Animal Defenders International, which argued that the denial of access to paid advertising on television or radio violated its right to freedom of expression.[60] In holding that there was self-evidently a violation, the United Kingdom's highest court also held that the restriction could be justified as being "necessary in a democratic society" for the protection of the "rights and freedoms of others," within Article 10(2). In reaching this decision, which the European Court of Human Rights upheld by a narrow margin, one of the judges in the House of Lords (Baroness Brenda Hale) opened her judgment in the following manner:

> There was an elephant in the committee room, always there but never mentioned, when we heard this case. It was the dominance of advertising, not only in elections but also in the formation of political opinion, in the United States of America. Enormous sums are spent, and therefore have to be raised, at election times: it is estimated that the disputed 2000 elections for President and Congress cost as much as U.S. $3 billion. Attempts to regulate campaign spending are struck down in the name of the First Amendment: "Congress shall make no law … abridging the freedom of speech, or of the press": see

[58] Communications Act 2003, § 321 (U.K.). On party political broadcast, see *id.* at § 333.

[59] Joint Committee on Human Rights, 19th Report, Draft Communications Bill, HL Paper 149, HC 1102 (2001–2002) para. 23 (U.K.). *Buckley* is referred to in this parliamentary committee report.

[60] R. (Animal Defenders International) v. Secretary of State for Culture, Media and Sport, [2008] UKHL 15 (U.K.).

> particularly *Buckley v Valeo* … *A fortiori* there is no limit to the amount that pressure groups can spend on getting their message across in the most powerful and pervasive media available. In the United Kingdom, and elsewhere in Europe, we do not want our government or its policies to be decided by the highest spenders. Our democracy is based upon more than one person one vote. It is based on the view that each person has equal value.[61]

Although not referred to by the European Court of Human Rights in its narrow majority decision subsequently to uphold the broadcasting ban, the ghost of *Buckley* nevertheless loomed large in the proceedings of *Animal Defenders International (ADI) v. United Kingdom*.[62] There was extensive reference to British parliamentary and other reports including "the differing freedom of expression traditions in the United States and Australia."[63] Indeed, the position in the United States was referred to on 11 occasions in the majority decision, the United Kingdom making it clear that this was a model of democracy it was seeking to avoid. One influential source relied on by the Court even referred to "the democratic right of UK citizens not to be subjected to a barrage of political propaganda at prime advertising time from the party with the richest backers,"[64] before continuing:

> If a court were in the future to rule to the contrary, this would potentially have a dramatic effect on the funding of the political parties. If free to do so, the parties would almost certainly feel obliged to make use of the opportunity to advertise themselves (or attack their opponents) on television and radio. In the United States a high percentage of the expenditure by the political parties at election times is devoted to television advertising. It is the pressure to advertise, as much as any other factor, which generates the demand for money and hence the arms race between Democrats and Republicans.[65]

The total ban on political advertising is nevertheless a far-reaching step to protect the integrity of elections which take place in the United Kingdom every five years (though there are also local government and devolved government elections in between). Questions arise as to whether it would not be possible to permit social advocacy and other groups to have access to paid TV advertising in non-election periods without undermining the integrity of the election process, and whether as a result a more proportionate and

[61] *Id.* at para. 47 (internal citations omitted).
[62] Animal Defenders Int'l v. United Kingdom, 2013 Eur. Ct. H.R. 491.
[63] *Id.* at para. 44.
[64] Committee on Standards in Public Life, The Funding of Political Parties in the United Kingdom, *Report*, Cm 4057-1, para. 13.11.
[65] *Id.*

less inclusive restriction should be introduced, as the government feared the European Court of Human Rights might demand when it reviewed the United Kingdom's position in 2002. Remarkably, the Strasbourg court thought this was not required.[66]

In a clear break with the thinking that dominated in *Buckley*, the European Court of Human Rights has thus embraced a total ban on political advertising, in order partly to protect electoral broadcasting arrangements. In place of the ban, the main political parties are guaranteed free time for party election broadcasts, with provisions made for small parties which contest a prescribed minimum number of seats at the election. It is a tough law reflecting an unequivocal commitment to the fairness of electoral opportunity and a determination to ensure that the airwaves are not dominated by those with an ability to pay. Like the United Kingdom's socialized healthcare system, it is a socialized electoral law, and as such the legacy of a very different political epoch.

VII

Returning finally to Australia, it will be recalled that the High Court struck down legislation on political advertising much less intrusive than that which the European Court of Human Rights upheld in the United Kingdom. Indeed, the Australian decision might usefully have been taken as a proportionate template for the European Court in Strasbourg, as it grappled with how to reconcile electoral integrity and free speech. One of the justifications given by the High Court of Australia in the *ACTV* case is that there were other ways of dealing with the mischief for which the broadcasting ban was designed. As the High Court of Australia explained:

> disclosure of contributions by donors as well as political parties, public funding, and limitations on contributions are but some of the remedies available to overcome the evil which arises not from the giving of information to the electorate or its content but from the conduct of contributors and political officials.[67]

The list of options notably did not include spending limits, and no significant changes to federal campaign finance law have been introduced since the *ACTV* decision, which ironically enabled the Australian trade union

66 Animal Defenders Int'l v. United Kingdom, 2013 Eur. Ct. H.R. 491 at para. 122.

67 Australian Capital Television Pty Ltd and New South Wales v. Commonwealth, [1992] HCA 45; (1992) 177 CLR 106 para. 37 (McHugh, J.) (Austral.).

movement to engage in the most expensive political advertising in Australia in the country's history. The advertising took place during the general election in 2008, which saw a massive air and ground war by trade unions organizing around the theme of labor rights to remove the incumbent right-wing Liberal-National government. The campaign was singularly effective and was not only credited with contributing to the defeat of Australia's governing party, but also with revealing that the Left could also use the broadcast media to good effect.[68]

But although no steps have been taken at the federal level to implement further campaign finance reforms since the *ACTV* case, pioneering legislation has been adopted at the state level, and in particular in New South Wales, which is important because New South Wales is Australia's most populous state.[69] Building on the regulatory regimes operating in Canada and the United Kingdom, New South Wales adopted a comprehensive regulatory system, based on transparency and disclosure, contribution caps, spending limits (applicable to candidates, political parties, and third parties), and the public funding of parties' general expenditures as well as election expenditures, while also creating an independent non-partisan agency (the NSW Electoral Commission) to administer, supervise, and enforce its legislation.[70]

This reads a bit like FECA revisited and strengthened, the legislation looking ripe for attack on liberal principles by a court that so enthusiastically embraced *Buckley*. As might be expected, an attack on the regulations in New South Wales took place in the High Court of Australia, indeed twice: first by trade unions which had been denied the right to make political donations to the Australian Labor Party (of which trade unions were a constituent part), and secondly by property developers who were one of a small category of businesses which were banned from making political donations (because of historic problems of corruption by colleagues who worked in this sector).[71] The other businesses excluded from making political donations were the gamblers, tobacco companies, and brewers.

The first of these applications succeeded, *Buckley* paradoxically being preyed in aid to restore the right of unions to make financial payments to the Australian Labor Party in what was the only occasion that the High Court has struck down legislation in any field since it took the power to do in the *ACTV* case in 1992.[72] The other case, however, is otherwise by some way the more

68 See generally the discussion in Kathie Muir, Worth Fighting For: Inside the Your Rights at Work Campaign (2008).

69 *See* New South Wales Electoral Commission, www.elections.nsw.gov.au.

70 *Id.*

71 *See* Unions NSW v. NSW, [2013] HCA 58; McCloy v. NSW, [2015] HCA 34 (Austral.).

72 *Unions* NSW, [2013] HCA 58 at para. 29 (citing *Buckley v. Valeo*, 424 U.S. 1, at 14, on the need to ensure the "unfettered interchange of ideas for the bringing about of political and social

interesting, even if the claims advanced by the property developer failed. The case is interesting because the Court: (i) appeared to reinterpret *ACTV* and somewhat narrowed its scope; while (ii) signaling its approval of the equality-based approach to campaign finance legislation to be found in British and Canadian legislation; while also (iii) indicating its repudiation of *Buckley* and its progeny.

In terms of the jurisprudence, what stands out in the general discussion of the majority judgment of the High Court of Australia in the case that resulted, *McCloy v. New South Wales*,[73] is the express reference to the *Harper* and *ADI* cases above. In referring to *Harper*, the High Court of Australia referred with approval to the passage concerning "the egalitarian model of elections adopted by Parliament as an essential component of our democratic society," appearing to approve also that "the premise for the model is equal opportunity for participation, and wealth is the major obstacle to equal participation."[74] Finally, the High Court expressly endorsed the suggestion in *Harper* that the state can equalize participation in the electoral process in two ways, as follows:

> First, the State can provide a voice to those who might otherwise not be heard.... Second, the State can restrict the voices which dominate the political discourse so that others may be heard as well.[75]

This is of course a direct repudiation of *Buckley*, as was the adoption by the High Court of the remarks by Lord Bingham in the *ADI* case, where he referred to the need for a level playing field in a democracy, stating that:

> This is achieved where, in public discussion, differing views are expressed, contradicted, answered and debated ... It is not achieved if political parties can, in proportion to their resources, buy unlimited opportunities to advertise in the most effective media, so that elections become little more than an auction.[76]

The idea of a level playing field is of course synonymous with the idea of an egalitarian model of elections on the one hand and equality of opportunity on the other. But as judges throughout the world now acknowledge, these are

changes desired by the people"). *See also* Joo-Cheong Tham, *NSW Election Funding Laws Are a Serious Attack on Freedom of Association*, GUARDIAN (Nov. 6, 2013) (drawing attention to the fact that *Buckley* was relied on by the union plaintiffs).

73 McCloy v. NSW, [2015] HCA 34 (Austral.).

74 *Id.*

75 *Id.*

76 *Id.* at para. 39.

principles that cannot be wished, but must be made to happen by the intervention of the regulatory power of the state.

There is thus no place here for the Burger Court's sentiment in *Buckley* that it is no business of the state to restrict the voice of some in order to enhance the relative voice of others (even though the state routinely does just that in other fields). On the contrary, the High Court of Australia expressly repudiated the jurisprudence of the United States that began with *Buckley*, understood as it was to mean that "the view that now prevails is that an attempt by the legislature to level the playing field to ensure that all voices may be heard is, prima facie, illegitimate."[77] According to the High Court, that is "not the case in Australia, where '[e]quality of opportunity to participate in the exercise of political sovereignty is an aspect of the representative democracy guaranteed by our Constitution.'"[78]

VIII

The United States has been on a remarkable jurisprudential journey since *Buckley*. But so too has the rest of the English-speaking world, as different countries play campaign finance catch-up.[79] As these journeys have been undertaken, the paths have diverged and continue to grow further and further apart, to such an extent that it is difficult to see how they could ever be reconnected. As a result, there are regulatory options taken for granted in the rest of the world that are simply not now within legislative contemplation in the United States (such as spending controls, broadcasting limits, and certain features of public funding). This is ironic in the sense that the United States helped to pioneer at least some of these options.

The legal limits on candidate spending in British law in particular are seen by overseas observers to be eye-wateringly low. The amount of permitted expenditure spending by candidates at a general election depends to some extent on the number of registered voters in the electoral district in question. But in a district with between 60,000 and 80,000 voters, the permitted amount would be in the region of £12,300 to £13,500 within the 25 days before an election.[80] American readers will be able to convert this into dollars and apply

77 *Id.* at para. 41.

78 *Id.* at para. 45.

79 It should be noted that *Buckley* has been considered in other jurisdictions as well. *See* Arthur Guerra Filho, *The Brazilian Supreme Court's ADI 4650 Decision: An Evolution Towards the End of Plutocracy?*, 28 King's L.J. 167 (2017).

80 This comes to about $15,000 to $16,000 in U.S. dollars. This is referred to as the "short campaign." There are additional caps on the "long campaign," the period of four months or so

it to their own electoral district. In addition to this cap on local spending, the main political parties are capped as to their national campaign spending at about £15 million in the year before the election, and this is in a country with about 45 million electors.[81]

The rejection of *Buckley* and its progeny has grown stronger as the courts in other jurisdictions have become more self-confident in constitutional or rights-based adjudication, having come to the genre much later than their American counterparts. But it is not only self-confidence that has led to a rejection of *Buckley*, so much as an awareness of different constitutional values, the importance of different constitutional actors in other systems, and the nauseating effect of the perceived consequences of *Buckley*—the "elephant in the committee room" of constitutional jurisprudence as Baroness Hale put in the *ADI* case in the British House of Lords, then the United Kingdom's highest court.[82]

The developments in other jurisdictions remind us that American democracy is different, not only because of its low levels of participation, but also to the extent that economic liberty translates so easily into political freedom. Constitutional form helps to reinforce that difference, with American liberty (as a constitutional principle if not as a living reality) much less equivocal than its counterpart elsewhere. We are most clearly reminded of this by the High Court of Australia in the *McCloy* case, where Chief Justice Robert French referred to counsel's mistake in equating:

> the freedom under our Constitution with an individual right such as is conferred by the First Amendment to the United States Constitution, which operates in the field of political donations and is in the nature of both a right of political expression and a right of political association.[83]

In the Australian system, "the freedom is not a personal right."[84] But even in those jurisdictions where it is—such as Canada under the Charter of Rights and Freedoms, and the United Kingdom under the Human Rights Act 1998—restrictions on that right are expressly accepted where there is a wider public

immediately before the "short campaign," so that tight constraints operate after 55 months from the election of the Parliament, which, under British law, is elected for a fixed term of 60 months. The "long campaign" limits were introduced by the Political Parties and Elections Act 2009, § 21.

[81] At the time of writing, this would be equivalent to about $100 million in U.S. dollars for each political party in a U.S. election.

[82] R. (Animal Defenders Int'l) v. Secretary of State for Culture, Media and Sport, [2008] UKHL 15 (U.K.).

[83] McCloy v. NSW, [2015] HCA 34 at para. 29.

[84] *Id.* at para. 30.

interest.[85] Apart from a more balanced approach to legal reasoning, this also allows for other other constitutional players to have a legitimate voice in constitutional design. Indeed, in these jurisdictions, the courts are willing to be impressed by the investigations conducted by independent non-partisan agencies, as well as by close and detailed scrutiny of legislation by legislatures themselves.[86]

These are influences on reasoning and decision-making that the Supreme Court of the United States would be unlikely to contemplate, as is the influence of foreign jurisprudence, with courts in all three jurisdictions considered here willing to rely on each other for support and authority.[87] This too is ironic, with the U.S. Supreme Court's introversion and isolation not being a feature of earlier generations of more outward-looking and intellectually curious justices.[88] A good example related to the subject matter of this chapter is *Railway Clerks v. Allen*,[89] where the Supreme Court not only referred to British legislation as a solution to the problem of agency shop fees being used for political purposes, but included British legislation as an appendix to its decision as a possible if not perfect solution.[90]

But although the jurisprudence in other jurisdictions is more permissive for reasons about which we can speculate at length, it does not follow that tighter regulation is more effective in containing the problem of economic power dominating the political agenda or competition for political office. So while the Australians, Canadians, and British smugly reflect on the superiority of their campaign finance regulatory systems, they nevertheless produce electoral outcomes curiously similar to those in the United States, which are contested on the terrain of economic markets that are very similar to that found in the

85 *Canadian Charter of Rights and Freedoms*, § 1, Pt. I of the Constitution Act, 1982, being Sch. B to the Canada Act 1982 (U.K.), 1982 (Can.), c. 11; European Convention on Human Rights (ECHR), art. 10(2).

86 *See* Harper v. Canada (Attorney General), [2004] 1 S.C.R. 827 (Can.). *See also* Animal Defenders International v. United Kingdom, 2013 Eur. Ct. H.R. 491.

87 The virtues of which are acknowledged at least by Justice Stephen Breyer. *See* Albert R. Hunt, *Breyer Sees Value in U.S. Supreme Court's Looking to Foreign Law*, N.Y. Times (Nov. 29, 2015).

88 *See, e.g.*, Atkins v. Virginia, 536 U.S. 304 (2002); Roper v. Simmons, 543 U.S. 551 (2005) (citing foreign and international sources en route to narrowing the constitutional scope of the death penalty in the United States).

89 Railway Clerks v. Allen, 373 U.S. 113 (1963). The jurisprudence has, however, taken a less progressive turn, *Allen* being perhaps an example of an unsuccessful transplant and a warning of the dangers as well as the creative opportunities of comparative law.

90 *Id.* at 123. The legislation in question was the Trade Union Act 1913, which required trade union political activity to be financed from a separate political fund, sustained by a separate political levy, from payment of which members had a right to claim exemption. This was seen to reconcile the interests of the majority with those of the dissenting minority.

United States. And while it is true that the United States lays claim to being one of the most unequal societies in the world, campaign finance regulation is not preventing the others from catching up.

While the lack of campaign finance regulation clearly matters, it is unclear how much it matters. Attempts to deal with political equality are unlikely to be effective in systems of great economic inequality. The problem of political inequality is greater than the palliative capacity of campaign finance regulation to deal with it, and the only solution may be radical surgery to address the problem that makes campaign finance reform necessary in the first place. The lesson from elsewhere is probably that the answer to the campaign finance problem is not campaign finance reform, but the equalization of personal incomes. To accomplish this, however, would require a public policy revolution that will be realized only when American currency speaks *to* us in a less strident tone.

We may have a long wait.

17

Equal Participation and Campaign Finance

Yasmin Dawood*

This chapter examines the concept of *equal participation* for the judicial review of campaign finance regulation. It draws on the jurisprudence of the Supreme Court of Canada on the "right to equal participation" in order to shed useful light on an alternate approach in the American context.

This chapter is organized in three parts. Part I argues for a general approach to campaign finance regulation under which the central challenge is to achieve a complex tradeoff between liberty and equality. Part II turns to the jurisprudence of the U.S. Supreme Court, and it focuses, first, on the role that political equality plays in election law, and second, on the Court's recent recognition of a new right to participation. It also shows how this right to participation is not rooted in a commitment to political equality. Part III sets out the general framework adopted by the Supreme Court of Canada with respect to campaign finance, and it identifies the lessons that might be learned from the right to equal participation as enunciated in Canada's jurisprudence. The chapter concludes with a discussion of the trend toward unequal participation in the U.S. Supreme Court's election law jurisprudence.

I. CAMPAIGN FINANCE REGULATION: TRADEOFFS BETWEEN LIBERTY AND EQUALITY

The debate over campaign finance regulation is often described as a choice between the libertarian approach and the egalitarian approach.[1] Under the

* Yasmin Dawood is the Canada Research Chair in Democracy, Constitutionalism, and Electoral Law and Associate Professor of Law and Political Science at the University of Toronto. She would like to thank Jennifer Che and Rachel Chan for excellent research assistance. The research for this chapter was supported by the Social Sciences and Humanities Research Council.

[1] *See* CASS R. SUNSTEIN, DEMOCRACY AND THE PROBLEM OF FREE SPEECH 1–51 (2d ed. 1995); *see also* OWEN M. FISS, THE IRONY OF FREE SPEECH 17 (1996).

libertarian approach, the state regulation of speech is viewed with suspicion. Free speech is crucial in a democracy because it enables citizens to criticize the government. People communicate ideas by donating money to candidates, parties, and other organizations that support their political viewpoints, or by spending money independently on electoral advertising. On this view, liberty is threatened if the state imposes restrictions on campaign finance.

Under the egalitarian approach, by contrast, some restrictions on speech are viewed as necessary to promote deliberation and political equality. Because the dissemination of viewpoints is expensive, private actors with the greatest wealth could monopolize the means of communication. On this view, campaign finance regulations are required to prevent inequalities in wealth from being translated into inequalities in political power. According to the egalitarian approach, regulations have a democratizing effect by equalizing the relative political power of all citizens.

Rather than treating campaign finance regulation as presenting a choice between the libertarian approach and the egalitarian approach, I have argued in my work that democracies should seek to incorporate both the values of liberty and equality within constitutional law.[2] Instead of emphasizing one value over the other, the ideal position is one that simultaneously recognizes the values of liberty and equality despite the irreconcilable tensions between them. Rather than resolving this tension between liberty and equality, I claim that it is vital to maintain it by instantiating the conflict in law. Democracy is better served when the law contains an explicit tension between these foundational values.

The decision to regulate electoral speech should thus be viewed as inevitably entailing a tradeoff between liberty and equality. Gains in liberty often result in losses to equality, while gains in equality often result in losses to liberty. As a result, the regulation of campaign finance requires a tradeoff between three competing goals: first, preventing the domination of the electoral process by the wealthy; second, allowing citizens to criticize the government; and third, enabling challengers to compete effectively against incumbents.[3] The objective of campaign finance regulation is to optimize all three goals by devising campaign finance restrictions that prevent the wealthy from dominating politics, while also allowing for free speech and political competition. Rather than taking one side or another (pro-regulation or anti-regulation),

[2] Yasmin Dawood, *Freedom of Speech and Democracy: Rethinking the Conflict Between Liberty and Equality*, 26 CAN. J. L. & JURIS. 293, 294 (2013).

[3] Yasmin Dawood, *Democracy, Power, and the Supreme Court: Campaign Finance Reform in Comparative Context*, 4 INT'L. J. CONST. L. 269, 272 (2006).

courts should openly discuss the power tradeoffs involved. The burden would be on the legislature to demonstrate that these objectives have been considered and that a reasonable balance has been achieved among them. Courts would then evaluate campaign finance regulations on the basis of how well the legislature has balanced these competing claims.

The implication of this approach is that the regulation of campaign finance is most effective when neither equality nor liberty is the dominant value expressed in a country's jurisprudence. What is required is a balance of values; hence, this chapter's discussion of equal participation is not meant to imply that equality is the only value that ought to be protected when considering how best to regulate campaign finance.

II. EQUALITY AND PARTICIPATION IN U.S. ELECTION LAW

A. *Political Equality and Campaign Finance Regulation*

Although at one time the U.S. Supreme Court's election law jurisprudence had a better balance between libertarian and egalitarian themes, the Court has in recent years increasingly adopted a libertarian approach to the regulation of campaign finance. In its first campaign finance case, *Buckley v. Valeo*,[4] the Court expressly rejected the egalitarian approach, declaring that the "the concept that government may restrict the speech of some elements of our society in order to enhance the relative voice of others is wholly foreign to the First Amendment."[5] Although the Court upheld the constitutionality of contribution limits in *Buckley*, its rationale was that such restrictions were needed to prevent the reality and appearance of corruption.[6] The Court struck down the restrictions on spending on the basis that these limits consisted of direct restraints on speech in violation of the First Amendment.[7]

In later decisions, however, the Court's anti-corruption rationale transformed into something close to an equalization rationale.[8] Although the Court did not openly embrace the equalization rationale, the meaning of corruption had broadened (for at least some of the justices) into a commitment to "anti-distortion," which overlapped in significant ways with the equalization

4 Buckley v. Valeo, 424 U.S. 1 (1976).

5 *Id.* at 48–49.

6 *Id.* at 26–27. For an analysis of the concept of corruption, see ZEPHYR TEACHOUT, CORRUPTION IN AMERICA: FROM BENJAMIN FRANKLIN'S SNUFF BOX TO CITIZENS UNITED (2014).

7 *Buckley*, 424 U.S. at 19–20.

8 Kathleen M. Sullivan, *Political Money and Freedom of Speech*, 30 U.C. DAVIS L. REV. 663, 679 (1997).

rationale.[9] In *Austin v. Michigan Chamber of Commerce*,[10] for instance, the Court found that large expenditures have "corrosive and distorting effects" since they do not necessarily reflect public support for the corporation's political ideas.[11] The overlap between the anti-corruption rationale and the equalization rationale was also evident in the Supreme Court's decision in *McConnell v. Federal Election Commission*.[12] In *McConnell*, a five-member majority found that corruption did not simply mean "cash-for-votes exchanges,"[13] but also encompassed the "undue influence on an officeholder's judgment, and the appearance of such influence."[14] Because the record contained many examples of political parties selling access to federal officeholders in exchange for large soft money donations, the Court concluded that Congress was justified in determining that such contributions give rise to the reality and appearance of corruption.[15]

The Supreme Court's decision in *Citizens United v. Federal Election Commission*[16] marked a turn toward a more exclusively libertarian approach.[17] In *Citizens United*, the Court majority struck down restrictions on independent spending by corporations and unions.[18] The majority narrowed the definition of corruption, holding that the only governmental interest strong enough to overcome First Amendment concerns is preventing *quid pro quo* corruption or the appearance thereof as stated in *Buckley v. Valeo*.[19] The Court also found, in a departure from its decision in *McConnell*, that access and influence do not amount to corruption.[20] The decision pointedly rejected *Austin*'s anti-distortion rationale on the basis that it was an equalization rationale that was inconsistent with the principle in *Buckley* that the government may not restrict

9 FEC v. Mass. Citizens for Life, 479 U.S. 238, 257 (1986).

10 Austin v. Mich. Chamber of Comm., 494 U.S. 652 (1990).

11 *Id.* at 660.

12 McConnell v. FEC, 540 U.S. 93 (2003).

13 *Id.* at 143.

14 *Id.* at 150.

15 *Id.* at 143–54.

16 Citizens United v. FEC, 558 U.S. 310 (2010).

17 For an analysis of the *Citizens United* decision, see Mark C. Alexander, Citizens United *and Equality Forgotten*, 35 N.Y.U. Rev. L. & Soc. Change 499 (2011); Richard Briffault, *Corporations, Corruption, and Complexity: Campaign Finance After* Citizens United, 20 Cornell J. L. & Pub. Pol'y 643 (2011); Richard L. Hasen, Plutocrats United: Campaign Money, the Supreme Court, and the Distortion of American Elections (2016); Samuel Issacharoff, *On Political Corruption*, 124 Harv. L. Rev. 118 (2010); Michael S. Kang, *The End of Campaign Finance Law*, 98 Va. L. Rev. 1 (2012); Kathleen M. Sullivan, *Two Concepts of Freedom of Speech*, 124 Harv. L. Rev. 143 (2010).

18 *Citizens United*, 558 U.S. at 365.

19 *Id.* at 367–71.

20 *Id.* at 360.

"the speech of some elements of our society in order to enhance the relative voice of others."[21] The Court's hostility to equality arguments was confirmed by a subsequent decision to strike down a law that provided matching funds to publicly financed candidates on the grounds that the law impermissibly leveled the playing field in violation of the First Amendment.[22]

B. *Participation and Campaign Finance Regulation*

The trend toward a libertarian approach to campaign finance regulation was reinforced by the Court's decision in *McCutcheon v. Federal Election Commission*. In *McCutcheon*, a 5-4 majority of the Court struck down aggregate limits on contributions.[23] The aggregate limits capped the total amount that donors could contribute to all federal candidates, political parties, and political action committees. The Court held that the aggregate limits were an unconstitutional restraint on the First Amendment. Chief Justice John Roberts issued a plurality opinion, which was joined by Justices Antonin Scalia, Anthony Kennedy, and Samuel Alito. While Justice Clarence Thomas agreed with the plurality that aggregate limits were unconstitutional, he wrote a concurring opinion.

Chief Justice Robert's plurality opinion in *McCutcheon* appears to have recognized a new right to participation, which subsumes within it various activities including voting and contributing money to candidates.[24] He opened his plurality opinion with the following statement: "There is no right more basic in our democracy than the right to participate in electing our political leaders."[25] He then stated the following: "Citizens can exercise that right in a variety of ways: They can run for office themselves, vote, urge others to vote for a particular candidate, volunteer to work on a campaign, and contribute to a candidate's campaign."[26] Chief Justice Roberts explained the decision in terms of the right to participate: the aggregate limits at issue in the case were struck down because they "seriously restrict[] participation in the democratic process."[27]

There are two important aspects of the Court's new "right to participate." First, the placement of these five activities under a common matrix of participation

[21] *Id.* at 349 (quoting Buckley v. Valeo, 424 U.S. 1, 48–49 (1976)).
[22] Ariz. Free Enter. Club's Freedom Club PAC v. Bennett, 564 U.S. 721 (2011).
[23] McCutcheon v. FEC, 134 S. Ct. 1434 (2014).
[24] Yasmin Dawood, *Democracy Divided: Campaign Finance Regulation and the Right to Vote*, 89 N.Y.U. L. Rev. Online 17, 17–20 (2014).
[25] *McCutcheon*, 134 S. Ct. at 1441.
[26] *Id.*
[27] *Id.* at 1442.

suggests that there is some equivalence in importance among these activities. By subsuming voting within the larger umbrella of the "right to participate," the right to *vote* is no longer the paramount way in which citizens participate in politics. Crucially, the right of wealthy individuals to contribute money is elevated as a normatively protected form of participation on par with voting. The Court majority found, for instance, that the aggregate contribution limits are a "special burden on broader participation in the democratic process."[28]

Second, the Court's new right to participate is not a right to participate *equally*. When the Court speaks of "broader participation," it does not mean participation by greater numbers of people, nor does it mean equal participation by *all* citizens; instead it means *more* participation by a tiny minority of wealthy individuals who have the financial means to exceed the aggregate limits.[29] By contrast, the idea of "broad participation" within democratic theory is usually understood as referring to increasing the participation of all citizens.

The Court plurality also found that wealthy donors' desire to influence the course of public policy as a result of their contributions is constitutionally protected activity. It stated that the First Amendment protects the participatory activity of "contributing to someone who will advocate for [the donor's] … policy preferences."[30] Far from amounting to corruption, ingratiation and access "embody a central feature of democracy—that constituents support candidates who share their beliefs and interests, and candidates who are elected can be expected to be responsive to those concerns."[31] According to the Court plurality, corruption only means *quid pro quo* corruption,[32] but even this kind of corruption does not arise simply because donors have influence over or access to elected officials.[33]

Instead of protecting equal participation, the Court plurality has effectively sanitized the disproportionate political influence of the wealthy.[34] This

[28] *Id.* at 1449.

[29] Spencer Overton argues that broader participation by citizens in contributing to electoral campaigns makes the government more responsive. *See* Spencer Overton, *The Participation Interest*, 100 GEO. L.J. 1259, 1260–61 (2012); *see also* Guy-Uriel E. Charles, *Corruption Temptation*, 120 CAL. L. REV. 25, 30–32 (2014) (arguing that there is insufficient political participation among citizens when it comes to the financing of our political campaigns).

[30] *McCutcheon*, 134 S. Ct. at 1448.

[31] *Id.* at 1441.

[32] *Id.*

[33] For an argument that corruption should be conceived of at the party level, see Michael Kang, *Party-Based Corruption and* McCutcheon v. FEC, 108 NW. U. L. REV. ONLINE 240 (2014).

[34] For an analysis of the connection between political inequality and money in politics, see Mark C. Alexander, *Money in Political Campaigns and Modern Vote Dilution*, 23 LAW & INEQ. J. 239 (2005).

so-called "donor class" funds the bulk of American politics.[35] The effect of the donor class on democratic functioning has become increasingly apparent. For instance, empirical research suggests that elected representatives are more responsive to the preferences of the affluent as compared to the preferences of most citizens.[36] The policy positions of elected representatives do not align with the policy positions of the median voter.[37] The net result of these developments is that the outsize political power of the wealthy few has distorted policy-making in Congress.[38]

Equal participation was also undermined by the Court's decision in *Shelby County v. Holder*,[39] which addressed the constitutionality of the preclearance process of the Voting Rights Act. In order to address longstanding discrimination in voting, Section 5 of the Voting Rights Act required certain states and local governments to obtain federal approval (technically called "preclearance") for any changes to their voting laws and practices in order to ensure that such changes did not deny or abridge the right to vote to racial minorities.[40] Section 4(b) of the Voting Rights Act contained the "coverage formula," which was used to determine which jurisdictions, in light of their histories of discrimination in voting, were subject to Section 5 preclearance.[41] Writing for a majority of the Court, Chief Justice Roberts struck down the constitutionality of Section 4(b) on the basis that the coverage formula was not responsive to current conditions and hence violated the principle of the equal sovereignty of states.[42] Although the Court majority did not strike down Section 5, the preclearance process was rendered inoperative without the coverage formula. In the wake of *Shelby County*, Republican-dominated states have enacted a variety of measures to make voting more difficult for racial minorities. According to one study, nearly half of the new restrictive

35 Spencer Overton, *The Donor Class: Campaign Finance, Democracy, and Participation*, 153 U. Pa. L. Rev. 73 (2004).

36 Larry Bartels, Unequal Democracy: The Political Economy of the New Gilded Age (2008); Martin Gilens, Affluence and Influence: Economic Inequality and Political Power in America (2012).

37 Nicholas Stephanopoulos, *Aligning Campaign Finance Law*, 101 Va. L. Rev. 1425 (2015); see also the chapter by Stephanopoulos that appears in this book.

38 Lawrence Lessig, Republic, Lost: How Money Corrupts Congress—and a Plan to Stop It 110 (2011).

39 Shelby County v. Holder, 570 U.S. 529 (2013).

40 *Id.* at 534.

41 *Id.* at 535.

42 *Id.* at 556–57. For a critique of the equal sovereignty principles, see James Blacksher & Lani Guinier, *Free at Last: Rejecting Equal Sovereignty and Restoring the Constitutional Right to Vote*, 8 Harv. L. & Pol'y Rev. 39, 43 (2014).

voting laws, such as strict voter ID laws, were passed in states that were formerly covered by Section 5.[43]

In sum, equal participation has a contradictory place in U.S. election law. On the one hand, equal participation is a central principle in the electoral redistricting cases, as evidenced by the one-person, one-vote standard.[44] On the other hand, unequal participation is increasingly protected by the conservative wing of the Supreme Court in both the campaign finance and voting rights arenas.

III. EQUAL PARTICIPATION AND CAMPAIGN FINANCE REGULATION IN CANADA

Campaign finance is also extensively regulated in Canada. There are strict reporting and administration rules that apply to political parties, candidates, and third parties. Political parties are subject to maximum election expenses which are determined by a complex statutory formula that takes into account various factors such as the number of electors and the duration of the election period.[45] Candidates are likewise subject to expense limits based on a statutory formula.[46] Political contributions may only be made by Canadian citizens or permanent residents; corporations and unions are banned from making political contributions.[47]

There are also a number of rules governing third-party election advertising, which refers to independent advertising expenditures by individuals or groups other than political parties and candidates. Third parties are not permitted to incur election advertising expenses of more than $150,000 with respect to a general election.[48] In addition, third parties may not spend more than $3,000 to promote or oppose the election of one or more candidates in an electoral district.[49] These limits apply only during the election period, which refers to the time between the announcement of an election and election day. The Canada Elections Act provides that the election period must be a minimum of 36 days.[50]

43 Brennan Center for Justice, *Election 2016: Restrictive Voting Laws by the Numbers* (Sept. 28, 2016), www.brennancenter.org/analysis/election-2016-restrictive-voting-laws-numbers.
44 Reynolds v. Sims, 377 U.S 535 (1964).
45 Canada Elections Act, S.C. 2000. c. 9, § 430(1)(a).
46 Canada Elections Act, S.C. 2000. c. 9, § 477.5(3).
47 Canada Elections Act, S.C. 2000. c. 9, § 363(1).
48 Canada Elections Act, S.C. 2000. c. 9, § 350(1).
49 Canada Elections Act, S.C. 2000. c. 9, § 350(2).
50 Canada Elections Act, S.C. 2000. c. 9, § 57.

The Supreme Court of Canada's campaign finance cases have considered the constitutionality of spending limits and limits on third party advertising. In these cases, the Court has recognized a right of equal participation. This next section describes the right of equal participation, in addition to identifying various lessons and challenges for the American context.

A. *The Right to Equal Participation*

One of the distinctive features of the Supreme Court of Canada's election law cases is that it has interpreted the right to vote, as protected by Section 3 of the Canadian Charter of Rights and Freedoms, as a plural right. This "bundle of rights" approach recognizes multiple democratic rights, each of which is concerned with a particular facet of democratic participation and representation.[51] The Supreme Court of Canada has recognized the following four subsidiary rights that are derived from the right to vote: (1) the right to effective representation; (2) the right to meaningful participation; (3) the right to equal participation; and (4) the right to a free and informed vote.[52]

The right to effective representation was recognized by the Supreme Court of Canada in a case concerning the constitutionality of a province's electoral redistricting map.[53] The majority opinion held that electoral districts do not have to adhere to the one-person, one-vote principle; the "purpose of the right to vote enshrined in s. 3 of the *Charter* is not equality of voting power *per se*, but the right to 'effective representation.'"[54] While the relative parity of voting power is a central consideration, effective representation is also based on additional considerations such as "geography, community history, community interests and minority representation."[55] In a later case involving the rules that apply to political parties, the Supreme Court of Canada held that the Section 3 right to vote includes "the right of each citizen to play a meaningful role in the electoral process."[56] The majority opinion stated that "the democratic rights entrenched in s. 3 ensure that each citizen has an opportunity to express an opinion about the formation of social policy and the functioning of public institutions through participation in the electoral process."[57]

51 Yasmin Dawood, *Democracy and the Right to Vote: Rethinking Democratic Rights Under the Charter*, 51 Osgoode Hall L.J. 251, 254–55 (2013).

52 *Id.*

53 Reference re Provincial Electoral Boundaries (Saskatchewan), [1991] 2 S.C.R. 158, 100 D.L.R. (4th) 212 (Can.).

54 *Id.* at para. 26.

55 *Id.* at para. 31.

56 Figueroa v. Canada (Attorney General), 2003 SCC 37, para. 25, [2003] 1 S.C.R. 912.

57 *Id.* at para. 29.

The Supreme Court of Canada first recognized a right to equal participation in *Libman v. Quebec* (A.G.),[58] a case which considered the constitutionality of independent spending limits set out in Quebec's referendum legislation.[59] Although the Supreme Court of Canada struck down the spending limits in *Libman* as a violation of the freedom of expression,[60] the Supreme Court of Canada adopted an egalitarian approach to rules governing spending during a referendum or an election.[61]

In particular, it endorsed several principles for the regulation of election spending. The first principle is fairness in the political sphere. The Court stated that in order to "ensure a right of equal participation in democratic government, laws limiting spending are needed to preserve the equality of democratic rights and ensure that one person's exercise of the freedom to spend does not hinder the communication opportunities of others."[62] Spending limits are required to "prevent the most affluent from monopolizing election discourse and consequently depriving their opponents of a reasonable opportunity to speak and be heard."[63]

The second principle emphasized was ensuring a free and informed vote.[64] Spending limits are required, claimed the Court, to "guarantee the right of electors to be adequately informed of all the political positions advanced by the candidates and by the various political parties."[65] It was important to prevent "the most affluent members of society from exerting a disproportionate influence by dominating the referendum debate through access to greater resources."[66] The Court argued that the "principle of electoral fairness flows directly from a principle entrenched in the Constitution: that of the political equality of citizens."[67] To ensure equality, spending limits prevent "the most affluent from monopolizing election discourse and consequently depriving their opponents of a reasonable opportunity to speak and be heard."[68]

[58] Libman v. Quebec, [1997] 3 S.C.R. 569, 51 D.L.R. (4th) 385 (Can).

[59] *Id.* at para. 1.

[60] *Id.* at paras. 35, 85. For an analysis of Canadian free speech law, see RICHARD MOON, THE CONSTITUTIONAL PROTECTION OF FREEDOM OF EXPRESSION (2000).

[61] *See* Colin Feasby, Libman v. Quebec (A.G.) *and the Administration of the Process of Democracy under the Charter: The Emerging Egalitarian Model*, 44 MCGILL L.J. 5, 8, 31–32 (1999).

[62] *Libman*, 3 S.C.R. 569 at para. 47.

[63] *Id.*

[64] *Id.*

[65] *Id.*

[66] *Id.* at para. 41.

[67] *Id.* at para. 47.

[68] *Id.*

At issue in its next campaign finance case, *Harper v. Canada*,[69] was the constitutionality of third-party spending limits as provided for in the Canada Elections Act.[70] Third-party spending refers to any spending by individuals and groups that are neither candidates nor political parties.[71] The lower courts had struck down the provisions as violation of the guarantees of freedom of expression and association as protected by the Canadian Charter of Rights and Freedoms.[72] A 6-3 majority of the Supreme Court of Canada upheld the constitutionality of the third-party spending limits. Writing for the majority, Justice Michel Bastarache confirmed that Parliament had adopted an egalitarian model of elections. Under this model, wealth is the main obstacle that prevents individuals from enjoying an equal opportunity to participate in the electoral process.[73]

The *Harper* majority endorsed the principles announced earlier in *Libman*, finding them consistent with the egalitarian model of elections adopted by Parliament.[74] Under an egalitarian model, "individuals should have an equal opportunity to participate in the political process."[75] According to the Court, "wealth is the main obstacle to equal participation."[76]

The Court majority noted that participation in the electoral process can be equalized in two ways. The first way is to "provide a voice to those who might otherwise not be heard," which is achieved through reimbursing candidates and political parties and by providing broadcast time.[77] The second way is to impose third-party spending limitations which "enables voters to be better informed" because "no one voice is overwhelmed by another."[78]

With respect to spending limitations, the Court described two objectives that would need to be met to achieve "equality in the political discourse."[79] First, voters must be adequately informed of all the political positions supported by candidates and parties.[80] To be adequately informed, a voter "must be able to weigh the relative strengths and weaknesses of each candidate

69 Harper v. Canada (Attorney General), 2004 SCC 33, [2004] 1 S.C.R. 827.

70 Canada Elections Act, S.C. 2000, c. 9 §§ 350(1)–351.

71 For an analysis of the *Harper* case, see Jamie Cameron, *Governance and Anarchy in the s 2(b) Jurisprudence: A Comment on* Vancouver Sun *and* Harper v. Canada, 17 NAT'L J. CONST. L. 71, 95 (2005).

72 [2001] 93 Alta LR (3d) 281; [2002] 14 Alta LR (4th) 4.

73 *Harper*, 2004 SCC 33 at para. 62.

74 *Id.*

75 *Id.*

76 *Id.*

77 *Id.*

78 *Id.*

79 *Id.* at para. 63.

80 *Id.* at para. 71.

and political party... [and] must also be able to consider opposing aspects of issues associated with certain candidates and political parties where they exist."[81] In order for "voters to be able to hear all points of view, the information disseminated by third parties, candidates, and political parties cannot be unlimited."[82] Without any spending limits, the affluent would be able to exert a disproportionate influence on the political discourse by "flood[ing] the electoral discourse with their message," thereby potentially drowning out certain voices.[83]

The second objective is to ensure that candidates would enjoy a level playing field in the sense that third-party spending would not disproportionately impact one of the candidates or political parties.[84] All candidates and political parties must be given a reasonable opportunity to present their positions to voters.[85] For this reason, the spending limits for third parties must be low enough so that a candidate has the resources to respond to an attack.[86] The majority stated that it "cannot be forgotten that small political parties, who play an equally important role in the electoral process, may be easily overwhelmed by a third party having access to significant financial resources."[87] An unequal dissemination of information will result in the voter not being adequately informed which in turn affects the voter's ability to participate meaningfully in the electoral process.[88]

The Court found that to "constitute an infringement of the right to vote, these spending limits would have to restrict information in such a way as to undermine the right of citizens to meaningfully participate in the political process and to be effectively represented."[89] The spending limits at issue, however, were not so low that they interfered with the right to meaningfully participate. Although the spending limits infringed upon the freedoms of expression and association guaranteed by the Canadian Charter of Rights and Freedoms, the provisions were nonetheless justifiable under Section 1 of the Charter as "a reasonable limit prescribed by law as can be demonstrably justified in a free and democratic society."[90]

[81] *Id.*
[82] *Id.* at para. 72.
[83] *Id.*
[84] *Id.* at para. 61.
[85] *Id.* at para. 81.
[86] *Id.* at para. 116.
[87] *Id.*
[88] *Id.* at para. 71.
[89] *Id.* at para. 73.
[90] *Id.* at para. 147.

B. Lessons and Challenges for the American Context

1. Rethinking Equality

The Supreme Court of Canada adopted a political equality rationale for justifying the constitutionality of campaign finance restrictions. The U.S. Supreme Court views itself as being bound to its pronouncement in *Buckley* that "the concept that government may restrict the speech of some elements of our society in order to enhance the relative voice of others is wholly foreign to the First Amendment."[91] The question, then, is whether there are any lessons in the Canadian experience for the American context, given *Buckley*'s pronouncement forbidding the restrictions of the speech of some individuals to enhance the relative voice of others. There are three possible avenues for rethinking political equality in the context of campaign finance regulation: first, equalizing voters; second, equalizing candidates; and third, equalizing access to politicians.

It is worth noting that in the Canadian context, the main thing that the courts have tried to equalize is the ability of *voters* to identify their true preferences and reach an informed decision prior to election day. In *Harper*, the Supreme Court of Canada stated that an individual's right to meaningful participation "includes a citizen's right to exercise his or her vote in an informed manner."[92] In order for a citizen to be well informed, "the citizen must be able to weigh the relative strengths and weaknesses of each candidate and political party."[93]

By contrast, the U.S. Supreme Court's "undue influence" standard in *McConnell* (which has since been rejected by the majority in *Citizens United*) was concerned with the undue influence exerted by various groups on the ability of *officeholders* to engage in fair and informed decision-making.[94] The Canadian justices, however, rejected the idea that equal participation is equivalent to "the ability to mount a media campaign capable of determining the outcome."[95] Instead, the concern is that third-party advertising may "systematically manipulate the voter" by making it difficult to "hear from all groups and thus promote a more informed vote."[96] In the era of fake news, the problem of misinformed and manipulated voters may have some traction.

[91] Buckley v. Valeo, 424 U.S. 1, 48–49 (1976).
[92] *Harper*, 2004 SCC 33 at para. 71.
[93] *Id.*
[94] McConnell v. FEC, 540 U.S. 93, 150 (2003).
[95] *Harper*, 2004 SCC 33 at para. 74.
[96] *Id.* at para. 80.

A second avenue is to equalize the conditions that apply to candidates. The Supreme Court of Canada found that campaign finance restrictions protect candidates and political parties by providing them with "an equal opportunity to present their positions to the electorate."[97] Elections often have rules establishing a level playing field among candidates, and it may be possible to devise a justification of certain campaign finance rules along these lines.

A third avenue is to restrict the pronouncement in *Buckley* as applying specifically to *speech*, but not to *access* to politicians. It is worth considering arguments that are concerned with the equality of access to politicians. The focus would be on the mechanics of access and influence that money affords, and on the exclusion of citizens from deliberative and decision-making processes that results from unequal access. It would be possible to describe this unequal access to politicians as a form of corruption by, for instance, reincorporating the "undue influence" standard from *McConnell*. As Mark Warren puts it, corruption results in "duplicitous exclusion" because it excludes those who have a right to be included in democratic decision-making, and does so in a manner that cannot be publicly justified.[98] Representatives may illegitimately empower wealthy donors in order to repay the debts of obligation they have amassed; by so doing, they may also ignore the best interests of their constituents, thereby disempowering them. The sale of special access to officeholders creates the perception that money buys influence. Selling access to the highest bidder undermines a central democratic tenet that all citizens in a democracy should have an equal opportunity to have their views heard by their representatives.

2. Political Equality as a Government Interest or a Right?

The Canadian experience sheds useful light on the question of whether political equality should be framed as a government interest or as a right in a litigation context. In the *Harper* case, political equality was described by the Supreme Court of Canada as both a government interest and as a right that voters enjoyed. The government gave three reasons why the restrictions were justified under Section 1 of the Charter: "first, to favor equality, by preventing those with greater means from dominating electoral debate; second, to foster informed citizenship, by ensuring that some positions are not drowned out by others (this is related to the right to participate in the political process by

97 *Id.* at para. 81.

98 Mark E. Warren, *What Does Corruption Mean in a Democracy?*, 48 AM. J. POL. SCI. 328, 333 (2004).

casting an informed vote); third, to enhance public confidence by ensuring equality, a better informed citizenship and fostering the appearance and reality of fairness in the democratic process."[99] As described above, the Court also recognized a right to equal participation as a logical extension of the right to vote as protected by Section 3 of the Charter. The Canadian experience suggests that it might be best to frame political equality as both a governmental interest and as an individual right.

3. The Evidentiary Record

Another important difference in terms of how campaign finance cases are handled in Canada concerns how the courts there rely on an evidentiary record. The type of evidence that is required to find that a restriction on the freedom of expression is justified differs in the Canadian context. In Canada, the legislature is not held to a standard of scientific proof when it is trying to solve a problem, particularly when the available social science evidence is inconclusive or conflicting. Instead, a court may rely on a "reasoned apprehension of harm" standard, under which it can consider logic, reason, and some social science evidence.[100]

The dissenting justices in *Harper* argued that the government had provided no evidence linking third-party spending and electoral fairness.[101] The dissent argued that the "dangers posited are wholly hypothetical" and that there is "no evidence that wealthier Canadians—alone or in concert—will dominate political debate during the electoral period absent limits."[102]

The majority, however, relied on past precedents that have established that the legislature is not required to provide scientific proof in order to act against a harm.[103] The majority stated that it was very difficult to measure scientifically either the nature of the harm (which it identified as electoral unfairness) or the efficaciousness of Parliament's remedy.[104] It found that the legislature had met its burden of demonstrating a reasoned apprehension of harm. The Court majority placed weight on the fact that the Royal Commission on Electoral Reform and Party Financing, also known as the Lortie Commission, recommended the enactment of spending limits in order to promote electoral

[99] *Harper*, 2004 SCC 33 at para. 23.
[100] *Id.* at para. 78.
[101] *Id.* at para. 29 (McLachlin, C.J. & Major, J., dissenting).
[102] *Id.* at para. 34 (McLachlin, C.J. & Major, J., dissenting).
[103] *Id.* at para. 77.
[104] *Id.* at para. 79.

fairness.[105] The Lortie Commission concluded that if the affluent dominate the political discourse, they could affect the outcome of the election and erode citizens' confidence in the fairness of the process.[106] Parliament relied on the Lortie Commission's findings when it enacted third-party spending limits.[107]

Still, the Supreme Court of Canada did identify four problems created by unlimited third-party advertising for which there was some expert evidence: (1) the dominance of the political discourse by the wealthy; (2) the circumvention of spending limits by candidates and parties; (3) an unfair impact on the outcome of an election; and (4) the erosion of public confidence in the electoral system.[108] For the last item, the Supreme Court of Canada noted the difficulty of measurement given the host of influences on voter behavior. It nonetheless concluded that "logic and reason assisted by some social science evidence is sufficient proof of the harm that Parliament seeks to remedy."[109] The majority concluded that even in the absence of any evidence that third-party advertising seeks to manipulate voters, the "danger that political advertising may manipulate or oppress the voter means that some deference chosen by Parliament is warranted."[110] The Supreme Court of Canada was particularly concerned about the perception of electoral fairness, stating that where "Canadians perceive elections to be unfair, voter apathy follows shortly thereafter."[111] For evidence, the majority relied on several surveys in which a large majority of Canadians view limits on third-party spending as an effective way to promote electoral fairness.[112]

The Canadian experience suggests that empirical evidence showing how money affects electoral fairness and democratic functioning could be helpful in the United States as well. It would be useful to develop a systematic account of how contributions, independent spending, and lobbying affect elections and the development of public policy.[113] More survey data on how Americans perceive the fairness of the electoral process, particularly with respect to the influence of wealthy donors, could also be helpful.[114]

[105] *See* ROYAL COMMISSION ON ELECTORAL AND PARTY FINANCING, FINAL REPORT: REFORMING ELECTORAL DEMOCRACY 332 (1991).

[106] *Harper*, 2004 SCC 33 at para. 79.

[107] *See* Canada Elections Act, R.S.C. 1985, c. E-2, §§ 259.1(1), 259.2(2).

[108] *Harper*, 2004 SCC 33 at para. 79.

[109] *Id.*

[110] *Id.* at para. 85.

[111] *Id.* at para. 82.

[112] *Id.* at para. 83.

[113] For an excellent example of this kind of research, see DANIEL P. TOKAJI & RENATA E. B. STRAUSE, THE NEW SOFT MONEY: OUTSIDE SPENDING IN CONGRESSIONAL ELECTIONS (2014).

[114] *But see* Nathaniel Persily & Kelli Lammie, *Perceptions of Corruption and Campaign Finance: When Public Opinion Determines Constitutional Law*, 153 U. PA. L. REV. 119 (2004)

4. The Election Period and Limitations on Free Speech

In their dissenting opinion in *Harper*, two justices of the Supreme Court of Canada, Chief Justice Beverley McLachlin and Justice John C. Major, expressed concern that the third-party spending limits impaired speech.[115] They contended that the spending limits imposed a virtual ban on third-party advertising during the election period.[116] The spending limits were so low that citizens could not take out a full-page advertisement in the national media or communicate through the national mail.[117] At most, they could distribute flyers and place ads in local papers.[118] The limits imposed on third parties are considerably lower than the limits imposed on candidates and parties; indeed, third parties were permitted to spend only 1.3 percent of the national advertising spending limits for political parties.[119] For these reasons, the dissenters wrote that spending limits violate "free expression where it warrants the greatest protection—the sphere of political discourse."[120] They noted that the "ability to engage in effective speech in the public square means nothing if it does not include the ability to attempt to persuade one's fellow citizens through debate and discussion."[121] For the dissent, "[f]reedom of expression must allow a citizen to give voice to her vision for her community and nation, to advocate change through the art of persuasion in the hope of improving her life and indeed the larger social, political and economic landscape."[122]

As the Supreme Court of Canada's majority pointed out, however, these spending limits applied only during the election period. Outside of the election period, a third party "may freely spend money or advertise to make its views known or to persuade others" and in fact many groups are "already organized and have a continued presence, mandate and political view which they promote."[123] The Supreme Court of Canada's majority found that the "legislature had to try to strike a balance between absolute freedom of individual expression and equality among the different expression for the benefit of all."[124] Although

(finding that while the campaign finance system contributes to public perceptions about corruption in government, campaign finance reform may not change these attitudes).

115 *Harper*, 2004 SCC 33 at para. 35 (McLachlin, C.J. & Major, J., dissenting).

116 *Id.*

117 *Id.* at paras. 4–5 (McLachlin, C.J. & Major, J., dissenting).

118 *Id.* at para. 7 (McLachlin, C.J. & Major, J., dissenting).

119 *Id.* at para. 8 (McLachlin, C.J. & Major, J., dissenting).

120 *Id.* at para. 2 (McLachlin, C.J. & Major, J., dissenting).

121 *Id.* at para. 16 (McLachlin, C.J. & Major, J., dissenting).

122 *Id.*

123 *Id.* at para. 112.

124 *Id.* at para. 86.

limits on third-party spending do restrict the freedom of speech, they enable citizens to meaningfully participate in the electoral process.[125] In addition, the design of the electoral system "reflects a political choice, the details of which are better left to Parliament."[126] The Supreme Court of Canada's majority emphasized that "[u]nder the egalitarian model of elections, Parliament must balance the rights and privileges of the participants in the electoral process: candidates, political parties, third parties and voters."[127]

One possible avenue for the American context would be to place time limitations on spending rules by adopting an election period.[128] However, there are some important differences between Canada and the United States with respect to election dates. In Canada, which has a parliamentary as opposed to a presidential system of government, a general election can be called at any time by the Governor General on the advice of the Prime Minister. The only restriction under the Constitution Act 1867, is that a given Parliament may sit for a maximum of five years. More recently, in 2007, Parliament adopted fixed election dates, which set general elections every four years. Despite these differences, it may be worth exploring the possibility of establishing an election period in the United States in which stricter campaign finance regulations could be applied for a limited period of time. Scholars have also argued for "electoral exceptionalism," which is the idea that elections should be treated as a distinct domain of democratic activity, subject to its own set of rules.[129] Such an approach could be used to justify expenditure limits.

5. Incumbency Protection

One drawback to campaign finance regulations is that they can help to entrench the power of officeholders.[130] Rules that make fundraising more difficult are

[125] *Id.* at para. 87.

[126] *Id.*

[127] *Id.*

[128] For arguments about the value of election periods, see Dennis Thompson, *Election Time: Normative Implications of Temporal Properties of the Electoral Process in the United States*, 98 AM. POL. SCI. REV. 51 (2004); Saul Zipkin, *The Election Period and the Regulation of the Democratic Process*, 18 WM. & MARY BILL RTS. J. 533 (2010).

[129] Frederick Schauer & Richard R. Pildes, *Electoral Exceptionalism and the First Amendment*, 77 TEXAS L. REV. 1803 (1999). Campaign finance regulation could be reframed as an effort to protect electoral integrity. For this argument, see ROBERT C. POST, CITIZENS DIVIDED: CAMPAIGN FINANCE REFORM AND THE CONSTITUTION (2014).

[130] For arguments against the democratizing effects of campaign finance regulations, see Bradley A. Smith, *Faulty Assumptions and Undemocratic Consequences of Campaign Finance Reform*, 105 YALE L.J. 1049, 1077 (1996); Bradley A. Smith, *Money Talks: Speech, Corruption, Equality, and Campaign Finance*, 86 GEO. L.J. 45, 93 (1997).

detrimental to challengers and therefore beneficial for incumbents.[131] For example, if contribution limits are set very low, challengers will find it difficult to gather sufficient funds from early supporters.[132] Because incumbents usually enjoy a far larger base of supporters, low contribution limits do not have the same impact on their electoral success. Incumbents also enjoy other built-in benefits such as free mailings to their constituents, name recognition, press coverage, and opportunities to help their constituents in an official capacity.[133] Given the significant advantages available to incumbents, challengers without significant financial resources find it difficult to win an election. Research has demonstrated that the more a challenger spends on a campaign, the more likely she is to win.[134] For this reason, campaign finance restrictions protect incumbents from challengers, particularly those challengers who do not have an independent source of funds.

The Supreme Court of Canada, however, has not raised the issue of incumbency protection when discussing campaign finance regulation. By contrast, in his dissenting opinion in *McConnell*, Justice Scalia stated that "first instinct of power is the retention of power, and, under a Constitution that requires periodic elections, that is best achieved by the suppression of election-time speech."[135] By regulating corporate speech, officeholders have insulated themselves "from the most effective speech that the major participants in the economy and major incorporated interest groups can generate."[136] If the United States ever implemented reforms like those in Canada, the problem of incumbency protection would have to be addressed in the American context. One possible argument is that incumbency protection could be mitigated by setting independent spending limits at a higher level so that officeholders are not insulated from critical speech.

IV. CONCLUSION: CONFRONTING UNEQUAL PARTICIPATION

The problem of unequal participation can have grave consequences for democratic legitimacy and functioning. As John Rawls argues in *A Theory of Justice*, the principle of participation "requires that all citizens are to have an equal

[131] *See* Lillian R. BeVier, *Money and Politics: A Perspective on the First Amendment and Campaign Finance Reform*, 73 CAL. L. REV. 1045, 1080 (1985).

[132] *See* Stephen E. Gottlieb, *The Dilemma of Election Campaign Finance Reform*, 18 HOFSTRA L. REV. 213, 220–21 (1989).

[133] *See id.* at 224.

[134] *See* FRANK J. SORAUF, MONEY IN AMERICAN ELECTIONS 162 (1988).

[135] McConnell v. FEC, 540 U.S. 93, 263 (2003) (Scalia, J., dissenting).

[136] *Id.* at 258 (Scalia, J., dissenting).

right to take part in, and to determine the outcome of, the constitutional process that establishes the laws with which they are to comply."[137] If private wealth can be converted into public power, the nature of democracy changes. Rawls argued that the "liberties protected by the principle of participation lose much of their value whenever those who have greater private means are permitted to use their advantages to control the course of public debate."[138] These liberties are undermined because the inequality of participation will "enable those better situated to exercise a larger influence over the development of legislation."[139] Eventually, the wealthy "are likely to acquire a preponderant weight in settling social questions, at least in regard to those matters upon which they normally agree, which is to say in regard to those things that support their favored circumstances."[140]

The U.S. Supreme Court's invocation of the right to participate in *McCutcheon* brings to the fore the problem of unequal participation. Since the civil rights era, participatory rights based on voting have been associated with the universal franchise and the principle of political equality. Participatory rights based on speech, however, are defended despite the increasing inequality with respect to which such rights are distributed in society.

The U.S. Supreme Court's right of participation also raises the question of whether the norm of unequal participation in the arena of campaign finance is imposing on voting rights. In *McCutcheon*, Chief Justice Roberts stated that the Court must protect "the First Amendment right of citizens to choose who shall govern them."[141] This is a striking declaration on its own terms because it indicates that the First Amendment is encroaching on territory that was once reserved exclusively for the right to vote.[142] This statement also poses a considerable challenge to the notion that the citizens' "right to choose who will govern them" is by definition a right that is distributed *equally* among citizens. Given *Buckley*'s key tenet that "the concept that government may restrict the speech of some elements of our society in order to enhance the relative voice of others is wholly foreign to the First Amendment,"[143] the Court's invocation of a First Amendment right of citizens to choose their representatives

[137] John Rawls, A Theory of Justice 194 (rev'd ed. 1999).

[138] *Id.* at 197–98.

[139] *Id.*

[140] *Id.*

[141] McCutcheon v. FEC, 134 S. Ct. 1434, 1439 (2014).

[142] *See* James A. Gardner, *Partition and Rights: The U.S. Supreme Court's Accidental Jurisprudence of Democratic Process*, 42 Fla. St. U. L. Rev. 61 (2014) (arguing that the First Amendment has been invoked for many disputes involving voting).

[143] Buckley v. Valeo, 424 U.S. 1, 48–49 (1976).

places equal participation under even greater threat. In conclusion, future work in the field must focus on strengthening the principle of equal participation in all dimensions of election law, and the difference between how the Supreme Court of Canada and the Supreme Court of the United States have approached this issue is instructive.

18

Political Finance and Political Equality: Lessons from Europe

Óscar Sánchez Muñoz*

I. INTRODUCTION

In most Western European democracies, one central purpose guides the regulation of political finance: guaranteeing the fairness of electoral competition.

Although it is controversial to speak of a single "European model," many of the political finance regulations that have been imposed in Western Europe's democracies share four similarities. First, they impose limits on expenditures, including third-party expenditures, and place significant restrictions, including sometimes even total bans, on paid political TV advertising. Second, they regulate private contributions to political parties, and in many cases the contribution limits are significant, such as the total ban on corporate donations in some countries. Third, these regulations provide for the public funding of political parties based on fair distribution criteria. Finally, many of these countries set rules to ensure there is public accountability in party financing.

After the fall of dictatorship in Greece, Portugal, and Spain in the 1970s, and after the fall of Communism in the countries of Central and Eastern Europe in the 1990s, the regulatory framework of the "European model" has been extended to the entire European continent. Of course, there remain differences between countries, and not all of the regulations mentioned above are found across the European continent with the same intensity. Still, we have seen a trend toward European countries adopting many common standards and harmonizing their political finance regulations. The Council of Europe's recommendations have been particularly relevant to this process.

* Óscar Sánchez Muñoz is Associate Professor of Constitutional Law at the University of Valladolid. He thanks the Fulbright-Schuman Program for funding his stay at the American University Washington College of Law, in Washington, D.C., where he conducted research on the topic of "Money and Politics: A United States-Europe Comparative Vision" and drafted much of this chapter.

In Europe, political parties play a much more important role in elections than they do in the United States. In addition, most European governments fund not only the electoral expenses of political parties, but also their ordinary expenses, which parties incur after they are awarded seats in parliament. Because the financial relationship with political parties persists long after the election ends, scholars in Europe prefer to use the term "political finance" instead of the term "campaign finance" to describe the complex and ongoing financial relationship that is formed between political parties and the state.

The greater dominance of political parties in Europe is linked to many factors. Most countries in Europe use a proportional representation (PR) electoral system. In many PR systems, voters cast ballots for parties rather than individual candidates. This tends to privilege and elevate the role of political parties in elections. Scholars also trace the dominance of political parties in Europe to the continent's "party-centric" model of political finance. There is a direct relationship between the continent's party-centric political finance model, on the one hand, and the dominance that parties play in Europe, on the other. Indeed, most aspects of the party system that scholars have recently studied in European party politics, particularly the phenomenon of the "cartel party,"[1] can be explained largely by the influence of Europe's political finance model.

The factors that have led many countries in Europe to reform their political finance systems were not that different from those that led other democracies, including Canada and the United States, to do the same. Two factors played a paramount role in particular in this regard. First, political finance reform was enacted in many European countries in response to deteriorating public confidence in government, which came about after various corruption scandals related to money in politics rocked the continent. Second, political finance reforms arose out of a concern that the playing field in European elections needed to be leveled, so as to prevent the distortion that money has on policy, namely by pulling its formation and expression away from the popular will.

Whenever European regulations have been challenged, courts in Europe, as in Canada, have found them to be fully compatible with the constitutional order. European courts have often given great value to arguments based on political equality and have justified placing limitations on the freedom of political actors in the name of equality. By contrast, the U.S. Supreme Court's decision in *Buckley v. Valeo*[2] adopted a radically different approach

[1] Richard S. Katz & Peter Mair, *Changing Models of Party Organization and Party Democracy: The Emergence of the Cartel Party*, 1 PARTY POL. 5 (1995).

[2] Buckley v. Valeo, 424 U.S. 1 (1976).

in the United States, promoting freedom of speech above other competing values. *Buckley* promoted the free speech interests of those seeking to inject large sums of money into elections above other interests, while completely disregarding competing concerns about electoral fairness. In the eyes of the U.S. Supreme Court, qualities like equality and fairness were "wholly foreign to the First Amendment."[3]

After *Buckley*, it might be said—albeit in a simplified way—that two dominant models of political finance regulation can now be found in the world. One of these is the "libertarian" model, and the other is the "egalitarian" model. The first model is dominant in the United States. The second model prevails, with modest variations, throughout most of Europe and in many other democracies in the world.

This chapter explains the political values and constitutional interpretations that underlie political finance regulation in Europe. It then analyzes the different kinds of regulations that have been introduced by various European countries, presenting some interesting case studies as a catalog of Europe's best practices. Finally, this chapter offers some critical perspectives on the effects of Europe's political finance regulations, focusing in particular on corruption and the weak connection between political parties and society as the main concerns that have arisen out of the European experience.

II. EQUALITY OF OPPORTUNITY: A GUIDING PRINCIPLE

The principle of equality of opportunity in electoral competition has become the inspiring principle that has guided much of contemporary election law in Europe.[4] As a constitutional principle, equality of opportunity has come to dominate the constitutional jurisprudence of many European courts. It deserves to be mentioned that the principle of equality of opportunity is itself based on two other major constitutional principles. The first of these is the principle of "freedom of electoral competition." This principle requires not only that parties have the freedom to compete, but also for citizens' votes to be free from undue influence. To ensure freedom of competition, parties must have equal access to media, government must be neutral, and so forth. The second principle on which equality of opportunity rests is the principle of political equality for all citizens. This requires every citizen to have an equal

3 *Id.* at 49–50.

4 Ann-Kristen Kölln, *Does Party Finance Regulation Create a Level Playing Field?*, 15 ELECTION L.J. 71 (2016).

opportunity to influence the outcome of an election and then to be given equal access to political power after it.[5]

At its core, the principle of equality of opportunity in electoral competition requires the legal system to provide sufficient guarantees to enable all political ideas present within the political community to compete with each other in the electoral arena. That translates into the freedom to create political parties and the freedom for these parties to be given access to the ballot, unencumbered by unreasonable restrictions.

The principle of equality of opportunity further stands for the idea that the law must guarantee to all "electoral competitors" a fair chance to be visible and to communicate their policies to the electorate. An electoral competitor can be a political party, an individual candidate, or another organization authorized to be on the ballot by law. Having a fair chance to communicate with the electorate, in turn, means that no competitor is able to take advantage of *de facto* superiority that may result from that competitor possessing more political power or access to greater economic resources.

Starting in the mid-twentieth century, the consensus began to form among elites across Europe that a basic tenet of democracy is that it should guarantee equality in the exercise of power. This consensus could be seen in the work of European legislatures, in the decisions of constitutional courts across much of the continent, and in the writings of various scholars who specialized in European politics. Imposing proportional limitations on the freedom of parties and candidates participating in election was often allowed by courts in order to guarantee equality among citizens when casting their votes. Indeed, this idea of equality of opportunity began to be viewed as being necessary to achieve a truly democratic mandate. The influence of money in politics was seen to be the main obstacle to political equality, and Europeans thought that influence must be counteracted. Otherwise, economic inequality would translate into uneven electoral competition, thus destroying any semblance of a level playing field.

A. *Germany: The* Chancengleichheit *Principle*

The first elaborate formulation of the principle of equality of opportunity was developed in Germany's jurisprudence following the adoption of the country's 1949 Basic Law. Germany's Federal Constitutional Court described the principle that has come to be known as *Chancengleichheit* in this way: "although

5 Óscar Sánchez Muñoz, La Igualdad de Oportunidades en las Competiciones Electorales [Equal Opportunities in Electoral Competitions] 3 (2008).

certainly not expressly stated in the Basic Law, [it] derives from the meaning of the freedom of creation of political parties and the principle of political pluralism for liberal democracy."[6]

As the Federal Constitutional Court has repeatedly asserted, the principle of equality of opportunity goes beyond a mere formal equality between candidates. It also extends to the political parties that support those candidacies. Essentially, it requires that those who compete for the people's vote should enjoy the same opportunities in their campaigns, and in the electoral process as a whole, and that they *in principle* should have the same resources or "arms" available to compete as all other competitors.[7]

It was only a matter of time before the Federal Constitutional Court eventually applied this principle to Germany's political finance regulations. The Court's first decision on this subject came in 1957,[8] when it declared unconstitutional Germany's system of making donations to political parties tax-deductible—because the tax deduction applied only to donations made by parties represented in parliament. One year later, in 1958,[9] in response to a complaint filed by the Social Democratic Party (SPD), the Federal Constitutional Court annulled the country's entire tax deduction scheme. Although all political parties were formally treated in the same way, the Federal Constitutional Court nonetheless reasoned that the tax scheme, because of the progressive nature of the tax system, favored parties with wealthier supporters. As the Court stated: "The legislature is not obliged to compensate for the existing *de facto* differences arising from the different sociological structures of the political parties. But it must not, without a compelling reason, adopt a regulation which exacerbates an existing factual inequality of the parties' competitive opportunities."[10]

How the jurisprudence of public financing evolved in Germany also deserves to be understood. The law was at first narrow and only allowed public financing to be used to pay for political parties' electoral expenses.[11] But the jurisprudence later achieved a broader interpretation as courts came to accept that having the state fund the ordinary expenses of political parties was also compatible with the Basic Law.[12] There is a significant difference between

6 Bundesverfassungsgericht [BVerfG] [Federal Constitutional Court] Decision of Feb. 21, 1957, 6 Entscheidungen des Bundesverfassungsgerichts [BVerfGE] 273 (280) (Ger.).

7 A brief summary of the early jurisprudence on this principle can be found, for example, in Hans-Uwe Erichsen, *Die Wahlrechtsgrundsätze des Grundgesetzes [Principles of Election Law in the Constitution]*, 5 JURA 635, 644.

8 BVerfG Decision of Feb. 21, 1957, 6 BVerfGE 273 (280) (Ger.).

9 BVerfG Decision of June 24, 1958, 8 BVerfGE 51 (Ger.).

10 *Id.* at 66.

11 BVerfG Decision of July 19, 1966, 20 BVerfGE 56 (168) (Ger.).

12 BVerfG Decision of Apr. 9, 1992, 85 BVerfGE 264 (Ger.).

electoral and ordinary expenses. Political parties incur fixed costs derived from their organizational structure that are not related to their electoral campaigns. Such costs include paying permanent staff salaries and pay rent for various real estate, such as the party's permanent headquarters. Legislation in Europe often distinguishes between the electoral and ordinary expenses of political parties, and public funding has traditionally been allocated for both types of expenses. However, in order to preserve the independence of political parties from the state and to ensure that the parties maintain their roots in civil society, the Federal Constitutional Court decided that public funding for political parties had to remain partial. This meant that parties could not be totally state-funded and still had to seek financial support from citizens.

Parties in Germany qualify for public funding based on their percentage of the vote. A party has to receive a minimum threshold percentage of the total vote to be eligible to receive public funding from the state. Originally, in 1967, Germany's Law on Political Parties fixed that threshold as 2.5 percent (the threshold was counted as a percentage of all valid ballots cast, within "invalid" ballots no counted), but the Federal Constitutional Court ruled that this percentage was too high, thus infringing on the equality of opportunity, and it ordered that the threshold be reduced to 0.5 percent.[13]

The Federal Constitutional Court has also issued several rulings on how the principle of equality of opportunity applies to private contributions to political parties. While the Court has warned that private donations made to political parties pose possible dangers of corruption to political decision-making, it has also found these dangers to be sufficiently ameliorated by Article 21.1 of the Basic Law, which requires parties to disclose their funding sources. Separately, another question that has come before the Court concerns whether the state is allowed to provide any tax incentives for the financial contributors made to parties. On this issue, the Court has ruled that donations from legal persons—corporations, associations, and foundations—are not to be favored by tax regulators, because the natural persons behind such donations would then enjoy a greater opportunity to influence political decisions than other citizens.[14]

B. *France: Electoral Fairness and the Fight against Corruption*

The French Constitution of 1958 states in Article 4, Paragraph 2 that the "[t]he law guarantees the pluralistic expression of opinions and the equitable

[13] BVerfG Decision of Dec. 3, 1968, 24 BVerfGE 300 (Ger.).

[14] BVerfG Decision of Apr. 9, 1992, 85 BVerfGE 264 (315) (Ger.).

participation of political parties and groups in the democratic life of the Nation."[15] But what is considered to be "equitable participation"? French jurisprudence has never explicitly elaborated on the principle of equality of opportunity to the same extent as the courts did in Germany. Nevertheless, after reforms in the 1980s and 1990s, legislation was adopted that has, along with the decisions emanating from French courts and other supervisory bodies, introduced greater guarantees of electoral fairness.

Although the important role of political parties has been enshrined in the French Constitution since 1958, for many years French law itself mostly ignored addressing the regulation of party activity. Political finance regulation did not become part of French public consciousness until the 1980s.[16] In fact, before 1988, the funding of political parties went completely unregulated. Leaving aside some limited electoral subsidies and public resources available for electoral campaigns, such as television airtime or mailing expenses, parties and candidates obtained their funding exclusively from the private contributions of their supporters. This posed serious problems for their independence, because those interest groups that provided significant party funding had the ability to exercise undue influence over public decisions. Too often the lack of public funding led parties and candidates to resort to illegal activities with private funders. Consequently, the number of political corruption scandals, not to mention the media attention afforded to them, began to undermine the public's confidence.

In France, the main regulators of political finance turned out to be the country's legislators, not its Constitutional Councils. A consensus began to mount around a few main principles, including that there should be a separation between economic and political life and fairness in electoral competition. The first French laws on political finance were adopted in 1988 and 1990.[17]

15 1958 CONST. art. 4, para. 2 (Fra.).

16 Nevertheless, from 1958 to 1988, there were various failed attempts to introduce legislation in this matter. On these proposals, see Éric Phélippeau, *Genese d'une Codification: L'Apprentissage Parlementaire de la Réforme du Financement de la Vie Politique Française, 1970–1987* [*Genesis of a Codification: What Parliament Learned in Reforming the Funding of French Political Life, 1970–1987*], 60 REV. FRANÇAISE SCI. POL. 519 (2010).

17 Loi org. 88–226 du 11 mars 1988 relative à la transparence financière de la vie politique, dispositions relatives au Président de la République [Organic Law 88–226 of Mar. 11, 1988 on the Financial Transparency of Political Life, Provisions Related to the President of the Republic], Journal Officiel de la République Française [J.O.], Mar. 12, 1988, p. 3288; loi 88–227 du 11 mars 1988 relative à la transparence financière de la vie politique, dispositions relatives à la declaration du patrimoine des membres du gouvernement et des titulaires de certaines fonctions electives [Law 88–227 of Mar. 11, 1988 on the Financial Transparency of Political Life, Provisions Relating to the Disclosure of Contributions to Members of the Government and the Holders of Certain Elected Positions], J.O., Mar. 12, 1988, p. 3290; loi

They established the five main pillars of the legislative framework regulating this issue in the country, and they were gradually refined afterwards through various reforms.[18] These five pillars included placing limits on election-related expenses; recognizing the need to limit (and limiting) private contributions to campaigns (for example, a prohibition was successfully put in place in 1995 banning all donations from corporations);[19] providing public funding for political parties and political candidates; creating a system of public accountability both for campaign expenses and campaign contributions; and instituting a system of campaign monitoring and control by independent French authorities (the reforms created a National Commission on Campaign Accounts and Political Finance, the CNCCFP).

90-55 du 15 janvier 1990 relative à la limitation des dépenses électorales et à la clarification du financement des activités politiques [Law 90-55 of Jan. 15, 1990 on the Limitation of Election Expenses and the Clarification of the Financing of Political Activities], J.O., Jan. 16, 1990, p. 639.

18 Loi 93–122 du 29 janvier 1993 relative à la prévention de la corruption et à la transparence de la vie économique et des procédures publiques [Law 93–122 of Jan. 29, 1993 on the Prevention of Corruption and the Transparency of Economic Life and Public Procedures], J.O., Jan. 30, 1993, p. 1588; loi org. 95-62 du 19 janvier 1995 modifiant diverses dispositions relatives à l'élection du Président de la République et à celle des députés à l'Assemblée nationale [Organic Law 95-62 of Jan. 19, 1995 Amending Various Provisions Relating to the Election of the President of the Republic and the Deputies to the National Assembly], J.O., Jan. 20, 1995, p. 1040; loi org. 95-63 du 19 janvier 1995 relative à la déclaration de patrimoine des membres du Parlement et aux incompatibilités applicables aux membres du Parlement et à ceux du Conseil constitutionnel [Organic Law 95-63 of Jan. 19, 1995 on the Declaration of Members of Parliament's Assets and on Conflicts of Interest for Members of Parliament and the Constitutional Council], J.O., Jan. 20, 1995, p. 1041; loi 95-65 du 19 janvier 1995 relative au financement de la vie politique [Law 95-65 of Jan. 19, 1995 on the Financing of Political Life], J.O., Jan. 21, 1995, p. 1105; loi org. 95-72 du 20 janvier 1995 relative au financement de la campagne en vue de l'élection du Président de la République [Organic Law 95-72 of Jan. 20, 1995 on Financing the Election Campaign of the President of the Republic], J.O., Jan. 24, 1995, p. 1249; loi org. 2006–404 du 5 avril 2006 relative à l'élection du Président de la République [Organic Law 2006–404 of Apr. 5, 2006 on Financing the Election Campaign of the President of the Republic], J.O., Apr. 6, 2006, p. 5192; loi org. 2011–410 du 14 avril 2011 relative à l'élection des députés et sénateurs [Organic Law 2011–410 of Apr. 14, 2011 on the Election of National Assembly Members and Senators], J.O., Apr. 19, 2011, p. 6826; loi 2011–412 du 14 avril 2011 portant simplification de dispositions du code électoral et relative à la transparence financière de la vie politique [Law 2011–412 of Apr. 14, 2011 on Simplifying Provisions of the Electoral Code on Financial Transparency in Politics], J.O., Apr. 19, 2011, p. 6831; loi org. 2013–906 du 11 octobre 2013 relative à la transparence de la vie publique [Organic Law 2013–906 of Oct. 11, 2013 on the Transparency of Political Life], J.O., Oct. 12, 2013, p. 16824; loi 2013–907 du 11 octobre 2013 relative à la transparence de la vie publique, la prévention des conflits d'intérêts et la transparence dans la vie publique [Law 2013–907 of Oct. 11, 2013 on the Transparency of Political Life, Preventing Conflicts of Interest and Promoting Transparency in Public Life], J.O., Oct. 12, 2013, p. 16829.

19 Loi 95-65 du 19 janvier 1995 relative au financement de la vie politique [Law 95-65 of Jan. 19, 1995 on the Financing of Political Life], J.O., Jan. 21, 1995, 1105; CODE ÉLECTORAL [C. ELECT.] [ELECTION CODE] art. 52–8, § 2 (Fr.).

The leitmotif of the various French reforms carried out since the late 1980s has been transparency and the fight against corruption. And while most reform efforts have come about in direct response to major scandals, this does not mean that the goal of achieving greater equality of opportunity among competitors has not also been on the minds of French legislators. The rules of the game laid down by the French legislature are clear. These rules are designed to ensure equality for opposing candidates, whom the system seeks to place in identical positions at the outset, subjecting each to the same forms of accountability, with the same right to reimbursement, and controlled by the same institutions.[20] As scholars have noted, it is clear that French reforms responded to a powerful idea: the need for fair and transparent electoral competition, independent from the influence of other spheres, and protected from plutocratic drift.[21]

Despite the fact that the Constitutional Council has played a circumscribed role in the development of France's political finance jurisprudence, unlike the case in Germany, it is nonetheless possible to point to some judicial decisions in France that serve to highlight the country's egalitarian orientation. For example, in 1990 the Constitutional Council held unconstitutional a law that required political parties to cross an electoral barrier of 5 percent of votes cast nationwide to qualify for state aid, claiming this barrier could "hinder the expression of new currents of opinion."[22] The law was declared unconstitutional under arts 2 and 4 of the French Constitution, which enshrine the principles of equality and the freedom of political parties to operate.

C. *Italy:* Par Condicio *in Access to Audiovisual Media by Political Parties*

In Italy, the principle that has embodied equality of opportunity in elections is known as *par condicio* (a Latin expression meaning "equal conditions" or "equal treatment"). In Italian election law, which has been marked by institutional turmoil since the beginning of the 1990s, this principle has mostly developed and been applied to the right of electoral competitors to receive access to audiovisual media.[23] The extraordinary Italian political turbulence witnessed under Silvio Berlusconi (in power from 1994–1995, 2001–2006, and

[20] Jean-Pierre Camby, *Les Candidats et L'Argent [Candidates and Money]*, 138 Pouvoirs: Rev. Français Études Const. & Pol. 85, 87 (2011).

[21] Phélippeau, *supra* note 16, at 521.

[22] Conseil constitutionnel [CC] [Constitutional Court] decision No. 89-271DC, Jan. 11, 1990, J.O., Jan. 13, 1990, p. 573 (Fr.).

[23] Legge 10 dicembre 1993, n. 515–1993, Gazzetta Ufficiale della Repubblica Italiana [G.U.] Dec. 14, 1993, n. 292; legge 22 febbraio 2000, n.28–2000, G.U. Feb. 22, 2000, n. 43 (It.).

2008–2011) involved having at the country's helm a prime minister who controlled a large portion of the Italy's private audiovisual media. That put the country's need to have equal conditions in elections not only at the center of its legal discussions, but also at the heart of its partisan political debates.

The jurisprudence of the Italian Constitutional Court has made consistent reference to the principle of equality of opportunity in elections. The Italian Constitutional Court's decision in 2002 concerning the right of political competitors to be given equal access to the media during their campaigns expressly speaks of "equal visibility" for political parties.[24] The Court recognized how, in most European countries, political communications have been regulated and oriented toward a model based on equality of opportunity, and that such regulations generally apply to a country's audiovisual media as well. Despite some disparity in the criteria for operationalizing this principle, the rule itself was made clear by the Italian courts.

D. *Equal Opportunity in International Organizations at the Regional Level*

Although there are no "hard law" rules in international law that apply to political finance, international law has played an important role in promoting the harmonization of legislation in various countries through its "soft law" standards. The final version of the United Nations Convention against Corruption deleted a draft article on political finance, and human rights treaties have barely scratched the surface.[25] Still, various international organizations at the European level have generated important soft law standards. They include the Council of Europe (CoE); its advisory body, the European Commission for Democracy through Law (also known as the Venice Commission); its anti-corruption monitoring body, the Group of States against Corruption (GRECO); and the Office for Democratic Institutions and Human Rights of the Organization for Security and Cooperation in Europe (OSCE/ODIHR). Together, these organizations have played an important role in standardizing country legislation and promoting best practices. The meaningful role played in this field by various non-governmental organizations, such as Transparency International, also deserves recognition.

[24] Corte Costituzionale (Corte Const.) [Constitutional Court], 24 aprile 2002, n. 155–2002, G.U. May 15, 2002, n. 19 (It.).

[25] For an argument about the applicability of human rights treaties to political finance and an account of how the UN Convention Against Corruption came up short, see Timothy K. Kuhner, *The Democracy to Which We Are Entitled: Human Rights and the Problem of Money in Politics*, 26 HARV. HUM. RTS. J. 39 (2013).

In the context of the transition processes the various Eastern European countries underwent in the 1990s, the "Copenhagen Document" of the OSCE, promulgated in 1990,[26] launched a basic catalogue of election standards. These encouraged member states to commit to holding campaigns "in a free and fair atmosphere" (Section 7.7) and ensuing "unimpeded access to the media on a non-discriminatory basis" (Section 7.8).

Some years later, in 2003, the same organization issued a report on the "Existing Commitments for Democratic Elections in OSCE Participating States."[27] The idea of fair elections, based in the equality of opportunity among competitors, is present in different places throughout the text of this report. Take, for example, Section 7.3's assertion that "the fair and free atmosphere needed for effective political campaigning requires the state to provide election contestants equal opportunity to convey their messages to the electorate." Relating specifically to campaign finance, the document contains a series of recommendations, including placing "reasonable limits on private financing of political parties and candidates in order to preserve fair competition during elections and lessen incentives for corruption and undue influence in politics" (Section 7.6); equitably distributing of public funding (Section 7.7); and instituting transparent disclosure and reporting requirements, including the directive to "publish [such] information in a suitable and timely manner" (Section 7.7).

But it is in pronouncements circulated by the Council of Europe where the principle of equality of opportunity has been reflected most clearly. The Venice Commission has extensively dealt with the issue of party financing in numerous documents since its first "Guidelines and Report on the Financing of Political Parties" was published in 2001.[28] In the same vein, the Parliamentary Assembly of the Council of Europe adopted, also in 2001, a "Recommendation on the Financing of Political Parties,"[29] a text that perfectly reflects the state of the public's opinion concerning political finance issues throughout Europe in the twenty-first century.

26 Off. for Dem. Inst. and Hum. Rts. of the Org. for Security and Cooperation in Eur. [hereinafter OSCE/ODIHR], *Document of the Copenhagen Meeting of the Conference on the Human Dimension of the CSCE* (June 29, 1990), www.osce.org/odihr/elections/14304.

27 OSCE/ODIHR, *Existing Commitments for Democratic Elections in OSCE Participating States* (June 30, 2003), www.osce.org/odihr/elections/13956.

28 Venice Commission, *Guidelines and Report on the Financing of Political Parties* (Mar. 23, 2001), www.osce.org/odihr/37843?download=true.

29 Council of Europe, Parl. Ass., *Recommendation 1516 on the Financing of Political Parties*, Doc. 9077 (2001), www.assembly.coe.int/nw/xml/XRef/Xref-XML2HTML-en.asp?fileid=16907&lang=en.

The Parliamentary Assembly of the Council of Europe, taking into account citizens' "concern with regard to corruption linked to political parties' gradual loss of independence and the occurrence of improper influence on political decisions through financial means" (Section 1), recommended that member states adopt rules based on several principles. There should exist, the Council of Europe stated:

> a reasonable balance between public and private funding, fair criteria for the distribution of state contributions to parties, strict rules concerning private donations, a threshold on parties' expenditures linked to election campaigns, complete transparency of accounts, the establishment of an independent audit authority and meaningful sanctions for those who violate the rules (Section 7).

The same basic principle of equality of opportunity has been maintained since 2001 in all documents emanating from institutions that comprise the Council of Europe. Thus, according to the "Code of Good Practice in Electoral Matters" that was adopted by the Venice Commission in 2002,[30] the principle of equality of opportunity is described as being connected directly to the freedom of voters to form an opinion and has numerous implications for political finance regulations.

In 2003, the Committee of Ministers of the Council of Europe adopted a Recommendation specifically focused on addressing the funding of political parties and electoral campaigns.[31] This document was considered a synthesis of the "European model" of political finance regulation, representing a clear adoption of the principle of equality of opportunity in political finance. Some of the relevant rules stated were:

1. States may provide financial support to their political parties, but this is limited to "reasonable contributions," "not interfer[ing] with [their] independence," and that support must be distributed according to "objective, fair and reasonable criteria" (Article 1).
2. "States should … consider the possibility of introducing rules limiting the value of donations to political parties" (Article 2.b.ii).
3. "States should consider adopting measures to prevent [the] excessive funding needs of political parties, such as establishing limits on the expenditures of electoral campaigns" (Article 9).

30 Venice Commission, *Code of Good Practice in Electoral Matters* (May 23, 2003), www.venice.coe.int/webforms/documents/default.aspx?pdffile=CDL-AD(2002)023rev-e. Regarding party funding, see in particular §§ I.2.3 and II.3.5.

31 Council of Europe, Eur. Comm. of Ministers, 835th Meeting of Committee of Ministers, *Recommendation Rec(2003)4 of the Comm. of Ministers to Member States*, Doc. No. 9774 App'x (April 8, 2003), https://rm.coe.int/168009 2b88.

4. "States should provide for independent monitoring in respect of the funding of political parties and electoral campaigns" (Article 14.a).

The more recent "Guidelines on Political Party Regulation," jointly drafted by the Venice Commission and the OSCE/ODIHR in 2010,[32] are also instructive. Rather than provide blanket solutions or establish a unified model, these Guidelines recognize the great diversity of legal traditions that exist in Europe, clarify key issues related to legislation regulating political parties, and provide recommendations for best election practices. Together with their interpretative notes, the Guidelines address a large number of issues concerning funding requirements and transparency. In this regard, this document, along with the Council of Europe's "Recommendation on the Financing of Political Parties" from 2003, best reflects the current common European vision for political finance that this chapter highlights. The section devoted to political finance opens with a paragraph summarizing the predominant European view:

> Political parties need appropriate funding to fulfill their core functions, both during and between election periods. The regulation of political party funding is essential to guarantee parties independence from undue influence created by donors and to ensure the opportunity for all parties to compete in accordance with the principle of equal opportunity and to provide for transparency in political finance. Funding of political parties through private contributions is also a form of political participation. Thus, legislation should attempt to achieve a balance between encouraging moderate contributions and limiting unduly large contributions. (Paragraph 159.)

Activity in this field by the Council of Europe's anti-corruption monitoring body, GRECO, which was established in 1999, also deserves mention. This body currently has 49 members and is open to non-members of the Council of Europe (such as the United States and Belarus). In the context of its Third Evaluation Round, in 2007, GRECO conducted on-site visits to the Council of Europe's member states and issued evaluation and compliance reports to monitor the implementation of the Council of Europe's 2003 "Recommendation on the Financing of Political Parties," which was actually issued by its Committee of Ministers. These evaluation reports[33] constitute a valuable source of information on best practices. They also document the political finance insufficiencies that exist in member states. On the whole,

[32] Venice Commission, *Guidelines on Political Party Regulation* (Oct. 25, 2010), www.venice.coe.int/webforms/documents/default.aspx?pdffile=CDL-AD(2010)024-e.

[33] Group of States against Corruption [GRECO], *Third Evaluation Round* (Jan. 1, 2007), www.coe.int/en/web/greco/evaluations. For a horizontal overview of evaluation results, see generally Yves-Marie Doublet, Political Financing (2010).

they have played a substantial role in reshaping political finance legislation in European countries.[34]

E. Equality of Opportunity and Freedom of Expression in the European Court of Human Rights

The European Court of Human Rights has repeatedly emphasized the close relationship between the right to free elections and the freedom of expression. In 1988, in *Bowman v. United Kingdom*, the Court found that these rights together "form the bedrock of any democratic system." The Court went on to state that:

> The two rights are inter-related and reinforce each other: for example, freedom of expression is one of the "conditions" necessary to "ensure the free expression of the opinion of the people in the choice of the legislature … For this reason, it is particularly important in the period preceding an election for opinions and information of all kinds to be permitted to circulate freely.[35]

However, the Court also explained that these "two rights may come into conflict." It resolved that tension in favor of the right to free elections, writing that "it may be considered necessary, in the period preceding or during an election, to place certain restrictions, of a type which would not usually be acceptable, on freedom of expression, in order to secure the 'free expression of the opinion of the people in the choice of the legislature.'"[36] Public intervention was justified in free elections because the Court recognized the role of the state as the "ultimate guarantor of pluralism."[37]

In terms of balancing these two rights, the Court specified that "states have a margin of appreciation" related to their discretion in how to run the overall "organization of their electoral systems."[38] In other words, for the European Court of Human Rights, when democratic governance and the freedom of expression came into conflict, the guarantee of democracy trumped the freedom of speech. Even though the Court did not use the term "equality of opportunity" in its jurisprudence, it is clear that it took the public interests

34 Daniela R. Piccio, The State of Political Finance Regulations in Western Europe 4 (2016), www.idea.int/sites/default/files/publications/the-state-of-political-finance-regulations-in-western-europe.pdf.

35 Bowman v. United Kingdom, 1998 Eur. Ct. H.R. at para. 42.

36 *Id.* at para. 43.

37 Özgürlük ve Dayanışma Partisi (ÖDP) v. Turkey, 2012 Eur. Ct. H.R. at para. 27.

38 *Bowman*, 1998 Eur. Ct. H.R. at para. 43.

protected by this principle as a legitimate aim. This explains its judgments allowing restrictions on the freedom of expression.

In *Bowman*, the United Kingdom maintained that the imposition of a spending limit in elections had a legitimate government purpose, since "it promoted fairness between competing candidates for election" and "helped to ensure that candidates remained independent of the influence of powerful interest groups."[39] The European Court of Human Rights agreed that the purpose of the United Kingdom's spending limits was "to contribute towards securing equality between candidates."[40] However, the Court also found that the restriction at issue—which "operated, for all practical purposes, as a total barrier to Mrs Bowman's publishing information with a view to influencing the voters"[41]—was disproportionate in relation to the purpose advanced by the government. Consequently, the Court found that the United Kingdom's spending limit infringed the freedom of expression protected by Article 10 of the European Convention on Human Rights.[42]

The Court has also examined whether the limits imposed by countries on political advertising in audiovisual media are compatible with the freedom of expression enshrined in the European Convention.[43] In a number of cases, the Court has accepted limits being placed on advertising in audiovisual media by member governments—especially when the arguments for these limits were premised on the need to preserve the equality of opportunity in electoral competition. However, given the particular circumstances of each case, the Court has not always considered the actual measures imposed to be proportionate and "necessary in a democratic society," as stipulated by the European Convention's provision on the permissible limitation of rights.[44]

In 2008, in *TV Vest AS and Rogaland Pensjonistparti v. Norway*,[45] the Court found that arguments made in support of a Norwegian ban on paid political TV advertising—including that the ban would safeguard the quality of political debate—were relevant, but not sufficient to justify a total prohibition of this form of advertising. The Court especially noted that the applicant in the

39 *Id.*

40 *Id.* at para. 38.

41 *Id.* at para. 47.

42 *Id.*

43 VgT Verein gegen Tierfabriken v. Switzerland, 2001 Eur. Ct. H.R.; TV Vest AS and Rogaland Pensjonistparti v. Norway, 2008 Eur. Ct. H.R.; Animal Defenders International v. United Kingdom, 2013 Eur. Ct. H.R.

44 Council of Europe, Convention for the Protection of Human Rights and Fundamental Freedoms, as amended by Protocols Nos. 11 and 14 (European Convention on Human Rights) (Nov. 4, 1950), E.T.S. No. 5, 213 U.N.T.S. 221, art. 10(2).

45 TV Vest AS and Rogaland Pensjonistparti v. Norway, 2008 Eur. Ct. H.R.

case, the Pensioners Party, received hardly any coverage in the Norwegian media, in contrast to the major political parties. Therefore, paid advertising on television became the only way for it to get its message across to the electorate. This judgment made it clear that any ban should be applied with sufficient flexibility, and that an exception to a ban would apply to smaller parties and political movements or organizations that receive very little media coverage.

In 2013, in *Animal Defenders International v. United Kingdom*,[46] the Court displayed greater deference to expenditure limits, accepting the broad prohibition on political advertisements established by the United Kingdom's Communications Act 2003. The Court considered the reasons cited by the United Kingdom to be relevant and sufficient. The British government contended that a prohibition on political advertising was necessary to avoid the kind of distorted debates on matters of public interest that result when financially powerful interests have unequal access to influential media. Only by limiting political advertising could pluralism and the democratic process be protected.[47] The Court noted that there is a lack of consensus among European countries on how to regulate paid political advertising when it comes to broadcasting; this results from differences in historical development, cultural diversity, political thought, and democratic vision in Europe's many countries. In the Court's view, however, these differences only served to broaden the otherwise narrow margin of appreciation enjoyed by these countries regarding their various restrictions on public interest expression.[48]

The Court has been exposed to arguments based on the principle of equality of opportunity in electoral competition in another area as well: access to the media during elections. Even though norms guarantee equal airtime to political candidates, the Court found that the European Convention does not guarantee any right, as such, for airtime on radio or television to be granted to political parties during electoral campaigns. However, the Court has conceded that difficult issues may arise in exceptional circumstances—for example, if in the run-up to an election one party was denied political broadcasting rights while other parties were granted them.[49] The Court has also found that the state is under an obligation to intervene to open up the media to differing viewpoints, especially when it comes to media coverage of campaigns.[50]

46 Animal Defenders Int'l v. United Kingdom, 2013 Eur. Ct. H.R.

47 *Id.* at paras. 99, 125.

48 *Id.* at para. 123.

49 Partija "Jaunie Demokrāti" and Partija "Mūsu Zeme" v. Latvia, 2007 Eur. Ct. H.R. (Decision of Inadmissibility, § III).

50 Communist Party of Russia and Others v. Russia, 2012 Eur. Ct. H.R. at para. 126.

In the 2012 case of *Özgürlük ve Dayanışma Partisi (ÖDP) v. Turkey*,[51] the European Court of Human Rights addressed how the principle of equality of opportunity impacted public funding for political parties. Turkey refused to provide public funding to the Freedom and Solidarity Party (ÖDP) on the grounds that the party did not qualify. To qualify for public funding, a party either had to hold seats in the Turkish Parliament or receive at least 7 percent of the vote in the previous election. The ÖDP did neither. The Court noted that requiring a party to obtain a minimum level of electoral support furthered a legitimate aim, namely strengthening pluralist democracy, while it avoided the excessive and dysfunctional fragmentation that resulted when voters were confronted with too many choices. The Court also examined Turkey's electoral threshold for public funding, which at 7 percent was the highest in Europe. The Court noted that despite this high threshold, it was not the case that public funding only went to parties with seats in parliament, for other parties that did not win parliamentary seats were also able to cross it and qualify for public funding. Meanwhile, the ÖDP's results in the 1999, 2002, and 2007 parliamentary elections were significantly lower than 7 percent. The European Court of Human Rights also found that the ÖDP had benefited from other forms of public support in the past, including tax exemptions offered by the government and broadcasting time offered during the election campaign. As a result, Turkey's refusal to grant direct financial support to the Freedom and Solidarity Party here was found to be objective and reasonable and did not impair the essence of the right to free expression or the will of the electorate.

What was most interesting in this case, beyond the decision itself, was the Court's observation that in Europe, as in the rest of the world, state funding for political parties is aimed at preventing corruption and avoiding excessive reliance by parties on private donors. It follows that such funding is intended to strengthen political pluralism and contributes to the proper functioning of democratic institutions.[52]

III. AN OVERVIEW OF REGULATIONS IN EUROPEAN STATES

Through its reception into the election laws of different countries, the principle of equality of opportunity has developed both negative and positive dimensions.

[51] Özgürlük ve Dayanışma Partisi (ÖDP) v. Turkey, 2012 Eur. Ct. H.R.
[52] *Id.* at para. 37.

The negative dimension requires the state to guarantee a level playing field by minimizing the influence of certain factors in electoral competition, such as financial superiority or pre-existing political power. This mandate shows up in the legal system through various measures aimed at restricting the activity of those involved in electoral competition—for instance, by placing limits on electoral expenditures and private contributions to parties. Some of these negative measures amount to limits on fundamental rights, like the freedom of expression. In these cases, the principle of equality of opportunity operates as a constitutional justification for limiting rights.

The positive dimension requires the state to optimize the visibility of different political options, which requires affirmative measures. This dimension must not be understood as compensating for pre-existing differences, but rather as facilitating communication between parties and electors through the allocation of public resources distributed in an equitable manner. The public funding of political parties, distributed according to fair criteria, is the best example of such a positive measure.

Both dimensions can be found in the election laws of most European countries, albeit in different formulations and to different degrees. Experience has shown that both are necessary to lay down a comprehensive and effective campaign finance framework. Along with substantive measures, it is also necessary to put in place instrumental measures to ensure compliance with the law, such as greater transparency, adequate election monitoring, and the creation of an election enforcement authority. A balanced mix of regulatory policies seems to be the most effective strategy.[53]

A. *Expenditure Limits*

Spending limits set a cap on the total amount a candidate or a political party (or that party's third-party supporters) can spend on the electoral campaign. Spending ceilings, when correctly set and strictly enforced, are the most powerful weapon to reduce the *de facto* advantage of political parties and candidates with access to large amounts of money, not to mention to reduce the likelihood of potentially corrupt exchanges. The logic of spending limits is very clear—the lower a political actor's expenditures, the lesser their dependence on large private contributors will be.

Most European countries have established caps on election campaign spending by political parties or candidates. According to the International

53 Checkbook Elections?: Political Finance in Comparative Perspective (Pippa Norris & Andrea Abel van Es eds., 2016).

IDEA Political Finance Database, which includes 44 European countries in its analysis, caps on party spending exist in 21 countries and caps on candidate spending in 29.[54] To evaluate this data, it is necessary to understand that campaigns in some countries are run by parties and in other countries by candidates. The different practices are often explained by a country's electoral system. In France, campaigns can be run by candidates or by the heads of party lists. Generally campaigns are run by candidates, and only candidates incur electoral expenses. Therefore, caps are placed on candidate spending. While there is technically no cap placed on the electoral expenses of political parties, if a party formally endorses a candidate in a given French district, then it must respect the spending cap placed on the candidate and that candidate is also required to disclose all the money received from the party. In Spain, by contrast, campaigns are not run by candidates. They are run exclusively by legal entities, which can be political parties, federations, coalitions, or groups of independent voters. These entities submit candidate lists to Spain's voters. Under the law, the entities engage in campaign spending, but candidates do not. As such, there is no need for Spain to impose spending cap on individual candidates.

In some countries where there are no spending caps, campaign costs are very limited because of the existence of prohibitions or limits on paid political TV advertising. This is the case of Germany and the Nordic countries, for instance.

This last consideration leads us to analyze the existence in many countries of so-called "qualitative spending limits." The phrase refers to a type of expenditure limit that works not by limiting the total amount of expenditures a candidate or party can spend, but rather places a ban or limit only on certain types of spending—in an effort to preserve equality of opportunity. The best example is a ban on paid political TV advertising, which exists in most European countries. The regulation of this type of advertising has to do with its greater influence, its high economic cost, and, consequently, its greater potential to allow wealth and wealthy interests to distort the democratic process.

There is wide consensus in Europe that paid political TV advertising requires regulation, but there is no consensus as to its form. A certain geographic divide among European countries is clearly evident.[55] The prohibition

[54] International IDEA Political Finance Database, www.idea.int/data-tools/data/political-finance-database.

[55] European Platform of Regulatory Authorities (EPRA), Political Advertising Case Studies and Monitoring (May 17, 2006), www.rtdh.eu/pdf/20060517_epra_meeting .pdf.

on paid political TV advertising is enshrined by law in the vast majority of Western Europe, including in Belgium, Denmark, France, Ireland, Malta, Norway, Portugal, Spain, Sweden, Switzerland, and the United Kingdom. By contrast, paid political TV advertising is allowed in many Central and Eastern European countries, such as Bosnia and Herzegovina, Bulgaria, Croatia, Hungary, Macedonia, Poland, and the Baltic States. Of course, many countries do not fit neatly into this geographical divide. Some countries in Central and Eastern Europe, such as the Czech Republic and Romania, have a prohibition on paid political TV advertising, while some countries in Western Europe, such as in Austria, Finland, Germany, and the Netherlands, happen to allow paid political TV advertising, although they also impose various types of restrictions on this practice.

Some countries that allow TV political advertising do so only with additional legal restrictions, such as placing limits on election expenditures (Greece, Latvia), placing limits on the prices paid for ads (Bosnia and Herzegovina), placing limits on the duration and frequency of ads (Bosnia and Herzegovina, Macedonia), regulating the scheduling of ads (Macedonia), instituting labeling or identification requirements for ads (Cyprus, Macedonia), and imposing equal conditions (ads must be the same price and appear during the same program or time period) for all parties (Hungary).[56] In a few countries, political advertising is permitted only during the limited time span during any given electoral campaign or pre-election period (Bosnia-Herzegovina, Croatia).

In France, Ireland, Malta, Spain and the United Kingdom, the law establishes a "wide-reaching ban" applied to any kind of paid political TV advertising (not only to electoral TV advertising), at all times (not just during campaigns), and carried out by any subjects (not only political parties or candidates).

Italy provides an interesting example of the evolution of regulations on paid TV advertising. The concentration of audiovisual media corporations and the massive use of TV spots led Italy to its first attempt at regulation in 1993,[57] when the country first began prohibiting the broadcast of these TV spots for one month prior to an election. A more complete regulation, adopted in 2000, distinguished the nuances between mere information and political communications, and within the latter category distinguished further between "spaces of confrontation" and "self-managed spaces," which can be free or paid.[58] So-called paid "self-managed spaces" are authorized on local TV

[56] *Id.*

[57] Legge 10 dicembre 1993, n. 515–1993, G.U. Dec. 14, 1993, n. 292 (It.).

[58] Legge 22 febbraio 2000, n. 28–2000, G.U. Feb. 22, 2000, n. 43 (It.).

channels but banned on national channels, a prohibition that is compensated by the allocation of free airtime. While the Italian regulations are detailed, the general idea is that political parties cannot buy ads for national channels, but they are allocated free airtime to promote their message. This allocation is mandatory for public channels and voluntary for private ones. Moreover, paid TV spots on local channels that are political in nature are subject to strict conditions regarding their timing, pricing, and scheduling.

A rather complex issue and an emerging challenge in most European countries concerns whether limits should be placed on the campaign spending of actors that are neither political parties nor candidates, but are so-called third parties. The absence of spending limits on third parties makes it possible for parties and candidates to evade spending caps by allowing for parallel campaigns to be run by supposedly independent organizations and interest groups. On the other hand, placing strict limits on the activities of these actors is often seen as restricting the freedom of expression, which itself is so vital to a democratic society. The broad prohibition of paid political TV advertising in force in many countries is intended to address this issue.

B. *Contribution Limits*

Placing limits on those who give funds to political parties and candidates is also an essential instrument. Contribution limits control the inflow of money and prevent inappropriate links between private interests and political decision-making.[59] Large donations to political parties or candidates, especially from corporations, are generally perceived as having a pernicious influence in the democratic process. This is why legal restrictions have been adopted in most European countries, whether through *quantitative limitations* (imposing a maximum that can be contributed by an individual in a given time period) or through *qualitative limitations* (imposing a ban on contributions from certain sources).

The sources of private funding that have been most frequently subject to qualitative restrictions include foreign entities, corporations, public and semi-public institutions,[60] and trade unions. A large number of states also prohibit candidates and political parties from accepting anonymous contributions and set limits on cash donations. The most interesting restrictions, for our purposes at least, are

59 Daniela R. Piccio, Public Funding to Political Parties (background paper prepared for the Global Conference on Money in Politics, Mexico City, Sept. 3–5, 2015), www.moneyinpolitics.info/wp-content/uploads/2015/05/Public_funding_GlobalConference_PICCIO.pdf.

60 Semi-public institutions are partially state-owned enterprises or foundations.

those imposed on corporations. Many countries in Europe have introduced a ban on donations from corporations, including Belgium, Bulgaria, Estonia, France, Greece, Hungary, Latvia, Lithuania, Luxembourg, Poland, Portugal, Russia, Slovenia, and Spain.[61] In Hungary, Slovenia, and Russia, corporate donations are banned for parties, but allowed for candidates; and in Estonia they are allowed only for independent candidates. In most of these countries, corporate donations bans were introduced in the wake of a series of corruption scandals in the attempt to limit plutocratic drift.[62] Still, it deserves to be noted that such corporate bans still exist in a minority of all European countries.

A large majority of European countries have also imposed caps on other kinds of donations, including individual donations. There are large differences in terms of the maximum cap that is allowed. Some countries have adopted relatively low caps, usually in combination with other measures, such as tax exemptions, in order to encourage grass-roots donations. That is the case of Ireland (where the maximum donation allowed is €2,500), Iceland (€2,800), Belgium (€4,000), France (€7,500), Cyprus (€8,000), Portugal (€10,650), and Greece (€15,000).[63] In other countries, however, the donation caps remain still quite high by European standards. For instance, in Spain the cap on donations happens to be €50,000, and in Italy it is €100,000.

The loans granted by banks to political parties represent another avenue of campaign funding—and one that carries a serious risk to democracy, especially because these loans are sometimes written off as a result of bargains struck between the parties that set policy once they are in government and the financial institutions that lend these loans and whom the government's policies affect. This phenomenon may be considered a form of hidden private funding. In Spain, the consistent and excessive indebtedness of the country's political parties has been highlighted by the Third Evaluation Round of GRECO. This indebtedness is seen as a challenge to the independence of Spanish political parties vis-à-vis their creditors. Loans made to political parties have also been a source of concern in the Czech Republic, Greece, Slovenia, and Romania.

C. *Public Funding*

Public funding for political parties has been introduced in almost all European countries. The aim of the continent's public funding systems is to provide sufficient and stable funds to parties, limit the influence of big and powerful

61 International IDEA Political Finance Database, *supra* note 54.
62 Piccio, *supra* note 59.
63 International IDEA Political Finance Database, *supra* note 54.

donors, prevent corruption, and avoid the excessive disparities that exist in political competition.[64]

Europe's first indirect public funding schemes came in the form of providing political parties with access to public resources—such as radio and TV, as well as billboards, meeting rooms, and mailings—and tax exemptions. The idea of giving public money directly to political parties and candidates themselves, however, is relatively newer. In Germany, campaign costs began being reimbursed to political parties by the state for the first time in 1959. However, though this practice began in 1959, it was not officially regulated by law until 1967. Other countries soon followed suit, including Finland in 1969, Sweden in 1972, Italy in 1974, Austria in 1975, Portugal and Spain in 1977, and Greece in 1981. Nowadays, every European country provides some form of public funding to political parties. There are only two exceptions, Malta and Switzerland.[65] Ukraine, one of the other last holdouts, passed a public financing law in October 2015 and now also provides public funding to parties.

Public funding of political parties or candidates can be direct or indirect. Direct funding refers to funds being directly transferred from the state to the accounts of parties or candidates for office. Those funds are meant to reimburse electoral expenses specifically or else to finance general or "ordinary" expenses of parties not used for campaigning. Indirect public funding refers to the state's assumption of parties' or candidates' costs. For example, the state may provide political parties with certain resources, such as broadcasting time, access to meeting venues, or free or subsidized postal services. Or the state may provide indirect funding by granting parties tax exemptions and tax deductions.

These various forms of state subsidies have become the most important source of public funds, at least from a quantitative point of view, for European political parties. Together, direct and indirect funding account for almost three-quarters of total revenue received.[66] In light of the ongoing regional trend of declining party membership,[67] state funding is likely to remain crucial to the survival of political parties in Europe.

64 Piccio, *supra* note 59.

65 In both countries, the introduction of public subsidies has recently been discussed. In Switzerland, two cantons (Geneva and Fribourg) have introduced legislation on the reimbursement of campaign expenses, and a number of recent initiatives at the national level have been rejected. FUNDING OF POLITICAL PARTIES AND ELECTION CAMPAIGNS: A HANDBOOK ON POLITICAL FINANCE 222 (Elin Falguera, Samuel Jones & Magnus Ohman eds., 2014), www.idea.int/sites/default/files/publications/funding-of-political-parties-and-election-campaigns.pdf.

66 *Id.*

67 Ingrid van Biezen et al., *Going, Going, … Gone? The Decline of Party Membership in Contemporary Europe*, 51 EUR. J. POL. RES. 24 (2012).

If the trend in Europe through the first decade of the twenty-first century has been to support the public funding of parties, a new trend has emerged in the last decade. European society is now characterized by increasing public suspicion of public funding. Naturally, this view has resulted from the growing disaffection that Europeans have with politics in general, as well as from their reaction to the 2008 global economic crisis and the financial austerity measures that were implemented thereafter, especially in Southern Europe. The result was that political finance laws had been "reformed" and the amounts by which the state subsidized political parties was reduced. This reduction happened after austerity measures were passed in Portugal (2010), Spain (2011), Ireland (2012), the Netherlands (2012), and Greece (2014). The subsidies available to political parties for either electoral or parliamentary activities were reduced in each country.[68] No country, however, has witnessed a greater reduction in public funding than Italy. An Italian law adopted in 2014 prohibited all forms of direct subsidies to political parties.[69] In place of direct subsidies, Italy now offers tax deductions and the possibility for individuals voluntarily to allocate 0.2 percent of their direct taxes to party funding.[70]

D. *Transparency*

Transparency and disclosure are core objectives for political finance regulations. They serve as an instrument not only and for ensuring there is compliance with the law and preventing corruption, but also, above all else, transparency provides information to the electorate, ensuring that the will of the people is truly being freely formed.

The goal of transparency measures is to provide citizens access to complete, user-friendly, and understandable information concerning the funding that stands behind political parties and candidates. For such information to be complete, it must allow citizens to know precisely how parties are financed. For it to be user-friendly, it must be available online and presented in a way that is understandable to most citizens, including being written in a language that is accessible. For it to be timely, this information must have immediacy,

[68] Piccio, *supra* note 34, at 9.

[69] In 2012, public funding was reduced to half by the Monti government. Legge 6 luglio 2012 n. 96–2012, in GU, July 9, 2012, n. 158 (It.). Finally, the Letta government decided to suppress it completely. The suppression is progressive and would be complete in 2017. Decreto legge 28 dicembre 2013, n. 149–2013, transformed in Legge 21 febbraio 2014, G.U. Feb. 26, 2014, n. 47 (It.).

[70] This mechanism was already experienced in Italy between 1997 and 1999. Each citizen can allocate 2 per 1,000 of his tax to a party of his choice by applying a code on his tax return; people not required to file the return can use a form to make their choice.

meaning the information must be made available so that is can serve to inform the will of the electorate. If this is not possible, then information must at least be made available at a time when citizens could still use it to hold officeholders and parties accountable. A policy of genuine transparency requires political parties and public authorities to be proactively involved.

In the last few years, GRECO, the Council of Europe's anti-corruption monitoring body, held a Third Evaluation Round and focused on transparency. Notable progress in improving regulation and compliance with transparency requirements was made in all of GRECO's member states, with the exception of Switzerland, which remains the only country without transparency legislation on the books.

During its Third Evaluation Round, GRECO examined the transparency of party funding in particular, as one of its themes. On the recommendation of the Committee of Ministers of the Council of Europe, GRECO issued "Recommendation (2003)4." It encouraged transparency standards to be taken on the following fronts:

- *Accounting*. Article 11 requires political parties and the entities related to them (such as foundations) to keep proper books and accounts. Article 12 requires that the accounts specify all donations received by the party, including the nature and value of each donation. In case of donations over a certain value, donors should be identified in the records.
- *Reporting*. Article 13 requires parties to present their accounts regularly, and at least annually, to an independent authority. Concerns have been raised in different countries about the level of detail of these reports and the lack of a standardized format for their presentation, which is needed to make comparisons over time and between different entities possible.[71]
- *Public access*. Article 13 requires political parties regularly, and at least annually, to make their accounts public, or to provide a summary of their accounts, including the information regarding electoral expenses, donations received, and the identity of donors giving above a certain level. Donors and the amount of their donations above a certain level are published in Bulgaria, Germany, Hungary, Ireland, Luxembourg, Norway, Poland, Spain and the United Kingdom. Donors, regardless of their level of giving, must be declared in the Czech Republic.[72]

Sweden stands out as an example of regulatory improvement after GRECO's recommendations.[73] Beforehand, no political finance transparency

[71] Doublet, *supra* note 33.
[72] *Id.* at 11.
[73] Piccio, *supra* note 34, at 4.

requirements were in force, though there was some voluntary disclosure being made by the country's political parties. In 2014, following the first visit to the country by GRECO, a new law was introduced that suddenly obligated Swedish political parties and candidates to disclose information about their revenues annually and to report donations above a certain value, including both the identity of donor and the amount of his donation. And all this information was made publicly accessible. Even so, Swedish political finance remains loosely regulated from a comparative perspective.[74]

Examples of best practices in political finance transparency include the experiences of the Central Register of Statistics of Norway, the French National Commission on Campaign Accounts and Political Finance (CNCCFP), and the Irish Standards in Public Office Commission. These bodies provide essential information to citizens, publishing the annual accounts of parties, political finance statistics, and analytical reports on the web in a timely, intelligible, and accessible manner.[75]

In other cases, despite any formal progress made, transparency requirements remain neglected in practice. This, for example, is the situation in Spain. After GRECO issued its Compliance Reports, reforms were introduced in Spain in 2012 and 2015. However, several issues remained unresolved. For instance, although donor identification is mandatory before the Spanish Court of Accounts, the information that must be reported only concerns donors who contribute more than €25,000. The average minimum contribution amount subject to disclosure in most of the rest of Western Europe is around €3,500.[76] In Spain, moreover, information on donations is only available to the public after a party's annual report is presented, which can be between seven and eleven months after the contribution is made. This does not satisfy the timeliness requirement. Similar problems concern the quest for information about bank loans to political parties, as well as contributions made to political party foundations.

E. *Oversight and Enforcement*

All political finance regulations risk being ineffective unless they are backed by a rigorous enforcement regime. There must be an entity responsible for monitoring the financial activities of political parties in accordance with preexisting rules, and that entity must be able to impose sanctions on those who

74 Checkbook Elections?, *supra* note 53, at 35–36.

75 Piccio, *supra* note 34, at 6.

76 Funding of Political Parties and Election Campaigns, *supra* note 65.

violate those rules. The fashion in which oversight bodies are designed shapes the eventual realities of enforcement. And these oversight bodies differ significantly, in their degree of independence, in the quality of their staffs, and in the degree of power granted to them in each entity.[77]

When it comes to regulating political finance, the greatest shortcoming in virtually all European countries arises in the area of oversight and enforcement.[78] Most of these enforcement bodies lack true or meaningful independence, and they are especially not free from political influence. This shortcoming can seriously affect the credibility and effectiveness of a country's political finance system. The dysfunction witnessed is most extreme in some of the countries of Central and Eastern Europe, but it also is present in more consolidated democracies.

Specialized bodies have been created to guarantee better oversight in several European nations. For example, this is the case in Belgium, France, Ireland, and Italy. In France, the National Commission on Campaign Accounts and Political Finance (*Commission nationale des comptes de campagne et des financements politiques*, or CNCCFP) has nine members. Three are active or honorary members of the State Council (*Conseil d'État*), the highest authority in French administrative law. Three are active or honorary members of the Supreme Court (*Cour de cassation*), the highest court within the French judiciary. The last three members of the CNCCFP are active or honorary members of the Court of Accounts (*Cour des comptes*), the supreme body charged with auditing the use of public funds in France. This structure leaves little doubt concerning the CNCCFP's independence. At the other end of the spectrum, consider the situation in Belgium, where the Commission created to oversee electoral expenditures and party funding in parliamentary elections is composed entirely of members of the Belgium's Chamber of Deputies and Senate.[79]

As with transparency mechanisms, we have seen substantial progress concerning the work of oversight bodies in most of the continent. Good examples of improvement are found in France, Italy, Portugal, and Spain, where greater powers and resources have recently been provided to such bodies. A 2013 amendment to French political finance law enabled the CNCCFP to compel political parties to provide any additional documents needed to ensure that the agency's monitoring duties are carried out successfully. In Italy, a new law adopted in 2015 has strengthened the Guarantee Commission on Political

77 Checkbook Elections?, *supra* note 53, at 43.

78 Piccio, *supra* note 34, at 7.

79 Doublet, *supra* note 71, at 35.

Parties (*Commissione di garanzia sui partiti politici*).[80] In Spain, legislative reforms in 2015 increased the power of the Court of Accounts, strengthened regulations, and enhanced the ability of regulators to impose sanctions.

Despite such signs of progress, a persistent problem remains in France, Spain and many other countries. Due to a lack of resources, supervisory bodies are not able to verify the accuracy of the information provided to them by political parties or candidates. Many evaluative reports show that oversight often fails to extend beyond the information supplied by political institutions, parties, and candidates themselves.[81]

However, there are examples of monitoring bodies that do function effectively. A good example of a monitoring body with effective supervisory powers is the Irish Standards Commission, which is authorized to carry out inquiries ex officio or following an individual complaint, and which under Irish law can then refer cases to the Director of Public Prosecutions or the police for further action.[82]

IV. CRITICAL REVIEW

Before closing this chapter, it is necessary to offer a critical assessment of how successful European political finance regulations have been. Any such critical assessment must take into account the four major objectives that European regulators worry about. These include preserving the stability of parties and their resources; promoting equal opportunities between electoral competitors; ensuring a connection between parties and civil society; and strengthening the fight against corruption.

In European society, there has been a certain degree of skepticism about the contributions that political finance law has made to the integrity of the electoral process and the public has less confidence these days in democratic politics. The skepticism now prevails among academics as well.[83] Reforms do not always deliver what they promise, and sometimes they are even counterproductive. There are still many weaknesses in Europe's regulatory framework, especially when it comes to oversight and enforcement provisions.

80 Maria Romana Allegri, *Statuti dei Partiti Politici e Trasparenza delle Fonti di Finanziamento* [Statutes on Transparency in the Funding of Political Parties], OSSERVATORIO COSTITUZIONALE [CONSTITUTIONAL OBSERVATORY] (2015), www.osservatorioaic.it/statuti-dei-partiti-politici-e-trasparenza-delle-fonti-di-finanziamento-fra-regole-inefficaci-correttivi-e-proposte-di-attuazione.html.

81 DOUBLET, *supra* note 71, at 39.

82 *Id.* at 42–43.

83 CHECKBOOK ELECTIONS? *supra* note 53, at 6.

Furthermore, official oversight is never sufficient on its own. It needs to be combined with oversight by the media and civil society. It is also clear that having political will on the part of the major players and having critical, rather than cynical, citizens are both essential for Europe's reforms to succeed in the long term.

A. *Sufficiency and Stability of Party Resources: Cheap Campaigns, but Big Bureaucratic Parties*

The main characteristic of the European model of campaign finance is that the continent now has relatively inexpensive campaigns. Political campaigns in the United States are remarkably long and expensive when compared with their European counterparts. One of the main reasons for the huge cost difference between American and European political campaigns is that European countries limit or prohibit paid TV political ads and, in their place, allocate free airtime to political parties.

But the fact that political campaigns are less expensive does not necessarily mean that European political parties need less funding. There are two basic ways to ensure that political parties have sufficient electoral resources. One involves providing them with a consistently stable income; the other involves reducing their expenditures. Both methods have been used in Europe. Because of public funding, the European model of campaign finance has largely been able to ensure the stability and professionalization of party structures. However, whether the funding and resources provided to parties are sufficient is a question that is hard to assess, since the real economic needs of parties, including what is necessary for them to be able to perform effectively, have not been studied reliably. Like any other organization, parties tend to expand over time. The more funding they receive, the larger they become and the greater their future needs become as well. In economic terms, parties are thought to be "insatiable," and their funding needs seem to increase in lock-step with their income. This, in turn, has led to the growing bureaucratization and hypertrophy in partisan party structures. As campaigns have become cheaper throughout Europe, in relatives terms at least, parties have ironically become bigger and more bureaucratic.

B. *Equality of Opportunity: Level Playing Field or Political Oligopoly?*

As we have seen, political finance regulations in Europe are meant to ensure healthy and pluralistic democratic competition. However, some studies suggest that regulations, particularly state subsidies, consolidate the *status quo* and stifle party competition, creating a kind of political oligopoly. They do this by penalizing smaller parties and making it difficult for newcomers to enter the fray. Views on this issue, as Kölln has shown,[84] are diverse, and the empirical findings are far from conclusive. For example, Scarrow does not find any systematic evidence that state subsidies impact the number of parties.[85] On the other hand, van Biezen and Rashkova's recent study shows that higher levels of state regulation hamper the entrance of new parties.[86]

To get to the heart of the matter, one must examine the criteria used to allocate public funding. Thresholds for accessing public funding and the criteria used to distribute public funds often work to determine whether the playing field will be level or continue to be slanted. Most European countries define eligibility for public funding based on two criteria: electoral support and parliamentary representation. This has led some courts, as we saw earlier in relation to France and Germany, to express concern over equality of opportunity, and to urge legislators to lower the threshold level of votes needed to qualify for public funding, so that public funding does not become the exclusive privilege only of those parties that have already obtained a presence in parliament. Indeed, this concern has not only been expressed by courts; it has also been expressed by international bodies like the Venice Commission and the OSCE/ODIHR.[87]

A few countries in Western Europe—including Spain, Belgium, Finland, the Netherlands, and the United Kingdom—provide direct public funding exclusively to parliamentary parties. This approach has been criticized on the grounds that it makes it harder for new parties to enter the political arena and compete under fair conditions with established parties. However, the actual harm to pluralism depends on the electoral threshold established in each case. In Finland and the Netherlands, where the electoral threshold is particularly low, the allocation of subsidies only to parliamentary parties does not pose the same problem for political pluralism that it does in other countries. The experience of Spain and Belgium, on the other hand, raises concerns, considering that the electoral threshold is 3 and 5 percent of the vote, respectively.[88]

Concern is much greater in some Central and Eastern European countries, particularly those that were former Soviet republics, about the counterproductive effects that party regulation has on equality of opportunity. In

84 Kölln, *supra* note 4, at 74.

85 Susan E. Scarrow, *Party Subsidies and the Freezing of Party Competition: Do Cartel Mechanisms Work?*, 29 W. Eur. Pol. 619, 635 (2006).

86 Ingrid van Biezen & Ekaterina R Rashkova, *Deterring New Party Entry? The Impact of State Regulation on the Permeability of Party Systems*, 20 Party Pol. 890 (2014).

87 Venice Commission, *Guidelines and Report on the Financing of Political Parties* § 188 (Mar. 23, 2001), www.osce.org/odihr/37843?download=true.

88 Funding of Political Parties and Election Campaigns, *supra* note 65, at 223.

the diverse countries of this region (and we can highlight the example of the Russian Federation),[89] political finance rules have been willfully designed to favor ruling parties. As recent findings have shown, in countries that lean toward authoritarianism, elaborate political finance regulation is actually used to weaken the opposition and prevent the emergence of new political actors.[90] Rigorous spending limits and abuse of the resources of the state together often combine to give ruling parties a very unfair advantage.

C. Connection between Parties and Society: Less Economic Power but More Reliance on Public Funding

The growth and availability of public money in Europe has generally contributed to an increase in equality of opportunity in electoral competition. It has also decreased the influence of big money on politics, particularly when public funding has been combined, as it has been in most countries, with limits or bans imposed on private contributions. New transparency requirements may also have had a positive effect, especially in educating the public of the dangers of linking politics and business.

As a sign of progress, researchers have reported witnessing a decline in corporate contributions as a source of funding in various European countries. Evidence of this decline has been observed in Germany and Sweden, and also in Italy, Ireland, and the United Kingdom. Big money has slowly been taken out of the political arena. The weight that big money played before has become quite small in Greece, the Netherlands, Sweden, and Norway.[91] In Sweden, the dominant political parties have voluntarily refused to accept any donations from corporations since the 1970s.

However, the news coming out of Europe is not entirely positive. Although the availability of public funding has helped political parties shield themselves from private economic powers, public funding has also increasingly made these same political parties financially dependent on state resources. For most European countries, the percentage of their funding that a country's political parties receive from the public (as opposed to from private sources) is between 60 and 80 percent. In some cases, including in Spain, Belgium, and Italy, that number ranges as high as 80 to 90 percent.[92]

The dependence of political parties on public subsidies has made parties less reliant on other, traditional sources of income, such as membership dues

[89] CHECKBOOK ELECTIONS? *supra* note 53, at 31–32.

[90] FUNDING OF POLITICAL PARTIES AND ELECTION CAMPAIGNS, *supra* note 65, at 173, 175.

[91] *Id.* at 216–17.

[92] Piccio, *supra* note 59.

and grass-roots funding. This, in turn, has decreased the incentives that parties had to maintain a strong presence on the ground. Scholars have observed that state-financed parties now are neglecting their constituents with increasing frequency.[93] To the extent this occurs, the phenomenon casts doubt on the most important justification for public subsidies, which is to "insulate parties and politicians from the undue pressures of wealthy donors" and to "permit them to be more responsive to the broader (non-wealthy) electorate."[94]

The weakening connection between political parties and civil society was observed by Germany's Federal Constitutional Court in its decision on public funding from 1992, which we discussed earlier in this chapter.[95] The Council of Europe has also stressed that having public financing be the only source of income for parties poses a danger, given that this weakens the link of parties to their voters.[96] This is why the Council of Europe's international guidelines instruct countries to support parties with "limited contributions," and to encourage parties to achieve a "reasonable balance between public and private funding."[97]

Scholars use the term "cartel party" to describe political parties that function in this new world of declining connectedness with the people and increasing closeness with the state. As Katz and Mair explain, the term "cartel party" is used to describe parties that have "become agents of the state and exploit state funds to ensure their collective survival."[98] By passing generous party funding legislation, parties serve their own interests first and foremost, ensuring their own survival, entrenching their continued role in the political system, and solidifying the *status quo*. When the state becomes a resource and the dominant source of revenue for parties, it is not long before a state's own legislation, which is dictated by parties of course, itself becomes an instrument to resist the challenges posed by new forms of social mobilization.

Still, some scholars question whether revenue maximization can really adequately explain the current state of political finance regulations in Europe. Though political parties do have self-serving interests, these interests alone cannot

93 Ingrid van Biezen, Financing Political Parties and Election Campaigns: Guidelines 13 (2003).

94 Susan E. Scarrow, *Political Finance in Comparative Perspective*, 10 Ann. Rev. Pol. Sci. 193, 205 (2007).

95 Bundesverfassungsgericht [BVerfG] [Federal Constitutional Court] July 19, 1966, 20 BVerfGE 56 (168) (Ger.); Bundesverfassungsgericht [BVerfG] [Federal Constitutional Court] Dec. 3, 1968, 24 BVerfGE 300 (Ger.).

96 Funding of Political Parties and Election Campaigns, *supra* note 65, at 225.

97 Council of Europe, Parl. Ass., *Recommendation 1516*, *supra* note 29.

98 Katz & Mair, *supra* note 1.

explain why Europe has experienced a convergence toward greater transparency of its political finance laws or a reduction in party subsidies in recent years.[99]

These days, the many signs of citizen dissatisfaction with representative institutions are impossible to miss. With the decline of electoral turnout throughout Europe, the rise of populist candidates and parties, and the emergence of protest movements, it is no surprise that trust in political parties has dropped significantly all over the European continent throughout the latest decade. Currently, the average percentage of citizens who say they trust political parties across the 28 states of the European Union stands at 16.7 percent. This is the lowest level of citizen trust for political parties ever recorded by the Eurobarometer surveys.[100]

In the wake of widespread disaffection, citizens are increasingly beginning to question the wisdom of providing state funding for political parties. Why should the state (and its taxpayers) support political parties if the connection of parties to citizens is weakening and parties are becoming unrecognizable bureaucratic structures? Italy's decision to end several direct forms of public funding for political parties comes as a warning sign. That decision arose from the dangerous combination of giving parties "lump sum" election reimbursements, which were not connected to the actual expenses these parties incurred, and having inadequate accounting and transparency measures.[101] Before citizens knew it, Italian parties became bloated and unresponsive to citizens. To put it mildly, that system failed to achieve the broader democratic goals it professed; instead, it undermined the credibility of this model of public funding.[102]

One proposal to counteract the excessive dependence of parties on public funding without letting parties succumb, at the same time, to the unwanted influence of big money, involves creating a public financing system that relies on small donations from individuals.[103] Most experts agree that small donations from private citizens play a positive role in funding democratic parties. Among other things, they strengthen parties' links to the electorate and do not threaten their access to policymakers.

Another proposal, which complements the one above, calls for the implementation of a matching funds system that links public funding to the ability of parties to demonstrate their connection to society—by showing they are also

[99] Funding of Political Parties and Election Campaigns, *supra* note 65, at 225.

[100] Standard Eurobarometer 83 (Spring 2015), European Commission Public Opinion, http://ec.europa.eu/commfrontoffice/publicopinion/archives/eb/eb83/eb83_en.htm.

[101] Piccio, *supra* note 59.

[102] *Id.*

[103] Óscar Sánchez Muñoz, *La Financiación de los Partidos Políticos en España: Ideas para un Debate [The Financing of Political Parties in Spain: Ideas for Debate]*, 99 Rev. Española Derecho Const. 161 (2013).

able to collect private contributions. Notably, the current funding allocation mechanisms in Germany and in the Netherlands include various incentives for political parties to maintain a social anchor to the society they seek to serve.[104] In Germany, public funding allocations are determined both by the proportion of vote a party won in the most recent elections and by the amount of private donations it received. Moreover, the amount of public funding received cannot exceed the total amount raised privately.

In the Netherlands, funds are distributed based on three criteria. First, a fixed amount is distributed to all parties represented in parliament; second, additional funds are distributed depending on the number of seats obtained; and, third, an additional amount is distributed in proportion to the number of party members who contribute privately to the party. It is not surprising that the level of dependency of political parties on the state in Germany and the Netherlands is the lowest in Western Europe[105].

D. *Corruption: The Scourge that Will Not Disappear*

In recent years, corruption scandals have rocked the European continent. Spain,[106] Greece,[107] Portugal,[108] Italy,[109] France,[110] and various Central and

104 Funding of Political Parties and Election Campaigns, *supra* note 65, at 223–24.

105 Piccio, *supra* note 59.

106 The "Gürtel" scandal in Spain was a major corruption scheme involving the country's ruling Popular Party (PP), while the "ERE" scandal involved the diversion of public funds from the socialist government of Andalusia. *See* Ignacio Zafra, *Key figures in Spain's huge Gürtel corruption case get 13-year jail terms*, El País (Feb. 10, 2017), http://elpais.com/elpais/2017/02/10/inenglish/1486716350_560840.html; María Fabra, *Supreme Court Calls Ex-Andalusian Premiers to Testify in ERE*, El País (Feb. 17, 2015), http://elpais.com/elpais/2015/02/17/inenglish/1424181545_702260.html.

107 Greece's many scandals have included tax fraud, kickbacks for public contracts, made up public accounts, and bribes or "fakelaki" in public services. *See, e.g.*, *Green Anti-Corruption Report*, Gan Business Anti-Corruption Portal, www.business-anti-corruption.com/country-profiles/greece.

108 In Portugal, Jose Socrates, who served as the country's socialist prime minister from 2005 to 2011, was accused of tax fraud and money laundering. Duarte Lima, former parliamentary leader of the center-right Social Democratic Party, was sentenced for fraud and money laundering.

109 Former Italian Prime Minister Silvio Berlusconi was accused of corruption numerous times. He was convicted of tax fraud in 2012 and found guilty of bribing a senator in 2015. Italy also witnessed the "Mafia Capitale" scandal, in which authorities uncovered a network of corrupt relationships between several politicians and criminals in Rome. *See* Rachel Donadio, *Berlusconi Convicted of Tax Fraud*, N.Y. Times (Oct. 26, 2012), www.nytimes.com/2012/10/27/world/europe/berlusconi-convicted-and-sentenced-in-tax-fraud.html; *Berlusconi Found Guilty of Bribing Italian Senator*, Reuters (July 8, 2015), www.reuters.com/article/us-italy-berlusconi-idUSKCN0PI2A520150708.

110 France's corruption scandals include the Libyan financing of President Nicolas Sarkozy's electoral campaign of 2007. In what came to be known as the "Bygmalion affair," Sarkozy allegedly

Eastern European countries have all had them and have been particularly affected. Transparency International's Corruption Perception Index (CPI) reveals that levels of perceived corruption in Europe have increased, not decreased. Europe's recent CPI scores have been some of the worst on record. Recent Eurobarometer surveys have given us similar results.[111]

The phenomenon of "corruption" is very broad and covers areas of social life that have little to do with politics, of course. But it is often enough related to politics. And whenever corruption seeps into the sphere of political finance, it becomes especially dangerous, for it undermines public trust in the political system writ large. Party funding regulations in Europe are meant to fight against corruption, although these regulations unfortunately do not seem to have delivered their intended results.

One glaring paradox in particular deserves mention. Countries that have adopted the most rigorous campaign finance regulations, including some of the countries in Southern Europe, are still perceived to have the most corrupt parties. By contrast, the countries of Northern Europe that have less rigorous regulations, such as Denmark, Sweden, and Switzerland, have the lowest levels of perceived corruption.[112] This is the case despite the fact that they do not have corporate donation bans and contribution limits. This fact may indicate that political culture may at times be a more important factor in minimizing corruption than the legal framework of a given country.

The case of Italy is probably extreme in this respect. Italy witnessed the collapse of its party system in the 1990s, thanks to widespread and repeated violations of Italian political finance regulations by Italy's political parties. At the same time, the state provided parties with a generous system of public financing. But the public financing system did not work like it should have. In Italy, the system did not contribute to the elimination of corruption, but rather led to its growth and development.[113]

Still, we must not ignore the role played by reform in making corruption visible and raising public awareness of it. Greater transparency works

used an events company to spend €23 million more on his presidential campaign than allowed by French law. *See* Angelique Chrisafis, *French Inquiry Opens into Allegations Gaddafi Funded Sarkozy 2007 Campaign*, GUARDIAN (Apr. 19, 2013), www.theguardian.com/world/2013/apr/19/french-inquiry-gaddafi-sarkozy-2007-campaign; Angelique Chrisafis, *Nicolas Sarkozy to face trial over 2012 campaign financing*, THE GUARDIAN (Feb. 7, 2017), www.theguardian.com/world/2017/feb/07/nicolas-sarkozy-to-face-trial-over-2012-campaign-financing.

[111] Piccio, *supra* note 59.

[112] FUNDING OF POLITICAL PARTIES AND ELECTION CAMPAIGNS *supra* note 65, at 208; EUROPEAN PARLIAMENT, *Party Financing and Referendum Campaigns in EU Member States*, 15.

[113] Eugeni Pizzimenti & Piero Ignazi, *Finanziamento Pubblico e Mutamenti Organizzativi nei Partiti Italiani [Public Financing and Organizational Changes in Italian Parties]*, 41 RIV. ITALIANA DI SCI. POL. 199, 200 (2011).

to educate the public about the link between big money and politics and thus increases popular awareness of corruption. And since reforms are often adopted in direct response to corruption scandals, we would expect to find more regulations being enacted in countries where the perception of corruption is high. Consequently, cases that combine high regulation with high corruption do not prove much about how effective such regulations are in combatting corruption.[114] Countries following this pattern could well have had even more corruption absent those regulations. And it may even be the case that regulations cause public outrage over previously tolerated behaviors, making it seem as though highly regulated countries have more corruption than lightly regulated ones.[115]

Corruption represents a very serious problem in Central and Eastern Europe, due to the close links that exist between political parties and specific corporate interests in many of these countries. Private-sector kickbacks in return for government favors have been behind serious party funding scandals in even some of the more consolidated democracies of this region, such as the Czech Republic, Hungary, and Poland.[116] Of course, the situation is even worse in Russia and other former Soviet republics. A particularly worrisome issue is the distortion in political competition created by "oligarchic parties" and by their abuse of state resources in electoral campaigns.[117]

Europe's concerns about corruption lead to a few final reflections. It is wrong—or at least incomplete—to link the regulation of party finance very closely to the fight against corruption. A country's political finance regulatory framework must be, above all, connected with the kind of political party system being promoted in that country, with the role that parties are expected to play within the democratic system, and, ultimately, with the kind of democracy in which its citizens want to live. And while corruption does pose a serious problem to Europe's political finance system, the persistence of corruption in Europe, despite the endless tightening of regulations concerning political finance, does not mean that these regulations are unnecessary or entirely ineffective. Rather, the persistence of corruption suggests mostly that political finance regulations alone are not sufficient and that broader measures are needed.

114 Magnus Ohman, How to Study the Impact of Political Finance Regulations 3 (Paper presented at the World Congress of International Political Science Association, Montreal, Canada, July 14–19, 2014).

115 Scarrow, *supra* note 94, at 201.

116 FUNDING OF POLITICAL PARTIES AND ELECTION CAMPAIGNS, *supra* note 65, at 175.

117 *Id.* at 185.

Index

www.ingramcontent.com/pod-product-compliance
Lightning Source LLC
LaVergne TN
LVHW100247210926
848480LV00003B/849
9781316630679